# Nation of Nations

## VOLUME TWO: SINCE 1865

Here is not merely a nation but a teeming nation of nations.
—*Walt Whitman*

# Nation of Nations

## A CONCISE NARRATIVE
## OF THE AMERICAN REPUBLIC

### VOLUME TWO: SINCE 1865

James West Davidson

William E. Gienapp
Harvard University

Christine Leigh Heyrman
University of Delaware

Mark H. Lytle
Bard College

Michael B. Stoff
University of Texas, Austin

OVERTURE
BOOKS
McGraw-Hill
College

Boston   Burr Ridge, IL   Dubuque, IA   Madison, WI   New York   San Francisco   St. Louis
Bangkok   Bogotá   Caracas   Lisbon   London   Madrid
Mexico City   Milan   New Delhi   Seoul   Singapore   Sydney   Taipei   Toronto

# McGraw-Hill College

*A Division of The McGraw-Hill Companies*

NATION OF NATIONS: VOLUME TWO A CONCISE NARRATIVE OF THE AMERICAN REPUBLIC, SECOND EDITION

This book is printed on acid-free paper.

1 2 3 4 5 6 7 8 9 0 DOC/DOC 9 3 2 1 0 9 8

ISBN 0–07–303386–3

Editorial director and publisher: *Jane E. Vaicunas*
Sponsoring editor: *Lyn Uhl*
Developmental editor: *Monica Freedman*
Senior marketing manager: *Suzanne Daghlian*
Senior project manager: *Marilyn Rothenberger*
Production supervisor: *Deborah Donner*
Designer: *Laurie Jean Entringer*
Photo research coordinator: *John C. Leland*
Supplement coordinator: *Rita Hingtgen*
Compositor: *York Graphic Services, Inc.*
Typeface: *10/12 Janson*
Printer: *R. R. Donnelley & Sons Company/Crawfordsville, IN*

The credits section for this book begins on page C.1 and is considered an extension of the copyright page.

**Library of Congress Has Cataloged the Volume Edition as Follows:**

Nation of nations : a concise narrative of the American republic /
  James West Davidson . . . [et al.]. —2nd ed.
    p. cm.
  Adapted from Nation of nations : a narrative history of the
American republic, 2nd ed. © 1994.
  Includes bibliographical references and index.
  ISBN 0–07–303375–8 (acid-free paper)
  1. United States—History.    I. Davidson, James West.
E178.4.N345  1999
973—dc21                                98–21631
                                                       CIP

www.mhhe.com

# Contents

# PART FOUR
## GLOBAL ESSAY: THE UNITED STATES IN AN INDUSTRIAL AGE

## CHAPTER EIGHTEEN
## The New Industrial Order

CHAPTER NINETEEN

# The Rise of an Urban Order

CHAPTER TWENTY
# Agrarian Domains: The South and the West 525

## CHAPTER TWENTY-TWO
# The Progressive Era

## CHAPTER TWENTY-THREE
# The United States and the Old World Order

# PART FIVE
## GLOBAL ESSAY: THE PERILS OF DEMOCRACY 656

### CHAPTER TWENTY-FOUR
# The New Era 658

## CHAPTER TWENTY-FIVE
# Crash and Depression

CHAPTER TWENTY-SIX
# The New Deal

CHAPTER TWENTY-SEVEN
# America's Rise to Globalism

# PART SIX
## GLOBAL ESSAY: THE UNITED STATES IN A NUCLEAR AGE

## CHAPTER TWENTY-EIGHT
# Cold War America

CHAPTER THIRTY
# Liberalism and Beyond

CHAPTER THIRTY-ONE
# The Vietnam Era

CHAPTER THIRTY-TWO
# The Age of Limits                                              897

CHAPTER THIRTY-THREE
# A Nation Still Divisible

# List of Maps and Charts

# About the Authors

**James West Davidson** received his Ph.D. from Yale University. A historian who has pursued a full-time writing career, he is the author of numerous books, among them *After the Fact: The Art of Historical Detection* (with Mark H. Lytle), *The Logic of Millennial Thought: Eighteenth-Century New England*, and *Great Heart: The History of a Labrador Adventure* (with John Rugge).

**William E. Gienapp** has a Ph.D. from the University of California, Berkeley. He taught at the University of Wyoming before going to Harvard University, where he is Professor of History. In 1988 he received the Avery O. Craven Award for his book *The Origins of the Republican Party, 1852–1856*. His essay "The Antebellum Era" appeared in the *Encyclopedia of Social History* (1992), and he is a coauthor of *Why the Civil War Came* (1996).

**Christine Leigh Heyrman** is Associate Professor of History at the University of Delaware. She received a Ph.D. in American Studies from Yale University and is the author of *Commerce and Culture: The Maritime Communities of Colonial Massachusetts, 1690–1750*. Most recently she received the Bancroft Prize for *Southern Cross: The Beginnings of the Bible Belt* (1997), a book about popular religious culture in the Old Southwest.

**Mark H. Lytle,** who was awarded a Ph.D. from Yale University, is Professor of History and Environmental Studies and Chair of the American Studies Program at Bard College. He is also Director of the Master of Arts in Teaching Program at Bard. His publications include *The Origins of the Iranian-American Alliance, 1941–1953* and *After the Fact: The Art of Historical Detection* (with James West Davidson), and most recently, "An Environmental Approach to American Diplomatic History," in *Diplomatic History*. He is at work on *The Uncivil War: America in the Vietnam Era*.

**Michael B. Stoff** is Associate Professor of History at the University of Texas at Austin, where he is Director of Graduate Studies. The recipient of a Ph.D. from Yale University, he wrote *Oil, War, and American Security: The Search for a National Policy on Foreign Oil, 1941–1947* and *Manhattan Project: A Documentary Introduction to the Atomic Age*. He has been honored many times for his teaching, most recently with the Friar's Centennial Teaching Excellence Award.

# Preface to the
# Second Concise Edition

*Nation of Nations* was written in the belief that students would be drawn more readily to the study of history if their text emphasized a narrative approach. Clearly, many of our readers agree, and to them we owe thanks for the warm reception the text has been given.

This edition provides a briefer alternative to the full-length text. In the belief that the original authors could best preserve both the themes and the narrative approach of the longer work, we have done the abridgment ourselves. Indeed, the task forced us to think again about the core elements of narrative history, for the task of condensing a full-length survey presents devilish temptations. Most teachers rightly resist sacrificing breadth of coverage; yet if an edition is to be concise, the words, the sentences, the paragraphs must go. The temptation is to excise the apparently superfluous "details" of a full-dress narrative: trimming character portraits, cutting back on narrative color, lopping off concrete examples. Yet too draconian a campaign risks producing either a barebones compendium of facts or a bloodless thematic outline, dispossessed of the tales that engaged the reader in the first place.

The intent, then, is to provide a text that remains a *narrative*—a history with enough contextual detail for readers to grasp the story. The fuller introductions to each chapter, a distinctive feature of the original text, have been preserved, though streamlined where possible. Within each chapter, we have attempted to maintain a balance between narrative and thematic analysis. Paradoxically, this has occasionally meant *adding* material to the concise edition: replacing longer stories with shorter emblematic sketches or recasting sections to ensure that students are not overwhelmed by the compression of too many details into too few paragraphs.

Each chapter of the concise edition also includes two additional features. The first, "Eyewitness to History," is designed to reinforce the centrality of narrative. Each Eyewitness is a primary source excerpt; some are written by eminent Americans, others by little-known folk who were intimately involved in the changes affecting their times. In either case, the vivid first-person accounts serve to draw readers further into the story. But we also hope that they will encourage students to recognize the hidden complexities of narrative. The diversity of materials and perspectives should make it clear that one of the historian's primary tasks is to step back and place the welter of overlapping, often conflicting narratives in a larger context.

A second feature, entitled "Counterpoint," is new to this concise edition. In it, we explore contrasting ways historians have interpreted a central topic covered by the chapter. We were led to do this, paradoxically, by the very success of the narrative approach, for some professors have written suggesting that precisely because the tale flows so smoothly, students may be seduced into thinking that the writing of history is without controversy—that the past must have occurred precisely as we have sketched it and that any questions of interpretations must be minor matters. To combat this misimpression, our Counterpoint discussions in each chapter are *not* separated out as boxed features; instead, they are integrated into the narrative so that students come to understand such debates as an inevitable (and productive) part of writing history.

In other ways, the approach of this concise edition remains the same as in the first edition. We continue to use marginal headings to help readers focus on key terms and concepts. Each chapter also concludes with a timeline of significant events. And each of the book's six parts begins with an essay setting American events in a global perspective. We believe it important to show that the United States did not develop in a geographic or cultural vacuum and that the broad forces shaping it also influenced other nations.

Over the past decade during which we have worked on this book we have been immensely grateful to the many reviewers generous enough to offer constructive comments and suggestions. To name them all would require more space than this preface itself occupies. But we cannot omit specific mention of those readers who have provided advice on the shaping of the concise edition of *Nation of Nations*. They include Janet Allured, McNeese State University; Virginia Paganelli Caruso, Henry Ford Community College; Kathryn Dabelow, Pasadena City College; Alan C. Downs, Georgia Southern University; Linda Killen, Radford University; Kenneth L. Kitchen, Trident Technical College; Michael J. Gillis, California State University–Chico; Shane Maddock, U.S. Coast Guard Academy; Jay Mullen, Southern Oregon University; Sydney Nathans, Duke University; Gary L. Shumway, California State University–Fullerton; Albert J. Smith, Modesto Junior College. The first concise edition also benefited from the advice of Michael Bellesiles, Emory University; James Crisp, North Carolina State University; Ann Ellis, Kennesaw State College; Norman Enhorning, Adirondack Community College; Jerry Felt, University of Vermont; Mary Ferrari, Radford University; Renee Shively Leonard; Steven White, Lexington Community College; James Woods, Georgia Southern; and William Woodward, Seattle Pacific University.

The division of labor for this book was determined by our respective fields of scholarship: Christine Heyrman, the colonial era, in which Europeans, Africans, and Indians participated in the making of both a new America and a new republic; William Gienapp, the 90 years in which the young nation first flourished, then foundered on the issues of section and slavery; Michael Stoff, the post–Civil War era, in which industrialization and urbanization brought the nation more centrally into an international system frequently disrupted by depression and war; and Mark Lytle, the modern era, in which Americans finally faced the reality that even the boldest dreams of national greatness are bounded by the finite nature of power and resources both natural and human. Finally, because the need to specialize inevitably imposes limits on any project as broad as this one, our fifth author, James Davidson, served as a general editor and writer, with the intent of fitting individual parts to the whole, as well as providing a measure of continuity, style, and overarching purpose. In producing this collaborative effort, all of us have shared the conviction that the best history speaks to a larger audience.

*James West Davidson*
*William E. Gienapp*
*Christine Leigh Heyrman*
*Mark H. Lytle*
*Michael B. Stoff*

# Introduction

History is both a discipline of rigor, bound by rules and scholarly methods, and something more: the unique, compelling, even strange way in which we humans define ourselves. We are all the sum of the tales of thousands of people, great and small, whose actions have etched their lines upon us. History supplies our very identity—a sense of the social groups to which we belong, whether family, ethnic group, race, class, or gender. It reveals to us the foundations of our deepest religious beliefs and traces the roots of our economic and political systems. It explores how we celebrate and grieve, sing the songs we sing, weather the illnesses to which time and chance subject us. It commands our attention for all these good reasons and for no good reason at all, other than a fascination with the way the myriad tales play out. Strange that we should come to care about a host of men and women so many centuries gone, some with names eminent and familiar, others unknown but for a chance scrap of information left behind in an obscure letter.

Yet we do care. We care about Sir Humphrey Gilbert, "devoured and swallowed up of the Sea" one black Atlantic night in 1583; about George Washington at Kips Bay, red with fury as he takes a riding crop to his retreating soldiers. We care about Octave Johnson, a slave fleeing through Louisiana swamps trying to decide whether to stand and fight the approaching hounds or take his chances with the bayou alligators; about Clara Barton, her nurse's skirts so heavy with blood from the wounded that she must wring them out before tending to the next soldier. We are drawn to the fate of Chinese laborers, chipping away at the Sierras' looming granite; a Georgian named Tom Watson seeking to forge a colorblind political alliance; and desperate immigrant mothers, kerosene in hand, storming Brooklyn butcher shops that have again raised prices. We follow, with a mix of awe and amusement, the fortunes of the quirky Henry Ford ("Everybody wants to be somewhere he ain't"), turning out identical automobiles, insisting his factory workers wear identical expressions ("Fordization of the Face"). We trace the career of young Thurgood Marshall, crisscrossing the South in his own "little old beat-up '29 Ford," typing legal briefs in the back seat, trying to get black teachers to sue for equal pay, hoping to get his people somewhere they weren't. The list could go on and on, spilling out as it did in Walt Whitman's *Leaves of Grass*: "A southerner soon as a northerner, a planter nonchalant and hospitable, A Yankee bound my own way . . . a Hoosier, a Badger, a Buckeye, a Louisianian or Georgian . . . ." Whitman embraced and celebrated them all, inseparable strands of what made him an American and what made him human:

> In all people I see myself, none more and not one a barleycorn less,
> And the good or bad I say of myself I say of them.

To encompass so expansive an America Whitman turned to poetry; historians have traditionally chosen narrative as their means of giving life to the past. That mode of explanation permits them to interweave the strands of economic, political, and social history in a coherent chronological framework. By choosing narrative, they affirm the multicausal nature of historical explanation—the insistence that events be portrayed in context. By choosing narrative, they are also acknowledging that, while long-term economic and social trends shape societies in significant ways, events often take on a logic (or an illogic) of their own, jostling one another, being deflected by unpredictable personal decisions, sudden deaths, natural catastrophes, and chance. There are literary reasons, too, for preferring a narrative approach, since it supplies a dramatic force usually missing from more structural analyses of the past.

In some ways, surveys like this one are the natural antithesis of narrative history. They strive, by definition, to be comprehensive: to furnish a broad, orderly exposition of their chosen field. Yet to cover so much ground in so limited a space necessarily deprives readers of the context of more detailed accounts. Then, too, the resurgence of social history—with its concern for class and race, patterns of rural and urban life, the spread of market and industrial economies—lends itself to more analytic, less chronological treatments. The challenge facing historians is to incorporate these areas of research without losing the story's narrative drive or the chronological flow that orients readers to the more familiar events of our past.

In the end, it is counterproductive to treat political and social history as distinct spheres. There is no simple way to separate the world of ordinary Americans or the marketplace of boom and bust from the corridors of political maneuvering or the ceremonial pomp of an inauguration. The primary question of this narrative—how the fledgling, often tumultuous confederation of "these United States" managed to transform itself into an enduring republic—is not only political but necessarily social. In order to survive, a republic must resolve conflicts among citizens of different geographic regions and economic classes, of diverse racial and ethnic origins, of competing religions and ideologies. The resolution of these conflicts has produced tragic consequences, perhaps, as often as noble ones. But tragic or noble, the destiny of these states cannot be understood without comprehending both the social and the political dimensions of the story.

# CHAPTER SEVENTEEN

# Reconstructing the Union

Joseph Davis had had enough. Well on in years and financially ruined by the war, he decided to quit farming. So, on November 19, 1866, he sold his Mississippi plantations Hurricane and Brierfield to Benjamin Montgomery and his sons. The sale of southern plantations was common enough after the war, but this transaction was bound to attract attention, since Joseph Davis was the elder brother of Jefferson Davis. Indeed, before the war the Confederate president had operated Brierfield as his own plantation, even though his brother retained legal title to it. But the sale was unusual for another reason—so unusual that the parties involved agreed to keep it secret. The plantation's new owners were black, and Mississippi law prohibited African Americans from owning land.

Though a slave, Benjamin Montgomery had been the business manager of the two Davis plantations before the war. He had also operated a store on Hurricane Plantation with his own line of credit in New Orleans. In 1863 Montgomery fled to the North, but when the war was over, he returned to Davis Bend, where the federal government had confiscated the Davis plantations and was leasing plots of the land to black farmers. Montgomery quickly emerged as the leader of the African American community at the Bend.

Then, in 1866, President Andrew Johnson pardoned Joseph Davis and restored his lands. Davis was now over 80 years old and lacked the will and stamina to rebuild, yet unlike many ex-slave holders, he felt bound by obligations to his former slaves. Convinced that with proper encouragement African Americans could succeed economically in freedom, he sold his land secretly to Benjamin Montgomery. Only when the law prohibiting African Americans from owning land was overturned in 1867 did Davis publicly confirm the sale to his former slave.

For his part, Montgomery undertook to create a model society at Davis Bend based on mutual cooperation. He rented land to black farmers, hired others to work his own fields, sold supplies on credit, and ginned and marketed the crops. To the growing African American community, he preached the gospel of hard work, self-reliance, and education.

Various difficulties dogged these black farmers, including the destruction caused by the war, several disastrous floods, insects, droughts, and declining cotton prices. Yet before long, cotton production exceeded that of the prewar years, and in 1870 the black families at Davis Bend produced 2500 bales. The

Montgomerys eventually acquired 5500 acres, which made them reputedly the third largest planters in the state, and they won national and international awards for the quality of their cotton. Their success demonstrated what African Americans, given a fair chance, might accomplish.

The experiences of Benjamin Montgomery during the years after 1865 were not those of most black southerners, who did not own land or have a powerful white benefactor. Yet Montgomery's dream of economic independence was shared by all African Americans. As one black veteran noted, "Every colored man will be a slave, and feel himself a slave until he can raise him own *bale of cotton* and put him own mark upon it and say dis is mine!" Blacks could not gain effective freedom simply through a proclamation of emancipation. They also needed economic power, including their own land that no one could unfairly take away.

For nearly two centuries the laws had prevented slaves from possessing such economic power. If such conditions were to be overturned, black Americans needed political power too. Thus the Republic would have to be reconstructed to give African Americans political power that they had been previously denied.

War, in its blunt way, had roughed out the contours of a solution, but only in broad terms. Clearly, African Americans would no longer be enslaved. The North, with its industrial might, would be the driving force in the nation's economy and retain the dominant political voice. But beyond that, the outlines of a reconstructed Republic remained vague. Would African Americans receive effective power? How would North and South readjust their economic and political relations? These questions lay at the heart of the problem of Reconstruction.

## PERSIDENTIAL RECONSTRUCTION

Throughout the war Abraham Lincoln had considered Reconstruction his responsibility. Elected with less than 40 percent of the popular vote in 1860, he was acutely aware that once the states of the Confederacy were restored to the Union, the Republicans would be weakened unless they ceased to be a sectional party. By a generous peace, Lincoln hoped to attract former Whigs in the South, who supported many of the Republicans' economic policies, and build up a southern wing of the party.

### Lincoln's 10 Percent Plan

Lincoln outlined his program in a Proclamation of Amnesty and Reconstruction, issued in December 1863. When a minimum of 10 percent of the qualified voters from 1860 took a loyalty oath to the Union, they could organize a state government. The new state constitution had to abolish slavery and provide for black education, but Lincoln did not insist that high-ranking Confederate leaders be barred from public life.

Lincoln indicated that he would be generous in granting pardons to prominent Confederate leaders and did not rule out compensation for slave property.

Moreover, while he privately advocated limited black suffrage in the disloyal southern states, he did not demand social or political equality for black Americans, and he recognized pro-Union governments in Louisiana, Arkansas, and Tennessee that allowed only white men to vote.

The Radical Republicans found Lincoln's approach much too lenient. Strongly antislavery, Radical members of Congress had led the struggle to make

*Radical Republicans*

emancipation a war aim. Now they led the fight to guarantee the rights of the freedpeople. The Radicals believed that it was the duty of Congress, not the president, to set the terms under which states would regain their rights in the Union. Though the Radicals often disagreed on other matters, they were united in a determination to readmit southern states only after slavery had been ended, black rights protected, and the power of the planter class destroyed.

Under the direction of Senator Benjamin Wade of Ohio and Representative Henry Winter Davis of Maryland, Congress formulated a much stricter plan of

*Wade–Davis bill*

Reconstruction. It required half the white adult males to take an oath of allegiance before drafting a new state constitution, and restricted political power to the hard-core Unionists. When the Wade–Davis bill passed on the final day of the 1864 congressional session, Lincoln exercised his right of a pocket veto.* Still, his own program could not succeed without the assistance of Congress, which refused to recognize his governments in Louisiana and Arkansas. As the war drew to a close, Lincoln appeared ready to make concessions to the Radicals, and at his final cabinet meeting he approved placing the defeated South temporarily under military rule. But only a few days later Booth's bullet found its mark, and Lincoln's final approach to Reconstruction would never be known.

## *The Mood of the South*

In the wake of defeat, the immediate reaction among white southerners was one of shock, despair, and hopelessness. Some former Confederates were openly antagonistic. A North Carolina innkeeper remarked bitterly that Yankees had stolen his slaves, burned his house, and killed all his sons, leaving him only one privilege: "To hate 'em. I git up at half-past four in the morning, and sit up till twelve at night, to hate 'em." Most Confederate soldiers were less defiant, having had their fill of war. Even among hostile civilians the feeling was widespread that the South must accept northern terms. A South Carolina paper admitted that "the conqueror has the right to make the terms, and we must submit."

This psychological moment was critical. To prevent a resurgence of resistance, the president needed to lay out in unmistakable terms what white southerners had to do to regain their old status in the Union. Perhaps even a clear and firm policy would not have been enough. But with Lincoln's death, the executive power came to rest in far less capable hands.

---

*If a president does not sign a bill after Congress has adjourned, it has the same effect as a veto.

## Johnson's Program of Reconstruction

Andrew Johnson, the new president, had been born in North Carolina and eventually moved to Tennessee, where he worked as a tailor. Barely able to read and write when he married, he rose to political power by portraying himself as the champion of the people against the wealthy planter class. "Some day I will

*Johnson's character and values*

show the stuck-up aristocrats who is running the country," he vowed as he began his political career. He had not opposed slavery before the war, and although he accepted emancipation as one consequence of the war, Johnson remained a confirmed racist with no concern for the welfare of African Americans. "Damn the negroes," he said during the war, "I am fighting these traitorous aristocrats, their masters."

During the war he had joined the Radicals in calling for stern treatment of southern rebels. "Treason must be made odious and traitors must be punished and impoverished," he proclaimed in 1864. After serving in Congress and as military governor of Tennessee following its occupation by Union forces, Johnson, a Democrat, was tapped by Lincoln in 1864 as his running mate on the rechristened "Union" ticket.

The Radicals expected Johnson to uphold their views on Reconstruction, and upon assuming the presidency he spoke of trying Confederate leaders and breaking up planters' estates. Unlike most Republicans, however, Johnson strongly supported states' rights and opposed government aid to business. Given such differences, conflict between the president and the majority in Congress was inevitable, but Johnson's political shortcomings made the situation worse. Scarred by his humble origins, he became tactless and inflexible when challenged or criticized, and he alienated even those who sought to work with him.

Johnson moved to quickly return the southern states to their place in the Union. He prescribed a loyalty oath white southerners would have to take to re-

*Johnson's program*

gain their civil and political rights and to have their property, except for slaves, restored. Excluded were high Confederate officials and those with property worth over $20,000, who had to apply for individual pardons. Johnson announced that once a state had drafted a new constitution and elected state officers and members of Congress, he would revoke martial law and recognize the new state government. Suffrage was limited to white citizens who had taken the loyalty oath. This plan was similar to Lincoln's, though more lenient. Only informally did Johnson stipulate that the southern states were to renounce their ordinances of secession, repudiate the Confederate debt, and ratify the proposed Thirteenth Amendment abolishing slavery.

## The Failure of Johnson's Program

The southern delegates who met to construct new governments soon demonstrated that they were in no frame of mind to follow Johnson's recommendations. Several states merely repealed instead of repudiating their ordinances of secession, rejected the Thirteenth Amendment, or refused to repudiate the Confederate debt.

Andrew Johnson was a staunch Unionist, but his contentious personality and inflexibility soured his relationship with Congress.

Nor did any of the new governments allow African Americans any political rights or provide in any effective way for black education. In addition, each state passed a series of laws, often modeled on its old slave code, that applied only to African Americans. These "black codes" did give African Americans some rights that had not been granted to slaves. They legalized marriages from slavery and allowed black southerners to hold and sell property and to sue and be sued in state courts. Yet their primary intent was to keep African Americans as propertyless agricultural laborers with inferior legal rights. The new freedpeople could not serve on juries, testify against whites, or work as they pleased. Mississippi prohibited them from buying or renting farmland, and most states ominously provided that black people who were vagrants could be arrested and hired out to landowners. Many northerners were incensed by the restrictive black codes, which violated their conception of freedom.

*Black codes*

Southern voters under Johnson's plan also defiantly elected prominent Confederate military and political leaders to office. At this point, Johnson could have called for new elections or admitted that a different program of Reconstruction was needed. Instead he caved in. For all his harsh rhetoric, he shrank from the prospect of social upheaval, and as the lines of ex-Confederates waiting to see him lengthened, he began issuing special pardons almost as fast as they could be printed. Publicly Johnson put on a bold face, announcing that Reconstruction had been successfully completed. But many members of Congress were deeply alarmed, and the stage was set for a serious confrontation.

*Elections in the South*

### Johnson's Break with Congress

The new Congress was by no means of one mind. A small number of Democrats and a few conservative Republicans backed the president's program of immediate and unconditional restoration. At the other end of the spectrum, a larger group of Radical Republicans, led by Thaddeus Stevens, Charles Sumner, Benjamin Wade, and others, was bent on remaking southern society in the image of the North. Reconstruction must "revolutionize Southern institutions, habits, and manners," thundered Representative Stevens, ". . . or all our blood and treasure have been spent in vain."

As a minority, the Radicals needed the aid of the moderate Republicans, the largest bloc in Congress. Led by William Pitt Fessenden and Lyman Trumbull, the moderates hoped to avoid a clash with the president, and they had no desire to foster social revolution or promote racial equality in the South. But they wanted to keep Confederate leaders from reassuming power, and they were convinced that the former slaves needed federal protection. Otherwise, Trumbull declared, the freedpeople would "be tyrannized over, abused, and virtually reenslaved."

The central issue dividing Johnson and the Radicals was the place of African Americans in American society. Johnson accused his opponents of seeking "to Africanize the southern half of our country," while the Radicals championed civil and political rights for African Americans. The only way to maintain loyal governments and develop a Republican party in the South, Radicals argued, was to give black men the ballot. Moderates agreed that the new southern governments were too harsh toward African Americans, but they feared that too great an emphasis on black civil rights would alienate northern voters.

*Issue of black rights*

In December 1865, when southern representatives to Congress appeared in Washington, a majority in Congress voted to exclude them. Congress also appointed a joint committee, chaired by Senator Fessenden, to look into Reconstruction.

The growing split with the president became clearer when Congress passed a bill extending the life of the Freedmen's Bureau. Created in March 1865, the Bureau provided emergency food, clothing, and medical care to war refugees (including white southerners) and took charge of settling freedpeople on abandoned lands. The new bill gave the Bureau the added responsibilities of supervising special courts to resolve disputes involving freedpeople and establishing schools for black southerners. Although this bill passed with virtually unanimous Republican support, Johnson vetoed it.

Johnson also vetoed a civil rights bill designed to overturn the more flagrant provisions of the black codes. The law made African Americans citizens of the United States and granted them the right to own property, make contracts, and have access to courts as parties and witnesses. For most Republicans Johnson's action was the last straw, and in April 1866 Congress overrode his veto. Congress then approved a slightly revised Freedmen's Bureau bill in July and promptly overrode the president's veto. Johnson's refusal to compromise drove the moderates into the arms of the Radicals.

*Johnson's vetoes*

## The Fourteenth Amendment

To prevent unrepentant Confederates from taking over the reconstructed state governments and denying African Americans basic freedoms, the Joint Committee on Reconstruction proposed an amendment to the Constitution, which passed both houses of Congress with the necessary two-thirds vote in June 1866.

The amendment guaranteed repayment of the national war debt and prohibited repayment of the Confederate debt. To counteract the president's whole-

*Provisions of the amendment*

sale pardons, it disqualified prominent Confederates from holding office and provided that only Congress by a two-thirds vote could remove this penalty. Because moderates balked at giving the vote to African Americans, the amendment merely gave Congress the right to reduce the representation of any state that did not have impartial male suffrage. The practical effect of this provision, which Radicals labeled a "swindle," was to allow northern states to retain white suffrage, since unlike southern states they had few African Americans in their populations and thus would not be penalized.

The amendment's most important provision, Section 1, defined an American citizen as anyone born in the United States or naturalized, thereby automatically making African Americans citizens. Section 1 also prohibited states from abridging "the privileges or immunities" of citizens, depriving "any person of life, liberty, or property, without due process of law," or denying "any person . . . equal protection of the laws." The framers of the amendment probably intended to prohibit laws that applied to one race only, such as the black codes, or that made certain acts felonies when committed by black but not white people, or that decreed different penalties for the same crime when committed by white and black lawbreakers. The framers probably did not intend to prevent segregation (the legal separation of the races) in schools and public places.

Johnson denounced the proposed amendment and urged southern states not to ratify it. Ironically, of the seceded states only the president's own state ratified the amendment, and Congress readmitted Tennessee with no further restrictions. The telegram sent to Congress by a longtime foe of Johnson officially announcing Tennessee's approval ended, "Give my respects to the dead dog in the White House."

## The Elections of 1866

When Congress blocked his policies, Johnson undertook a speaking tour of the East and Midwest in the fall of 1866 to drum up popular support. But Johnson found it difficult to convince northern audiences that white southerners were fully repentant. Only months earlier white mobs in Memphis and New Orleans had attacked black residents and killed nearly 100 in two major race riots. "The negroes now know, to their sorrow, that it is best not to arouse the fury of the white man," boasted one Memphis newspaper. When the president encountered hostile audiences during his northern campaign, he only made matters worse by trading insults and proclaiming that the Radicals were traitors.

Not to be outdone, the Radicals vilified Johnson as a traitor aiming to turn the country over to former rebels. Resorting to the tactic of "waving the bloody shirt," they appealed to voters by reviving bitter memories of the war. In a classic example of such rhetoric, Governor Oliver Morton of Indiana proclaimed that "every bounty jumper, every deserter, every sneak who ran away from the draft" was a Democrat; every "New York rioter in 1863 who burned up little children in colored asylums called himself a Democrat. In short, the Democratic party may be described as a common sewer. . . ."

Voters soundly repudiated Johnson, as the Republicans won more than a two-thirds majority in both houses of Congress. The Radicals had reached the height of their power, propelled by genuine alarm among northerners that Johnson's policies would lose the fruits of the Union's victory. Johnson was a president virtually without a party.

*Repudiation of Johnson*

## CONGRESSIONAL RECONSTRUCTION

With a clear mandate in hand, congressional Republicans passed their own program of Reconstruction, beginning with the first Reconstruction Act in March 1867. Like all later pieces of Reconstruction legislation, it was repassed over Johnson's veto.

Placing the 10 unreconstructed states under military commanders, the act provided that in enrolling voters, officials were to include black adult males but not former Confederates who were barred from holding office under the Fourteenth Amendment. Delegates to the state conventions were to frame constitutions that provided for black suffrage and disqualified prominent ex-Confederates from office. The first state legislatures to meet under the new constitution were required to ratify the Fourteenth Amendment. Once these steps were completed and Congress approved the new state constitution, a state could send representatives to Congress.

White southerners found these requirements so obnoxious that officials took no steps to register voters. Congress then enacted a second Reconstruction Act, also in March, ordering the local military commanders to put the machinery of Reconstruction into motion. Johnson's efforts to limit the power of military commanders produced a third act, passed in July, that upheld their superiority in all matters. When elections were held to ratify the new state constitutions, white southerners boycotted them in sufficient numbers to prevent a majority of voters from participating. Undaunted, Congress passed the fourth Reconstruction Act (March 1868), which required ratification of the constitution by only a majority of those voting rather than those who were registered.

*Resistance of white southerners*

By June 1868 Congress had readmitted the representatives of seven states. Texas, Virginia, and Mississippi did not complete the process until 1869. Georgia finally followed in 1870.

### The Land Issue

While the political process of Reconstruction proceeded, Congress debated whether land should be given to former slaves to foster economic independence. At a meeting with Secretary of War Edwin Stanton near the end of the war,

African American leaders declared, "The way we can best take care of ourselves is to have land, and till it by our own labor." The Second Confiscation Act of 1862 had authorized the government to seize and sell the property of supporters of the rebellion. In June 1866, however, President Johnson ruled that confiscation laws applied only to wartime.

For over a year Congress debated land confiscation off and on, but in the end it rejected all proposals to give land to former slaves. Even some Radicals were opposed. Given Americans' strong belief in self-reliance, little sympathy existed for the idea that government should support any group. In addition, land redistribution represented an attack on property rights, another cherished American value. "A division of rich men's lands amongst the landless," argued the *Nation*, a Radical journal, "would give a shock to our whole social and political system from which it would hardly recover without the loss of liberty." By 1867 land reform was dead.

*Failure of land redistribution*

Few freedpeople acquired land after the war, a development that severely limited African Americans' economic independence and left them vulnerable to white coercion. It is doubtful, however, that this decision was the basic cause of the failure of Reconstruction. In the face of white hostility, African Americans probably would have been no more successful in protecting their property than they were in maintaining the right to vote.

## Impeachment

Throughout 1867 Congress routinely overrode Johnson's vetoes, but the president had other ways of undercutting congressional Reconstruction. He interpreted the new laws as narrowly as possible and removed military commanders who vigorously enforced them. Congress responded by restricting his power to issue orders to military commanders in the South. It also passed the Tenure of Office Act, which forbade Johnson from removing any member of the cabinet without the Senate's consent. The intention of this law was to prevent him from firing Secretary of War Edwin Stanton, the only remaining Radical in the cabinet.

*Tenure of Office Act*

When Johnson tried to dismiss Stanton in February 1868, the House of Representatives angrily approved articles of impeachment. The articles focused on the violation of the Tenure of Office Act, but the charge with the most substance was that Johnson had conspired to systematically obstruct Reconstruction legislation. In the trial before the Senate, his lawyers argued that a president could be impeached only for an indictable crime, which Johnson clearly had not committed. The Radicals countered that impeachment applied to political offenses and not merely criminal acts. In May 1868 the Senate voted 36 to 19 to convict, one vote short of the two-thirds majority needed. The seven Republicans who joined the Democrats in voting for acquittal were uneasy about using impeachment as a political weapon.

*Johnson's acquittal*

## COUNTERPOINT *Should Johnson Have Been Removed from Office?*

For the first half of the twentieth century, most historians viewed Reconstruction as an undertaking that was tragically flawed at best or vindictive and misconceived at worst. Since 1960, however, historians increasingly have found much to praise in the experiment of Reconstruction and much to condemn in Andrew Johnson's leadership. (It is no coincidence that this reevaluation gained momentum just as the civil rights movement was forcing Americans to rethink attitiudes about segregation, racism, and equality.)

Controversy persists, however, over the issue of whether congressional Republicans were wise to pursue impeachment. Some historians point out that when the Constitution was drafted, James Madison argued that impeachment should apply to political misdeeds as well as crimes. Johnson, after all, had not been elected president in his own right. Voters in the 1866 congressional elections had rejected his clumsy attempts to gain support. Furthermore, as president he had taken an oath to uphold the laws of the nation. Yet time after time Johnson interpreted those laws as narrowly as possible, refusing to enforce them in a manner that Congress clearly intended. When Congress voted to not convict the president, these historians argue, it lessened the threat that impeachment would ever be used. Yet that was one of the legislative branch's most important weapons to control presidential abuse of power.

Other historians, while not sympathetic to Johnson's policies, believe that his acquittal was fortunate. The Constitution states only that a president may be removed for "Treason, Bribery, or other high Crimes and Misdemeanors." Johnson's lawyers ably argued that whatever his "misdeeds" in the eyes of Congress, he had not comitted "high Crimes." Historians who sympathize with that view argue that a conviction would have upset the constitutional doctrine of separation of powers. Removing Johnson from office would have seriously weakened the presidency, placed too much power in the hands of Congress, and provided a dangerous precedent for the future. The best course, they conclude, was the one Congress finally followed: to let Johnson finish his term as an ineffective president.

## RECONSTRUCTION IN THE SOUTH

The waning power of the Radicals in Congress, evident in the failure to remove Johnson, meant that the success or failure of Reconstruction increasingly hinged on developments in the southern states themselves. Power in these states rested with the new Republican parties, representing a coalition of black and white southerners and transplanted northerners.

## Black Officeholding

Almost from the beginning of Reconstruction, African Americans had lobbied for the right to vote. After they received the franchise, black men constituted as much as 80 percent of the Republican voters in the South. They steadfastly opposed the Democratic party with its appeal to white supremacy. As one Tennessee Republican explained, "The blacks know that many conservatives [Democrats] hope to reduce them again to some form of peonage. Under the impulse of this fear they will roll up their whole strength and will go entirely for the Republican candidate whoever he may be."

Throughout Reconstruction, African Americans never held office in proportion to their voting strength. No African American was ever elected governor, and only in South Carolina, where more than 60 percent of the population was black, did they control even one house of the legislature. During Reconstruction between 15 and 20 percent of the state officers and 6 percent of members of Congress (2 senators and 15 representatives) were black. Only in South Carolina did black officeholders approach their proportion of the population.

Those who held office came from the top levels of African American society. Among state and federal officeholders, perhaps four-fifths were literate, and over a quarter had been free before the war, both marks of distinction in the black community. Their occupations also set them apart: two-fifths were professionals (mostly clergy), and of the third who were farmers, nearly all owned land. In their political and social values, African American leaders were more conservative than the rural black population, and they showed little interest in land reform.

*Black political leadership*

## White Republicans in the South

Black citizens were a majority of the voters only in South Carolina, Mississippi, and Louisiana. Thus in most of the South the Republican party had to secure white votes to stay in power. Opponents scornfully labeled white southerners who allied with the Republican party scalawags, yet an estimated

*Scalawags*

A black politician addresses former slaves at a political meeting in the South during the 1868 presidential campaign. Although only men could vote, black women are also in the audience.

quarter of white southerners at one time voted Republican. They were primarily Unionists from the upland counties and hill areas who were largely yeoman farmers. Such voters were attracted by Republican promises to rebuild the South, restore prosperity, create public schools, and open isolated areas to the market with railroads.

The other group of white Republicans in the South were known as carpet-baggers. Originally from the North, they allegedly had arrived with all their

*Carpetbaggers* worldly possessions stuffed in a carpetbag, ready to loot and plunder the defeated South. Some did, certainly, but northerners moved south for a variety of reasons. Though carpetbaggers made up only a small percentage of Republican voters, they controlled almost a third of the offices. More than half of all southern Republican governors and nearly half of Republican members of Congress were originally northerners.

The Republican party in the South had difficulty maintaining unity. Scalawags were especially susceptible to the race issue and social pressure. "Even my own kinspeople have turned the cold shoulder to me because I hold office under a Republican administration," testified a Mississippi white Republican. As black southerners pressed for greater recognition, white southerners increasingly defected to the Democrats. Carpetbaggers, by contrast, were less sensitive to race, although most felt that their black allies should be content with minor offices. The animosity between scalawags and carpetbaggers, which grew out of their rivalry for party honors, was particularly intense.

## Reforms Under the New State Governments

The new southern state constitutions enacted several significant reforms. They devised fairer systems of legislative representation and made many previously ap-

*Reconstruction state constitutions* pointive offices elective. The Radical state governments also assumed some responsibility for social welfare and established the first statewide systems of public schools in the South. Although the Fourteenth Amendment prevented high Confederate officials from holding office, only Alabama and Arkansas temporarily forbade some ex-Confederates from voting.

All the new constitutions proclaimed the principle of equality and granted black adult males the right to vote. On social relations they were much more

*Race and social equality* cautious. No state outlawed segregation, and South Carolina and Louisiana were the only ones that required integration in public schools (a mandate that was almost universally ignored). Sensitive to status, mulattoes pushed for prohibition of social discrimination, but white Republicans refused to adopt such a radical policy.

## Economic Issues and Corruption

With the southern economy in ruins at the end of the war, problems of economic reconstruction were severe. The new Republican governments sought to encourage industrial development by providing subsidies, loans, and even temporary exemptions from taxes. These governments also largely rebuilt the southern railroad system, often offering lavish aid to railroad corporations. In the two decades after 1860, the region doubled its manufacturing establishments, yet the South steadily slipped further behind the booming industrial economy of the North.

The expansion of government services offered temptations for corruption. In many southern states, officials regularly received bribes and kickbacks for

*Corruption*

their award of railroad charters, franchises, and other contracts. By 1872 the debts of the 11 states of the Confederacy had increased $132 million, largely because of railroad grants and new social services such as schools. The tax rate grew as expenditures went up, so that by the 1870s it was four times the rate of 1860.

Corruption, however, was not only a southern problem: the decline in morality affected the entire nation. During these years, the Democratic Tweed Ring in New York City alone stole more money than all the Radical Republican governments in the South combined. Moreover, corruption in the South was hardly limited to Republicans. Many Democrats and white business leaders participated in these corrupt practices, both before and after the Radical governments were in power. Louisiana Governor Henry Warmoth, a carpetbagger, told a congressional committee, "Everybody is demoralizing down here. Corruption is the fashion."

Corruption in Radical governments undeniably existed, but southern Democrats exaggerated its extent for partisan purposes. They opposed honest Radical regimes just as bitterly as notoriously corrupt ones. In the eyes of most white southerners, the real crime of the Radical governments was that they allowed black citizens to hold some offices and tried to protect the civil rights of black Americans. Race was white conservatives' greatest weapon. And it would prove the most effective means to undermine Republican power in the South.

## BLACK ASPIRATIONS

Emancipation came to slaves in different ways and at different times. Betty Jones's grandmother was told about the Emancipation Proclamation by another slave while they were hoeing corn. Mary Anderson received the news from her master near the end of the war when Sherman's army invaded North Carolina. And for Louis Napoleon, emancipation arrived after the war when Union troops occupied Tallahassee, Florida. Whatever the timing, freedom meant a host of precious blessings to people who had been in bondage all their lives.

### Experiencing Freedom

The first impulse was to think of freedom as a contrast to slavery. Emancipation immediately released slaves from the most oppressive aspects of bondage—the whippings, the breakup of families, the sexual exploitation. Freedom also meant movement, the right to travel without a pass or white permission. Above all,

*Meaning of freedom*

freedom meant that African Americans' labor would be for their own benefit. One Arkansas freedman, who earned his first dollar working on a railroad, recalled that when he was paid, "I felt like the richest man in the world."

Freedom included finding a new place to work. Changing jobs was one concrete way to break the psychological ties of slavery. Even planters with reputations for kindness sometimes found that most of their former hands had departed. The cook who left a South Carolina family, even though they offered her higher wages than her new job did, explained, "I must go. If I stays here I'll never know I'm free."

Symbolically, freedom meant having a full name. African Americans now adopted last names, most commonly the name of the first master in the family's oral history as far back as it could be recalled. Most, on the other hand, retained their first name, especially if the name had been given to them by their parents (as most often had been the case). Whatever name they took, it was important to black Americans that they made the decision themselves.

## The Black Family

African Americans also sought to strengthen the family in freedom. Since slave marriages had not been recognized as legal, thousands of former slaves insisted on being married again by proper authorities, even though this was not required

*Upholding the family*

by law. Those who had been forcibly separated in slavery and later remarried confronted the dilemma of which spouse to take. Laura Spicer, whose husband had been sold away in slavery, received a series of wrenching letters from him after the war. He had thought her dead, had remarried, and had a new family. "You know it never was our wishes to be separated from each other, and it never was our fault. I had rather anything to had happened to me most than ever have been parted from you and the children," he wrote. "As I am, I do not know which I love best, you or Anna." Declining to return, he closed, "Laura, truly, I have got another wife, and I am very sorry. . . ."

As in white families, black husbands deemed themselves the head of the family and acted legally for their wives. They often insisted that their wives would not work in the fields as they had in slavery. "The [black] women say they never mean to do any more outdoor work," one planter reported, "that white men support their wives and they mean that their husbands shall support them." In negotiating contracts, a father also demanded the right to control his children and their labor. All these changes were designed to insulate the black family from white control.

## The Schoolhouse and the Church

In freedom, the schoolhouse and the black church became essential institutions in the black community. "My Lord, Ma'am, what a great thing learning is!" a

*Black education*

South Carolina freedman told a northern teacher. "White folks can do what they likes, for they know so much more than we." At first, northern churches and missionaries, working with the Freedmen's

Bureau, set up black schools in the South. Tuition at these schools represented 10 percent or more of a laborer's monthly wages, yet these schools were full. Eventually, states established public school systems, which by 1867 enrolled 40 percent of African American children.

Black adults, who often attended night classes, had good reasons for seeking literacy. They wanted to be able to read the Bible, to defend their newly gained civil and political rights, and to protect themselves from being cheated. Both races saw that education would undermine the old servility that slavery had fostered.

The teachers in the Freedmen's Bureau schools were primarily northern middle-class white women sent south by northern missionary societies. "I feel that

*Teachers in black schools*

it is a precious privilege," Esther Douglass wrote, "to be allowed to do something for these poor people." Many saw themselves as peacetime soldiers, struggling to make emancipation a reality. Indeed, hostile white southerners sometimes destroyed black schools and threatened and even murdered white teachers. Then there were the everyday challenges: low pay, dilapidated buildings, insufficient books, classes of 100 or more children, and irregular attendance. Meanwhile, the Freedmen's Bureau undertook to train black teachers, and by 1869 a majority of the teachers in these schools were black.

Most slaves had attended white churches or services supervised by whites. Once free, African Americans quickly established their own congregations led by

*Independent black churches*

black preachers. Mostly Methodist and Baptist, black churches were the only major organizations in the African American community they controlled. A white missionary reported that "the Ebony preacher who promises perfect independence from White control and direction carried the colored heart at once." Just as in slavery, religion offered African Americans a place of refuge in a hostile white world and provided them with hope, comfort, and a means of self-identification.

## New Working Conditions

As a largely propertyless class, blacks in the postwar South had no choice but to work for white landowners. Except for paying wages, whites wanted to retain the old system of labor, including close supervision, gang labor, and physical punishment. Determined to remove all emblems of servitude, African Americans refused to work under these conditions, and they demanded time off to devote to their own interests. Because of shorter hours and the withdrawal of children and women from the fields, blacks' output declined by an estimated 35 percent in freedom. They also refused to live in the old slave quarters located near the master's house and instead erected cabins on distant parts of the plantation. Wages initially were $5 or $6 a month plus provisions and a cabin; by 1867, they had risen to an average of $10 a month.

These changes eventually led to the rise of sharecropping. Under this arrangement African American families farmed separate plots of land and then

*Sharecropping*

at the end of the year divided the crop, normally on an equal basis, with the white landowner. Sharecropping had higher status

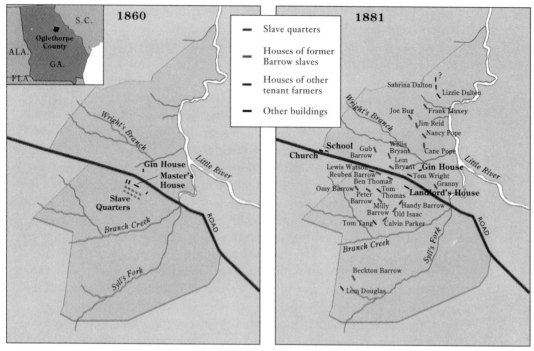

A GEORGIA PLANTATION AFTER THE WAR   After emancipation, sharecropping became
the dominant form of agricultural labor in the South. Black families no longer lived in
the old slave quarters but dispersed themselves to separate plots of land that they
farmed themselves. At the end of the year each sharecropper turned over part
of the crop to the white landowner.

and offered greater personal freedom than being a wage laborer. "I am not
working for wages," one black farmer declared in defending his right to leave
the plantation at will, "but am part owner of the crop and as I have all the rights
that you or any other man has. . . ." Although black per capita agricultural income increased 40 percent in freedom, sharecropping was a harshly exploitative
system in which black families often sank into perpetual debt.

## The Freedmen's Bureau

The task of supervising the transition from slavery to freedom on southern
plantations fell to the Freedmen's Bureau, a unique experiment in social policy
supported by the federal government. Assigned the task of protecting freedpeople's economic rights, approximately 550 local agents regulated working
conditions in southern agriculture after the war. The racial attitudes of Bureau
agents varied widely, as did their commitment and competence. Then, too, they
had to depend on the army to enforce their decisions.

Most agents required written contracts between white planters and black laborers, specifying not only wages but also the conditions of employment.

*Bureau's mixed record*

Although agents sometimes intervened to protect freedpeople from unfair treatment, they also provided important help to planters. They insisted that black laborers not leave at harvest time, they arrested those who violated their contracts or refused to sign new ones at the beginning of the year, and they preached the gospel of hard work and the need to be orderly and respectful. Given such attitudes, freedpeople increasingly complained that Bureau agents were mere tools of the planter class. One observer reported, "Doing justice seems to mean seeing that the blacks don't break contracts and compelling them to submit cheerfully."

The primary means of enforcing working conditions were the Freedmen's Courts, which Congress created in 1866 in order to avoid the discrimination African Americans received in state courts. These new courts functioned as military tribunals, and often the agent was the entire court. The sympathy black laborers received varied from state to state. In 1867 one agent summarized the Bureau's experience with the labor contract system: "It has succeeded in making the freedman work and in rendering labor secure and stable—but it has failed to secure to the Freedman his just dues or compensation."

Opposed to any permanent welfare agency, Congress in 1869 decided to shut down the Bureau, and by 1872 it had gone out of business. Despite its mixed record, it was the most effective agency in protecting blacks' civil and political rights. Its disbanding signaled the beginning of the northern retreat from Reconstruction.

## Planters and a New Way of Life

Planters and other white southerners faced emancipation with dread. "All the traditions and habits of both races had been suddenly overthrown," a Tennessee planter recalled, "and neither knew just what to do, or how to accommodate themselves to the new situation."

The old ideal of a paternalistic planter, which required a facade of black subservience and affection, gave way to an emphasis on strictly economic relationships. When two black laborers falsely accused her of trickery and hauled her into court, Mary Jones, a Georgia slaveholder before the war, told her assembled employees that she had previously "considered them friends and treated them as such but now they were only laborers under contract, and only the law would rule between us." Only with time did planters develop new norms to judge black behavior. What in 1865 had seemed insolence was viewed by the 1870s as the normal attitude of freedom.

Slavery had been a complex institution that welded black and white southerners together in intimate relationships. After the war, however, planters increasingly embraced the ideology of segregation. Since emancipation significantly reduced the social distance between the races, white southerners sought psychological separation and kept dealings with African Americans to a minimum. By the time Reconstruction ended, white planters had developed a new way of life based on the institutions of sharecropping and segregation and undergirded by a militant white supremacy.

*Planters' new values*

While most planters kept their land, they did not regain the economic prosperity of the prewar years. Cotton prices began a long decline, and southern per capita income suffered as a result. By 1880 the value of southern farms had slid 33 percent below the level of 1860.

## THE ABANDONMENT OF RECONSTRUCTION

On Christmas Day 1875 a white acquaintance approached Charles Caldwell in Clinton, Mississippi, and invited him to have a drink. A former slave, Caldwell was a state senator and the leader of the Republican party in Hinds County. But the black leader's fearlessness made him a marked man. Only two months earlier, Caldwell had fled the county to escape an armed white mob. Despite threats against him, he had returned home to vote in the November state election. Now, as Caldwell and his "friend" raised their glasses in a holiday toast, a gunshot exploded through the window and Caldwell collapsed, mortally wounded. He was taken outside, where his assassins riddled his body with bullets. He died alone in the street.

Charles Caldwell shared the fate of a number of black Republican leaders in the South during Reconstruction. Resorting to violence and terror, southern whites challenged the commitment of the federal government to sustain Reconstruction. But following Johnson's acquittal, the Radical's influence waned, and the Republican party was increasingly drained of its crusading idealism. Ulysses S. Grant was hardly the cause of this change, but he certainly came to symbolize it.

### The Election of Grant

In 1868 Republicans nominated Grant for president. Although he was elected, Republicans were shocked that his popular margin was only 300,000 votes and that, with an estimated 450,000 black Republican votes cast in the South, a majority of whites had voted Democratic. The 1868 election helped convince Republican leaders that an amendment securing black suffrage throughout the nation was necessary.

In February 1869 Congress sent the Fifteenth Amendment to the states for ratification. It forbade any state from denying the right to vote on grounds of race, color, or previous condition of servitude. It did not forbid literacy and property requirements, as some Radicals wanted, because the moderates feared that only a conservative version could be ratified. As a result, the final amendment left loopholes that eventually allowed southern states to disfranchise African Americans. Furthermore, advocates of women's suffrage like Lucy Stone and Susan B. Anthony were bitterly disappointed when Congress refused to prohibit voting discrimination on the basis of sex as well as race. The amendment was ratified in March 1870, aided by the votes of the four southern states that had not completed the process of Reconstruction and thus were also required to endorse this amendment before being readmitted to Congress.

*Fifteenth Amendment ratified*

## The Grant Administration

Ulysses Grant was ill at ease with the political process: his simple, quiet manner, while superb for commanding armies, did not serve him as well in public life, and his well-known resolution withered when he was uncertain of his goal.

A series of scandals wracked Grant's presidency, so much so that "Grantism" soon became a code word in American politics for corruption, cronyism, and venality. Although Grant did not profit personally, he remained loyal to his friends and displayed little zeal to root out wrongdoing. James W. Grimes, one of the party's founders, denounced the Republican party under Grant as "the most corrupt and debauched political party that has ever existed."

*Corruption under Grant*

Nor was Congress immune from the lowered tone of public life. In such a climate ruthless state machines, led by men who favored the status quo, came to dominate the party. Office and power became ends in themselves, and party leaders worked in close cooperation with northern industrial interests.

As corruption in both the North and the South worsened, reformers became more interested in cleaning up government than in protecting black rights. Congress in 1872 passed an amnesty act, removing the restrictions of the Fourteenth Amendment on officeholding, except for about 200 to 300 ex-Confederate leaders. That same year liberal Republicans broke with the Republican party and nominated for president Horace Greeley, the editor of the New York *Tribune*. A one-time Radical, Greeley had become disillusioned with Reconstruction and urged a restoration of

*Liberal Republican movement*

Grant swings from a trapeze while supporting a number of associates accused of corruption. While not personally involved in the scandals during his administration, Grant was reluctant to dismiss from office supporters accused of wrongdoing.

home rule in the South as well as adoption of civil service reform. Democrats decided to back the Liberal Republican ticket. The Republicans renominated Grant, who, despite the defection of a number of prominent Radicals, won an easy victory with 56 percent of the popular vote.

## Growing Northern Disillusionment

During Grant's second term, Congress passed the Civil Rights Act of 1875, the last major piece of Reconstruction legislation. This law prohibited racial discrimination in public accommodations, transportation, places of amusement, and juries. At the same time, Congress rejected a ban on segregation in public schools, which was almost universally practiced in the North as well as the South. The federal government made little attempt to enforce the law, however, and in 1883 the Supreme Court struck down its provisions, except the one relating to juries.

*Civil Rights Act of 1875*

Despite passage of the Civil Rights Act, many northerners were growing disillusioned with Reconstruction. They were repelled by the corruption of the southern governments, they were tired of the violence and disorder in the South, and they had little faith in black Americans. William Dodge, a wealthy New York capitalist and an influential Republican, wrote in 1875 that the South could never develop its resources "till confidence in her state governments can be restored, and this will never be done by federal bayonets." It had been a mistake, he went on, to make black southerners feel "that the United States government was their special friend, rather than those . . . among whom they must live and for whom they must work. We have tried this long enough," he concluded. "Now let the South alone."

As the agony of the war became more distant, the Panic of 1873, which precipitated a severe depression that lasted four years, diverted public attention from Reconstruction to economic issues. Battered by the panic and the corruption issue, the Republicans lost a shocking 77 seats in Congress in the 1874 elections, and along with them control of the House of Representatives for the first time since 1861.

*Depression and Democratic resurgence*

"The truth is our people are tired out with the worn out cry of 'Southern outrages'!!" one Republican concluded. "Hard times and heavy taxes make them wish the 'ever lasting nigger' were in hell or Africa." Republicans spoke more and more about cutting loose the unpopular southern governments.

## The Triumph of White Supremacy

As northern commitment to Reconstruction waned, southern Democrats set out to overthrow the remaining Radical governments. Already white Republicans in the South felt heavy pressure to desert their party. In Mississippi one party member justified his decision to leave on the grounds that otherwise he would have "to live a life of social isolation" and his children would have no future.

To poor white southerners who lacked social standing, the Democratic appeal to racial solidarity offered great comfort. Explained one, "I may be poor

*Racism*

and my manners may be crude, but . . . because I am a white man, I have a right to be treated with respect by Negroes. . . . no Negro is ever going to forget that he is not a white man." The large landowners and other wealthy groups that led southern Democrats objected less to black southerners voting, since they were confident that if outside influences were removed, they could control the black vote.

Democrats also resorted to economic pressure to undermine Republican power. In heavily black counties, newspapers published the names of black res-

*Terror and violence*

idents who cast Republican ballots and urged planters to discharge them. But terror and violence provided the most effective means to overthrow the radical regimes. A number of paramilitary organizations broke up Republican meetings, terrorized white and black Republicans, assassinated Republican leaders, and prevented black citizens from voting. The most famous of these organizations was the Ku Klux Klan, which with similar groups functioned as an unofficial arm of the Democratic party.

What became known as the Mississippi Plan was inaugurated in 1875, when Democrats decided to use as much violence as necessary to carry the state elec-

*Mississippi Plan*

tion. Several local papers trumpeted, "Carry the election peaceably if we can, forcibly if we must." Recognizing that northern public opinion had grown sick of repeated federal intervention in southern elections, the Grant administration rejected the request of Republican Governor Adelbert Ames for troops to stop the violence. Bolstered by terrorism, the Democrats swept the election in Mississippi. Violence and intimidation prevented as many as 60,000 black and white Republicans from voting, converting the normal Republican majority into a Democratic majority of 30,000. Mississippi had been "redeemed."

Two Ku Klux Klan members pose in full regalia. Violence played a major role in overthrowing the Radical governments in the South.

### The Disputed Election of 1876

With Republicans on the defensive across the nation, the 1876 presidential election was crucial to the final overthrow of Reconstruction. The Republicans nominated Ohio Governor Rutherford B. Hayes to oppose Samuel Tilden of New York. Once again, violence prevented an estimated quarter of a million Republican votes from being cast in the South. Tilden had a clear majority of 250,000 in the popular vote, but the outcome in the Electoral College was in doubt because both parties claimed South Carolina, Florida, and Louisiana, the only reconstructed states still in Republican hands.

To arbitrate the disputed returns, Congress established a 15-member electoral commission. By a straight party vote of 8 to 7, the commission awarded the disputed electoral votes—and the presidency—to Hayes.

When angry Democrats threatened a filibuster to prevent the electoral votes from being counted, key Republicans met with southern Democrats and reached an informal understanding, later known as the Compromise of 1877. Hayes's supporters agreed to withdraw federal troops from the South and not oppose the new Democratic state

*Compromise of 1877*

---

E Y E W I T N E S S   T O   H I S T O R Y

### *The Mississippi Plan in Action*

**S**eeing that nothing but intimidation would enable them [the Democrats] to carry the election they resorted to it in every possible way, and the republicans at once found themselves in the midst of a perfect organized armed opposition that embraced the entire democratic party. . . . At Sulphur Springs they came very near precipitating a bloody riot by beating colored men over the heads with pistols. . . . The republicans . . . revoked the balance of their appointments running up to the election, and did not attempt to hold any more meetings in the Co[unty]. . . . On the night before the election armed bodies of men visited almost every neighborhood in the county, threatening death to all who voted the "radical" ticket. . . .

On the morning of the election in Aberdeen . . . the White-Liners took possession of the polls. . . . The colored men who had gathered . . . to vote were told if they did not leave the town within five minutes that the last man would be shot dead in his tracks, and that not a man could vote that day unless he voted the democratic ticket. . . . The cannon was placed in position bearing on the large crowd, . . . when the whole crowd broke & run in confusion, then the infantry & cavalry had no trouble in driving everything from town; and there are over 1,300 men in this county . . . who will swear that they were driven from the polls & could not vote.

James W. Lee to Adelbert Ames, Aberdeen, Miss., February 7, 1876, 44th Cong., 1st Sess., Senate Report 527, v. 2, pp. 67–68.

governments. For their part, southern Democrats dropped their opposition to Hayes's election and pledged to respect African Americans' rights.

Without federal support, the last Republican governments collapsed, and Democrats took control of the remaining states of the Confederacy. By 1877, the entire South was in the hands of the Redeemers, as they called themselves. Reconstruction and Republican rule had come to an end.

### Racism and the Failure of Reconstruction

Reconstruction failed for a multitude of reasons. The reforming impulse that had created the Republican party in the 1850s had been battered and worn down by the war. The new materialism of industrial America inspired a jaded cynicism in many Americans. In the South, African American voters and leaders inevitably lacked a certain amount of education and experience; elsewhere, Republicans were divided over policies and options.

Yet beyond these obstacles, the sad fact remains that the ideals of Reconstruction were most clearly defeated by a deep-seated racism that permeated American life. Racism stimulated white southern resistance, undercut northern support for black rights, and eventually made northerners willing to write off Reconstruction, and with it the welfare of African Americans. While Congress might pass a constitutional amendment abolishing slavery, it could not overturn at a stroke the social habits of two centuries.

Certainly the political equations of power, in the long term, had been changed. The North had secured the power to dominate the economic and political destiny of the nation. With the overthrow of Reconstruction, the white South had won back some of the power it had lost in 1865—but not all. Even with white supremacy triumphant, African Americans did not return to the social position they had occupied before the war. They were no longer slaves, and black southerners who walked dusty roads in search of family members, sent their children to school, or worshiped in churches they controlled knew what a momentous change this was. Even under the exploitative sharecropping system, black income rose significantly in freedom. Then, too, the guarantees of "equal protection" and "due process of law" had been written into the Constitution and would be available for later generations to use in championing once again the Radicals' goal of racial equality.

But this was a struggle left to future reformers. For the time being, the clear trend was away from change or hope—especially for former slaves like Benjamin

*An end to the Davis Bend experiment*

Montgomery and his sons, the owners of the old Davis plantations in Mississippi. In the 1870s bad crops, lower cotton prices, and falling land values undermined the Montgomerys' financial position, and in 1875 Jefferson Davis sued to have the sale of Brierfield invalidated.

A lower court ruled against Davis, since he had never received legal title to the plantation. Davis appealed to the state supreme court, which, following the overthrow of Mississippi's Radical government, had a white conservative majority. In a politically motivated decision, the court awarded Brierfield to Davis in 1878, and the Montgomerys lost Hurricane as well. The final outcome was not without bitter irony. In applying for restoration of his property after the war, Joseph Davis had convinced skeptical federal officials that he—and not his younger brother—held legal title to Brierfield. Had they decided instead that the plantation belonged to Jefferson Davis, it would have been confiscated.

But the waning days of Reconstruction were times filled with such ironies: of governments "redeemed" by violence, of Fourteenth Amendment rights designed to protect black people being used by conservative courts to protect giant corporations, of reformers taking up other causes. Disowned by its northern supporters and unmourned by public opinion, Reconstruction was over.

SIGNIFICANT EVENTS

| | |
|---|---|
| 1863 | Lincoln outlines Reconstruction program |
| 1864 | Lincoln vetoes Wade–Davis bill; Louisiana, Arkansas, and Tennessee establish governments under Lincoln's plan |
| 1865 | Freedmen's Bureau established; Johnson becomes president; presidential Reconstruction completed; Congress excludes representatives of Johnson's governments; Thirteenth Amendment ratified; Joint Committee on Reconstruction established |
| 1865–1866 | Black codes enacted |
| 1866 | Civil Rights bill passed over Johnson's veto; Memphis and New Orleans riots; Fourteenth Amendment passes Congress; Freedmen's Bureau extended; Ku Klux Klan organized; Tennessee readmitted to Congress; Republicans win decisive victory in congressional elections |
| 1867 | Congressional Reconstruction enacted; Tenure of Office Act |
| 1867–1868 | Constitutional conventions in the South; blacks vote in southern elections |
| 1868 | Johnson impeached but acquitted; Fourteenth Amendment ratified; Grant elected president |
| 1869 | Fifteenth Amendment passes Congress |
| 1870 | Last southern states readmitted to Congress; Fifteenth Amendment ratified |
| 1872 | General Amnesty Act; Freedmen's Bureau dismantled; Liberal Republican revolt |
| 1873–1877 | Panic and depression |
| 1874 | Democrats win control of the House |
| 1875 | Civil Rights Act; Mississippi Plan |
| 1876 | Disputed Hayes–Tilden election |
| 1877 | Compromise of 1877; Hayes declared winner of electoral vote; last Republican governments in South fall |

## The United States in an Industrial Age

With some justice, the United States has been called a nation of immigrants. Looking back today, most Americans tend to view the "huddled masses" passing the Statue of Liberty as part of the stream of newcomers stretching back to the English Pilgrims, the French fur traders of Canada, and the Spanish friars of Old California. But the tide of immigration that swelled during the mid-nineteenth century was strikingly different.

Before 1820 most new arrivals in North and South America did not come voluntarily. Nearly 8 million Africans were brought to the Americas during those years, virtually all as slaves. That number was four to five times the number of Europeans who came during the same period. In contrast, between 1820 and 1920 nearly 30 million free immigrants arrived from Europe.

Nor was this new flood directed only toward America. At least as many Europeans settled in other regions of Europe or the world. From Eastern Europe millions followed the Trans-Siberian Railway (completed in 1905) into Asiatic Russia. The Canadian prairie provinces of Manitoba and Saskatchewan competed for homesteaders with Montana and the Dakotas. Before 1900 two out of three emigrating Italians booked passage not for the United States but for Brazil and Argentina.

This broad movement could not have taken place without a global network of communication, markets, and transportation. By midcentury, urbanization and industrialization were well under way in both America and Europe. The British, who led in revolutionizing industry, also discovered its harsh side effects. Urban factory workers in Britain jammed into dark, dingy row houses built with few windows along streets and alleys where open sewers flowed with garbage. Spurred by a deadly cholera epidemic in 1848, social reformer Edwin Chadwick led a campaign to install water and sewer systems throughout major cities.

Other urban planners admired the radical renovation of Paris begun in the 1850s by Baron Georges Haussmann. Haussmann's workers tore down the city's medieval fortress walls, widened major streets into boulevards, and set aside land for pleasant green parks. American innovations inspired Europeans to adopt horse-drawn streetcars and, later, electric trolleys.

As hubs of the new industrial networks, cities needed efficient links to raw materials. Much of the late nineteenth century can be seen as a scramble of Western nations for those natural resources. Miners combed the hills of California for gold in 1849, as they did two years later in Victoria, Australia. In Canada, Argentina, Australia, and New Zealand, farmers and cattle ranchers moved steadily toward larger commercial operations. All these enterprises extracted value from previously untapped natural resources.

The end result of the scramble was the age of imperialism, as the European powers sought to dominate newly acquired colonies in Africa and Asia. The United States joined the rush somewhat late, in part because it was still extracting raw materials from its own "colonial" regions, the booming West and the defeated South.

European imperialists sometimes justified their rule over nonwhite races as a noble sacrifice made on behalf of their subject peoples—"the White Man's Burden," British poet Rudyard Kipling called it. But the burdens were far greater for the coolie laborers of Kipling's India, who died by the thousands clearing jungles for tea plantations. Imperialism's costs were also harsh for black miners laboring in South Africa and for Chinese workers in Australia and the United States who found themselves excluded and segregated after both gold rushes. A similar racism thwarted Southern black sharecroppers in the United States and made it easier for successive waves of prospectors, cowhands, and sodbusters to drive American Indians off their lands.

The social strains arising out of such changes forced political systems to adjust as well. In the United States both the Populists and the Progressives called on the government to take a more active role in managing the excesses of the new industrial order. In Europe, industrializing nations went further, passing social legislation that included the first social security systems and health insurance. In the end, however, the political system was unable to manage the new global order of commerce and imperialism. With the coming of World War I, it was shaken to its roots.

# CHAPTER EIGHTEEN

# The New Industrial Order

It was so dark Robert Ferguson could not see his own feet. Inching along the railroad tracks, he suddenly pitched forward as the ground vanished beneath him. To his dismay, he found himself wedged between two railroad ties, his legs dangling in the air. Scrambling back to solid ground, he retreated to the railroad car, where he sat meekly until dawn.

Ferguson, a Scot visiting America in 1866, had been in Memphis only two days earlier, ready to take the "Great Southern Mail Route" east some 850 miles to Washington. Things had gone badly from the start. About 50 miles down the track, a broken river bridge had forced him to take a ferry and then spend 10 miles bumping along in a mule-drawn truck before learning that the rail line did not resume for another 40 miles. Disheartened, he had decided to return to Memphis to try again.

The train to Memphis had arrived six hours late, dawdled its way home, and then, three miles outside the city, derailed in the middle of the night. When a few passengers decided to hike the remaining distance into town, Ferguson had tagged along. It was then that he had fallen between the tracks. At dawn he discovered to his horror that the tracks led onto a flimsy, high river bridge. Ferguson had trouble managing the trestle even in daylight.

Before he finally reached Washington, Robert Ferguson faced six more days of difficult travel. One rail line would end, and passengers and freight would be forced to transfer to another because rail gauges—the width of the track—differed from line to line. Or a bridge would be out. Or there would be no bridge at all. Trains had no meals "on board"–or any sleeping cars. "It was certainly what the Americans would call 'hard travelling,'" Ferguson huffed; "—they do not make use of the word 'rough,' because roughness may be expected as a natural condition in a new country."

Less than 20 years later, rail passengers traveled in relative luxury. T. S. Hudson, another British tourist, launched a self-proclaimed "Scamper Through America" in 1882. It took him just 60 days to go from England to San Francisco and back. He crossed the continent on a ticket booked by a single agent in Boston. Such centralization would have been unthinkable in 1866 when, in any case, the transcontinental railroad was still three years from completion.

Hudson's trains had Pullman Palace cars with posh sleeping quarters, full meals, and installed air brakes. Bridges appeared where none had been before, including a "magnificent" span over the Mississippi at St. Louis. It had three arches of "five hundred feet each, approached by viaducts, and, on the western shore, also by a tunnel." Hudson also found himself in the midst of a communications revolution. Traveling across the plains, he was struck by the number of telephone poles along the route.

What made America in the 1880s so different from the 1860s was a new industrial order. The process of industrialization had begun at least three decades

*An industrial transformation*

before the Civil War. Small factories had produced light consumer goods like clothing, shoes, and furniture. They catered to local markets in an economy of farmers and merchants. After the 1850s the industrial economy matured, with larger factories, more machines, greater efficiency, and national markets.

The transformation, remarkable as it was, brought pain along with the progress. Virgin forests vanished from the Pacific Northwest, the hillsides of Pennsylvania and West Virginia were scarred by open-pit mines, and the rivers of the Northeast grew toxic with industrial wastes. In 1882, the year Hudson scampered by rail across America, an average of 675 people were killed on the job every week. Like most Americans, workers scrambled—sometimes literally—to adjust.

## THE DEVELOPMENT OF INDUSTRIAL SYSTEMS

The new industrial order can best be understood as a web of complex industrial systems. Look, for example, at the bridge across the Mississippi that Hudson so admired. When James B. Eads constructed his soaring arches in 1874, he needed steel, most likely made from iron ore mined in northern Michigan. Giant steam shovels scooped up the ore and loaded whole freight cars in a few strokes. A transportation system—railroads, boats, and other carriers—moved the ore to Pittsburgh, where the factory system furnished the labor and machinery to finish the steel. The capital to create such factories came itself from a system of finance, linking investment banks and stock markets to entrepreneurs in need of money. Only with a national network of industrial systems could the Eads bridge be built and a new age of industry arise.

E Y E W I T N E S S      T O      H I S T O R Y

## *An Englishman Visits Pittsburgh in 1898*

**P**ittsburgh is not an Eastern City. . . . A cloud of smoke hangs over it by day. The glow of scores of furnaces light[s] the riverbanks by night. It stands at the junction of two great rivers, the Monongahela which flows down today in a turbid yellowy stream, and the Allegheny which is blackish. They join at the nose of the city where Fort Duquesne stood. A hundred and fifty years ago the whole country was desolate except for the little French blockhouse at the river junction. Today the old block-house stands in a little green patch off a filthy slum-street. . . .

I spent today seeing the [steel] works where the Bessemer rails are turned out. On the other side of the river is Homestead where the great strike was and the Duquesne works, all three of them under Carnegie and Co. . . . All nations are jumbled up here, the poor living in tenement dens or wooden shanties thrown up or dumped down (better expression) with very little reference to roads or situation, whenever a new house is wanted. It is a most chaotic city, and as yet there is no public spirit or public consciousness to make the conditions healthy or decent. Carnegie has given libraries, a Park and organs to several dozen churches. Some of the other millionaires have done the same. Otherwise the town is chaos. . . . It is industrial greatness with all the worst industrial abuses on the grandest scale.

The class of manufacturer I have met is not pleasing. There is profound contempt and dislike of Unions and all their ways, much worse than in England. A certain De Armit was recommended to me to tell me about mining, being a great controller of pits and 'having fought the unions like the devil'. He was well-nigh drunk with whiskey at 5 in the afternoon at the best town club, and as coarse a fighting-cock as I have often seen. Not much chance of conciliation with such a man. His fierce competence was evident. But he was nothing but a selfish, violent money-maker. All the men I meet here are rough; but they are a good breed and shrewd and friendly. With their immense natural resources they will do great things. I absolutely trust them to evolve order out of their social disorder in time.

Charles Philips Trevelyan, April 15, 1898. *Letters from North America and the Pacific* (London: Chatto & Windus, 1969), pp. 31–33.

## Natural Resources and Industrial Technology

The earliest European settlers had marveled at the "merchantable commodities" of America, from the glittering silver mines of the Spanish empire to the continent's hardwood forests. What set the new industrial economy apart from that older America was the scale and efficiency of using resources. New technologies made it possible to employ natural riches in ways undreamed of only decades earlier.

Iron, for example, had been forged into steel swords as far back as the Middle Ages. In the 1850s, inventors in England and America discovered a cheaper way—called the Bessemer process—to convert large quantities of iron into steel. By the late 1870s, the price of steel had dropped by more than half. Steel was lighter than iron, could support 20 times as much weight, and lasted 20 years instead of 3. Steel tracks soon carried most rail traffic; steel girders replaced the old cast-iron frames; steel cables supported new suspension bridges.

*Bessemer process*

Industrial technology made some natural resources more valuable. New distilling methods transformed a thick, smelly liquid called petroleum into kerosene for lighting lamps, oil for lubricating machinery, and paraffin for making candles. Beginning in 1859, new drilling techniques began to tap vast pools of petroleum below the surface. About the same time, Frenchman Etienne Lenoir constructed the first practical internal combustion engine. After 1900, new vehicles like the gasoline-powered carriage turned the oil business into a major industry.

*Petroleum industry*

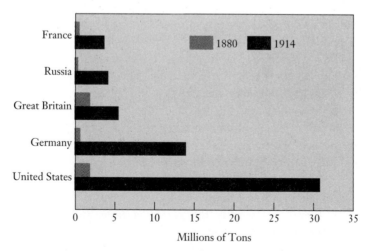

STEEL PRODUCTION, 1880 AND 1914 While steel production jumped in western industrial nations from 1880 to 1914, it skyrocketed in the United States because of rich resources, cheap labor, and aggressive management.

The environmental price of industrial technology soon became evident. Coal mining, logging, and the industrial wastes of factories produced only the most obvious environmental degradation. In California, as giant water cannons blasted away hillsides in search of gold, rock and gravel washed into rivers, raising their beds and threatening those downstream with floods. When engineers tried to cleanse the Chicago River by reversing its flow, so that it emptied into the Illinois River instead of Lake Michigan, they only succeeded in shifting pollution to rivers downstate. Some industrialists had greater success in limiting the damage. Meatpackers, for example, stretched their imaginations to use every conceivable part of the animals that came into their plants. Even blood was dried and sold as powder.

## Systematic Invention

Industrial technology rested on invention. For sheer inventiveness, the 40 years following the Civil War have rarely been matched in American history. Between 1790 and 1860, 36,000 patents had been registered with the government. Over the next three decades, the U.S. Patent Office granted more than half a million. The process of invention became systematized as small-scale inventors were replaced by orderly "invention factories"—forerunners of expensive research labs.

No one did more to bring system, order, and profitability to invention than Thomas Alva Edison. In 1868, at the age of 21, Edison went to work for a New

*Edison's contributions*

York brokerage house and promptly improved the design of the company's stock tickers. Granted a $40,000 bonus, he set himself up as an independent inventor. For the next five years, Edison patented a new invention almost every five months.

Edison was determined to bring system and order to the process of invention. Only then could breakthroughs come in a steady and profitable stream. He moved 15 of his workers to Menlo Park, New Jersey, where in 1876 he created an "invention factory." Like a manufacturer, Edison subdivided the work among gifted inventors, engineers, toolmakers, and others.

This orderly bureaucracy soon evolved into the Edison Electric Light Company. Its ambitious owner aimed at more than perfecting his new electric lightbulb. Edison wanted to create a unified electrical power system—central stations to generate electric current, wired to users, all powering millions of small bulbs in homes and businesses. To launch his enterprise, Edison won the backing of several large banking houses by lighting up the Wall Street district in 1882. By 1898 there were nearly 3000 power stations, lighting some 2 million bulbs across America. By then, electricity was also running trolley cars, subways, and factory machinery.

George Eastman revolutionized photography by making the consumer a part of his inventive system. In 1888 Eastman marketed the "Kodak" camera. The small black box weighed two pounds and contained a strip of celluloid film that replaced hundreds of pounds of photography equipment. After 100 snaps of the shutter, the owner simply sent the camera back to the factory and waited for the developed photos, along with a reloaded camera, to return by mail. "You press the button—we do the rest" was Eastman Kodak's apt slogan.

What united these innovations was the notion of rationalizing inventions—of making a systematic business out of them. By 1913, Westinghouse Electric, General Electric, U.S. Rubber Company, and other firms had set up research laboratories. And by the middle of the century research labs had spread beyond business to the federal government, universities, trade associations, and labor unions.

*The research laboratory*

## Transportation and Communication

Abundant resources and new inventions remained worthless to industry until they could be moved to processing plants, factories, and offices. With more than 3.5 million square miles of land in the United States, distance alone was daunting. Where 100 miles of railroad track would do for shipping goods in Germany and England, 1000 miles was necessary in America.

*The problem of scale*

An efficient internal transportation network tied the country into an emerging international system. By the 1870s railroads crisscrossed the country, and steam-powered ships (introduced before the Civil War) were pushing barges down rivers and carrying passengers and freight across the oceans. Between 1870 and 1900, the value of American exports tripled. Eventually the rail and water transportation systems fused. By 1900 railroad companies owned nearly all of the country's domestic steamship lines.

A thriving industrial nation also required effective communication. Information was a precious commodity, as essential as resources or technology to industry. In the early 1840s, it took newspapers as many as 10 days to reach Indiana from New York and 3 months to arrive by ship in San Francisco. In 1844 Samuel Morse succeeded in sending the first message over an electrical wire between cities. By 1861 the Western Union Company had strung 76,000 miles of telegraph lines across the country. If a bank collapsed in Chicago, bankers in Dallas knew of it that day. Railroads could keep traffic unsnarled through the dots and dashes of Morse's code. So useful to railroads was the telegraph that they allowed poles and wires to be set along their rights of way in exchange for free telegraphic service. By the turn of the century a million miles of telegraph wire handled some 63 million messages a year, not to mention those flashing across underwater cables to China, Japan, Africa, and South America.

*Telegraph*

A second innovation in communication, the telephone, vastly improved on the telegraph. Alexander Graham Bell, a Scottish immigrant, was teaching the deaf when he began experimenting with ways to transmit speech electrically. In 1876, he transmitted his famous first words to his

*Telephone*

young assistant: "Mr. Watson, come here! I want you." No longer did messages require a telegraph office, the unwieldy Morse code, and couriers to deliver them. Communication could be instantaneous *and* direct. New York and Boston were linked in 1877 by the first intercity telephone line, and before the turn of the century, the Bell-organized American Telephone and Telegraph Company had combined more than 100 local companies to furnish business and government with long-distance service. The telephone patent proved to be the most valuable ever granted.

Along with other advances like the typewriter (1868), carbon paper (1872), and the mimeograph machine (1892), telephones modernized offices and eased business transactions. When rates dropped after the turn of the century, the telephone entered homes and helped to bring on a social revolution. Like the railroad and the telegraph, it compressed distances and reduced differences across the country.

## Finance Capital

As industry grew, so did the demand for investment capital—the money spent on land, buildings, and machinery. The need for capital was great especially because so many new industrial systems were being put into place at once. In the old days, a steamboat could be set afloat for the price of the boat itself. A railroad, on the other hand, had enormous start-up costs. Track had to be laid, workers hired, engines and cars bought, depots constructed. Industrial processes involving so many expensive systems could not take shape until someone raised the money to build them.

For the first three-quarters of the nineteenth century, investment capital had come mostly from the savings of firms. In the last half of the century "capital deepening"—a process essential for industrialization—took place. Simply put, as national wealth increased, people began to save and invest more of their money. This meant that more funds could be lent to companies seeking to start up or expand.

*Sources of capital*

Savings and investment grew more attractive with the development of a complex network of financial institutions. Commercial and savings banks, investment houses, and insurance companies gave savers new opportunities to channel money to industry. The New York Stock Exchange, in existence since 1792, linked eager investors with money-hungry firms. By the end of the nineteenth century the stock market had established itself as the basic means of making capital available to industry.

## The Corporation

For those business leaders with the skill to knit the industrial pieces together, large profits awaited. This was the era of the notorious "robber baron." And to be sure, sheer ruthlessness went a long way in the fortune-building game. "Law?

Who cares about law!" railroad magnate Cornelius Vanderbilt once boasted. "Hain't I got the power?"

But to survive in the long term, business leaders could not depend on ruthlessness alone. They needed ingenuity, an eye for detail, and the gift of foresight. The growing scale of enterprise and need for capital, for example, led them to adapt an old device, the corporation, to new needs.

The corporation had several advantages over more traditional forms of ownership, the single owner and the partnership. A corporation could raise

*Advantages of the corporation*

large sums quickly by selling "stock certificates" or shares in its business. It could also outlive its owners (or stockholders) because it required no legal reorganization if one died. It limited liability, since owners were no longer personally responsible for corporate debts. And it separated owners from day-to-day management of the company. Professional managers could now operate complex businesses. So clear were these advantages that before the turn of the century, corporations were making two-thirds of all manufactured products in the United States.

## A Pool of Labor

Last, but hardly least important for the new industrial order, was a pool of labor. In the United States the demand for workers was so great that the native-born could not fill it. In 1860 it took about 4.3 million workers to run all the factories, mills, and shops in the United States. By 1900 there were approximately 20 million industrial workers in America.

Europe was one recruiting ground. Mechanization, poverty, and oppression pushed many laborers from farms into cities and finally off the continent en-

*European sources*

tirely. To lure them across the Atlantic, industrialists advertised in newspapers, distributed pamphlets, and sent agents to Europe. In the 1880s incoming iron workers from Sweden often knew only three words of English: "Charlie—Deere—Moline" (Charlie was the president of the John Deere Plow Company in Moline, Illinois).

More than 8 million immigrants arrived in the United States between 1870 and 1890, another 14 million by 1914. Most settled in industrial cities in hopes of returning home with fatter purses. Often unskilled, many of them peasants, they found jobs in factories and mines or on construction and road gangs. And they were willing to work harder for less than those they replaced. "Immigrants work for almost nothing," complained a native-born laborer, "and seem to be able to live on wind."

To get those jobs, immigrants relied on well-defined migration chains of friends and family. A brother might find work with other Slavs in the mines of

*Migration chains*

Pennsylvania; or the daughter of Greek parents, in a New England textile mill filled with relatives. Labor contractors also served as a funnel to industry. Tough and savvy immigrants themselves, they met newcomers at the docks and train stations with contracts.

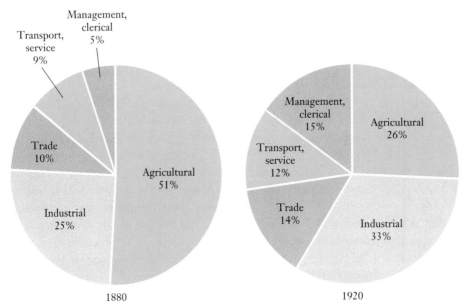

OCCUPATIONAL DISTRIBUTION, 1880 AND 1920   Between 1880 and 1920, management
and industrial work—white- and blue-collar workers—
grew at the expense of farmwork.

Among Italians they were known as *padrones;* among Mexicans, as *enganchistas.*
By 1900 they controlled two-thirds of the labor in New York.

A massive migration of rural Americans—some 11 million between 1865 and
1920—provided a home-grown source of labor. Driven from the farm by machines or bad times or just following dreams of a new life, they
moved first to small, then to larger cities. Most lacked the skills
for high-paying work. But they spoke English, and many could read and write.
In iron and steel cities as well as in coal-mining towns, the better industrial jobs
and supervisory positions went to them. Others found work in retail stores or offices and slowly entered the new urban middle class of white-collar workers.

*Domestic sources*

Most African Americans continued to work the fields of the South. About
300,000 moved to northern cities between 1870 and 1910. Like the new immigrants, they were trying to escape discrimination and follow opportunity. One
by one, they brought their families. Discrimination still dogged them, but they
found employment. Usually they worked in low-paying jobs as day laborers or
laundresses and domestic servants. Black entrepreneurship also thrived as black-
owned businesses served growing black communities.

Mexicans, too, came in search of jobs, mainly in agriculture but also in industry. They helped to build the transcontinental railroad. After the turn of the
century, a small number turned farther north for jobs in the tanneries, meatpacking plants, foundries, and rail yards of Chicago and other midwestern industrial cities.

RAILROADS: AMERICA'S FIRST BIG BUSINESS

The system was a mess: any good railroad man knew as much. All across the country, each town—each rail station—set its clocks separately by the sun. In 1882, the year T. S. Hudson scampered across America, New York and Boston were 11 minutes and 45 seconds apart. Stations often had several clocks showing the time on different rail lines, along with one displaying "local mean time." So in 1883, without consulting anyone, the railroad companies divided the country into four time zones. Congress did not get around to making the division official until 1916.

*Railroad time*

At the center of the new industrial systems were the railroads, moving people and freight, spreading communications, reinventing time, ultimately tying the nation together. Railroads also stimulated economic growth, simply because they required so many resources to build—coal, wood, glass, rubber, brass, and, by the 1880s, 75 percent of all U.S. steel. By lowering transportation costs railroads allowed manufacturers to reduce prices, attract more buyers, and increase business. Perhaps most important, as America's first big business they devised new techniques of management, soon adopted by other companies.

## A Managerial Revolution

To the men who ran them, railroads provided a challenge in organization and finance. In the 1850s, one of the largest industrial enterprises in America, the Pepperell textile mills of Maine, employed about 800 workers. By the early 1880s the Pennsylvania Railroad had nearly 50,000 people on its payroll. From setting schedules and rates to determining costs and profits, everything required a level of coordination unknown in earlier businesses.

The so-called trunk lines pioneered in devising new systems of management. Scores of early companies had serviced local networks of cities and communities, often with less than 50 miles of track. During the 1850s trunk lines emerged east of the Mississippi to connect the shorter branches, or "feeder" lines. By the outbreak of the Civil War, with four great trunk lines under a single management, railroads linked the eastern seaboard with the Great Lakes and western rivers. After the war, trunk lines grew in the South and West until the continent was spanned in 1869.

*Pioneering trunk lines*

The operations of large lines spawned a new managerial elite, beneath owners but with wide authority over operations. Daniel McCallum, superintendent of the New York and Erie in the 1850s, laid the foundation for this system by drawing up the first table of organization for an American company. A tree trunk with roots represented the president and board of directors; five branches constituted the main operating divisions; leaves stood for the local agents, train crews, and others. Information moved up and down the trunk so that managers could get reports to and from the separate parts.

*The new managers*

By the turn of the century, these managerial techniques had spread to other industries. Local superintendents were responsible for daily activities. Central offices served as corporate nerve centers, housing divisions for purchases, production, transportation, sales, and accounting. A new class of middle managers ran them and imposed new order on business operations. Executives, managers, and workers were being taught to operate in increasingly precise and coordinated ways.

## Competition and Consolidation

While managers made operations more systematic, the fierce struggle among railroad companies to dominate the industry was anything but precise and rational. In the 1870s and 1880s the pain of railroad progress began to tell.

By their nature, railroads were saddled with enormous fixed costs: equipment, payrolls, debts. These remained constant regardless of the volume of traffic. To generate added revenue, railroads constructed more lines in hopes of increasing their traffic. Soon the railroads had overbuilt. With so much extra capacity, railroad owners schemed to win new accounts. They gave free passes to favored shippers, promised them free sidings at their plants, offered free land to lure businesses to their territory.

*Railroad problems*

The most savage and costly competition came over the rates charged for shipping goods. Managers lowered [rates] prices for freight that was shipped in bulk, on long hauls, or on return routes (since the cars were empty anyway). They used "rebates"—secret discounts to preferred customers—to drop prices below the posted rates of competitors (and then recouped the losses by overcharging small shippers like farmers). When the economy plunged or a weak line sought to improve its position, rate or price wars broke out. By 1880, 65 lines had declared bankruptcy.

*Rebates*

Consolidation worked better than competition. During the 1870s railroads created regional federations to pool traffic, set prices, and divide profits among members. Pooling—informal agreements among competing companies to act together—was designed to remove the incentive for cutting rates. Without the force of law, however, pools failed. Members broke ranks by cutting prices in hopes of quick gain. In the end, rate wars died down only when weaker lines failed or stronger ones bought up competitors.

*Pooling*

## The Challenge of Finance

Earlier in the nineteenth century, many railroads relied on state governments for financial help. Backers also looked to counties, cities, and towns for bonds and other forms of aid. People living near the ends of rail lines, who stood to gain from construction, were persuaded to take stock in exchange for land or labor. In the 1850s and 1860s western promoters went to Washington for

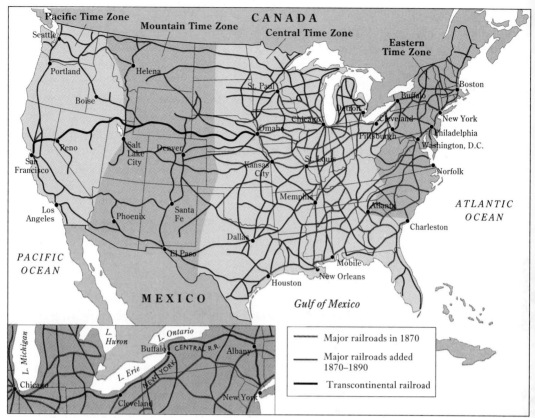

RAILROADS, 1870–1890  By 1890, the railroad network stretched from one end of the country to the other, with more miles of track than all of Europe combined. New York and Chicago, linked by the New York Central trunk line, became the new commercial axis.

federal assistance. Congress loaned $65 million to six western railroads and granted some 131 million acres of land.

Federal aid helped to build only part of the nation's railroads. Most of the money came from private investors. The New York Stock Exchange expanded rapidly as railroad corporations began to trade their stocks there. Large investment banks developed financial networks to track down money at home and abroad. By 1898 a third of the assets of American life insurance companies had gone into railroads, while Europeans owned nearly a third of all American railroad securities.

*New ways of raising money*

Because investment bankers played such large roles in funding railroads, they found themselves advising companies about their business affairs. If a company fell into bankruptcy, bankers sometimes served as the "receivers" who oversaw the property until financial health returned. By absorbing smaller lines into larger ones, eliminating rebates, and stabilizing rates, the bankers helped to reduce competition and impose order and centralization. In the process, they often gained control of the companies they advised.

By 1900, the new industrial systems had transformed American railroads. Some 200,000 miles of track were in operation, 80 percent of it owned by only six groups of railroads. Time zones allowed for coordinated schedules; standardized track permitted easy cross-country freighting. Soon passengers were traveling 16 billion miles a year. To that traffic could be added farm goods, raw materials, and factory-finished products. Everything moved with new regularity that allowed businesses to plan and prosper.

## THE GROWTH OF BIG BUSINESS

In 1865, near the end of the Civil War, 26-year-old John D. Rockefeller sat blank-faced in the office of his Cleveland oil refinery, about to conclude the biggest deal of his life. Rockefeller's business was thriving, but he had fallen out with his partner over how quickly to expand. Rockefeller was eager to grow fast; his partner was not. They dissolved their partnership and agreed to bid for the company. Bidding opened at $500, rocketed to $72,500, and abruptly stopped. "The business is yours," said the partner. The men shook hands, and a thin smile crept across Rockefeller's angular face.

Twenty years later, Rockefeller's Standard Oil Company controlled 90 percent of the nation's refining capacity and an empire that stretched well beyond Cleveland. Day and night, trains whisked Standard executives to New York, Philadelphia, and other eastern cities. The railroads were a fitting form of transportation for Rockefeller's company, for they were the key to his oil empire. They pioneered the business systems upon which he was building. And they carried his oil products for discounted rates, giving him the edge to squeeze out rivals. Like other American firms, Standard Oil was improving on the practices of the railroads in order to do bigger and bigger business.

### Growth in Consumer Goods

But first a great riddle had to be solved: how to control the ravages of competition? In Michigan in the 1860s, salt producers found themselves fighting for their existence. The presence of too many salt makers had begun an endless round of price-cutting that was driving them all out of business. Seeing salvation in combination, they drew together in the nation's first pool. In 1869 they formed the Michigan Salt Association. They voluntarily agreed to allocate production, divide markets, and set prices—at double the previous rate.

Salt processing and other industries that specialized in consumer goods had low start-up costs, so they were often plagued by competition. Horizontal combination—joining together loosely with rivals—had saved Michigan salt producers. By the 1880s there was a whiskey pool, a cordage pool, and countless rail and other pools. Such

*Horizontal growth*

informal pools ultimately proved to be unenforceable and therefore unsatisfactory. (After 1890 they were also considered illegal restraints on trade.) But other forms of horizontal growth, such as formal mergers, spread in the wake of an economic panic in the 1890s.

Some makers of consumer products worried less about direct competition and concentrated on boosting efficiency and sales. They adopted a vertical-growth strategy that integrated several different activities under one company. Gustavus Swift, a New England butcher, moved to Chicago in the mid-1870s. Aware of the demand for fresh beef in the East, he acquired new refrigerated railcars to ship meat from western slaughterhouses and a network of ice-cooled warehouses in eastern cities to store it. By 1885 he had created the first national meatpacking enterprise, Swift and Company.

*Vertical integration*

Swift moved upward, closer to consumers, by putting together a fleet of wagons to distribute his beef to retailers. He moved down toward raw materials, extending and coordinating the purchase of cattle at the Chicago stockyards. By the 1890s Swift and Company was a fully integrated, vertically organized corporation operating on a nationwide scale. Soon Swift, Armour and Company, and three other giants—together called the "Big Five"—controlled 90 percent of the beef shipped across state lines.

Vertical growth generally moved producers of consumer goods closer to the marketplace in search of high-volume sales. The Singer Sewing Machine Company and the McCormick Harvesting Machine Company created their own retail sales arms. Manufacturers began furnishing ordinary consumers with technical information, credit, and repair services. Advertising expenditures grew, to some $90 million by 1900, in an effort to identify markets, shape buying habits, and increase sales.

## Carnegie Integrates Steel

Industrialization encouraged vertical integration in heavy industry but more often in the opposite direction, toward reliable sources of raw materials. These firms made products for big users like railroads and factory builders. Their markets were easily identified and changed little. For them, success lay in securing limited raw materials and in holding down costs.

Andrew Carnegie led the way in steel. A Scottish immigrant, he worked his way up from bobbin boy to expert telegrapher to superintendent of the Pennsylvania Railroad's western division at the age of 24. A string of wise investments paid off handsomely. He owned a share of the first sleeping car and the first iron railroad bridge as well as a locomotive factory and an iron factory that became the nucleus of his steel empire.

In 1872, on a trip to England, Carnegie chanced to see the Bessemer process in action. Awestruck, he rushed home to build the biggest steel mill in the world. It opened in 1875, in the midst of a severe depression. Over the next 25 years, Carnegie added mills at Homestead and elsewhere in Pennsylvania and moved from railroad building to city building. He supplied steel for the Brooklyn Bridge, New York City's elevated railway, and the Washington Monument.

Carnegie succeeded, in part, by taking advantage of the boom-and-bust business cycle. He jumped in during hard times, building and buying when equipment and businesses were cheap. But he also found skilled managers, who employed the administrative techniques of the railroads. And Carnegie knew how to compete. He scrapped machinery, workers, even a new mill to keep costs down and undersell competitors.

*Keys to Carnegie's success*

The final key to Carnegie's success was expansion. His empire spread horizontally by purchasing rival steel mills and constructing new ones. It spread vertically, buying up sources of supply, transportation, and eventually sales. Controlling such an integrated system, Carnegie could ensure a steady flow of materials from mine to mill and market, as well as profits at every stage. In 1900 his company turned out more steel than Great Britain and netted $40 million.

Integration of the kind Carnegie employed expressed the logic of the new industrial age. More and more, the industrial activities of society were being linked in one giant, interconnected process.

### Rockefeller and the Great Standard Oil Trust

John D. Rockefeller accomplished in oil what Carnegie achieved in steel. And he went further, developing an innovative business structure—the trust—that promised greater control than even Carnegie's integrated system. At first Rockefeller grew horizontally by buying out or joining other refiners. To cut costs, he also expanded vertically, with oil pipelines, warehouses, and barrel factories. By 1870, when he and five partners formed the Standard Oil Company of Ohio, his high-quality, low-cost products could compete with any other.

*Rockefeller's methods of expansion*

Since the oil refining business was a jungle of competitive firms, Rockefeller proceeded to compete ferociously. He bribed rivals, spied on them, created phony companies, and slashed prices. His decisive edge came from the railroads. Desperate for business, they granted Standard Oil not only rebates on shipping rates but also "drawbacks," a fee for any product shipped by a rival oil company. Within a decade Standard dominated American refining with a vertically integrated empire that stretched from drilling to selling.

Throughout the 1870s Rockefeller kept his empire stitched together through informal pools and other business combinations. But they were weak and afforded him too little control. He could try to expand further, except that corporations were restricted by state law. In Rockefeller's home state of Ohio, for example, corporations could not own plants in other states or own stock in out-of-state companies.

In 1879 Samuel C. T. Dodd, chief counsel of Standard Oil, came up with a new device, the "trust." The stockholders of a corporation surrendered their

*The trust*

shares "in trust" to a central board of directors with the power to control all property. In exchange, stockholders received certificates of trust that paid hefty dividends. Since it did not literally own other companies, the trust violated no state law.

In 1882 the Standard Oil Company of Ohio formed the country's first great trust. It brought Rockefeller what he sought so fiercely: centralized management of the oil industry. Other businesses soon created trusts of their own—in meatpacking, wiremaking, farm machinery, and elsewhere. Just as quickly, trusts became notorious for crushing rivals and controlling prices.

## The Mergers of J. Pierpont Morgan

The trust was only a stepping-stone to an even more effective means of avoiding competition, managing people, and controlling business: the corporate merger. The merging of two corporations—one buying out another—remained impossible until 1889, when New Jersey began to permit corporations to own other companies.

In 1890, the need to find a substitute for the trust grew urgent. Congress outlawed trusts under the Sherman Antitrust Act (see p. 485). The Sherman Act

*The holding company*

specifically banned business from "restraining trade" by setting prices, dividing markets, or engaging in other unfair practices. The ever-inventive Samuel Dodd came up with the "holding company." It had the power to own other companies. Many industries converted their trusts into holding companies, including Standard Oil, which moved to New Jersey in 1899.

Two years later came the biggest corporate merger of the era. It was the creation of a financial wizard named J. Pierpont Morgan. His orderly mind detested the chaotic competition that threatened his profits. "I like a little competition," Morgan used to say, "but I like combination more." After the Civil War he had taken over his father's powerful investment bank. For the next 50 years, the House of Morgan played a part in consolidating almost every major industry in the country.

Morgan's greatest triumph came in steel. In 1901, a colossal steel war loomed between Andrew Carnegie and other steelmakers. Morgan convinced Carnegie to put a price tag on his company. When a messenger brought the scrawled reply back—over $400 million—Morgan merely nodded and said, "I accept this price." He then bought Carnegie's eight largest competitors and announced the formation of the United States Steel Corporation.

U. S. Steel gobbled up over 200 manufacturing and transportation companies, 1000 miles of railways, and the whole Mesabi iron range. The mammoth holding company produced nearly two-thirds of all American steel. Its value of $1.4 billion exceeded the national debt and made it the country's first billion-dollar corporation.

What Morgan helped to create in steel was rapidly coming to pass in other industries. A wave of mergers swept through American business after the de-

*The merger movement*

pression of 1893. As the economy plunged, cutthroat competition bled businesses until they were eager to sell out. Giants sprouted almost overnight. By 1904, in each of 50 industries one firm came to account for 60 percent or more of the total output.

## Corporate Defenders

As Andrew Carnegie's empire grew, his conscience turned troubled. Preaching a "gospel of wealth," he urged the rich to act as agents for the poor, "doing for them

*The gospel of wealth*

better than they would or could do for themselves." He devoted his time to philanthropy by creating foundations and endowing libraries and universities with some $350 million in contributions.

Defenders of the new corporate order were less troubled than Carnegie about the rough-and-tumble world of big business. They justified the system by stressing the opportunity created for individuals by economic growth. Through frugality, acquisitiveness, and discipline—the sources of cherished American individualism—anyone could rise like Andrew Carnegie.

When most ordinary workers failed to follow in Carnegie's footsteps, defenders blamed the individual. Failures were lazy, ignorant, or morally de-

*Social Darwinism*

praved, they said. British philosopher Herbert Spencer added the weight of science by applying Charles Darwin's theories of evolution to society. He maintained that in society, as in biology, only the "fittest" survived. The competitive social jungle doomed the unfit to poverty and rewarded the fit with property and privilege.

Spencer's American apostle, William Graham Sumner, argued that competition was natural and had to proceed without any interference, including government regulation. Millionaires were simply the "product of natural selection." Such "Social Darwinism" found strong support among turn-of-the-century business leaders. The philosophy certified their success even as they worked to destroy the very competitiveness it celebrated.

## Corporate Critics

Meanwhile a group of radical critics mounted a powerful attack on corporate capitalism. Henry George, a journalist and self-taught economist, proposed a way to redistribute wealth in *Progress and Poverty* (1879). George attacked larger landowners as the source of inequality. They bought property while it was cheap and then held it until the forces of society—labor, technology, and speculation

*Henry George's single tax*

on nearby sites—had increased its value. George proposed to do away with all taxes except a single tax on these "unearned" profits, to end monopoly landholding. "Single-tax" clubs sprang up throughout the country, and George nearly won the race for mayor of New York in 1886.

The journalist Edward Bellamy tapped the same popular resentment against the inequalities of corporate capitalism. In his utopian novel, *Looking Backward* (1888), a fictional Boston gentleman falls asleep in 1887 and awakens Rip Van Winkle-like in the year 2000. The competitive, caste-ridden society of the nineteenth century is gone. In its place is an orderly utopia, managed by a benevolent government trust. Competition, exploitation, and class divisions have been replaced by "fraternal cooperation" and shared abundance. Like George's ideas, Bellamy's philosophy inspired a host of clubs around the nation. His followers demanded redistribution of wealth, civil service reform, and nationalization of railroads and utilities.

Less popular but equally hostile to capitalism was the Socialist Labor party, formed in 1877. Under Daniel De Leon, a West Indian immigrant, it stressed

*Socialist Labor party*

class conflict and called for a revolution to give workers control over production. De Leon refused to compromise his radical beliefs, and the socialists ended up attracting more intellectuals than workers. Some immigrants found its class consciousness appealing, but most rejected its radicalism and rigidity. A few party members, bent on gaining greater support, revolted and in 1901 founded the more successful Socialist Party of America. Workers were beginning to organize their own responses to industrialism.

By the mid-1880s, in response to the growing criticism of big business, several states in the South and West had enacted laws limiting the size of corporations. But state laws proved all too easy to evade when states such as New Jersey and Delaware eased their rules to cover the whole nation.

In 1890, the public clamor against trusts finally forced Congress to act. The Sherman Antitrust Act relied on the only constitutional authority Congress had

*Sherman Antitrust Act*

over business: its right to regulate interstate commerce. The act outlawed "every contract, combination in the form of trust or otherwise, or conspiracy, in restraint of trade or commerce." The United States stood practically alone among industrialized nations in regulating business combinations.

Its language was purposefully vague, but the Sherman Antitrust Act did give the government the power to break up trusts and other big businesses. So high was the regard for the rights of private property, however, that few in Congress expected the government to exercise that power or the courts to uphold it. They were right. Before 1901, the Justice department filed only 14 antitrust suits against big businesses, virtually none of them successful. And in 1895, the Supreme Court dealt the law a major blow by severely limiting its scope. *United States v. E. C. Knight Co* held that businesses involved in manufacturing (as opposed to "trade or commerce") lay outside the authority of the Sherman Act. Not until after the turn of the century would the law be used to bust a trust.

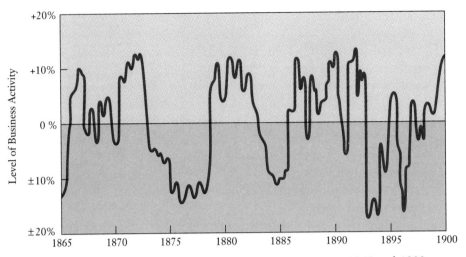

BOOM AND BUST BUSINESS CYCLE, 1865–1900   Between 1865 and 1900, industrialization produced great economic growth but also wild swings of prosperity and depression. During booms, productivity soared, and near-full employment existed. But the rising number of industrial workers meant high unemployment during deep busts.

## The Costs of Doing Business

The heated debates between the critics and defenders of industrial capitalism made clear that the changes in American society were two-edged. Big businesses helped to rationalize the economy, increase national wealth, and tie the country together. Yet they also concentrated power, corrupted politics, and made the gap between rich and poor more apparent than ever. In 1890, the richest 9 percent of Americans held nearly three-quarters of all wealth in the United States. By 1900, one American in eight (nearly 10 million people) lived below the poverty line.

More to the point, the practices of big business subjected the economy to enormous disruptions. The banking system could not always keep pace with the demand for capital, and businesses failed to distribute enough of their profits to sustain the purchasing power of workers. The supply of goods periodically outstripped demand, and then the wrenching cycle of boom and bust set in. Three severe depressions—1873–1879, 1882–1885, and 1893–1897—rocked the economy in the last third of the nineteenth century. With hard times came fierce competition as managers searched frantically to cut costs, and the industrial barons earned their reputations for ruthlessness.

*The boom-and-bust cycle*

*American Business Leaders: Robber Barons or Captains of Industry?*

Attacks and celebrations have continued to characterize portraits of the Carnegies, Rockefellers, and Morgans. Some historians have followed the lead of nineteenth-century critics and depicted them as hypocrites who extolled the virtues of competition while crushing it to pursue profits. Financiers and industrialists acted like medieval barons, robbing workers of the fruits of their labors, concentrating power, and threatening democracy.

Other historians see them as captains of industry: leaders and innovators who created an economy of abundance. Business historians have shown little interest in questions of morality or democracy versus economic concentration. They emphasize instead the strategies, structures, and forms of doing business.

## THE WORKERS' WORLD

At seven in the morning, Sadie Frowne sat at her sewing machine in a Brooklyn garment factory. Her boss, a man she barely knew, dropped a pile of unfinished skirts next to her. She pushed one under her needle and began to rock her foot on the pedal that powered her machine. Sometimes Sadie pushed the skirts too quickly, and the needle pierced her finger. "The machines go like mad all day because the faster you work the more money you get," she explained of the world of industrial work in 1902.

The cramped sweatshops, the vast steel mills, the dank tunnels of the coal fields—all demanded workers and required them to work in new ways. Farmers or peasants who had once timed themselves by the movement of the sun now lived by the clock and labored by the twilight of gaslit factories. Instead of being self-employed, they had to deal with supervisors and were paid by the piece or hour. Not the seasons but the relentless cycle of machines set their pace. Increasingly, workers bore the brunt of depressions, faced periodic unemployment, and toiled under dangerous conditions as they struggled to bring the new industrial processes under their control.

### Industrial Work

In 1881, the Pittsburgh Bessemer Steel Company opened its new mill in Homestead, Pennsylvania. Nearly 400 men and boys went to work on its 60 acres of sheds. They kept the mill going around the clock by working in two shifts: 12 hours a day the first week, 12 hours a night the next. In the furnace room, some men fainted from the heat, while the vibration and screeching of machinery deafened others. There were no breaks, even for lunch. "Home is just the place where I eat and sleep," said a steelworker. "I live in the mills."

Few industrial laborers worked under such conditions, but the Homestead mill reflected common characteristics of industrial work: the use of machines for mass production; the division of labor into intricately organized, menial tasks; and the dictatorship of the clock. At the turn of the century, two-thirds of all industrial work came from large-scale mills.

*Pattern of industrial work*

Under such conditions labor paid dearly for industrial progress. By 1900, most of those earning wages in industry worked 6 days a week, 10 hours a day. They held jobs that required more machines and fewer skills. Repetition of small chores replaced fine craftwork. In the 1880s, for example, almost all the 40 different steps that had gone into making a pair of shoes by hand could be performed by a novice or "green hand" with a few days of instruction at a simple machine.

With machines also came danger. Tending furnaces in a steel mill or plucking tobacco from cigarette-rolling machines was tedious. If a worker became bored or tired, disaster could strike. Each year from 1880 to 1900 industrial mishaps killed an average of 35,000 wage earners and injured over 500,000. Workers and their families could expect no payment from employers or government for death or injury.

Carnegie Furnaces, Braddock, Pennsylvania

Industrial workers rarely saw an owner. The foreman or supervisor exercised complete authority over the unskilled in his section, hiring and firing them, even setting their wages. Skilled workers had greater freedom; yet they too felt the pinch of technology and organization. Carpenters found that machine-made doors were replacing the ones they used to construct at the site. Painters no longer mixed their own paints.

Higher productivity and profits were the aims, and for Frederick W. Taylor, efficiency was the way to achieve them. During the 1870s and 1880s, Taylor un-

*Taylorism* dertook careful time-and-motion studies of workers' movements in the steel industry. He set up standard procedures and offered pay incentives for beating his production quotas. On one occasion, he designed 15 ore shovels, each for a separate task. One hundred forty men were soon doing the work of 600. By the early twentieth century "Taylorism" was a full-blown philosophy, complete with its own professional society. "Management engineers" prescribed routines from which workers could not vary.

For all the high ideals of Taylorism, ordinary laborers refused to perform as cogs in a vast industrial machine. In a variety of ways, they worked to maintain control. Many European immigrants continued to observe the numerous saint's days and other religious holidays of their homelands, regardless of factory rules. When the pressure of six-day weeks became too stifling, workers took an unauthorized "blue Monday" off. Or they slowed down to reduce the

grueling pace. Or they simply walked off the job. Come spring and warm weather, factories reported turnover rates of 100 percent or more.

For some, seizing control of work was more than a matter of survival or self-respect. Many workers regarded themselves as citizens of a democratic re-

*Worker citizens* public. They expected to earn a "competence"—enough money to support and educate their families and enough time to stay up with current affairs. Few but highly skilled workers could realize such democratic dreams. More and more, labor was being managed as another part of an integrated system of industry.

## Children, Women, and African Americans

In the mines of Pennsylvania, nimble-fingered eight-year-olds snatched bits of slate from amid the chunks of coal. In Illinois glass factories, "dog boys" dashed with trays of red-hot bottles to the cooling ovens. By 1900, the industrial labor force included some 1.7 million children, more than double the number 30 years earlier. Parents often had no choice. As one union leader observed, "Absolute necessity compels the father . . . to take the child into the mine to assist him in winning bread for the family." On average, children worked 60 hours a week and carried home paychecks a third the size of those of adult males.

Women had always labored on family farms, but by 1870 one out of every four nonagricultural workers was female. In general they earned one-half of what men did. Nearly all were single and young, anywhere from their mid-teens to their mid-twenties. Most lived in boardinghouses or at home with their parents. Usually they contributed their wages to the family kitty. Once married, they took on a life of full-time housework and child rearing.

Only 5 percent of married women held jobs outside the home in 1900. Married black women—in need of income because of the low wages paid their husbands—were four times more likely than married whites to work away from home. Industrialization inevitably pushed women into new jobs. Mainly they worked in industries considered extensions of housework: food processing, textiles and clothing, cigar making, and domestic service.

New methods of management and marketing opened positions for white-collar women as "typewriters," "telephone girls," bookkeepers, and secretaries.

*Feminization of work* On rare occasions women entered the professions, though law and medical schools were reluctant to admit them. Such discrimination drove ambitious, educated women into nursing, teaching, and library work. Their growing presence soon "feminized" these professions, pushing men upward into managerial slots or out entirely.

Even more than white women, all African Americans faced discrimination in the workplace. They were paid less than whites and given menial jobs. Their greatest opportunities in industry often came as strikebreakers to replace white workers. Once a strike ended, however, black workers were replaced themselves—

Clerks' jobs, traditionally held by men, came to be filled by women as growing industrial networks created more managerial jobs for men. In this typical office, male managers literally oversee female clerks.

and hated by the white regulars all the more. The service trades furnished the largest single source of jobs. Craftworkers and a sprinkling of black professionals could usually be found in cities. After the turn of the century, black-owned businesses thrived in the growing black neighborhoods of the North and South.

### The American Dream of Success

Whatever their separate experiences, working-class Americans did improve their overall lot. Though the gap between the very rich and the very poor

*Rising real wages*

widened, most wage earners made some gains. Between 1860 and 1890 real daily wages—pay in terms of buying power—climbed some 50 percent as prices gradually fell. And after 1890, the number of hours on the job began a slow decline.

Yet most unskilled and semiskilled workers in factories continued to receive low pay. In 1890, an unskilled laborer could expect about $1.50 for a 10-hour day; a skilled one, perhaps twice that amount. It took about $600 to make ends meet, but most manufacturing workers made under $500 a year. Native-born white Americans tended to earn more than immigrants, those who spoke English more than those who did not, men more than women, and all others more than African Americans and Asians.

Few workers repeated the rags-to-riches rise of Andrew Carnegie. But some did rise, despite periodic unemployment and ruthless wage cuts. About one-quarter of the manual laborers in one study entered the lower middle class in their own lifetimes. More often such unskilled workers climbed in financial status within their own class. And most workers, seeing some improvement, believed in the American dream of success, even if they did not fully share in it.

## THE SYSTEMS OF LABOR

Putting in more hours to save a few pennies, walking out in exhaustion or disgust, slowing down on the job—these were the ways individual workers coped with industrial America. Sporadic and unorganized, such actions had little chance of bringing the new industrial order under the control of labor. For ordinary workers to begin to control industrialization they had to combine, just as businesses did. They needed to join together horizontally—organizing not just locally but on a national scale. They needed to integrate vertically by coordinating action across a wide range of jobs and skills, as Andrew Carnegie coordinated the production of steel. For workers, unions were their systematic response to industrialization.

### Early Unions

In the United States unions began forming before the Civil War. Skilled craft-workers—carpenters, iron molders, cigar makers—united to counter the growing power of management. Railroad "brotherhoods" also furnished insurance for those hurt or killed on the accident-plagued lines. Largely local and exclusively male, these early craft unions remained weak and unconnected to each other, as well as to the growing mass of unskilled workers.

After the war, a group of craft unions, brotherhoods, and reformers united skilled and unskilled workers in a nationwide organization. The National Labor

*National Labor Union*

Union (NLU) hailed the virtues of a simpler America, when workers controlled their workday, earned a decent living, and had time to be good informed citizens. NLU leaders attacked the wage system as unfair and enslaving and urged workers to manage their own factories. By the early 1870s, NLU ranks swelled to more than 600,000.

Among other things, the NLU pressed for the eight-hour workday, the most popular labor demand of the era. Workers saw it as a way not merely of limiting their time on the job but of limiting the power of employers over their lives. "Eight hours for work; eight hours for rest; eight hours for what we will!" proclaimed a banner at one labor rally. Despite the popularity of the issue, the NLU wilted during the depression of 1873.

## The Knights of Labor

More successful was a national union born in secrecy. In 1869 Uriah Stephens and nine Philadelphia garment cutters founded the Noble and Holy Order of the Knights of Labor. They draped themselves in ritual and regalia to deepen their sense of solidarity and met in secret to evade hostile owners. The Knights remained small and fraternal for a decade. Their strongly Protestant tone repelled Catholics, who made up almost half the workforce in many industries.

In 1879 the Knights elected Terence V. Powderly as their Grand Master Workman. Handsome, dynamic, Irish, and Catholic, Powderly threw off the Knights' secrecy, dropped their rituals, and opened their ranks.

*Terence Powderly*

He called for "one big union" to embrace the "toiling millions"— skilled and unskilled, men and women, natives and immigrants, all religions, all races. By 1886, membership had leaped to over 700,000, including nearly 30,000 African Americans and 3000 women.

Like the NLU, the Knights of Labor looked to abolish the wage system and in its place create a cooperative economy of worker-owned mines, factories, and railroads. The Knights set up more than 140 cooperative workshops, where workers shared decisions and profits, and sponsored some 200 political candidates. To tame the new industrial order, they supported the eight-hour workday and the regulation of trusts. Underlying this program was a moral vision of society. If only people renounced greed, laziness, and dishonesty, Powderly argued, corruption and class division would disappear. Democracy would flourish. To reform citizens, the Knights promoted the prohibition of child and convict labor and the abolition of liquor.

It was one thing to proclaim a moral vision for his union, quite another to coordinate the activities of so many members. Locals resorted to strikes and violence, actions Powderly condemned. In the mid-1880s, such stoppages wrung concessions from the western railroads, but the organization soon became associated with unsuccessful strikes and violent extremists. Even the gains against the railroads were wiped out when the Texas and Pacific Railroad broke a strike by local Knights. By 1890, the Knights of Labor teetered near extinction.

## The American Federation of Labor

The Knights' position as the premier union in the nation was taken by the rival American Federation of Labor (AFL). The AFL reflected the practicality of its leader, Samuel Gompers. Born in a London tenement, the son

*Samuel Gompers*

of a Jewish cigar maker, he had immigrated in 1863 with his family to New York's Lower East Side. Unlike the visionary Powderly, Gompers accepted capitalism and the wage system. What he wanted was "pure and simple unionism"—higher wages, fewer hours, improved safety, more benefits.

Gompers chose to organize highly skilled craftworkers because they were difficult to replace. He then bargained with employers, using strikes and boycotts only as last resorts. With the Cigar Makers' Union as his base, Gompers helped create the first national federation of craft unions in 1881. In 1886, it was reorganized as the American Federation of Labor. Twenty-five labor groups joined, representing some 150,000 workers.

Gompers fought off radicals and allied himself with whatever candidate supported labor. Stressing gradual, concrete gains, he made the AFL the most powerful union in the country. By 1901 it had more than a million members, almost a third of all skilled workers in America.

Gompers was less interested in vertical integration: combining skilled and unskilled workers. For most of his career, he preserved the privileges of craftsmen and accepted their prejudices against women, blacks, and immigrants. Only two locals—the Cigar Makers' Union and the Typographers' Union—enrolled women. Most affiliates restricted black membership through high entrance fees and other discriminatory practices.

Despite the success of the AFL, the laboring classes did not organize themselves as systematically as the barons of industrial America. At the turn of the

*Failure of organized labor*

century, union membership included less than 10 percent of industrial workers. Separated by different languages and nationalities, divided by issues of race and gender, workers resisted unionization during the nineteenth century. In fact, a strong strain of individualism often made them regard all collective action as un-American.

## The Limits of Industrial Systems

As managers sought to increase their control over the workplace, workers often found themselves at the mercy of the new industrial order. Even in boom times, one in three workers was out of a job at least three or four months a year. But it was in hard times that the industrial system was driven to its limits.

When a worker's pay dropped and frustration mounted, when a mother worked all night and fell asleep during the day while caring for her children,

*Spontaneous protests*

when food prices suddenly jumped—violence might erupt. "A mob of 1,000 people, with women in the lead, marched through the Jewish quarter of Williamsburg last evening and wrecked half a dozen butcher shops," reported the New York *Times* in 1902. In the late nineteenth century a wave of labor activism swept the nation. More often than mob violence, it was strikes and boycotts that challenged the authority of employers and gave evidence of working-class identity and discontent.

Most strikes broke out spontaneously, organized by informal leaders in a factory. "Malvina Fourtune and her brother Henry Fourtune it was them who started the strike," declared a company informer in Chicopee, Massachusetts. "They go from house to house and tells the people to keep up the strike." Thousands of rallies and organized strikes were staged as well, often on behalf of the eight-hour workday, in good times and bad, by union and nonunion workers alike.

In 1877 the country's first nationwide strike opened an era of confrontation between labor and management. When the Baltimore and Ohio Railroad cut

*Great Railroad Strike*

wages by 20 percent, a crew in Martinsburg, West Virginia, seized the local depot and blocked the line. Two-thirds of the nation's track shut down in sympathy. When strikebreakers were brought in, striking workers torched rail yards, smashed engines and cars, and tore up track. Local police, state militia, and federal troops finally crushed the strike after 12 bloody days. In its wake, the Great Railroad Strike of 1877 left 100 people dead and $10 million worth of railroad property in rubble.

In 1886, tension between labor and capital exploded in the "Great Upheaval"—a series of strikes, boycotts, and rallies. One of the most violent

*Haymarket Square riot*

episodes occurred at Haymarket Square in Chicago. A group of anarchists was protesting the recent killing of workers by police at the McCormick Harvesting Company. As rain drenched the small crowd, police moved in and ordered everyone out of the square. Suddenly a bomb exploded. One officer was killed, and 6 others mortally wounded. When police opened fire, the crowd fired back. Nearly 70 more policemen were injured, and at least 4 civilians died.

Conservatives charged that radicals were responsible for the "Haymarket Massacre." Ordinary citizens who had supported labor grew fearful of its power

In this painting by Robert Koehler, entitled *The Strike* (1886), labor confronts management in a strike that may soon turn bloody. One worker reaches for a stone as an anxious mother and her children look on. Barely visible on the desolate horizon is a smoke-enshrouded factory.

to spark violence and disorder. Though the bomb thrower was never identified, a trial of questionable legality found eight anarchists guilty of conspiracy to murder. Seven were sentenced to death. Cities enlarged their police forces, and states built more National Guard armories on the borders of working-class neighborhoods.

## Management Strikes Again

The strikes, rallies, and boycotts of 1886 were followed by a second surge of labor activism in 1892. In the silver mines of Coeur d'Alene, Idaho, at the Carnegie steel mill in Homestead, Pennsylvania, in the coal mines near Tracy City, Tennessee, strikes flared. Often state and federal troops joined company guards and Pinkerton detectives to crush these actions.

The broadest confrontation between labor and management took place two years later. A terrible depression had shaken the economy for almost a year

*Pullman strike* when George Pullman, owner of the Palace Car factory and inventor of the plush railroad car, laid off workers, cut wages (but kept rents high on company-owned housing), and refused to discuss grievances. In 1894 workers struck and managed to convince the new American Railway Union (ARU) to support them by boycotting all trains that used Pullman cars. Quickly the strike spread to 27 states and territories. Anxious railroad owners appealed to President Grover Cleveland for federal help. On the slim pretext that the strike obstructed mail delivery (strikers had actually been willing to handle mail trains without Pullman cars), Cleveland secured a court order halting the strike. He then called several thousand special deputies into Chicago to enforce it. In the rioting that followed, 12 people died and scores were arrested. But the strike was quashed.

In all labor disputes the central issue was the power to shape the new industrial systems. Employers always enjoyed the advantage. They hired and fired

*Management weapons* workers, set the terms of employment, and ruled the workplace. They fought unions with "yellow dog" contracts that forced workers to refuse to join. Blacklists circulated the names of labor agitators. Lockouts kept protesting workers from plants, and labor spies infiltrated their organizations. With a growing pool of labor, employers could replace strikers and break strikes.

Management could also count on local, state, and federal authorities to send troops to break strikes. In addition, businesses used a powerful new legal weapon, the injunction. These court orders prohibited certain actions, including strikes, by barring workers from interfering with their employer's business. It was just such an order that had brought federal deputies into the Pullman strike and put Eugene Debs, head of the railway union, behind bars.

In a matter of only 30 or 40 years, the new industrial order had transformed the landscape of America. Whether rich or poor, workers, entrepreneurs, or industrial barons, Americans were drawn closer by the new industrial systems. Ore scooped from Mesabi might end up in a steel girder on James Eads's Mississippi bridge, in a steel needle for Sadie Frowne's sewing machine in Brooklyn, or in a McCormick reaper slicing across the Nebraska plains. When a textile worker in Massachusetts struck, a family in Alabama might well pay more for clothes. A man in Cleveland now set his watch to agree with the time of a man in New York, regardless of the position of the sun.

Such changes might seem effortless to someone like T. S. Hudson, scampering across the rails of America in 1882. But as the nineteenth century drew to a close, material progress went hand in hand with social pain and upheaval.

## SIGNIFICANT EVENTS

1859 — First oil well drilled near Titusville, Pennsylvania
1866 — National Labor Union founded
1869 — Knights of Labor created
1870 — John D. Rockefeller incorporates Standard Oil Company of Ohio
1873 — Carnegie Steel Company founded; Panic of 1873
1874 — Massachusetts enacts first 10-hour workday law for women
1876 — Alexander Graham Bell invents telephone
1877 — Railroad wage cuts lead to violent strikes; Thomas Edison invents phonograph
1879 — Edison develops incandescent lightbulb; Henry George's *Progress and Poverty* published
1882 — Rockefeller's Standard Oil Company becomes nation's first trust; Thomas Edison's electric company begins lighting New York City
1883 — Railroads establish standard time zones
1886 — American Federation of Labor organized; Haymarket Square bombing
1892 — Homestead Steel strike
1893 — Panic of 1893
1894 — Pullman strike
1901 — U.S. Steel Corporation becomes nation's first billion-dollar company

# CHAPTER NINETEEN

# The Rise of an Urban Order

Graziano's bootblack stand was jammed with people, mulling about, looking for help. Above the crowd, enthroned like an Irish king, sat George Washington Plunkitt, ward boss of Manhattan's Fifteenth Assembly District. There to help, Plunkitt asked little in return, only votes on election day. Plunkitt understood the close relationship between help and votes. "There's got to be in every ward," another boss explained, "somebody that any bloke can come to—no matter what he's done—and get help. *Help, you understand; none of your law and justice, but help.*" The reverse was also true: to maintain power, bosses like Plunkitt had to be able to count on the political support of those they helped.

For years Plunkitt had been a leader of Tammany Hall, the Democratic party organization that ruled New York City politics from 1850 to 1930. Much of his daily routine was taken up with helping. One typical day began when a bartender roused him at two in the morning to get a friend out of jail. Plunkitt succeeded but didn't get back to bed until after three. Howling fire sirens woke him at six. Before dawn he was assisting burned-out tenants with food, clothing, and shelter. Home by eleven, he found four unemployed men waiting for him. Within hours each had a job. A quick bite of lunch and it was off again, this time to a pair of funerals. Plunkitt brought flowers for the bereaved and offered consolation, all in full view of the assembled. From there he rushed to attend a "Hebrew confirmation." Early evening found him at district headquarters, helping his election captains plot ways of "turning out the vote."

*A boss at work*

After a quick stop at a church fair, it was back to the party clubhouse where he helped some local teams by buying tickets for their next game. Before leaving, he pledged to stop the police from harassing two dozen pushcart peddlers.

He arrived at a wedding reception at half past ten (having already bestowed on the bride and groom "a handsome wedding present"). Finally, at midnight, he crawled into bed, after a day of helping all he could.

Such relentless effort helped Plunkitt as well. Born to Irish immigrants, he died a millionaire in 1924. His pluck and practicality would have made him the envy of any industrialist. Like the Carnegies and Rockefellers, fierce ambition fueled his rise from butcher boy to political boss. City politics was his way out of the slums in a world that favored the rich, the educated, and the well-established.

In the late nineteenth century the needs of rapidly growing cities gave political bosses like George Washington Plunkitt their chance. "I seen my opportunities and I took 'em," Plunkitt used to say. Every city contract and bond issue, every tax assessment, every charter for a new business offered Plunkitt and his cronies an opportunity to line their pockets. Money made from inside

*Boodle*

knowledge of city projects was known as "boodle." How much boodle bosses collected depended on how well their organization managed to elect sympathetic officials. And that explained why Plunkitt spent so much time helping his constituents in order to get out the vote.

Plunkitt's New York was the first great city in history to be ruled by men of the people in an organized and continuing way. Bosses and their henchmen came from the streets and saloons, the slums and tenements, the firehouses and funeral homes. Many of their families had only recently arrived in America. While the Irish of Tammany Hall ran New York, Germans governed St. Louis, Scandinavians Minneapolis, and Jews San Francisco.

In an earlier age political leadership had been drawn from the ranks of the wealthy and native-born. America had been an agrarian republic, in which most personal relationships were grounded in small communities. By the late nineteenth century, the country was in the midst of an urban explosion. Industrial cities of unparalleled size and diversity were transforming American life. They lured people from all over the globe, created tensions between natives and newcomers, reshaped the social order. For Plunkitt, as for so many Americans, the golden door of opportunity opened onto the city.

## A NEW URBAN AGE

The modern city was the product of industrialization. Cities contained the great investment banks, the smoky mills and dingy sweatshops, the spreading railroad yards, the grimy tenements and sparkling mansions, the new department stores and skyscrapers. People came from places as near as the countryside and as far away as Italy, Russia, Armenia, and China. By the end of the nineteenth century America had entered a new urban age, with tens of millions of "urbanites," an urban landscape, and a growing urban culture.

### The Urban Explosion

During the 50 years after the Civil War, the population of the United States quadrupled—from 31 million to 92 million. Yet the number of Americans living in cities increased nearly sevenfold. In 1860, only one American in six lived in a city with a population of 8000 or more; in 1900, one in three did. By 1910 nearly half the nation lived in cities large and small.

Cities grew in every region of the country. In the Northeast and upper Midwest early industrialization created more cities than in the West and the South, although a few big cities sprouted there as well. Atlanta, Nashville, and later Dallas and Houston boomed under the influence of railroads. Los Angeles had barely 6000 people in 1870. By 1900 it was the second-largest city on the Pacific coast, with 100,000 residents.

Large urban centers dominated whole regions, tying the country together in a vast urban network. New York, the nation's banker, printer, and chief

Realist painters like George Bellows, who were scorned by critics as the "Ashcan School," captured the grittiness and vibrancy of teeming cities, here in Bellows's *Cliff Dwellers*.

*Cities' relations to regions around them*

marketplace, ruled the East. Smaller cities operated within narrower spheres of influence and often specialized. Milwaukee was famous for beer, Tulsa for oil, and Hershey, Pennsylvania, for chocolate. Cities even shaped the natural environment hundreds of miles beyond their limits. Chicago became not only the gateway to the West but also a powerful agent of ecological change. As its lines of commerce and industry radiated outward, the city transformed the rich ecosystems of the West. Wheat to feed Chicago's millions replaced sheltering prairie grasses. Great stands of white pine in Wisconsin vanished, only to reappear in the furniture and frames of Chicago houses, or as fence rails shipped to prairie farms.

## The Great Global Migration

Between 1820 and 1920, some 60 million people across the globe left farms and villages for cities. Mushrooming population gave them a powerful push. In Europe the end of the Napoleonic Wars in 1815 launched a cycle of baby booms that continued at 20-year intervals for the rest of the century. Improved diet and sanitation, aided by Louis Pasteur's discovery that bacteria cause infection and disease, reduced deaths. Meanwhile machinery cut the need for farmworkers. In 1896 one man in a wheat field could do what had taken 18 men just 60 years earlier.

Surplus farmworkers became a part of a vast international labor force, pulled by industry to cities in Europe and America. The prospect of factory work for better pay and fewer hours especially lured the young. In America, young farm women spearheaded the urban migration. Mechanization and the rise of commercial agriculture made them less valuable in the fields, while mass-produced goods from mail-order houses made them less useful at home.

Earlier in the century, European immigrants had come from northern and western Europe. In the 1880s, however, "new" immigrants from southern and

*The "new" immigration*

eastern Europe began to arrive. Some, like Russian and Polish Jews, were fleeing religious and political persecution. Others left to evade famine or diseases such as cholera, which swept across southern Italy in 1887. But most came for the same reasons that motivated migrants from the countryside: a job, more money, a fresh start.

Ambitious, hardy, and resourceful, immigrants found themselves tested every step of the way to America. They left behind the comforting familiarity of families, friends, and old ways. The price of one-way passage by steamship—about $50 in 1904—was far too high for most to bring relatives, at least at first. And the trip was dangerous. Wayfarers often stole across heavily guarded borders. They traveled for weeks just to reach a port like Le Havre in France. At dockside, shipping lines vaccinated, disinfected, and examined them to ensure against their being returned at company expense.

It took from one to two weeks to cross the Atlantic. Immigrants spent most of the time below decks in cramped, filthy compartments called "steerage."

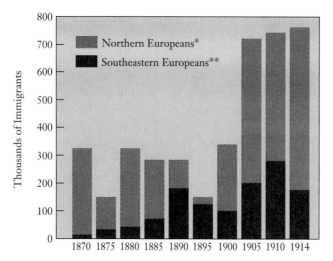

*Includes immigrants from Great Britain, Ireland, Germany, and the Scandinavian countries.

**Includes immigrants from Poland, Russia, Italy, and other Baltic and east European countries.

IMMIGRATION, 1860–1920   Between 1860 and 1920 immigration increased dramatically as the sources of immigrants shifted from northern Europe to southeastern Europe. Despite fears to the contrary, the proportion of newcomers as a percentage of population increases did not show nearly the same jump.

Most landed at New York's Castle Garden or the newer facility on nearby Ellis Island, opened in 1892. If arriving from Asia, they landed at Angel Island in San Francisco Bay. They had to pass another medical examination, have their names recorded by customs officials, and pay an entry tax. At any point, they could be detained or shipped home.

Immigrants arrived in staggering numbers—by 1900 they made up nearly 15 percent of the population. Most newcomers were young, between the ages of 15 and 40. Few spoke English or had skills or much educa-

*Immigrant profile*

tion. Unlike earlier arrivals, who were mostly Protestant, these new immigrants worshiped in Catholic, Greek, or Russian Orthodox churches and Jewish synagogues. Almost two-thirds were men. A large number came to make money to buy land or start businesses back home. Some changed their minds and sent for relatives, but those returning home were common enough to be labeled "birds of passage."

Jews were an exception. Between 1880 and 1914, a third of eastern Europe's Jewry left in the face of growing anti-Semitism. They made up 10 percent of all immigration to the United States. Almost all stayed and brought their families, often one by one. They had few choices. As one Jewish immigrant wrote of his Russian homeland, "Am I not despised? Am I not urged to leave? . . . Do I not rise daily with the fear lest the hungry mob attack me?"

## The Shape of the City

In colonial days, Benjamin Franklin could walk from one end of Boston to the other in an hour. Only Franklin's adopted home, Philadelphia, spilled into suburbs. Over the years these colonial "walking cities" developed ringed patterns of settlement. Merchants, professionals, and the upper classes lived near their shops and offices in the city center. As one walked outward, the income and status of the residents gradually declined.

Cities of the late nineteenth century still exhibited this ringed pattern, except that industrialization had reversed the order and increased urban sprawl.

*Patterns of settlement*

As the middle and upper classes moved out of a growing industrial core, the poor, some immigrants, African Americans, and laborers filled the inner void. They took over old factories and brownstones, shanties and cellars. By sheer weight of numbers they transformed these areas into the slums of the central city.

Curled around the slums was the "zone of emergence," an income-graded band of those on their way up. It contained second-generation city dwellers, factory workers, skilled laborers, and professional mechanics. They lived in progressively better tenements and neater row houses. Poverty no longer imprisoned them, but they could still slip back in hard times.

Farther out was the suburban fringe, home to the new class of white-collar managers and executives. They lived in larger houses with individual lots on neat, tree-lined streets. The very wealthy still maintained mansions on fashionable city avenues, but by the 1870s and 1880s, they too began to keep suburban homes.

## Urban Transport

For all their differences, the circles of settlement held together as a part of an interdependent whole. One reason was an evolving system of urban transportation. By the mid-nineteenth century horse-drawn railways were conveying some 35 million people a year in New York. Their problems were legendary: so slow, a person could walk faster; so crowded (according to Mark Twain), you "had to hang on by your eyelashes and your toenails"; so dirty, tons of horse manure were left daily in the streets.

Civic leaders came to understand that the modern city could not survive, much less grow, without improved transportation. San Francisco installed trolley cars pulled by steam-driven cables. The innovation worked so well in hilly San Francisco that Chicago, Seattle, and other cities installed cable systems in the 1880s. Still other cities experimented with elevated trestles, to carry steam locomotives or cable lines high above crowded streets. But none of the breakthroughs quite did the trick. Cables remained slow and unreliable; the elevated railways, or "els," were dirty, ugly, and noisy.

Electricity rescued city travelers. In 1888 Frank Julian Sprague, a naval engineer who had once worked for Thomas Edison, installed the first electric

*Role of electricity* trolley line in Richmond, Virginia. Electrified streetcars were soon speeding along at 12 miles an hour, twice as fast as horses. By 1902 electricity drove nearly all city railways. Sprague's breakthroughs also meant that "subways" could be built without having to worry about tunnels filled with a steam engine's smoke and soot. Between 1895 and 1897 Boston built the first underground electric line. New York followed in 1904 with a subway that ran from City Hall on the southern tip of Manhattan north to 145th Street.

The rich had long been able to keep homes outside city limits, traveling to and fro in private carriages. New systems of mass transit freed the middle class and even the poor to live miles from work. For a nickel or two, anyone could ride from central shopping and business districts to the suburban fringes and back. A network of moving vehicles held the segmented and sprawling city together and widened its reach out to "streetcar suburbs."

## Bridges and Skyscrapers

Since cities often grew along rivers and harbors, their separate parts sometimes had to be joined over water. The principles of building large river bridges had already been worked out by the railroads. It remained for a German immigrant and his son, John and Washington Roebling, to make the bridge a symbol of urban growth. The Brooklyn Bridge, linking Manhattan with Brooklyn, took 13 years to complete. It cost $15 million and 20 lives, including that of designer John. When it opened in 1883, it stretched more than a mile across the East River, with passage broad enough for a footpath, two double carriage lanes, and two railroad lines. Its arches were cut like giant cathedral windows, and its supporting cables hung, said an awestruck observer, "like divine messages from above." Soon other suspension bridges were spanning the railroad yards in St. Louis and the bay at Galveston, Texas.

Even as late as 1880 church steeples dominated the urban landscape. They towered over squat factories and office buildings. But growing congestion and the increasing value of land pushed architects to search for ways to make buildings taller. In place of thick, heavy walls of brick that restricted factory floor space, builders used cast iron columns. The new "cloudscrapers" were strong, durable, and fire-resistant, ideal for warehouses and also for office buildings and department stores.

Steel, tougher in tension and compression, turned cloudscrapers into skyscrapers. William LeBaron Jenney first used steel in his 10-story Home Insurance Building (1885) in Chicago. By the end of the century steel frames and girders raised buildings to 30 stories or more. New York City's triangular Flatiron building (on page 505) used the new technology to project an angular, yet remarkably delicate elegance. In Chicago, Daniel Burnham's Reliance Building (1890) made such heavy use of new plate glass windows that contemporaries called it "a glass tower fifteen stories high."

The Flatiron building

It was no accident that many of the new skyscrapers arose in Chicago. The city had burned nearly to the ground in 1871. The "Chicago school" of archi-

*Louis Sullivan and the "Chicago school"*

tects helped to rebuild it. The young maverick Louis H. Sullivan promised a new urban profile in which the skyscraper would be "every inch a proud and soaring thing." In the Wainwright Building (1890) in St. Louis and the Carson, Pirie, and Scott department store (1889–1904) in Chicago, Sullivan produced towering structures that symbolized the modern industrial city.

## Slum and Tenement

Far below the skyscrapers lay the slums and tenements of the inner city. In cramped rooms and sunless hallways, along narrow alleys and in flooded basements, lived the city poor. They often worked there, too. In "sweaters' shops" as many as 18 people labored and slept in foul two-room flats.

In New York, whose slums were among the nation's worst, crime thrived in places called "Bandit's Roost" and "Hell's Kitchen." Bands of young toughs with

*Perils of the slum neighborhood*

names like the "Sewer Rats" and the "Rock Gang" stalked the streets in search of thrills and easy money. Gambling, prostitution, and alcoholism all claimed their victims most readily in the slums. The poor usually turned to crime in despair. A 20-year-old prostitute supporting a sickly mother and four brothers and sisters made no apologies: "Let God Almighty judge who's to blame most, I that was driven, or them that drove me to the pass I'm in."

Slum dwellers often lived on poor diets that left them vulnerable to epidemics. Cholera, typhoid, and an outbreak of yellow fever in Memphis in the 1870s killed tens of thousands. Tuberculosis was deadlier still. Slum children—all city children—were most vulnerable to such diseases. Almost a quarter of the children born in American cities in 1890 never lived to see their first birthday.

The installation of new sewage and water purification systems helped. The modern flush toilet came into use only after the turn of the century. Until then people relied on water closets and communal privies. Some catered to as many as 800. All too often cities dumped waste into old private vaults or rivers used for drinking water. In 1881 the exasperated mayor of Cleveland called the Cuyahoga River "an open sewer through the center of the city."

Slum housing was often more dangerous than the water. The tubercle bacillus flourished in musty, windowless tenements. In 1879 New York enacted a

*The dumbbell tenement*

new housing law requiring a window in all bedrooms of new tenements. Architect James E. Ware won a competition with a creative design that contained an indentation on both sides of the building. When two tenements abutted each other, the indentations formed a narrow shaft for air and light. From above, the buildings looked like giant dumbbells. Up to 16 families lived on a floor, with two toilets in the hall.

Originally hailed as an innovation, Ware's dumbbell tenement spread over such cities as Cleveland, Cincinnati, and Boston "like a scab," said an unhappy reformer. Ordinary blocks contained 10 tenements and housed as many as 4000 people. The airshafts became giant silos for trash, which blocked what little light had entered and, worse still, carried fires from one story to the next. When the New York housing commission met in 1900, it concluded that conditions were worse than when reformers had started 33 years earlier.

## RUNNING AND REFORMING THE CITY

Every new arrival to the city brought dreams and altogether too many needs. Schools and houses had to be built, streets paved, garbage collected, sewers dug, fires fought, utility lines laid. Running the city became a full-time job, and a new breed of full-time politician rose to the task. So, too, did a new breed of reformer, determined to help the needy cope with the ravages of urban life.

The need for reform change was clear. Many city charters dating from the eighteenth century included a paralyzing system of checks and balances. Mayors

*The weaknesses of city government*

vetoed city councils; councils ignored mayors. Jealous state legislatures allowed cities only the most limited and unpopular taxes, such as those on property. At the same time, city governments were often decentralized: fragmented, scattered, at odds with one another. By 1890, Chicago had 11 branches of government. Each was a tiny kingdom with its own regulations and taxing authority. As immigrants and rural newcomers flocked to factories and tenements, the structures of urban government strained to adapt.

## Boss Rule

"Why must there be a boss," journalist Lincoln Steffens asked Boss Richard Croker of New York, "when we've got a mayor—and a city council?" "That's why," Croker broke in. "It's because we've got a mayor and a council and judges—*and*—a hundred other men to deal with." The boss was right. He and his system furnished cities with the centralization, authority, and services they sorely needed.

Bosses ruled through the political machine. Often, as with New York's Tammany Hall, machines dated back to the late eighteenth and early nineteenth centuries. They began as fraternal and charitable organizations. Over the years they became centers of political power. In New York the machine was Democratic; in Philadelphia, Republican. Some were less centralized, as in Chicago; some less ethnically mixed, as in Detroit. Machines could even be found in rural areas such as Duval County, Texas, where the Spanish-speaking Anglo boss Archie Parr molded a powerful alliance with Mexican American landowners.

In an age of enterprise, the boss operated his political machine like a corporation. His office might be a saloon, a funeral home, or, like George

*The boss as entrepreneur*

Washington Plunkitt's, a shoeshine stand. His managers were party activists, connected in a corporate-like chain of command. Local committeemen reported to district captains, captains to district leaders, district leaders to the boss or bosses who directed the machine.

The goods and services of the machine were basics: a Christmas turkey, a load of coal for the winter, jobs for the unemployed, English-language classes for recent immigrants. Bosses sponsored fun too: sports teams, glee clubs, balls and barbecues.

This system, rough and uneven as it was, served as a form of public welfare at a time when private charity could not cope with the crush of demands. To

*Crude welfare system*

the unskilled, the boss doled out jobs in public construction. For bright, ambitious young men, he had places in city offices or in the party. These represented the first steps into the middle class.

In return, citizens expressed their gratitude at the ballot box. Sometimes the votes of the grateful were not enough. "Little Bob" Davies of Jersey City was adept at mobilizing the "graveyard vote." He drew names from tombstones to pad lists of registered voters and hired "repeaters" to vote under the phony names. When reformers introduced the Australian (secret) ballot in the 1880s to prevent fraud, bosses pulled the "Tasmanian dodge" by premarking election tickets. Failing that, they dumped whole ballot boxes into the river or used hired thugs to scare unpersuaded voters away from the polls.

## Rewards, Accomplishments, and Costs

Why did bosses go to such lengths? Some simply loved the game of politics. More often bosses loved money. Their ability to get it was limited only by their

*Boss William Tweed*

ingenuity or the occasional success of an outraged reformer. The record for brassiness must go to Boss William Tweed. During his reign in the 1860s and 1870s, Tweed swindled New York City out of a fortune. His masterpiece of graft was a chunky three-story courthouse in lower Manhattan originally budgeted at $250,000. When Tweed was through, the city had spent more than $13 million—and the building was still not finished! Tweed died in prison, but with such profits to be made, it was small wonder that bosses rivaled the pharaohs of Egypt as builders.

In their fashion bosses played a vital role in the industrial city. Rising from the bottom ranks, they guided immigrants into American life and helped some of the underprivileged up from poverty. They changed the urban landscape with a massive construction program. They modernized city government by uniting it and making it perform. Choosing the aldermen, municipal judges, mayors, and administrative officials, bosses exerted new control to provide the contracts and franchises to run cities. Such accomplishments fostered the notion that government could be called on to help the needy. The welfare state, still decades away, had some roots here.

The toll was often outrageous. Inflated taxes, extorted revenue, unpunished vice and crime were only the obvious costs. A woman whose family enjoyed Plunkitt's Christmas turkey might be widowed by an accident to her husband in a sweatshop kept open by timely bribes. Filthy buildings might claim her children, as corrupt inspectors ignored serious violations. Buying votes and selling favors, bosses turned democracy into a petty business—as much a "business," said Plunkitt, "as the grocery or dry-goods or the drug business." Yet they were the forerunners of the new breed of professional politicians who would soon govern the cities and the nation as well.

## Nativism, Revivals, and the Social Gospel

Urban blight and the condition of the poor inspired social as well as political activism, especially within churches. Not all of it was constructive. The popular Congregationalist minister Josiah Strong concluded that the city was "a menace to society." Along with anxious economists and social workers, he blamed everything from corruption to unemployment on immigrant city dwellers and urged restrictions on their entry.

In the 1880s and 1890s, two depressions sharpened such anxieties. Nativism, a defensive and fearful nationalism, peaked as organizations like the new

*Nativist restrictions*

Immigration Restriction League attacked Catholics and foreigners. Already the victims of racial prejudice, the Chinese were an easy target. In 1882 Congress enacted the Chinese Exclusion

Act. It banned the entry of Chinese laborers and represented an important step in the drive to restrict immigration. In 1897 the first bill requiring literacy tests for immigrants passed Congress, but President Grover Cleveland vetoed it.

Some clergy took their missions to the slums to bridge the gap between the middle class and the poor. Beginning in 1870 Dwight Lyman Moody, a 300-pound former shoe salesman, won armies of lowly converts with revivals in Boston, Chicago, and other cities. Evangelists helped to found American branches of the British Young Men's Christian Association and the Salvation Army. By the end of the century the Salvation Army had grown to 700 corps staffed by some 3000 officers. They ministered to the needy with food, music, shelter, and simple good fellowship.

A small group of ministers rejected the traditional notion that weak character explained sin and that society would be perfected only as individual sin-

*The Social Gospel*

ners were converted. They spread a new "Social Gospel" that focused on improving the conditions of society in order to save individuals. In *Applied Christianity* (1886), the influential Washington Gladden preached that the church must be responsible for correcting social injustices in the political and economic order, including dangerous working conditions and unfair labor practices. Houses of worship, such as William Rainford's St. George's Episcopal Church in New York, became centers of social activity, with boys' clubs, gymnasiums, libraries, glee clubs, and industrial training programs.

*Billy Sunday* (1923), by George Bellows, depicts a revival meeting of William Ashley "Billy" Sunday. Sunday, a hard-drinking professional baseball player turned evangelist, began his religious revivals in the 1890s and drew thousands.

## The Social Settlement Movement

Church-sponsored programs often repelled the immigrant poor, who saw them as thinly disguised missionary efforts. Immigrants and other slum dwellers were more

*The settlement house*

receptive to a bold experiment called the settlement house. Situated in the worst slums, often in renovated old houses, these early community centers were run by middle-class women and men to help the poor and foreign-born. At the turn of the century there were more than 100 of them, the most famous being Jane Addams's Hull House in Chicago. In 1898 the Catholic church sponsored its first settlement house in New York, and in 1900 Bronson House opened its doors to the Latino community in Los Angeles.

High purposes inspired settlement workers, who actually lived in the settlement houses. They left comfortable middle-class homes and dedicated themselves (like the "early Christians," said one) to service and sacrifice. They aimed to teach immigrants American ways and to create a community spirit that would foster "right living through social relations." But immigrants were also encouraged to preserve their heritages through festivals, parades, and museums. Like political bosses, settlement reformers furnished help, from day nurseries to English-language and cooking classes to playgrounds and libraries. Armed with statistics and personal experiences, they also lobbied for social legislation to improve housing, women's working conditions, and public schools.

### CITY LIFE

City life reflected the stratified nature of American society in the late nineteenth century. Every city had its slums and tenements but also its fashionable avenues, where many-roomed mansions housed the rich. The rich constituted barely 1 percent of the population but owned a fourth of all wealth. In between tenement and mansion lived the broad middle of urban society, which made up nearly a third of the population and owned about half of the nation's wealth. With more money and leisure time, the middle class was increasing its power and influence.

In the impersonal city of the late nineteenth century, class distinctions, as ever, continued to be based on wealth and income. But no longer were dress and man-

*Urban social stratification*

ners enough to distinguish one class from another. Such differences were reflected in where people lived, what they bought, which organizations they joined, and how they spent their leisure time.

## The Immigrant in the City

When they put into port, the first thing immigrants were likely to see was a city. Perhaps it was Boston or New York or Galveston, Texas, where an overflow of Jewish immigrants was directed after the turn of the century. Most immigrants, exhausted physically and financially, settled in cities.

Cities developed a well-defined mosaic of ethnic communities, since immigrants usually clustered together on the basis of their villages or provinces. But

*Ethnic neighborhoods*

these neighborhoods were in constant flux. As many as half the residents moved every 10 years, often because they got better-paying jobs or had more of their family working. Though one nationality usually dominated a neighborhood, there was always a sprinkling of others. Despite popular misconceptions, no other immigrants lived like the Chinese in urban ghettos of just one ethnic group. Racial prejudice forced the Chinese together, and local ordinances kept them from buying their way out like other immigrants.

Ethnic communities served as havens from the strangeness of American society and springboards to a new life. From the moment they stepped off the boat, newcomers felt pressed to learn English, don American clothes, and drop their "greenhorn" ways. Yet in their neighborhoods they also found comrades who spoke their language, theaters that performed their plays and music, restaurants that served their food.

The *Jewish Daily Forward* and scores of other foreign-language newspapers reported events from the homeland but also gave eager readers profiles of local

Entertainment in immigrant neighborhoods often resulted in a cross-fertilization of cultures. The Cathay Boys Club Band (pictured above), a marching band of Chinese Americans, was formed in San Francisco's Chinatown in 1911. It was inspired by the Columbia Park Boys Band of Italians from nearby North Beach and played American music only.

leaders, advice on voting, and tips on adjusting to America. Immigrant aid societies like the Polish National Alliance and the Society for the Protection of Italian Immigrants furnished fellowship and assistance in the newcomers' own languages. They fostered assimilation by sponsoring baseball teams, insurance programs, libraries, and English classes.

Sometimes immigrants combined the old and the new in creative ways. Italians developed a pidgin dialect called Italglish. It permitted them to communicate quickly with Americans and to absorb American customs. So the Fourth of July became "*Il Forte Gelato*" (literally "The Great Freeze"), a play on the sound of the words. Other immigrant groups invented similar idioms, like *Chuco*, a dialect that developed among border Mexicans in El Paso.

Houses of worship were always at the center of immigrant life. They often catered to the practices of individual towns or provinces. Occasionally they changed their ways under the cultural pressures of American life. Where the Irish dominated the American Catholic church other immigrants formed new churches with priests from their homelands. Eastern European Jews began to break the old law against sitting next to their wives and daughters in synagogues. The Orthodox churches of Armenians, Syrians, Romanians, and Serbians gradually lost their national identifications.

The backgrounds and cultural values of immigrants influenced their choice of jobs. Because Chinese men did not scorn washing or ironing, more than 7500 of them could be found in San Francisco laundries by 1880. Sewing ladies' garments seemed unmanly to many native-born Americans but not to Russian and Italian tailors. Slavs tended to be physically robust and valued steady income over education. They pulled their children out of school, sent them to work, and worked themselves in the mines for better pay than in factories.

On the whole, immigrants married later and had more children than the native-born. Greeks and eastern European Jews prearranged marriages according to tradition. They imported "picture brides," betrothed by mail with a photograph. After marriage men ruled the household, but women *Family life* managed it. Although child-rearing practices varied, immigrants resisted the relative permissiveness of American parents. Youngsters were expected to contribute like little adults to the welfare of the family.

In these "family economies" of working-class immigrants, key decisions—over whether and whom to marry, over work and education, over when to leave home—were made on the basis of collective rather than individual needs. Though immigrant boys were more likely to work outside the home than girls, daughters often went to work at an early age so sons could continue their education. It was customary for one daughter to remain unmarried so she could care for younger siblings or aged parents.

The Chinese were an exception to the pattern. The ban on the immigration of Chinese laborers in the 1880s (pages 508–509) had frozen the gender ratio of Chinese communities into a curious imbalance. Like other immigrants,

EYEWITNESS TO HISTORY

## A Chinese Immigrant Names
## His Children

As we children arrived, Father was confronted with a vexatious problem. It perplexed not only him, but every other Chinatown father. What names should he give us children born in this country? . . . He winced at the prospect of saddling his children with names which could be ridiculously distorted into pidgin English. He had had enough, he said, of Sing High, Sing Low, Wun Long Hop, Ching Chong, Long Song.

. . . For him the problem, when I arrived, was immensely simplified. According to the Barbarian calender, I was born on "The Double Ninth," or the ninth day of the ninth month . . . a holiday commemorating California's admission into the Union. "Why not," suggested Dr. [Mabel] LaPlace [who delivered his daughter and for whom she was named] . . . , "name your son after the Governor?" . . . At that time the Governor of California bore the name of Dr. George C. Pardee. . . . I was named for a fellow Republican.

I doubt whether Father ever quite realized the tremendous burden he placed upon our shoulders. Sister Mabel . . . never had to live up to her name in school, although she did have to live down among her playmates the discreditable fact that her brothers and sisters bore the socially forbidding names of George C. Pardee, Alice Roosevelt, Helen Taft, Woodrow Wilson, and Thomas Riley Marshall.

. . . As we grew up, our Chinese names were used less and less. When we visited Chinatown and were addressed, as always happened, by these Chinese names, it gave us a weird, uncomfortable feeling as though someone other than ourselves were being addressed . . . Our lives never seemed to be ours to do with as we saw fit. . . . In our Chinese world we had to order our lives for the happiness of our parents and the dignity of our clan; while in the American one it was no different. It was obvious that we not only had to "make a name" for ourselves, but acquit with distinction our namesakes as well.

Pardee Lowe, *Father and Glorious Descendant* (Boston: Little, Brown, and Company, 1943), pp. 12–25. Copyright renewed in 1971 by Pardee Lowe. All rights reserved.

most Chinese newcomers had been single men. In the wake of the ban, those in the United States could not bring over their wives and families. Nor by law in 13 states could they marry white Americans. With few women, Chinese communities suffered from high rates of prostitution, large numbers of gangs and secret societies, and low birth totals. When the San Francisco earthquake and fire destroyed birth records in 1906, resourceful Chinese immigrants created "paper sons" (and less often "paper daughters") by forging birth certificates and claiming their China-born children as American citizens.

Caught between past and present, immigrants clung to tradition and assimilated slowly. Their children adjusted more quickly. They soon spoke English like natives, married whomever they pleased, and worked their way out of old neighborhoods. Yet the process was not easy. Children faced heartrending clashes with parents and rejection from peers.

*Assimilation*

## COUNTERPOINT   *The "New" Immigrants: Who Came and Why?*

With so many immigrants coming to America, it is no wonder historians have disagreed over who came and why. Early historians of immigration focused specifically on the United States and the European arrivals. The newcomers were depicted as an undifferentiated mass of peasants in search of economic opportunity and freedom from persecution. These immigrants, according to early interpretations, helped to make the American experience unique.

More recently, historians have placed immigration to the United States in global perspective by examining both receiving and sending countries. In an international framework, the United States moves from the center of immigration action to the fringes of the narrative as one of many components in an expanding world economy. Immigration to America thus becomes part of international labor exchange and the American experience less exceptional and more comparable to that of other receiving nations such as Argentina and Australia. As for the immigrants themselves, the international perspective makes the pool from which they were drawn more diverse economically and ethnically and less poverty-stricken than originally thought.

### Urban Middle-Class Life

Life for the urban middle class revolved around home and family. By the turn of the century just over a third of middle-class urbanites owned their homes. Often two or three stories, made of brick or brownstone, these houses were a measure of their owners' social standing. The plush furniture, heavy drapes, antiques, and curios all signaled status and refinement.

Such homes, usually on their own lots, also served as havens to protect and nourish the family. Seventeenth-century notions of children as inherently sinful had given way to more modern theories about the shaping influence of environment. Calm and orderly households with nurturing mothers would launch children on the right course. "A clean, fresh, and well-ordered house," stipulated a domestic adviser in 1883, "exercises over its inmates a moral, no less than physical

*The home as haven and status symbol*

influence, and has a direct tendency to make members of the family sober, peaceable, and considerate of the feelings and happiness of each other."

A woman was judged by the state of her home. The typical homemaker pre-pared elaborate meals, cleaned, laundered, and sewed. Each task took time.

*The middle-class homemaker*

Baking a loaf of bread required nearly 24 hours, and in 1890, four of five loaves were still made at home. Perhaps 25 percent of urban households had live-in servants to help with the work. They were on call about 100 hours a week, were off but one evening and part of Sunday, and averaged $2 to $5 a week in salary.

By the 1890s a wealth of new consumer products eased the burdens of housework. Brand names trumpeted a new age of commercially prepared food—Campbell's soup, Quaker oats, Pillsbury flour, Jell-O, and Cracker Jacks, to name a few. New appliances such as "self-working" washers offered mechanical assistance but often shredded shirts. Aching arms testified to how far short mechanization still fell.

Toward the end of the century, Saturday became less of a workday and more of a family day. Sunday mornings remained a time for church, still an impor-tant center of family life. Afternoons had a more secular flavor. There were shopping trips (city stores often stayed open) and visits to lakes, zoos, and amusement parks (usually built at the end of trolley lines to attract more rid-ers). Outside institutions—fraternal organizations, uplift groups, athletic teams, and church groups—were becoming part of middle-class urban family life.

## Victorianism and the Pursuit of Virtue

Middle-class life reflected a rigid social code called Victorianism, named for Britain's long-reigning Queen Victoria. It emerged in the 1830s and 1840s as part of an effort to tame the turbulent urban-industrial society developing in Europe.

Victorianism dictated that personal conduct be based on orderly behavior and disciplined moralism. It stressed sobriety, industriousness, self-control, and sexual modesty and taught that demeanor, particularly proper manners, was the backbone of society. According to its sexual precepts, women were "pure ves-sels," devoid of carnal desire. Their job was to control the "lower natures" of their husbands by withholding sex except for procreation.

Women's fashion mirrored Victorian values. Strenuously laced corsets ("an instrument of torture," according to one woman ) pushed breasts up, stomachs in, and rear-ends out. The resulting wasplike figure accentuated the breasts and hips, promoting the image of women as child bearers. Ankle-length skirts were draped over bustles, hoops, and petticoats to make hips look even larger and suggest fertility. Such elegant dress set off middle- and upper-class women from those below, whose plain clothes signaled lives of drudgery and want.

When working-class Americans failed to follow Victorian cues, reformers helped them to pursue virtue. In 1874 Frances Willard, fearing the ill effects of

*WCTU*

alcohol on the family, helped to organize the Woman's Christian Temperance Union. Under her leadership the WCTU worked relentlessly to stamp out alcohol and promote sexual purity and other middle-class virtues. By the turn of the century it was the largest women's organization in the country, with 500,000 members.

Anthony Comstock crusaded with equal vigor against what he saw as moral pollution, ranging from pornography and gambling to the use of nude art models. In 1873 President Ulysses S. Grant signed the so-called

*Comstock Law*

Comstock Law, a statute banning from the mails all materials "designed to incite lust." Two days later Comstock went to work as a special agent for the Post Office. In his 41-year career, he claimed to have made more than 3000 arrests and destroyed 160 tons of vice-ridden books and photographs.

Victorian crusaders like Comstock were not simply missionaries of a stuffy morality. They were apostles of a middle-class creed of social control, responding to an increasing incidence of alcoholism, venereal disease, gambling debts, prostitution, and unwanted pregnancies. No doubt they overreacted in warning that the road to ruin lay behind the door of every saloon, gambling parlor, or bedroom. Yet the new urban environment did indeed reflect the disorder of a rapidly industrializing society.

The insistence with which moralists warned against "impropriety" suggests that many people did not heed their advice. Three-quarters of the women surveyed toward the turn of the century reported that they enjoyed sex. The growing variety of contraceptives—including spermicidal douches, sheaths made of animal intestines, rubber condoms, and forerunners of the diaphragm—testified to the desire for pregnancy-free intercourse. Abortion, too, was available. According to one estimate, a third of all pregnancies were aborted, usually with the aid of a midwife. (By the 1880s abortion had been made illegal in most states following the first antiabortion statute in England in 1803.) Despite Victorian marriage manuals, middle-class Americans became more conscious of sexuality as an emotional dimension of a satisfying union.

## Challenges to Convention

A few bold men and women challenged convention more openly. Victoria Woodhull, publisher of *Woodhull & Claflin's Weekly*, divorced her husband, ran

*Victoria Woodhull*

for president in 1872 on the Equal Rights Party ticket, and pressed the case for sexual freedom. "I am a free lover!" she shouted to a riotous audience in New York. "I have the inalienable, constitutional, and natural right to love whom I may, to love as long or as short a period as I can, to change that love every day if I please!" Woodhull made a strong public case for sexual freedom. In private, however, she believed in strict monogamy and romantic love for herself.

The same cosmopolitan conditions that provided protection for Woodhull's unorthodox beliefs also made possible the growth of self-conscious communi-

*Urban homosexual communities*

ties of homosexual men and women. Earlier in the century, Americans had idealized romantic friendships among members of the same sex, without necessarily attributing to them sexual overtones. But for friendships with an explicitly sexual dimension, the anonymity of large cities provided new meeting grounds. Single factory workers and clerks, living in furnished rooms rather than with their families in small towns and on farms, were freer to seek others who shared their sexual orientation. Homosexual men and women began forming social networks: on the streets where they regularly met, at specific restaurants and clubs, which, to avoid controversy, sometimes passed themselves off as athletic associations or chess clubs. Such places could be found in New York City's Bowery, around the Presidio military base in San Francisco, and at Lafayette Square in Washington, D.C.

Only toward the end of the century did physicians begin to notice homosexual behavior, usually to condemn it as a disease or an inherited infirmity. Indeed, not until the turn of the century did the term *homosexual* come into existence. Certainly homosexual love itself was not new. But for the first time in the United States, the conditions of urban life allowed gays and lesbians to define themselves in terms of a larger, self-conscious community, even if they were stoutly condemned by the prevailing Victorian morality.

## CITY CULTURE

"We cannot all live in cities," the reformer Horace Greeley lamented just after the Civil War, "yet nearly all seemed determined to do so. . . ." Economic opportunity drew people to the teeming industrial city. But so, too, did a vibrant urban culture.

By the 1890s, cities had begun to clean up downtown business districts, pave streets, widen thoroughfares, erect fountains and buildings of marble. This "city beautiful" movement aimed also to elevate public tastes and, like Victorian culture itself, refine the behavior of urbanites. Civic leaders built museums, libraries, and parks to uplift unruly city masses. Public parks followed the model of New York's Central Park. When it opened in 1858, Central Park was meant to serve as pastoral retreat from the turbulent industrial city. Its rustic paths, woodsy views, and tranquil lakes, said designer Frederick Law Olmsted, would have "a distinctly harmonizing and refining influence" on even the rudest fellow.

For those in search of lower-brow entertainment, cities offered dance halls and sporting events, amusement parks and vaudeville shows, saloons and arcades. In the beckoning cities of the late nineteenth century, Americans sought to realize their dreams of fun and success.

## Public Education in an Urban Industrial World

Those at the bottom and in the middle of city life found in public education one key to success. Although the campaign for public education began in the Jacksonian era, it did not make much headway until after the Civil War, when industrial cities began to mushroom. As late as 1870 half the children in the country received no formal education at all, and one American in five could not read.

Between 1870 and 1900, an educational awakening occurred. As more and more businesses required better-educated workers, attendance in public schools more than doubled. The length of the school term rose from 132 to 144 days. Illiteracy fell by half. By the turn of the century, nearly all the states outside the South had enacted mandatory education laws. Almost three of every four school-age children were enrolled. Even so, the average American adult still attended school for only about five years, and less than 10 percent of those eligible continued beyond the eighth grade.

The average school day started early, but by noon most girls were released under the assumption that they needed less formal education. Curricula stressed the fundamentals of reading, writing, and arithmetic. Courses in manual training, science, and physical education were added as the demand for technical knowledge grew and opportunities to exercise shrank. Students learned by memorization, sitting in silent study with hands clasped or standing erect while they repeated phrases and sums. Few schools encouraged creative thinking. "Don't stop to think," barked a Chicago teacher to a class of terrified youngsters in the 1890s, "tell me what you know!"

A strict social philosophy underlay the harsh routine. In an age of industrialization, massive immigration, and rapid change, schools taught conformity and values as much as facts and figures. Teachers acted as drillmasters, shaping their charges for the sake of society. "Teachers and books are better security than handcuffs and policemen," wrote a New Jersey college professor in 1879.

As Reconstruction faded, so did the impressive start made in black education. Most of the first generation of former slaves had been illiterate. So eager were they to learn that by the end of the century nearly half of all African Americans could read. But discrimination soon took *African Americans* its toll. For nearly 100 years after the Civil War, the doctrine of "separate but equal," upheld by the Supreme Court in *Plessy v. Ferguson* (1896), kept black and white students apart but scarcely equal (page 534). By 1882 public schools in a half dozen southern states were segregated by law, the rest by practice. Underfunded and ill-equipped, black schools served dirt-poor families whose every member had to work.

Like African Americans, immigrants saw education as a way of getting ahead. Some educators saw it as a means of Americanizing newcomers. They *Immigrant education* assumed that immigrant and native-born children would learn the same lessons in the same language and turn out the same way. Only toward the end of the century, as immigration mounted, did eastern cities begin to offer night classes that taught English, along with civics lessons, for foreigners. When public education proved inadequate, immigrants established their own schools. Catholics, for example, started an elaborate expansion of their parochial schools in 1884.

By the 1880s educational reforms were helping schools respond to the needs of an urban society. Opened first in St. Louis in 1873, American versions of innovative German "kindergartens" put four- to six-year-olds in orderly classrooms while parents went off to work. "Normal schools" multiplied to provide teachers with more professional training. And in the new industrial age, science and manual training supplemented more conventional subjects in order to supply industry with educated workers.

### Higher Learning and the Rise of the Professional

Colleges served the urban industrial society, too, not by controlling mass habits but by providing leaders and managers. Early in the nineteenth century, most Americans had regarded higher learning as unmanly and irrelevant. The few who sought it often preferred the superior universities of Europe to those in the United States.

As American society grew more organized, mechanized, and complex, the need for professional, technical, and literary skills brought greater respect for

*Postgraduate education*

college education. The Morrill Act of 1862 generated a dozen new state colleges and universities, eight mechanical and agricultural colleges, and six black colleges. Private charity added more. Railroad barons like Johns Hopkins and Leland Stanford used parts of their fortunes to found colleges named after them (Hopkins in 1873, Stanford in 1890). The number of colleges and universities nearly doubled between 1870 and 1910, though less than 5 percent of college-age Americans enrolled in them.

A practical impulse inspired the founding of several black colleges. In the late nineteenth century, few institutions mixed races. Church groups and private foundations, such as the Peabody and Slater funds (supported by white donors from the North), underwrote black colleges after Reconstruction. By 1900, a total of 700 black students were enrolled. About 2000 had graduated. Through hard work and persistence, some even received degrees from institutions reserved for whites.

In keeping with the new emphasis on practical learning, professional schools multiplied to provide training beyond a college degree. American universities adopted the German model requiring young scholars to perform research as part of their education. The number of law and medical schools more than doubled between 1870 and 1900; medical students almost tripled. Ten percent of them were women, though their numbers shrank as physicians became more organized and exclusive.

Professionals of all kinds—in law, medicine, engineering, business, academics—swelled the ranks of the middle class. Slowly they were becoming a new force in urban America, replacing the ministers and gentlemen freeholders of an earlier day as community leaders.

## Higher Education for Women

Before the Civil War women could attend only three private colleges. After the war they had new ones all their own, including Smith (1871), Wellesley (1875), and Bryn Mawr (1885). Such all-women schools, with their mostly female faculties and administrators, deepened an emerging sense of membership in a special community of women. Many land-grant colleges, chartered to serve all people, also admitted women. By 1910 some 40 percent of college students were women, almost double the 1870 figure. Only one college in five refused to accept them.

Potent myths of gender continued to plague women in college. As Dr. Edward Clarke of the Harvard Medical School told thousands of students in *Sex in Education* (1873), the rigors of a college education could lead the "weaker sex" to physical or mental collapse, infertility, and early death. Women's colleges therefore included a program of physical activity to keep students healthy. Many offered an array of courses in "domestic science"—cooking, sewing, and other such skills—to counter the claim that higher education would be of no value to women.

College students, together with office workers and female athletes, became role models for ambitious young women. These "new women," impatient with custom, cast off Victorian restrictions. Fewer of them married, and more—perhaps 25 percent—were self-supporting. They shed their corsets and bustles and donned lighter, more comfortable clothing, such as "shirtwaist" blouses (styled after men's shirts) and lower-heeled shoes. And they showed that women could move beyond the domestic sphere of home and family.

## A Culture of Consumption

The city spawned a new material culture built around consumption. As standards of living rose, American industries began providing "ready-made" clothing to replace garments that had once been made at home. Similarly, food and furniture were mass-produced in greater quantities. The city became a giant market for these goods, the place where new patterns of mass consumption took hold. Radiating outward to more rural areas, this urban consumer culture helped to level American society. Increasingly city businesses sold the same goods to farmer and clerk, rich and poor, native-born and immigrant.

Well-made, inexpensive merchandise in standard sizes and shapes found outlets in new palaces of consumption known as "department stores," so called

*Department stores* because they displayed their goods in separate sections or departments. Unlike the small exclusive shops of Europe, department stores were palatial, public, and filled with inviting displays of furniture, housewares, and clothing.

The French writer Emile Zola claimed that department stores "democratized luxury." Anyone could enter free of charge, handle the most elegant and expensive goods, and buy whatever was affordable. When consumers found goods too pricey, department stores pioneered lay-away plans with deferred payments. The department store also educated people by showing them what "proper" families owned and the correct names for things like women's wear and parlor furniture. This process of socialization was occurring not only in cities but in towns and villages across America. Mass consumption was giving rise to a mass culture.

"Chain stores" (a term coined in America) spread the culture of consumption without frills. They catered to the working class, who could not afford department stores, and operated on a cash-and-carry basis. Owners

*Chain stores and mail-order houses* kept their costs down by buying in volume to fill the small stores in growing neighborhood chains. Founded in 1859, the Great Atlantic and Pacific Tea Company (later to become A&P supermarkets) was the first of the chain stores. By 1876 its 76 branch stores had added groceries to the original line of teas.

Far from department and chain stores, rural Americans joined the community of consumers by mail. In 1872, Aaron Montgomery Ward sent his first price sheet to farmers from a livery stable loft in Chicago. Ward avoided the middleman and promised savings of 40 percent on fans, needles, trunks, harnesses, and scores of other goods. By 1884, his catalog boasted 10,000 items, each illustrated by a lavish woodcut. Similarly, Richard W. Sears and Alvah C. Roebuck built a $500 million mail-order business by 1907. Schoolrooms that had no encyclopedia used a Ward's or Sears' catalog instead. When asked the source of the Ten Commandments, one farm boy replied that they came from Sears, Roebuck.

## Leisure

As mechanization gradually reduced the number of hours on the job, factory workers found themselves with more free time. So did the middle class, with free weekends, evenings, and vacations. A new, stricter division between work and play developed in the more disciplined society of industrial America. City dwellers turned leisure into a consumer item that often reflected differences in class, gender, and ethnicity.

Sports, for example, had been a traditional form of recreation for the rich. They continued to play polo, golf, and the newly imported English game of ten-

*Sports and class distinctions* nis. Croquet had more middle-class appeal. It required less skill and special equipment. Perhaps as important, it could be enjoyed in mixed company, like the new craze of bicycling. Bicycles evolved from unstable contraptions with large front wheels into "safety" bikes with equal-sized wheels, a dropped middle bar, pneumatic tires, and coaster brakes. A good one cost about $100, far beyond the reach of a factory worker. On Sunday afternoons city parks became crowded with cyclists. Women rode the new safety bikes too, although social convention prohibited them from riding alone. But cycling broke down conventions too. It required looser garments, freeing women from corsets. And lady cyclists demonstrated that they were hardly too fragile for physical exertion.

Organized spectator sports attracted crowds from every walk of life. Baseball overshadowed all others. For city dwellers with dull work, cramped quarters,

*Spectator sports for the urban masses*

and isolated lives, baseball offered the chance to join thousands of others for an exciting outdoor spectacle. The first professional teams appeared in 1869, and slowly the game evolved. Umpires began to call balls and strikes, the overhand replaced the underhand pitch, and fielders put on gloves. Teams from eight cities formed the National League of Professional Baseball Clubs in 1876, followed by the American League in 1901. League players were distinctly working class. At first, teams featured some black players. When African Americans were barred in the 1880s, black professionals formed their own team, the Cuban Giants of Long Island, New York, looking to play anyone they could.

Horse racing, bicycle tournaments, and other sports of speed and violence helped to break the monotony, frustration, and routine of the industrial city. In 1869, without pads or helmets, Rutgers beat Princeton in the first intercollegiate football match. By the 1890s the service academies and state universities fielded teams. Football soon attracted crowds of 50,000 or more. Beginning in 1891 when Dr. James Naismith nailed a peach basket to the gymnasium wall at the YMCA Training School in Springfield, Massachusetts, "basketball" became the indoor interlude between the outdoor sports of spring and fall.

### Arts and Entertainment

Variety also marked social life in the city. The saloon served as a workingman's club, while young working women escaped the drudgery of factory, office, or sweatshop at vaudeville shows and the new amusement parks. Coney Island's Luna Park, opened in 1903, drew 5 million customers in a single season. Jostling with crowds, eating ice cream and hot dogs, riding "Shoot-the-Chutes," young women and men, even the newest immigrants, could feel gloriously American. Instead of the Victorian values of orderly conduct and sober industry, amusement parks encouraged abandon, fantasy, and gaiety.

Workingmen took their dates to dance halls and boxing exhibitions, staged in small rings used for variety acts between fights. Wealthier couples went to concerts given by local symphony orchestras, which played a mixture of popular tunes, John Philip Sousa marches, and the music of classical European composers. At the theater, popular melodramas gave patrons a chance to avoid the

From balconies at theaters (like the one depicted in Charles Dana Gibson's pen-and-ink drawing *The Villain Dies*) rowdy patrons cheered, whistled, and booed at performers. Around the turn of the century, theater owners imposed strict rules of behavior on audiences in an effort to attract middle-class families.

ambiguities of modern life. Theatergoers booed villains and cheered heroes, as seen in the illustration above; they shuddered for heroines and marveled at tricky stage mechanics that made ice floes move and players float upward to heaven.

In villages and cities music of every tempo and style filled the air. Organ grinders churned out Italian airs on street corners. Steam-powered calliopes tooted spirited waltzes from amusement parks and riverboat decks. In bandstands brass ensembles played German-style concerts. By 1900 the sale of phonograph records had reached 3 million. Popular music became a big business, as companies hawked sentimental ballads like "My Mother Was a Lady" or topical tunes celebrating the discovery of oil or the changing styles of women's clothing. In Scott Joplin's "Maple Leaf Rag" (1899) the lively syncopation of ragtime heralded the coming of jazz.

As the nineteenth century drew to a close, the city was reshaping the country, just as the industrial system was creating a more specialized, diversified, and interlocking economy. Cities beckoned migrants from the countryside and immigrants from abroad with unparalleled opportunities for work and pleasure. The playwright Israel Zangwill celebrated the city's transforming power in his 1908 Broadway hit *The Melting Pot*. "The real American," one of his characters explained, "is only in the Crucible, I tell you—he will be the fusion of all the races, the coming superman."

Where Zangwill saw a melting pot with all its promise for a new super race, champions of traditional American values like the widely read Protestant minister Josiah Strong saw "a commingled mass of venomous filth and seething sin, of lust, of drunkenness, of pauperism, and crime of every sort." Both the champions and the critics of the late nineteenth century had a point. Corruption, crudeness, and disorder were no more or less a part of the cities than the vibrancy, energy, and opportunities that drew people to them. The gap between rich and poor yawned most widely in cities. As social critic Henry George observed, progress and poverty seemed to go hand in hand.

In the end moral judgments, whether pro or con, missed the point. Cities stood at the nexus of the new industrial order. All Americans, whatever they thought about the new urban world, had to search for ways to make that world work.

## SIGNIFICANT EVENTS

| | |
|---|---|
| 1869 | Cincinnati Red Stockings become first professional baseball team; Rutgers beats Princeton in first intercollegiate football game |
| 1870 | Elevated railroad begins operation in New York City |
| 1872 | William "Boss" Tweed convicted of defrauding city of New York |
| 1873 | Comstock Law enacted |
| 1874 | Woman's Christian Temperance Union founded |
| 1875 | Dwight Moody begins urban evangelical revivals |
| 1876 | Central Park completed in New York City; Johns Hopkins University opens nation's first graduate school |
| 1882 | Chinese Exclusion Act |
| 1883 | Brooklyn Bridge opens |
| 1885 | Home Life Insurance Building, world's first skyscraper, built in Chicago; first all-black professional baseball team, the Cuban Giants, organized |
| 1888 | Nation's first electric trolley line begins operation in Richmond, Virginia |
| 1889 | Hull House opens in Chicago |
| 1891 | Basketball invented |
| 1892 | Ellis Island opens as receiving station for immigrants |
| 1894 | Immigration Restriction League organized |
| 1897 | Boston opens nation's first subway station |

# CHAPTER TWENTY

# Agrarian Domains:
# The South and the West

**T**he news spread across the South during the late 1870s. Perhaps a man came around with a handbill, telling of cheap land; or a letter might arrive from friends or relatives and be read aloud at church. The news spread in different ways, but in the end, the talk always spelled *Kansas*.

Few black farmers had been to Kansas themselves. But more than a few knew that the abolitionist Old John Brown had lived there before coming east to raid Harpers Ferry. Black folks, it seemed, might be able to live more freely in Kansas. "You can buy land at from a dollar and a half to two dollars an acre," wrote one settler to his friend in Louisiana. There was another distinct advantage: "They do not kill Negroes here for voting."

In 1878 such prospects excited hundreds of black families already stretched to their limits by hardship and violence. With Rutherford Hayes president, Reconstruction was at an end. Southern state governments had been "redeemed" by conservative whites, and the future seemed uncertain. "COME WEST," concluded *The Colored Citizen*, a newspaper in Topeka. "COME TO KANSAS."

St. Louis learned of these rumblings in the first raw days of March 1879, as steamers from downriver began unloading freedmen in large numbers. While the weather was still cold, they sought shelter beneath tarpaulins along the river levee, built fires by the shore, and got out frying pans to cook meals while their children jumped rope nearby. By the end of 1879, more than 20,000 had arrived.

When the crowds overwhelmed the wharves and temporary shelters, the city's black churches banded together to house the "refugees," feed them, and

*The Exodusters* help them continue toward Kansas. Repeated rumors that rail passage would not be free failed to shake their hopes. "We's like de chilun ob Israel when dey was led from out o' bondage by Moses," one explained, referring to the Bible's tale of exodus from Egypt. "If we sticks togeter an' keeps up our faith we'll git to Kansas and be out o' bondage for shuah." So the "Exodusters," as they became known, pressed onward.

In the end, most of the black emigrants settled in growing towns like Topeka, Lincoln, and Kansas City. Men worked as hired hands; women did laundry. With luck, couples made $350 a year, saved a bit for a home, and put down roots.

The host of Exodusters who poured into Kansas were part of a human flood westward. It had many sources: played-out farms of New England and the South, crowded cities, all of Europe. Special trains brought the settlers to the plains, all eager to start anew. During the 1880s the number of Kansans jumped from a million to a million and a half. Other western states experienced similar booms.

Yet the boomers' optimistic spirits could not mask serious strains in the rapidly expanding nation, especially in the South and West. The boom economies of cotton, cattle, and grain all depended on city markets. Especially during hard times, westerners and southerners saw themselves as the victims of a colonial economic system, in which their fortunes were controlled by the industries of northeastern cities and their hardships ignored by Washington.

*Relations between the South, West, and Northeast*

But these self-styled victims themselves exploited both people and land. Whether locking former slaves into new forms of economic bondage or conquering land from Indians and Hispanics, both Southerners and Westerners built societies of racial caste. Violence became a common means of carving out and sustaining these societies. Imbalances emerged as drought, exhausted mines, overcut timberlands, and overproduction strained these regional economies to their limits.

## THE SOUTHERN BURDEN

Henry Grady, the editor of the Atlanta *Constitution*, often liked to tell the story of the poor cotton farmer buried in a pine coffin in the pine woods of Georgia. Only the coffin hadn't been made in Georgia but in Cincinnati. The nails in the coffin had been forged in Pittsburgh, though an iron mine lay near the cemetery. Even the farmer's cotton coat was made in New York and his trousers in Chicago. The "South didn't furnish a thing on earth for that funeral but the corpse and the hole in the ground!" fumed Grady. The irony of the story was the tragedy of the South. The region had human and natural resources aplenty but, alas, few factories to manufacture the goods it needed.

In the 1880s Grady campaigned to bring about a "New South" based on bustling industry, cities, and commerce. The business class and its values would displace the old planter class as southerners raced "to out-Yankee the Yankee." Grady and other publicists recognized the South's potential. Extending from Delaware south to Florida and west to Texas, the region took in a third of the nation's total area. It held a third of its arable farmlands, vast tracts of lumber, and rich deposits of coal, iron, oil, and fertilizers. To overcome the destruction of the Civil War and the loss of slave-

*The gospel of a "New South"*

holding wealth, apostles of the New South campaigned to catch up with the industrial North. But well into the twentieth century, Grady's New South remained the poorest section of the country. And it suffered as well the burden of an unwieldy labor system that was largely unskilled and racially divided.

## Agriculture in the New South

For all the hopeful talk of industry, the economy of the postwar South remained agricultural, tied to crops like tobacco, rice, sugar, and especially cotton. By us-

*A cotton-dominated economy*

ing fertilizers, planters were able to introduce cotton into areas once considered marginal. The number of acres planted in cotton more than doubled between 1870 and 1900. Some southern farmers sought prosperity in crops other than cotton. George Washington Carver, of Alabama's Tuskegee Institute (page 574), persuaded many poor black farmers to plant peanuts. But most southern soils were too acidic and the spring rains too heavy for other legumes and grains to flourish. Parasites and diseases plagued cattle herds. Try as southerners might to diversify, cotton still dominated their economy.

Yet from 1880 to 1900 world demand for cotton grew slowly, and prices fell. As farms in other parts of the country were becoming larger, more efficient, and tended by fewer workers per acre, southern farms decreased in size. This reflected the breakup of large plantations, but it also resulted from a high birthrate. Across the country, the number of children born per mother was dropping, but in the South, large families remained common because more children meant more farmhands. Each year, fewer acres of land were available for each person to cultivate. Even though the southern economy kept pace with national growth, per capita income fell behind.

## Tenancy and Sharecropping

To freedpeople across the South, the end of slavery brought hopes of economic independence. John Solomon Lewis was one farmer with such hopes. After the war Lewis rented land to grow cotton in Tensas Parish, Louisiana. A depression in the 1870s dashed his dreams. "I was in debt," Lewis explained, "and the man I rented land from said every year I must rent again to pay the other year, and so I rents and rents and each year I gets deeper and deeper in debt."

Lewis was impoverished like most small farmers in the cotton South. The South's best lands remained in the hands of large plantation owners. Few freed-

*Tenancy*

men or poor white southerners had money to acquire property. Like Lewis, most rented land—perhaps a plot of 15 to 20 acres— as tenants. Since cotton was king and money scarce, rents were generally set in pounds of cotton rather than dollars. Usually the amount added up to between one-quarter and one-half the value of the crop.

Among the most common and exploitative forms of farm tenancy in the South was sharecropping. Unlike renters, who leased land and controlled what

*Sharecropping and crop liens*

they raised, sharecroppers simply worked a parcel of land in exchange for a share of the crop, usually a third after debt was deducted. It was rarely enough to make ends meet and, like other forms of tenancy, left the farmer in perpetual debt. But this system would not have proved so ruinous if the South had possessed a fairer system of credit. Before selling crops in the fall, farmers without cash had to borrow money in the spring to buy seeds, tools, and other necessities. Most often, the only source of supplies was the local store. When John Solomon Lewis and other tenants entered the store, they saw two prices, one for cash and one for credit. The credit price might be as much as 60 percent higher. (By contrast, merchants in New York City seldom charged over 6 percent to buy on credit.) As security for the merchant's credit, the only asset most renters and sharecroppers could offer was a mortgage or "lien" on their crops. The lien gave the shopkeeper first claim on the crop until the debt was paid off.

Across the South, sharecropping and crop liens reduced many farmers to virtual slavery by shackling them to debt. Year after year, they rented land and

*Debt peonage*

borrowed against their harvests. This economic dependence, known as debt peonage, robbed small farmers of their freedom. The landlord or shopkeeper (often the same person) could insist that sharecroppers grow profitable crops like cotton rather than things they could eat. Most landlords also required that raw cotton be ginned, baled, and marketed

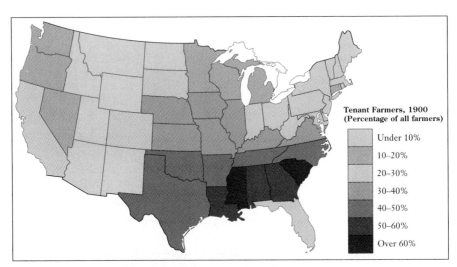

TENANT FARMERS, 1900   Tenant farming dominated southern agriculture after the Civil War. But notice that by 1900 it accounted for much of the farm labor in the trans-Mississippi West, where low crop prices, high costs, and severe environmental conditions forced independent farmers into tenancy.

through their mills—at a rate they controlled. "The white people do not allow us to sell our own crops," one black sharecropper remarked. "When we do, we do it at risk of our lives, getting whipped, shot at, and often some get killed." Sharecropping, crop liens, and monopolies on ginning and marketing added up to inequality and crushing poverty for the South's small farmers, black or white.

## Southern Industry

The crusade for a New South did bring change. From 1869 to 1909, industrial production grew faster than the national rate. A boom in railroad building af-

*Boom in textiles*

ter 1879 furnished the region with good transportation. In two areas, cotton textiles and tobacco, southern advances were striking. With cotton fiber and cheap labor close at hand, 400 cotton mills were humming by 1900, when they employed almost 100,000 workers.

Most new textile workers were white southerners escaping competition from black farm laborers or fleeing the hardscrabble life of the mountains. Entire families worked in the mills. Older men had the most trouble adjusting. They lacked the experience, temperament, and dexterity to tend spindles and looms in cramped mills. Only over time, as farm folk adapted to the tedious rhythm of factories, did southerners become competitive with workers from other regions of the United States and western Europe.

The tobacco industry also thrived in the New South. Before the Civil War, American tastes had run to cigars, snuff, and chewing tobacco. In 1876, James

*Tobacco and cigarettes*

Bonsack invented a machine to roll cigarettes. That was just the device Washington Duke and his son James needed to boost the fortunes of their growing tobacco business. Cigarettes suited the new urban market in the North. Unlike chewing tobacco and snuff, they were, in the words of one observer, "clean, quick, and potent."

Between 1860 and 1900, Americans spent more money on tobacco than on clothes or shoes. The sudden interest in smoking offered southerners a rare opportunity to control a national market. But the factories were so hot, the stench of tobacco so strong, and the work so unskilled that native-born white southerners generally refused the jobs. Duke solved the labor problem by hiring Jewish immigrants, expert cigar makers, to train black southerners in the techniques of tobacco work. Then he promoted cigarettes in a national advertising campaign, using gimmicks like collectible picture cards. By the 1890s his American Tobacco Company led the industry.

## Timber and Steel

In the postwar era, the South possessed over 60 percent of the nation's timber resources. With soaring demand from towns and cities, lumber and turpentine became the South's chief industries and employers. Aggressive lumbering, however, added little to local economies. Logging camps were isolated and temporary. Visitors described the lumberjacks as "single, homeless, and possession-less." Once loggers leveled the forests around their camps, they moved on to another site. Sawmills followed a similar pattern. Thus loggers and millers had little time to put down roots and invest their cash in the community.

The environmental costs were equally high. In the South as elsewhere, overcutting and other logging practices stripped hillsides bare. As spring rains

*Environmental costs*

eroded soil and unleashed floods, forests lost their capacity for self-renewal. With them went the golden eagles, peregrine fal-cons, and other native species.

Turpentine mills, logging, and lumbering provided young black southern-ers with their greatest source of employment. Occasionally an African American rose to be a supervisor, though most were white. Because the work was dirty and dangerous and required few skills, turnover was high and morale low. Workers usually left the mills for better wages or for sharecropping in order to marry and support families.

The iron and steel industry most disappointed promoters of the New South. The availability of coke as a fuel made Chattanooga, Tennessee, and Birming-

*Birmingham steel*

ham, Alabama, major centers for foundries. By the 1890s the Tennessee Coal, Iron, and Railway Company (TCI) of Birming-ham was turning out iron pipe for gas, water, and sewer lines vi-tal to cities. Unfortunately Birmingham's iron deposits were ill suited to pro-duce the kinds of steel in demand. In 1907 TCI was sold to the giant U.S. Steel Corporation, controlled by northern interests.

The pattern of lost opportunity was repeated in other southern industries. Under the campaign for a New South, all grew dramatically in employment and value, but not enough to end poverty. The South remained largely rural, agri-cultural, and poor.

## The Sources of Southern Poverty

Why did poverty persist in the New South? Many southerners claimed that the region was exploited by outside interests. In effect, they argued, the South be-came a colonial economy, controlled by business interests in New York or Pittsburgh, rather than Atlanta or New Orleans. Raw materials such as miner-als, timber, and cotton were shipped to other regions, which earned larger prof-its by turning them into finished goods.

Three factors peculiar to the South offer a better explanation for the re-gion's poverty. First, the South began to industrialize later than the Northeast,

*Late start in industrializing*

so northerners had a head start on learning new manufacturing techniques. Once southern workers overcame their inexperience, they competed well. Second, the South commanded only a small technological community to guide its industrial development. Northern engi-neers and mechanics seldom followed northern capital into the region. Few experts were available to adapt modern technology to southern conditions or to teach southerners how to do it themselves.

Education might have overcome the problem by upgrading the region's workforce. But no region in the nation spent less on schooling than the South.

*Undereducated labor*

Southern leaders, drawn from the ranks of the upper class, cared little about educating ordinary white residents and openly resisted educating black southerners. Education, they contended, "spoiled" otherwise contented workers by leading them to demand higher wages and better conditions. In fact, the region's low wages encouraged educated workers to leave the South in search of higher pay.

Lack of education aggravated the third and central source of southern poverty: the isolation of its labor force. In 1900 agriculture still dominated the

*The isolated southern labor market*

southern economy. It required unskilled, low-paid sharecroppers and wage laborers. Southerners feared outsiders, whether capitalists, industrialists, or experts in technology, who might spread discontent among workers. So southern states discouraged social services and opportunities that might have attracted human and financial resources, keeping their workforce secluded and uneducated. The South remained poor because it received too little, not too much, outside investment.

## LIFE IN THE NEW SOUTH

Many a southern man, noted a son of the region, loved "to toss down a pint of raw whiskey in a gulp, to fiddle and dance all night, to bite off the nose or gouge out the eye of a favorite enemy, to fight harder and love harder than the next man, to be known far and wide as a hell of a fellow. . . ." Life in the New South was a constant struggle to balance this love of sport and leisure with the powerful pull of Christian piety.

Divided in its soul, the South was also divided by race. After the Civil War, some 90 percent of African Americans continued to live in the rural South. Without slavery, however, white southerners lost the system of social control that had defined race relations. Over time they substituted a new system of racial separation that eased, but never eliminated, white fear of black Americans.

### Rural Life

Pleasure, piety, race—all divided southern life, in town and country alike. And in the country especially, where most southerners lived, life separated along lines of gender as well.

Southern males loved hunting. For rural people a successful hunt could add meat and fish to a scanty diet. Hunting also offered welcome relief from heavy

*Hunting*

farmwork. One South Carolinian recalled that possum hunting "gave you a wild feeling of being free." Through hunting many boys found a path to manhood. Seeing his father and brothers return with wild turkeys, young Edward McIlhenny longed "for the time when I would be old enough to hunt this bird."

The thrill of illicit pleasure drew many southern men to events of violence and chance, including cockfighting. They were convinced that their champions fought more boldly than northern bantams. Gambling between bird owners and among spectators only heightened the thrills. Such sport offended churchgoing southerners. They condemned as sinful "the beer garden, the baseball, the low theater, the dog fight and cock fight and the ring for the pugilist and brute."

On the other hand, many southern customs involved no such disorderly behavior. Work-sharing festivals celebrated the harvest and offered relief from the daily burdens of farm life. A Mississippian spoke of "neighborhood gatherings such as house raisings, log rollings, quiltings, and road workings." These events, too, were generally segregated along gender lines. Men did the heavy chores and competed in contests of physical prowess. Women shared more domestic tasks. Quilting was a favorite, for it brought women an opportunity to work together and enjoy one another's company. Community gatherings also offered young southerners an opportunity for courtship. In one courting game, the young man who found a rare red ear of corn "could kiss the lady of his choice"—although in the school, church, or home under adult supervision, such behavior was discouraged.

*Farm entertainments*

For rural folk, a trip to town brought special excitement and a bit of danger. Saturdays, court days, and holidays provided an occasion to mingle. For men the saloon, the blacksmith shop, or the storefront was a place to do business and to let off steam. Few men went to town without participating in social drinking. When they turned to roam the streets, the threat of brawling and violence drove most women away. One Tennessee woman claimed that "it was never considered safe for a lady to go down on the streets on Saturdays."

*Town*

Court week drew the biggest crowds as a district judge arrived to mete out rough justice. Some people came to settle disputes; most came to enjoy the spectacle or do some business like horse trading. Peddlers and entertainers worked the crowds with magic tricks, patent medicines, and other wares. Town also offered a chance to attend the theater or a traveling circus.

## The Church

At the center of southern life stood the church as a great stabilizer and custodian of social order. "When one joined the Methodist church," a southern woman recalled, "he was expected to give up all such things as cards, dancing, theatres, in fact all so called worldly amusements." Many devout southerners pursued these ideals, although such restraint asked more of people, especially men, than most were willing to show, except perhaps on Sunday.

For Baptists in the South, the ceremony of adult baptism included immersion, often in a nearby river. The ritual symbolized the waters of newfound faith washing away sins. Here, a black congregation looks on, some holding umbrellas to protect against the sun.

Congregations were often so small and isolated they could attract a preacher only once or twice a month. Evangelicals counted on the Sunday sermon to steer them from sin. In town, a sermon might last 30 to 45 minutes, but in the country, a preacher could go on for two hours or more, whipping up his congregation until "even the little children wept."

*Rural religion*

By 1870 southern churches were segregated by race (see page 455). Congregations, particularly in rural areas, were separated by gender, too. Upon seeing a man and woman seated together, a Virginia Baptist claimed "they were from Richmond or Lynchburg, or some other city where folks did not know any better." Churches were female domains. Considered guardians of virtue, women made up a majority of members, attended church more often, and ran many church activities.

Church was a place to socialize as well as worship. Church picnics and all-day sings brought people together for hours of eating, talk, services, and hymn singing. Still, these occasions could not match the fervor of a week-long camp meeting. In the late summer or early fall, town and countryside alike emptied as folks set up tents in shady groves and listened to two or three ministers preach day and night, in the largest event of the year. The camp meeting re-fired evangelical faith while celebrating traditional values of home and family.

## Segregation

After Reconstruction, white northerners and southerners achieved sectional harmony by sacrificing the rights of black citizens. White southerners were assured that in matters of race they would be "left alone" by the federal govern-

*Laissez-faire race relations*

ment. The hands-off, or laissez-faire, approach also suited even white northerners who had once championed black rights. The editor of one magazine published in New York told northern readers that he doubted whether former slaves were capable of participating in "a system of government for which you and I have much respect." In the New South, African Americans would remain free but scarcely equal.

During the 1880s, Redeemer governments (pages 461–462) moved to formalize a new system of segregation or racial separation. The pressure to do so increased as more African Americans moved into southern towns and cities, competing for jobs with poor whites. One way to preserve the social and economic superiority of white southerners, poor as well as rich, was to separate blacks as an inferior caste. But federal laws designed to enforce the Civil Rights Act of 1866 and the Fourteenth Amendment stood in the way. In effect, they established social equality for all races in public places such as hotels, theaters, and railroads.

In 1883, however, the Supreme Court ruled in the *Civil Rights Cases* that hotels and railroads were not "public" institutions because private individuals owned them. The Fourteenth Amendment was thus limited to protecting citizens from violations of their civil rights only by states, not by private individuals. The national policy of laissez faire in race relations could not have been made any clearer.

Within 20 years every southern state had enacted segregation as law. The earliest laws legalized segregation in trains and other public conveyances. Soon

*Jim Crow laws*

a web of "Jim Crow" statutes separated the races in almost all public places except streets and stores. (The term "Jim Crow," to denote a policy of segregation, originated in a song of the same name sung in minstrel shows of the day.) In 1896, the Supreme Court again upheld the policy of segregation. *Plessy v. Ferguson* upheld a Louisiana law requiring segregated railroad facilities. Racial separation did not constitute discrimination, the Court

*Plessy v. Ferguson*

argued, so long as accommodations for both races were equal. In reality, of course, such separate facilities were seldom equal and always stigmatized African Americans.

By the turn of the century segregation was firmly in place, stifling economic competition between the races and reducing African Americans to second-class citizenship. Many kinds of employment, such as work in the textile mills, went largely to whites. Skilled and professional black workers generally served black clients only. Blacks could enter some white residences only as servants and hired help, and then only by the back door. They were barred from juries and usually received far stiffer penalties than whites for the same crimes. Any African

American who crossed the color line risked violence. Some were tarred and feathered, others whipped and beaten, and many lynched. Of the 187 lynchings averaged each year of the 1890s, some 80 percent occurred in the South, where the victims were usually black.

## WESTERN FRONTIERS

The black Exodusters flooding into the treeless plains of Kansas in the 1870s and 1880s were only part of the vast migration west. Looking beyond the Mississippi in the 1840s and 1850s, "overlanders" had set their sights on California and Oregon and the promise of land. So they headed into the trans-Mississippi West, pushing the frontier of Anglo settlement to the edge of the continent. They rolled over the Great Plains, through the snow-capped Rockies, and across the Great Basin, with deserts so dry rain sometimes evaporated before hitting the ground. When they reached the fertile valleys of the coast, they were ready, as one Oregonian immigrant proclaimed, "to seek their fortunes and settle an empire."

The overlanders went west in search of opportunity and "free" land. In the trans-Mississippi West, however, opportunity proved elusive to those without

*Moving frontiers*

money or power. They also found Indians and "Hispanos" (settlers of Spanish descent), who hardly considered the land free for use by Anglos. They discovered that the West was not one region but many, each governed by a different ecology. And its frontiers moved in many directions, not just from east to west. Before the Civil War, the frontier for easterners had moved beyond the Mississippi to the timberlands of Missouri, but skipped over the Great Plains, as the overlanders settled in California and Oregon. Another frontier then pushed east from the Pacific coast, following miners into the Sierra Nevadas. For Texans, the frontier moved from south to north as cattle ranchers sought new grazing land, as had the ancestors of the Hispanic *rancheros* of the Southwest. And for American Indians, the frontier was constantly shifting and disrupting their ways of life.

---

COUNTERPOINT   *How to Define the Frontier*

For historian Frederick Jackson Turner, writing in the 1890s, the West was not many frontiers but one. He defined it as a westward-moving line, "the meeting point of savagery and civilization." For Turner, the frontier represented the march of progress into isolated areas of "free land." Its significance in American history—as social safety valve, as cradle of democracy, as fountain of American self-reliance and sense of community—could no longer be ignored.

Modern historians have rejected this "Turner thesis," though not the importance of the West in American history. In the ethnocentric fashion of his day, Turner ignored the presence of rich Hispanic and Indian cultures beyond the bounds of Anglo settlement, just as he ignored the important role of women in the West. Where Turner saw a westward-moving frontier along which savagery met civilization, modern historians see a "new West" of conflict and conquest, of opportunity and cultural interplay along a series of shifting borders.

## The Western Landscape

Early travellers from the United States labelled the vast lands beyond the Mississippi the "Great American Desert"—with good reason. Most of the region between the 98th meridian and the West Coast receives fewer than 20 inches of rain a year, making the Great Plains a treeless expanse of prairie grass and dunes. But the plains are only part of the trans-Mississippi West. And even they can be divided. The Great Plains west of the 98th meridian are semi-arid, but the eastern Prairie Plains are favored with good soil and abundant rain. Beyond the plains the jagged peaks of the Rocky Mountains stretch from Alaska to New Mexico. And beyond the mountains lies the Great Basin of Utah, Nevada, and eastern California, where temperatures climb above 100 degrees and the ground cracks. Near the coast rise the Sierra Nevadas and Cascades, rich in minerals and lumber and sloping to the temperate shores of the Pacific.

Already by the 1840s, the Great Plains and mountain frontier comprised a complex web of cultures and environments. The horse, for example, had been introduced into North America by the colonial Spanish. By the eighteenth century horses were grazing on prairie grass across the Great Plains. By the nineteenth century the Comanche, Cheyenne, Apache, and other tribes had become master riders and hunters, who could shoot their arrows with deadly accuracy at a full gallop. The new mobility of the Plains Indians far extended the area in which they could hunt buffalo. Their lives shifted from settled, village-centered agriculture to a more nomadic existence.

## Indian Peoples and the Western Environment

Some whites embraced the myth of the Indian as "noble savage" who lived in perfect harmony with the natural world. To be sure, Plains Indians were inventive in using scarce resources. Cottonwood bark fed horses in winter, while the buffalo supplied not only meat but also bones for tools, fat for cosmetics, and sinews for thread. Yet Indians could not help but alter their environment. Plains Indians hunted buffalo by stampeding herds over cliffs, which often led to waste. They irrigated crops and set fires to improve vegetation. By the mid-nineteenth century some tribes had become so enmeshed in the white fur trade that they overtrapped their own hunting grounds. In these and other ways, Indians altered the ecological systems around them.

Ecosystems, in turn, helped shape Indian cultures. Although big-game hunting was common among many western tribes, the nomadic buffalo culture

*Variety of Indian cultures*

of the Plains Indians was hardly representative. In the lush forests and mountain ranges of the Pacific Northwest, Yuroks, Chinook, and other tribes hunted bear, moose, elk, and deer. Along the rocky coast they took whales, seals, and a variety of fish from the ocean. The Yakimas and Walla Wallas moved into the river valleys for the great salmon runs. Elsewhere, with land less bountiful, Indian tribes lived close to starvation. Utes, Shoshones, Paiutes, and Pavistos scoured the deserts of the Great Basin to eke out a diet of rabbits, snakes, insects, roots, and berries.

Despite their diversity, Indian peoples shared certain values. Most tribes were small kinship groups of 300 to 500 people in which the well-being of all

*Shared values*

outweighed the needs of each member. Although some tribes were materially better off than others, the gap between rich and poor within tribes was seldom large. Such small material differences often promoted communal decision making. The Cheyenne, for example, employed a council of 44 to advise the chief.

Most of all, Indians shared a reverence for nature, whatever their actual impact on the natural world. They believed human beings were part of an interconnected world of animals, plants, and other natural elements. All had souls of their own but were bound together, as if by contract, to live in balance through the ceremonial life of the tribe and the customs related to specific plants and animals. The Taos of New Mexico believed that each spring the pregnant earth issued new life. To avoid disturbing "mother" earth, they removed the hard shoes from their horses and walked themselves in bare feet or soft moccasins.

Such regard for the land endowed special places with religious meaning utterly foreign to most whites. Where the Sioux saw in the Black Hills the sacred home of Wakan Tanka, the burial place of the dead, and the site of their "vision quests," whites saw grass for grazing and gold for the taking. From such contrasting views came conflict.

## Whites and the Western Environment: Competing Visions

As discoveries of gold and silver lured white settlers into Indian territory, many adopted the confident outlook of Missouri politician William Gilpin. Only a

*William Gilpin, a western booster*

lack of vision prevented the opening of the West for exploitation, Gilpin told an Independence, Missouri, audience in 1849. What was most needed were cheap lands and a railroad linking the two coasts "like ears on a human head." In his expansive view, Indians were just another impediment to overcome.

By 1868 a generous Congress had granted western settlers their two greatest wishes: free land under the Homestead Act of 1862, and a transcontinental railroad. As the new governor of Colorado, Gilpin crowed about the region's limitless resources. One day, he believed, the West would support more than a billion peo-

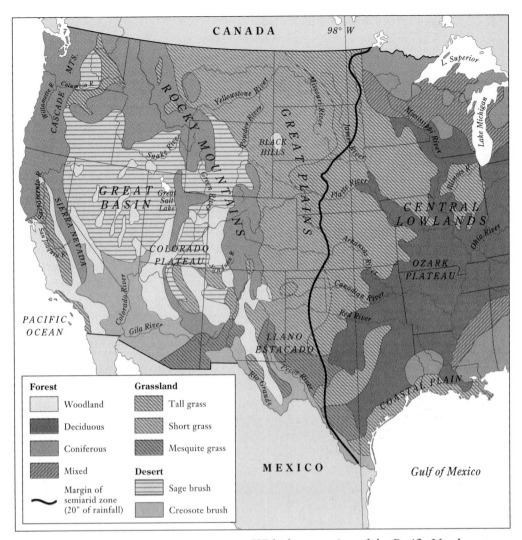

NATURAL ENVIRONMENT OF THE WEST   With the exception of the Pacific Northwest, few areas west of the 20-inch rainfall line receive enough annual precipitation to support agriculture without irrigation. Consequently water has been the key to development west of the 98th meridian, encompassing more than half the country.

ple. Scarce rainfall and water did not daunt him, for in his eyes the West was an Eden-like garden, not a desert. Once the land had been planted, Gilpin assured listeners, the rains would develop naturally. He subscribed to the popular notion that "rain follows the plow."

Unlike the visionary Gilpin, John Wesley Powell knew something about water and farming. After losing an arm in the Civil War, geologist Powell came

*John Wesley Powell*

west. In 1869 and 1871 he led scientific expeditions down the Green and Colorado rivers through the Grand Canyon. Navigating the swirling rapids that blocked his way, he returned to warn Congress that developing the West required more scientific planning. Much of the region had not yet been mapped nor its resources identified.

In 1880 Powell became director of the recently formed U.S. Geological Survey. He, too, had a vision of the West, but one based on the limits of its environment. The key was water, not land. In the water-rich East, the English legal tradition of river rights prevailed. Whoever owned the banks of a river or stream controlled as much water as they might take, regardless of the consequence for those downstream. Such a practice in the West, Powell recognized, would enrich the small number with access to water while spelling ruin for the rest.

*Water as a key resource*

The alternative was to treat water as community property. The practice would benefit many rather than a privileged few. To that end Powell suggested that the federal government establish political boundaries defined by watersheds and regulate the distribution of the scarce resource. But his scientific realism could not overcome the popular vision of the West as the American Eden. Powerful interests ensured that development occurred with the same laissez-faire credo that ruled the East.

## THE WAR FOR THE WEST

Beginning in 1848, a series of gold and silver discoveries signaled the first serious interest by white settlers in the arid and semiarid lands beyond the Mississippi. To open more land, federal officials introduced in 1851 a policy of "concentration." Tribes were pressured into signing treaties limiting the boundaries of their hunting grounds—the Sioux to the Dakotas, the Crow to Montana, the Cheyenne to the foothills of Colorado. Such treaties often claimed that their provisions would last "as long as waters run," but time after time, land-hungry pioneers broke the promises of their government by squatting on Indian lands and demanding federal protection. The government, in turn, forced more restrictive agreements on the western tribes. This cycle of promises made and broken was repeated, until a full-scale war for the West raged between whites and Indians.

*Policy of concentration*

### Contact and Conflict

By 1862 the lands of the Santee Sioux had been whittled down to a strip 10 miles wide and 150 miles long along the Minnesota River. Lashing out in frustration, the tribe attacked several undefended white settlements along the Minnesota frontier. In response, General John Pope arrived in St. Paul declaring his intention to wipe out the Sioux. "They are to be treated as maniacs or

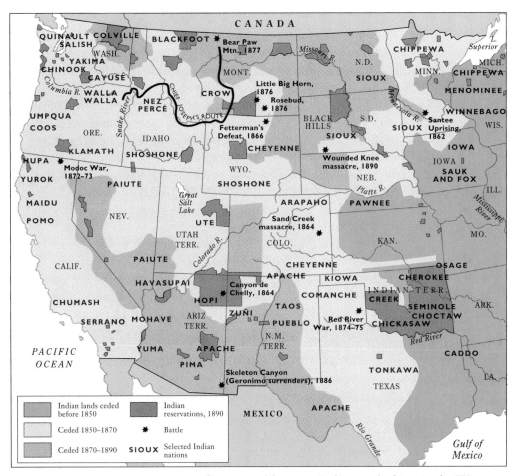

THE INDIAN FRONTIER   As conflict erupted between Indians and whites in the West, the government pursued a policy of concentrating tribes on reservations. Indian resistance helped unite the Sioux and Cheyenne, traditionally enemies, in the Dakotas in the 1870s.

wild beasts and by no means as people," he instructed his officers. When Pope's forces captured 1800 Sioux, white Minnesotans were outraged that President Lincoln ordered only 38 hanged.

The campaign under General Pope was the opening of a guerrilla war that continued off and on for some 30 years. The conflict gained momentum in

*Chivington massacre*

November 1864, when a force of Colorado volunteers under Colonel John Chivington fell upon a band of friendly Cheyenne gathered at Sand Creek under army protection. Chief Black Kettle raised an American flag to signal friendship, but Chivington would have none of it. "Kill and scalp all, big and little," he told his men. The troops massacred well over 100, including children holding white flags of truce and mothers with babies in their arms. In 1865 virtually all Plains Indians joined in the First Sioux War to drive whites from their lands.

War was only one of several ways in which contact with whites undermined tribal cultures. Liquor and disease, including smallpox, measles, and cholera, killed more Indians than combat. On the Great Plains the railroad disrupted the migratory patterns of the buffalo and thus the patterns of the hunt. Tourist parties came west to bag the buffalo from railside. When hides became popular back East, commercial companies hired hunters who killed more than 100 bison an hour. Military commanders promoted the butchery as a way of weakening Indian resistance. In three short years, from 1872 to 1874, approximately 9 million members of the herd were slaughtered. By 1883 bison had nearly disappeared from the plains. In other areas mines, crops, grazing herds, and fences disturbed traditional hunting and farming lands of many tribes.

### Custer's Last Stand—And the Indians

The Sioux War ended in 1868 with the signing of the Treaty of Fort Laramie. It established two large Indian reservations, one in Oklahoma and the other in the Dakota Badlands. Only six years later, however, Colonel George Armstrong Custer led an expedition into *Paha Sapa*, the sacred Black Hills of the Sioux. In doing so, he flagrantly disregarded the treaty of 1868. Custer, a Civil War veteran, already had a reputation as a "squaw killer" for his cruel warfare against Indians in western Kansas. To open the Black Hills to whites, his expedition spread rumors of gold "from the grass roots down." Prospectors poured into Indian country. Federal authorities tried to force yet another treaty to gain control of the Black Hills. When negotiations failed, President Grant ordered all "hostiles" in the area driven onto the reservations.

In reaction the Cheyenne for the first time allied with the Sioux, who were led by the young war chief Crazy Horse and medicine man Sitting Bull. Against

*Battle of Little Big Horn*

them in the summer of 1876 marched several army columns, including Custer's Seventh Cavalry of about 600 troops. Custer, eager for glory, arrived at the Little Big Horn River a day earlier than the other columns. Hearing of a native village nearby, he attacked, only to discover that he had stumbled onto an encampment of more than 12,000 Sioux and Cheyenne, extending for almost three miles. From a deep ravine Crazy Horse charged Custer, killing him and some 250 soldiers.

As he led the attack, Crazy Horse yelled "It is a good day to die!"—the traditional war cry. Even in the midst of victory he spoke truly. Although Custer had been conquered, railroads stood ready to extend their lines, prospectors to make fortunes, and soldiers to protect them. By late summer the Sioux were forced to split into small bands in order to evade the army. While Sitting Bull barely escaped to Canada, Crazy Horse and 800 with him surrendered in 1876 after a winter of suffering and starvation.

The battles along the Platte and upper Missouri rivers did not end the war between whites and Indians, but never again would it reach such proportions. Even peaceful tribes like the Nez Percé of Idaho found no security once whites began to hunger for their land. The Nez Percé had become breeders of livestock, rich in horses and cattle that they grazed in the meadows west of the Snake River canyon. That did not prevent the government from trying to force them onto a small reservation in 1877.

Rather than see his people humiliated, Chief Joseph led almost 600 Nez Percé toward Canada, pursued by the U.S. Army. In 75 days they traveled more than 1300 miles. Every time the army closed to attack, Chief Joseph's warriors drove them off. But before they could reach the border, they were trapped and forced to surrender. The government then shipped the defeated tribe to the bleak Indian Country of Oklahoma. There disease and starvation finished the destruction the army had begun.

*Chief Joseph*

## *Killing with Kindness*

By 1887 reformers recognized that the policy of concentrating Indians on reservations had failed. With a mix of good intentions and unbridled greed, Congress adopted the Dawes Severalty Act in 1887. It ended reservation policy with the goals of drawing Indians into white society as farmers and small property owners and (less high-mindedly) their lands into the marketplace. Lands held by tribes would now be parceled out to individuals: 160 acres to the head of a family and 80 acres to single adults or orphans.

*The Dawes Act*

In practice, the Dawes Act was more destructive than any blow struck by the army. It undermined the communal structure upon which Indian tribal life was based. And as John Wesley Powell had warned, small homestead farms in the West could not support a family—white or Indian—unless they were irrigated. Most Indians, moreover, had no experience with farming, managing money, or other white ways. The sponsors of the Dawes Act, knowing that whites might swindle Indians out of their private holdings, arranged for the government to hold title to the land for 25 years, but that did not stop unscrupulous speculators from "leasing" lands. Furthermore, all reservation lands not allocated to Indians were opened to non-Indian homesteaders.

Against such a dismal future, some Indians sought solace in the past. In 1890 a religious revival spread when word came from the Nevada desert that a humble Paiute named Wovoka had received revelations from the Great Spirit. Wovoka preached that if his followers adopted his mystical rituals and lived together in love and harmony, the Indian dead would come back, whites would be driven from the land, and game would be thick again. As the rituals spread, alarmed settlers called the strange shuffling and chanting the "Ghost Dance." The army moved to stop the proceedings among the Sioux for fear of another uprising. At Wounded Knee in South Dakota the

*Wounded Knee*

E Y E W I T N E S S    T O    H I S T O R Y

## An Indian Girl Is Shorn at Boarding School

L ate in the morning, my friend Judewin gave me a terrible warning. . . . She heard the paleface woman talk about cutting our long, heavy hair. Our mothers had taught us that only unskilled warriors who were captured had their hair shingled by the enemy. Among our people, short hair was worn by mourners, and shingled hair by cowards!

We discussed our fate some moments, and when Judewin said, "We have to submit, because they are strong," I rebelled.

"No, I will not submit! I will struggle first!" I answered.

I watched my chance, and when no one noticed I disappeared, I crept up the stairs as quietly as I could in my squeaking shoes—my moccasins had been exchanged for shoes. . . . Turning aside to an open door, I found a large room with three white beds in it. . . . On my hands and knees I crawled under [a] bed, and cuddled myself in the dark corner.

From my hiding place I peered out. . . . Loud voices were calling my name, and I knew that even Judewin was searching for me. . . . Then the steps were quickened and the voices became excited. . . . Women and girls entered the room. I held my breath and watched them open closet doors and peep behind large trunks. . . . What caused them to stoop and look under the bed I do not know. I remember being dragged out, though I resisted by kicking and scratching wildly. In spite of myself, I was carried downstairs and tied fast in a chair.

I cried aloud, shaking my head all the while until I felt the cold blades on the scissors against my neck, and heard them gnaw off one of my thick braids. Then I lost my spirit. Since the day I was taken from my mother I had suffered extreme indignities. People had stared at me. I had been tossed about in the air like a wooden puppet. And now my long hair was shingled like a coward's! In my anguish I moaned for my mother, but no one came to comfort me. Not a soul reasoned quietly with me, as my own mother used to do; for now I was only one of many little animals driven by a herder.

Zitkala-Sa (Gertrude Simmons Bonnin), "The School Days of an Indian Girl," *Atlantic Monthly*, Vol. 89 (1900) January–March, pp. 45–47, 190, 192–194.

cavalry fell upon one band and with devastating artillery fire killed at least 146 men, women, and children.

Wounded Knee was a final act of violence against an independent Indian way of life. After 1890 the battle was over assimilation, not extinction. The system of markets, rail networks, and extractive industries was linking the Far West with the rest of the nation. Free-roaming bison were replaced by herded cattle and sheep, nomadic tribes by prairie sodbusters, and sacred hunting grounds by gold fields. Reformers relied on education, citizenship, and allotments to move Indians from their communal lives into white society. Most Indians were equally determined to preserve their tribal ways and separateness as a people.

## Borderlands

The coming of the railroad in the 1880s and 1890s brought wrenching changes to the Southwest as well, with a twist. As new markets and industries sprang up, new settlers poured in from the east but also from the south, across the Mexican border. Indians like the Navajo and the Apache thus faced the hostility of Anglos *and* Hispanos, those settlers of Spanish descent already in the region.

Like Indians, Hispanos discovered that they had either to embrace or to resist the flood of new Anglos. The elite, or *Ricos*, often aligned themselves with

*Juan José Herrera and the White Caps*

Anglos against their countryfolk to protect their status and property. Others, including Juan José Herrera, resisted the newcomers. When Anglo cattle ranchers began forcing Hispanos off their lands near Las Vegas, Herrera assembled a band of masked night riders known as *Las Gorras Blancas* (the White Caps). In 1889 and 1890 as many as 700 White Caps burned Anglo fences, haystacks, and occasionally barns and houses, and attacked railroads that refused to raise the low wages of Hispano workers.

New Anglos frequently fought Hispanos. But it was western lawyers and politicians, using legal tactics, who deprived Hispanos of most of their property. Thomas Catron, an ambitious New Mexico lawyer, squeezed out many Hispanos by contesting land titles so aggressively that his holdings grew to 3 million acres. In those areas of New Mexico and California where they remained a majority, Hispanos continued to play a role in public life. During the early 1890s Herrera and his allies formed a "People's Party," swept local elections, and managed to defeat a bid by Catron to represent the territory in Congress.

With the railroads came more white settlers, as well as Mexican laborers from south of the border. Just as the southern economy depended on African

*Mexican immigrants*

American labor, the Southwest grew on the labor of Mexicans. Mexican immigrants worked mostly as contract and seasonal laborers for railroads and large farms. Many of them settled in the growing cities along the rail lines: El Paso, Albuquerque, Tucson, Phoenix, and Los Angeles. They lived in segregated *barrios*, Spanish towns, where their cultural traditions persisted. But by the late nineteenth century, most

Hispanics, whether in barrios or on farms and ranches, had been excluded from power.

Yet to focus on cities alone would distort the experience of most southwesterners of Spanish descent, who lived in small villages like those in northern New Mexico and southern Colorado. There a pattern of adaptation and resistance to Anglo penetration developed. As the market economy advanced, Hispanic villagers turned to migratory labor to adapt. While women continued to work in the old villages, men traveled from job to job in mining, in farming, and on the railroads. The resulting "regional communities" of village and migrant workers allowed Hispanic residents to preserve the communal culture of the village, incorporating those aspects of Anglo culture—like the sewing machine—that suited their needs. At the same time, the regional community also sustained migrant workers with a base of operations and a haven to which they could return in protest against harsh working conditions.

## BOOM AND BUST IN THE WEST

Opportunity in the West lay in land and resources, but wealth also accumulated in the towns. Each time a speculative fever hit a region, new communities sprouted to serve those who rushed in. The western boom began in mining— with the California Gold Rush of 1849 and the rise of San Francisco (see page 367). In the decades that followed, new hordes threw up towns in Park City, Utah; Tombstone, Arizona; Deadwood in the Dakota Territories; and other promising sites. All too often, busts followed booms, transforming boom towns into ghost towns.

### Mining Sets a Pattern

The gold and silver strikes of the 1840s and 1850s set a pattern followed by other booms. Stories of easy riches attracted single prospectors with their shovels and wash pans. Almost all were male and nearly half foreign-born. Muddy mining camps sprang up, where a prospector could register a claim, get provisions, bathe, and buy a drink or a companion. Outfitting these boom societies siphoned riches into the pockets of storeowners and other suppliers. Once the quick profits were gone, a period of consolidation brought more order to towns and larger scale to regional businesses.

In the mine fields, that meant corporations with the capital for hydraulic water jets to blast ore loose and other heavy equipment to crush rock and ex-

*Environmental costs*

tract silver and gold from deeper veins. In their quest for quick profits, such operations often led to environmental disaster. Floods, mud slides, and dirty streams threatened the livelihood of farmers in the valleys below.

In corporate mining operations, paid laborers replaced the independent prospectors of earlier days. As miners sought better wages and working conditions, along with shorter hours, management fought back. In Coeur d'Alene, Idaho, troops crushed a strike in 1892, killing seven miners. The miners, in turn, created the Western Federation of Miners. In the decade after 1893 the union attracted some 50,000 members and gained a reputation for militancy. In a cycle repeated elsewhere, the rowdy mining frontier of small-scale prospectors was integrated into the industrial system of wage labor, large-scale resource extraction, and high finance capital.

## The Transcontinental Railroad

As William Gilpin predicted in 1849, the development of the West awaited the railroads. Before the Central and Union Pacific railroads were joined in 1869, travel across the West was slow and dusty. Vast distances and sparse population gave entrepreneurs little chance to follow the eastern practice of building local railroads from city to city.

In 1862 Congress granted the Central Pacific Railroad the right to build the western link of the transcontinental railroad eastward from Sacramento. To

*Railroad land grants*

the Union Pacific Corporation fell responsibility for the section from Omaha westward. Generous loans and gifts of federal and state lands made the venture wildly profitable. For every mile of track completed, the rail companies received between 200 and 400 square miles of land—some 45 million acres by the time the route was completed. Fraudulent stock practices, corrupt accounting, and wholesale bribery (involving a vice president of the United States and at least two members of Congress) swelled profits even more. More than 75 western railroads eventually benefited from such government generosity before the lines were linked at Promontory Point, Utah, on May 10, 1869.

General Grenville Dodge, an army engineer on leave to the Union Pacific, recruited his immense labor force from Irish and other European immigrants. Charles Crocker of the Central Pacific relied on some 10,000 Chinese laborers. With wheelbarrows, picks, shovels, and baskets they inched eastward, building trestles like the one at Secrettown (see page 547) and chipping away at the Sierras' looming granite walls.

As the railroads pushed west in the 1860s, they helped to spawn cities like Denver and later awakened sleepy communities such as Los Angeles.

*The power of the railroads*

Railroads opened the Great Plains to cattle drives that in the 1870s brought great herds to "cow towns" like Sedalia, Missouri, and Cheyenne, Wyoming, where cattle could be shipped to market. The rail companies recognized the strategic position they held. Just by threatening to bypass a town, a railroad could extract concessions on rights of way, taxes, and loans. If a key to profiting from the gold rush was supplying miners, one way to prosper from the West was to control transportation. That was why westerners developed such mixed feelings toward the railroads.

Trestles for the transcontinental railroad at Secrettown. Nearly 10,000 Chinese laborers, some pictured above, chipped away with picks and shovels at the granite walls of the Sierra Nevadas.

## Cattle Kingdom

Westerners recognized that railroads were crucial components of the cattle industry. Cow towns like Abilene, Denver, and Cheyenne flourished from the business of the growing cattle kingdom. By 1860, some 5 million head of longhorn cattle were wandering the grassy plains of Texas. Ranchers allowed their herds to roam the unbroken or "open" range freely, identified only by a distinctive brand. Each spring cowboys rounded up the herds, branded the calves, and selected the steers to send to market.

Anglo-Americans who came to Texas readily adopted the Mexican equipment: the tough mustangs and broncos (horses suited to managing mean-

*Mexican ranching techniques*

spirited longhorns), the branding iron for marking the herds, the corral for holding cattle, and the *riata*, or lariat, for roping. The cowboys also wore Mexican chaps, spurs, and broad-brimmed sombrero, or "hat that provides shade." After the Civil War, veterans of the Confederate army made up the majority of the cowhands in Texas. But at least a third of all cowboys were Mexicans and black freedmen.

In 1866, as rail lines swept west, Texas ranchers began driving their herds north to railheads for shipment to market. These "long drives" lasted two to three months and might cover more than 1000 miles. When early routes to Sedalia, Missouri, proved unfriendly, ranchers scouted alternatives. The

Chisholm Trail led from San Antonio to Abilene and Ellsworth in Kansas. More westerly routes ran to Dodge City and even Denver and Cheyenne.

Since cattle grazed on the open range, early ranches were primitive. Most had a house for the rancher and his family, a bunkhouse for the hired hands, and about 30 to 40 acres per animal. Women were scarce in the cattle kingdom. Most were ranchers' wives, who cooked, nursed the sick, and helped run things. Some women ranched themselves. When Helen Wiser Stewart of Nevada learned that her husband had

*Home on the range*

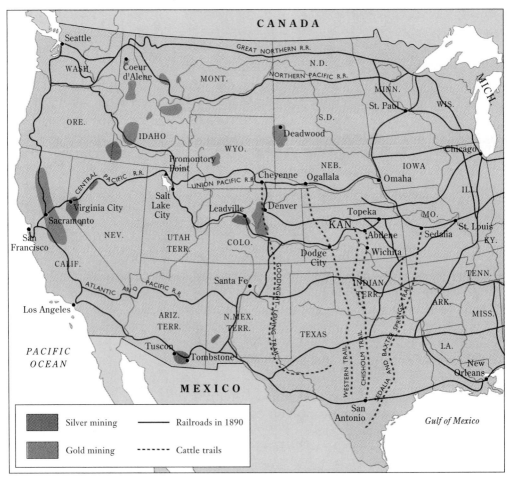

THE MINING AND CATTLE FRONTIERS   Railroads, cattle trails, and gold mines usually preceded the arrival of enough settlers to establish a town. Cattle trails ended at rail lines, where cattle could be shipped to city markets. By transecting the plains, railroads disrupted the migratory patterns of the buffalo, undermining Indian cultures and opening the land to grazing and farming.

been murdered, she took over the ranch. Her life was an endless round of buying and selling cattle, managing the hands, and tending to family and crops.

Farmers looking for their own homesteads soon became rivals to the cattle ranchers. The "nesters," as ranchers disdainfully called them, fenced off their lands, thus shrinking the open range. Vast grants to the railroads also limited the area of free land, while ranchers intent on breeding heavier cattle with more tender beef began to fence in their stock to prevent them from mixing with inferior strays. Conflicts also arose between cattle ranchers and herders of another animal introduced by the Mexicans: sheep. Sheep cropped grasses so short that they ruined land for cattle grazing. On one occasion enraged cattlemen clubbed 8000 sheep to death along the Green River in Wyoming. The feuds often burst into range wars, some more violent than those between farmers and ranchers.

Ranchers came to expect profits of 25 to 40 percent a year. As in all booms, however, forces were at work bringing the inevitable bust. High profits soon

*Western boom and bust*

swelled the size of the herds and led to overproduction. Increased competition from cattle producers in Canada and Argentina caused beef prices to fall. And in the end, nature imposed its own limits on the boom. There was simply not enough grass along the trails to support the millions of head on their way to market. Then in 1886 and 1887 came two of the coldest winters in recorded history. The winds brought blizzards that drove wandering herds up against fences, where they either froze or starved to death. Summer brought no relief. Heat and drought scorched the grasslands and dried up waterholes. In the Dakotas, Montana, Colorado, and Wyoming, losses ran as high as 90 percent.

By the 1890s the open range and the long drives had largely vanished. What prevailed were the larger cattle corporations like the King Ranch of Texas. Only they had enough capital to acquire and fence vast grazing lands, hire ranchers to manage herds, and pay for feed during winter months. As for the cowboys, most became wage laborers employed by the ranching corporations. As with mining, the eastern pattern of economic concentration and labor specialization was being applied in the West.

## THE FINAL FRONTIER

In the 1860s they had come in a trickle; in the 1870s they became a torrent. They were farmers from the East and Midwest, black freedmen from the rural South, and peasant-born immigrants from Europe. What bound them together was a craving for land. They had read railroad and steamship advertisements and heard stories from friends about millions of free acres in the plains west of the 98th meridian. Hardier strands of wheat like the "Turkey Red" (imported from Russia) improved machinery, and new farming methods made it possible to raise crops in what once had been called the "Great American Desert." The number of farms in the United States jumped from around 2 million on the eve of the Civil War to almost 6 million in 1900.

## Farming on the Plains

Farmers looking to plow the plains faced a daunting task. Under the Homestead Act, government land could be bought for $1.25 an acre, or claimed free if a homesteader worked it for five years. But the best parcels—near a railroad line, with access to eastern markets—were owned by the railroads themselves or by speculators, and sold for around $25 an acre. Furthermore, successful farming on the plains demanded expensive machinery. Steel-tipped plows and harrows (which left a blanket of dust to keep moisture from evaporating too quickly) permitted "dry farming" in arid climates. Threshers, combines, and harvesters brought in the crop, while steam tractors pulled the heavy equipment.

With little rain, many farmers had to install windmills and pumping equipment to draw water from deep underground. The threat of cattle trampling the fields forced farmers to erect fences. Lacking wood, they found the answer in barbed wire, first marketed in 1874. When all was said and done, the average farmer spent what was for the poor a small fortune, about $785 on machinery and another $500 for land. Bigger operators invested 10 or 20 times as much.

Tracts of 160 acres granted under the Homestead Act might be enough for eastern farms, but in the drier West more land was needed to produce the same

*Bonanza farms*
harvest. Farms of more than 1000 acres, known as "bonanza farms," were most common in the wheatlands of the northern plains. A steam tractor working a bonanza farm could plow, harrow, and seed up to 50 acres a day—20 times more than a single person could do without machinery. Against such competition, small-scale farmers could scarcely survive. As in the South, many westerners became tenants on land owned by others. Bonanza farmers hired as many as 250 laborers to work each 10,000 acres in return for room, board, and 50 cents a day in wages.

## A Plains Existence

For poor farm families, life on the plains meant sod houses or dugouts carved from hillsides for protection against the wind. Tough, root-bound sod was cut into bricks a foot wide and three feet long and laid edgewise to create walls; sod bricks covered rafters for a roof. The average house was seldom more than 18 by 24 feet and in severe weather had to accommodate animals as well as people. One door and a single window provided light and air. The thick walls kept the house warm in winter and cool in summer, but a heavy, soaking rain or snow could bring the roof down, or drip mud and water into the living area.

The heaviest burdens fell to women. With stores and supplies scarce, they spent long days over hot tubs preparing tallow wax for candles or soaking ashes

*Plains women* and boiling lye with grease and pork rinds to make soap. In the early years of settlement wool was in such short supply that resourceful women used hair from wolves and other wild animals to make cloth. Buttons had to be fashioned from old wooden spoons. Without doctors, women learned how to care for the hurt and sick, treating anything from frostbite to snakebite to burns and rheumatism.

Nature imposed added hardships. Blizzards swept the plains, piling snow to the rooftops and halting all travel. Weeks would pass before farm families saw an outsider. In the summers, searing winds blasted the plains for weeks. Grasses grew so dry that a single spark could ignite thousands of acres. Farmers in the Southwest lived in dread of stinging centipedes and scorpions that inhabited wall cracks. From Missouri to Oregon, nothing spelled disaster like locusts. They descended without warning in swarms 100 miles long. Beating against houses like hailstones, they stripped all vegetation, including the bark of trees. An entire year's labor might be destroyed in a day.

In the face of such hardships many westerners found comfort in religion. Indians turned to traditional spiritualism, Hispanics to the Catholic Church, as *Religion* a means of coping with nature and change. Though Catholics and Jews came West, evangelical Protestants dominated the Anglo frontier in the mining towns and in other western communities. Worship offered an emotional outlet, intellectual stimulation, a means of preserving old values and sustaining hope. As in the rural South, circuit riders compensated for the shortage of preachers, while camp meetings offered the chance to socialize. Both brought contact with a world beyond the prairie. In many communities it was the churches that first instilled order on public life. Through church committees westerners could deal with local problems like the need for schools or charity for the poor.

## The Urban Frontier

Not all westerners lived in such isolation. By 1890, the percentage of those living in cities of 10,000 or more was greater than in any other section of the country except the Northeast.

Some western cities—San Antonio, El Paso, Los Angeles—were old Spanish towns whose growth had been reignited by the westward march of Anglo migrants, the northward push of Mexican immigrants, and the spread of railroads. Other cities, like Portland near the Columbia River in Oregon, blossomed because they stood astride commercial routes. Still others, such as Witchita, Kansas, arose to serve the cattle and mining booms. As technology freed people from the need to produce their own food and clothing, westerners turned to the business of supplying goods and services, enterprises that required the labor of densely populated cities.

Denver was typical. Founded in 1859, the city profited from the discovery of gold in nearby Cherry Creek. The completion of the Denver Pacific and Kansas Pacific railroads sparked a second growth spurt in the 1870s. By the 1890s, with a population of over 100,000, it ranked behind only Los Angeles and Omaha among western cities. Like much of the urban West, Denver grew outward rather than upward, breaking the pattern set by the cramped cities of the East. In the West, such urban sprawl produced cities with sharply divided districts for business, government, and industry. Workers lived in one section of town; managers, owners, and wealthier citizens in another.

Examining the returns from 1890, the superintendent of the census noted that landed settlements stretched so far that "there can hardly be said to be a frontier line." One after another, territories became states: Nebraska in 1867; Colorado in 1876; North Dakota, South Dakota, Montana, and Washington in 1889; Wyoming in 1890; Utah in 1896; Oklahoma in 1907; and New Mexico and Arizona in 1912. A new West was emerging as a mosaic of ethnicities, races, cultures, and climates, but with the shared identity of a single region.

That sense of a regional identity was heightened for both westerners and southerners, because so many of them felt isolated from the mainstream of industrial America. Ironically, it was not their isolation from northern industry but their links to it that marginalized them. The campaign for a New South to out-Yankee the industrial Yankee could not overcome the low wages and high fertility rates of an older South. The promoters of the West had greater success in adapting large-scale industry and investment to mining, cattle ranching, and farming. But they too confronted the limits of their region, whose resources were not endless and whose rainfall did not follow the plow. Like easterners, citizens of the West found that large corporations with near-monopoly control over markets and transportation bred inequality, corrupt politics, and resentment.

These sectional upheavals inevitably affected the political system, as conflicts of class, race, and region spilled into the national arena. By the 1890s, an agrarian revolt was sweeping the South and West. In both sections disillusionment and despair turned to bitterness as more small farmers, black and white, found themselves enslaved to debt and driven toward bankruptcy, tenancy, and wage labor. It was small wonder, then, that the South and the West gave rise to a "People's party," determined to end the "business as usual" approach of the Democratic and Republican parties.

# SIGNIFICANT EVENTS

| | |
|---|---|
| 1849–1859 | Gold and silver strikes open western mining frontier |
| 1862 | Homestead Act; Minnesota Sioux uprising begins Plains Indian wars |
| 1864 | Chivington massacre |
| 1866 | Drive to Sedalia, Missouri, launches cattle boom |
| 1869 | Completion of first transcontinental railroad; Powell explores the Grand Canyon |
| 1872–1874 | The great buffalo slaughter |
| 1874 | Black Hills gold rush; barbed wire patented |
| 1876 | Battle of Little Big Horn; Nez Percé resist relocation |
| 1877 | Compromise of 1877 ends Reconstruction; Crazy Horse surrenders |
| 1879 | Height of Exoduster migration to Kansas |
| 1880 | Bonsack cigarette-rolling machine invented |
| 1883 | *Civil Rights Cases* |
| 1886–1887 | Severe winter and drought cycle in the West |
| 1887 | Dawes Severalty Act |
| 1889 | Oklahoma opened to settlement |
| 1890 | Ghost Dance Indian religious revival; Wounded Knee |
| 1892 | Union violence at Coeur d'Alene, Idaho; Wyoming range wars |
| 1896 | *Plessy v. Ferguson* upholds separate but equal doctrine |

# CHAPTER TWENTY-ONE

# The Political System Under Strain

On May 1, 1893, an eager crowd of nearly half a million people jostled into a dramatic plaza fronted on either side by gleaming white buildings. Named the Court of Honor, the plaza was the center of a strange, ornamental city that was at once both awesome and entirely imaginary.

At one end stood a building whose magnificent white dome exceeded even the height of the Capitol in Washington. Unlike the marble-built Capitol, however, this building was all surface: a stucco shell plastered onto a steel frame and then sprayed with white oil paint to make it glisten. Beyond the Court of Honor stretched thoroughfares encompassing over 200 colonaded buildings, piers, islands, and watercourses. Located five miles south of Chicago's center, this city of the imagination proclaimed itself the "World's Columbian Exposition" to honor the 400th anniversary of Columbus's voyage to America.

President Grover Cleveland opened the world's fair in a way that symbolized the nation's industrial transformation. He pressed a telegrapher's key. Instantly electric current set 7000 feet of shafting into motion—motion that in turn unfurled flags, set fountains pumping, and lit 10,000 electric bulbs. The lights played over an array of exhibition buildings soon known as the "White City."

In Cleveland's judgment the neoclassical architecture was both "magnificent" and "stupendous." Surely the sheer size was astonishing, for the buildings had been laid out not by the square foot but by the acre. The Hall of Manufactures and Liberal Arts alone spread its roof over 30 acres, twice the area of Egypt's Great Pyramid.

One English visitor dismissed the displays within as "the contents of a great dry goods store mixed up with the contents of museums." In a sense he was right. Visitors paraded by an unending stream of typewriters, pins, watches, agricultural machinery, cedar canoes, and refrigerators, to say nothing of a map of the United States fashioned entirely out of pickles. But this riot of mechanical marvels, gewgaws, and bric-a-brac was symbolic, too, of the nation's industrial transformation. The fair resembled nothing so much as a living, breathing version of the new department store mail-order catalogues whose pages were now introducing the goods of the city to the hinterlands.

The connections made by the fair were international as well. This was the *World's* Columbian Exposition, with exhibits from 36 nations. Germany's famous manufacturer of armaments, Krupp, had its own separate building. It housed a 120-ton rifled gun 46 feet long, "said to be able to throw a projectile weighing one ton a distance of twenty miles." Easily within the range of its gunsights was a replica of the U.S. battleship *Illinois*, whose own bristling turrets stood just offshore of the exposition, on Lake Michigan. At the fair's amusement park, visitors encountered exotic cultures—and not just temples, huts, and totems, but exhibits in the living flesh. The Arabian village featured Saharan camels, veiled ladies, elders in turbans, and beggar children. Nearby, Irish peasants boiled potatoes over turf fires and Samoan men threw axes.

Like all such fairs, the Columbian Exposition created a fantasy. Beyond its boundaries, the real world was showing serious signs of strain. Early in 1893 the Philadelphia and Reading Railroad had gone bankrupt, setting off a financial panic. By the end of the year, nearly 500 banks and 15,000 businesses had failed. Although tourists continued to marvel at the fair's wonders, crowds of worried and unemployed workers also gathered in Chicago. On Labor Day, Governor John Altgeld of Illinois told one such assemblage that the government was powerless to avoid or even soften "suffering and distress" that this latest economic downturn would bring.

In truth, the political system was ill equipped to cope with the economic and social revolutions reshaping America. The executive branch remained weak, while Congress and the courts found themselves easily swayed by the financial interests of the industrial class. The crises of the 1890s forced the political order to try to address such inequities.

The political system also had to take into account developments abroad. Industrialization had sent American businesses around the world searching for raw materials and new markets. As that search intensified, many influential Americans argued that the United States needed, like European nations, to acquire territory overseas. By the end of the century, the nation's political system had taken its first steps toward modernization. That included a major political realignment at home and a growing empire abroad. Both changes launched the United States into the twentieth century and an era of prosperity and power.

## THE POLITICS OF PARALYSIS

During the 1880s and 1890s, as the American political system came under strain, Moisei Ostrogorski was traveling across the United States. Like other foreign visitors, the Russian political scientist had come to see the new democratic experiment in action. His verdict was as blunt as it was widely shared: "the constituted authorities are unequal to their duty." It seemed that the experiment had fallen victim to private greed, middle-class indifference, and political mediocrity.

In fact, there were deeper problems: a great gulf between rich and poor; the growing power of corporate industry; the wretched poverty of city and farm; an endless cycle of boom and bust; the unmet needs of African Americans, women, Indians, and other Americans. These problems had scarcely been addressed, let alone resolved. Politics was the traditional medium of resolution, but it was grinding into a dangerous stalemate.

### Political Stalemate

From 1877 to 1897 American politics rested on a delicate balance of power that left neither Republicans nor Democrats in control. Republicans inhabited the White House for 12 years; Democrats, for 8. Margins of victory in presidential elections were paper thin. And no president could count on having a majority of his party in both houses of Congress for his entire term. Usually Republicans controlled the Senate, while Democrats controlled the House of Representatives.

With elections so tight, both parties worked hard to bring out the vote. Brass bands, parades, cheering crowds of flag-wavers "are the order of the day and night from end to end of the country," reported a British visitor. In cities

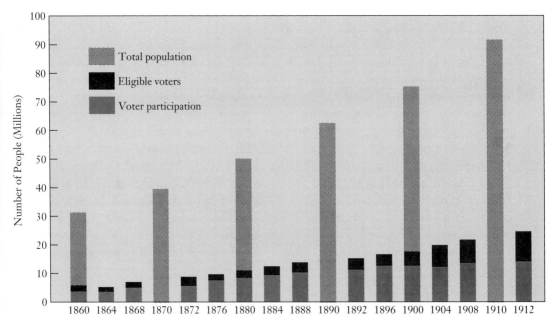

THE VOTING PUBLIC, 1860–1912    Between 1860 and 1910 the population and the number of eligible voters increased nearly threefold. As reforms of the early twentieth century increased the number of eligible voters but reduced the power of political machines to mass voters, the percentage of participation actually declined.

party workers handed out leaflets and pinned campaign buttons on anyone who passed. When Election Day arrived, stores closed and businesses shut down. At political clubs and corner saloons men lined up to get voting orders (along with free drinks) from ward bosses. In the countryside, fields went untended as farmers took their families to town, cast their ballots, and bet on the outcome.

An average of nearly 80 percent of eligible voters turned out for presidential elections between 1860 and 1900, a figure higher than at any time since. In

*Voter turnout*

that era, however, the electorate made up a smaller percentage of the population. About one American in five actually voted in presidential elections from 1876 to 1892. Virtually all were white males. Women could vote in national elections only in a few western states, and beginning in the 1880s, the South erected barriers that eventually disfranchised many African American voters.

Party loyalty rarely wavered. In every election, 16 states could be counted on to vote Republican and 14 Democratic. In only six states—the most important being New York and Ohio—were the results in doubt.

## The Parties

What inspired such loyalty? Republicans and Democrats did have similarities but also had differences. Both parties supported business and condemned radicalism; neither offered embattled workers and farmers much help. But Democrats believed in states' rights and limited government, while Republicans

*Democrats and Republicans compared*

favored federal activism to foster economic growth. The stronghold of Democrats lay in the South, where they continually reminded voters that they had led the states of the Old Confederacy, "redeemed" them from Republican Reconstruction, and championed white supremacy. Republicans dominated the North with strong support from industry and business. They, too, invoked memories of the Civil War to secure voters, black as well as white. "Not every Democrat was a rebel," they chanted, "but every rebel was a Democrat."

Ethnicity and religion also cemented voter loyalty. Republicans drew on old-stock Protestants, who feared new immigrants and put their faith in promoting pious behavior. In the Republican party, they found support for immigration restriction, prohibition, and English-only schools. The Democratic party attracted urban political machines, their immigrant voters, and the working poor. Often Catholic, they saw salvation in following religious rituals, not in dictating the conduct of all society. For them, the Democratic party defended liberty because it opposed the very restrictions sought by native-born Protestants.

Region, religion, and ethnicity thus bound voters to each party. Some citizens weighed their purses at election time, but many more thought of their pastors or their parents or their communities when they went to the polls. Year after year, these cultural loyalties shaped political allegiances.

Outside the two-party system, impassioned reformers often fashioned political instruments of their own. Some formed groups that aligned themselves behind issues rather than parties. Opponents of alcohol created the Woman's Christian Temperance Union (1874) and the Anti-Saloon League (1893). Champions of women's rights joined the National American Woman Suffrage Association (1890), a reunion of two branches of the women's suffrage movement that had split in 1869.

Third political parties might also crystallize around a single concern or a particular group. Those who sought inflation of the currency formed the

*Third parties*

Greenback party (1874). Angry farmers in the West and South created the Populist, or People's, party (1892). All drew supporters from both conventional parties, but as single-interest groups they mobilized minorities, not majorities.

## The Issues

In the halls of Congress, attention focused on well-worn issues: veterans' benefits, appointments, tariffs, and money. The presidency had been weakened by the impeachment of Andrew Johnson, the scandals of Ulysses S. Grant, and the contested victory of Rutherford B. Hayes in 1876 (see pages 462–463). So Congress enjoyed the initiative in making policy.

Some divisive issues were the bitter legacy of the Civil War. Republicans and Democrats waved symbolic "bloody shirts," each tarring the other with re-

*Legacies of the Civil War*

sponsibility for the war. The politics of the Civil War also surfaced in the lobbying efforts of veterans. The Grand Army of the Republic, an organization of more than 400,000 Union soldiers, petitioned Congress for pensions to make up for poor wartime pay and to support the widows and orphans of fallen comrades. By the turn of the century Union army veterans and their families were receiving $157 million annually. It was one of the largest public assistance programs in American history and laid the foundation for the modern welfare state.

---

COUNTERPOINT    *Origins of the Welfare State*

Historians disagree over the origins of the American welfare state. Some maintain that the United States followed the lead of industrial nations in Europe, where the first social insurance laws were passed in the 1880s and 1890s. Similar laws were not enacted in the United States until the Great Depression of the 1930s. Marxist historians see their emergence as a way for capitalism to control the working class and head off more radical change.

Other historians and social scientists place the origins of the welfare state in late nineteenth-century America. These scholars focus on the activities of interest groups, especially veterans', women's, and other voluntary organizations. Their lobbying resulted in an extensive aid program for Civil War veterans and, by the first two decades of the twentieth century, benefits for mothers and pensions for widows in over 40 states, many of them more elaborate than those in Europe.

More important than public welfare was the campaign for a new method of staffing federal offices. Since the early nineteenth century, political victors had practiced patronage by rewarding loyal followers with government or party jobs, regardless of their qualifications. After elections, winners faced an army of office seekers, "lying in wait . . . like vultures for a wounded bison."

A growing federal bureaucracy aggravated the problem. From barely 53,000 employees at the end of the Civil War, the federal government had grown to 166,000 by the early 1890s, with far more jobs requiring special skills. But dismantling this "spoils system" proved difficult. American politics rested on patronage. Without it, politicians—from presidents to lowly ward captains—feared that they could attract neither workers nor money. Reacting to the scandals of the Grant administration, a group of independents formed the National Civil Service Reform League in 1881. The league promoted the British model of civil service based on examination and merit. But in Congress neither party was willing to take action when it held power (and thus controlled patronage).

One July morning in 1881, a frustrated office seeker named Charles Guiteau unwittingly broke the log jam. As President James Garfield hurried to catch a train, Guiteau jumped from the shadows and shot him twice. Garfield's death *Pendleton Act* finally produced reform. In 1883 the Civil Service Act, or Pendleton Act, created a bipartisan civil service commission to administer competitive examinations for some federal jobs. Later presidents expanded the jobs covered. By 1896 almost half of all federal workers came under civil service jurisdiction.

As much as any issue, the protective tariff stirred Congress. As promoters of economic growth, Republicans usually championed this tax on manufactured imports. Democrats, with their strength in the agrarian South, generally sought tariff reduction to encourage foreign trade, reduce prices on manufactured goods, *McKinley Tariff* and cut the federal surplus. In 1890, when Republicans controlled the House, Congress enacted the McKinley Tariff. It raised schedules to an all-time high. The McKinley Tariff also contained a novel twist known as reciprocity: the president could lower rates if other countries did the same. In 1894 House Democrats succeeded in reducing rates, only to be thwarted by some 600 Senate amendments restoring most cuts. In 1897 the Dingley Tariff raised rates still higher but soothed reductionists by broadening reciprocity.

Just as divisive was the issue of currency. Until the mid-1800s money was coined from both gold and silver. The need for more money during the Civil *Currency debates* War had led Congress to issue "greenbacks"—currency printed on paper with a green back. For the next decade and a half Americans argued over whether to print more paper money (not backed by gold or silver) or take it out of circulation. Farmers and other debtors favored green-backs as a way of inflating prices and reducing their debts. For the opposite reasons, bankers and creditors stood for "sound money" backed by gold. Fear of inflation led Congress first to reduce the number of greenbacks and then in 1879 to make all remaining paper money convertible into gold.

A more heated battle was developing over silver-backed money. By the early 1870s so little silver was being used that Congress stopped coining it. A silver

*Bland–Allison Act*

mining boom in Nevada soon revived demands for more silver money. In 1878 the Bland–Allison Act inaugurated a limited form of silver coinage. But pressure for unlimited coinage of silver—coining all silver presented at U.S. mints—mounted as silver production quadrupled between 1870 and 1890. In 1890 pressure for silver peaked in the Sherman Silver Purchase Act. It obligated the government to buy 4.5 million ounces of silver every month. Paper tender called "treasury notes," redeemable in either gold or silver, would pay for it. The compromise satisfied both sides only temporarily.

### The White House from Hayes to Harrison

From the 1870s through the 1890s a string of nearly anonymous presidents presided over the country. Not all were mere caretakers. Some tried to revive the office, but Congress continued to rein in the executive.

Republican Rutherford B. Hayes was the first of the "Ohio dynasty," which included three presidents from 1876 to 1900. As president, Hayes moved quickly to end Reconstruction and tried unsuccessfully to woo southern Democrats with promises of economic support. His pursuit of civil service reform ended only in splitting his party between "Stalwarts" (who favored the spoils systems) and "Half-Breeds" (who opposed it). Hayes left office after a single term, happy to be "out of a scrape."

In 1880, Republican James Garfield, another Ohioan, succeeded Hayes by a handful of votes. He spent his first hundred days in the White House besieged by office hunters and failing to placate the rival sections of his party. After Garfield's assassination only six months into his term, Chester A. Arthur, the "spoilsman's spoilsman," became president.

To everyone's surprise, the dapper Arthur turned out to be an honest president. He broke with machine politicians, including his mentor and Stalwart leader Roscoe Conkling. He worked to lower the tariff, warmly endorsed the new Civil Service, or Pendleton, Act, and reduced the federal surplus by beginning construction of a modern navy. Such even-handed administration left him little chance for renomination divided by party leaders.

The election of 1884 was one of the dirtiest ever waged. Senator James Blaine, the beloved "Plumed Knight" from Maine and leader of the Half-

*The dirty election of 1884*

Breeds, ran against Democrat Grover Cleveland, the former governor of New York. Despite superb talents as a leader and vote-getter, Blaine was haunted by old charges of illegal favoritism for the Little Rock and Fort Smith Railroad. For his part, "Grover the Good" had built a reputation for honesty by fighting corruption and the spoils system in New York. So hard a worker was the portly Cleveland, sighed a reporter, that he "remains within doors constantly, eats and works, eats and works, and works and eats." The bachelor Cleveland spent enough time away from his desk to father an illegitimate child. The country rang with Republican taunts of "Ma, ma, where's my pa?"

In the last week of the tight race, Cleveland supporters in New York circulated the statement of a local Protestant minister that labeled Democrats the party of "Rum, Romanism, and Rebellion" (alcohol, Catholicism, and the Civil War). The Irish-Catholic vote swung to the Democrats. New York went to Cleveland, and with it, the election. Democrats crowed with delight over where to find the bachelor "pa": "Gone to the White House, ha, ha, ha!"

Cleveland was the first Democrat elected to the White House since James Buchanan in 1856, and he was more active than many of his predecessors. He pleased reformers by expanding the civil service, and his devotion to gold, economy, and efficiency earned him praise from business. He supported the growth of federal power by endorsing the Interstate Commerce Act (1887), new agricultural research, and federal arbitration of labor disputes.

Still, Cleveland's presidential activism remained limited. He vetoed two of every three bills brought to him, more than twice the number vetoed by all his predecessors. Toward the end of his term, embarrassed by the large federal surplus, Cleveland finally reasserted himself by attacking the tariff, but to no avail. The Republican-controlled Senate blocked his attempt to lower it.

In 1888 Republicans nominated a sturdy defender of tariffs, Benjamin Harrison, the grandson of President William Henry Harrison. President Cleveland won a plurality of the popular vote but lost in the Electoral College. The "human iceberg" (as Harrison's colleagues called him) worked hard, rarely delegated management, and turned the White House into a well-regulated office. He helped to shape the Sherman Silver Purchase Act (1890), kept up with the McKinley Tariff (1890), and accepted the Sherman Antitrust Act (1890) to limit the power and size of big businesses.

By the end of Harrison's term in 1892, Congress had completed its most productive session of the era, including the first billion-dollar peacetime budget. To Democratic jeers of a "Billion Dollar Congress," Republican House Speaker Thomas Reed shot back, "This is a billion-dollar country!"

### Ferment in the States and Cities

Despite growing expenditures and more legislation, most people expected little from the federal government. Few newspapers even bothered to send correspondents to Washington. Public pressure to curb the excesses of the new industrial order mounted closer to home, in state and city governments. Experimental and often effective, state programs began to grapple with the problems of corporate power, discriminatory shipping rates, political corruption, and urban disorder.

Starting in 1869 with Massachusetts, states established commissions to investigate and regulate industry, especially railroads, America's first big business.

*State commissions*

By the turn of the century, almost two-thirds of the states had them. The first commissions gathered and publicized information on shipping rates and business practices and furnished advice about public policy.

In the Midwest, on the Great Plains, and in the Far West, merchants and farmers pressed state governments to reduce railroad rates and stop the rebates given to large shippers. In California, one newspaper published a schedule of freight rates to Nevada, showing that lower rates had been charged by wagon teams before the railroads were built. On the West Coast and in the Midwest, state legislatures empowered commissions to end rebates and monitor rates. In 1870 Illinois became the first of several states to define railroads as public highways subject to regulation, including setting maximum rates.

Concern over cities led to state municipal conventions, the first in Iowa in 1877. Philadelphia sponsored a national conference on good city government

*National Municipal League*

in 1894. A year later reformers founded the National Municipal League. It soon had more than 200 branches. Its model city charter advanced such farsighted reforms as separate city and state elections, limited contracts for utilities, and more authority for mayors. Meanwhile cities and states in the Midwest enacted laws closing stores on Sundays, prohibiting the sale of alcohol, and making English the language of public schools—all in an effort to standardize social behavior and control the habits of new immigrants.

## THE REVOLT OF THE FARMERS

In 1890, the politics of stalemate cracked, as did the patience of farmers across the South and the western plains. Beginning in the 1880s, a sharp depression drove down agricultural prices, pushed up surpluses, and forced thousands from their land. Farmers also suffered from a great deal more, including heavy mortgages, widespread poverty, and railroad rates that discriminated against them. In 1890 their resentment boiled over. An agrarian revolt—called Populism—swept across the political landscape and broke the stalemate of the previous 20 years.

### The Harvest of Discontent

The revolt of the farmers stirred first on the southern frontier, spreading eastward from Texas through the rest of the Old Confederacy, then west across the

*Targets of farm anger*

plains. Farmers blamed their troubles on obvious inequalities: manufacturers protected by the tariff, high railroad rates, bankers who held their mounting debts, and expensive middlemen who

Mary Shelley's novel of a man-made creature who turns against its creator strikes the theme for this antirailroad cartoon entitled "The American Frankenstein" (1874). "Agriculture, commerce, and manufacture are all in my power," bellows the mechanical monster with the head of a locomotive.

stored and processed their commodities. All seemed to profit at the expense of farmers.

The true picture was fuzzier. The tariff protected industrial goods but also supported some farm commodities. Railroad rates, however high, actually fell from 1865 to 1890. And while mortgages were heavy, most were short, no more than four years. Farmers often refinanced them, using the money to buy more land and machinery, which only increased their debt. Millers and operators of grain elevators earned handsome profits; yet every year more of them came under state regulation.

In hard times, of course, none of this mattered. And in the South many poor farmers seemed condemned to hard times forever. Credit lay at the root of the

*Credit crunch* problem, since most southern farmers had to borrow money in order to plant and harvest their crops. The inequities of sharecropping and the crop–lien system (page 528) forced them deeper into debt. When crop prices fell, they borrowed still more, stretching the financial resources of the South beyond their meager limits. Within a few years after the

E Y E W I T N E S S     T O     H I S T O R Y

## A Nebraska Farmer Laments His Plight

**T**his season is without a parallel in this part of the country. The hot winds burned up the entire crop, leaving thousands of families wholly destitute, many of whom might have been able to run through this crisis had it not been for the galling yoke put on them by the money loaners and sharks— not by charging 7 per cent per annum, which is the lawful rate of interest, or even 10 per cent, but the unlawful and inhuman country destroying rate of 3 per cent a month, some going still farther and charging 50 per cent per annum. We are cursed, many of us financially, beyond redemption, not by the hot winds so much as by the swindling games of the bankers and money loaners, who have taken the money and now are after the property, leaving the farmer moneyless and homeless. . . . I have borrowed for example $1,000. I pay $25 besides to the commission man. I give my note and second mortgage of 3 per cent of the $1,000, which is $30 more. Then I pay 7 per cent on the $1,000 to the actual loaner. Then besides all this I pay for appraising the land, abstract, recording, etc., so when I have secured my loan I am out the first year $150. Yet I am told by the agent who loans me the money, he can't stand to loan at such low rates. This is on the farm, but now comes the chattel loan. I must have $50 to save myself. I get the money; my note is made payable in thirty or sixty days for $35, secured by chattel of two horses, harness and wagon, about five times the value of the note. The time comes to pay, I ask for a few days. No I can't wait; must have the money. If I can't get the money, I have the extreme pleasure of seeing my property taken and sold by this iron handed money loaner while my family and I suffer.

W. M. Taylor to editor, *Farmer's Alliance* (Lincoln), January 10, 1891, Nebraska Historical Society, reprinted in Robert D. Marcus and David Burner, eds., *America Firsthand*, Vol. II (New York: St. Martin's Press, 1992), p. 90.

Civil War, Massachusetts' banks had five times as much money as all the banks of the Old Confederacy.

Beginning in the 1870s, nearly 100,000 debt-ridden farmers a year picked up stakes across the Deep South and fled to Texas to escape the system, only to find it waiting for them. Others stood and fought, as one pamphlet exhorted in 1889, "not with glittering musket, flaming sword and deadly cannon, but with the silent, potent and all-powerful ballot."

## The Origins of the Farmers' Alliance

Before farmers could vote together, they had to get together. Life on the farm was harsh, drab, and isolated. Such conditions shocked Oliver Hudson Kelley as he traveled across the South after the Civil War. In 1867 the young govern-

*Patrons of Husbandry*

ment clerk founded the Patrons of Husbandry to brighten the lives of farmers and broaden their horizons. Local chapters, called granges, brought farmers and their families together to pray, sing, and learn new farming techniques. The Grangers sponsored fairs, picnics, dances, lectures—anything to break the bleakness of farm life. After a slow start the Grange grew quickly. By 1875 there were 800,000 members in 20,000 locals, most in the Midwest, South, and Southwest.

At first the Grangers swore off politics. But in a pattern often repeated, socializing led to economic and then political action. By pooling their money for supplies and equipment to store and market their crops, Grangers could avoid the high charges of middlemen. By the early 1870s they also were lobbying midwestern legislatures to adopt "Granger laws" regulating rates charged by railroads, grain elevator operators, and other middlemen.

Eight "Granger cases" came before the Supreme Court in the 1870s to test the new regulatory measures. *Munn v. Illinois* (1877) upheld the right of Illinois to

*Granger cases*

regulate private property (in this case, giant elevators used for storing grain) "devoted to a public use." Later decisions allowed state regulation of railroads but only within state lines. Congress responded in 1887 by creating the Interstate Commerce Commission, a federal agency that could regulate commerce across state boundaries. In practice, it had little power, but it was a key step toward establishing the public right to regulate private corporations.

Slumping prices in the 1870s and 1880s bred new farm organizations. Slowly they blended into what the press called the "Alliance Movement." The Southern

*Southern Alliance*

Alliance, formed in Texas in 1875, spread rapidly after Dr. Charles W. Macune took command in 1886. A doctor and lawyer as well as a farmer, Macune planned to expand Texas's network of local chapters, or suballiances, into a national network of state Alliance Exchanges. Like the Grangers, the exchanges pooled their resources in cooperatively owned enterprises for buying and selling, milling and storing, banking and manufacturing.

Soon the Southern Alliance was publicizing its activities in local newspapers, publishing a journal, and sending lecturers across the country. For a brief period, between 1886 and 1892, the Alliance cooperatives multiplied throughout the South, grew to more than a million members, and challenged accepted ways of doing business. Macune claimed that his new Texas Exchange saved members 40 percent on plows and 30 percent on wagons. But most Alliance cooperatives were managed by farmers without the time or experience to succeed. Usually opposed by irate local merchants, the ventures eventually failed.

Although the Southern Alliance admitted no African Americans, it encouraged them to organize. A small group of black and white Texans founded the

*Colored Farmers' Alliance*

Colored Farmers' National Alliance and Cooperative Union in 1886. By 1891 a quarter of a million farmers had joined. Its operations were largely secret, since public action often brought swift retaliation from white supremacists. When the Colored Farmers' Alliance organized a strike of black cotton pickers near Memphis in 1891, white mobs hunted down and lynched 15 strikers. The murders went unpunished, and the Colored Alliance began to founder.

## The Alliance Peaks

Farmer cooperation reached northward to the states of the Midwest and Great Plains in the National Farmers' Alliance, created in 1880. In June 1890 Kansas organizers formed the first People's party to compete with Democrats and Republicans. Meanwhile the Southern Alliance changed its name to the National Farmers' Alliance and Industrial Union, incorporated the strong Northern Alliances in the Dakotas and Kansas, and made the movement truly national.

The key to Alliance success was not organization but leadership, both at the top and in the middle. Alliance lecturers fanned out across the South and the Great Plains, organizing suballiances and teaching new members about finance and cooperative businesses. Women were often as active as men. "Wimmin is everywhere," noted one observer of the Alliance. The comment seemed to apply literally to Mary Elizabeth Lease, who in the summer of 1890 alone gave 160 speeches.

In 1890 members of the Alliance met in Ocala, Florida, and issued the "Ocala Demands." The manifesto reflected the populists' deep distrust of "the

*Ocala Demands*

money power"—large corporations and banks, whose financial power gave them the ability to manipulate the "free" market. The Ocala Demands called on government to correct such abuses by reducing tariffs, abolishing national banks, regulating railroads, and coining silver money freely. The platform also demanded a federal income tax and the popular election of senators, to make government more responsive to the public. The most innovative feature came from Charles Macune. His "subtreasury system" would require the federal government to furnish warehouses for harvested crops and low-interest loans to tide farmers over until prices rose. Under such a system farmers would no longer have to sell in a glutted market, as they did under the crop–lien system. And they could expand the money supply simply by borrowing at harvest time.

In the elections of 1890 the old parties faced hostile farmers across the nation. In the South, the Alliance worked within the Democratic party and elected four governors, won eight legislatures, and sent 44 members of Congress and three senators to Washington. In the Great Plains, Alliance candidates drew farmers from the Republican party. Newly created farmer parties elected five representatives and two senators in Kansas and South Dakota and took over both houses of the Nebraska legislature.

In the West especially, Alliance organizers began to dream of a national third party that would be free from the corporate influence, sectionalism, and

*The People's Party*
racial tensions that split Republicans and Democrats. It would be a party not just of farmers but of the downtrodden, including industrial workers.

In February 1892, as the presidential election year opened, a convention of 900 labor, feminist, farm, and other reform delegates (100 of them black) met in St. Louis. They founded the People's, or Populist, party and called for another convention to nominate a presidential ticket. Initially southern Populists held back, clinging to their strategy of working within the Democratic party. But when newly elected Democrats failed to support Alliance programs, southern leaders like Tom Watson of Georgia abandoned the party and began recruiting black and white farmers for the Populists.

The national convention of Populists met in Omaha, Nebraska, on Independence Day, July 4, 1892. Their impassioned platform promised to return government "to the hands of 'the plain people.'" Planks advocated the subtreasury plan, unlimited coinage of silver and an increase in the money supply, direct election of senators, an income tax, and government ownership of railroads, telegraph, and telephone. To attract wage earners the party endorsed the eight-hour workday, restriction of immigration, and a ban on the use of Pinkerton detectives in labor disputes—for the Pinkertons had engaged in a savage gun battle with strikers that year at Andrew Carnegie's Homestead steel plant. Delegates rallied behind the old greenbacker and Union general James B. Weaver, carefully balancing their presidential nomination with a one-legged Confederate veteran as his running mate.

## The Election of 1892

The Populists enlivened the otherwise dull campaign, as Democrat Grover Cleveland and Republican incumbent Benjamin Harrison refought the election of 1888. This time, however, Cleveland won, and for the first time since the Civil War, Democrats gained control of both houses of Congress. The Populists too enjoyed success. Weaver polled over a million votes, the first third-party candidate to do so. Populists elected 3 governors, 5 senators, 10 representatives, and nearly 1500 members of state legislatures.

Despite these victories, the election revealed dangerous weaknesses in the People's party. Across the nation thousands of voters changed political affilia-

*Populist weaknesses*
tions, but most often from the Republicans to the Democrats, not to the Populists. No doubt the campaign of intimidation and repression hurt the People's party in the South, where white conservatives had been appalled by Tom Watson's open courtship of black southerners. In the North, Populists failed to win over labor and most city dwellers. Both were more concerned with family budgets than with the problems of farmers and the downtrodden.

The darker side of Populism also put off many Americans. Its rhetoric was often violent and laced with naturist slurs; it spoke ominously of conspiracies and stridently in favor of immigration restriction. In fact, the Alliance lost members, an omen of defeats to come. But for the present, the People's party had demonstrated two conflicting truths. It showed how far from the needs of many ordinary Americans the two parties had drifted, and how difficult it would be to break their power.

## THE NEW REALIGNMENT

On May 1, 1893, President Cleveland was in Chicago to throw the switch that set ablaze 10,000 electric bulbs and opened the World's Columbian Exposition (pages 554–555). The gleaming "White City" with its grand displays stood as a monument to the nation's glorious progress. Four days later a wave of bankruptcies destroyed major firms across the country, and stock prices sank to all-time lows, setting off the depression of 1893.

At first Chicago staved off the worst, thanks to the business generated by the exposition. But when that closed in October, thousands of laborers found themselves out of a job. Chicago's mayor estimated the number of unemployed in the city to be near 200,000. He had some firsthand experience on which to base his calculations, for every night desperate men slept on the floors and stairways of City Hall and every police station in the city put up 60 to 100 additional homeless. Children as well as their parents rifled the city's garbage dumps for food.

### The Depression of 1893

The sharp contrast between the exposition's White City and the nation's economic misery demonstrated the inability of the political system to smooth out the economy's cycle of boom and bust. The new industrial order had brought prosperity by increasing production, opening markets, and tying Americans closer together. But in 1893, the price of interdependence became obvious. A major downturn in one area affected the other sectors of the economy. And with no way to control swings in the business cycle, depression came on a scale as large as that of the booming prosperity.

The depression of 1893, the deepest the nation had yet experienced, lasted until 1897. Railroad baron and descendant of two presidents Charles Francis Adams, Jr., called it a "convulsion," but the country experienced it as crushing idleness. In August 1893, unemployment stood at 1 million; by the middle of 1894, it was 3 million. At the end of the year nearly one worker in five was out of a job.

The federal government had no program at all. "While the people should patriotically and cheerfully support their Government," President Cleveland

Charles Dana Gibson, famous for his portraits of well-bred young women in the 1890s, tackles a different subject in this drawing, a breadline of mixed classes during the depression of 1893.

declared, "its functions do not include the support of the people." The states offered little more. Relief, like poverty, was considered a private matter. The burden fell on local charities, benevolent societies, churches, labor unions, and ward bosses. In city after city, citizens organized relief committees to distribute bread and clothing until their meager resources gave out.

Others were less charitable. As the popular preacher Henry Ward Beecher told his congregation, "No man in this land suffers from poverty unless it be more than his fault—unless it be his sin." But the scale of hardship was so great, its targets so random, that anyone could be thrown out of work—an industrious neighbor, a factory foreman with 20 years on the job, a bank president. Older attitudes about personal responsibility for poverty began to give way to new ideas about its social origins and the obligation of public agencies to help.

## The Rumblings of Unrest

Even before the depression, rumblings of unrest had begun to roll across the country. The Great Railroad Strike of 1877 had ignited nearly two decades of labor strife (page 495). After 1893 discontent mounted as wages were cut, employees laid off, and factories closed. During the first year of the depression, 1400 strikes sent more than half a million workers from their jobs.

Uneasy business executives and politicians saw radicalism and the possibility of revolution in every strike. But the depression of 1893 had unleashed an-

*Coxey's Army*

other force: simple discontent. And in the spring of 1894, it focused on government inaction. On Easter Sunday, "General"

Jacob Coxey, a 39-year-old Populist and factory owner, launched the "Tramps' March on Washington" from Massillon, Ohio. His "Commonweal Army of Christ"—some 500 men, women, and children—descended on Washington at the end of April to offer "a petition with boots on" for a federal program of public works. Cleveland's staff tightened security around the White House, as other "armies" of unemployed mobilized: an 800-person contingent left from Los Angeles; a San Francisco battalion of 600 swelled to 1500 by the time it reached Iowa.

On May 1, Coxey's troops, armed with "clubs of peace," massed at the foot of the capitol. When Coxey entered the capitol grounds, 100 mounted police routed the demonstrators and arrested the general for trespassing on the grass. Nothing came of the protest, other than to signal a growing demand for federal action.

Federal help was not to be found. Grover Cleveland had barely moved into the White House when the depression struck. The country blamed him; he blamed silver. In his view the Sherman Silver Purchase Act of 1890 had shaken business confidence by forcing the government to use its shrinking reserves of gold to purchase (though not coin) silver. Repeal of the act, Cleveland believed, was the way to build gold reserves and restore confidence. After bitter debate, Congress complied. But this economic tinkering only strengthened the resolve of "silverites" in the Democratic party to overwhelm Cleveland's conservative "gold" wing.

*Democrats under fire*

Worse for the president, repeal of silver purchases brought no economic revival. In the short run abandoning silver hurt the economy by contracting the money supply just when expansion might have stimulated it by providing needed credit. As panic and unemployment spread across the country, Cleveland's popularity wilted. Democrats were buried in the congressional elections of 1894. Dropping moralistic reforms and stressing national activism, Republicans won control of both the House and the Senate.

With the Democrats confined to the South, the politics of stalemate was over. All that remained for the Republican party was to capture the White House in 1896.

## The Battle of the Standards

The campaign of 1896 quickly became a "battle of the standards." Both major parties obsessed over whether gold alone or gold and silver should become the nation's monetary standard. Most Republicans saw gold as the stable base for building business confidence and economic prosperity. They adopted a platform calling for "sound money" supported by gold. Their candidate, Governor William McKinley of Ohio, cautiously supported the gold plank and firmly believed in high tariffs to protect American industry.

Silverites, on the other hand, campaigned for "free and independent" coinage of silver, in which the Treasury freely minted all the silver presented to

*Free silver*    it, independent of other nations. The supply of money would increase, prices would rise, and the economy would revive—or so
their theory said.

But the free silver movement was more than a monetary theory. It was a
symbolic protest of region and class—of the agricultural South and West against
the commercial Northeast, of debt-ridden farm folk against industrialists and financiers. Silverites pressed their case like preachers exhorting their flocks,
nowhere more effectively than in William Harvey's best-selling pamphlet, *Coin's
Financial School* (1894). It reached tens of thousands of readers with the common sense of Coin, its young hero, fighting for silver.

At the Democratic convention in Chicago, William Jennings Bryan of
Nebraska was ready to fight, as well. Just 36 years old, Bryan looked "like a
young divine"—"tall, slender, handsome," with a rich melodic voice that reached
the back rows of the largest halls (no small asset in the days before electric am-
plification). He had served two terms in Congress and worked as a journalist.
He favored low tariffs, opposed Cleveland, and came out belatedly for free silver. Systematically, he coordinated a quiet fight for his nomination.

Silverites controlled the convention from the start. They paraded with silver banners, wore silver buttons, and wrote a plank into the anti-Cleveland platform calling for free and unlimited coinage of the metal. The high point came
when Bryan stepped to the lectern, threw back his head, and offered himself to
"a cause as holy as the cause of liberty—the cause of humanity." The crowd was
in a near-frenzy as he reached the dramatic climax and spread his arms in mock
crucifixion: "You shall not crucify mankind upon a cross of gold." The next day
the convention nominated him for the presidency.

Populists were in a quandary. They had expected the Democrats to stick
with Cleveland and gold, sending unhappy silverites headlong into their camp.
Instead, the Democrats had stolen their thunder by endorsing silver and nominating Bryan. "If we fuse [with the Democrats] we are sunk," complained one
Populist. "If we don't fuse, all the silver men we have will leave us for the more
powerful Democrats." At a bitter convention, fusionists nominated Bryan for
president. The best antifusionists could do was drop the Democrats' vice presidential candidate in favor of a fiery agrarian rebel from Georgia, Tom Watson.

## Campaign and Election

Bryan knew he faced an uphill battle. Adopting a more active style that would
be imitated in future campaigns, he traveled 18,000 miles by train, gave as many
as 30 speeches a day, and reached perhaps 3 million people in 27 states. The
nomination of the People's party actually did more harm than good by labeling
Bryan a Populist (which he was not) and a radical (which he definitely was not).
Devoted to the "plain people," the Great Commoner spoke for rural America
and Jeffersonian values: small farmers, small towns, small government.

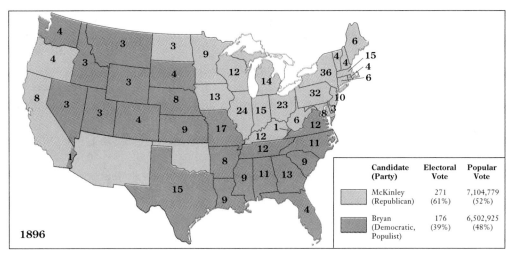

| Candidate (Party) | Electoral Vote | Popular Vote |
|---|---|---|
| McKinley (Republican) | 271 (61%) | 7,104,779 (52%) |
| Bryan (Democratic, Populist) | 176 (39%) | 6,502,925 (48%) |

1896

THE ELECTION OF 1896 The critical election of 1896 established the Republicans as the majority party, ending two decades of political gridlock with a new political realignment. Republican victor William McKinley dominated the large industrial cities and states, as the returns of the electoral college show.

McKinley knew he could not compete with Bryan's barnstorming, so he contented himself with sedate speeches from his front porch in Canton, Ohio. The folksy appearance of the campaign belied its reality. From the beginning, it had been engineered by Marcus Alonzo Hanna, a talented Ohio industrialist. Hanna relied on modern techniques of organization and marketing. He advertised McKinley, said Theodore Roosevelt, "as if he were patent medicine." His well-financed campaign brought to Canton tens of thousands, who cheered the candidate's promises of a "full dinner pail." Hanna also saturated the country with millions of leaflets, along with 1400 speakers attacking free trade and free silver.

On election night, Bryan sat at home in Lincoln, Nebraska, as three telegraph operators brought him bulletin after bulletin spelling defeat. Both candidates tallied more votes than any of their predecessors: Bryan, 6.5 million; McKinley, 7.1 million (making him the first president since Grant to receive a popular majority).

The election proved to be one of the most critical in the republic's history.[*] Over the previous three decades, political life had been characterized by vibrant

---

[*] Five elections, in addition to the contest of 1896, are often cited as critical shifts in voter allegiance and party alignments: the Federalist defeat of 1800, Andrew Jackson's rise in 1828, Lincoln's Republican triumph of 1860, Al Smith's Democratic loss in 1928, and—perhaps—Ronald Reagan's conservative tide of 1980.

*Republican coalition* campaigns, slim party margins, high voter turnout, and low-profile presidents. The election of 1896 signaled a new era of dwindling party loyalties and voter turnout, stronger presidents, and Republican rule. McKinley's victory broke the political stalemate and forged a powerful coalition that dominated politics for the next 30 years. It rested on the industrial cities of the Northeast and Midwest and combined old support from businesses, farmers, and Union Army veterans with broader backing from industrial wage earners. The Democrats controlled little but the South, and the Populists virtually vanished from the political scene.

## The Rise of Jim Crow Politics

In 1892, despite the stumping of Populists like Tom Watson, African Americans cast their ballots for Republicans, when they were permitted to vote freely. But increasingly, their voting rights were being curtailed across the South.

As the century drew to a close, long-standing racism deepened. The arrival of "new" immigrants from eastern and southern Europe and the acquisition of new overseas colonies encouraged prejudices that stridently rationalized segregation and other forms of racial control (pages 534–535). In the South racism was enlisted in a political purpose: preventing an alliance of poor blacks and whites that might topple white conservative Democrats. So the white supremacy campaign, ostensibly directed at African Americans, also had a broader target in the world of politics: rebellion from below, whether black or white.

Mississippi, whose Democrats had led the move to "redeem" their state from Republican Reconstruction, in 1890 took the lead in disfranchising African Americans. A new state constitution required voters to pay a poll tax and pass a literacy test, requirements that eliminated the great majority of black voters. Conservative Democrats favored the plan because it also reduced the voting of poor whites, who were most likely to join opposition parties. Before the new constitution went into effect, Mississippi contained more than 250,000 eligible voters. By 1892, after its adoption, there were fewer than 77,000. Soon an all-white combination of conservatives and "reformers"—those disgusted by frequent election stealing with blocks of black votes—passed disfranchisement laws across the South. Between 1895 and 1908, disfranchisement campaigns won out in every southern state.

Sometimes disfranchisement laws relied on the complicated procedure of charging poll taxes and demanding receipts at the polls, as in Mississippi. (To *Disfranchisement* trick voters who had paid, local politicians arranged for circuses to tour black districts before elections and collect poll tax receipts as the price of admission. Without them, black voters could not cast their ballots.) Sometimes literacy tests were used as a barrier. Where African American voters were concentrated in large numbers, some states gerrymandered, or remapped the boundaries of election districts, to split up black votes. "Grandfather clauses" allowed citizens to vote only if their grandfathers had voted in elections held before 1860 (or 1866 in some cases). The provision excluded most African Americans.

The disfranchisement campaign also succeeded in barring many poor whites from the polls. In Louisiana, for example, under the new provisions the number of citizens voting was cut by more than two-thirds, excluding almost all the black voters and almost half the whites. The disfranchisement campaign had one final consequence: splitting rebellious whites from blacks, as the fate of Tom Watson demonstrated.

Only a dozen years after his biracial campaign of 1892, Watson was promoting black disfranchisement in Georgia. Like other southern Populists, Watson returned to the Democratic party still hoping to help poor whites. But he turned against black southerners. Only by playing a powerful race card could he hope to win election. "What does civilization owe the negro?" he asked bitterly. "Nothing! Nothing!! NOTHING!!!" In 1920, after a decade of baiting blacks (as well as Catholics and Jews), the Georgia firebrand was elected to the Senate. Watson, who began with such high racial ideals, gained power only by abandoning them.

## The African American Response

To mount a successful campaign for disfranchisement, white conservatives inflamed racial passions. They staged "White Supremacy Jubilees" and peppered newspaper editorials with complaints of "bumptious" and "impudent" African Americans. The number of lynchings peaked during the 1890s, averaging over a hundred a year for the decade. Most took place in the South. In Atlanta and New Orleans, white mobs terrorized blacks for days in the new, heightened atmosphere of tension.

Under such circumstances, African Americans worked out responses to the climate of intolerance. One came from Booker T. Washington, a former slave

*Booker T. Washington*

and founder of an industrial and agricultural school for blacks in Tuskegee, Alabama. "I love the South," he reassured an audience of white and black southerners in Atlanta in 1895. He conceded that white prejudice existed throughout the region but nonetheless counseled African Americans to work for their economic betterment through manual labor. Every laborer who learned a trade, every farmer who tilled the land could increase his savings. And those earnings would amount to "a little green ballot" that "no one will throw out or refuse to count." Thus Tuskegee's curriculum stressed vocational skills for farming, manual trades, and industrial work.

Many white Americans hailed Washington's "Atlanta Compromise," for it struck the note of patient humility they were so eager to hear. For African Americans, it made the best of a bad situation. Washington, an astute politician, discovered that philanthropists across the nation hoped to make Tuskegee an example of their generosity. He was the honored guest of Andrew Carnegie at his imposing Skibo Castle. California railroad magnate Collis Huntington became his friend, as did other business executives eager to discuss "public and so-cial questions."

Throughout, Washington preached accommodation to the racial caste sys-tem. He accepted segregation (so long as separate facilities were equal) and qual-ifications on voting (if they applied to white citizens as well). Above all Washington sought economic self-improvement for common black folk in fields and factories. In 1900 he organized the National Negro Business League to help establish black businessmen as the leaders of their people. The rapid growth of local chapters (320 by 1907) extended his influence across the country.

Not all black leaders accepted Washington's call for accommodation. W. E. B. Du Bois, a professor at Atlanta University, leveled the most stinging attack in

*W. E. B. Du Bois*

*The Souls of Black Folk* (1903). Du Bois saw no benefit for African Americans in sacrificing intellectual growth for narrow vocational training. Nor was he willing to abide the humiliating stigma that came from the South's discriminatory caste system. A better future would come only if black citizens struggled politically to achieve suffrage and equal rights.

Instead of exhorting African Americans to pull themselves up slowly from the bottom, Du Bois called on the "talented tenth," a cultured black vanguard,

*NAACP*

to blaze a trail of protest. In 1905 he founded what became known as the Niagara movement for political and economic equality. In 1909 a coalition of blacks and sympathetic whites transformed the Niagara movement into the National Association for the Advancement of Colored People (NAACP). Middle class and elitist, it mounted legal challenges to the Jim Crow system of segregation. But for sharecroppers in southern cot-ton fields and laborers in northern factories—the mass of African Americans—the strategy offered little relief.

Neither accommodation nor legal agitation would suffice. But in the "Solid South" (as well as an openly racialized North) it was Washington's restrained approach that articulated an agenda for most African Americans. The ferment of the early 1890s, among black Populists and white, was replaced by an all-white Democratic party that dominated the region but remained in the minor-ity on the national level.

## McKinley in the White House

In William McKinley, Republicans found a skillful chief with a national agenda and personal charm. He cultivated news reporters, openly walked the streets of Washington, and courted the public with handshakes and flowers from his own lapel. Firmly but delicately, he curbed the power of old-time state bosses. When necessary, he prodded Congress to action. In all these ways, he foreshadowed "modern" presidents, who would act as party leaders rather than as executive caretakers.

Fortune at first smiled on McKinley. When he entered the White House, the economy had already begun its recovery, as the cycle of economic retrenchment hit bottom. Factory orders were slowly increasing, and unemployment dropped. Farm prices climbed. New discoveries of gold in Alaska and South Africa expanded the supply of money without causing "gold bugs" to panic that it was being destabilized by silver.

Freed from the burdens of the economic crisis, McKinley called a special session of Congress to revise the tariff. In 1897 the Dingley Tariff raised protective rates still higher but allowed the tariffs to come down if other nations lowered theirs. McKinley also sought a solution for resolving railroad strikes, like the Pullman conflict, before they turned violent. The Erdman Act of 1898 set up machinery for government mediation. McKinley even began laying plans for stronger regulation of trusts.

But the same expansiveness that had pushed an industrial nation across the continent and shipped grain and cotton abroad was also drawing the country into a race for empire and a war with Spain. Regulation—and an age of reform—would have to await the next century.

## VISIONS OF EMPIRE

The crisis with Spain was only the affair of the moment that turned American attention abroad. Underlying the conflict were larger forces linking the United States with international events. By the 1890s, southern farmers were exporting half their cotton crop to factories worldwide, while western wheat farmers earned some 30 to 40 percent of their income from markets abroad. John D. Rockefeller's Standard Oil Company shipped about two-thirds of its refined products overseas, and Cyrus McCormick supplied Russian farmers with the reaper.

More than commerce turned American eyes overseas. Since the 1840s expansionists had spoken of a divine destiny to overspread the North American continent from the Atlantic to the Pacific. Some Americans still cast covetous glances at Canada to the north and Mexico and Cuba to the south. More often, however, they dreamed of empire in more distant lands.

### Imperialism, European-Style and American

The scramble for empire was well under way by the time the Americans, Japanese, and Germans entered in the late nineteenth century. Spain and Portugal still clung to the remnants of colonial empires dating from the fifteenth and sixteenth centuries. Meanwhile, England, France, and Russia accelerated their drive to control foreign peoples and lands. But the late nineteenth century became the new age of imperialism because the technology of arms and the networks of communication, transportation, and commerce brought the prospect of effective, truly global empires within much closer reach.

The naked force with which Europeans took possessions in Africa in the 1880s prompted many Americans to argue for this European-style imperialism

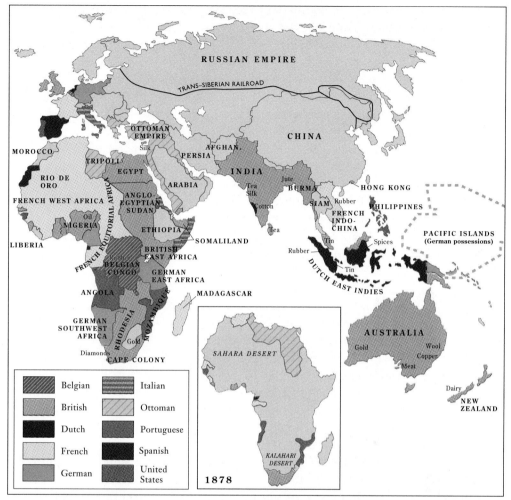

IMPERIALIST EXPANSION, 1900   Often resource-poor countries like Great Britain sought colonies for their raw materials, such as South African diamonds and tin from Southeast Asia. While China appears to be undivided, the major powers were busy establishing spheres of influence there.

*American values* of conquest and possession. But others preferred the more indirect imperialism that exported products, ideas, and influence. To them, this American imperialism seemed somehow purer, for they could portray themselves as bearers of their long-cherished values: democracy, free-enterprise capitalism, and Protestant Christianity. No doubt most Americans felt the world's far reaches would benefit as a result.

While Americans tried to justify imperial control in the name of democracy, social, economic, and political forces were drawing them rapidly into the impe-

*Forces of imperialism*

rial race. The growth of industrial networks linked them to international markets as never before. This was true whether they were Arkansas sharecroppers dependent on world cotton prices or Pittsburgh steelworkers whose jobs were made possible by orders for railroad steel from entrepreneurs like Isaac Singer, whose agents sold sewing machines from Europe to Asia. As economic systems became more tightly knit and political systems more responsive to industrialists and financiers, a rush for markets and distant lands was perhaps unavoidable.

But in 1880, the United States still lacked the military might of an imperial power. Its once-proud Civil War fleet of more than 600 warships was rotting and rusted with neglect. The U.S. Navy ranked twelfth in the world, behind Denmark and Chile. The United States had a coastal fleet but in effect no functional navy to protect its interests overseas.

Discontented navy officers joined with trade-hungry business leaders to lobby Congress for a modern navy with steam-powered, steel-hulled ships.

*Alfred Thayer Mahan and the new navy*

Alfred Thayer Mahan, a Navy captain and later admiral, formulated their ideas into a widely accepted theory of navalism. In *The Influence of Sea Power Upon History* (1890), Mahan argued that great nations were seafaring powers that relied on foreign trade for wealth and might. In times of overproduction and depression, as had occurred repeatedly in the United States after the Civil War, overseas markets assumed even greater importance.

The only way to gain and protect foreign markets, Mahan argued, was with large cruisers and battleships, not small coastal defenders. These ships, operating far from American shores, would need coaling stations and other resupply facilities throughout the world.

Mahan's logic was persuasive. So too were the profits a shipbuilding program would bring to American factories. In the 1880s, Congress launched a program to rebuild the navy with steam vessels made of steel rather than the wooden sailing ships of old. By 1900, the U.S. Navy ranked third in the world. With a modern navy, the country had the means to become an imperial power.

## The Shaping of Foreign Policy

Although the climate for expansion and imperialism was present at the end of the nineteenth century, the small farmer or steelworker was little concerned with how the United States advanced its goals abroad. An elite group—Christian missionaries, intellectuals, business leaders, and commercial farmers—joined with navy careerists to push for a more active American imperialism.

Protestant missionaries provided a spiritual rationale that complemented Mahan's navalism. As American Protestant missionaries sought to convert "heathen" unbelievers in faraway lands, they encountered people whose cultural differences often made them unreceptive to the Christian message. Many came to believe that the natives first had to become Western in culture before becoming Christian in belief. They introduced Western goods, education, and systems of government administration—any "civilizing medium," as one minister remarked when he encouraged Singer to bring his sewing machines to China. Yet most American missionaries were not territorial imperialists. They eagerly took up what they called "the white man's burden" of introducing civilization to the "colored" races of the world. But they opposed direct military or political intervention.

From scholars, academics, and scientists came racial theories to justify European and American expansion. Charles Darwin's *On the Origin of Species*

*Social Darwinism*

(1859) had popularized the notion that among animal species, the fittest survived through a process of natural selection. Social Darwinists (page 484) argued that the same laws of survival governed the social order. When applied aggressively, Social Darwinism was used to justify theories of white supremacy as well as the slaughter and enslavement of nonwhite native populations that resisted conquest. When combined with the somewhat more humane "white man's burden" of Christian missionaries, conquest included uplifting natives by spreading Western ideas, religion, and government.

Perhaps more compelling than either racial or religious motives for American expansion was the need for trade. The business cycle of boom and

*Commercial factors*

bust reminded Americans of the unpredictability of their economy. In hard times, people sought salvation wherever they could, and one obvious road to recovery lay in markets abroad. With American companies outgrowing the home market, explained the National Association of Manufacturers, "expansion of our foreign trade is [the] only promise of relief."

In and out of government, leading public figures called for a campaign to "find markets in every part of the habitable globe." Imperialist policies, whether defined as an expansion of U.S. boundaries, the acquisition of colonies, or merely the achievement of a controlling influence, offered the chance to spread American values, increase foreign trade, enhance American prestige, and guarantee future security.

## William Henry Seward

No one did more to initiate the idea of a "New Empire" for the United States than William Henry Seward. Secretary of state under Lincoln and Andrew Johnson, he had employed skillful diplomacy to avert European intervention in the Civil War. Following the war, the breadth of his vision led him to dream dreams beyond those of most politicians.

Seward rested his expansionism on his two central political laws. The first was that "empire has . . . made its way constantly westward . . . until the tides

*Seward's laws of empire*

of the renewed and decaying civilizations of the world meet on the shores of the Pacific Ocean." The United States must thus be prepared to win supremacy in the Far East. Seward's second maxim underscored how the battle could be won: the great empires of the future would be commercial, not military. The American empire required not colonies but markets. Equal access to foreign markets, often called the "open door," guided both British and American policy in Asia.

While he pursued ties to Japan, Korea, and China, Seward promoted a transcontinental railroad at home and a canal across the Central American isthmus. Link by link, he was trying to connect eastern factories to western ports and, from there, to markets in the Far East. But his dreams of opening Asia to American commerce bore little result in his lifetime. The transcontinental railroad, Atlantic cable, and high tariffs that he supported did come to pass. But his attempts to buy Iceland, Greenland, and a few Caribbean islands (and to annex Cuba) ran into opposition both at home and abroad.

Seward made two notable territorial acquisitions. An American naval officer raised the Stars and Stripes over the Pacific island of Midway in 1867 as a result of Seward's efforts. Unimportant by itself, the value of

*Midway and Alaska purchases*

Midway lay as a way station to Asia and a Pacific toehold near Hawaii, where missionary planters were already establishing an American presence. Seward also engineered the purchase of Alaska in 1867. Critics called it "Seward's Folly" and the "Polar Bear Garden." But the Alaskan purchase turned out to be a bargain. The United States paid Russia $7.2 million, or about 2 cents an acre, for a mineral-rich territory twice the size of Texas.

## The United States and Latin America

Many Americans did not accept Seward's conviction that their future lay in Asia. After the Civil War, some expansionists renewed talk of annexing Canada or provoking a border war with Mexico to gain territory. By the early 1870s, however, most Americans had decided that it was more profitable to trade with their northern neighbor than to possess it. Similarly, commercial and business interests pushed for friendly economic ties with Mexico. In 1881 Secretary of State James G. Blaine made it clear that the United States was not looking for the chance to acquire new territory there, only the opportunity to invest its "large accumulation of capital."

Elsewhere in Latin America, Blaine looked for ways to expand American trade and influence. One obstacle was the British presence in Central America.

*James G. Blaine*

Blaine launched a campaign to cancel the Clayton–Bulwer Treaty (1850) sharing rights with Great Britain to any canal built in the region. At the same time, he tried to shift Central American imports from British to American goods by promoting hemispheric cooperation and stability. For years Latin America had endured political rivalries, governments rising and falling, and British and American meddling. International conflicts pitted Mexico against Guatemala, Chile against Argentina, Nicaragua against Honduras, Chile against Peru and Bolivia, and even resulted in near-war between Chile and the United States in 1891.

To promote regional trade and ease tensions Blaine helped organize the Pan-American Congress. He presided over the opening session as representa-

*Blaine's Pan-American Congress*

tives from 18 nations gathered in October 1889. Blaine immediately proposed a "customs union" to reduce trade barriers in the Americas and a set of arbitration procedures to prevent disputes from erupting into war. Deep suspicions over American motives hamstrung delegates, who in the end established only the weak Pan-American Union to foster peaceful understanding.

Blaine thus found himself forced to pursue separate talks and sometimes to strong-arm his way to the tariff reductions he wanted. If Latin American nations refused to lower their tariffs, he threatened to ban the products of their often single-crop economies under provisions of the 1890 McKinley Tariff. Only three nations—Colombia, Haiti, and Venezuela—had the will to resist.

## Prelude in the Pacific

In the Pacific, the United States faced Great Britain and Germany as they vied for control of the strategically located islands of Samoa. In 1878 a treaty gave America the rights to the fine harbor at Pago Pago. When the Germans sent marines to secure their interests in 1889, the British and Americans sent gunboats. As tensions peaked, a typhoon struck, sinking the rival fleets and staving off conflict. Ten years later the three powers finally carved up the islands, with the United States retaining Pago Pago.

If American expansionists wanted to extend trade across the Pacific to China, Hawaii was the crucial link. The islands had been settled some 2000

*Ambitions in Hawaii*

years earlier by visitors from the Polynesian Islands. In the 1780s an American merchant ship had stopped there, and by the 1840s American merchants and missionaries dominated the port at Honolulu.

Whereas the missionaries had been God-fearing idealists, their descendants were a practical lot: they saw the possibilities for a harvest in sugarcane, not Polynesian souls. Thus they acquired thousands of acres on which they produced sugar for export to the United States. In 1879 the total value of sugar estates in Hawaii was less than $10 million, but by 1898 that figure had jumped to over $40 million. Planters imported cheap laborers from China, Japan, the Philippines, Korea, and Puerto Rico to work the sugarcane fields. Soon Japanese immigrants alone made up a fourth of the population. Native Hawaiians were rapidly becoming a minority on their own islands.

By the 1880s the United States had asserted virtual control over the islands, including naval rights to a base at Pearl Harbor. European imperialists found

Polynesians were culturally ill-suited to the backbreaking labor of sugarcane cultivation in Hawaii. English and American planters, who dominated the sugar plantations, instead recruited Japanese workers like this one.

themselves hopelessly outmaneuvered. The Hawaiian sugar planters had forged particularly close ties with the U.S. because a treaty in 1875 allowed Hawaiian sugar to enter the states duty-free.

In 1890, the planters received a jolt when the McKinley Tariff added a bounty of 2 cents a pound to home-grown sugarcane. Of course, if the Hawaiian Islands

*McKinley Tariff* were annexed by the United States, their growers would gain this advantage—a thought that set more than a few planters to scheming. Unfortunately for them, Queen Liliuokalani ascended to the Hawaiian throne the very next year. A strong nationalist, she tried to limit foreign influence and restore the power of the monarchy.

As a nationalist, Queen Liliuokalani believed that Hawaii should remain in the hands of its native peoples. And as a monarchist, she believed those hands should be hers, not those of sugar planters who might dominate a constitutional legislature. In 1893, the planters overthrew her. Their success was ensured when a contingent of marines arrived ashore on the pretense of protecting American lives. In the face of heavily armed opposition, the queen capitulated. A commission of planters—four American and one British—took over.

Eager to dampen any British designs on the islands, President Benjamin Harrison signed an annexation treaty with the American-dominated commis-

*Hawaii revolts* sion early in 1893. But before the Senate could ratify it, Grover Cleveland took office and put the treaty on hold. Cleveland was no foe of expansion but was, as his secretary of state noted, "unalterably opposed to stealing territory, or of annexing people against their consent, and the people of Hawaii do not favor annexation." The idea of incorporating the non-white population also troubled Cleveland. For a time, matters stood at a stalemate.

## Crisis in Venezuela

Gold, with its capacity to muddy the waters from which it is panned, stirred trouble in the jungles of Venezuela. In the 1880s prospectors unearthed a 32-pound nugget along the border between Venezuela and the colony of British Guiana. Venezuela and Britain both laid claim to the territory, which also included the mouth of the Orinoco River. The river was a gateway to trade in the interior of South America's northern coast.

For years the United States pressed Britain to submit the dispute to arbitration. In 1895 an exasperated President Cleveland warned the British that their expansive claims against Venezuela impinged on the "safety," "honor," and "welfare" of the United States. Facing an economic depression, neither the president nor Congress wanted to chance having Great Britain close off a promising market. Arbitration, Cleveland insisted, was the only way to avoid armed American intervention.

When the British rejected arbitration, Cleveland fired off what amounted to an ultimatum. The United States would send a commission to set the boundary, and if the British still refused to arbitrate, more forceful action—perhaps even war—would follow. In the end, cool heads prevailed. After all, Cleveland did not want war with Britain, only British consent to terms acceptable to the United States. In that he succeeded. Eager to avoid conflict, the British agreed to arbitration, which in the end left Venezuela with what it wanted most, control of access to the Orinoco, and the United States what it wanted, an opportunity to assert its supremacy in the hemisphere.

Tensions between the United States and Great Britain eased in the wake of the crisis. The British had no choice but to make up. In Europe, they faced a formidable rival: newly unified Germany, rapidly industrializing, seeking colonies, and building a navy. In Asia, Japan and Russia threatened to exclude Britain from important markets. In South Africa, the Boer War—with the descendants of old Dutch settlers—was draining British blood and resources. Granting the United States a free hand in the Western Hemisphere was a small price to pay for cementing Anglo-American relations.

The treaty concluded by Secretary of State John Hay and British Ambassador Sir Julian Pauncefote in 1901 symbolized the new era of Anglo-American friend-

*Hay–Pauncefote Treaty*

ship. It also ended a campaign begun by James Blaine years earlier. Under the Hay–Pauncefote Treaty, Britain ceded its interest in building a canal across the Central American isthmus, while the United States pledged to leave such a canal open to ships of all nations.

## THE IMPERIAL MOMENT

In 1895, after almost 15 years of planning from exile in the United States, José Martí returned to Cuba to renew the struggle for independence from Spain.

*Cuba in revolt* With cries of *Cuba libre*, Martí and his rebels cut railroad lines, destroyed sugar mills, and set fire to the cane fields. Within a year, rebel forces controlled more than half the island. But even as they fought the Spanish, the rebels worried about the United States. Their island, just 90 miles off the coast of Florida, had long been a target of American expansionists and business interests. "I have lived in the bowels of the monster," Martí said in reference to the United States, "and I know it."

The Spanish overlords struck back at Martí and his followers with brutal violence. Governor-General Valeriano Weyler herded a half million Cubans from their homes into fortified camps where filth, disease, and starvation killed perhaps 200,000. Outside these "reconcentration" camps, Weyler chased the rebels across the countryside, polluting drinking water, killing farm animals, burning crops.

### Mounting Tensions

Cleveland had little sympathy for the Cuban revolt. He doubted that the mostly black population was capable of self-government and feared that independence from Spain might lead to chaos on the island. Already the revolution had caused widespread destruction of American-owned property. The president settled on a policy that would throw American support neither to Spain nor to the rebels: opposing the rebellion, but pressing Spain to grant Cuba some freedoms.

In the Republican party, expansionists like Theodore Roosevelt and Massachusetts senator Henry Cabot Lodge urged a more forceful policy. In 1896 they

*Republican imperialism* succeeded in writing an imperial wish list into the Republican national platform: annexation of Hawaii, the construction of a Nicaraguan canal, purchase of the Virgin Islands, and more naval expansion. They also called for recognition of Cuban independence, a step that, if taken, would likely provoke war with Spain. When the victorious William McKinley entered the White House, however, his Republican supporters found only a moderate expansionist. Cautiously, privately, he lobbied Spain to stop cracking down on the rebels and destroying American property.

In 1897 Spain promised to remove the much-despised Weyler, end the reconcentration policy, and offer Cuba greater autonomy. The shift encouraged McKinley to resist pressure at home for more hostile action. But leaders of the Spanish army in Cuba had no desire to compromise. Although Weyler was removed, the military renewed efforts to crush the rebels and stirred pro-army riots in the streets of Havana. Early in 1898, McKinley dispatched the battleship *Maine* to show that the United States meant to protect its interests and its citizens.

A grisly depiction of the explosion that sank the battleship *Maine* in Havana harbor
in 1898, complete with a panel entitled "Recovering the Dead Bodies" (upper right).
The causes of the explosion remain a mystery, but illustrations like this one helped
jingoists turn the event into a battle cry.

Then in February 1898 the State Department received a stolen copy of a
letter to Cuba sent by the Spanish minister in Washington, Enrique Dupuy de

*De Lôme letter*

Lôme. So did William Randolph Hearst, a pioneer of sensation-
alist, or "yellow," journalism who was eager for war with Spain.
"WORST INSULT TO THE UNITED STATES IN ITS HISTORY,"
screamed the headline of Hearst's New York *Journal.* What had de Lôme actually written? After referring to McKinley as a mere "would-be politician," the
letter admitted that Spain had no intention of changing its policy of crushing
the rebels. Red-faced Spanish officials immediately recalled de Lôme, but most
Americans now believed that Spain had deceived the United States.

On February 15, 1898, as the *Maine* lay peacefully at anchor in the Havana
harbor, explosions ripped through the hull. Within minutes the ship sank to the

*Sinking of the Maine*

bottom, killing some 260 American sailors. The cause of the
blasts remains unclear, but most Americans, inflamed by hysterical news accounts, concluded that Spanish agents had sabotaged
the ship. McKinley sought a diplomatic solution but also a $50 million appro-
priation "to get ready for war."

Pressures for war proved too great, and on April 11, McKinley asked Congress to authorize "forceful intervention" in Cuba. Nine days later Congress recognized Cuban independence, insisted on the withdrawal of Spanish forces, and gave the president authority to use military force. In a flush of idealism, Congress also adopted the Teller Amendment, renouncing any aim to annex Cuba.

*Teller Amendment*

Certainly both idealism and moral outrage led many Americans down the path to war. But in the end, the "splendid little war" (as Secretary of State John Hay called it) came as a result of less lofty ambitions: empire, trade, glory.

## The Imperial War

For the 5462 men who died, there was little splendid about the Spanish–American War. Only 379 gave their lives in battle. The rest succumbed to accidents, disease, and the mismanagement of an unprepared army. As war began, the American force totaled only 30,000, none trained for fighting in tropical climates. The sudden expansion to 60,000 troops and 200,000 volunteers overtaxed the graft-ridden system of supply. Rather than tropical uniforms troops were issued winter woolens and sometimes fed on rations that were diseased, rotten, or poisoned. Some soldiers found themselves fighting with weapons from the Civil War.

*Military disorganization*

The Navy fared better. Decisions in the 1880s to modernize the fleet paid handsome dividends. Naval battles largely determined the outcome of the war. As soon as war was declared, Admiral George Dewey ordered his Asiatic battle squadron from China to the Philippines. Just before dawn on May 1, he opened fire on the Spanish ships in Manila Bay. Five hours later the entire Spanish squadron lay at the bottom of the bay. Three hundred eighty-one Spaniards were killed but only one American, a ship's engineer who died of a heart attack. Dewey had no plans to follow up his stunning victory with an invasion. His fleet carried no marines with which to take Manila. So ill-prepared was President McKinley for war, let alone victory, that only after learning of Dewey's success did he order 11,000 American troops to the Philippines.

*Dewey at Manila*

Halfway around the globe, another Spanish fleet had slipped into Santiago harbor in Cuba just before the arrival of the U.S. Navy. The Navy, under Admiral William Sampson, blockaded the island, expecting the Spanish to flee under the cover of darkness. Instead, on July 3, the Spanish fleet made a desperate dash for the open seas in broad daylight. So startled were the Americans that several of their ships nearly collided as they rushed to attack their exposed foes. All seven Spanish ships were sunk, with 474 casualties. Only one American was killed and one wounded. With Cuba cut off from Spain, the war was virtually won.

## *War in Cuba*

Few Americans had heard of the Philippine Islands; fewer still could locate them on a globe. McKinley himself followed news from the Pacific front on an old textbook map. But most Americans knew the location of Cuba and how close it lay to the Florida coast.

Before the outbreak of hostilities, Tampa, Florida, was a sleepy coastal town with a single railroad line. As the port of embarkation for the Cuban expeditionary force, it became a hive of activity. In the spring of 1898 alone, some 17,000 troops arrived. Tampa's overtaxed facilities soon broke down, spawning disease, tension, and racial violence as well.

President McKinley had authorized the army to raise five volunteer regiments of black soldiers. By the time war was declared, over 8000 African

*Racial tensions* Americans had signed up. Like most southern towns, Tampa and nearby Lakeland were largely segregated. The 4000 black soldiers stationed there could sail off to die freeing the peasants of Cuba, but they could not buy a soda at the local drugstore. "Is America any better than Spain?" one dismayed black chaplain wondered. As the expeditionary force prepared to

Black veterans of the western Indian wars along with volunteers, segregated and commanded by white officers, made up almost a quarter of the American force that invaded Cuba. Members of the Tenth Calvary, shown here, were clearly in no mood to be subjected to the harrassment they and other black troops encountered around Tampa. Later the Tenth Calvary supported a charge by Colonel Teddy Roosevelt's Rough Riders at the battle of San Juan Hill.

leave in early June, anger turned to violence. After drunken white troops shot at a black child, black troops in Tampa rioted. Three white and 27 black Americans were wounded in the melee.

Matters were scarcely less chaotic as 17,000 disorganized troops and hundreds of reporters finally scrambled aboard ships. There they sat for a week, until finally sailing for Santiago and battle. By June 30, the Americans had landed to challenge some 24,000 Spanish, many equipped with modern rifles. The following day 7000 Americans—including the black soldiers of the Ninth and Tenth Cavalry regiments—stormed up heavily fortified San Juan Hill and nearby Kettle Hill. Their objective was the high ground north and east of Santiago.

Among them Lieutenant Colonel Theodore Roosevelt thrilled at the experience of battle. He had raised a cavalry troop of cowboys and college polo play-

*The Rough Riders*

ers, originally called "Teddy's Texas Tarantulas." By the time they arrived in Cuba, the volunteers were answering to the nickname "Rough Riders." As they charged toward the high ground, Roosevelt yelled: "Gentlemen, the Almighty God and the just cause are with you. Gentlemen, *charge!*" The withering fire drowned out his shrill, squeaky voice, so he repeated the call. Charge they did and conquer the enemy, though the battle cost more than 1500 American casualties.

Without a fleet for cover or any way to escape, the Spanish garrison surrendered on July 17. In the Philippines, a similar brief battle preceded the American taking of Manila on August 13. The "splendid little war" had ended in less than four months.

## Peace and the Debate over Empire

Conquering Cuba and the Philippines proved easier than deciding what to do with them. The Teller Amendment had renounced any American claim to Cuba. But clearly the United States had not freed the island to see chaos reign or American business and military interests excluded. And what of the Philippines—and Spanish Puerto Rico, which American forces had taken without a struggle? Powerful public and congressional sentiment pushed McKinley to claim empire as the fruits of victory.

The president himself favored such a course. The battle in the Pacific highlighted the need for naval bases and coaling stations. "To maintain our flag in

*Annexing Hawaii*

the Philippines, we must raise our flag in Hawaii," the New York *Sun* insisted. On July 7 McKinley signed a joint congressional resolution annexing Hawaii, as planters had wanted for nearly a decade.

The Philippines presented a more difficult problem. Filipinos had greeted the American forces as liberators, not new colonizers. The popular leader of the

*Aguinaldo*

rebel forces fighting Spain, Emilio Aguinaldo, had returned to the islands on an American ship. To the rebels' dismay, McKinley

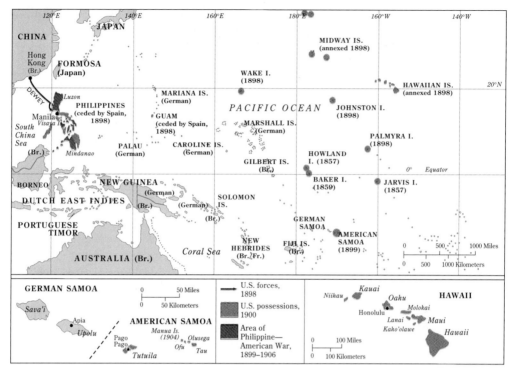

**THE UNITED STATES IN THE PACIFIC** In the late nineteenth century, Germany and the United States emerged as Pacific naval powers and contestants for influence and trade in China. The island groups of the Central and Southwest Pacific were of little economic value but had great strategic worth as bases and coaling stations along the route to Asia.

insisted that the islands were under American authority until the peace treaty settled matters.

Many influential Americans—former president Grover Cleveland, steel baron Andrew Carnegie, novelist Mark Twain—opposed annexation of the Philippines. Yet even these anti-imperialists favored expansion, if

*Anti-imperialists* only in the form of trade. Business leaders especially believed that the country could enjoy the economic benefits of the Philippines without the costs of maintaining it as a colony. Annexation would mire the United States too deeply in the quicksands of Asian politics, they argued. More important, a large, costly fleet would be necessary to defend the islands. To the imperialists that was precisely the point: a large fleet was crucial to the interests of a powerful commercial nation.

Racist ideas shaped both sides of the argument. Imperialists believed that the racial inferiority of nonwhites made occupation of the Philippines necessary,

*The role of racism*

and they were ready to assume the "white man's burden" and govern. Gradually, they argued, Filipinos would be taught the virtues of Western civilization, Christianity,* democracy, and self-rule. Anti-imperialists, on the other hand, feared racial intermixing and the possibility of Asian workers' flooding of the American labor market. They also maintained that dark-skinned people would never develop the capacity for self-government. An American government in the Philippines could be sustained only at the point of bayonets—yet the U.S. Constitution made no provision for governing people without representation or equal rights. Such a precedent, the anti-imperialists warned, might one day threaten American liberties at home.

Still, when the Senate debated the Treaty of Paris ending the Spanish–American War in 1898, the imperialists had the support of the president, most of Congress, and the majority of public opinion. Even an anti-imperialist like William Jennings Bryan, defeated by McKinley in 1896, supported the treaty. In it Spain surrendered title to Cuba, ceded Puerto Rico and Guam to the United States, and in return for $20 million turned over the Philippines as well.

Eager to see war ended, Bryan and other anti-imperialists believed that once the United States possessed the Philippines, it could free them. The imperialists had other notions. Having acquired an empire and a modern navy to protect it, the United States could now assert its new status as one of the world's great powers.

## America's First Asian War

Managing an empire turned out to be even more devilish than acquiring one. As the Senate debated annexation of the Philippines in Washington, rebels clashed

*The Philippine insurrection*

with an American patrol outside of Manila, igniting a guerrilla war. The few Americans who paid attention called it the "Filipino insurrection," but to those who fought, it was a brutal war. When it ended more than three years later, nearly 5000 Americans, 25,000 rebels, and perhaps as many as 200,000 civilians lay dead.

Racial antagonism spurred the savage fighting. American soldiers tended to dismiss Filipinos as nearly subhuman. Their armed resistance to American occupation often transformed the frustrations of ordinary troops into brutality and torture. To avenge a rebel attack, one American officer swore he would turn the surrounding countryside into a "howling wilderness." Before long the American force was resorting to a garrison strategy of herding Filipinos into concentration camps, while destroying their villages and crops. The policy was embarrassingly reminiscent of "Butcher" Weyler (page 584) in Cuba. In 1902, only after the Americans captured Aguinaldo himself, did the war end.

In contrast to the bitter guerrilla war, the United States ruled its new island territory with relative benevolence. Under William Howard Taft, the first civil-

*In point of fact, most Filipinos were already Catholic after many years under Spanish rule.

*U.S. rule in the Philippines* ian governor, the Americans built schools, roads, sewers, and factories and inaugurated new farming techniques. The aim, said Taft, was to prepare the Philippines for independence, and in keeping with it, he granted great authority to local officials. These advances—social, economic, and political—benefited the Filipino elite and thus earned their support. Finally, on July 4, 1946, the Philippines were granted independence.

The United States played a similar role in Puerto Rico. As in the Philippines, executive authority resided in a governor appointed by the U.S. president. *Puerto Rico* Under the Foraker Act of 1900 Puerto Ricans received a voice in their government, as well as a nonvoting representative in the U.S. House of Representatives, and certain tariff advantages. All the same, many Puerto Ricans chafed at the idea of such second-class citizenship. Some favored eventual admission to the United States as a state while others advocated independence, a division of opinion that persists even today.

## An Open Door in China

Interest in Asia drove the United States to annex the Philippines; and annexation of the Philippines only whetted American interest in Asia. As ever, the possibility of markets in China—whether for Christian souls or consumer goods—proved an irresistible lure.

Both the British, who dominated China's export trade, and the Americans, who wanted to, worried that China might soon be carved up by other powers. Japan had defeated China in 1895, encouraging Russia, Germany, and France to join in demanding trade concessions. Each nation sought to establish an Asian "sphere of influence" in which its commercial and military interests reigned. Often this ended in commercial and other restrictions against rival powers. Since Britain and the United States wanted the benefits of trade rather than actual colonies, they tried to limit foreign demands while leaving China open to all commerce.

In 1899, at the urging of the British, Secretary of State John Hay circulated the first of two "open door" notes among the imperial powers. He did not ask *The "open door" notes* them to relinquish their spheres of influence in China, only to keep them open to free trade with other nations. The United States could hardly have enforced even so modest a proposal, for it lacked the military might to prevent the partitioning of China. Still, Japan and most of the European powers agreed in broad outline with Hay's policy, out of fear that the Americans might tip the delicate balance by siding with a rival. Hay seized on the tepid response and brashly announced that the open door in China was international policy.

Unrest soon threatened to close the door. Chinese nationalists, known to Westerners as Boxers for their clenched fist symbol, formed secret societies to

*Boxer Rebellion* drive out the *fon kwei*, or foreign devils. Encouraged by the Chinese empress, Boxers murdered hundreds of Christian missionaries and their followers and besieged foreign diplomats and citizens at the British Embassy in Beijing. European nations quickly dispatched troops to quell the uprising and free the diplomats, while President McKinley sent 2500 Americans to join the march to the capital city. Along the way, the angry foreign armies plundered the countryside and killed civilians before reaching Beijing and breaking the siege.

Hay feared that once in control of Beijing the conquerors might never leave. So he sent a second open-door note in 1900, this time asking foreign powers to respect China's territorial and administrative integrity. They endorsed the proposal in principle only. In fact, the open-door notes together amounted to little more than an announcement of American desires to maintain stability and trade in Asia. Yet they reflected a fundamental purpose to which the United States dedicated itself across the globe: to open closed markets and to keep open those markets that other empires had yet to close. The new American empire would have its share of colonies, but in Asia as elsewhere it would be built primarily on trade.

To expansionists like Alfred Thayer Mahan, Theodore Roosevelt, and John Hay, American interests would be secure only when they had been established worldwide, a course of action they believed to be blessed by divine providence. "We will not renounce our part in the mission of the race, trustee under God of the civilization of the world," declared Senator Albert Beveridge. But to one French diplomat, more accustomed to wheeling and dealing in the corridors of international power, it seemed that the Americans had tempted fate rather than destiny. With a whiff of Old World cynicism or perhaps a prophet's eye, he remarked, "The United States is seated at the table where the great game is played, and it cannot leave it."

On New Year's Eve at the State House in Boston a midnight ceremony ushered in the twentieth century. The crowd celebrated with psalms and hymns. There was a flourish of trumpets, and in the absence of a national anthem everyone sang "America."

Solemn and patriotic, the dawn of the new century brought an end to an era of political uncertainty and a decade of social upheaval. Prosperity returned at home; empire beckoned abroad. But deep divisions—between rich and poor, farmers and factory workers, men and women, native-born and immigrant, black and white—split America. A younger generation of leaders stood in the wings, fearful of the schisms but confident it could bridge them. As Theodore Roosevelt looked eagerly toward war with Spain and the chance to expand American horizons, he did not mince words with an older opponent. "You and your generation have had your chance. . . . Now let us of this generation have ours!"

SIGNIFICANT EVENTS

1850 — Clayton–Bulwer Treaty

1867 — Patrons of Husbandry ("Grange") founded; Alaska acquired

1869 — Prohibition party founded; Massachusetts establishes first state regulatory commission

1874 — Greenback party organized; Woman's Christian Temperance Union formed

1875 — First Farmers' Alliance organized

1877 — *Munn v. Illinois* establishes the right of states to regulate private property in the public interest

1881 — President James Garfield assassinated; Chester Arthur sworn in; Booker T. Washington founds Tuskegee Normal and Industrial Institute in Alabama

1887 — Interstate Commerce Commission created

1889 — First Pan-American Congress

1890 — National American Woman Suffrage Association created; Sherman Antitrust Act; Wyoming enters the Union as first state to give women the vote; Sherman Silver Purchase Act; McKinley Tariff; Southern and Northwestern Alliances adopt Ocala Demands; Mahan's *The Influence of Sea Power Upon History, 1660–1783* published

1892 — Populist party formed; Grover Cleveland elected president

1893 — Panic of 1893; Sherman Silver Purchase Act repealed; Anti-Saloon League created; controversy over annexation of Hawaii

1894 — Coxey's Army marches on Washington to demand public works for the unemployed

1895 — National Municipal League founded; Venezuelan boundary dispute; Martí revives Cuban revolution

1896 — League for the Protection of the Family organized; William McKinley elected president

1898 — Sinking of the USS *Maine;* war with Spain; Teller Amendment; Dewey captures the Phillipines; Tampa riots; Treaty of Paris; Hawaii formally annexed; Anti-Imperialist League established

1898–1902 — Philippine insurrection

1899 — First open-door notes

1900 — Boxer Rebellion; second open-door notes; Foraker Act establishes civil government in Puerto Rico

1903 — W. E. B. Du Bois's *The Souls of Black Folk* published

1909 — National Association for the Advancement of Colored People founded

# CHAPTER TWENTY-TWO

# The Progressive Era

Quitting time, March 25, 1911. The long day had almost come to an end at the Triangle Shirtwaist Company in New York City. The deafening whir of some 1500 sewing machines would soon be silenced as hundreds of workers—mostly young immigrant women and their daughters—were set free. To some quitting time seemed like an emancipation. Twelve-hour days in stifling, unsafe workrooms, weekly paychecks of but $3 to $15, fines for the tiniest mistakes, deductions for needle and thread—even for electricity—made seamstresses angry. Two years earlier, their frustrations had boiled over into an industrywide strike for better wages and working conditions. Despite a union victory, the only change visible at Triangle was that every morning the doors were locked to keep workers in and labor organizers out.

The fire started in the lofts as the workers were leaving their machines. In minutes the top stories were ablaze. Terrified seamstresses groped through the black smoke, only to find exits locked or clogged with bodies. All but one of the few working fire escapes collapsed. When the fire trucks arrived, horrified firefighters discovered that their ladders could not reach the top stories. "Spectators saw again and again pitiable companionships formed in the instant of death—girls who placed their arms around each other as they leaped," read one news story. Their bodies hit the sidewalk with a sickening thud or were spiked on the iron guard rails. One hundred forty-six people died, most of them young working-class women.

A few days later 80,000 New Yorkers joined the silent funeral procession snaking slowly up Fifth Avenue in the rain. A quarter of a million watched. At the Metropolitan Opera House, union leader Rose Schneiderman told a rally, "This is not the first time that girls have been burned alive in the city. Every year thousands of us are maimed." A special state commission investigated the tragedy. Over the next four years its recommendations produced 56 state laws regulating fire safety, hours, machinery, and homework. They amounted to the most far-reaching labor code in the country.

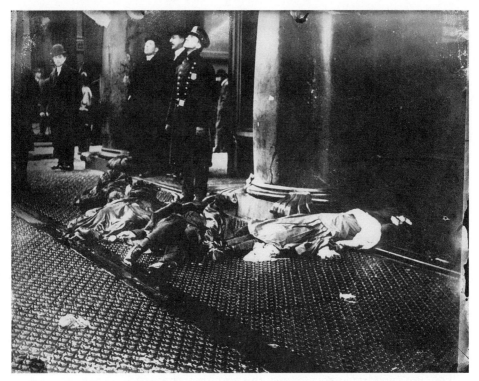

On a street littered with the bodies of dead workers, a policeman looks up at the blazing Triangle Shirtwaist factory, unable to stop more people from jumping. Firefighters arrived within minutes, but their ladders could not reach the top stories.

The Triangle fire shocked the nation and underscored a growing fear: modern industrial society had created profound strains, widespread misery, and deep class divisions. Corporations grew to unimagined size, bought and sold legislators, dictated the terms of their own profit. Men, women, and children worked around the clock in unsafe factories for wages that barely supported them. In cities across America, tenement-bred disease took innocent lives, criminals threatened people and property, saloons tied the working poor to dishonest political bosses. Even among the middle class, inflation was shrinking their wallets at the rate of 3 percent a year. "It was a world of greed," concluded one garment worker; "the human being didn't mean anything."

But human beings did mean something to followers of an influential reform movement sweeping the country. Progressivism had emerged in the mid-1890s and would last through World War I. The movement sprang *The rise of progressivism* from many impulses, mixing a liberal concern for the poor and working class with conservative efforts to stabilize business and avoid social chaos. Liberal or conservative, most progressives shared a desire to soften the harsh impact of industrialization, urbanization, and immigration.

Progressivism thus began in the cities, where those forces converged. It was organized by an angry, idealistic middle class and percolated up from neighborhoods to city halls, state capitals, and, finally, Washington. Though usually pursued through politics, the goals of progressives were broadly social—to create a "good society," where people could live decently, harmoniously, and prosperously, along middle-class guidelines.

Unlike earlier reformers, progressives saw government as a protector, not an oppressor. Only government possessed the resources for the broad-based reforms they sought. Progressivism spawned the modern activist state, with its capacity to regulate the economy and manage society. And because American society had become so interdependent, progressivism became the first nationwide reform movement. No political party monopolized it; no single group controlled it. It flowered in the presidencies of Republican Theodore Roosevelt and Democrat Woodrow Wilson. In 1912 it even spawned its own party, the Progressive, or "Bull Moose," party. By then progressivism had filtered well beyond politics into every realm of American life.

## THE ROOTS OF PROGRESSIVE REFORM

Families turned from their homes; an army of unemployed on the roads; hunger, strikes, and bloody violence across the country—the wrenching depression of 1893 forced Americans to take a hard look at their new industrial order. They found common complaints that cut across lines of class, religion, and ethnicity. If streetcar companies raised fares while service deteriorated, if food processors doctored their canned goods with harmful additives, if politicians skimmed money from the public till, everyone suffered. And no one alone could stop it.

The result was not a coherent progressive movement but a set of loosely connected goals. Some progressives fought for efficient government and honest politics. Others called for greater regulation of business and

*Aims of progressives*

a more orderly economy. Some sought social justice for the urban poor; others, social welfare to protect children, women, workers, and consumers. Still other progressives looked to purify society by outlawing alcohol and drugs, stamping out prostitution and slums, and restricting the flood of new immigrants.

Paternalistic by nature, progressives often imposed their solutions no matter what the less "enlightened" poor or oppressed saw as their own best interests. And they acted partly out of nostalgia. Progressives wanted to redeem such traditional American values as democracy, opportunity for the individual, and the spirit of public service. Yet if their ends were traditional, their means were distinctly modern. They used the systems and methods of the new industrial order—the latest techniques of organization, management, and science—to fight its excesses.

## COUNTERPOINT  *What Was Progressivism?*

Embracing such diversity, progressivism has generated a host of interpretations. Historians writing during the movement depicted it as progressives did: a democratic crusade by the "good people" to curb big business, fight political corruption, and promote social justice. A later generation of historians, examining individual progressives, concluded that they were a small group of once-powerful, upper-middle-class families anxious to reassert the status they had lost to rising industrialists and corporate executives.

To explain the often strong support of corporations, historians of the "New Left" have portrayed progressivism as the "triumph of conservatism," whose aim was to protect corporations from strict regulation and competition. Still others have looked at progressivism as a widespread effort by the "new middle class" of professionals, business leaders, and others to secure their power by bringing order and efficiency to the new industrial economy.

Historians with interests in women, consumers, and African Americans have all found in progressivism an opportunity for these groups to advance their separate, sometimes conflicting goals. Perhaps the most useful interpretation comes from those who see progressivism as part of the broad process of adjustment to the new industrial order. They emphasize the weakening of political parties and the growing influence of "interest groups" of workers, industrialists, consumers, and others who campaigned for the reforms they wanted.

## *Progressive Beliefs*

Progressives were moderate modernizers. They accepted the American system as sound, only in need of adjustment. Many drew on the increasingly popular Darwinian theories of evolution to buttress this gradual approach to change. With its notion of slowly changing species, evolution undermined the acceptance of fixed principles that had guided social thought in the Victorian era. Progressives saw an evolving landscape of shifting values. They denied the old Calvinist doctrine of inborn sinfulness and instead saw people as having a greater potential for good than for evil.

Yet progressives somehow had to explain the existence of evil and wrong-doing. Most agreed that they were "largely, if not wholly, products of society or environment." People went wrong, wrote one progressive, because of "what happens to them." By changing what happened, the human potential for good could be released.

With an eye to results, progressives asked not "Is it true?" but "Does it work?" Philosopher Charles Peirce called this new way of thinking "pragma-

*Pragmatism*

tism." William James, the Harvard psychologist, became its most famous popularizer. For James, pragmatism meant "looking towards last things, fruits, consequences, facts."

## The Pragmatic Approach

Pragmatism led educators, social scientists, and lawyers to adopt new approaches to reform. John Dewey, the master educator of the progressive era, believed that environment shaped the patterns of human thought. Instead of demanding mindless memorization of abstract and unconnected facts, Dewey tried to "make each one of our schools an embryonic community life." At his School of Pedagogy, founded in 1896, he let students unbolt their desks from the floor, move about, and learn by doing so that they could train for real life.

Psychologist John B. Watson believed that human behavior could be shaped at will. Give him control of an infant's world from birth, Watson boasted, "and

*Behaviorism*

I'll guarantee to take any one at random and train him to become any specialist I might select, doctor, lawyer, artist, merchant, chief, and yes, even beggarman and thief." "Behaviorism" swept the social sciences and later advertising, where Watson himself eventually landed.

Lawyers and legal theorists applied their own blend of pragmatism and behaviorism. Justice Oliver Wendell Holmes, Jr., appointed to the Supreme Court in 1902, rejected the idea that the traditions of law were constant and universal. Law was a living organism to be interpreted according to experience and the needs of a changing society.

This environmental view of the law, known as "sociological jurisprudence," found a skilled practitioner in Louis Brandeis. Shaken by the brutal suppression of the Homestead steel strike of 1892, Brandeis quit his corporate practice and proclaimed himself the "people's lawyer." The law must "guide by the light of reason," he wrote, which meant bringing everyday life to bear in any court case. When laundry owner Curt Muller challenged an Oregon law limiting his laun-

*Brandeis Brief*

dresses to a 10-hour workday, Brandeis defended the statute before the Supreme Court in 1908. His famous brief contained 102 pages describing the damaging effects of long hours on working women and only 2 pages of legal precedents. *In Muller v. Oregon*, the Supreme Court upheld Oregon's right to limit the working hours of laborers and thus legitimized the "Brandeis Brief."

## The Progressive Method

Seeing the nation torn by conflict, progressives tried to restore a sense of community through the ideal of a single public interest. Christian ethics were the guide, to be applied after using the latest scientific methods to gather and analyze data about a social problem. The modern corporation furnished an appealing model for organization. Like corporate executives, progressives relied on careful management, coordinated systems, and specialized bureaucracies to carry out reforms.

Between 1902 and 1912 a new breed of journalists provided the necessary evidence and fired public indignation. They investigated wrongdoers, named them in print, and described their misdeeds in vivid detail. Most exposés began as articles in mass-circulation magazines such as *McClure's*. It stirred controversy (and boosted circulation) when publisher Samuel McClure sent reporter Lincoln Steffens to uncover the crooked ties between business and politics. "Tweed Days in St. Louis," which *McClure's* published in October 1902, was followed in the November issue by the first of Ida M. Tarbell's stinging, well-researched indictments of John D. Rockefeller's oil empire, collected later as the *History of the Standard Oil Company* (1904). Soon a full-blown literature of exposure was covering every ill from unsafe food to child labor.

A disgusted Theodore Roosevelt thought the new reporters had gone too far and called them "muckrakers," after the man who raked up filth in the

*Muckrakers*

seventeenth-century classic *Pilgrim's Progress*. But by documenting dishonesty and blight, muckrakers not only aroused people but educated them. No broad reform movement of American institutions would have taken place without them.

To move beyond exposure to solutions, progressives stressed volunteerism and collective action. They drew on the organizational impulse that seemed

*Voluntary organizations*

everywhere to be bringing people together in new interest groups. Between 1890 and 1920 nearly 400 organizations were founded, many to combat the ills of industrial society. Some, like the National Consumers' League, grew out of efforts to promote general causes—in this case protecting consumers and workers from exploitation. Others, such as the National Tuberculosis Association, aimed at a specific problem.

When voluntary action failed, progressives looked to government to protect the public welfare. They mistrusted legislators, who might be controlled by corporate interests or political machines. So they strengthened the executive branch by increasing the power of individual mayors, governors, and presidents. Then they watched those executives carefully.

Progressives also drew on the expertise of the newly professionalized middle class. Confident, cosmopolitan professionals—doctors, engineers, psychia-

*Professionals*

trists, city planners—mounted campaigns to stamp out venereal disease and dysentery, to reform prisons and asylums, and to beautify cities. At local, state, and federal levels, new agencies and commissions staffed by experts began to investigate and regulate lobbyists, insurance and railroad companies, public health, even government itself.

## THE SEARCH FOR THE GOOD SOCIETY

If progressivism ended in politics, it began with social reform: the need to reach out, to do something to bring the "good society" a step closer. Ellen Richards had just such ends in mind in 1890 when she opened the New England Kitchen in downtown Boston. Richards, a chemist and home economist, designed the Kitchen to sell cheap, wholesome food to the working poor. For a few pennies, customers could choose from a nutritious menu, every dish of which had been tested in Richards's laboratory at the Massachusetts Institute of Technology.

The New England Kitchen promoted social as well as nutritional reform. Women freed from the drudgery of cooking could seek gainful employment. And as a "household experiment station" and center for dietary information, the Kitchen tried to educate the poor and Americanize immigrants by showing them how the middle class prepared meals. According to philanthropist Pauline Shaw, it was also a "rival to the saloon." A common belief was that poor diets fostered drinking, especially among the lower classes.

In the end, the New England Kitchen served more as an inexpensive eatery for middle-class working women and students than as a resource for the poor

*Pattern of reform*

or an agency of Americanization. Still, Ellen Richards's experiment reflected a pattern typical of progressive social reform: the mix of professionalism with uplift, socially conscious women entering the public arena, the hope of creating a better world along middle-class lines.

### Poverty in a New Light

During the 1890s crime reporter and photographer Jacob Riis introduced middle-class audiences to urban poverty. Writing in vivid detail in *How the Other Half Lives* (1890), he brought readers into the teeming tenement. Accompanying the text were shocking photos of poverty-stricken Americans—Riis's "other half." He also used lantern slide shows to publicize their plight. His pictures of slum life appeared artless, merely recording the desperate poverty before the camera. But Riis used them to tell a moralistic story, as the earlier English novelist Charles Dickens had used his melodramatic tales to attack the abuses of industrialism in England. People began to see poverty in a new, more sympathetic light—the fault less of the individual than of social conditions.

A haunting naturalism in fiction and painting followed Riis's gritty photographic essays. In *McTeague* (1899) and *Sister Carrie* (1900), novelists like Frank

*Naturalism*

Norris and Theodore Dreiser spun dark tales of city dwellers struggling to keep body and soul intact. The "Ashcan school" painted urban life in all its grimy realism. Photographer Alfred Stieglitz and painters John Sloan and George Bellows chose slums, tenements, and dirty streets as subjects. Poverty began to look less ominous and more heartrending.

Between 1908 and 1914 the Russell Sage Foundation produced six large volumes of facts and figures documenting a vicious cycle of urban poverty that trapped its victims for generations. The children of paupers were likely to be paupers themselves, not because of heredity or sin but because of deprivation.

A new profession—social work—proceeded from this new view of poverty. Social work developed out of the old settlement house movement (page 510).

*Social work*  Like the physicians from whom they drew inspiration, social workers studied hard data to diagnose the problems of their "clients" and worked with them to solve their problems. A social worker's "differential casework" attempted to treat individuals case by case, each according to the way the client had been shaped by environment.

In reality poverty was but a single symptom of deep-rooted personal and social ills. Most progressives, however, continued to see it as a by-product of political and corporate greed.

## Expanding the "Woman's Sphere"

Progressive social reform attracted a great many women seeking what Jane Addams called "the larger life" of public affairs. In the late nineteenth century, women found that protecting their traditional sphere of home and family forced them to move beyond it. Bringing up children, making meals, keeping house, and caring for the sick now involved community decisions about schools, public health, and countless other matters.

Many middle- and upper-middle-class women received their first taste of public life from women's organizations, including mothers' clubs, temperance

*Women's organizations*  societies, and church groups. By the turn of the century, some 500 women's clubs boasted over 160,000 members. Through the General Federation of Women's Clubs, they funded libraries and hospitals, and supported schools, settlement houses, compulsory education, and child labor laws. Eventually they moved beyond the concerns of home and family to endorse such controversial causes as woman suffrage and unionization. To that list the National Association of Colored Women added the special concerns of race, none more urgent than the fight against lynching.

The dawn of the century saw the rise of a new generation of women. Longer lived, better educated, and less often married than their mothers, they

*New woman*  were also willing to pursue careers for fulfillment. Usually they turned to professions that involved the traditional role of nurturer—nursing, library work, teaching, and settlement housework. Custom and prejudice still restricted these new women. The faculty at the Massachusetts Institute of Technology, for example, refused to allow Ellen Richards to pursue a doctorate. Instead they hired her to run the gender-segregated "Woman's Laboratory" for training public school teachers. At the turn of the century, only about 1500 female lawyers practiced in the United States, and in 1910 women made up barely 6 percent of licensed physicians. That figure rapidly declined as

By 1900 one-fourth of the nonfarm labor force was female. On average, women earned $3 less a week than unskilled men. Here at a Labor Day parade in San Diego in 1910 women demand equal pay for equal work.

male-dominated medical associations grew in power and discouraged the entry of women.

Despite the often bitter opposition of families, some feminists tried to destroy the boundaries of the woman's sphere. In *Women and Economics* (1898) Charlotte Perkins Gilman condemned the conventions of womanhood—femininity, marriage, maternity, domesticity—as enslaving and obsolete. She argued for a radically restructured society with large apartment houses, communal arrangements for child rearing and housekeeping, and cooperative kitchens to free women from economic dependence on men.

Margaret Sanger sought to free women from chronic pregnancy. Sanger, a visiting nurse on the Lower East Side of New York, had seen too many poor

*Margaret Sanger*

women overburdened with children, pregnant year after year, with no hope of escaping the cycle. The consequences were crippling. "Women cannot be on equal footing with men until they have complete control over their reproductive functions," she argued.

The insight came as a revelation one summer evening in 1912 when Sanger was called to the home of a distraught immigrant family on Grand Street. Sadie Sachs, mother of three, had nearly died a year earlier from a self-induced abortion. In an effort to terminate another pregnancy, she had killed herself. Sanger

## Jane Addams Fights Child Labor

Our very first Christmas at Hull-House, when we as yet knew nothing of child labor, a number of little girls refused the candy which was offered them as part of the Christmas good cheer, saying simply that they "worked in a candy factory and could not bear the sight of it." We discovered that for six weeks they had worked from seven in the morning until nine at night, and they were exhausted as well as satiated. The sharp consciousness of stern economic conditions was thus thrust upon us in the midst of the season of good will. . . .

The visits we made in the neighborhood constantly discovered women sewing upon sweatshop work, and often they were assisted by incredibly small children. I remember a little girl of four who pulled out basting threads hour after hour, sitting on a stool at the feet of her Bohemian mother, a little bunch of human misery. But even for that there was no legal redress, for the only child-labor law in Illinois with any provision for enforcement had been secured by the coal miners' unions, and was confined to children employed in mines. . . .

While we found many pathetic cases of child labor and hard-driven victims of the sweating system who could not possibly earn enough in the short busy season to support themselves during the rest of the year, it became evident that we must add carefully collected information to our general impression of neighborhood conditions if we would make it of genuine value.

There was at the time no statistical information on Chicago industrial conditions, and Mrs. Florence Kelley, an early resident of Hull-House, suggested to the Illinois State Bureau of Labor that they investigate the sweating system in Chicago with its attendant child labor. The head of the Bureau adopted this suggestion and engaged Mrs. Kelley to make the investigation. When the report was presented to the Illinois Legislature, a special committee was appointed to look into the Chicago conditions. . . .

As a result of its investigations, this committee recommended to the Legislature the provisions which afterward became those of the first factory law of Illinois, regulating the sanitary conditions of the sweatshop and fixing fourteen as the age at which a child might be employed. . . .

Although this first labor legislation was but bringing Illinois into line with the nations in the modern industrial world, which "have long been obliged for their own sakes to come to the aid of the workers by which they live—that the child, the young person and the woman may be protected from their own weakness and necessity—" nevertheless from the first it ran counter to the instinct and tradition, almost to the very religion of the manufacturers, who were for the most part self-made men.

Jane Addams, *Twenty Years at Hull-House* (New York: The Macmillan Company, 1910), pp. 148–153.

vowed that night "to do something to change the destiny of mothers whose miseries were as vast as the sky." She became a crusader for what she called "birth control." By distributing information on contraception, she hoped to free women from unwanted pregnancies and the fate of Sadie Sachs.

Single or married, militant or moderate, professional or lay, white or black, more and more middle-class urban women thus became "social housekeepers." From their own homes they turned to the homes of their neighbors and from there to all of society.

## Social Welfare

In the "bigger family of the city," as one woman reformer called it, settlement house workers found that they alone could not care for the welfare of the poor. If industrial America, with its sooty factories and overcrowded slums, was to be transformed into the good society, individual acts of charity would have to be supplemented by government. Laws had to be passed and agencies created to promote social welfare, including improved housing, workplaces, parks, and playgrounds, the abolition of child labor, and the enactment of eight-hour day laws for working women.

By 1910 the more than 400 settlement houses across the nation had organized into a loose affiliation, with settlement workers ready to help fashion government policy. With greater experience than men in the field, women led the way. Julia Lathrop, a Vassar College graduate, spent 20 years at Jane Addams's Hull House before becoming the first head of the new federal Children's Bureau in 1912. By then two-thirds of the states had adopted some child labor legislation, although loopholes exempted countless youngsters from coverage. Under Lathrop's leadership, Congress was persuaded to pass the Keating–Owen Act (1916), forbidding goods manufactured by children to cross state lines.[*]

*Keating–Owen Act*

---

*The Supreme Court struck down the law in 1918 as an improper regulation of local labor; nonetheless, it focused greater attention on the abuses of child labor.

Florence Kelley, who had also worked at Hull House (page 510), spear-headed a similar campaign in Illinois to protect women workers by limiting their workday to eight hours. As general secretary of the National Consumers' League, she also organized boycotts of companies that treated employees inhumanely. Eventually most states enacted laws restricting the number of hours women could work.

## Woman Suffrage

Ever since the conference for women's rights held at Seneca Falls in 1848, women reformers had pressed for the right to vote on the grounds of simple justice and equal opportunity. They adopted the slogan *"woman* suffrage*"* to emphasize the solidarity of women, regardless of class, ethnicity, or race. Progressives embraced woman suffrage by stressing what they saw as the practical results: protecting the home and increasing the voting power of native-born whites. The "purer sensibilities" of women—an ideal held by Victorians and progressives alike—would help cleanse the political process of selfishness and corruption.

The suffrage movement benefited, too, from new leadership. In 1900 Carrie Chapman Catt became president of the National American Woman Suffrage

*Catt's "winning plan"*

Association, founded by Susan B. Anthony in 1890. Politically astute and a skilled organizer, Catt mapped a grass-roots strategy of education and persuasion from state to state. She called it "the winning plan." As the map shows, victories came first in the West, where women and men had already forged a more equal partnership to overcome the hardships of frontier life. By 1914, 10 western states (and Kansas) had granted women the vote in state elections, as Illinois had in presidential elections.

The slow pace of progress drove some women to militancy. In England, turn-of-the-century suffragists had chained themselves to lampposts, refused to

*Militant suffragists*

eat when imprisoned, and assaulted politicians. A young American Quaker named Alice Paul had been with them and brought the aggressive tactics to America. In 1913 she organized 5000 women to parade in protest at President Woodrow Wilson's inauguration. Half a million people watched as a near-riot ensued. The suffragists were hauled to jail, stripped naked, and thrown into cells with prostitutes.

A year later Paul formed the Congressional Union, dedicated to enacting a suffrage amendment at any cost. She soon allied her organization with western women voters in the militant National Woman's party. In 1917, they picketed the White House. When Paul was thrown into jail, she refused to eat in protest. "This is a spirit like Joan of Arc," concluded the doctor who examined her.

*Nineteenth Amendment*

Prison officials declared her insane. But public anger over such treatment, along with the need for broad-based support for World War I, led the House of Representatives to pass a woman suffrage amendment in 1918. In 1920 it became the Nineteenth Amendment.

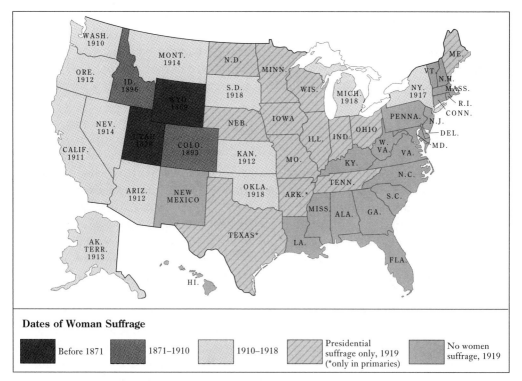

**Dates of Woman Suffrage**

| | | | | |
|---|---|---|---|---|
| Before 1871 | 1871–1910 | 1910–1918 | Presidential suffrage only, 1919 (*only in primaries) | No women suffrage, 1919 |

WOMAN SUFFRAGE   Western states were the first to grant women the right to vote. Sparsely populated and more egalitarian than the rest of the nation, the West was used to women participating more fully in settlement and work.

## CONTROLLING THE MASSES

"Observe immigrants," wrote one American in 1912; "you are struck by the fact that from ten to twenty percent are hirsute, low-browed, big-faced persons of obviously low mentality. . . . They clearly belong in skins, in wattled huts at the close of the Ice Age." The writer was neither an uneducated fanatic nor a stern opponent of change. He was Professor Edward A. Ross, a progressive from Madison, Wisconsin, who prided himself on his scientific study of sociology.

Faced with the chaos of urban life, more than a few progressives feared they were losing control of their country. Saloons and dance halls lured youngsters and impoverished laborers; prostitutes walked the streets; vulgar amusements pandered to the uneducated. And worse—strange Old World cultures clashed with "all-American" customs, and races jostled uneasily. The city challenged middle-class reformers to convert this riot of diverse customs into a more uniform society. To maintain control they sometimes moved beyond education and regulation and sought restrictive laws to control the new masses.

## Stemming the Immigrant Tide

A rising tide of nonwhite and ethnic Americans, often settling in cities, aggravated the fears of many progressives and native-born whites. During the 1890s, segregation laws had already begun to restrict the opportunities of African Americans in the South (page 534); after 1900, the rhetoric of reform was used to support white supremacy. Southern progressives won office by promising to disfranchise black southerners, in order to break the power of corrupt political machines that rested on the black vote, much as northern machines marshaled the immigrant vote.

The South was hardly the only region in which discrimination flourished. Asians, Latinos, and Indians faced similar curbs in the West, as did the new arrivals from southern and eastern Europe in the North. The sharp increase in immigration especially chilled native-born Americans, including reformers anxious over the changing ethnic complexion of the country. In northern cities progressives often succeeded in reducing immigrant voting power by increasing residency requirements.

The infant science of "eugenics" lent respectability to the idea that newcomers were biologically inferior. Eugenicists believed that heredity deter-

*Eugenics* mined everything and advocated selective breeding for human improvement. By 1914 magazine articles discussed eugenics more than slums, tenements, and living standards combined. In *The Passing of the Great Race* (1916), upper-crust New Yorker and amateur zoologist Madison Grant helped to popularize the notion that the "lesser breeds" threatened to "mongrelize" America. So powerful was the pull of eugenics that it captured the support of many reformers, including birth control advocate Margaret Sanger.

More enlightened reformers such as Jane Addams stressed the "gifts" immigrants brought: folk rituals, dances, music, and handicrafts. With character-

*Americanization* istic paternalism, these reformers hoped to "Americanize" the foreign-born (the term was newly coined) by teaching them middle-class ways. Education was one key. Progressive educator Peter Roberts, for example, developed a lesson plan for the Young Men's Christian Association that taught immigrants to dress, tip, buy groceries, and vote.

Less tolerant citizens (usually native-born and white) sought to restrict immigration as a way of reasserting control and achieving social harmony. Usually not progressives themselves, they employed progressive methods of organization, investigation, education, and legislation. Active since the 1890s, the Immigration Restriction League pressed Congress in 1907 to require a liter-

*Literacy test* acy test for admission into the United States. Presidents Taft and Wilson vetoed it in 1913 and 1915, but Congress overrode Wilson's second veto in 1917 as war fever raised fears of foreigners to a new peak.

## The Curse of Demon Rum

Tied closely to concern over immigrants was an attack on saloons. Part of a broader crusade to clean up cities, the antisaloon campaign drew strength from the century-old drive to lessen the consumption of alcohol. Women made up a disproportionate number of alcohol reformers. In some ways, the temperance movement reflected their growing campaign to storm male domains, in this case the saloon, and to contain male violence, particularly the wife and child abuse associated with drinking.

Reformers considered a national ban on drinking unrealistic and intrusive. Instead they concentrated on prohibiting the sale of alcohol at local and state

*Anti-Saloon League*

levels. Led by the Anti-Saloon League (1893), a massive publicity campaign bombarded citizens with pamphlets and advertisements. Doctors cited scientific evidence linking alcohol to cirrhosis, heart disease, and insanity. Social workers connected drink to the deterioration of the family; employers, to accidents on the job and lost efficiency.

By 1917 three out of four Americans lived in dry counties. Nearly two-thirds of the states had adopted laws outlawing the manufacture and sale of alcohol. Not all progressives were prohibitionists, but by curtailing the liquor business those who were breathed a sigh of relief at having taken some of the profit out of human pain and corruption.

## Prostitution

No urban vice worried reformers more than prostitution. In their eyes it was a "social evil" that threatened young city women. The Chicago Vice Commission of 1910 estimated that 5000 full-time and 10,000 occasional prostitutes plied their trade in the city. Other cities, small and large, reported similar results.

An unlikely group of reformers united to fight the vice: feminists who wanted husbands to be as chaste as their wives, social hygienists worried about the spread of venereal disease, immigration restrictionists who regarded the growth of prostitution as yet another sign of corrupt newcomers. Progressives condemned prostitution but saw the problem in economic and environmental terms. "Poverty causes prostitution," concluded the Illinois Vice Commission in 1916.

Some reformers saw more active agents at work. Rumors spread of a vast and profitable "white slave trade." Men armed with hypodermic needles were

*White slave trade*

said to be lurking about streetcars, amusement parks, and dance halls in search of young women. Although the average female rider of the streetcar was hardly in danger of villainous abduction, every city had locked pens where women were held captive and forced into prostitution. By conservative estimates they constituted some 10 percent of all prostitutes.

As real abuses blended with sensationalism, Congress passed the Mann Act (1910), prohibiting the interstate transport of women for immoral purposes. By

1918 reformers succeeded in banning previously tolerated "red light" districts in most cities. As with the liquor trade, progressives went after those who made money from misery.

## THE POLITICS OF MUNICIPAL AND STATE REFORM

Reform the system. In the end, so many urban problems came back to over-hauling government. Jane Addams learned as much outside the doors of her beloved Hull House in Chicago. For months during the early 1890s, garbage had piled up in the streets. The filth and stench drove Addams and her fellow workers to city hall in protest—700 times in one summer—but to no avail. In Chicago, as elsewhere, a corrupt band of city bosses had made garbage collection a plum to be awarded to the company that paid the most for it.

In desperation, Addams submitted a bid for garbage removal in the ward. When it was thrown out on a technicality, she won an appointment as garbage inspector. For almost a year she dogged collection carts, but boss politics kept things dirty. So Addams ran candidates in 1896 and 1898 against the local ward boss. They lost, but Addams kept up the fight for honest government and social reform—at city hall, in the Illinois legislature, and finally in Washington. Politics turned out to be the only way to clean things up.

### The Reformation of the Cities

In the smokestack cities of the Midwest, where the frustrations of industrial and agricultural America fed each other, the urban battleground furnished the first test of political reform. A series of colorful and independent mayors demonstrated that cities could be run humanely without changing the structure of government.

In Detroit, shoe magnate Hazen Pingree turned the mayor's office into an agency of reform when elected in 1889. By the end of his fourth term, Detroit had new parks and public baths, fairer taxes, ownership of the local light plant, and a work-relief program for victims of the depression of 1893. In 1901, Cleveland mayor Tom Johnson launched a similar reform campaign. Before he

*Gas and water socialism*

was through, municipal franchises had been limited to a fraction of their previous 99-year terms, and the city ran the utility company. By 1915 nearly two out of three cities in the nation had copied some form of this "gas and water socialism" to control the runaway prices of utility companies.

Tragedy sometimes dramatized the need to alter the very structure of government. On a hot summer night in 1900 a tidal wave from the Gulf of Mexico

*Commission plan*

smashed the port city of Galveston, Texas. Floods killed one of every six residents. The municipal government sank into confusion. Business leaders stepped in with a new charter that replaced the mayor and city council with a powerful commission. Each of five commissioners controlled a municipal department, and together they ran the city. Nearly 400 cities had adopted the plan by 1920. Expert commissioners enhanced efficiency and helped to check party rule in municipal government.

In other cities, elected officials appointed an outside expert or "city manager" to run things, the first in Staunton, Virginia, in 1908. Within a decade,

*City manager plan*

45 cities had them. At lower levels experts took charge of services: engineers oversaw utilities; accountants, finances; doctors and nurses, public health; specially trained firefighters and police, the safety of citizens. Broad civic reforms attempted to break the corrupt alliance between companies doing business with the city and the bosses who controlled the wards. Citywide elections replaced the old ward system, and civil service laws helped to create a nonpartisan bureaucracy. Political machines and ethnic voters lost power, while city government gained efficiency.

## Progressivism in the States

"Whenever we try to do anything, we run up against the charter," complained the reform-minded mayor of Schenectady, New York. Charters granted by state governments defined the powers of cities. The rural interests that generally dominated state legislatures rarely gave cities adequate authority to levy taxes, set voting requirements, draw up budgets, or legislate reforms. State legislatures, too, found themselves under the influence of business interests, party machines, and county courthouse rings. Reformers therefore tried to place their candidates where they could do some good: in the governors' mansions.

As with urban reform, state progressivism enjoyed its earliest success in the Midwest, under the leadership of Robert La Follette of Wisconsin. La Follette first won election to Congress in 1885 by toeing the Republican line of high tariffs and the gold standard. When a Republican boss offered him a bribe in a railroad case, La Follette pledged to break "the power of this corrupt influence." In 1900 he won the governorship of Wisconsin as an uncommonly independent Republican.

Over the next six years "Battle Bob" La Follette made Wisconsin, in the words of Theodore Roosevelt, "the laboratory of democracy." La Follette's

*La Follette's Wisconsin idea*

"Wisconsin idea" produced the most comprehensive set of state reforms in American history. There were new laws regulating railroads, controlling corruption, and expanding the civil service. His direct primary weakened the hold of party bosses by transferring nominations from the party to the voters. Among La Follette's notable "firsts" were a state income tax, a state commission to oversee factory safety and sanitation, and a Legislative Reference Bureau at the University of Wisconsin. University-trained experts poured into state government.

Other states copied the Wisconsin idea or hatched their own. All but three had direct primary laws by 1916. To cut the power of party organizations and

*Reforming politics*

make officeholders directly responsible to the public, progressives worked for three additional reforms: initiative (voter introduction of legislation), referendum (voter enactment or repeal of laws), and recall (voter-initiated removal of elected officials). By 1912 a dozen states had adopted initiative and referendum; seven, recall. A year later the Seventeenth Amendment to the Constitution permitted the direct election of senators. Previously they had been chosen by state legislatures, where political machines and corporate lobbyists controlled the selections.

Almost every state established regulatory commissions with the power to hold public hearings, examine company books, and question officials. Some

*Regulating business*

could set maximum prices and rates. Yet it was not always easy to define, let alone serve, the "public good." All too often commissioners found themselves refereeing battles within industries—between carriers and shippers, for example—rather than between what progressives called "the interests" and "the people." Regulators had to rely on the advice of experts drawn from the business community itself. Many commissions thus became captured by the industries they regulated.

Social welfare received special attention from the states. The lack of workers' compensation for injury, illness, or death on the job had long drawn fire

*Seeds of the welfare state*

from reformers and labor leaders. American courts still operated on the common-law assumption that employees accepted the risks of work. Workers or their families could collect damages only if they proved employer negligence. Most accident victims received nothing. In 1902 Maryland finally adopted the first workers' compensation act. By 1916 most states required insurance for factory accidents, and over half had employer liability laws. Thirteen states also provided pensions for widows with dependent children.

More and more it was machine politicians and women's organizations that pressed for working-class reforms. Despite the progressive attack on machine politics, political bosses survived, in part by adapting the climate of reform to the needs of their working-class constituents. After the Triangle fire of 1911, for example, it was Tammany Democrats Robert F. Wagner and Alfred E. Smith who led the fight for a new labor code.

This working-class "urban liberalism" also found advocates among women's associations, especially those concerned with mothers, children, and working women. The Federation of Women's Clubs opened a crusade for mothers' pensions (a forerunner of aid to dependent children). When in 1912 the National Consumers' League and other women's groups succeeded in establishing the Children's Bureau, it was the first federal welfare agency and the only female-run national bureau in the world. At a time when women lacked the vote, they nonetheless sowed the seeds of the welfare state and helped to make urban liberalism a powerful instrument of social reform.

## PROGRESSIVISM GOES TO WASHINGTON

On September 6, 1901, at the Pan-American Exposition in Buffalo, New York, Leon Czolgosz stood nervously in line. He was waiting among well-wishers to meet President William McKinley. Unemployed and bent on murder, Czolgosz shuffled toward McKinley. As the president reached out, Czolgosz fired two bullets into his chest. McKinley slumped into a chair. Eight days later the president was dead. The mantle of power passed to Theodore Roosevelt. At 42 he was the youngest president ever to hold the office.

Roosevelt's succession was a political accident. Party leaders had seen the weak office of vice president as a way of removing him from power, but the tragedy in Buffalo foiled their plans. "It is a dreadful thing to come into the presidency this way," Roosevelt remarked, "but it would be a far worse thing to be morbid about it." Surely progressivism would have come to Washington without him, and while there, he was never its most daring advocate. In many ways he was quite conservative. He saw reform as a way to avoid more radical change. Yet without Theodore Roosevelt, progressivism would have had neither the broad popular appeal nor the buoyancy he gave it.

### TR

TR, as so many Americans called him, was the scion of seven generations of wealthy, aristocratic New Yorkers. A sickly boy, he built his body through rigorous exercise, sharpened his mind through constant study, and pursued a life so strenuous that few could keep up. He learned to ride and shoot, roped cattle in the Dakota Badlands, mastered judo, and later in life climbed the Matterhorn, hunted African game, and explored the Amazon.

In 1880, driven by an urge to lead and serve, Roosevelt won election to the New York State Assembly. In rapid succession he became a civil service commissioner in Washington, New York City police commissioner, assistant secretary of the navy, and the Rough Rider hero of the Spanish–American War. At the age of 40 he won election as reform governor of New York and two years later as vice president. Through it all, TR remained a loyal Republican, personally flamboyant but committed to mild change only.

To the Executive Mansion (he renamed it the "White House"), Roosevelt brought a passion for order, a commitment to the public, and a sense of presidential possibilities. Most presidents believed that the Constitution set specific limits on their power. Roosevelt thought that the president could do anything not expressly forbidden in the document. Recognizing the value of publicity, he

Bull-necked and barrel-chested, Theodore Roosevelt was "pure act," said one admirer. Critics, less enthused with his perpetual motion, charged him with having the attention span of a golden retriever.

gave reporters the first press room in the White House and favored them with all the stories they wanted. He was the first president to ride in an automobile, fly in an airplane, and dive in a submarine—and everyone knew it.

To dramatize racial injustice, Roosevelt invited black educator Booker T. Washington to lunch at the White House in 1901. White southern journalists called such mingling with blacks treason, but for Roosevelt the gesture served both principle and politics. His lunch with Washington was part of a "black and tan" strategy to build a biracial coalition among southern Republicans. He denounced lynching and appointed black southerners to important federal offices in Mississippi and South Carolina.

Sensing the limits of political possibility, Roosevelt went no further. Perhaps his own racial narrowness stopped him too. In 1906, when Atlanta exploded in

*Brownsville incident*

a race riot that left 12 people dead, he said nothing. Later that year he discharged "without honor" three entire companies of African American troops because some of the soldiers were unjustly charged with having "shot up" Brownsville, Texas. All lost their pensions, including six winners of the Medal of Honor. The act stained Roosevelt's record.

(Congress acknowledged the wrong in 1972 by granting the soldiers honorable discharges.)

## A Square Deal

Roosevelt could not long follow the cautious course McKinley had charted. He had more energetic plans in mind for the country. He accepted growth—
*Philosophy of the Square Deal* whether of business, labor, or agriculture—as natural. In his pluralistic system, big labor would counterbalance big capital, big farm organizations would offset big food processors, and so on. Standing astride them all, mediating when needed, was a big government that could ensure fairness for all. Later, as he campaigned for a second term in 1904, Roosevelt named his program the "Square Deal."

In a startling display of presidential initiative, Roosevelt in 1902 intervened in a strike that idled 140,000 miners and paralyzed the anthracite (hard) coal in-
*Anthracite coal strike* dustry. As winter approached, public resentment with the operators mounted when they refused even to recognize the miners' union, let alone negotiate. Roosevelt summoned both sides to the White House. John A. Mitchell, the young president of the United Mine Workers, agreed to arbitration, but mine owners balked. Roosevelt leaked word to Wall Street that the army would take over the mines if management did not yield.

Seldom had a recent president acted so decisively, and never had one acted on behalf of strikers. In late October 1902 the owners settled by granting miners a 10 percent wage hike and a nine-hour day in return for increases in coal prices and no recognition of the union. Roosevelt was equally prepared to intervene on the side of management, as he did when he sent federal troops to end strikes in Arizona in 1903 and Colorado in 1904. His aim was to establish a vigorous presidency ready to deal squarely with both sides.

Roosevelt especially needed to face the issue of economic concentration. Financial power had become consolidated in giant trusts following a wave of mergers at the end of the century. As large firms swallowed smaller ones, Americans feared that such consolidation would destroy individual enterprise and free competition. A series of government investigations revealed rampant corporate abuses: rebates, collusion, "watered" stock, payoffs to government officials. The conservative courts showed little willingness to break up the giants
*United States v. E. C. Knight* or blunt their power. In *United States v. E. C. Knight* (1895), the Supreme Court crippled the Sherman Antitrust Act by ruling that the law applied only to commerce and not to manufacturing. The decision left the American Sugar Refining Company in control of 98 percent of the nation's sugar factories.

In his first State of the Union message, Roosevelt told Congress that he did not oppose business concentration. As he saw it, large corporations were not only inevitable but more productive than smaller operations. He wanted to regulate them to make them fairer and more efficient. Only then would the economic order be humanized, its victims protected, and class violence avoided. Like individuals, trusts had to be held to strict standards of morality. Conduct, not size, was the yardstick TR used to measure "good" and "bad" trusts.

With a progressive's faith in the power of publicity and a regulator's need for the facts, Roosevelt moved immediately to strengthen the federal power of investigation. He called for the creation of a Department of Labor and Commerce with a Bureau of Corporations that could force companies to hand over their records. Congressional conservatives shuddered at the prospect of putting corporate books on display. Finally, after Roosevelt charged that John D. Rockefeller was orchestrating the opposition, Congress enacted the legislation and provided the Justice Department with additional staff to prosecute antitrust cases.

In 1902, to demonstrate the power of government, Roosevelt had his attorney general file an antitrust suit against the Northern Securities Company.

*Northern Securities*　The mammoth holding company virtually monopolized railroads in the Northwest. Worse still, it had bloated its stock with worthless certificates. Here, clearly, was a symbol of the "bad" trust. A trust-conscious nation cheered as the Supreme Court ordered the company to dissolve in 1904. Ultimately, the Roosevelt administration brought suit against 44 giants, including Standard Oil Company, American Tobacco Company, and Du Pont Corporation.

Despite his reputation for trustbusting, Roosevelt always preferred regulation. The problems of the railroads, for example, were newly underscored by a

*Railroad regulation*　recent round of consolidation that had contributed to higher freight rates. Roosevelt pressed Congress to revive the ineffective Interstate Commerce Commission (ICC). In 1903 Congress passed the Elkins Act, which gave the ICC power to end rebates. Even the railroads supported the act because it saved them from the costly practice of granting special reductions to large shippers.

By the election of 1904 the president's iniatives had won him broad popular support. He trounced his two rivals, Democrat Alton B. Parker, a jurist from New York, and Eugene V. Debs of the Socialist party. No longer was he a "political accident," Roosevelt boasted.

Conservatives in his own party opposed Roosevelt's meddling in the private sector. But progressives demanded still more regulation of the railroads, in particular a controversial proposal for making public the value of all rail property. In 1906, the president finally reached a compromise typical of his restrained approach to reform. The Hepburn Railway Act allowed the ICC to set maximum rates and to regulate sleeping car companies, ferries, bridges, and terminals. Progressives did not gain the provision of disclosure of company value, but the Hepburn Act drew Roosevelt nearer to his goal of continuous regulation of business.

## Bad Food and Pristine Wilds

Extending the umbrella of federal protection to consumers, Roosevelt belatedly threw his weight behind two campaigns for healthy foods and drugs. In 1905 Samuel Hopkins Adams of *Collier's Weekly* wrote that in its patent medicines "Gullible America" would get "huge quantities of alcohol, an appalling amount of opiates and narcotics," and worse—axle grease, acid, and glue. Adams sent the samples he had collected to Harvey Wiley, chief chemist at the Agriculture Department. Wiley's "Poison Squad" produced scientific evidence of Adams's charges.

Several pure food and drug bills had already died at the hands of lobbyists, despite a presidential endorsement. The appearance of Upton Sinclair's *The Jungle* in 1906 spurred Congress to act. Sinclair intended to recruit people to socialism by exposing the plight of workers in the meatpacking industry. The novel contained a brief but dramatic description of the slaughter of cattle infected with tuberculosis, of meat covered with rat dung, and of men falling into cooking vats. Readers paid scant attention to the workers, but their stomachs turned at what they might be eating for breakfast. The Pure Food and Drug Act of 1906 sailed through Congress, and the Meat Inspection Act soon followed.

Roosevelt came late to the consumer cause, but on conservation he led the nation. An outdoors enthusiast, he galvanized public concern over the reckless use of natural resources. His chief forester, Gifford Pinchot, persuaded him that planned management under federal guidance was needed to protect the natural domain. Cutting trees must be synchronized with tree plantings, oil pumped from the ground must be under controlled conditions, and so on.

*Conservation through planned management*

In the western states water was the problem. Economic growth, even survival, depended on it. As uneven local and state water policies sparked controversy, violence, and waste, many progressives campaigned for a federal program to replace the chaotic web of rules. Democratic senator Frederick Newlands of Nevada introduced the Reclamation Act of 1902 to set aside proceeds from the sale of public lands for irrigation projects. The Reclamation Act signaled a progressive step toward the conservationist goal of rational resource development.

Conservation often conflicted with the more radical vision of preservationists, led by naturalist and wilderness philosopher John Muir. Muir founded the Sierra Club (1892) in hopes of maintaining such natural wonders as Yosemite and its neighboring Hetch-Hetchy valley in a state "forever wild" to benefit future generations. Many conservationists saw such valleys as sites for dams and reservoirs. Controversy flared after 1900 when San Francisco announced plans to create a city reservoir flooding the Hetch-Hetchy valley. For 13 years Muir waged a publicity campaign against the "devotees of ravaging commercialism." Pinchot enthusiastically backed San Francisco's claim. Roosevelt, torn by his friendship with Muir, did so less loudly.

*John Muir and preservation*

The Sierra Club, founded by naturalist John Muir, believed in the importance of preserving wilderness in its natural state. Muir helped to persuade President Theodore Roosevelt to double the number of national parks. Here a group of Sierra clubbers lounges at the base of a giant redwood in Big Basin in 1905.

Not until 1913 did President Woodrow Wilson finally decide the issue in favor of San Francisco. Conservation had won over preservation.

Roosevelt nonetheless advanced many of Muir's goals. Over the protests of cattle and timber interests, he added nearly 200 million acres to government forest reserves; placed coal and mineral lands, oil reserves, and water-power sites in the public domain; and enlarged the national park system. When Congress balked, he appropriated another 17 million acres of forest before the legislators could pass a bill limiting him. Roosevelt also set in motion national congresses and commissions on conservation and mobilized governors across the country. Like a good progressive, he sent hundreds of experts to work applying science, education, and technology to environmental problems.

As Roosevelt acted more forcefully, conservatives lashed back. So far his record had been modest, but his chief accomplishment—invigorating the presidency—could lead to deeper reform. When another spike in the business cycle produced financial panic on Wall Street in 1907, business leaders and conservative politicians blamed the president. An angry Roosevelt blamed the "speculative folly and the flagrant dishonesty of a few men of great wealth."

Clearly shaken, however, Roosevelt assured business leaders that he would do nothing to interfere with their efforts at recovery. That included a pledge not to file an antitrust suit if the giant U.S. Steel bought the Tennessee Coal and Iron Company. The economy recovered, and having declared he would not run in 1908, the 50-year-old Roosevelt prepared to give over his office to William Howard Taft, his handpicked successor.

### The Troubled Taft

On March 4, 1909, as snow swirled outside the White House, William Howard Taft readied himself for his inauguration. Over breakfast with Roosevelt, he warmed in the glow of recent Republican victories. He had beaten Democrat William Jennings Bryan in the "Great Commoner's" third and last bid for the presidency. Republicans had retained control of Congress as well as a host of northern legislatures. Reform was at high tide, and Taft was eager to continue the Roosevelt program.

"Will," as Roosevelt liked to call him, was a distinguished jurist and public servant, the first American governor-general of the Philippines, and Roosevelt's secretary of war. Taft had great administrative skill and personal charm. But he disliked the political maneuvering of Washington and preferred conciliation to confrontation. Even Roosevelt had doubts. "He's all right," TR had told a reporter on inauguration day. "But he's weak. They'll get around him. They'll"— and here Roosevelt pushed the reporter with his shoulder—"lean against him."

Trouble began early when progressives in the House moved to curb the near-dictatorial power of the conservative Speaker, Joseph Cannon. Taft waffled, first supporting them, then abandoning them to preserve the tariff reductions he was seeking. When progressives later broke Cannon's power without Taft's help, they scorned him. And Taft's compromise was wasted. Senate protectionists peppered the tariff bill with so many amendments that rates jumped nearly to their old levels.

Late in 1909, the rift between Taft and the progressives reached the breaking point in a dispute over conservation. Taft had appointed Richard Ballinger

*Ballinger–Pinchot affair*

secretary of the interior over the objections of Roosevelt's old friend and mentor, Chief Forester Pinchot. When Ballinger opened a million acres of public lands for sale, Pinchot charged that shady dealings led Ballinger to transfer Alaskan public coal lands to a syndicate that included J. P. Morgan. Early in 1910, Taft fired Pinchot for insubordination. Angry progressives saw the Ballinger–Pinchot controversy as another betrayal by Taft. They began to look longingly across the Atlantic, where TR was stalking big game in Africa.

Despite his failures, Taft was no conservative pawn. For the next two years he pushed Congress to enact a progressive program regulating safety standards

*Taft's accomplishments*

for mines and railroads, creating a federal children's bureau, and setting an eight-hour workday for federal employees. Taft's support of a graduated income tax—sometimes heated, sometimes tepid—was finally decisive. Early in 1913 it became the Sixteenth Amendment. Historians view it as one of the most important reforms of the century, for it eventually generated the revenue for many new social programs.

Yet no matter what Taft did, he managed to alienate conservatives and progressives alike. That spelled trouble for the Republicans as the presidential election of 1912 approached.

### Roosevelt Returns

In June 1910 Roosevelt came home, laden with hunting trophies and exuberant as ever. He found Taft unhappy and progressive Republicans threatening to defect. Party loyalty kept Roosevelt quiet through most of 1911, but in October, Taft pricked him personally on the sensitive matter of busting trusts. Like TR, Taft accepted trusts as natural, but he failed to make Roosevelt's distinction between "good" and "bad" ones. He demanded, more impartially, that all trusts be prevented from restraining trade. In four years as president, Taft had brought nearly twice the antitrust suits Roosevelt had in seven years.

In October 1911 the Justice Department charged U. S. Steel with having violated the Sherman Act by acquiring the Tennessee Coal and Iron Company. Roosevelt regarded the action as a personal rebuke, since he himself had allowed U. S. Steel to proceed with the acquisition. Taft, complained TR, "was playing small, mean, and foolish politics."

Roosevelt decided to play big, high-minded, and presidential. Already, in a speech at Osawatomie, Kansas, in 1910, he had outlined a program of sweep-

*New Nationalism*

ing national reform. His "New Nationalism" recognized the value of consolidation in the economy—whether big business or big labor—but insisted on protecting the interests of individuals through big government. The New Nationalism went further, stressing planning and efficiency under a powerful executive, "a steward of the public welfare." It promised taxes on incomes and inheritances and greater regulation of industry. And it embraced social justice, specifically workers' compensation for accidents, minimum wages and maximum hours, child labor laws, and "equal suffrage"—a nod to women and loyal black Republicans. Roosevelt, a cautious reformer as president, now grew daring as he campaigned for the White House.

### The Election of 1912

"My hat is in the ring!" Roosevelt announced in February 1912, to no one's surprise. Taft responded by claiming that the New Nationalism had won support only from "radicals," "emotionalists," and "neurotics." In fact, the enormously popular Roosevelt won most of the primaries; but by the time Republicans met in Chicago in June 1912, Taft had used presidential patronage and promises to secure the nomination.

A frustrated Roosevelt bolted and took progressive Republicans with him. Two months later, amid choruses of "Onward Christian Soldiers," delegates to

*Progressive party*

the newly formed Progressive party nominated Roosevelt for the presidency. "I'm feeling like a bull moose!" he bellowed. Progressives suddenly had a symbol for their new party.

The Democrats met in Baltimore, jubilant over the prospect of a divided Republican party. Delegates chose as their candidate Woodrow Wilson, the progressive governor of New Jersey. Wilson wisely concentrated his fire on

*New Freedom*

Roosevelt. He countered the New Nationalism with his "New Freedom." It rejected the economic consolidation that Roosevelt embraced. Bigness was a sin, crowding out competition, promoting inefficiency, and reducing opportunity. Only by strictly limiting the size of businesses could the free market be preserved. And only by keeping government small could individual freedom be preserved. "Liberty," Wilson cautioned, "has never come from government," only from the "limitation of governmental power."

Increasingly voters found Taft beside the point. And in an age of reform, even the Socialists looked good. Better led, financed, and organized than ever, the Socialist party had increased its membership to nearly 135,000 by 1912. Socialist mayors ran 32 cities. The party also had an appealing candidate in Eugene V. Debs, a homegrown Indiana radical. He had won 400,000 votes for president in 1904. Now, in 1912, he summoned voters to make "the working class the ruling class."

On election day voters gave progressivism a resounding endorsement. Wilson won 6.3 million votes; Roosevelt, 4.1 million; Taft, just 3.6 million. Debs received almost a million votes. Together the two progressive candidates amassed a three to one margin. But the Republican split had broken the party's

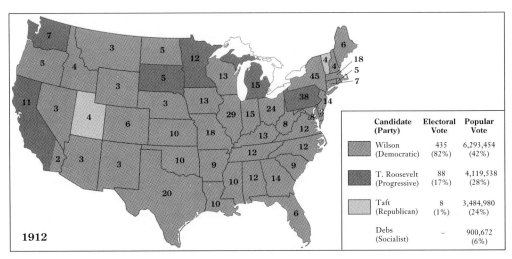

| Candidate (Party) | Electoral Vote | Popular Vote |
|---|---|---|
| Wilson (Democratic) | 435 (82%) | 6,293,454 (42%) |
| T. Roosevelt (Progressive) | 88 (17%) | 4,119,538 (28%) |
| Taft (Republican) | 8 (1%) | 3,484,980 (24%) |
| Debs (Socialist) | – | 900,672 (6%) |

1912

THE ELECTION OF 1912

hold on national politics. For the first time since 1896, a Democrat would sit in the White House—and with his party in control of Congress.

## WOODROW WILSON AND THE POLITICS OF MORALITY

Soon after the election Woodrow Wilson made a proud if startling confession to the chairman of the Democratic National Committee: "God ordained that I should be the next President of the United States." To the White House, Wilson brought a sense of destiny and a passion for reform. All his life, he believed he was meant to accomplish great things, and he did. Under him, progressivism peaked.

### Early Career

From the moment of his birth in 1856, Woodrow Wilson felt he could not escape destiny. It was all around him. In his family's Presbyterian faith, in the sermons of his minister father, in dinnertime talk ran the unbending belief in a world predetermined by God and ruled by saved souls, an "elect." Wilson ached to be one of them and behaved as though he were.

To prepare to lead, Wilson studied the fiery debates of the British Parliament and wandered the woods reciting them from memory. Like most southerners, he loved the Democratic party, hated the tariff, and accepted racial separation. (Under his presidency, segregation returned to Washington for the first time since Reconstruction.)

An early career in law bored him, so he turned to history and political science and became a professor. His studies persuaded him that a modern president must act as a "prime minister," directing and uniting his party, molding legislation and public opinion, exerting continuous leadership. In 1910, after a stormy tenure as head of Princeton University, Wilson was helped by Democratic party bosses to win the governorship of New Jersey. In 1912 they helped him again, this time to the presidency of the country.

### The Reforms of the New Freedom

As governor, Wilson had led New Jersey on the path of progressive reform. As president, he was a model of progressive leadership. More than Theodore Roosevelt, he shaped policy and legislation. He went to Congress to let members know he intended to work personally with them. He kept party discipline tight and mobilized public opinion when Congress refused to act.

Lowering the high tariff was Wilson's first order of business. Progressives had long attacked the tariff as another example of the power of trusts. By pro-

*Underwood–
Simmons Tariff*

tecting American manufacturers, Wilson argued, such barriers weakened the competition he cherished. When the Senate threatened to raise rates, the new president appealed directly to the public. "Industrious" and "insidious" lobbyists were blocking reform, he cried to reporters. A "brick couldn't be thrown without hitting one of them."

The Underwood–Simmons Tariff of 1913 marked the first downward revision in 19 years and the biggest since before the Civil War. To compensate for lost revenue, Congress enacted a graduated income tax under the newly adopted Sixteenth Amendment. It applied solely to corporations and the tiny fraction of Americans who earned more than $4000 a year. It nonetheless began a momentous shift in government revenue from its nineteenth-century base—public lands, alcohol taxes, and customs duties—to its twentieth-century base: personal and corporate incomes.

Wilson turned next to the perennial problems of money and banking. Early in 1913 a congressional committee under Arsène Pujo revealed that a few powerful banks controlled the nation's credit system. They could choke Wilson's free market by raising interest rates or tightening the supply of money. As a banking reform bill moved through Congress in 1913, opinion divided among conservatives, who wanted centralized and private control, rural Democrats, who wanted regional banks under local bankers, and Populists and progressives— including Bryan and La Follette—who wanted government control.

Wilson split their differences in the Federal Reserve Act of 1913. The new Federal Reserve System contained 12 regional banks scattered across the coun-

*Federal
Reserve Act*

try. But it also created a central Federal Reserve Board in Washington, appointed by the president, to supervise the system. The board could regulate credit and the money supply by setting the interest rate it charged member banks, by buying or selling government bonds, and by issuing paper currency called Federal Reserve notes. Thus the Federal Reserve System sought to stabilize the existing order by increasing federal control over credit and the money supply.

When Wilson finally took on the trusts, he inched toward the New Nationalism of Theodore Roosevelt. The Federal Trade Commission Act of

*Federal Trade
Commission*

1914 created a bipartisan executive agency to oversee business activity. The end—to enforce orderly competition—was distinctly Wilsonian, but the means—an executive commission to regulate commerce—were pure Roosevelt.

Roosevelt would have stopped there, but Wilson made good on his campaign pledge to attack trusts. The Clayton Antitrust Act (1914) barred some of

*Clayton
Antitrust Act*

the worst corporate practices: price discrimination, holding companies, and interlocking directorates (directors of one corporate board sitting on others). Yet despite Wilson's bias against size, the advantages of large-scale production and distribution were inescap-able. In practice his administration chose to regulate rather than break up bigness. The

Justice Department filed fewer antitrust suits than it had under the Taft administration.

## Labor and Social Reform

For all of Wilson's impressive accomplishments, voters seemed lukewarm toward the New Freedom. In the elections of 1914 Republicans cut Democratic majorities in the House and won important industrial and farm states. To strengthen his hand in the presidential election of 1916, Wilson began edging toward the social reforms of the New Nationalism he had once criticized as paternalistic and unconstitutional. He signaled the change early in 1916 when he nominated his close adviser Louis D. Brandeis to the Supreme Court. The progressive Brandeis had fought for the social reforms lacking from Wilson's agenda. His appointment also broke the tradition of anti-Semitism that had previously kept Jews off the Court.

In other ways, Wilson showed a new willingness to intervene more actively in the economy. He helped pass laws improving the working conditions of merchant seamen and setting an eight-hour day for workers on interstate railroads. He supported the Keating–Owen Child Labor Act (page 604). Farmers benefited from legislation providing them with low-interest loans. And just before the election Wilson intervened to avert a nationwide strike of rail workers.

## The Limits of Progressive Reform

Woodrow Wilson's administration capped a decade and a half of heady reform. Seeing chaos in the modern industrial city, progressive reformers had worked to reduce the damage of poverty and the hazards of industrial work, control rising immigration, and spread a middle-class ideal of morality. In city halls and state legislatures, they tried to break the power of corporate interests and entrenched political machines. In Washington, they enlarged government and broadened its mission from caretaker to promoter of public welfare.

Progressivism did not always succeed. Reformers sometimes betrayed their high ideals by denying equality to African Americans, Asians, and other minorities and by attempting to Americanize foreigners rather than accepting the contributions of their cultures. Too often government commissions meant to be "watchdog" agencies were captured by the interests they were supposed to oversee. Heavy regulation of industries like the railroads crippled them for decades. Although the direct primary, the popular election of senators, and other reforms weakened the power of political machines, boss rule survived.

For all its claims of sweeping change, progressivism left the system of market capitalism intact. Neither the New Nationalism of Theodore Roosevelt, with its emphasis on planning and regulation, nor Woodrow Wilson's New

Freedom, which promoted competition through limits on corporate size, aimed to do more than improve the system. But the Gilded Age philosophy of laissez faire—of giving private enterprise a free hand—had clearly been rejected. Both state and federal governments established their right to regulate the actions of private corporations for the public good.

The reforms thus achieved, including the eight-hour day, woman suffrage, direct election of senators, graduated income taxes, and public ownership of utilities, began to address the problems of an urban industrial society. Under progressive leadership, the modern state—active and interventionist—was born.

SIGNIFICANT EVENTS

| | |
|---|---|
| 1890 | New England Kitchen opens; General Federation of Women's Clubs organized |
| 1892 | Sierra Club founded |
| 1893 | Illinois legislature enacts eight-hour workday law for women; Anti-Saloon League created |
| 1895 | *United States v. E. C. Knight* |
| 1899 | National Consumers' League founded |
| 1900 | Robert La Follette elected governor of Wisconsin; Galveston, Texas, creates first commission form of government |
| 1901 | Leon Czolgosz assassinates President McKinley; Theodore Roosevelt becomes president; Socialist Party of America founded |
| 1902 | Northern Securities Company dissolved under Sherman Antitrust Act; anthracite coal miners strike in Pennsylvania; Maryland adopts first workers' compensation law |
| 1903 | Department of Labor and Commerce created; Elkins Act passed; Wisconsin first state to enact direct primary |
| 1904 | Lincoln Steffens's *The Shame of the Cities* published; Theodore Roosevelt elected president |
| 1906 | Hepburn Act strengthens Interstate Commerce Commission; Upton Sinclair's *The Jungle* published; Meat Inspection and Pure Food and Drug acts passed |
| 1907 | William James's *Pragmatism* published |
| 1908 | *Muller v. Oregon*; William Howard Taft elected president |
| 1909 | Ballinger–Pinchot controversy |
| 1910 | Mann Act passed |
| 1911 | Triangle Shirtwaist fire |
| 1912 | Progressive ("Bull Moose") party nominates Theodore Roosevelt for presidency; Woodrow Wilson elected president |
| 1913 | Sixteenth and Seventeenth amendments passed; Underwood–Simmons Tariff enacted; Federal Reserve Act passed |
| 1914 | Clayton Antitrust Act passed; Federal Trade Commission created |
| 1916 | Margaret Sanger organizes New York Birth Control League; Keating–Owen Child Labor Act passed; Woodrow Wilson reelected president |
| 1917 | Congress enacts literacy test for new immigrants |
| 1920 | Nineteenth Amendment ratified |

# CHAPTER TWENTY-THREE

# The United States and the Old World Order

In 1898, as tens of thousands of eager young men signed up to kill Spaniards in Cuba, the USS *Oregon* left San Francisco Bay on a roundabout route toward its battle station in the Caribbean. It first headed south through the Pacific, passing Central America and leaving it thousands of miles behind. Then in the narrow Strait of Magellan at South America's tip, the ship encountered a gale so ferocious the shore could not be seen. All communication ceased, and Americans at home feared the worst. But the *Oregon* passed into the Atlantic and steamed north until finally, after 68 days and 13,000 miles at sea, it helped win the Battle of Santiago Bay.

The daring voyage electrified the nation but worried its leaders. Since the defeat of Mexico in 1848, the United States had stretched from the Atlantic to the Pacific without enough navy to go around. As an emerging power, the country needed a path between the seas, a canal across the narrow isthmus of Colombia's Panamanian province in Central America, to defend itself and to promote its growing trade.

"I took the isthmus," President Theodore Roosevelt later told a cheering crowd. In a way he did. In 1903 he reached an agreement with Colombia to lease the needed strip of land. Hoping for more money and greater control over the canal, the Colombians refused to ratify the agreement.

Privately, TR talked of seizing Panama. But when he learned of a budding independence movement there, he let it be known that he would welcome a revolt. On schedule and without bloodshed, the Panamanians rebelled late in 1903. The next day a U.S. cruiser dropped anchor offshore to prevent Colombia from landing troops. The United States quickly recognized the new Republic of Panama and signed a treaty for a renewable lease on a canal zone 10 miles wide. Panama received $10 million plus an annual rent of $250,000, the same terms offered to Colombia. Critics called it "a rough-riding assault upon another republic." (In 1921, after oil had been discovered in Colombia, Congress voted $25 million to the country.)

In November 1906 Roosevelt pulled into port at Panama City aboard the *Louisiana*, newly launched and the biggest battleship in the fleet. He spent the next three days traveling the length of the canal in the pouring rain. Soaked from head to toe, his huge Panama hat and white suit sagging about his body, he splashed through labor camps, asking workers for their complaints. He toured the hospital at Ancon and met Dr. William Gorgas, conqueror of the yellow-fever–bearing mosquito. He walked railroad ties at the cuts and made speeches in the mud. "This is one of the great works of the world," he told an assembly of black diggers.

The Panama Canal embodied Roosevelt's muscular policy of respect through strength. TR modernized the army and tripled its size, created a general staff for planning and mobilization, and established the Army War College. As a pivot point between the two hemispheres, his canal allowed the United States to flex its strength across the globe.

These expanding horizons came about largely as an outgrowth of American commercial and industrial expansion, just as the imperialist empires of Great Britain, France, Germany, Russia, and Japan reflected the spread of their own industrial and commercial might. The Americans, steeped in democratic ideals, frequently seemed uncomfortable with the naked ambitions of European empire builders. Roosevelt's embrace of the canal, however, showed how far some Americans had come in being willing to shape the world.

Expansionist diplomats at home and abroad assured each other that global order could be maintained by balancing power through a set of carefully crafted alliances. But that system of alliances did not hold. In 1914, the year the Panama Canal opened, the old world order shattered in a terrible war.

## PROGRESSIVE DIPLOMACY

As the Panama Canal was being built, progressive diplomacy was taking shape. Like progressive politics, it stressed moralism and order as it stretched executive power to new limits, molding and remaking now the international envi-

*Foundations of progressive diplomacy*

ronment. "Of all our race, [God] has marked the American people as His chosen nation to finally lead in the redemption of the world," said one senator in 1900. At the core of this missionary faith lay a belief in the superiority of Anglo-American institutions. Every western leader assumed that northern Europeans were racially superior, too. The darker peoples of the tropical zones, observed a progressive educator, dwelled in "nature's asylum for degenerates." In this global vision of Manifest Destiny, few progressives questioned the need to uplift them.

Economic expansion underlay the commitment to a "civilizing" mission. The depression of 1893 had encouraged American manufacturers and farmers to look overseas for markets, and that expansion continued after 1900. By 1918, at the end of World War I, the United States had become the largest creditor in the world. Every administration committed itself to opening doors of trade and keeping them open.

## Big Stick in the Caribbean

Theodore Roosevelt liked to invoke the old African proverb, "Walk softly and carry a big stick." But in the Caribbean he moved both loudly and mightily. The Panama Canal gave the United States a commanding position in the Western Hemisphere. Its importance required the country to "police the surrounding premises," explained Secretary of State Elihu Root. Before granting Cuba independence in 1902, the United States reorganized its finances and included in the Cuban constitution the Platt Amendment. It gave American authorities the right to intervene if Cuban independence or internal order were threatened. Claiming that power, U.S. troops occupied the island twice between 1906 and 1923.

*Platt Amendment*

In looking to enforce a favorable environment for trade in the Caribbean, Roosevelt also worried about European intentions. The Monroe Doctrine of 1823 declared against further European colonization of the Western Hemisphere, but in the early twentieth century the rising debts of Latin Americans to Europeans invited intrusion. "If we intend to say hands off to the power of Europe, then sooner or later we must keep order ourselves," Roosevelt warned.

Going well beyond Monroe's concept of resisting foreign penetration, Roosevelt asserted American command of the Caribbean. He convinced Britain and Germany to arbitrate a debt dispute with Venezuela in 1902. Two years later, when the Dominican Republic defaulted on its debts, he added the "Roosevelt Corollary" to the Monroe Doctrine by claiming the right to police the Americas. Under it, the United States assumed responsibility for several Caribbean states, including the Dominican Republic, Cuba, and Panama.

*Roosevelt Corollary to the Monroe Doctrine*

## A "Diplomatist of the Highest Rank"

In the Far East Roosevelt exercised ingenuity rather than force, since he considered Asia beyond the American sphere of influence. Like McKinley, TR committed himself only to maintaining an "open door" of equal access to trade in China and to protecting the Philippines, "our heel of Achilles."

The key lay in offsetting Russian and Japanese ambitions in the region. When Japan attacked Russian holdings in the Chinese province of Manchuria in 1904, Roosevelt offered to mediate. He worried that if unchecked, Japan might threaten American interests in China and the Philippines. Both sides met at the U.S. Naval Base near

*Treaty of Portsmouth*

Portsmouth, Maine, and, under Roosevelt's guidance, produced the Treaty of Portsmouth in 1905. It recognized the Japanese victory (the first by an Asian power over a European country) and ceded to Japan Port Arthur, the southern half of Sakhalin Island, and, in effect, control of Korea. Japan promised to leave Manchuria as part of China and keep trade open to all foreign nations. Both the balance of power in Asia and the open door in China had been preserved. Roosevelt's diplomacy earned him the Nobel Peace Prize in 1906.

Some Japanese nationalists resented the peace treaty for curbing Japan's ambitions in Asia. Their anger surfaced in a protest lodged, of all places, against the San Francisco school board. In 1906, rising Japanese immigration led San Francisco school authorities to place the city's 93 Asian students in a separate school. In Japan citizens talked of war over the insult. Roosevelt, fuming at the "infernal fools in California," summoned the mayor of San Francisco and seven school board members to the White House. In exchange for an end to the segregation order, Roosevelt offered to arrange a mutual restriction of immigration between Japan and the United States. In 1907 all sides accepted his "gentlemen's agreement."

*Gentlemen's agreement*

The San Francisco school crisis sparked wild rumors that Japan was bent on taking Hawaii, or the Philippines, or the Panama Canal. In case Japan or any other nation thought of upsetting the Pacific balance, Roosevelt sent 16 gleaming white battleships on a world tour. "By George, isn't it magnificent!" he crowed, as the "Great White Fleet" steamed out of Hampton Roads, Virginia, in 1907. The fleet made its most conspicuous stop in Japan. Some Europeans predicted disaster. Instead, cheering crowds turned out in Tokyo and Yokohama, where a group of Japanese children sang "The Star Spangled Banner" in English. The show of force heralded a new age of American naval might but had an unintended consequence that haunted Americans for decades: it spurred Japanese admirals to expand their own navy.

*Great White Fleet*

Watching Roosevelt in his second term, an amazed London *Morning Post* dubbed him a "diplomatist of the highest rank." Abroad as at home, his brand of progressivism was grounded in an enthusiastic nationalism that mixed force with finesse to achieve balance and order. Yet despite TR's efforts, imperial rivalries, an unchecked naval arms race, and unrest in Europe threatened to plunge the world into chaos.

## Dollar Diplomacy

Instead of force or finesse, William Howard Taft relied on private investment to promote economic stability, keep peace, and tie debt-ridden nations to the United States. "Dollar diplomacy" simply amounted to "substituting dollars for bullets," Taft explained. He and Philander Knox, his prickly secretary of state, treated the restless nations of Latin America like ailing corporations, injecting capital and reorganizing management. By the time Taft left office in 1913, half of all American investments abroad were in Latin America.

In Nicaragua dollar diplomacy was not enough. In 1909, when the Nicaraguan legislature balked at American demands to take over its customshouse and national bank, a U.S. warship dropped anchor off the coast. The lawmakers changed their minds, but in 1912 a revolution led Taft to dispatch 2000 marines to protect American lives and property. Sporadic American intrusions lasted more than a dozen years.

Failure dogged Taft overseas as it did at home. In the Caribbean his dollar diplomacy was linked so closely with unpopular regimes, corporations, and banks that Woodrow Wilson scrapped it as soon as he entered the White House. Taft's efforts to strengthen China with investments and trade only intensified rivalry with Japan and made China more suspicious of all foreigners, including Americans. In 1911 the southern Chinese provinces rebelled against foreign intrusion and overthrew the monarchy. Only persistent pressure from the White House kept dollar diplomacy in Asia alive at all.

## WOODROW WILSON AND MORAL DIPLOMACY

The Lightfoot Club had been meeting in the Reverend Wilson's hayloft for months when the question of whether the pen was mightier than the sword came up. Young Tommy Wilson, who had organized the debating society, jumped at the chance to argue that written words were more powerful than armies. But when the boys drew lots, Tommy ended up on the other side. "I can't argue for something I don't believe in," he protested. Thomas Woodrow Wilson eventually dropped his first name, but he never gave up his boyhood conviction that morality, at least as he defined it, should guide conduct.

### Missionary Diplomacy

As president, Woodrow Wilson revived and enlarged Jefferson's notion of the United States as a beacon of freedom. The country had a mission: "We are chosen, and prominently chosen, to show the way to the nations of the world how they shall walk in the paths of liberty." Such paternalism only thinly masked Wilson's assumption of Anglo-American superiority and his willingness to spread western-style democracy and Christian morality through force.

Wilson's missionary diplomacy had a practical side. In the twentieth century foreign markets would serve as America's new frontier. American industries "will burst their jackets if they cannot find free outlets in the markets of the world," he cautioned in 1912. Wilson's genius lay in reconciling this commercial self-interest with a global idealism. In his eyes, exporting American democracy and capitalism would promote stability and progress throughout the world.

In Asia and the Pacific, Wilson moved to put "moral and public considerations" ahead of the "material interests of individuals." He pulled American bankers out of a six-nation railroad project in China backed by President Taft.

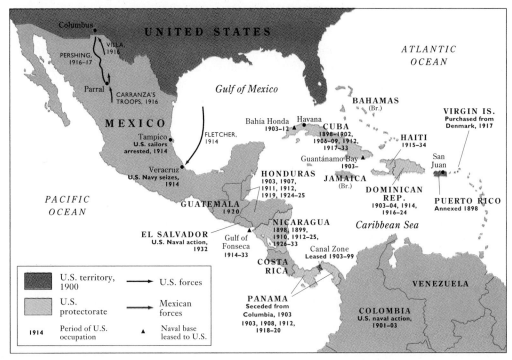

AMERICAN INTERVENTIONS IN THE CARIBBEAN, 1898–1930   In the first three decades
of the twentieth century, armed and unarmed interventions by the United States
virtually transformed the Caribbean into an American lake.

The scheme encouraged foreign intervention and undermined Chinese sovereignty, Wilson said. The United States became the first major power to recognize the new democratic Republic of China in 1911 and in 1915 strongly opposed Japan's "Twenty-One Demands" for control of the country.

In the Caribbean and Latin America, Wilson discovered that interests closer
to home could not be pursued through principles alone. In August 1914 he convinced Nicaragua, already occupied by American troops, to yield control of a
naval base and grant the United States an alternative canal route. Upheavals in
Haiti and the Dominican Republic brought in the U.S. Marines. By the end of
his administration American troops were still stationed there and also in Cuba.
All four nations were economically dependent on the United States and virtual
protectorates. Missionary diplomacy, it turned out, could spread its gospel with
steel as well as cash.

## Intervention in Mexico

A lingering crisis turned Wilson's "moral diplomacy" into a mockery in Mexico.
A common border, 400 years of shared history, and millions of dollars in investments made what happened in Mexico of urgent importance to the United

*Mexican Revolution*

States. In 1910 a revolution plunged Mexico into turmoil. Just as Wilson was entering the White House in 1913, the ruthless general Victoriano Huerta emerged as head of the government. Wealthy landowners and foreign investors endorsed Huerta, who was likely to protect their holdings. Soon a bloody civil war was raging.

Most European nations recognized the Huerta regime, but Wilson refused to accept the "government of butchers." (Huerta had murdered the popular leader Francisco Madero with the approval of the Taft administration.) When Huerta proclaimed himself dictator, Wilson banned arms shipments to Mexico. He threw his support to rebel leader Venustiano Carranza, on the condition that Carranza participate in American-sponsored elections. No Mexican was ready to tolerate such interference. Carranza and his "constitutionalists" rejected the offer. With few options, Wilson armed the rebels anyway.

Wilson's distaste for Huerta was so great that he used a minor incident as a pretext for an invasion. In April 1914 the crew of the USS *Dolphin* landed without permission in the Mexican port city of Tampico. Local police arrested the sailors, only to release them with an apology. Unappeased, their squadron commander demanded a 21-gun salute to the American flag. Agreed, replied the Mexicans, but only if American guns returned the salute to Mexico. Learning of a German shipload of weapons about to land at Veracruz, Wilson broke the impasse by ordering American troops to take the city. Instead of the bloodless occupation they expected, U.S. marines encountered stiff resistance as they stormed ashore; 126 Mexicans and 19 Americans were killed before the city fell.

Only the combined diplomacy of Argentina, Brazil, and Chile staved off war between Mexico and the United States. When a bankrupt Huerta resigned in 1914, Carranza formed a new constitutionalist government but refused to follow Wilson's guidelines. Wilson threw his support to Francisco "Pancho" Villa, a wily, peasant-born general who had broken from Carranza. Together with Emiliano Zapata, another peasant leader, Villa kept rebellion flickering.

*Pancho Villa*

A year later, when Wilson finally recognized the Carranza regime, Villa turned against the United States. In January 1916 he abducted 18 Americans from a train in Mexico and slaughtered them. In March, he galloped into Columbus, New Mexico, killed 19 people, and left the town in flames. Wilson ordered 6000 troops into Mexico to capture Villa. A reluctant Carranza agreed to yet another American invasion.

For nearly two years, General John "Black Jack" Pershing (nicknamed for the all-black unit he commanded in the Spanish–American War) chased Villa on horseback, in automobiles, and with airplanes. There were bloody skirmishes with government troops, but not a single one with Villa and his rebels. As the chase turned wilder and wilder, Carranza withdrew his consent for U.S. troops on Mexican soil. Early in 1917 Wilson pulled Pershing home. The "punitive expedition," as the president called it, poisoned Mexican–American relations for the next 30 years.

## THE ROAD TO WAR

In early 1917, around the time that Wilson recalled Pershing, the British liner *Laconia* was making its way home across the Atlantic. As it steamed through the black night, passengers below decks talked almost casually of the war raging in Europe since 1914. "What do you think are our chances of being torpedoed?" asked Floyd Gibbons, an American reporter. Since Germany had stepped up its submarine attacks, the question was unavoidable. "I should put our chances at 250 to 1 that we don't meet a sub," replied a British diplomat.

"At that minute," recalled Gibbons, "the torpedo hit us." As warning whistles blasted the passengers abandoned ship, watching in horror from lifeboats as a second torpedo struck. The *Laconia*'s bow rose straight in the air as its stern sank; then the entire ship slid beneath icy waters. After a miserable night spent bobbing in the waves, Gibbons was rescued. But by 1917 other neutral Americans had already lost their lives at sea. Despite its best efforts, the United States found itself dragged into war.

### *The Guns of August*

For a century, profound strains had been pushing Europe toward war. Its population tripled, its middle and working classes swelled, and discontent with industrial society grew. Nationalism surged and with it, militarism and an aggressive imperialism. Led by Kaiser Wilhelm II and eager for empire, Germany aligned itself with Turkey and Austria–Hungary. The established imperial powers of England and France looked to contain Germany by supporting its foe, Russia. By the summer of 1914 Europe bristled with weapons, troops, and armor-plated navies. And these war machines were linked to one another through a web of diplomatic alliances—all of them committed to war, should someone or some nation set chaos in motion.

*Causes of World War I*

That moment came on June 28, 1914, in the streets of Sarajevo, the provincial capital of Bosnia in southwest Austria–Hungary. There, the heir to the Austro-Hungarian throne, Archduke Franz Ferdinand, was gunned down with his wife. The young assassin who carried out the deed belonged to the Black Hand, a terrorist group that had vowed to reunite Bosnia with Serbia in yet another Slavic nation on Austria–Hungary's border.

*Assassination of Archduke Ferdinand*

Austria–Hungary mobilized to punish all of Serbia. In response, rival Russia called up its 6 million-man army to help the Serbs. Germany joined with Austria–Hungary; France, with Russia. On July 28, after a month of insincere demands for apologies, Austria–Hungary attacked Serbia. On August 1, Germany declared war on Russia and, two days later, on France.

The guns of August heralded the first global war. Like so many dominoes, nations fell into line: Britain, Japan, Romania, and later Italy to the side of

"Allies" France and Russia; Bulgaria and Turkey to the "Central Powers" of Germany and Austria–Hungary. Armies fought from the deserts of North Africa to the plains of Flanders. Fleets battled off the coasts of Chile and Sumatra. Soldiers came from as far away as Australia and India. Nearly 8 million never returned.

### Neutral but Not Impartial

The outbreak of war in Europe shocked most Americans. Few knew Serbia as anything but a tiny splotch on a world map. Fewer still were prepared to go to war in its defense. President Wilson issued an immediate declaration of neutrality and approved a plan for evacuating Americans stranded in Belgium. "The more I read about the conflict," Wilson wrote a friend, "the more open it seems to me to utter condemnation."

Wilson came to see the calamity as an opportunity. Neutral America would lead warring nations to "a peace without victory" and a new world order. Selfish

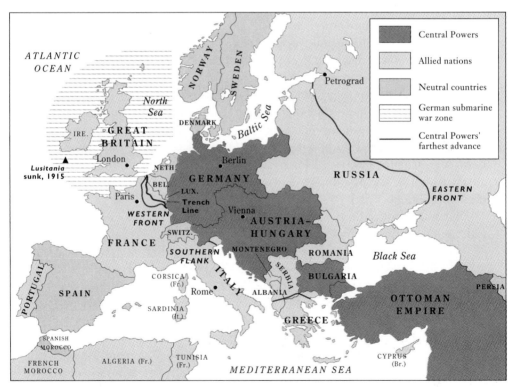

THE WAR IN EUROPE, 1914–1917   When World War I erupted, few countries in Europe remained neutral. The armies of the Central Powers penetrated as far west as France and as far east as Russia. By 1917, the war in Europe had settled into a hideous standoff along a deadly line of trenches on the western front.

nationalism would give way to cooperative internationalism; power politics, to collective security and Christian charity. Progressive faith in reason would triumph over violence. Everything hinged on maintaining neutrality. Only if America stood above the fray could it lead the way to a higher peace. Americans must remain "impartial in thought as well as action," Wilson insisted in 1914.

But true impartiality was impossible. Americans of German and Austrian descent naturally sympathized with the Central Powers, as did Irish-Americans, on the grounds of England's centuries-old domination of Ireland. But the bonds of language, culture, and history tied most Americans to Great Britain. Even Wilson, who had long admired British institutions, could not escape the tug of loyalty. And gratitude for French aid during the American Revolution still lived. When the first American division marched through Paris years later, its commander stopped to salute Lafayette's tomb with the cry, "Nous voilà, Lafayette!"—Lafayette, we are here!

Germany aroused different sentiments. Although some progressives admired German social reforms, Americans generally saw Germany as an iron military power bent on conquest. Americans read British propaganda of spike-helmeted "Huns" raping Belgian women, bayoneting their children, pillaging their towns. Some of the stories were true, some embellished, some manufactured, but all worked against Germany.

Then, too, American economic ties to Britain and France created an investment in Allied victory. After faltering briefly in 1914, the American economy boomed with the flood of war orders. Between 1914 and 1916 trade with the Allies rocketed from $800 million to $3 billion. The Allies eventually borrowed more than $2 billion from American banks to finance their purchases. By contrast, a British blockade reduced American "contraband" commerce with the Central Powers to a trickle.

## The Diplomacy of Neutrality

Wilson had admired Great Britain all his life. Try as he might, he could not contain his sympathies. Although he insisted that all warring powers respect the right of neutrals to trade with any nation, he hesitated to retaliate against Great Britain's blockade. Britain's powerful navy was its key to victory over Germany, a land power. By the end of 1915 the United States had all but accepted the British blockade of Germany, while American supplies continued to flow to England. True neutrality was dead. America became the quartermaster of the Allies.

Early in 1915, Germany turned to a dreadful new weapon to even the odds at sea. It mounted a counterblockade of Great Britain with two dozen sub-

*Submarine warfare*

marines, or *Unterseeboote*, called U-boats. Before submarines, sea raiders usually gave crews and passengers the chance to escape. But if thin-skinned U-boats surfaced to obey these conventions, they risked being rammed or blown from the water. So submarines attacked without warning and spared no lives. Invoking international law and national honor, President Wilson threatened to hold Germany to "strict accountability" for any American losses. Germany promised not to sink any American ships, but soon a new issue grabbed the headlines: the safety of American passengers on belligerent vessels.

On the morning of May 7, 1915, the British passenger liner *Lusitania* appeared out of a fog bank off the coast of Ireland on its way from New York to Southampton. The commander of the German U-20 could hardly believe his eyes: the giant ship filled the viewfinder of his periscope. He fired a single torpedo. A tremendous roar followed as one of the *Lusitania*'s main boilers exploded. The ship listed so badly that lifeboats could barely be launched before the vessel sank. Nearly 1200 men, women, and children perished, including 128 Americans.

Former President Theodore Roosevelt charged that such an "act of piracy" demanded war against Germany. Wilson, though horrified at this "murder on the high seas," urged restraint. "There is such a thing as a nation being so right that it does not need to convince others by force," he said a few days later. He sent notes of protest but did little more.

Secretary of State Bryan, an advocate of what he called "real neutrality," wanted equal protests lodged against both German submarines and British blockaders. He suspected that the *Lusitania* carried munitions and was thus a legitimate target. (Much later, evidence proved him right.) Relying on passengers for protection against attack, Bryan argued, was "like putting women and children in front of an army." Rather than endorse Wilson's policy, Bryan resigned.

Battling on two fronts in Europe, Germany wanted to keep the United States out of the war. But in February 1916 a desperate Germany declared submarine warfare on all *armed* vessels, belligerent or neutral. A month later a U-boat commander mistook the French steamer *Sussex* for a mine layer and torpedoed the unarmed vessel as it ferried passengers and freight across the English Channel. Several Americans were injured.

In mid-April, Wilson issued an ultimatum. If Germany refused to stop sinking nonmilitary vessels, the United States would break off diplomatic relations.

*Sussex pledge*

War would surely follow. Without enough U-boats to control the seas, Germany agreed to Wilson's terms, all but abandoning its counterblockade. This *Sussex* pledge gave Wilson a major victory but carried a grave risk. If German submarines resumed unrestricted attacks, the United States would have to go to war. "Any little German [U-boat] commander can put us into the war at any time," Wilson admitted to his cabinet.

## Peace, Preparedness, and the Election of 1916

While hundreds of young Yanks slipped across the border to enlist in the Canadian army, most Americans agreed that neutrality was the wisest course. Before the war a peace movement had taken seed in the United States, nourished in 1910 by a gift of $10 million from Andrew Carnegie. In 1914 social reformers Jane Addams, Charlotte Perkins Gilman, and Lillian Wald founded the Women's International League for Peace and Freedom and the American Union Against Militarism. Calling on Wilson to convene a peace conference, they lobbied for open diplomacy, disarmament, an end to colonial empires, and an international organization to settle disputes. These would become the core of Wilson's peace plan.

Pacifists might condemn the war, but Republicans and corporate leaders argued that the nation was woefully unprepared to keep peace. The army numbered only 80,000 men in 1914; the navy, just 37 battleships and a handful of new "dreadnoughts," or supercruisers. Advocates of "preparedness" called for a navy larger than Great Britain's, an army of millions of reservists, and universal military training.

By the end of 1915, frustration with German submarines led Wilson to join the cause. He toured the country promoting preparedness and promising a "navy second to none." In Washington, he pressed Congress to double the army, increase the National Guard, and begin construction of the largest navy in the world. To foot the bill progressives pushed through new graduated taxes on higher incomes and on estates as well as additional levies on corporate profits.

Whoever paid for it, most Americans were thinking of preparedness for peace, not war. The Democrats discovered the political power of peace early in the presidential campaign of 1916. As their convention opened in St. Louis in June, the keynote speaker began what he expected to be a dull description of Wilson's recent diplomatic maneuvers—only to have the crowd roar back in each case, "What did we do? What did we do?" The speaker knew the answer

*"He kept us out of war"* and shouted it back: "We didn't go to war! We didn't go to war!" The next day Wilson was renominated by acclamation. "He Kept Us Out of War" became his campaign slogan.

The Republicans had already nominated Charles Evans Hughes, the former governor of New York. He endorsed "straight and honest" neutrality and peace. But despite his moderate stand, Democrats succeeded in painting him as a warmonger, partly because Theodore Roosevelt had rattled his own sabers so loudly. As the election approached, Democrats took full-page advertisements in newspapers across the country: "If You Want WAR, Vote for HUGHES! If You Want Peace with Honor, VOTE FOR WILSON!"

By the time the polls closed, Wilson had squeaked out a victory. He carried the South and key states in the Midwest and West on a tide of prosperity, progressive reform, and, most of all, promises of peace.

## Wilson's Final Peace Offensive

Twice since 1915 Wilson had sent his trusted advisor Colonel Edward House to Europe to negotiate a peace between the warring powers, and twice House had failed. With the election over, Wilson opened his final peace offensive. But when he asked the belligerents to state their terms for a cease-fire, neither side responded. Frustrated, fearful, and genuinely agonized, Wilson called for "peace without victory." There could only be "a peace among equals," he told the Senate in January 1917.

As Wilson spoke, a fleet of U-boats was cruising toward the British Isles. Weeks earlier German military leaders had persuaded the Kaiser to take one last gamble to starve the Allies into submission. On January 31, 1917, the German ambassador in Washington announced that unrestricted submarine warfare would resume the next day.

Wilson's dream of keeping the country from war collapsed. He asked Congress for authority to arm merchant ships and early in February severed re-

*Zimmermann telegram*

lations with Germany. Then British authorities handed him a bombshell—an intercepted telegram from the German foreign secretary, Arthur Zimmermann, to the Kaiser's ambassador in Mexico. In the event of war, the ambassador was instructed to offer Mexico guns, money, and its "lost territory in Texas, New Mexico, and Arizona" to attack the United States. Hot with rage, Wilson released the Zimmermann telegram to the press. Soon after, he ordered gun crews aboard merchant ships and directed them to shoot U-boats on sight.

The momentum of events now propelled a reluctant Wilson toward war. On March 12, U-boats torpedoed the American merchant vessel *Algonquin*. On March 15, a revolution in Russia toppled Czar Nicholas II. A key ally was crumbling from within. By the end of the month U-boats had sunk nearly 600,000 tons of Allied and neutral shipping. For the first time reports came to Washington of cracking morale in the Allied ranks.

On April 2, accompanied by armed cavalry, Wilson rode down Pennsylvania Avenue. He trudged up the steps of the capitol and delivered to Congress a stirring war message, full of idealistic purpose. "We shall fight for the things we have always carried nearest our hearts—for democracy, for the right of those who submit to authority to have a voice in their own governments, for the rights and liberties of small nations."

Pacifists held up the war resolution until it finally passed on April 6. Six senators and 50 House members opposed it, including the first woman in Congress, Jeannette Rankin. Cultural, economic, and historical ties to the Allies, along with the German campaign of submarine warfare, had tipped the country toward war. Wilson had not wanted it, but now the battlefield seemed the only path to a higher peace.

---

## COUNTERPOINT    *Why Did the United States Go to War?*

Because the country was never attacked, the question of why the United States went to war has sparked heated debate. Within a decade of the First World War, an early generation of "revisionists" rejected the official explanation that for moral and practical reasons Germany's campaign of submarine warfare compelled American entry. They pointed to a conspiracy of greedy munitions makers, financiers, and others who stood to profit from Allied victory. A school of "realists" emphasized the importance of strategic, diplomatic, and other pragmatic considerations by arguing that Wilson had rightly gone to war in 1917 but for the wrong reasons: abstract moral principals such as "making the world safe for democracy."

Other historians have painted a more complex portrait that underscores the pressures from all sides limiting Wilson's choices, including the German submarine campaign and Allied blockade but also interventionists, preparedness groups, and advocates of continued trade. Finally, "New Left" historians of the 1960s and 1970s placed blame for American entry on capitalism, which required a stable, peaceful world for the United States to exert its commercial supremacy.

## WAR AND SOCIETY

In 1915 the German zeppelin LZ-38, hovering at 8000 feet, dropped a load of bombs that killed 7 Londoners. For the first time in history, civilians died in an air attack. Few aerial bombardments occurred during the First World War, but they signaled the growing importance of the home front in modern combat. Governments not only fielded armies but also mobilized industry, controlled labor, even rationed food. In the United States, traditions of cooperation and volunteerism helped to organize the home front and the battlefront, often in ways that were peculiarly progressive.

### The Slaughter of Stalemate

While the United States debated entry into the Great War, the Allies were coming perilously close to losing it. Following the initial German assault in 1914, the war had settled into a grisly stalemate. A continuous, immovable front stretched south from Flanders to the border of Switzerland. Troops dug ditches,

*Trench warfare* six to eight feet deep and four to five feet wide, to escape bullets, grenades, and artillery. Twenty-five thousand miles of these "trenches" slashed a muddy scar across Europe. Men lived in them for years, prey to disease, lice, and a plague of rats.

War in the machine age gave the advantage to the defense. When soldiers bravely charged "over the top" of the trenches, they were shredded by machine guns that fired 600 rounds a minute. Poison gas choked them in their tracks. Giant howitzers lobbed shells on them from positions too distant to see. Even in quiet times 7000 British soldiers died or were wounded every day. In the Battle of the Somme River in 1916 a million men were killed in just four months of fighting. Only late in the war did new armored "landships"—

Trench warfare, wrote one general, is "marked by uniform formations, the
regulation of space and time by higher commands . . . fixed distances between
units and individuals." The reality of life in the trenches
(as pictured here) was something else again.

code-named "tanks"—return the advantage to the offense by surmounting the
trench barriers with their caterpillar treads.

By then Vladimir Lenin was speeding home to Russia where food riots, coal
shortages, and protests against the government had led to revolution. Lenin had
been exiled to Switzerland during the early stages of the Russian Revolution but
returned to lead the Bolshevik party to power in November 1917. Soon the
Russians negotiated a separate peace with Germany, which then transferred a
million soldiers to the western front for the coming spring offensive.

### "You're in the Army Now"

The Allies' plight forced the army into a crash program to send a million men
to Europe by the spring of 1918. The United States had barely 180,000 men in
uniform. To raise the force, Congress passed the Selective Service

*Selective
Service Act*

Act in May 1917. Feelings about the draft ran high. "There is
precious little difference between a conscript [draftee] and a convict," protested the House Speaker in 1917. Progressives were more inclined to
see military service as an opportunity to unite America and promote democracy:

"Universal [military] training will jumble the boys of America all together, . . . smashing all the petty class distinctions that now divide, and prompting a brand of real democracy."

At ten in the morning on July 20, 1917, Secretary of War Newton Baker tied a blindfold over his eyes, reached into a huge glass bowl, and drew the first number in the new draft lottery. Some 24 million men were registered. Almost 3 million were drafted; another 2 million volunteered. Most were white, and all were young, between the ages of 21 and 31. Several thousand women served as clerks, telephone operators, and nurses. In a nation of immigrants, nearly one draftee in five had been born in another country. Training often aimed at educating and Americanizing these ethnic recruits. In special "development battalions" drill sergeants barked out orders while volunteers from the YMCA taught American history and English.

African Americans volunteered in disproportionately high numbers and quickly filled the four all-black army and eight National Guard units already in existence. Abroad, where 200,000 black troops served in France, only 42,000

Members of the 369th Regiment, one of the few all-black units permitted to fight, are pictured in front of their barracks. Still in World War I commanded by whites (at center), these black troops were among the first Americans to see action and initially were attached to the French army. The unit displays the Croix de Guerre, the French medal of honor.

were permitted in combat. Southern Democrats in Congress had opposed training African Americans to arms, fearful of putting "arrogant, strutting representatives of black soldiery in every community." But four regiments of the all-black Ninety-Third Division, brigaded with the French army, were among the first Americans in the trenches and among the most decorated units in the U.S. Army.

Racial violence sometimes flared among the troops. The worst episode occurred in Houston in the summer of 1917. Harassed by white soldiers and by the city's Jim Crow laws, seasoned black regulars rioted and killed 17 white civilians. Their whole battalion was disarmed and sent under arrest to New Mexico. Thirteen troopers were condemned to death and hanged within days, too quickly for appeals even to be filed.

*Houston riot*

Black or white, recruits learned the ways of the army—rising before dawn, drilling in close order, marching for miles. But many of them also learned to wash regularly, use indoor toilets, and read. To fight sexually transmitted disease, the army produced thousands of pamphlets, films, and lectures. The drive constituted the first serious sex education young Americans ever received.

Progressive reformers did not miss the chance to put the social sciences to work in the army. Most recruits had fewer than seven years of education; yet they had to be classified and assigned quickly to units. Psychologists saw the chance to use new intelligence tests to help the army and prove their own theories about the value of "IQ" (intelligence quotient) in measuring the mind. In fact, these new "scientific" IQ tests often measured little more than class origins. Questions such as "Who wrote 'The Raven'?" exposed background rather than intelligence. More than half the Russian, Italian, and Polish draftees and almost 80 percent of the black draftees showed up as "inferior." The army stopped the testing program in January 1919, but schools across the country adopted it after the war, reinforcing many ethnic and racial prejudices.

## Mobilizing the Economy

Armed against the enemy, clothed and drilled, the doughboys marched up the gangplanks of the "Atlantic Ferry"—the ships that conveyed them to Europe. (Infantrymen were called "doughboys," most likely because of the clay dough used by soldiers in the 1850s to clean their belts.) To equip, feed, and transport an army of nearly 5 million required a national effort.

At the Treasury Department, Secretary William Gibbs McAdoo fretted over how to finance the war, which cost, finally, $32 billion. At the time the entire national debt ran to only $2 billion. New taxes paid about a third of the war costs. The rest came from loans financed through "Liberty" and "Victory" bonds and war savings certificates. By 1920 the national debt had climbed to $20 billion.

With sweeping grants of authority provided by Congress, President Wilson constructed a massive bureaucracy to mobilize the home front. What emerged

War Industries
Board

was a managed economy, similar to the New Nationalism envisioned by Theodore Roosevelt. A War Industries Board (WIB) coordinated production through networks of industrial and trade associations. Although it had the authority to order firms to comply, the WIB relied instead on persuasion through publicity and "cost-plus" contracts that covered all production costs, plus a guaranteed profit. Corporate profits tripled, and production soared.

The Food Administration encouraged farmers to grow more and citizens to eat less wastefully. Publicity campaigns promoted "wheatless" and "meatless" days and exhorted families to plant "victory" gardens. Spurred by rising prices, farmers brought more marginal lands into cultivation, as their real income jumped 25 percent.

A Fuel Administration met the army's energy needs by increasing production and limiting domestic consumption. Transportation snarls required more drastic action. In December 1917 the U.S. Railroad Administration simply took over rail lines for the duration of the war. Government coordination, together with a new system of permits, got freight moving and kept workers happy. Rail workers saw their wages grow by $300 million. Railroad unions won recognition, an eight-hour day, and a grievance procedure. For the first time in decades labor unrest subsided, and the trains ran on schedule.

The modern bureaucratic state received a powerful boost during the 18 months of American participation in the war. Speeding trends already under

Bureaucratic
state

way, some 5000 new federal agencies centralized authority and cooperated with business and labor. The number of federal employees more than doubled between 1916 and 1918, to over 850,000. The wartime bureaucracy was quickly dismantled at the end of the war, but it set an important precedent for the future.

## War Work

The war benefited working men and women, though not as much as their employers. Government contracts guaranteed high wages, an eight-hour day, and equal pay for comparable work. To encourage people to stay on the job, federal contracting agencies set up special classes to teach employers the new science of personnel management in order to supervise workers more efficiently and humanely. American industry moved one step closer to the "welfare capitalism" of the 1920s, with its profit sharing, company unions, and personnel departments to forestall worker discontent.

Personnel management was not always enough to guarantee industrial peace. In 1917 American workers called over 4000 strikes, the most in American

National War
Labor Board

history. To keep factories running smoothly, President Wilson created the National War Labor Board (NWLB) early in 1918. The NWLB arbitrated more than 1000 labor disputes, helped to increase wages, and established overtime pay. In return for pledges not to strike,

Wartime needs brought more women into the labor force, often on jobs that challenged assumptions about gender roles. These women work on a production line manufacturing bullets. The novelty of the situation seems evident from the fashionable high-button, high-heeled shoes that they wear.

the board guaranteed the rights of unions to organize and bargain collectively. Membership in the American Federation of Labor jumped from 2.7 million in 1916 to nearly 4 million by 1919.

As doughboys went abroad, the war brought about a million new women into the labor force. Most were young and single. Sometimes they took over jobs once held by men as railroad engineers, drill press operators, and electric lift truck drivers. The prewar trend toward higher-paying jobs intensified, though most women still earned less than the men they replaced. And some of the most spectacular gains in defense and government work evaporated after the war as male veterans returned and the country demobilized. Tens of thousands of army nurses, defense workers, and war administrators lost their jobs. Agencies such as the Women's Service Section of the Railroad Administration, which fought sexual harassment and discrimination, simply went out of business.

## Great Migrations

War work sparked massive migrations of laborers. As the fighting abroad choked off immigration and the draft depleted the workforce, factory owners scoured the country for workers. Industrial cities, no matter how small, soon swelled with newcomers. Between 1917 and 1920, some 150,000 Mexicans crossed the border into Texas, California, New Mexico, and Arizona. Some *Mexican migrations* Mexican Americans left segregated *barrios* of western cities for war plants in Chicago, Omaha, and other northern cities, pushed out by the cheaper labor from Mexico and seeking higher paying jobs. But most worked on farms and ranches, freed from military service by the deferment granted to agricultural labor.

Northern labor agents fanned out across the rural South to recruit young African Americans, while black newspapers like the Chicago *Defender* sum-

*African Americans*

moned them up to the "Land of Hope." During the war more than 400,000 moved to the booming industries of the North. Largely unskilled and semiskilled, they worked in the steel mills of Pennsylvania, the war plants of Massachusetts, the brickyards of New Jersey. Southern towns were decimated by the drain. Finally, under pressure from southern politicians, the U.S. Employment Service suspended its program to assist blacks moving north.

These migrations of African Americans—into the army as well as into the city—aggravated racial tensions. Lynching parties murdered 38 black southerners in 1917 and 58 in 1918. In 1919, after the war ended, more than 70 were hanged, some still in uniform. Housing shortages and job competition helped to ignite race riots across the North. In almost every city black citizens, stirred by war rhetoric of freedom and democracy, showed new militancy. During the bloody "red summer" of 1919 race wars broke out in Washington, D.C., Omaha, Nebraska, New York City, and Chicago, where thousands of African Americans were burned out of their homes and hundreds injured as they fought white mobs.

## Propaganda and Civil Liberties

"Once lead this people into war," President Wilson warned before American entry into the conflict, "and they'll forget there ever was such a thing as tolerance." Americans succumbed to a ruthless hysteria during World War I, but they had help. Wilson knew how reluctant Americans had been to enter the war, and in 1917 he created the Committee on Public Information (CPI) to cement American commitment to the war.

Under George Creel, a California journalist, the CPI launched a zealous publicity campaign that produced colorful war posters, 75 million pamphlets,

*Committee on Public Information*

and patriotic "war expositions" in two dozen cities across the country. An army of 75,000 fast-talking "Four-Minute Men" invaded theaters, schools, and churches to keep patriotism at "white heat" with four minutes of war tirades. The CPI organized "Loyalty Leagues" in ethnic communities and sponsored rallies, including a much-publicized immigrant "pilgrimage" to the birthplace of George Washington.

As war fever mounted, voluntary patriotism blossomed into an orgy of "100 percent Americanism" that distrusted all aliens, radicals, pacifists, and dissenters. German Americans became special targets. In Iowa the governor made it a crime to speak German in public. Hamburgers were renamed "Salisbury steak"; German measles, "liberty measles." When a mob outside of St. Louis lynched a naturalized German American who had tried to enlist in the navy, a jury found the leaders not guilty.

E Y E W I T N E S S    T O    H I S T O R Y

## An African American Woman's
## View of the 1919 Race Riots

he Washington riot gave me the *thrill that comes once in a life time.* I . . . read between the lines of our morning paper that at last our men had stood like men, struck back, were no longer dumb driven cattle. When I could no longer read for my streaming tears, I stood up, alone in my room, held both hands high over my head and exclaimed aloud: "Oh I thank God, thank God." . . . Only colored women of the South know the extreme in suffering and humiliation.

We know how many insults we have borne silently, for we have hidden many of them from our men because we did not want them to die needlessly in our defense . . ., the deep humiliation of sitting in the Jim Crow part of a street car and hear the white men laugh and discuss us, point out the good and bad points of our bodies. . . .

And, too, a woman loves a strong man, she delights to feel that her man can protect her, fight for her if necessary, save her.

No woman loves a weakling, a coward be she white or black, and some of us have been near thinking our men cowards, but thank God for Washington colored men! All honor to them, for they first blazed the way and right swiftly did Chicago men follow [during the 1919 race riot]. They put new hope, a new vision into their almost despairing women.

God Grant that our men everywhere refrain from strife, provoke no quarrel, but they protect their women and homes at any cost.

*A Southern Colored Woman*

*The Crisis*, Vol. 19 (November 1919), p. 339. Reprinted in William Loren Katy, ed., *Eyewitness: The Negro in American History* (New York: Pittman Publishing, 1976), p. 403.

---

Congress gave hysteria more legal bite by passing the Espionage and the Sedition acts of 1917 and 1918. Both set harsh penalties for any actions that hindered the war effort or that could be viewed as even remotely unpatriotic. Following passage, 1500 citizens were arrested for offenses that included denouncing the draft, criticizing the Red Cross, and complaining about wartime taxes.

*Espionage and Sedition acts*

Radical groups received especially severe treatment. The Industrial Workers of the World (IWW), a militant union centered in western states, saw the war as a battle among capitalists and threatened to strike mining and lumber companies in protest. Federal agents raided IWW headquarters in Chicago and arrested 113 members. The crusade destroyed the union. Similarly, the Socialist party opposed the "capitalist" war. In response, the postmaster general banned a dozen Socialist publications from the mail, though the party was a legal organization that had elected mayors, municipal officials, and members of Congress. In June 1918 government agents arrested Eugene V. Debs, the Socialist candidate for president in 1912, for an anti-war speech. A jury found him guilty of sedition and sentenced him to 10 years in jail.

The Supreme Court endorsed such actions. In *Schenck v. United States* (1919), the Court unanimously affirmed the conviction of a Socialist party officer who had mailed pamphlets urging resistance to the draft. The pamphlets, wrote Justice Oliver Wendell Holmes, created "a clear and present danger" to a nation at war.

*Schenck v. United States*

## Over There

The first American doughboys landed in France in June 1917, but few saw battle. General John Pershing held back his raw troops until they could receive more training. He also separated them in a distinct American Expeditionary Force to preserve their identity and avoid Allied disagreements over strategy.

In the spring of 1918, as the Germans pushed toward Paris, Pershing rushed 70,000 American troops to the front. American units helped block the Germans both at the town of Château-Thierry and, a month later in June, at Belleau Wood. Two more German attacks, one at Amiens and the other just east of the Marne River, ended in costly German retreats. On September 12, 1918, half a million American soldiers and a smaller number of French troops overran the German stronghold at Saint-Mihiel in four days.

With their army in retreat and civilian morale low, Germany's leaders sought an armistice. They hoped to negotiate terms along the lines laid out by Woodrow Wilson in a speech to Congress in January 1918. Wilson's bright vision of peace had encompassed "Fourteen Points." The key provisions called for open diplomacy, free seas and free trade, disarmament, democratic self-rule, and an "association of nations" to guarantee collective security. It was nothing less than a new world order to end selfish nationalism, imperialism, and war.

*Fourteen Points*

Allied leaders were not impressed. "President Wilson and his Fourteen Points bore me," French Premier Georges Clemenceau said. "Even God Almighty has only ten!" But Wilson's idealistic platform was also designed to save the Allies deeper embarrassment. Almost as soon as it came to power in 1917, the new Bolshevik government in Moscow had begun publishing secret treaties from the czar's archives. They revealed that the Allies had gone to war

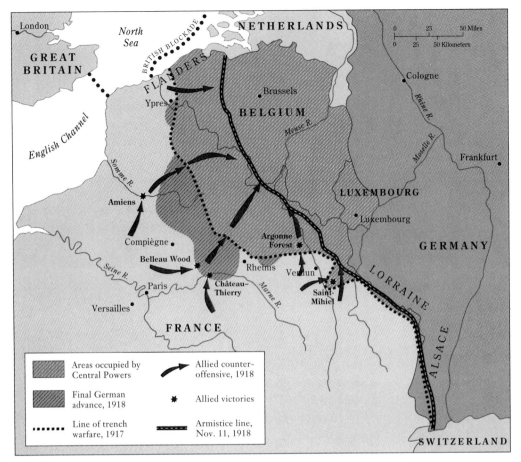

THE FINAL GERMAN OFFENSIVE AND ALLIED COUNTERATTACK, 1918 On the morning of March 21, 1918, over 60 German divisions sliced through Allied lines and plunged within 50 miles of Paris before being stopped at the Marne River in July. The Allied counterattack was marked by notable American victories at Château-Thierry, Belleau Wood, Saint-Mihiel, and Meuse-Argonne.

for territory and colonies, not for high principles. Wilson's Fourteen Points had given their cause a nobler purpose.

Wilson's ideals also stirred German liberals. On October 6 he received a telegram from Berlin requesting an immediate truce. Within a month Turkey and Austria–Hungary surrendered. Early in November the Kaiser was overthrown and fled to neutral Holland. On November 11, 1918, German officers filed into Allied headquarters in a converted railroad car near Compiègne, France, and signed the armistice.

Of the 2 million Americans who served in France, over 50,000 were killed in combat, fewer than had died in the influenza pandemic of 1918. By comparison, the war claimed 2.2 million Germans, 1.7 million Russians, 1.4 million

French, 1.2 million Austro-Hungarians, and nearly a million Britons. The American contribution had nonetheless been crucial, providing vital convoys at sea and fresh, confident troops on land. The United States emerged from the war stronger than ever. Europe, on the other hand, looked forward—as one newspaper put it—to "Disaster . . . Exhaustion . . . Revolution."

## THE LOST PEACE

As the USS *George Washington* approached the coast of France in mid-December 1918, the mist suddenly lifted in an omen of good hope. Woodrow Wilson had come to represent the United States at the Paris peace conference at Versailles, once the glittering palace of Louis XIV. A world of problems awaited him and the other Allied leaders. Europe had been shelled into ruin and scarred with the debris of war. Fifty million people lay dead or maimed from the fighting. Throughout the Balkans and the old Turkish empire, ethnic rivalries, social chaos, and revolution loomed.

With the old world order so evidently in shambles, Wilson felt the need to take vigorous action. Thus the president handpicked the Peace Commission of experts that accompanied him. It included economists, historians, geographers, and political scientists—but not a single member of the Republican-controlled Senate. What promised to make peace negotiations easier created a crippling liability in Washington, where Republicans were already casting hostile eyes on the mirrored halls of Versailles.

### The Treaty of Versailles

Everywhere Wilson went, cheers greeted him. In Paris 2 million people showered him with flowers. In Italy they hailed him as the "peacemaker from America." And everywhere he went, Woodrow Wilson believed what he heard, unaware of how determined the victors were to punish the vanquished. David Lloyd George of England, Georges Clemenceau of France, Vittorio Orlando of Italy, and Wilson constituted the Big Four at the conference that included some 27 nations. War had united them; now peacemaking threatened to divide them.

Wilson's sweeping reforms had taken Allied leaders by surprise. Hungry for new colonies, eager to see Germany crushed and disarmed, their secret treaties had already divided up the territories of the Central Powers. Germany had offered to surrender on the basis of Wilson's Fourteen Points, but the Allies refused to accept them. When Wilson threatened to negotiate peace on his own, Allied leaders finally agreed—but only for the moment.

Noticeably absent when the peace conference convened in January 1919 were the Russians. None of the Western democracies had recognized the Bolshevik regime in Moscow, out of fear that the communist revolution might spread. Instead, France and Britain were helping to finance a civil war to overthrow the Bolsheviks. Even Wilson had been persuaded to send several thousand American troops to join the Allied occupation of some northern Russian ports and to Siberia. The Soviets would neither forgive nor forget this intrusion.

Grueling negotiations forced Wilson to yield several of his Fourteen Points. Britain, with its powerful navy, refused even to discuss the issues of free trade and freedom of the seas. Wilson's "open diplomacy" was conducted behind closed doors by the Big Four. The only mention of disarmament involved Germany, which was permanently barred from rearming. Wilson's call for "peace without victory" gave way to a "guilt clause" that saddled Germany with responsibility for the war. Worse still, the victors imposed on the vanquished a burdensome debt of $33 billion in reparations.

Wilson did achieve some successes. His pleas for national self-determination led to the creation of a dozen new states in Europe, including Yugoslavia, Hungary, and Austria. (Poland and newly created Czechoslovakia, however, contained millions of ethnic Germans.) Former colonies gained new status as "mandates" of the victors, who were obligated to prepare them for independence. The old German and Turkish empires in the Middle East and Africa became the responsibility of France and England, while Japan took over German possessions in the Far East.

Wilson never lost sight of his main goal: a League of Nations. He had given so much ground precisely because he believed this new world organization would

*League of Nations*

correct any mistakes in the peace settlement. As constituted, the League was composed of a general Body of Delegates, a select Executive Council, and a Court of International Justice. Members promised to submit all war-provoking disagreements to arbitration and to isolate aggressors by cutting off commercial and military trade. Article X (Wilson called it "the heart of the covenant") bound members to respect one another's independence and territory and to join together against attack. "It is definitely a guarantee of peace," the president told the delegates in February 1919.

## The Battle for the Treaty

Wilson left immediately for home to address growing opposition in Congress. In the off-year elections of 1918, voters unhappy with wartime controls, new taxes, and attacks on civil liberties gave both houses to the opposition Republicans. A slim Republican majority in the Senate put Wilson's archrival, Henry Cabot Lodge of Massachusetts, in the chairman's seat of the all-important Foreign Relations Committee.

While most of the country favored the League, Lodge was against it. For decades he had fought to preserve American freedom of action in foreign af-

*Lodge opposes the League*

fairs. Now he worried that the League would force Americans to subject themselves to "the will of other nations." And he certainly did not want Democrats to win votes by taking credit for the treaty. Securing the signatures of enough senators to block any treaty, Lodge rose in the Senate just before midnight on March 3 to read a "round robin" resolution against the League. "Woodrow Wilson's League of Nations died in the Senate tonight," concluded the New York *Sun*.

Wilson formally presented the treaty in July. "Dare we reject it and break the heart of the world?" he asked the senators. Fourteen Republicans and two Democrats were ready to do just that. "Irreconcilable" opponents of internationalism, they vowed to kill "the unholy thing with the holy name." Over 20 "strong reservationists," led by Lodge, sought to amend the treaty with major changes requiring yet another round of Allied negotiations. Twelve "mild reservationists" wanted minimal alterations, mainly interpretive in nature.

Wilson's only hope of winning the necessary two-thirds majority lay in compromise. Worn out by the concessions already wrung from him in Paris, afflicted by numbing headaches and a twitch in his left eye, he resisted all changes. Despite his doctor's warnings, Wilson took his case to the people in a month-long stump across the nation in 1919.

In Pueblo, Colorado, a crowd of 10,000 heard perhaps the greatest oration of his career. Wilson spoke of American soldiers killed in France and American *Wilson's stroke* boys whom the League one day would spare from death. Listeners wept openly. That evening, utterly exhausted, he collapsed in a spasm of pain. On October 2, four days after being rushed to the White House, he fell to the bathroom floor, knocked unconscious by a stroke.

For six weeks Wilson could do no work at all and for months after worked little more than an hour a day. His second wife, Edith Bolling Wilson, handled the routine business of government along with the president's secretary and his doctor. The country knew nothing of the seriousness of his condition. Wilson recovered slowly but never fully. More and more the battle for the treaty consumed his fading energies.

Late in 1919 Lodge finally reported the treaty out of committee with 14 amendments to match Wilson's Fourteen Points. The most important asserted that the United States assumed no obligation under Article X to aid League members unless Congress consented. Wilson believed Lodge had delivered a "knife thrust at the heart of the treaty" and refused to accept any change. Whatever ill will Lodge bore Wilson, his objections did not destroy the treaty, but only weakened it by protecting the congressional power to declare war.

Wilson and Lodge refused to compromise. When the amended treaty finally came before the Senate in March 1920, enough Democrats broke from the president to produce a majority—but not the required two-thirds. The Treaty of Versailles was dead in America. Not until July 1921 did Congress enact a joint resolution ending the war. The United States, which had fought separately from the Allies, made a separate peace as well.

## Red Scare

Peace abroad did not bring peace at home. On May Day 1919, six months after the war ended, mobs in a dozen cities broke up Socialist parades, injured hundreds, and killed three people. Later that month, when a spectator at a Victory Loan rally in Washington refused to stand for the national anthem, a sailor shot him in the back. The stadium crowd applauded.

The spontaneous violence and extremism occurred because Americans believed they were under attack. Millions of soldiers had returned home, now unemployed and looking for jobs. With prices rising and war regulations lifted, laborers were demanding higher wages and striking when they failed to get them. In Boston even the police walked off their jobs. When a strike by conservative trade unionists paralyzed Seattle for five days in January, Mayor Ole Hanson draped his car in an American flag and led troops through the streets in a show of force. Hanson blamed radicals, while Congress ascribed the national ills to Bolshevik agents, inspired by the revolution in Russia.

*Radicals and labor unrest*

The menace of radicalism was entirely overblown. With Socialist Eugene Debs in prison, his dwindling party numbered only about 30,000. Radicals at first hoped that the success of the Russian Revolution would help reverse their fortunes in the United States. But most Americans found the prospect of "Bolshevik" agitators threatening, especially after March 1919, when the new Russian government formed the Comintern to spread revolution abroad. Furthermore, the Left itself splintered. In 1919 dissidents deserted the Socialists to form the more radical Communist Labor party. About the same time, a group of mostly Slavic radicals created a separate Communist party. Both organizations together counted no more than 40,000 members.

On April 28 Mayor Hanson received a small brown parcel at his office, evidently another present from an admirer of his tough patriotism. It was a homemade bomb. Within days, 20 such packages were discovered, including ones sent to John D. Rockefeller, Supreme Court Justice Oliver Wendell Holmes, and the Postmaster General. On June 2 bombs exploded simultaneously in eight different cities. One of them demolished the front porch of A. Mitchell Palmer, attorney general of the United States. The bomb thrower was blown to bits, but enough remained to identify him as an Italian anarchist from Philadelphia. Already edgy over Bolshevism and labor militancy, many Americans assumed that an organized conspiracy was being mounted to overthrow the government.

*Palmer raids*

Palmer, a Quaker and a progressive, hardened in the wake of the bombings. In November 1919 and again in January 1920, he launched raids in over 30 cities across the United States. Government agents invaded private homes, meeting halls, and pool parlors, taking several thousand alleged communists into custody without warrants and beating those who resisted. Prisoners were marched through streets in chains, crammed into di-

On September 16, 1920, a wagonload of bombs exploded at the corner of Broad and Wall streets, killing 33 people and injuring more than 200. The nation was horrified but saw no communist plot behind the mysterious blast, as Attorney General A. Mitchell Palmer charged.

lapidated jails, held without hearings. Over two hundred aliens, most of whom had no criminal records, were deported to the Soviet Union.

Arrests continued at the rate of 200 a week through March. State after state passed new statutes outlawing radical unions. In Centralia, Washington, vigilantes spirited radical labor organizer Wesley Everest from jail, castrated him, and hanged him from the Chehalis River bridge as they riddled his body with bullets. The county coroner ruled it a suicide.

Such abuses of civil liberties provoked a backlash. After the New York legislature expelled five duly-elected Socialists in 1919, responsible politicians—from former presidential candidate Charles Evans Hughes to Ohio Senator Warren Harding—denounced the action. The "deportation delirium" ended early in 1920. Palmer finally overreached himself by predicting a revolutionary uprising for May 1, 1920. Buildings were put under guard and state militia called to readiness. Nothing happened. Four months later, when a wagonload of bombs exploded on Wall Street, Palmer blamed a Bolshevik conspiracy. Despite 33 deaths and more than 200 injuries, Americans saw it as the work of a few demented radicals (which it probably was) and went about business as usual.

Not for another 20 years would the United States assume a responsible position in international affairs. And the spirit of reform at home dimmed as well. When war came, progressivism had furnished the bureaucratic weapons to organize the fight, but its push for social justice and toleration had been overshadowed by a patriotic frenzy.

War changed Americans. They experienced a planned economy for the first time. Propaganda shaped diverse ethnic, racial, class, and gender differences into the uniform purpose of victory. War work drew millions from country to city, from farm to factory. The army mixed millions more, who returned from Europe with tales of its wonders. Provincial America thus became more cosmopolitan and urban. But the corrosive effects of war and the cynicism of the European victors led to disillusionment. Americans turned from idealistic crusades to the practical business of getting and spending.

## SIGNIFICANT EVENTS

| | |
|---|---|
| 1901 | Canal authorized across the Central American isthmus |
| 1902 | Platt Amendment ratified |
| 1904 | Roosevelt Corollary to Monroe Doctrine |
| 1905 | Treaty of Portsmouth ends Russo-Japanese War |
| 1907 | "Gentlemen's agreement" with Japan; "Great White Fleet" embarks on world tour |
| 1910 | Mexican Revolution erupts |
| 1914 | U.S. Navy invades Veracruz; Archduke Franz Ferdinand assassinated; World War I begins; Panama Canal opens |
| 1915 | Japan issues Twenty-One Demands; Germany proclaims war zone around British Isles; *Lusitania* torpedoed; Secretary of State Bryan resigns; Wilson endorses preparedness |
| 1916 | *Sussex* pledge; General John Pershing invades Mexico in pursuit of Pancho Villa; Wilson reelected president |
| 1917 | Wilson calls for "peace without victory"; Germany resumes unrestricted submarine warfare; Zimmermann telegram released; Russian Revolution breaks out; U.S. enters World War I; Selective Service Act passed; War Industries Board created |
| 1918 | Wilson's Fourteen Points for peace; Eugene Debs jailed under Sedition Act; influenza epidemic; Germany sues for peace; armistice declared |
| 1919 | Paris Peace Conference; *Schenck v. United States* affirms Espionage Act; red summer; Chicago race riot; Senate rejects Treaty of Versailles |
| 1920 | Palmer raids; red scare |

## The Perils of Democracy

In the wake of World War I, the editors of *The New Republic* despaired that "the war did no good to anybody. Those of its generation whom it did not kill, it crippled, wasted, or used up." But by the mid-1920s, with a post-war recession lifting, despair gave way to hope. Woodrow Wilson's vision of a world made safe for democracy no longer seemed so naive.

In both political and material terms democracy seemed to be advancing. Great Britain eliminated restrictions on suffrage for men and by 1928 gave the vote to women as well. Hapsburg Germany transformed itself into the Weimar Republic, whose constitution provided universal suffrage and a bill of rights. Across central and eastern Europe, the new nations carved out of the old Russian and Austro-Hungarian empires, along with the previously independent Romania, Bulgaria, Greece, and Albania, attempted to create governments along similarly democratic lines.

The winds of reform also blew through Asia. Some Asians, like Mao Zedong in China and Ho Chi Minh in Indochina, saw communism as the means to liberate their peoples from imperialist rule. But even Asian Marxists aligned themselves with the powerful force of nationalism. In India, the Congress party formed by Mohandas K. Gandhi united socialists and powerful industrial capitalists in a campaign of nonviolence and boycotts of British goods that ultimately brought self-government to India. In Turkey, Kemal Atatürk in 1923 abolished the sultanate and established the Turkish Republic with all the trappings of a Western democratic state.

The spread of democracy had a material side as well. Indeed, the respect given parliamentary governments depended heavily on their ability to restore prosperity. As the world economy expanded, some optimists suggested that innovations in manufacturing, like Henry Ford's moving assembly line, would usher in an era in which plenty would replace want. Increased earnings encouraged a democratic culture of consumption, whether it was buying radios in France or Western-style fashions in Tokyo. Culture too was being spread globally, with the coming of mass media. Movies, radio, and mass-circulation magazines made once-remote people and places accessible and familiar.

But democracy's foundations were fragile. In the new Soviet Union, communists led by Lenin and the ruthless Joseph Stalin demonstrated that talk of "the masses" and "democratic socialism" could mask an iron totalitarianism. In Japan, democracy was hampered by feudal traditions. By the late 1920s nationalists from the old samurai class had joined with the nation's economically powerful families in a militarist quest for a Japanese East Asian empire.

Fear of communist revolution led some nationalists in Europe to reject democracy. With Italy's parliamentary government seemingly paralyzed by postwar unrest, Benito Mussolini and his *Fasci di Combattimento*, or fascists, used terrorism and murder to create an "all-embracing" single-party state. During the 1920s Italian fascists rejected the liberal belief in political parties in favor of a glorified nation-state dominated by the middle class, small businesspeople, and small farmers. In Germany Adolf Hitler trumpeted similar ideals and relied on equally brutal tactics to gain power in 1933. His Nazi party used its Gestapo, or secret police, to ensure that Germans expressed only ideas that conformed to the views of their national leader, the *Führer*.

Hitler succeeded partly because the prosperity of the 1920s was shattered worldwide by the Great Depression. Farmers ruined by overproduction, urban workers out of a job, shopkeepers facing bankruptcy—such people found it easy to believe that only the forceful leadership of one could unite the many. Even in the United States, the business newspaper *Barron's* mused that "a mild species of dictatorship" might "help us over the roughest spots in the road ahead."

Thus the Depression shook both the political and the material pillars of democratic culture. On the eve of World War II the number of European democracies had been reduced from 27 to 10. Latin America was ruled by a variety of dictators and military juntas, China by the corrupt one-party dictatorship of Chiang Kai-shek. Almost alone, the New Deal attempted to combat the Depression through the methods of parliamentary democracy. The totalitarian states had promised stability, national glory, and an end to the communist menace. Instead they led the world to chaos and war from which both communism and democracy emerged triumphant.

# CHAPTER TWENTY-FOUR

# The New Era

J ust before Christmas 1918 the "Gospel Car" pulled into Los Angeles. Bold letters on the side announced: "JESUS IS COMING—GET READY." Aimee Semple McPherson, the ravishing redheaded driver, had completed a cross-country trip to seek her destiny in the West. With only "ten dollars and a tambourine" to her name, destiny at first proved hard to find. But after three years of wandering the state, she landed in San Diego, a city with the highest rates of illness and suicide in California. It was the perfect place to preach the healing message of Sister Aimee's "Foursquare Gospel." Her revival attracted 30,000 people, who witnessed her first miracle: a paralytic walked.

Sister Aimee had a Pentecostal message for her flock: "Jesus is the healer. I am only the little office girl who opens the door and says, 'Come in.'" After the miracle in San Diego, her fame spread. She returned triumphantly to Los Angeles, where nearly three-quarters of a million people, many from the nation's heartland, had migrated in search of opportunity, sun, and perhaps salvation. In heading west, more than a few had lost touch with the traditional Protestant denominations at home. Sister Aimee put her traveling gospel tent away. She would minister to the lost flock at her doorstep.

To the blare of trumpets on New Year's Day, 1923, she unveiled the $1.5 million Angelus Temple, graced by a 75-foot rotating electronic cross. It was visible at night from 50 miles away. Inside was a 5000-seat auditorium, radio station KFSG (Kall Four Square Gospel), a "Cradle Roll Chapel" for babies, and a "Miracle Room" filled with the many aids discarded by the cured faithful. Services were not simply a matter of hymn, prayer, and sermon. Sister added pageants, Holy Land slide shows, circuses, and healing sessions.

Aimee Semple McPherson succeeded because she was able to blend old and new. Her lively sermons carried the spirit of what people were calling the "New Era" of productivity and consumerism. Country preachers menaced their congregations with visions of eternal damnation, but Sister Aimee, wrote a reporter,

Sister Aimee Semple McPherson, billed as the "world's most pulchritudinous evangelist," in her robes

offered "flowers, music, golden trumpets, red robes, angels, incense, nonsense, and sex appeal." Her approach revealed a nose for publicity and a sophisticated understanding of the booming media industries of the 1920s. Here was one brand of evangelism suited to a new consumer age.

Modernizing the gospel was just one symptom of the New Era. Writing in 1931, journalist Frederick Lewis Allen found the changes of the preceding decade so overwhelming that it hardly seemed possible 1919 was *Only Yesterday*, as he titled his book. To give some sense of the transformation, Allen followed an average American couple, the fictitious "Mr. and Mrs. Smith," through the decade. Among the most striking changes was the revolution in women's fashions and behavior. Mrs. Smith's corset vanished, her hemline jumped from her ankle to her knee, and she "bobbed," or cut, her long hair to the popular near-boyish length and flattened her breasts for greater freedom of movement.

With Prohibition in full force, Mrs. Smith and other women of her day walked into illegal "speakeasy" saloons as readily as men. In the trendy hotels she and her husband danced to jazz and sprinkled their conversations with references to "repressed sexual drives" and the best methods of contraception.

*Urban role in the New Era*
But perhaps the most striking change about these "average" Americans was that they lived in the city. The census of 1920 showed that for the first time just over half the population were urbanites. Here, in urban America, the New Era worked its changes and sent them rippling outward.

Yet the Smiths of Frederick Allen's imagination were hardly average. Nearly as many Americans still lived on isolated farms, in villages, and in small towns as in the cities. In fact, many "city" dwellers lived there too. By defining cities

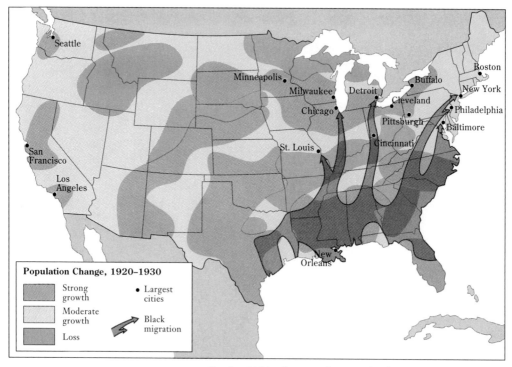

AREAS OF POPULATION GROWTH   In the 1920s the population of urban America grew by some 15 million people—at the time, the greatest 10-year jump in American history. Cities grew largely by depopulating rural areas. In the most dramatic manifestation of the overall trend, more than a million African Americans migrated from the rural South to the urban North.

as incorporated municipalities with 2500 people or more, the Census Bureau had created hundreds of statistical illusions. New York with its millions of in-habitants ranked in the census tables alongside Sac Prairie, Wisconsin, whose population hovered barely above the mystical mark of 2500, and tiny Hyden, a town along the Cumberland plateau of eastern Kentucky.

Most citizens, the Smiths aside, dwelled in an earlier America and clung to many of its values. The poet August Derleth grew up in Sac Prairie. As a 10-year-old in 1919 he could hear the "howl of wolves" at night. The town observed changing seasons not with new fashions but by the appearance and disappearance of plants and animals. In Hyden, Kentucky, Main Street was still unpaved. By 1930 there were still only 10 automobiles in the county. God-fearing Baptists worshiped together as their parents had before them and still repaired to the Middle Fork of the Kentucky River for an open-air baptism when they declared their new birth in Christ. They would have nothing to do with flapper girls or the showy miracles of Aimee McPherson.

As much as some Americans resisted the transforming forces of modern life, the New Era could not be walled out. New industrial technologies stimulated a host of consumer goods, while large corporations developed more "modern" bureaucracies to make workers and production lines more efficient. Whether Americans embraced the New Era or condemned it, change came nonetheless, in the form of a mass-produced consumer economy, a culture shaped by mass media, and a more materialistic society.

## THE ROARING ECONOMY

In the 1920s, the United States was in the midst of a revolution in production. Manufacturing rose 64 percent; output per workhour, 40 percent. The sale of electricity doubled; the consumption of fuel oil more than doubled. Between 1922 and 1927 the economy grew by 7 percent a year—the largest peacetime rate ever. If anything roared in the "Roaring Twenties," it was industry and commerce.

### Technology and Consumer Spending

Technology was partly responsible. Steam turbines and shovels, electric motors, belt and bucket conveyors, and countless other new machines became commonplace at work sites. Machines replaced 200,000 workers each year, and a new phrase—"technological unemployment"—entered the vocabulary. Even so, demand, especially for new consumer goods, kept the labor force growing at a rate faster than that of the population. And pay improved. Between 1919 and 1927, average income climbed nearly $150 for each American.

As the industrial economy matured, more consumer goods appeared on store shelves: cigarette lighters, wristwatches, radios, panchromatic film. The improvement in productivity helped to keep prices down. The cost of a tire and an inner tube, for example, dropped by half between 1914 and 1929. Meanwhile, the purchasing power of wage earners jumped by 20 percent. Americans enjoyed the highest standard of living any people had ever known.

Yet for all the prosperity, a dangerous imbalance in the economy developed. Most Americans were putting very little of their savings into the bank. Personal debt was rising two and a half times faster than personal income, an unhealthy sign of consumers scrambling to spend.

### The Booming Construction Industry

Along with technology and consumer spending, new "boom industries" promoted economic growth. Construction was one. In a rebound after the war years, even cities the size of Beaumont, Texas, Memphis, Tennessee, and Syracuse, New York, were constructing buildings of 20 stories or more. Residential construction doubled as people moved from cities to suburbs. Suburban Grosse Point, near Detroit, grew by 700 percent; and Beverly Hills, on the outskirts of Los Angeles, by 2500 percent. Road construction made suburban life possible and pumped millions of dollars into the economy. In 1919 Oregon, New Mexico, and Colorado hit on a novel idea for financing roads: a tax on gasoline. Within a decade every state had one.

Construction stimulated other businesses too: steel, concrete, lumber, home mortgages, and insurance. It even helped change the nation's eating habits. The limited storage space of small "kitchenettes" in new apartments boosted supermarket chains and the canning industry. And as shipments of fresh fruits and vegetables sped across new roads, interest in nutrition grew. Vitamins, publicized with new zeal, appeared on breakfast tables.

### The Automobile

No industry boomed more than auto manufacturing. Although cars had first appeared on streets at the turn of the century, for many years they remained little more than expensive toys. By 1920 there were 10 million in America, a sizable number. But by 1929 the total had jumped to 26 million, one for every 5 people (compared with one for every 43 in Britain). Automakers bought one-seventh of the nation's steel and more rubber, plate glass, nickel, and lead than any other industry. By the end of the decade, one American in four somehow earned a living from automobiles.

Henry Ford made it possible by pushing standardization and mass production to such ruthless extremes that the automobile became affordable. Trading

*Henry Ford*

on his fame as a race-car manufacturer, he founded the Ford Motor Company in 1903 with the dream of building a "motor car for the multitude." "Everybody wants to be somewhere he ain't," Ford said. The way to succeed was to reduce manufacturing costs by making all the cars alike, "just like one pin is like another pin." In 1908 Ford perfected the Model T. It had a 20-horsepower engine and a body of steel. It was high enough to ride the worst roads, and it came in only one color: black.

Priced at $845, the Model T was cheap by industry standards but still too costly and too time-consuming to build. Two Ford engineers suggested copying a practice of Chicago meatpacking houses, where beef carcasses were carried on moving chains past meat dressers. In 1914 Ford introduced the moving assembly line. A conveyor belt, positioned waist high to eliminate bending or walking, propelled the chassis at six feet per minute as stationary workers put the cars together. The process cut assembly time in half. In 1925 new Model Ts were rolling off the line every 10 seconds. At $290, almost anybody could buy one. By 1927 Ford had sold 15 million of his "tin lizzies."

Ford was also a social prophet. Breaking with other manufacturers, he preached a "doctrine of high wages." According to it, workers with extra money

*Doctrine of high wages*

in their pockets would buy enough to sustain a booming prosperity. In 1915 Ford's plants in Dearborn established the "Five-Dollar Day," twice the wage rate in Detroit. He reduced working hours from 48 to 40 a week and cut the workweek to five days.

Yet Ford workers were not happy. Ford admitted that the repetitive operations on his assembly line made it scarcely possible "that any man would care to continue long at the same job." The Five-Dollar Day was designed, in part, to reduce the turnover rate of 300 percent a year at Ford plants. Ford recouped his profits by speeding up the assembly line and enforcing ruthless efficiencies. Ford workers could not talk, whistle, smoke, or sit on the job. They wore frozen expressions called "Fordization of the Face" and communicated in the "Ford Whisper" without moving their lips. A "Sociological Department" spied on workers in their homes, and the "Education Department" taught plant procedures and also "Americanization" classes where immigrant workers learned English, proper dress, even etiquette.

By making automobiles available to nearly everyone, the industry changed the face of America. The spreading web of paved roads fueled urban sprawl, real

*A car culture*

estate booms in California and Florida, and a new roadside economy of restaurants, service stations, and motels. Thousands of "auto camps" opened to provide tourists with tents and crude toilets. Automobile travel broke down rural isolation and advanced common dialects and manners. By 1930 almost two farm families in three had cars.

Across the country the automobile gave the young unprecedented freedom from parental authority. After hearing 30 cases of "sex crimes" (19 had occurred in cars), an exasperated juvenile court judge declared that the automobile was "a house of prostitution on wheels." It was, of course, much more. The automobile was to the 1920s what the railroad had been to the nineteenth century: the catalyst for economic growth, a transportation revolution, and a cultural symbol.

## The Business of America

In business, said Henry Ford, the "fundamentals are all summed up in the single word, 'service.'" President Calvin Coolidge echoed the theme of service to society in 1925: "The business of America is business. The man who builds a factory builds a temple. The man who works there worships there." A generation earlier, progressives had criticized business for its social irresponsibility. But the wartime contributions of business managers and the return of prosperity in 1922 gained them a renewed respect.

Encouraged by federal permissiveness, a wave of mergers swept the economy. Between 1919 and 1930, some 8000 firms disappeared as large gobbled

*Corporate consolidation*

small. Oligopolies (where a few firms dominated whole industries) grew in steel, meatpacking, cigarettes, and other businesses. National chains began to replace local "mom and pop" stores. By 1929, one bag of groceries in ten came from the 15,000 red-and-gold markets of the Great Atlantic and Pacific Tea Company, commonly known as A & P.

This expansion and consolidation meant that national wealth was being controlled not by affluent individuals, but by corporations. The model of modern business was the large, bureaucratic corporation, in which those who actually managed the company had little to do with those who owned it, the shareholders. Stocks and bonds were becoming so widely dispersed that few individuals held more than 1 or 2 percent of any company.

A salaried bureaucracy of executives and plant managers formed a new elite, which no longer set their sights on becoming swashbuckling entrepreneurs like

*Managerial elite* the Carnegies and Rockefellers of old. The new managers looked to work their way up a corporate ladder. They were less interested in risk than in productivity and stability. Managers subdivided operations and put experts in charge. Corporate leaders learned the techniques of "scientific management" taught at Harvard and other new schools of business, through journals, professional societies, and consulting firms. And they channeled earnings back into their companies to expand factories and carry on research. By the end of the decade more than a thousand firms had research laboratories.

## *Welfare Capitalism*

The new scientific management also stressed good relations between managers and employees. There was reason to, for the rash of postwar strikes had left business leaders suspicious as ever of labor unions and determined to find ways to limit their influence.

Some tactics were more strong-armed than scientific. In 1921 the National Association of Manufacturers, the Chamber of Commerce, and other em-

*The American* ployer groups launched the "American Plan," aimed at ending
*Plan* "closed shops," factories where only union members could work. Employers made workers sign agreements disavowing union membership. Labor organizers called them "yellow dog contracts." Companies infiltrated unions with spies, locked union members out of factories if they protested, and boycotted firms that hired union labor.

The benevolent side of the American Plan involved a social innovation called "welfare capitalism." Companies like General Electric and Bethlehem Steel pledged to care for their employees and give them incentives for working hard. They built clean, safe factories, installed cafeterias, hired trained dietitians, formed baseball teams and glee clubs. Several hundred firms encouraged perhaps a million workers to buy company stock. And they had more enroll in company unions. Called "Kiss-Me Clubs" for their lack of power, they nonetheless offered what few independent unions could match: health and safety insurance; a grievance procedure; and representation for African Americans, women, and immigrants.

But welfare capitalism embraced barely 5 percent of the workforce and often gave benefits only to skilled laborers, the hardest to replace. Most companies cared more for production than for contented employees. In the 1920s a family of four could live in "minimum health and decency" on $2000 a year. The average industrial wage was $1304. Thus working-class families often needed more than one wage earner just to get by. Over a million children, ages 10 to 15, still worked full-time in 1920. Some received as little as 20 cents an hour.

In 1927, in the most famous strike of the decade, 2500 mill hands in the textile town of Gastonia, North Carolina, left their jobs. Even strikebreakers walked out. Eventually, authorities broke the strike, presaging a national trend. A year later there were only 629 strikes, a record low for the nation. Union membership sank from almost 5 million in 1921 to less than 3.5 million in 1929. "The AF of L [American Federation of Labor] machinery has practically collapsed," reported one union official.

## The Consumer Culture

During the late nineteenth century the economy had boomed too, but much of its growth went into nonconsumer goods: huge steel factories and rail, telephone, and electric networks. By World War I, these industrial networks had penetrated enough of the country to create mass markets. As a greater percentage of the nation's industries turned out consumer goods, prosperity hinged increasingly on consumption. If consumers purchased more goods, production would increase, at the same time bringing down costs. The lower production costs would allow for lower prices, which would lift sales still higher, increase employment, and repeat the cycle again.

Everything in this cycle of prosperity depended on consumer purchases. In the consumer economy, wives ceased to be homemakers who canned fruit and baked their own bread to become buyers of processed food and manufactured goods. Husbands were not merely workers but, equally important, consumers of mortgages and other forms of credit. Even vacationers became consumers— in this case, consumers of leisure time, as more employees got two-week (unpaid) vacations. Consumption was the key to prosperity, and increased consumption rested on two innovations: advertising to encourage people to buy and credit to help them pay.

Before World War I advertising had been a grubby business, hawking the often exaggerated virtues of products. Around the turn of the century, advertisers began a critical shift from emphasizing *products* to stressing a consumer's *desires:* health, popularity, social prestige. During the war, the Committee on Public Information demonstrated the power of emotional appeals as an instrument of mass persuasion. Behavioral psychologists like John B. Watson, who left Johns Hopkins University for an advertising agency in the 1920s, helped to develop more sophisticated techniques for attracting customers.

*Role of advertising*

Albert Lasker, the owner of Chicago's largest advertising firm, Lord and Thomas, created modern advertising in America. His eye-catching ads were hard-hitting, positive, and often preposterous. To expand the sales of Lucky Strike cigarettes Lord and Thomas advertisements claimed that smoking made

E Y E W I T N E S S   T O   H I S T O R Y

## A Mexican Laborer Sings of the Sorrows of the New Era

| | |
|---|---|
| Desde Morelia vine enganchado | I came under contract from Morelia |
| ganar los dólars fué mi ilusión | To earn dollars was my dream, |
| compré zapatos, compré sombrero, | I bought shoes and I bought a hat |
| y hasta me puse de pantalón. | And even put on trousers. |
| | |
| Pues me decían que aquí los dólars | For they told me that here the dollars |
| se pepenaban y de a montón | Were scattered about in heaps; |
| que las muchachas y que los teatros | That there were girls and theaters |
| y que aquí todo era vacilón. | And that here everything was good fun. |
| | |
| Y ahora me encuentro ya sin resuello | And now I'm overwhelmed— |
| soy zapatero de profesión | I am a shoemaker by trade |
| pero aquí dicen que soy camello | But here they say I'm a camel |
| y a pura pala y puro azadón. | And good only for pick and shovel. |
| | |
| De qué me sirve saber mi oficio | What good is it to know my trade |
| si fabricantes hay de a montón | If there are manufacturers by the score, |
| y en tanto que hago yo dos botines | And while I make two little shoes |
| ellos avientan más de un millón | They turn out more than a million. |
| | |
| Hablar no quieren muchos paisanos | Many Mexicans don't care to speak |
| lo que su mamá les enseñó | The language their mothers taught them |
| y andan diciendo que son hispanos | And go about saying they are Spanish |
| y renegando del pabellón | And denying their country's flag. |

people slimmer and more courageous. "Lucky's" became one of the most popular brands in America. Bogus doctors and dentists endorsed all kinds of products, including toothpaste containing potassium chloride—eight grams of which was lethal. "Halitosis" was plucked from the pages of an obscure medical dictionary and used to sell Listerine mouthwash.

Advertisers encouraged Americans to borrow against tomorrow to purchase what advertising convinced them they wanted today. Installment buying had

*Installment buying as credit*

once been confined to sewing machines and pianos. In the 1920s it grew into the tenth-biggest business in the United States. In 1919 automaker Alfred Sloan created millions of new customers by establishing the General Motors Acceptance Corporation, the nation's first consumer credit organization. By 1929 Americans were buying most of their

Los hay mas prietos que el chapote
pero presumen de ser sajón
andan polveados hasta el cogote
y usan enaguas por pantalón

Some are darker than *chapote*
But they pretend to be Saxon;
They go about powdered to the back of
  the neck
And wear skirts for trousers.

Van las muchachas casi encueradas
y a la tienda llaman estor
llevan las piernas rete chorreadas
pero con medias de esas chifón.

The girls go about almost naked
And call *la tienda* "estor" ["store"]
They go around with dirt-streaked legs
But with those stockings of chiffon.

Hasta me vieja me la han cambiado
viste de seda rete rabón
anda pintada como piñata
y va en las noches al dancing jol.

Even my old woman has changed on
  me—
She wears a bob-tailed dress of silk,
Goes about painted like a *piñata*
And goes at night to the dancing hall.

Mis chilpallates hablan puro "inglis"
ya no les cuadra nuestro español
me llaman fader y no trabajan
y son reguënos pa'l chárleston.

My kids speak perfect English
And have no use for our Spanish
They call me "fader" and don't work
And are crazy about the Charleston.

Ya estoy cansado de esta tonteada
yo me devuëlvo para Michoacán
hay de recuerdo dejo a la vieja
a ver si alguno se la quiere armar.

I am tired of all this nonsense
I'm going back to Michoacán;
As a parting memory I leave the old
  woman
To see if someone else wants to burden
  himself.

Paul S. Taylor, *Mexican Labor in the United States*, Vol. II (Berkeley: University of California Press, 1932), pp. vi–vii.

cars, radios, and furniture on the installment plan. Consumer debt had jumped 250 percent to $7 billion, almost twice the federal budget.

## A MASS SOCIETY

In the evening after a day's work in the fields—perhaps in front of an adobe house built by one of the western sugar-beet companies—Mexican American workers might gather to chat or sing a *corrido* or two. The *corrido*, or ballad, was an old Mexican folk tradition. But the subjects changed over time, to match the concerns of those who sang them. One *corrido* during the 1920s told of a field laborer distressed that his family had rejected Mexican customs in favor of new

American fashions (see "Eyewitness to History"). His wife, he sang, now dressed in "a bob-tailed dress of silk" and, wearing makeup, went about "painted like a *piñata.*" As for his children, they spoke English, not Spanish, and loved all the new dances. It was enough to make him long for Mexico.

For Americans from all backgrounds, the New Era was witness to "a vast dissolution of ancient habits," commented columnist Walter Lippmann. Mass marketing and mass distribution led not simply to a higher standard of living but to a life less regional and diverse. In place of moral standards set by local communities and churches came "modern" fashions and attitudes, spread by the new mass media of movies, radio, and magazines. In the place of "ancient habits" came the forces of mass society: independent women, freer love, standardized culture, urban energy and impersonality, and growing alienation.

### The New Woman

The "New Woman," charged critics, was at the bottom of what Frederick Lewis Allen called the "revolution in manners and morals" of the twenties. The most flamboyant of them wore makeup, close-fitting felt hats, long-waisted dresses, strings of beads, and unbuckled galoshes. They called themselves "flappers." Cocktail in hand, cigarette in mouth, footloose and economically free, the New Woman became a symbol of liberation to some. To others she represented the decline of civilization.

World War I had served as a powerful social catalyst. Before the war women could be arrested for smoking cigarettes openly, using profanity, appearing on public beaches without stockings, and driving automobiles without men beside them. Wartime America ended many of these restrictions. With women bagging explosives, running locomotives, and drilling with rifles, the old taboos often seemed silly.

Disseminating birth control information by mail had also been a crime before the war. By the armistice there was a birth control clinic in Brooklyn, a National Birth Control League, and later an American Birth Control League led by Margaret Sanger. Sanger's crusade had begun as an attempt to save poor women from the burdens of unwanted pregnancies (page 602). By the 1920s her message had found a receptive middle-class audience. Surveys showed that by the 1930s nearly 90 percent of college-educated couples practiced contraception.

*Margaret Sanger*

Being able to a degree to control the matter of pregnancy, women felt less guilt about enjoying sex. In 1909 Sigmund Freud had come to America to lecture on his theories of coping with the unconscious and overcoming harmful repressions. Some of Freud's ideas, specifically his emphasis on childhood sexuality, shocked Americans, while most of his complex theories sailed over their heads. As popularized in the 1920s, Freudian psychology stamped sexuality as a key to health.

*Freudian psychology*

"Street selling was torture for me,"
Margaret Sanger recalled of her efforts
to promote the *Birth Control Review*. A
heckler once shouted: "Have you ever
heard God's word to be fruitful and
multiply?" The reply came back,
"They've done that already."

Such changes in the social climate were real enough, but the life of a flapper girl hardly mirrored the lives and work routines of most American women.

*Women
and labor*

Over the decade, the female labor force grew by only 1 percent.
As late as 1930 nearly 60 percent of all working women were
African American or foreign-born and generally held low-paying
jobs in domestic service or the garment industry. At home, women found that
even new, "labor-saving" appliances could increase their burdens by raising
standards of household cleanliness.

The New Era did spawn new careers for women. The consumer culture
capitalized on a preoccupation with appearance and led to the opening of some
40,000 beauty parlors staffed by hairdressers, manicurists, and cosmeticians.
"Women's fields" carved out by progressive reformers expanded opportunities
in education, libraries, and social welfare. Women earned a higher percentage
of doctoral degrees (from 10 percent in 1910 to 15.4 percent in 1930) and held
more college teaching posts than ever (32 percent). But in most areas, professional men resisted the "feminization" of the workforce. The number of female
doctors dropped by half. Medical schools imposed restrictive quotas, and 90
percent of all hospitals rejected female interns.

In 1924 two women—Nellie Ross in Wyoming and Miriam ("Ma") Ferguson
in Texas—were elected governors, the first female chief executives. For the most

part, though, women continued to be marginalized in party politics while remaining widely involved in educational and welfare programs. Operating outside male-dominated political parties, women activists succeeded in winning passage of the Sheppard–Towner Federal Maternity and Infancy Act in 1921 to fight high rates of infant mortality with rural prenatal and baby care centers. It was the first federal welfare statute. Yet by the end of the decade the Sheppard–Towner Act had lapsed.

In the wake of their greatest success, the hard-won vote for women, feminists splintered. The National Woman Suffrage Association disbanded in 1920.

*Equal Rights Amendment*     In its place the League of Women Voters was begun to encourage informed voting. For the more militant Alice Paul and her allies, that was not enough. Their National Woman's party pressed for a constitutional Equal Rights Amendment (ERA). Social workers and others familiar with the conditions under which women labored opposed it. Death and injury rates for women were nearly double those for men. To them the ERA meant losing the protection as well as the benefits women derived from mothers' pensions and maternity insurance. Joined by most men and a majority of Congress they fought the amendment to a standstill.

## Mass Media

In balmy California, where movies could be made year-round, Hollywood helped give the New Woman notoriety as a temptress and trendsetter. When sexy Theda Bara (the "vamp") appeared in *The Blue Flame* in 1920, crowds mobbed theaters. And just as Hollywood dictated standards of physical attractiveness, it became the judge of taste and fashion in countless other ways because motion pictures were a virtually universal medium. There was no need for literacy or fluency, no need even for sound, given the power of the pictures parading across the screen.

Motion pictures, invented in 1889, had first been shown in tiny neighborhood theaters called "nickelodeons." For only a nickel, patrons watched a silent

*Motion pictures*     screen flicker with moving images as an accompanist played music on a tinny piano. The audience was anything but silent. The theater reverberated with the cracking of Indian nuts, the day's equivalent of popcorn, while young cowboys shot off their Kilgore repeating cap pistols during dramatic scenes. Often children read the subtitles aloud to their immigrant parents, translating into Italian, Yiddish, or German.

After the first feature-length film, *The Great Train Robbery* (1903), productions became rich in spectacle, attracted middle-class audiences, and turned into America's favorite form of entertainment. By 1926 more than 20,000 movie houses offered customers lavish theaters with overstuffed seats, live music, and a celluloid dream world—all for 50 cents or less. At the end of the decade, they were drawing over 100 million people a week, roughly the equivalent of the national population.

In the spring of 1920 Frank Conrad of the Westinghouse Company in East Pittsburgh rigged up a research station in his barn and started transmitting phonograph music and baseball scores to local wireless operators. An ingenious Pittsburgh newspaper began advertising radio

*Radio*

equipment to "be used by those who listen to Dr. Conrad's programs." Six months later Westinghouse officials opened the first licensed broadcasting station in history, KDKA, to stimulate sales of their supplies. By 1922 the number of licensed stations had jumped to 430. Nearly one home in three had a radio ("furniture that talks," comedian Fred Allen called it) by 1930.

At first radio was seen as a civilizing force. "The air is your theater, your college, your newspaper, your library," exalted one ad in 1924. But with the growing number of sets came commercial broadcasting, catering to more common tastes. Almost the entire nation listened to "Amos 'n' Andy," a comedy about African Americans created by two white vaudevillians in 1929. At night families gathered around the radio instead of the hearth, listening to a concert, perhaps, rather than going out to hear music. Ticket sales at vaudeville theaters collapsed. The aged, the sick, and the isolated, moreover, could be "at home but never alone," as one radio ad declared. Linked by nothing but airwaves, Americans were finding themselves part of a vast new community of listeners.

Print journalism also broadened its audience during the 1920s. In 1923 Yale classmates Henry R. Luce and Briton Hadden rewrote news stories in a snappy style, mixed them with photographs, and created the country's

*Mass circulation weeklies*

first national weekly, *Time* magazine. Fifty-five giant newspaper chains distributed 230 newspapers with a combined circulation of 13 million by 1927. Though they controlled less than 10 percent of all papers, the chains pioneered modern mass news techniques. Editors relied on central offices and syndicates to prepare editorials, sports, gossip, and Sunday features for a national readership.

## A Youth Culture

By the 1920s, the drive for public education had placed a majority of teenagers in high school for the first time in American history. College enrollment reached 10 percent of the eligible population by 1928; in 1890 it had been less than 3 percent. A "peer culture" of adolescents emerged as children and teens spent more time outside the family among people their own age. Revolving around school and friends, its components were remarkably modern—athletics, clubs, sororities and fraternities, dating, proms, "bull sessions," and moviegoing.

Tolerance for premarital sex seems to have grown in the 1920s ("necking" and "petting" parties replaced sedate tea parties), but the new subculture of youth still tied sexual relations to love. Casual sex remained rare; what changed was the point at which sexual intimacy occurred. A growing minority of young women reported having premarital intercourse, for example, but only with their future husbands. Unsupervised dating and "going together" replaced chaperoned courting.

For all the frivolity and rebelliousness it promoted, the new youth culture tended to fuse the young to the larger social culture by promoting widely held values: competitiveness, merit through association, service, prestige. Even notorious young flappers, if they wed, found themselves defined by home and family.

### *"Ain't We Got Fun?"*

"Ev'ry morning, ev'ry evening, ain't we got fun?" ran the 1921 hit song. As the average hours on the job each week decreased from 47.2 in 1920 to 42 by 1930,

*Spectator sports*

spending on amusement and recreation shot up 300 percent. Spectator sports came of age. In 1921, some 60,000 fans paid $1.8 million to see Jack Dempsey, the "Manassas Mauler," knock out French champion Georges Carpentier. Millions more listened as radio took them ringside for the first time in sports history. Universities constructed huge stadiums for football, such as Ohio State's 64,000 seater. By the end of the decade college football games were outdrawing major league baseball.

Baseball still remained the national pastime but became a bigger business. An ugly World Series scandal in 1919 led owners to appoint Judge Kenesaw Mountain Landis "czar" of the sport early in the decade. His strict rule reformed the game. In 1920 the son of immigrants revolutionized it. George Herman "Babe" Ruth hit 54 home runs and made the New York Yankees the first club to attract a million fans in one season. A heroic producer in an era of consumption, Ruth was also baseball's bad boy. He smoked, drank, cursed, and chased every skirt in sight. Under the guidance of the first modern sports agent, Christy Walsh, Ruth became the highest-paid player in the game and made a fortune endorsing everything from automobiles to clothing.

At parties old diversions—charades, card tricks, recitations—faded in popularity as dancing took over. The ungainly camel walk, the sultry tango, and in 1924 the frantic Charleston were the urban standards. Country barns featured a revival of square dancing with music provided by Detroit's WBZ, courtesy of Henry Ford. And from the turn-of-the-century brothels and gaming houses of New Orleans, Memphis, and St. Louis came a rhythmic, compelling music that swept into nightclubs and over the airwaves: jazz.

Jazz was a remarkably complex blend of several older African American musical traditions, combining the soulfulness of the blues with the brighter synco-

*Jazz*

pated rhythms of ragtime music. The distinctive style of jazz bands came from a marvelous improvising as the musicians embellished melodies and played off one another. The style spread when the "Original Dixieland Jazz Band" (hardly original but possessed of the commercial advantage of being white) recorded a few numbers for the phonograph. The music became a sensation in New York in 1917 and spread across the country. Black New Orleans stalwarts like Joe "King" Oliver's Creole Jazz Band began touring, and in 1924 Paul Whiteman inaugurated respectable "white" jazz in a concert at Carnegie Hall. When self-appointed guardians of good taste denounced such music as "intellectual and spiritual debauchery," Whiteman disagreed: "Jazz is the folk music of the machine age."

## The Art of Alienation

Before World War I a generation of young writers had begun rebelling against Victorian purity. The savagery of the war drove many of them even further from any faith in reason or progress. Instead they embraced a "nihilism" that denied all meaning in life. When the war ended, they turned their resentment against American life, especially its small towns, big businesses, conformity, technology, and materialism. Some led unconventional lives in New York City's Greenwich

*Expatriates* Village. Others, called expatriates, left the country altogether for the artistic freedom of London and Paris. Their alienation helped produce a literary outpouring unmatched in American history.

On the eve of World War I the poet Ezra Pound had predicted an "American Risorgimento" that would "make the Italian Renaissance look like a tempest in a teapot." From Europe the expatriate Pound began to make it happen. Abandoning rhyme and meter in his poetry, he decried the "botched civilization" that had produced the war. Another voluntary exile, T. S. Eliot, bemoaned the emptiness of modern life in his epic poem *The Waste Land* (1922). Ernest Hemingway captured the disillusionment of the age in *The Sun Also Rises* (1926) and *A Farewell to Arms* (1929), novels in which resolution came as it had in war—by death.

At home Minnesota-born Sinclair Lewis, the first American to win a Nobel prize in literature, sketched a scathing vision of midwestern small-town life in *Main Street* (1920). The book described "savorless people . . . saying mechanical things about the excellence of Ford automobiles, and viewing themselves as the greatest race in the world." His next novel, *Babbitt* (1922), dissected small-town businessman George Follansbee Babbitt, a peppy realtor from the fictional city of Zenith. Faintly absurd and supremely dull, Babbitt was the epitome of the average.

The novels of another Minnesotan, F. Scott Fitzgerald, glorified youth and romantic individualism but found redemption nowhere. Fitzgerald's heroes, like Amory Blaine in *This Side of Paradise* (1920), spoke for a generation "grown up to find all Gods dead, all wars fought, all faiths in man shaken." Like most writers of the decade, Fitzgerald saw life largely as a personal affair—opulent, self-absorbing, and ultimately tragic.

## A "New Negro"

As World War I seared white intellectuals, so too did it galvanize black Americans. Wartime labor shortages had spurred a migration of half a million African Americans out of the rural South into northern industrial cities. But postwar unemployment and racial violence quickly dashed black hopes for equality. Common folk in these urban enclaves found an outlet for their alienation in a charismatic nationalist from Jamaica named Marcus Garvey.

Garvey brought his organization, the Universal Negro Improvement Association (UNIA), to America in 1916 in hopes of restoring black pride by

*Marcus Garvey*

returning Africans to Africa and Africa to Africans. "Up you mighty race," he told his followers, "you can accomplish what you will." When Garvey spoke at the first national UNIA convention in 1920, over 25,000 supporters jammed Madison Square Garden in New York to listen. Even his harshest critics admitted there were at least half a million members in more than 30 branches of his organization. It was the first mass movement of African Americans in history. But in 1925 Garvey was convicted of mail fraud for having oversold stock in his Black Star Line, the steamship company founded to return African Americans to Africa. His dream shattered.

As Garvey rose to prominence, a renaissance of black literature, painting, and sculpture was brewing in Harlem. The first inklings came in 1922 when

*Harlem Renaissance*

Claude McKay, another Jamaican immigrant, published a book of poems entitled *White Shadows*. In his most famous poem, "If We Must Die," McKay mixed defiance and dignity: "Like men we'll face the murderous, cowardly pack/Pressed to the wall, dying but fighting back!"

Often supported by white patrons, or "angels," young black writers and artists found their subjects in the street life of cities, the folkways of the rural South, and the primitivism of preindustrial cultures. Poet Langston Hughes reminded his readers of the ancient heritage of African Americans in "The Negro Speaks of Rivers," while Zora Neale Hurston collected folktales, songs,

Born in Jamaica in 1887, Marcus Garvey founded his "Back to Africa" movement in 1914 and brought it to the United States in 1916. In 1925 he went to prison for mail fraud, before being deported two years later.

and prayers of black southerners. Though generally not a racial protest, the Harlem Renaissance drew on the growing assertiveness of African Americans as well as on the alienation of white intellectuals. In 1925 Alain Locke, a black professor from Howard University, collected a sampling of their works in *The New Negro*. The title reflected not only an artistic movement but also a new racial consciousness.

## DEFENDERS OF THE FAITH

As mass society pushed the country into a future of machines, organization, middle-class living, and cosmopolitan diversity, not everyone approved. Dr. and Mrs. Wilbur Crafts, the authors of *Intoxicating Drinks and Drugs in All Lands and Times*, set forth a litany of modern sins that tempted young people in this "age of cities." "Foul pictures, corrupt literature, leprous shows, gambling slot machines, saloons, and Sabbath breaking. . . . *We are trying to raise saints in hell.*"

The changing values of the New Era seemed especially threatening to traditionalists like the Crafts. Their deeply held beliefs reflected the rural roots of so many Americans: an ethic that valued neighborliness, small communities, and a homogeneity of race, religion, and ethnicity. Opponents of the new ways could be found among not only country folk but also rural migrants to cities as well as an embattled Protestant elite. All were determined to defend the older faiths against the modern age.

### Nativism and Immigration Restriction

In 1921, two Italian aliens and admitted anarchists presented a dramatic challenge to those older faiths. Nicola Sacco and Bartolomeo Vanzetti were sentenced to death for a shoe company robbery and murder in South

*Sacco and Vanzetti*

Braintree, Massachusetts. Critics charged that they were innocent and convicted only of being foreign-born radicals. During the trial, the presiding judge had scorned them in private as "anarchist bastards," and in 1927, they were executed. For protesters around the world, the execution was a symbol of American bigotry and prejudice.

By then, nativism—a rabid hostility to foreigners—had produced the most restrictive immigration laws in American history. In the aftermath of World War I immigration was running close to 1 million a year, almost as high as prewar levels. Most immigrants came from eastern and southern Europe and from Mexico; most were Catholics and Jews. Alarmed white native-born Protestants warned that if the flood continued, Americans might become "a hybrid race of people as worthless and futile as the good-for-nothing mongrels of Central America and Southeastern Europe." Appreciating the benefits of a shrunken labor pool, the American Federation of Labor supported restriction too.

In the Southwest, Mexicans and Mexican Americans became a target of concern. The Spanish had inhabited the region for nearly 400 years, producing a rich blend of European and Indian cultures. By 1900 about 300,000 Mexican Americans lived in the United States. In the following decade Mexicans fleeing poverty and a revolution in 1910 almost doubled the Latino population of Texas and New Mexico. In California it quadrupled. During World War I, labor shortages led authorities to relax immigration laws, and in the 1920s American farmers opened a campaign to attract Mexican farmworkers.

*Mexican Americans*

Thousands of single young men, known as *solos*, also crossed the border to catch trains for Detroit, Kansas City, and other industrial cities. By the end of the 1920s, northern industrial cities had thriving communities of Mexicans. In these *barrios* Spanish-speaking newcomers settled into an immigrant life of family and festivals, churchgoing, hard work, and slow adaptation. Like other immigrants, many returned home, but others brought their families. The census of 1930 listed nearly 1.5 million Mexicans living in the United States, not including an untold number who had entered the country illegally.

In 1921 Senators Henry Cabot Lodge of Massachusetts and Hiram Johnson of California sponsored legislation that cut off the flood of immigrants at 350,000 a year. A quota parceled out available spaces by admitting up to 3 percent of each nationality living in the United States as of 1910. Asian immigration was virtually banned. In 1924 a new National Origins Act reduced the quota to 150,000 and pushed the base year back to 1890, before the bulk of southern and eastern Europeans arrived.

*National Origins acts*

The National Origins Act fixed the pattern of immigration for the next four decades. Immigration from southern and eastern Europe was reduced to a trickle. The free flow of Europeans to America, a migration of classes and nationalities that had been unimpeded for 300 years, came to an end.

## The "Noble Experiment"

Nativists who distrusted immigrants usually viewed alcohol as a particular problem of the immigrant lower classes. Progressive prohibitionists stressed the need for efficiency and public health, which they contrasted with the corrupting influence of the immigrant saloon culture. German brewers and their beer gardens came under special suspicion during World War I.

For nearly a hundred years reformers had tried—with sporadic success—to reduce the consumption of alcohol. Their most ambitious campaign climaxed in January 1920, when the Eighteenth Amendment to the Constitution went into effect. It outlawed the sale of liquor. Prohibition was not total: private citizens could still drink. They simply could not make, sell, transport, or import any "intoxicating beverage"

*Eighteenth Amendment*

containing 0.5 percent alcohol or more. By some estimates, consumption was reduced by as much as half.

From the start, however, enforcement was underfunded and understaffed. In large cities "speakeasies"—taverns operating undercover—were plentiful. Rural stills continued to turn out "moonshine." Even so, the consequences of

*Consequences of Prohibition*

so vast a social experiment were significant and often unexpected. Prohibition reversed the prewar trend toward beer and wine, since hard liquor brought greater profits to bootleggers. It also advanced women's rights. While saloons had discriminated against "ladies," having them enter by a separate door, speakeasies welcomed them. Prohibition helped to line the pockets—and boost the fame—of gangsters, including "Scarface" Al Capone. Like Capone, thousands of poor immigrants looked to illegal bootlegging to move them out of the slums. As rival gangs fought over territory, cities erupted in a mayhem of violence.

Prohibition can be best understood as cultural and class legislation. Support had run deepest in Protestant churches, especially the evangelical Baptists and Methodists. And there had always been a strong antiurban and anti-immigrant bias among reformers. As it turned out, the steepest decline in drinking occurred among working-class ethnics. Only the well-to-do had enough money to drink regularly without risking death or blindness, the common effects of cheap, tainted liquor. Traditionalists might celebrate the triumph of the "noble experiment," but modern urbanites either ignored or resented it.

## KKK

On Thanksgiving Day 1915, just outside Atlanta, 16 men trudged up a rocky trail to the crest of Stone Mountain. There, as night fell, they set ablaze a huge wooden cross and swore allegiance to the Invisible Empire, Knights of the Ku Klux Klan. The KKK was reborn.

The modern Klan, a throwback to the hooded order of Reconstruction days (page 461), reflected the insecurities of the New Era. Klansmen worried about the changes and conflicts in American society, which they attributed to the rising tide of immigrants, "uppity women," and African Americans who refused to "recognize their place." Whereas any white man could join the old Klan, the new one admitted only "native born, white, gentile [Protestant] Americans." And the reborn Klan was not confined to the South, like the hooded night riders of old. By the 1920s its capital had become Indianapolis, Indiana. More than half of its leadership and over a third of its members came from cities of more than 100,000 people.

The new Klan drew on the culture of small-town America. It was patriotic, gave to local charities, and boasted the kind of outfits and rituals adopted by many fraternal lodges. Klansmen wore white hooded sheets and satin robes, sang songs called "klodes," and even used a secret hand-"klasp." A typical gathering brought the whole family to a barbecue with fireworks and hymn singing, the evening capped by the burning of a giant cross.

Members came mostly from the middle and working classes: small businesspeople, clerical workers, independent professionals, farmers, and laborers

*Social composition of the Klan*

with few skills. Sometimes they lived on the edge of unemployment and poverty. The Klan offered them status, security, and the promise of restoring an older America. It touted white supremacy, chastity, fidelity, and parental authority and fought for laissez-faire capitalism and fundamental Protestantism. When boycotts and whispering campaigns failed to cleanse communities of Jews, Mexicans, Japanese,

A brutal form of racial violence, lynching continued to be a national scourge well into the 1920s and 1930s, when Paul Cadmus drew this searing study entitled *To the Lynching!* In 1921, after a long campaign by the National Association for the Advancement of Colored People, an antilynching bill was introduced in Congress but fell victim to a Senate filibuster.

or others who offended their social code, the Klan resorted to floggings, kidnappings, acid mutilations, and murder.

Using modern methods of promotion, two professional fund-raisers, and an army of 1000 salesmen (called "kleagles"), the Klan enrolled perhaps 3 million dues-paying members by the early 1920s. Moving into politics, its candidates captured legislatures in Indiana, Texas, Oklahoma, and Oregon. The organization was instrumental in electing six governors, three senators, and thousands of local officials. In the end, however, the Klan was undone by sex scandals and financial corruption. In November 1925 David Stephenson, grand dragon of the Indiana Klan and the most powerful leader in the Midwest, was sentenced to life imprisonment for rape and second-degree murder. Across the country in elections for mayor, governor, or senator, Klan-backed candidates lost as conventional politicians fought back with hard-hitting campaigns for office.

## Fundamentalism versus Darwinism

Although Aimee Semple McPherson embraced the fashions of the New Era, many Protestants, especially in rural areas, felt threatened by the secular aspects of modern life. Scientists and intellectuals spoke openly about the relativity of moral values and questioned the possibility of biblical miracles. Darwinism, pragmatism, and other scientific and philosophical theories left traditional religious teachings open to skepticism and scorn.

As early as the 1870s anxious conservatives had combined to combat modernist influences. Between 1909 and 1912 two wealthy Los Angeles churchgoers, Lyman and Milton Stewart, subsidized a series of booklets

*The Fundamentals*

known as *The Fundamentals*. The 3 million copies sent across the country stressed the "verbal inerrancy" of scripture: every word of the Bible was literally true. Advocates of this view, who after 1920 were increasingly known as "fundamentalists," saw themselves as defenders of traditional religion. Yet their literal reading of scripture was hardly traditional, for over the centuries many Christian theologians had interpreted various passages of scripture symbolically.

Fundamentalists maintained effective ministries nationwide, but especially among Southern Baptists. Nothing disturbed them more than Darwinian theories of evolution. By definition Darwinism denied the divine origin of humankind and made the creation story of Adam and Eve at best a parable. In 1925 a part-time schoolteacher and clerk of the Round Lick Association of Primitive Baptists convinced his fellow Tennessee legislators to make it illegal to teach that "man has descended from a lower order of animals." Oklahoma, Florida, Mississippi, and Arkansas soon passed similar statutes.

Encouraged by the newly formed American Civil Liberties Union, a number of skeptics in the town of Dayton, Tennessee, decided to test the law. In the

*Scopes trial*

spring of 1925 a bespectacled biology teacher named John T. Scopes was arrested for teaching evolution. Behind the scenes,

Scopes's sponsors were preoccupied as much with the commercial boost a sensational trial could give their town as with the defense of academic freedom.

When the Scopes trial opened in July, millions listened over the radio to the first trial ever broadcast. Inside the courtroom Clarence Darrow, the renowned defense lawyer from Chicago and a professed agnostic, acted as co-counsel for Scopes. Opposing him was William Jennings Bryan, the three-time presidential candidate who had recently joined the antievolution crusade. It was urban Darrow against rural Bryan in what Bryan described as a "duel to the death" between Christianity and evolution.

The presiding judge ruled that scientists could not be used to defend evolution. He considered their testimony "hearsay" because they had not been present at the Creation. The defense virtually collapsed, until Darrow called Bryan to the stand as an "expert on the Bible." Under withering examination Bryan admitted, to the horror of his followers, that the Earth might not have been made "in six days of 24-hours." Even so, the Dayton jury took only eight minutes to find Scopes guilty and fine him $100.

By then the excesses of the Scopes trial had transformed it into more of a national joke than a confrontation between darkness and light. But the debate over evolution raised a larger question that continued to reverberate throughout the twentieth century. As scientific, religious, and cultural standards clashed, how much should religious beliefs influence public education in a nation where church and state were constitutionally separated?

## REPUBLICANS ASCENDANT

"The change is amazing," wrote a Washington reporter after the inauguration of Warren G. Harding in March 1921. Woodrow Wilson had been ill, reclusive, and austere. Harding was handsome, warm, lovable. Wilson had kept his own counsel; Harding promised to bring the "best minds" into the cabinet to run things. Sentries disappeared from the gates of the White House, tourists again walked the halls, and reporters freely questioned the president. The reign of "normalcy," as Harding called it, had begun. "By 'normalcy,'" he explained, ". . . I mean normal procedure, the natural way, without excess."

### The Politics of Normalcy

"Normalcy" turned out to be anything but normal. After eight years of Democratic rule, Republicans controlled the White House from 1921 to 1933 and both houses of Congress from 1918 to 1930. Fifteen years of reform gave way to eight years of cautious governing. The presidency, strengthened by Wilson, now fell into weak hands. The cabinet and the Congress set the course of the nation.

*Warren G. Harding*

Harding and his successor, Calvin Coolidge, were content with delegating power. Harding appointed to the cabinet some men of quality: Charles Evans Hughes as secretary of state, Henry C. Wallace as secretary of agriculture, and Herbert Hoover as secretary of commerce. He also made, as one critic put it, some "unspeakably bad appointments": his old crony Harry Daugherty as attorney general and New Mexico Senator Albert Fall as interior secretary. Daugherty sold influence for cash and resigned in 1923. Only a divided jury saved him from jail. In 1929 Albert Fall became the first cabinet member to be convicted of a felony. In 1922 he had accepted bribes of more than $400,000 for secretly leasing naval oil reserves at Elk Hill, California, and Teapot Dome, Wyoming, to private oil companies.

Harding died suddenly in August 1923, before most of the scandals came to light. Though he would be remembered as lackluster, his tolerance and moderation had a calming influence on the strife-ridden nation. Slowly he had even begun to lead. In 1921 he created a Bureau of the Budget that brought modern accounting techniques to the management of federal revenues. Toward the end of his administration he cleared an early scandal from the Veterans' Bureau and set an agenda for Congress that included expanding the merchant marine.

To his credit Calvin Coolidge handled Harding's sordid legacy with skill and dispatch. He created a special investigatory commission, prosecuted wrong-

*Calvin Coolidge*

doers, and restored the confidence of the nation. Decisiveness, when he chose to exercise it, was one of Coolidge's hallmarks. As governor of Massachusetts, he had ended the Boston police strike in 1919 with a firm declaration: "There can be no right to strike against the public safety by anybody, anywhere, anytime." He believed in small-town democracy and minimalist government. "One of the most important accomplishments of my administration has been minding my own business," he boasted. Above all Coolidge worshiped wealth. "Civilization and profits," he once said, "go hand in hand."

Coolidge had been in office barely a year when voters returned him to the White House by a margin of nearly two to one in the election in 1924. It was yet another sign that Americans had wearied of reform and delighted in surging prosperity. Whether the business-dominated policies served the economy or the nation well in the long term was open to question.

## The Policies of Mellon and Hoover

Coolidge retained most of Harding's cabinet, including his powerful treasury secretary, Andrew Mellon. The former head of aluminum giant Alcoa, Mellon believed that prosperity "trickled down" from rich to poor through investment, which raised production, employment, and wages. In 1921 Mellon persuaded Congress to repeal the excess-profits tax on corporations; under Coolidge he convinced legislators to end all gift taxes, to halve estate and income taxes, and to reduce corporation and consumption taxes even further.

Business leaders applauded the Mellon tax program for reversing the progressive tax policies of the Wilson era. They, after all, paid the most in taxes and profited most from the tax cuts as well as from the protectionism of a new tariff. In 1922 the Fordney–McCumber Tariff increased rates on manufactured and farm goods.

Unlike Mellon, Commerce Secretary Herbert Hoover (also a Harding holdover) was not a traditional Republican. Dedicated to efficiency, distribution, cooperation, and service, Hoover advocated a progressive capital-

*Associationalism*

ism called "associationalism." It sought to bring order to the economy through the industrywide trade associations that had proved so helpful in organizing war production. Government provided advice, statistics, and forums. Business leaders exchanged ideas, set industry standards, and developed markets. Hoover also promoted the ideals of welfare capitalism by encouraging firms to sponsor company unions, pay employees decent wages, and protect workers from factory hazards and unemployment. Meanwhile the Commerce Department worked to expand foreign markets and fight international cartels.

Both Hoover and Mellon, each in his own way, placed government in the service of business. As a result, the role of government in the economy grew. So did its size, by more than 40,000 employees between 1921 and 1930. Building on their wartime partnership, government and business dropped all pretense of a laissez-faire economy. Efficiency increased, production soared, and prosperity reigned.

---

COUNTERPOINT   *Were the 1920s a Sharp Break with the Past?*

Historians have long argued over the meaning of the 1920s. Initially most took their cues from Frederick Lewis Allen's *Only Yesterday* and concluded that the decade represented a sharp, if frivolous, break from the serious past of reform and war. Later historians have seen the 1920s as more continuous with the past, more complex, and more important. Business historians have pointed to the trade association movement as an innovative attempt to achieve the old progressive goals of efficiency and equity in a modern industrial economy. Political historians have emphasized the remnant progressives who continued the fight for social justice and social welfare. Social historians have stressed the search for continuity amid dramatic change by fastening on the theme of shared anxiety over the future and nostalgia for a mythic past. In their eyes, the rise of nativism and religious fundamentalism, along with the drive toward Prohibition and creationism, represented reactions to the intrusion of secularism, science, and social pluralism on an older, more homogeneous America. Cultural historians have seen both change and continuity in the decade. Some see the intellectual revolt of the 1920s as having originated a decade earlier, while others have highlighted the emergence of a new American culture radiating outward from "mongrel Manhattan," with its hybrid mix of ethnicities, races, and sexes.

## *Distress Signals*

Some economic groups remained outside the magic circle of Republican prosperity. Ironically, they included those people who made up the biggest business in America: farmers. In 1920 agriculture still had an investment value greater than manufacturing, all utilities, and all railroads combined. A third of the population made a living from farming.

Yet the farmers' portion of the national income shrank by almost half during the 1920s. The government withdrew wartime price supports for wheat and
*Decline of farm prosperity*
ended its practice of feeding refugees with American surpluses. As European farms began producing again, the demand for American exports dropped. New dietary habits meant that average Americans of 1920 ate 75 fewer pounds of food annually than they had 10 years earlier. New synthetic fibers drove down demand for natural wool and cotton.

In 1921 a group of southern and western senators organized the "farm bloc" in Congress, to coordinate relief for farmers. Over the next two years they succeeded in bringing stockyards, packers, and grain exchanges under federal supervision. Other legislation exempted farm cooperatives from antitrust actions and created a dozen banks for low-interest farm loans. But regulation and credit were not enough. Over the decade, farmers' purchasing power continued to slide.

For the four years that Coolidge ran a "businessman's government," workers reaped few gains in wages, purchasing power, and bargaining rights. Although welfare capitalism promised benefits, only a handful of companies put it into practice. And those that did often used it to weaken independent unions. As dangerous imbalances in the economy developed, Coolidge ignored them.

If most Americans disregarded the distress signals at home, they paid almost no heed to economic unrest abroad. At the end of World War I, Europe's vic-
*Economic unrest abroad*
tors had forced Germany to take on $33 billion in war costs or reparations, partly to repay their own war debts to the United States. When Germany defaulted in 1923, French forces occupied the Ruhr valley in Germany's industrial heartland. Germany struck back by printing more money, a move that dramatized the crushing burden of its debt. Runaway inflation wiped out the savings of the German middle class, shook confidence in the new Weimar Republic, and soon threatened the economic structure of all Europe.

In 1924 American business leader Charles G. Dawes persuaded the victorious Europeans to scale down reparations. In return the United States promised
*The Dawes plan*
to help stabilize the German economy. Encouraged by the State Department, American bankers made large loans to Germany, with which the Germans paid their reparations. The European victors then used those funds to repay *their* war debts to the United States. It amounted to taking money out of one American vault and depositing it in another. In 1926 the United States also reduced European war debts. Canceling them altogether would have made more sense, but few Americans were that forgiving.

Despite Europe's debt problems, an arms race continued among the great powers. The United States vied with Britain, France with Italy, and Japan with nearly everyone for naval supremacy. Within the United States two factions sought to end military escalation, but for different reasons. Pacifists and peace activists blamed the arms race between Germany and England for having brought the world to war in 1914. They believed disarmament would secure a permanent peace. Saber-rattling Republicans had few qualms about military rivalry but worried about the high cost of maintaining navies in the Pacific as well as the Atlantic Ocean.

Two grand diplomatic gestures reflected the twin desires for peace and economy. In 1921, following the lead of the United States, the world's sea powers agreed to freeze battleship construction for 10 years and set ratios on the tonnage of each navy. The Five-Power Agreement was the first disarmament treaty in modern history. A more extravagant gesture came seven years later, in

*Kellogg–Briand Pact* 1928, when the major nations of the world (except the Soviet Union) signed an agreement outlawing war, the Kellogg–Briand Pact. "Peace is proclaimed," announced Secretary of State Frank Kellogg as he signed the document with a foot-long pen of gold.

But what seemed so bold on paper proved to be ineffective in practice. The French resented the lower limits set on their battleships under the Five-Power Agreement and began building smaller warships such as submarines, cruisers, and destroyers. The arms race now concentrated on these vessels. And the Kellogg–Briand Pact remained a hollow proclamation, with no means of enforcement.

## The Election of 1928

On August 2, 1927, in a small classroom in Rapid City, South Dakota, Calvin Coolidge handed a terse typewritten message to reporters: "I do not choose to run for President in nineteen twenty-eight." Republicans honored the request and nominated Herbert Hoover. Hoover was not a politician but an administrator and had never once campaigned for public office. It didn't matter. Republican prosperity made it difficult for any Democrat to win. Hoover, perhaps the most admired public official in America, made it impossible.

The Democratic party continued to be polarized between its rural supporters in the South and West and urban laborers in the Northeast. The two factions had clashed during the 1924 convention, scuttling the presidential candidacy of New York governor Al Smith. By 1928 the shift in population toward cities had given an edge to the party's urban wing. Al Smith won the nomination on the first ballot, even though his handicaps were evident. For one, he sounded like a city slicker. When the New York City–bred Smith spoke "poisonally" on the "rha-dio," voters across America winced. Though he pledged to enforce Prohibition, he campaigned against it and even took an occasional drink

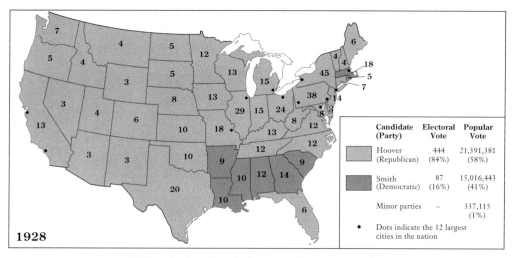

**1928**

| Candidate (Party) | Electoral Vote | Popular Vote |
|---|---|---|
| Hoover (Republican) | 444 (84%) | 21,391,381 (58%) |
| Smith (Democratic) | 87 (16%) | 15,016,443 (41%) |
| Minor parties | – | 337,115 (1%) |
| ● Dots indicate the 12 largest cities in the nation | | |

THE ELECTION OF 1928  In the pivotal election of 1928, Republican Herbert Hoover cracked the solidly Democratic South, which would return to the Democrats in 1932. Democrat Al Smith won the 12 largest cities in the country, all of which had voted Republican in 1924 but would stay with the Democrats in 1932.

(which produced the false rumor that Smith was a hopeless alcoholic). Most damaging of all, he was Catholic, at a time when anti-Catholicism remained strong in many areas of the country.

In the election of 1928, nearly 60 percent of the eligible voters turned out to give all but eight states to Hoover. The solidly Democratic South cracked for the first time. Still, the stirrings of a major political realignment were buried in the returns. The 12 largest cities in the country had gone to the Republicans in 1924; in 1928 the Democrats won them. The Democrats were becoming the party of the cities and of immigrants, a core around which they would build the most powerful vote-getting coalition of the twentieth century.

Early on a May morning in 1927, a silver monoplane streaked into the skies above Long Island and headed east. At the controls sat the young pilot Charles Lindbergh. Thirty-three hours and thirty minutes later, he landed just outside of Paris. An ecstatic mob swamped him and nearly tore his plane to pieces in search of souvenirs. Eight other flyers had died trying to cross the ocean. Lindbergh alone succeeded.

Lindbergh, dubbed the "Lone Eagle," and his plane, the *Spirit of St. Louis,* returned home aboard the warship *Memphis.* As he sailed up the Potomac, he received an honor previously reserved only for heads of state, a 21-gun salute. Lindbergh, wrote one reporter, "fired the imagination of mankind." Never had one person mastered a machine so completely or conquered nature so heroically. To Americans ambivalent about mass production, mass consumption, and mass society, here was a sign. Perhaps they could control the New Era without losing their cherished individualism. For a brief moment it seemed possible.

## SIGNIFICANT EVENTS

| | |
|---|---|
| 1903 | First feature-length film, *The Great Train Robbery*, released |
| 1909 | Sigmund Freud comes to America |
| 1914 | Henry Ford introduces moving assembly line |
| 1915 | Modern Ku Klux Klan founded |
| 1916 | Marcus Garvey brings Universal Negro Improvement Association to America |
| 1920 | First commercial radio broadcast; Eighteenth Amendment outlaws alcohol use; Nineteenth Amendment grants women right to vote; Warren Harding elected president |
| 1921 | Congress enacts quotas on immigration; Sheppard–Towner Federal Maternity and Infancy Act; American Birth Control League organized |
| 1921–1922 | Washington Naval Disarmament Conference |
| 1922 | Fordney–McCumber Tariff raises rates; Sinclair Lewis's *Babbitt* published; T. S. Eliot's *The Waste Land* published |
| 1923 | *Time* magazine founded; Harding dies; Calvin Coolidge becomes president; Harding scandals break |
| 1924 | Dawes plan to stabilize German inflation; Coolidge elected president |
| 1925 | John T. Scopes convicted of teaching evolution in Tennessee; Alain Locke's *The New Negro* published |
| 1927 | Charles Lindbergh's solo flight across the Atlantic; Sacco and Vanzetti executed |
| 1928 | Herbert Hoover elected president; Kellogg–Briand Pact signed |

# CHAPTER TWENTY-FIVE

# Crash and Depression

**H**igh above Columbus Circle in New York City a gigantic electric sign blinked out the happy decree: "You should have $10,000 at the age of 30; $25,000 at the age of 40; $50,000 at the age of 50." In the pages of the *Ladies Home Journal* John J. Raskob, who had run the Finance Committee at General Motors and listed his profession as "capitalist," told people how. "Everyone ought to be rich," he declared: $15 a month, "wisely invested," would be worth $80,000 in 20 years. In the 1920s, when 40 percent of American families earned less than $1500 a year, that was rich.

Possibilities for profit seemed to be everywhere, including far-off Florida. Land fever hit southern Florida in the mid-1920s. Before World War I Miami

*Florida land boom*

sat on mangrove jungle and bug-infested swamp. Attracted by 80-degree temperatures in winter, developers cleared the jungle, drained the swamp, put up a sea wall, and built a three-mile causeway from the beach to the mainland. Miami became the fastest-growing city in America as land speculators poured in. So many people arrived in the summer that famine threatened the state, and ice could be obtained only by doctor's prescription.

One mid-September night in 1926, Miami barometers dropped to 27.75—the lowest reading North America had ever recorded. Wind howled through the city at 130 miles per hour. Twenty-foot waves pounded sea walls and washed away beaches. Flooded swamps reclaimed landfills. Speculators discovered an awful truth: south Florida lay in the middle of the hurricane belt. In one night 100 Miamians drowned; 40,000 lost their homes. Reality punctured the vast speculative bubble. The value of oceanfront lots dropped by two-thirds. Hundreds went bankrupt; thousands lost their land to foreclosures.

The Florida land boom of the 1920s laid the foundation for later development, but stock market scams and speculation did nothing except turn the financial center of the nation into a gambling den. Phony stock deals (oil wells and mines were the most popular) netted swindlers more than $600 million a year. Some stock maneuvering was legal but deceptive. Favored "insiders"

In the 1930s Dorothea Lange pioneered a new realism in
photography—grim, unvarnished, and poignant. Nowhere did she
better capture the shattering effects of the Great Depression than
in this picture of a heavily mortgaged Georgia cotton farmer
overcome by despair.

(including President Calvin Coolidge) were placed on "preferred lists" at brokerage houses and tipped off about impending issues.

The desire for quick riches obsessed the nation. The volume of sales on the
New York Stock Exchange jumped 400 percent from 1923 to 1928. Other exchanges in Chicago, St. Louis, San Francisco, and Los Angeles registered similar gains. Buyers were less concerned about wise investments—about profit and
loss statements or market shares of a company—than about rising stock prices.
A simple dictum governed all strategy: buy low, sell high; buy high, sell higher.
"Everybody ought to be rich"—and anyone could be.

So it seemed in the late 1920s, as the New Era careened toward disaster.
Behind electric signs directing the pursuit of wealth and slogans exhorting it,
beneath land booms and stock deals, the economy was honeycombed with
weaknesses, and in 1929 it shattered.

## THE GREAT BULL MARKET

Strolling across the felt-padded floor of the New York Stock Exchange,
Superintendent William Crawford greeted the New Year with swaggering confidence. Nineteen twenty-eight had been a record setter, with more than

90,500,000 shares traded. The "bulls"—buyers of stock—had routed the "bears"—those who sell. It was the greatest bull market in history as eager purchasers drove prices to new highs. At the end of the last business day of the year, Crawford surveyed the floor and declared flatly, "The millennium's arrived."

Veteran financial analyst Alexander Noyes knew better. Speculation—buying and selling on the expectation that rising prices will yield quick gains—had taken over. "Something has to give," said Noyes in September 1929. Less than a month later, the Great Bull Market collapsed in a heap.

### The Rampaging Bull

No one knows exactly what caused the wave of speculation that boosted the stock market to dizzying heights. Driven alternately by greed and fear, the market succumbed to greed in a decade that considered it a virtue. A new breed of aggressive outsiders helped to spread the speculative fever. William Durant of General Motors, the Fisher brothers from Detroit, and others like them bought millions of shares, crowded out more conservative investors from the East, and helped to send prices soaring.

Money to fuel the market became plentiful. From 1922 to 1929, some $900 million worth of gold flowed into the country. The money supply expanded by

*New money*

$6 billion. Over the decade corporate profits grew by 80 percent. At interest rates as high as 25 percent, more could be made from lending money to brokers (who made "brokers' loans" to clients for stock purchases) than from constructing new factories. Borrowed over the phone, lent with the purchased stock as collateral, this "call money" could be collected, or called in, at any time and was usually renewable. By 1929 Bethlehem Steel had more than $157 million invested in the "call money market," and brokers' loans had almost tripled from two years earlier.

"Margin requirements," the cash actually put down to purchase stock, hovered around 50 percent for most of the decade. Thus buyers had to come up

ON THE FLOOR - N.Y. STOCK EXCHANGE    REGINALD MARSH

with only half the price of a share. The rest came from brokers' loans. As trading reached record heights in August 1929, the Federal Reserve Board tried to dampen speculation by raising the interest, or "rediscount," rate charged for loans to member banks. Higher interest rates made borrowing more expensive and, authorities hoped, would rein in the galloping bull market. But it was already too late.

## The Great Crash

On Thursday morning, October 24, 1929, the gallery of the New York Stock Exchange was packed with visitors. Trouble was in the air. The day before, a sharp break downward had capped a week of falling prices. Speculators had begun to sell their stocks and take their profits.

At the opening bell, a torrent of sell orders flooded the Exchange. Prices plunged as panic set in. By the end of "Black Thursday" nearly 13 million shares had been traded—a record. Losses stood at $3 billion, another record. Thirty-five of the largest brokerage houses on Wall Street issued a joint statement of reassurance: "The worst has passed."

The worst had only begun. Prices rallied for the rest of the week, buoyed by a bankers' buying pool organized at the House of Morgan. The following Tuesday, October 29, 1929, the bubble burst. Stockholders lost $10 billion in a single day. Within a month industrial stocks lost half of what they had been worth in September. And the downward spiral continued for almost four years. At their peak in 1929 stocks had been worth $87 billion. In 1933 they bottomed out at $18 billion.

The Great Crash did not cause the Great Depression, but it did damage the economy. Although only about 500,000 people were actually trading stocks by
*Role of the crash*    the end of the decade, their investments had helped to sustain prosperity. Thousands of middle-class investors lost their savings and their futures. Commercial banks—some loaded with corporate stocks, others deeply in the call money market—reeled in the wake of the crash. As historian Robert McElvaine has suggested, the shock of the stock market's fall "lowered the economy's resistance to the point where already existing defects could multiply rapidly and bring down the whole organism."

## The Causes of the Great Depression

What, then, were the defects in the American economy? With national attention riveted on the stock market, hardly anyone had paid them heed. But by 1928 the booming construction and automobile industries began to lose vitality as consumer demand for housing and cars sagged. In fact, increases in consumer spending for all goods and services slowed to a lethargic 1.5 percent for 1928–1929. Warehouses began to fill as business inventories climbed, from $500 million in 1928 to $1.8 billion in 1929.

In one sense, businesses had done all too well. They had increased profits during the 1920s by keeping the cost of labor and raw materials low, as well as by increasing productivity (producing more goods using fewer

*Overexpansion and decline in mass purchasing power*

workers). But most of the profits reaped by business were used to expand factories rather than to pay workers higher wages. Without strong labor unions or government support to help buoy them, real wages never kept pace with productivity. And this led to a paradox. As consumers, workers did not have enough money to buy the new products so many factories were turning out. The American economy was overexpanding at the same time that purchasing power was declining.

People made up the difference between earnings and purchases by borrowing. Consumers bought "on time," paying for merchandise a little each month.

*Consumer debt and uneven distribution of wealth*

During the decade consumer debt rose by 250 percent. Few could afford to keep spending at that rate. Nor could the distribution of wealth sustain prosperity. By 1929, 1 percent of the population owned 36 percent of all personal wealth. The wealthy had more money than they could possibly spend and saved too much. The working and middle classes had not nearly enough to keep the economy growing, spend though they might.

Another problem lay with the banking system. Mismanagement, greed, and the emergence of a new type of executive—half banker, half stockbroker—led

*Banking system*

banks to divert more funds into more speculative investments. The uniquely decentralized American banking system left no way to set things right if a bank failed. At the end of the decade half of the 25,000 banks in America lay outside of the Federal Reserve System. Its controls even over member banks were weak. During the decade, 6000 banks failed.

Added to the weak banking structure was a shaky corporate structure. No government agency monitored the stock exchanges at all, while big business

*Corporate structure and public policy*

operated largely unchecked. Insider trading, shady deals, and outright fraud ran rampant. Meanwhile public policy encouraged corporate consolidation and control by discouraging antitrust suits. High profits and the Mellon program of tax reduction (see page 681) helped make many corporations wealthy enough to avoid borrowing. Thus changes in interest rates had little influence on them. Free from government regulation, fluctuating prices, and the need for loans, huge corporations ruled the economy. And they ruled badly.

Unemployment began to increase as early as 1927, revealing a growing softness in the economy. By the fall of 1929 nearly 2 million people were out of work.

*"Sick" industries*

Many of them were in textiles, coal mining, lumbering, and railroads. All were "sick" industries that had suffered from overexpansion, reduced demand, and weak management. Farmers were in trouble too. As European agriculture revived after World War I, farm prices tumbled. American farmers earned 16 percent of the national income in 1919 but only 9 percent in 1929. As more of them went bust, so did the rural banks that had lent them money.

Finally, plain economic ignorance contributed to the calamity. High tariffs protected American industries but discouraged foreign trade, making it harder

*Economic
ignorance*

for European businesses to sell to the world's most profitable market. Since Europeans weren't profiting, they lacked the money to spend on American goods being shipped to Europe. Only American loans and investments supported demand for American goods abroad; when the economy began to collapse, those were withdrawn.

Furthermore, the Federal Reserve had been stimulating the economy both by expanding the money supply and by lowering interest rates. That only fed the speculative fever. A decision to raise interest rates in 1929 to stem speculation ended up speeding the slide.

---

## COUNTERPOINT   *What Caused the Great Depression?*

Not all scholars see the causes of the Depression just so. Most historians follow the thinking of British economist John Maynard Keynes. His revolutionary ideas challenged traditional notions that the economy was a self-adjusting mechanism that would eventually recover on its own. "Keynesians" argue that the capitalist economy must expand to survive. Economic expansion requires spending by both consumers and investors. Without such spending, the economy could stagnate at low levels of productivity and employment, as was the case in the 1930s. What caused the Great Depression, according to this school, was a decline in both investments and consumption as markets for producer and consumer goods reached saturation. Simply put, not enough income was being distributed to sustain consumer purchasing power and to encourage expansion and investment.

Followers of American economist Milton Friedman disagree. Called "monetarists," they point to the money supply as the root of the problem. In the crucial years between 1930 and 1932 the money supply shrank at an annual rate of 10 percent, reversing the pre-1929 period of expansion. The failure of the Federal Reserve System to increase the supply of money, argue monetarists, fatally weakened banks and set off a "great contraction" in the economy. More money in circulation and lower interest rates on loans would have promoted a quick recovery in the wake of the stock market crash of 1929.

---

### The Sickening Slide

The Great Crash signaled the start of a 10-year depression, the worst in the history of the nation. The gains of the twenties were wiped out in a few years. In the first three years after the crash total productivity dropped from $103 billion to $56 billion. National income fell by half; factory wages, by almost half; foreign trade, by more than two-thirds. Some 85,000 businesses failed.

The shock waves helped to topple already fragile economies in Europe. American loans, investments, and purchases had propped up Europe since the end of World War I. When they stopped, European governments defaulted on war debts. More European banks failed; more businesses collapsed; unemployment surged. Europeans scrambled to protect themselves. Led by Great Britain in 1931, 41 nations abandoned the gold standard. Foreign governments hoped to devalue their currencies by expanding their supplies of money. Exports would be cheaper, and foreign trade would increase. But at the same time, each country raised tariffs to protect itself from foreign competition, and devaluation failed. The resulting trade barriers only deepened the crisis.

Declining sales abroad sent crop prices in the United States to new lows. Farm income dropped by more than half—to a paltry $5 billion. The epidemic of rural bank failures spread to the cities as nervous depositors rushed to withdraw their cash. Even healthy banks could not bear the strain. Between 1929 and 1933 collapsing banks took more than $20 billion in assets with them. The economy was spiraling downward, and no one could stop it.

## THE AMERICAN PEOPLE IN THE GREAT DEPRESSION

Long bread lines snaked around corners. Vacant-eyed apple sellers stood shivering in the wind. A man with his hat in his hand came to the back door asking for food in exchange for work. Fewer automobiles rode the streets; more hobos rode the rails. Trains were shorter and the air was cleaner as factories cut back or shut down. Between 1929 and 1932 an average of 100,000 people lost their jobs every week until some 13 million Americans were jobless. At least one worker in four could find no work at all.

The Great Depression was a great leveler that reduced differences in the face of common want. The New York seamstress without enough piecework to pay her rent felt the same frustration and anger as the Berkeley student whose college education was cut short when the bank let her father go. Not everyone was devastated. Most husbands had some job. Most wives continued as homemakers. Most Americans got by, often cooperating with one another, practicing a ruthless underconsumption to make ends meet. "We lived lean," recalled one Depression victim. So did most of the American people—northern and southern; urban and rural; black, white, yellow, and brown.

### Hard Times

Even before the Great Crash many Americans were having trouble making a living. In the golden year of 1929, economists calculated that for necessities alone a family of four required $2000 a year—more money than 60 percent of American families earned. By 1932 the average family had an annual income of $1348, barely enough to survive.

*Subsistence incomes*

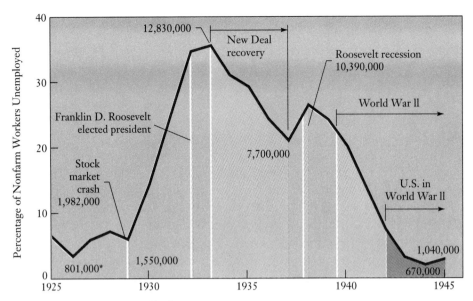

UNEMPLOYMENT, 1925–1945   Unemployment mushroomed in the wake of the stock market crash of 1929. The success of the New Deal in increasing employment did not nearly match World War II, which turned out to be the unintended agent of recovery.

As soup kitchens opened and bread lines formed in cities across the nation, survival often became the primary goal. Millions stayed alive by foraging like animals, and city hospitals began receiving new patients ill from starvation. In the coal-mining regions of West Virginia and Illinois almost every child fed by the American Friends Service Committee was underweight. Pellagra and other diseases associated with malnutrition increased. Despite official claims that "no one has starved," the New York City Welfare Council reported 29 victims of starvation and 110 dead of malnutrition in 1932. Most were children.

Unable to pay mortgages or rent, many families lived off the generosity of forgiving landlords. Some traded down to smaller quarters or simply lost their homes. By 1932 between 1 million and 2 million Americans were homeless wanderers, among them an estimated 25,000 nomadic families. For the first time, emigration out of the United States exceeded immigration into it because Americans could find so little work in their own country.

Victims of the Depression overthrew the governments of seven Latin American countries, but in the United States most citizens turned their anger

*Psychological impact*

inward. "People blamed themselves, not the system," explained one woman. "They felt they had been at fault: . . . 'if we hadn't bought that old radio' . . . 'if we hadn't bought that second-hand car.'" Shame, self-doubt, and pessimism became epidemic. "I'm just no good, I

Shantytowns (called "Hoovervilles" after the president) sprang up around most cities as the Depression deepened.

guess," a Houston woman lamented in 1934. Most tried to keep up appearances. Men resharpened old razor blades, rolled their own cigarettes, used 25-watt bulbs to save electricity. Women retailored their dresses for their daughters and sewed together lengths of sheets to equalize wear. Under the strain, rates of mental illness and suicide rose.

Some never forgot the humiliation of life in the Depression. "Shame? You tellin' me?" recalled a businessman. "I would go stand on that relief line [and] bend my head low so nobody would recognize me. The only scar that is left on me is my pride, my pride." The lasting legacy of humiliation and fear—that the bottom would fall out again, that life would be leveled once more, that the next depression might not end—this was what one writer called an "invisible scar."

## The Depression Family

Jane Addams, 81 years old in 1931 and a tireless fighter for social justice, saw the anxiety in the faces of those living around her beloved Hull House in Chicago—"men and women who have seen their margin of savings disappear; heads of families who see and anticipate hunger for their children before it occurs. That clutch of cold fear is one of the most hideous aspects."

The "clutch of cold fear" led many young couples to put off having children: births per 1000 women of childbearing age dropped from 97.4 in 1929 to

*Baby shortage*

75.7 in 1933. For the first time in three centuries the curve of population growth was leveling off. The marriage rate slumped as well and did not begin to recover until 1934. Although divorce declined throughout the 1930s, desertion—the "poor man's divorce"—increased.

Studies found that the Depression did not split families so much as it magnified tendencies already present. Weak families languished or fell apart. Strong

*Impact on families*

ones hung together and grew closer. But in all families the Depression took a toll, especially on men. Work had defined them as productive members of society. Suddenly they had nothing to do. Husbands without jobs grew listless and discouraged after a few weeks at home. Some put on ties and jackets each morning, but instead of going to the office they sold Two-in-One shoe polish or cheap neckties door to door. In a culture that stressed self-reliance and male breadwinning, such men felt like failures.

During the Depression the routines of most of the country's 28 million homemakers were less disrupted than their husbands', but demands on them

*Importance of homemaking*

grew as homemaking took on added importance. Between 1929 and 1933 living costs dropped almost 25 percent, but family incomes tumbled by 40 percent. Homemakers watched family budgets with a close eye. They substituted less expensive fish for red meat or dropped meat from their menus altogether. Jell-O, the cheapest all-purpose dessert, enjoyed new popularity. Corn, tomatoes, and pole beans sprang up in backyards and vacant city lots. Families took in relatives and boarders. Some homemakers sold baked goods, made dresses, or opened kitchen beauty parlors.

After a decade of being drawn from home by automobiles and mass entertainment, the middle-class family turned inward. Church attendance declined, and a third of the Grange and rural women's clubs vanished. Home and family emerged as the center of recreation and companionship. People dreamed of the outdoors—playing tennis, swimming, or boating—but surveys showed that they spent their free time indoors, reading, listening to the radio, and going to the movies, in that order.

The Great Depression marked a generation. Countless women came to associate working outside the home with financial distress. The middle-class dream of a wife freed from working for wages, which had weakened in the 1920s, reasserted itself. Whether in the renewed importance of homemaking and family life or in the reemergence of home industries, Americans retreated into traditionalism.

## Working Women, Anxious Children

As the Depression deepened, more women worked outside their homes to supplement meager family incomes. Some critics claimed they took jobs from men, and one offered a simple solution: "Fire the women, who shouldn't be working

## A Salesman Loses Everything

I was in business for myself, selling clothing on credit, house to house. And collecting by the week. Up to that time, people were buying very good and paying very good. But they started to speculate, and I felt it. My business was dropping from the beginning of 1928. They were mostly middle-class people. They weren't too rich, and they weren't too poor.

All of a sudden, in the afternoon, October 1929 . . . I was going on my business and I heard the newspaper boys calling, running all around the streets and giving news and news: stock market crashed, stock market crashed. It came out just like lightning.

I remember vividly. I was on my route, going to see my customer. It didn't affect me much at the time. I wasn't speculating in the market. Of course, I had invested some money in some property and some gold bonds, they used to call it. Because I have more confidence in the gold bonds than the stock market. Because I know the stock market goes up and down. But the gold bond, I was told from the banks, is just like gold. Never lose its value. Later we found to our sorrow that it was fake. . . .

We lost everything. It was the time I would collect four, five hundred dollars a week. After that, I couldn't collect fifteen, ten dollars a week. I was going around trying to collect enough money to keep my family going. It was impossible. Very few people could pay you. Maybe a dollar if they would feel sorry for you or what.

Finally people started to talk me into going into the relief. They had open soup kitchens. Al Capone, he had open soup kitchens somewhere downtown, where people were standing in line. And you had to go two blocks, stand there, around the corner, to get a bowl of soup.

Ben Issacs in Studs Terkel, *Hard Times: An Oral History of the Great Depression* (New York: Pantheon, 1986), pp. 423–427. Copyright © 1970 by Studs Terkel. Reprinted by permission of Pantheon Books, a division of Random House, Inc.

anyway, and hire the men. Presto! No unemployment. No relief rolls. No depression."

Such thinking reflected the prejudice still dogging female wage earners. Past discrimination had relegated many women to jobs as secretaries,

*Working outside the home* schoolteachers, and social workers. Over half the female labor force worked in domestic service or the garment trades. Live-in maids, the elite of domestic servants, got $8 a week; pieceworkers in the textile mills of Lawrence, Massachusetts, $4. Most unemployed men would have been reluctant to take such "women's work," even if it were available.

Married women who sought employment faced special obstacles. Opinion polls showed that more than three in four Americans believed wives belonged at home. Few school districts would hire them, and half had a policy of firing them first. Between 1932 and 1937 federal regulations prohibited more than one family member from holding a civil service job. Three-quarters of those forced to resign were women. The proportion of women in the workforce rose anyway because they were willing to take almost any job. By 1940 it approached 25 percent. Wages for women rose too, until they were 63 percent of men's.

The nation's 21 million children could not escape anxiety. Teachers reported even kindergartners being "excitable and high-strung." Many of them were as uncertain of their future as they were of their next meal.

*Childhood anxiety* Initially some 250,000 children took to the road, often to relieve families of their support or just to escape. But school enrollments grew as prospects for employment shrank. By 1940 three-quarters of high school-aged children were attending, compared with less than half in 1930. Extended schooling kept children out of the labor force, and the Depression fed the long-term trend toward a highly educated public.

## Play

Somber faces fill the photographs of the Depression decade, but in fact Americans still had fun, although play was often conditioned by the crisis. In the midst of fear and uncertainty, games built on rationality captured middle-class imaginations: contract bridge with its systematic bidding and play; Parker Brothers' board game Monopoly, which rewarded orderly investing in real estate; pinball, the ultimate machine-age game that carried the injunction "Do Not Tilt." All relied on rules and skill as well as luck. In more physical games, endurance became a virtue. Six-day bicycle races staged a comeback. Dance marathons, another contest for survival, kept partners on the floor 45 minutes out of every hour, 24 hours a day, sometimes for weeks on end.

The Depression produced more traditional fashions for women: longer skirts and hair and more curves. A desire to escape the here-and-now helped to make bestsellers of *The Good Earth* (1931), Pearl Buck's saga of China, and Margaret Mitchell's Civil War epic, *Gone with the Wind* (1936). New skepticism about business led Fred Schlink to write *100,000,000 Guinea Pigs*, a sequel to *Your Money's Worth* (1927), his earlier exposé of false advertising. By 1935 the two books had sold half a million copies.

Hungry for diversions, people still flocked to spectacles, as they had in the 1920s. A world's fair in Chicago in 1933 and another in New York in 1939 drew millions. Families living on a limited budget took up cheaper pursuits, such as stamp collecting, knitting, and jigsaw puzzles. Boxtop contests and other games of chance held out hope of turning bad financial luck good. Inaugurated in 1930, the Irish Sweepstakes became the most successful lottery in the world within five years.

With a wider audience than ever, record sales jumped a hundredfold between 1934 and 1937. Classical music enjoyed new popularity as tastes turned to a more controlled, full-bodied sound. By 1939 there were more than 270 symphony orchestras in the country; only 17 had existed in 1915. More than 10 million families listened to symphonic music and opera each weekend on radio. Popular music became more melodic and cheerful. "Swing," a commercialized jazz, dominated the charts, and big-band orchestras played popular favorites at nightclubs and theaters.

### The Golden Age of Radio and Film

By the end of the decade almost 9 out of 10 families owned radios. (The cost of one had dropped from $100 in 1929 to about $50 by the mid-1930s.) People depended on them for nearly everything—news, sports, and weather; music and entertainment; advice on how to bake a cake or find God. Radio entered a

*Commercial programming*

golden age of commercialism, as sponsors hawked their products on variety programs like "Major Bowes' Amateur Hour" and comedy shows with George Burns and Gracie Allen. Daytime melodramas, called "soap operas" because they were sponsored by soap companies, aimed at women with stories of the personal struggles of ordinary folk. The hair-raising adventures of "The Lone Ranger" drew young listeners. By 1939 it was being heard three times a week on 140 stations.

Radio continued to bind the country together. A teenager in Splendora, Texas, could listen to the same wisecracks from Jack Benny, the same music from Guy Lombardo, as kids in New York and Los Angeles. In 1938 Orson Welles broadcast H. G. Wells's classic science fiction tale, *The War of the Worlds.* Americans everywhere listened to breathless reports of an "Invasion from Mars," and some believed them. In Newark, New Jersey, cars jammed roads as families rushed to evacuate the city. The nation, bombarded with reports of impending war in Europe, was prepared to believe anything, even invaders from Mars.

In Hollywood an efficient but dictatorial "studio system" churned out a record number of feature films. Eight motion picture companies produced

*Studio system*

more than two-thirds of them. Color, first introduced in features in *Becky Sharp* (1935), soon complemented sound, which had debuted in the 1927 version of *The Jazz Singer.* Neither alone could keep movie theaters full. As attendance waned early in the Depression, big studios like Metro-Goldwyn-Mayer and Universal sought to lure audiences back with films that shocked, titillated, and just plain entertained.

Popular movies often played upon deep national emotions. Early Depression gangster movies like *Little Caesar* (1931) and *Scarface* (1932) allowed Americans ambivalent about the ethic of success to root for misfits who challenged it and still applaud their just demise. The Marx Brothers made fun of social disorder in *Monkey Business* (1931) and *Duck Soup* (1933), while teamwork and cooperation were stressed in the elaborately choreographed musicals of Busby Berkeley and in the dancing routines of Fred Astaire and Ginger Rogers. Only toward the end of the decade did Hollywood develop a social conscience in such films as *Dead End* (1937) and *The Grapes of Wrath* (1941).

By the mid-1930s more than 60 percent of Americans were going to the movies at least once a week. They saw tamer films as the industry regulated movie content in the face of growing criticism. To avoid censorship and boycotts, studios stiffened their own regulations.

*Production code*

According to the Motion Picture Production Code of 1934, producers could not depict homosexuality, abortion, drug use, or sex. (Even the word *sex* was banned.) If couples were shown in bed, they had to be clothed and one foot of each partner had to touch the floor. Middle-class morality reigned on the screen, and most Depression movies, like most of popular culture, preserved traditional social and economic values.

## *"Dirty Thirties": An Ecological Disaster*

On Armistice Day 1933, the wind began to blow through Beadle County, South Dakota, not just briskly but at 60 miles an hour. "By noon," reported R. D. Lusk from a local farmhouse, "it was darker than night." When the wind finally died down, the farm, like the rest of Beadle County, was transformed. Lusk saw no fields, "only sand drifting into mounds. . . . Fences, machinery, and trees were gone, buried. The roofs of sheds stuck out through drifts deeper than a man is tall."

Between 1932 and 1939 an average of nearly 50 "black blizzards" a year turned 1500 square miles between the Oklahoma panhandle and western Kansas into a gigantic "Dust Bowl." It was one of the worst ecological disasters in modern history, and its baleful effects were felt as far

*Dust Bowl*

north as the Dakotas and as far south as Texas. Nature played its part, scorching the earth and whipping the winds. But the "dirty thirties" were mostly man-made. The semiarid lands west of the 98th meridian were not suitable for agriculture or livestock. Sixty years of intensive farming and grazing had stripped the prairie of its natural vegetation and rendered it defenseless against the elements. When the dry winds came, one-third of the Great Plains just blew away.

The dust storms lasted anywhere from hours to days. Walking into one, as R. D. Lusk discovered when he stepped outside, was like walking into "a wall of dirt." For protection people wore gauze masks, swabbed their nostrils with Vaseline, covered their windows with paraffin-soaked rags. Nothing worked. Tiny particles of dust covered everything, and food crunched to the bite.

"Black blizzards" dwarfed all man-made structures. The drought that helped to bring them about lasted from 1932 to 1936. In a single day in 1934, dust storms dumped 12 million tons of western dirt on Chicago.

Some 3.5 million plains people abandoned their farms. Landowners or corporations forced off about half of them, as large-scale commercial farming slowly spread east from California into the heartland of America. The Great Plains contained the only states that suffered a net loss of residents during the decade. No one knows how many of these rural refugees became migrants, but relief offices around the country reported a change in migrant families. No longer black or brown, more and more were white and native-born, typically a young married couple with one child.

Most did not travel far, perhaps to the next county. Long-distance migrants—the "Exodusters" from Oklahoma, Arizona, and Texas—usually set

*Exodusters*

their sights on California. Handbills and advertisements promised jobs picking fruit and harvesting vegetables. If they were like the Joad family in John Steinbeck's classic novel *The Grapes of Wrath* (1939), they drove west along Route 66 through Arizona and New Mexico, their belongings piled high atop rickety jalopies, heading for the West Coast.

More than 350,000 Oklahomans migrated to California, so many that "Okie" came to mean any Dust Bowler, even though most of Oklahoma lay outside the Dust Bowl. The poor were only a small minority of new arrivals, but Californians grew edgy. By the middle of the decade Los Angeles police had formed "bum blockades" to keep out migrants. "Negroes and Okies upstairs," read one sign in a San Joaquin Valley theater. Native-born whites had never encountered such discrimination before.

Only one in two or three migrants actually found work. The labor surplus allowed growers to set their own terms. A migrant family earned about $450 a year, less than a third of the subsistence level. Those who did not work formed wretched enclaves called "little Oklahomas." The worst were located in the fertile Imperial Valley. There at the end of the decade relief officials discovered a family of 10 living in a 1921 Ford.

## Mexican Americans and African Americans

The Chavez family lost their farm in the North Gila River valley of Arizona in 1934. They had owned a small homestead near Yuma for two generations, but the
*Cesar Chavez* Depression pushed them out. Cesar, barely six years old at the time, remembered only images of the departure: a "giant tractor" leveling the corral, the loss of his room and bed, a beat-up Chevy hauling the family west, his father vowing to buy another plot in Arizona someday.

The elder Chavez could never keep his promise. Instead he and his family lived on the road, "following the crops" in California. In eight years Cesar went to 37 schools. The family was forced to sell their labor to unscrupulous *enganchistas*, or contractors, for less than $10 a week. The father joined strikers in the Imperial Valley in the mid-1930s, but they were crushed. "Some people put this out of their minds and forget it," said Cesar Chavez years later. "I don't." Thirty years later he founded the United Farm Workers of America, the first union of migratory workers in the country.

The Chavezes resembled the Joads in every way but one: they were Mexican Americans. The Joads had encountered at least a few sympathetic store clerks on their way west. When the Chavezes found a roadside restaurant, the sign outside read: "White trade only." In an America still strictly segregated, the owner never thought twice about refusing service to Americans who were brown or black. "Every time we thought of it, it hurt us," remembered Cesar.

A deep ambivalence had always characterized American attitudes toward Mexicans, but the Great Depression turned most Anglo communities against
*Repatriation* them. Cities like Los Angeles, fearing the burden of relief, found it cheaper to ship them home. Some migrants left voluntarily. Others were driven out by frustrated officials or angry neighbors. Beginning in 1931 the federal government launched a series of deportations, or "repatriations," of Mexicans back to Mexico. These included their American-born children, who by law were citizens of the United States.

During the decade the Spanish-speaking population of the Southwest declined by 500,000. In a city like Chicago, the Mexican community shrank almost by half. Staying often turned out to be as difficult as leaving. The average income of Mexican American families in the Rio Grande valley of Texas was $506 a year. The sum represented the combined income of parents and children. Following the harvest made schooling particularly difficult: fewer than 2 Mexican American children in 10 completed five years of school.

Hard times were nothing new to African Americans. "The Negro was born in depression," opined one man. "It only became official when it hit the white man." Still, when the Depression struck, black unemployment surged. By 1932 it reached 50 percent, twice the national level. By 1933 several cities reported between 25 and 40 percent of their black residents with no support but relief payments. Even skilled black workers who retained their jobs saw their wages cut in half, according to one study of Harlem in 1935.

Migration from the rural South, up 800,000 over the 1920s, dropped by 50 percent during the 1930s. As late as 1940 three of four African Americans still lived in rural areas; yet conditions there were as bad as in cities. Forty percent of all black workers in the United States were farm laborers or tenants. In 1934 one study estimated the average income for black cotton farmers at under $200 a year.

Millions of African Americans made do by stretching meager incomes as they had for years. "Our wives could go to the store and get a bag of beans or a sack of flour and a piece of fat meat, and they could cook this. And we could eat it," explained another man. "Now you take the white fella, he couldn't do this."

Like many African Americans, George Baker refused to be victimized by the Depression. Baker had moved from Georgia to Harlem in 1915. He changed

*Father Divine and Elijah Muhammad*

his name to M. J. Divine and founded a religious cult that promised followers an afterlife of full equality. In the 1930s "Father Divine" preached economic cooperation and opened shelters, or "heavens," for regenerate "angels," black and white. In Detroit, Elijah Poole changed his name to Elijah Muhammad and in 1931 established the Black Muslims, a blend of Islamic faith and black nationalism. He exhorted African Americans to celebrate their African heritage, to live a life of self-discipline and self-help, and to strive for a separate all-black nation.

The Depression inflamed racial prejudice. "Dust has been blown from the shotgun, the whip, and the noose," reported *The New Republic* in 1931, "and Ku

*Scottsboro boys*

Klux Klan practices were being resumed in the certainty that dead men not only tell no tales but create vacancies." Lynchings tripled between 1932 and 1933. In 1932 the Supreme Court ordered a retrial in the most celebrated racial case of the decade. A year earlier nine black teenagers had been accused of raping two white women on a train bound for Scottsboro, Alabama. Within weeks all-white juries had sentenced eight of them to death. The convictions rested on the testimony of the women, one of whom later admitted the boys had been framed. Appeals kept the case alive for almost a decade. In the end charges against four of the "Scottsboro boys" were dropped. The other five received substantial prison sentences.

Elsewhere the Depression divided black and white Americans, but in the Arkansas delta hard times drew them together. In Arkansas poor black and white farmers joined forces to organize the Southern Tenant Farmers Union in 1934. The union published its own newspaper, the *Sharecropper's Voice*, and attracted national support from Socialists and other radicals. Landlords became uneasy with union demands for federal subsidies and an end to arbitrary evictions. Planters and riding bosses broke up union meetings and horsewhipped organizers. Although they won few concessions, union members hung together.

## THE TRAGEDY OF HERBERT HOOVER

A cold, gray morning sent shivers through the crowd huddled in front of the capitol on March 4, 1929. Herbert Hoover had just been sworn in as the thirty-first president of the United States. His monotone came booming over the loudspeakers: "I have no fears for the future of our country. It is bright with hope." Within seven months a "depression" had struck. (Hoover coined the term himself to minimize the crisis.) Try as he might, he could not beat it, and the nation turned against him. "People were starving because of Herbert Hoover," cried an angry mother in 1932. "Men were killing themselves because of Herbert Hoover, and their fatherless children were being packed away to orphanages . . . because of Herbert Hoover."

The charge was unfair, but it stuck. Hoover's presidency, begun with such bright hope, became the worst ordeal of his life. Near the end of his term in 1932 he lamented that "all the money in the world could not induce me to live over the last nine months." He nonetheless felt duty-bound to accept his party's renomination for the presidency. His ordeal soon turned into a tragic and humiliating rejection.

### *The Failure of Relief*

By the winter of 1931–1932 the story was the same everywhere: relief organizations with too little money and too few resources to combat the Depression.

*Private charity* — Once-mighty private charity had dwindled to 6 percent of all relief funds. Hull House in Chicago, the model of progressive benevolence, was overwhelmed by the needs of the neighborhood it served. New York City employees had been donating 1 percent of their salaries to feed the needy since 1930, yet many New Yorkers were starving to death.

Ethnic charities made similar efforts to stave off disaster. Mexican Americans and Puerto Ricans turned to *mutualistas*, traditional societies that provided members with social support, life insurance, and sickness benefits. The stress of the Depression quickly bankrupted most *mutualistas*. In San Francisco, the Chinese Six Companies offered food and clothing to needy Chinese Americans. But as one charity head warned, private efforts were failing. The government would be "compelled, by the cruel events ahead of us, to step into the situation and bring relief on a large scale."

An estimated 30 million needy people nationwide quickly depleted city treasuries, already pressed by delinquent tax rates of nearly 30 percent. In

*City services* — Philadelphia relief payments to a family of four totaled $5.50 a week. It was the highest rate in the country. Some cities gave nothing to unmarried people or childless couples, no matter how impoverished they were. Oklahoma City began arresting unemployed men, charging them with vagrancy and ordering them out of town. Roads went unpaved in summer; snow, unplowed in winter. By the end of 1931, Detroit, Boston, Buffalo, and scores of other cities were bankrupt.

Cities clamored for help from state capitals, but after a decade of extravagant spending and sloppy bookkeeping, many states were already running in the red. As businesses and property values collapsed, tax bases shrank and with them state revenues. Michigan, one of the few states to provide any relief, reduced

*TERA* funds by more than half between 1931 and 1932. Until New York established its Temporary Emergency Relief Administration (TERA) in 1931, no state had any agency at all to handle the problem.

Some people refused to accept help even when they qualified. To go on relief, said one man, was to endure a "crucifixion." Before applications could even be considered, all property had to be sold, all credit exhausted, all relatives declared flat broke. After a half-hour grilling about his family, home, and friends, one applicant left, "feeling I didn't have any business living any more." Hostile officials attached every possible stigma to aid. In 1932 residents of Lewiston, Maine, voted to bar all welfare recipients from the polls. Ten states wrote property requirements for voting into their constitutions. The destitute were being disfranchised.

## Herbert Hoover

Trumpets blared, servants bowed, and the president of the United States sat down to dinner. One after another, seven full courses were set before him. When he finished, the uniformed buglers sounded his departure. Every night he stayed at the White House during the Great Depression, Herbert Hoover dined in such splendor. He thought about economizing but decided against it. If he changed his habits one bit, it might be taken as a sign of lost confidence.

It was not that Herbert Hoover was insensitive—far from it. He never visited a bread line or a relief shelter because he could not bear the sight of suffering. Yet he was doing all he could to promote recovery, more than any of his predecessors, and still he was scorned. His natural sullenness turned to self-pity. Calvin Coolidge advised patience: "You can't expect to see calves running in the field the day after you put the bull to the cows." "No," said an exasperated Hoover, "but I would expect to see contented cows."

Hoover's frustration was understandable. He had never failed before. Orphaned at nine, he graduated from the newly opened Stanford University in 1895, an engineer and soon the owner of one of the most successful mining firms in the world. Before he turned 40, he was a millionaire. As a good Quaker he balanced private gain with public service. He saved starving refugees in war-torn Europe and flood victims at home and became known as the greatest humanitarian of his generation. The people of Finland added a new word to their vocabulary: to *hoover* meant to help.

## The Hoover Depression Program

From the fall of 1930 onward, Hoover took responsibility for ending the crisis—and as humanely as possible. He understood the vicious cycle of rising unemployment and falling demand and knew the necessity for investment. His unprecedented Depression program rested on his associational philosophy (see page 682), with its commitment to voluntary efforts, faith in the power of capitalism, and conviction that too much government action would undermine freedoms and initiative.

Despite Hoover's best efforts, the program failed. He secured pledges from business leaders to maintain employment, wages, and prices, only to have them back down as the economy sputtered. To bolster public confidence, he reassured Americans that "conditions are fundamentally sound," but the sagging economy quickly proved him wrong. When Hoover tax cuts to increase the purchasing power of consumers led to an unbalanced federal budget, Hoover tax increases followed in 1932, further undermining investment and consumption. Presidential commissions to discover the number of unemployed and spark local relief did neither, and Hoover's Federal Farm Board, created to stimulate the sale of farm commodities, lacked the funds to make it effective. The president endorsed the Smoot–Hawley Tariff (1930) to protect the United States from cheap foreign goods, but the new tariff ended up bringing a wave of retaliation that choked world trade. Even Hoover's spending on public works—at $1 billion, more than all the presidents before him—did not approach the $10 billion needed to put only half the unemployed to work.

Under pressure from Congress, Hoover took his boldest action to save the banks. Without the credit they supplied, there could be no recovery. Between 1930 and 1932 some 5100 banks failed as panicky depositors withdrew their funds. Losses in deposits alone amounted to more than $3.2 billion. In 1932 Hoover endorsed the Reconstruction Finance Corporation (RFC), an agency that could lend money to banks and their chief corporate debtors—insurance companies and railroads. Modeled on a similar organization that had been created during World War I, the RFC had a capital stock of $500 million and the power to borrow four times that amount. Within three months bank failures dropped from 70 a week to 1 every two weeks. The Glass–Steagall Banking Act (1932) made it easier for banks to lend money by adding $2 billion of new currency to the money supply, backed by Federal Reserve government bonds.

*Reconstruction Finance Corporation*

Yet in spite of this success, Hoover drew criticism for rescuing banks and not people. From the start he rejected the idea of direct federal relief for the unemployed. He feared that a dole or giveaway program (of the kind being used in Britain) would damage the character of recipients. Federal experiments with relief could have unhealthy results for the whole nation, he argued, perhaps creating a permanent underclass. The program, moreover, would be expensive, and a bureaucracy would be needed to police recipients. Inevitably it would meddle

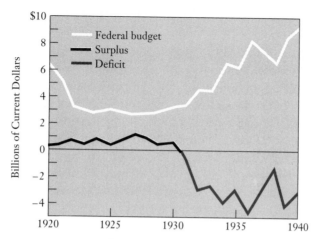

FEDERAL BUDGET AND SURPLUS/DEFICIT, 1920–1940   During the 1920s, the federal government ran a modest surplus. Beginning in 1930, federal deficits mounted as spending for Depression programs climbed and revenues from taxes and tariffs sank.

in the lives of citizens and bring a "train of corruption and waste." Hoover assumed that neighborliness and cooperation would be enough.

In 1930, as unemployment topped 4 million, Americans sent a new Congress to Washington. The off-year elections reduced the Republican majority to one in the Senate and gave Democrats a slim lead in the House. After rejecting Democratic proposals for more public works and a federal employment service, Hoover slowly retreated on federal relief. In 1932 he finally dictated the terms of his surrender in the Emergency Relief and Construction Act. It authorized the RFC to lend up to $1.5 billion for "reproductive" public works like toll bridges and slum clearance. Another $300 million went to states as loans for the direct relief of the unemployed. They were hardly adequate: when the governor of Pennsylvania requested funds to furnish the destitute with 13 cents a day for a year, the RFC sent only enough for 3 cents a day.

*Unemployment relief*

## Stirrings of Discontent

Hoover had given ground on relief, but like the rest of his Depression program it was too little and came too late. "The word revolution is heard at every hand," one writer warned in 1932. Some wondered if capitalism itself had gone bankrupt.

Here and there the desperate took matters into their own hands in 1932. In Wisconsin the Farm Holiday Association, under the leadership of Milo Reno, dumped thousands of gallons of milk on highways in a vain attempt to raise prices. Ten thousand striking miners formed a 48-mile motor car "Coal Caravan" that worked its way in protest across southern Illinois. In March a demonstration turned ugly when

*Farm Holiday Association*

communist sympathizers led a hunger march on Henry Ford's Rouge Assembly Plant in Dearborn, Michigan. As 3000 protesters surged toward the gates, Ford police drenched them with hoses, then opened fire at point-blank range. Four marchers were killed and more than 20 wounded.

For all the stirrings of discontent, revolution was never a danger. By 1932 the Communist party of the United States had only 20,000 members, up from 6500 in 1929 but hardly a political force. Under the slogan "Starve or Fight!" the Communists staged dozens of food, unemployment, and eviction protests. They led unionizing drives and courted intellectuals and the oppressed with their commitment to labor and civil rights.

*Communist party*

Deeply suspicious of Marxism, most Americans were unsympathetic. Fewer than 1000 African Americans joined the party in the early 1930s, despite a vigorous campaign to recruit them. In the election of 1932 Communist presidential candidate William Z. Foster polled just over 100,000 votes. At first hostile to established politics, the Communists adopted a more cooperative strategy to

Labor pickets, such as the one in Joe Jones'
*We Demand*, highlighted the failures of
capitalism. Here workers and their children, white
and black, display solidarity and new
"militancy" as they march in protest.

contain Adolf Hitler when his Nazi party won control of Germany in 1933. The Soviet Union ordered Communist parties in Europe and the United States to join with liberal politicians in a "popular front" against Nazism. Thereafter party membership peaked in the mid-1930s at about 80,000.

Hoover sympathized with the discontented but only to a point. When 1600 Communist-led hunger marchers came to Washington in December 1931, he was determined to protect their right to protest. The president ordered blankets, tents, a field kitchen, and medical aid for them. Washington police stood guard over their parade. Hoover himself received their petitions at the White House. But the following summer, the "Bonus Army" received a far different reception.

## The Bonus Army

The "army," a ragtag collection of World War I veterans, was looking to cash in certificates they had received from Congress in 1924, as a reward for wartime service. Called "bonuses," the certificates were due to mature at an average of $1000 each in 1945. Penniless and hungry, the veterans wanted their bonuses now, whatever they were worth.

In May 1932 Congressman Wright Patman of Texas introduced a bill for immediate payment of bonuses. Three hundred veterans set out from Portland, Oregon, on a march for the bonus bill. By the time they reached Washington in June, the "Bonus Expeditionary Force" had swelled to 15,000, the biggest protest in the city's history. Bonus Army leaders met with congressional representatives, but the president refused to see them. For the first time since the end of World War I the gates of the Executive Mansion were chained shut.

Hoover dismissed the veterans as a special-interest lobby eager to feather an already soft nest. Veterans' benefits accounted for a quarter of the federal budget, the largest single item. At a cost of $2.3 billion, their bonuses would have nearly doubled the deficit. The Senate spared Hoover the trouble of vetoing the bonus bill by blocking it.

Some veterans went home, but about 10,000 stayed to dramatize their plight. When Washington police tried to evict the veterans from buildings in the Federal Triangle, Hoover called in the army to help. He wanted nothing more than unarmed military support; instead Army Chief of Staff General Douglas MacArthur arrived with four troops of cavalry brandishing sabers, followed by six tanks and a column of infantry.

On July 28, 1932, soldiers cleared the Federal Triangle with bayonets and tear gas. Major George S. Patton, Jr., rode down a crowd of marchers in the last mounted charge of the U.S. Cavalry. MacArthur then turned to the Bonus encampment on the Anacostia Flats across the Potomac River. Despite Hoover's orders to halt, the general burned the camp to the ground. As the smoke drifted over the capitol the next morning, the Bonus marchers had vanished, except for some 300 wounded veterans. Among them was Joseph T. Angelino. In 1918 he had received the Distinguished Service Cross for saving the life of a young officer—none other than George Patton.

Hoover took full responsibility. He offered the lame excuse that Bonus marchers were "not veterans" but "Communists and persons with criminal records" bent on insurrection. (A survey conducted by the Veterans Administration later belied the claim.) In Albany, New York, Governor Franklin Roosevelt exploded at the president's performance: "There is nothing inside the man but jelly." Hoover's fear of big government and commitment to private initiative and voluntarism overcame his humanitarian impulses. Like the hero of a classical tragedy, Herbert Hoover came tumbling down.

## The Election of 1932

The Republicans refused to abandon Hoover. In June 1932 their national convention opened in Chicago and supported his Depression program to the last detail. Hoover was renominated, and rather thoughtlessly, the band struck up "California, here I come/Right back where I started from."

With an opportunity to recapture the White House for the first time since 1920, buoyant Democrats also gathered in Chicago. Their platform blamed the Depression on the Republicans, called for a 25 percent cut in federal spending, and promised a balanced budget. It also vowed somehow to provide federal public works and unemployment relief.

Franklin D. Roosevelt swept all challengers aside on the fourth ballot. Effervescent and inspiriting, Roosevelt broke tradition by accepting the nomination in person: "I pledge you, I pledge myself, to a new deal for the American people." In that instant, Roosevelt found his slogan—"the New Deal."

The campaign was over before it began, but Hoover fought on. He viewed the contest as a fight between two philosophies of government: the dangerous federal activism of Democrats against the voluntarism and prudent leadership of Republicans. Roosevelt, Hoover warned, would increase federal spending, inflate the currency, reduce the tariff, and "build a bureaucracy such as we have never seen in our history."

Without a national following, Roosevelt tailored his appeal to as broad a constituency as possible. In Iowa he said he was a "farmer"; in San Francisco, an economic planner. He called for a balanced budget one minute, more unemployment relief the next. He attacked Hoover as a "profligate spender," then went on to describe his own costly program for expanding public works.

Despite such fuzzy promises, election day brought a thundering rejection of Hoover and the Republicans. Roosevelt received nearly 58 percent of the popular vote. Norman Thomas won for the Socialists proportionately fewer votes than in 1912 or 1920. Democrats held majorities in both houses of Congress.

As telling as the magnitude of the victory were the returns themselves. Roosevelt carried the South and West and almost all the industrial states.

*Roosevelt coalition*    Dissatisfaction with Republican rule was galvanizing immigrants, Catholics and Jews, farmers and industrial laborers, city dwellers, and the rural poor into a broad coalition. With them the Democratic party would dominate politics for decades to come.

Early the next morning, Franklin Roosevelt returned to his townhouse from victory celebrations at the Biltmore Hotel in New York, only to experience a rare moment of doubt. As his son James helped him to bed, he confessed, "I am afraid I may not have the strength to do this job. After you leave me tonight, Jimmy, I am going to pray. . . . I hope you will pray for me, too."

The challenge was daunting: more than 12 million unemployed, 30 banks a week failing, factories idle, farms on the auction block, prices plummeting. People who had scorned government, including businessmen, were baffled and now looked to Washington. The nation awaited Roosevelt, but not even Roosevelt knew whether he would be equal to the job. All he knew was that he would try anything to help. In the progressive tradition, he would rely on the power of government. In one of his first acts, Roosevelt ordered that no one telephoning the White House for aid should be shut off. Someone in the administration would be found to answer every call.

## SIGNIFICANT EVENTS

1926 — Miami real estate bust

1927 — First "talking" film, *The Jazz Singer,* released

1928 — Great Bull Market begins to peak

1929 — Herbert Hoover inaugurated; stock market crash; Federal Farm Board created

1930 — Smoot–Hawley Tariff raises rates

1931 — Repatriation of Mexicans; Scottsboro boys arrested; New York establishes Temporary Emergency Relief Administration

1932 — Glass–Steagall Banking Act; Reconstruction Finance Corporation established; Emergency Relief and Construction Act; Farm Holiday Association formed; Bonus Army marches on Washington, D.C.; Franklin Roosevelt elected president

1933 — Legion of Decency formed; "black blizzards" begin to create Dust Bowl

1934 — Southern Tenant Farmers Union organized

1935 — *Becky Sharp,* first color film; Communist party announces popular front

1936 — Margaret Mitchell's *Gone with the Wind* published

1938 — Orson Welles's radio broadcast of "Invasion from Mars"

1939 — John Steinbeck's *The Grapes of Wrath* published

# CHAPTER TWENTY-SIX

# The New Deal

**W**inner, South Dakota, November 10, 1933. "Dammit, I don't WANT to write to you again tonight. It's been a long, long day, and I'm tired." All the days had been long since Lorena Hickok began her cross-country trek. Four months earlier Harry Hopkins, the new federal relief administrator, had hired the newspaper journalist to report on the relief efforts of the New Deal. Forget about statistics or the "social worker angle," he told her. "Talk with the unemployed, those who are on relief and those who aren't, and when you talk to them," he added, "don't ever forget that but for the grace of God you, I, any of our friends might be in their shoes."

In 1933 and 1934, Hickok found that Roosevelt's relief program was falling short. Its half-billion-dollar subsidy to states, localities, and charities was still leaving out too many Americans, like the sharecropper Hickok discovered near Raleigh, North Carolina. He and his daughters had been living in a tobacco barn for two weeks on little more than weeds and table scraps. "Seems like we just keep goin' lower and lower," said the blue-eyed 16-year-old. To Hickok's surprise, hope still flickered in those determined eyes. Hick couldn't explain it until she noticed a pin on the girl's chest. It was a campaign button from the 1932 election—"a profile of the President." Hope sprang from the man in the White House.

Before Franklin D. Roosevelt and the New Deal, the White House was far removed from ordinary citizens. The only federal agency with which they had any contact was the post office. And these days it usually delivered bad news. But as Hickok traveled across the country in 1933, she detected a change. People were talking about government programs. Perhaps it was long-awaited contributions to relief or maybe reforms in securities and banking or the new recovery programs for industry and agriculture. Just as likely it was Franklin Roosevelt. Hickok seldom heard voters call themselves "Republicans" or "Democrats" any more. Instead, she wrote, they were "for the president."

Lorena Hickok (left) met Eleanor Roosevelt (right) in 1928.
Thereafter she served as Mrs. Roosevelt's unofficial press adviser
and became her closest friend. (In the center of this photograph
is Paul Person, governor of the Virgin Islands.)

The mail to Washington carried other signs that plain people were looking to the president. During the first weekend after the inauguration nearly half a million letters and telegrams poured into the White House. For years the average remained a record 5000 to 8000 a day. Over half the letters came from those at the bottom of the economic heap. Most sought help, offered praise, or just expressed their gratitude.

Whatever the individual messages, their collective meaning was clear: Franklin D. Roosevelt and the New Deal had begun to restore national confidence. Though it never brought full recovery, the New Deal did improve economic conditions and provided relief to millions of Americans. Equally significant, it made lasting reforms in the nation's economic system and committed the federal government to a more active role in managing the ups and downs of the business cycle. In doing so it extended the progressive drive to soften industrialization and translated decades of growing concern for the disadvantaged into a federal aid program. For the first time, Americans believed Washington would help them through a terrible crisis. In short, during the Roosevelt years the liberal state came of age: active, interventionist, and committed to social welfare.

## THE EARLY NEW DEAL (1933–1935)

On March 4, 1933, as the clocks struck noon, Eleanor Roosevelt wondered if it were possible to "do anything to save America now." She looked at her husband, who had just been sworn in as thirty-second president of the United States. Franklin faced the crowd of over 100,000. Heeding the nation's call for "action, and action now," he promised to exercise "broad Executive power to wage a war against the emergency." The crowd cheered. Eleanor was terrified: "One has the feeling of going it blindly because we're in a tremendous stream, and none of us know where we're going to land."

The early New Deal unfolded in the spring of 1933 with a chaotic 100-day burst of legislation. It stressed recovery through planning and cooperation with business but also tried to aid the unemployed and reform the economic system. Above all, the early New Deal broke the cycle of despair. With Roosevelt in the White House, most Americans believed that they were in good hands, wherever they landed.

### The Democratic Roosevelts

From the moment they entered it in 1933, Franklin and Eleanor—the Democratic Roosevelts—transformed the White House. No more footmen; no more buglers; above all, no more seven-course meals like those Hoover had served. Instead visitors got fare fit for a boardinghouse. Roosevelt's lunches of hash and a poached egg cost 19 cents. The gesture was symbolic, but it made the president's point of ending business as usual.

Such belt-tightening was new to Franklin Roosevelt. Born of an old Dutch family in New York, he grew up rich and pampered. He idolized his Republican cousin Theodore Roosevelt and mimicked his career, except as a Democrat. Like Theodore, Franklin was graduated from Harvard University (in 1904), won a seat in the New York State legislature (in 1910), secured an appointment as assistant secretary of the navy (in 1913), and ran for the vice presidency (in 1920). Then disaster struck. On vacation in the summer of 1921, Roosevelt fell ill with poliomyelitis. The disease paralyzed him from the waist down. For the rest of his life, he walked only with the aid of crutches and heavy steel braces.

*Franklin Roosevelt*

Roosevelt emerged from the ordeal to win the governorship of New York in 1928. When the Depression struck, he created the first state relief agency in 1931, the Temporary Emergency Relief Administration. Aid to the jobless "must be extended by Government, not as a matter of charity, but as a matter

Most photographers acceded to White House wishes that President Roosevelt, a victim of polio, never be shot from the waist down. The president sits poolside at Warm Springs, Georgia, a polio treatment center that he helped to fund. Notice the newspaper held over his stricken legs.

of social duty," he explained. He considered himself a progressive but moved well beyond the cautious federal activism of most progressives. He adopted no single ideology. He cared little about economic principles. What he wanted were results. Experimentation became a hallmark of the New Deal.

Eleanor Roosevelt redefined what it meant to be First Lady. Never had a president's wife been so visible, so much of a crusader, so cool under fire. She

*Eleanor Roosevelt*

was the first First Lady to hold weekly press conferences. Her column, "My Day," appeared in 135 newspapers, and her twice-weekly broadcasts made her a radio personality rivaling her husband. She became his eyes, ears, and legs, traveling 40,000 miles a year. Secret Service men code-named her "Rover."

Eleanor believed she was only a spur to presidential action. But she was active in her own right, as a teacher and social reformer before Franklin became president and afterwards as a tireless advocate of the underdog. In the White House, she pressed him to hire more women and minorities but also supported antilynching and anti–poll tax measures, when he would not, and experimental towns for the homeless. By 1939 more Americans approved of her than of her husband.

### Saving the Banks

Before the election Roosevelt had gathered a group of economic advisers called the "Brains Trust." Out of their recommendations came the early or "first" New

*The Brains Trust*

Deal of government planning, intervention, and experimentation. Brains Trusters disagreed over the means of achieving their goals, but those goals they broadly shared: economic recovery,

# E Y E W I T N E S S   T O   H I S T O R Y

## "My Day":
## The First Lady Tours Tennessee

Johnson City, Tenn., May 31 [1939]—I looked out of the window of the train this morning while I was waiting for my breakfast, and it suddenly occurred to me that scenes from a train window might give a rather good picture of the variety in the conditions and occupations of our people in different parts of the country. I saw a little girl, slim and bent over, carrying two heavy pails of water across a field to an unpainted house. How far that water had to be carried, I do not know, but it is one thing to carry water on a camping trip for fun during a summer's holiday, and it is another thing to carry it day in and day out as part of the routine of living. On the outskirts of the town, I saw a wash line. On it hung two brown work shirts, a pair of rather frayed and faded blue dungarees, two child's sun suits and a woman's calico dress. Not much sign of wasteful living here.

Through its open door, I had a glimpse of the inside of a cabin in the hollow below us. It was divided into two rooms, one of them the bedroom with two beds in it. These two beds took up about all the available space in the room and it must have been necessary to leave the door open for air. There was a pad which looked rather like the cotton mattresses that have been made on WPA [Works Progress Administration], and a quilt neatly over each bed. I didn't notice any sheets or pillows.

There has been rain down here and the fields look in good condition. We passed a man plowing in a field with two women not far away hoeing. Beyond, in a grove of trees, there stood a stately house and under the trees was a baby carriage. I caught sight of someone in a flowered dress sitting on the porch. Then I again saw a yard of an unpainted house in the outskirts of a small town and a happy looking woman rocking a baby on the porch while a group of youngsters played in the yard. Happiness may exist under all conditions, given the right kind of people and sufficient economic security for adequate food and shelter.

Rochelle Chadakoff, ed., *Eleanor Roosevelt's My Day: Her Acclaimed Columns, 1936–1945* (New York: Pharos Books, 1989), pp. 119–120. Reprinted by permission of UFS, Inc.

relief for the unemployed, and sweeping reform to ward off future depressions. All concurred that the first step was to save the banks. By the eve of the inauguration governors in 38 states had temporarily closed their banks to stem the withdrawal of deposits. Without a sound credit structure, there could be no recovery.

On March 5, the day after his inauguration, Roosevelt ordered every bank in the country closed for four days. He shrewdly called it a "bank holiday." On March 9, the president introduced emergency banking legislation. The House passed the measure, sight unseen, and the Senate endorsed it later in the day. Roosevelt signed it that night.

Rather than nationalizing the banks as radicals wanted, the Emergency Banking Act followed the modest course of extending federal assistance to them.

*Emergency Banking Act* Sound banks would reopen immediately with government support. Troubled banks would be handed over to federal "conservators," who would guide them to solvency. On Sunday, March 12, Roosevelt explained what was happening in the first of his many informal "fireside-chat" radio broadcasts. When banks reopened the next day, deposits exceeded withdrawals.

To guard against another stock crash, financial reforms gave government greater authority to manage the currency and regulate stock transactions. In April 1933, Roosevelt dropped the gold standard and began experimenting with the value of the dollar to boost prices. Later that spring the Glass–Steagall Banking Act restricted speculation by banks and, more important, created federal insurance for bank deposits of up to $2500. Under the

*Federal Deposit Insurance* Federal Deposit Insurance Corporation, fewer banks failed for the rest of the decade than in the best year of the 1920s. The Securities Exchange Act (1934) established a new federal agency, the Securities and Exchange Commission, to oversee the stock market.

### Relief for the Unemployed

Saving the banks and financial markets meant little if human suffering could not be relieved. Mortgage relief for the millions who had lost their homes came eventually in 1934 in the Home Owners' Loan Act. But the urgent need to alleviate starvation led Roosevelt to propose a bold new giveaway program. The Federal Emergency Relief Administration (FERA) opened its door in May 1933. Sitting amid unpacked boxes, gulping coffee and chain-smoking, former social worker Harry Hopkins spent $5 million of a $500 million appropriation in his first two hours as head of the new agency. In its two-year existence, FERA furnished more than $1 billion in grants to states, local areas, and private charities.

As the winter of 1933–1934 approached, Hopkins persuaded Roosevelt to expand relief with an innovative shift from government giveaways to a

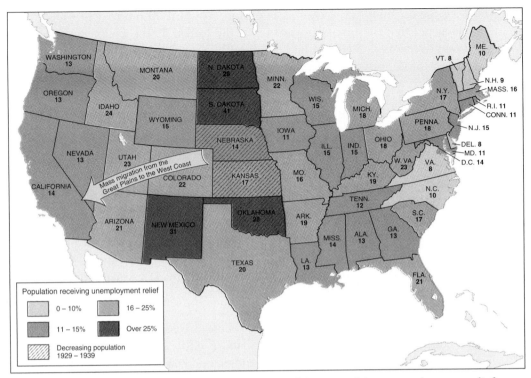

UNEMPLOYMENT RELIEF, 1934   The percentage of those receiving unemployment relief differed markedly throughout the nation. The farm belt of the plains was especially hard-hit, with 41 percent of South Dakota's citizens receiving federal benefits. In the East, the percentage dropped as low as 8 percent in some states.

*Work relief*     work program. Paying someone "to do something socially useful," Hopkins explained, "preserves a man's morale." The Civil Works Administration (CWA) employed 4 million Americans. Alarmed at the high cost of the program, Roosevelt disbanded the CWA in the spring of 1934. It nonetheless furnished a new weapon against unemployment and an important precedent for future relief programs.

Another work relief program established in 1933 proved even more creative. The Civilian Conservation Corps (CCC) was Roosevelt's pet project. It combined his concern for conservation with compassion for youth. The CCC took unmarried 18- to 25-year-olds from relief rolls and sent them into the woods and fields to plant trees, build parks, and fight soil erosion. During its 10 years, the CCC provided 2.5 million young men with jobs (which prompted some critics to chant, "Where's the she, she, she?").

New Dealers intended relief programs to last only through the crisis. But the Tennessee Valley Authority (TVA)—a massive public works project created

*Tennessee Valley Authority* in 1933—made a continuing contribution to regional planning. For a decade, planners had dreamed of transforming the flood-ridden basin of the Tennessee River, one of the poorest areas of the country, with a program of regional development and social engineering. The TVA constructed a series of dams along the seven-state basin to control flooding, improve navigation, and generate cheap electric power. In cooperation with state and local officials, it also launched social programs to stamp out malaria, provide library bookmobiles, and create recreational lakes.

Like many New Deal programs, the TVA produced a mixed legacy. It saved 3 million acres from erosion, multiplied the average income in the valley ten-fold, and repaid its original investment in federal taxes. Its cheap electricity helped to bring down the rates of private utility companies. But the experiment in regional planning also pushed thousands of families from their land, failed to end poverty, and created an agency that became one of the worst polluters in the country.

## The Riddle of Recovery

Planning, not just for regions but for the whole economy, seemed to many New Dealers the key to recovery. Some held that if businesses were allowed to plan and cooperate with one another, the ruthless competition that was driving down prices, wages, and employment could be controlled and the riddle of recovery solved. Business leaders had been urging such a course since 1931. In June 1933, under the National Industrial Recovery Act (NIRA), Roosevelt put planning to work for industry.

The legislation created two new agencies. The Public Works Administration (PWA) was designed to boost industrial activity and consumer spending with a *Public Works Administration* $3.3 billion public works program. The companies put under contract and unemployed workers hired would help stimulate the economy and leave a legacy of capital improvement. Harold Ickes, the prickly interior secretary who headed PWA, built the Triborough Bridge and Lincoln Tunnel in New York, the port city of Brownsville, Texas, and two aircraft carriers. But he was so fearful of waste and corruption that he never spent funds quickly enough to jumpstart the economy.

A second federal agency, the National Recovery Administration (NRA), aimed directly at controlling competition. Under NRA chief Hugh Johnson, *National Recovery Administration* representatives from government and business (and also from labor and consumer groups) drew up "codes of fair practices." Industry by industry, the codes established minimum prices, minimum wages, and maximum hours. No company could seek a competitive edge by cutting prices or wages below certain levels or by working a few employees mercilessly and firing the rest. It also required business to accept key demands of labor, including union rights to organize and bargain with management (thus ensuring that if prices jumped, so too might wages). And each code promised improved working conditions and outlawed such practices as child labor and sweatshops.

No business was forced to comply, for New Dealers feared that such government coercion might be ruled unconstitutional. The NRA relied on voluntary participation. A publicity campaign of parades, posters, and public pledges exhorted businesses to join the NRA and consumers to buy only NRA-sanctioned products. More than 2 million employers eventually signed up. In store windows and on merchandise, shiny decals with blue-eagle crests alerted customers that "We Do Our Part."

### The NRA in Trouble

For all the hoopla, the NRA failed to bring recovery. Big businesses shaped the codes to their advantage. Often they limited production and raised prices, sometimes beyond what they normally had been. Not all businesses joined, and those that did often found the codes too complicated or costly to follow. The NRA tried to cover too many businesses, and its relatively few inspectors had trouble keeping up with all the complaints. Even NRA support for labor tottered, for it had no means of enforcing its guarantee of union rights. Business survived under the NRA, but without increasing production there was no incentive for expansion and new investment. Under such conditions hard times could last indefinitely. And in the short run, despite an enthusiastic start, the NRA was soon spawning little but evasion and criticism.

On May 27, 1935, the Supreme Court struck down the floundering NRA in *Schecter Poultry Corp. v. United States*. The justices unanimously ruled that the NRA had exceeded federal power over commerce among the states by regulating the Schecter brothers' poultry business in New York. Privately Roosevelt was relieved to be rid of the NRA. But he and other New Dealers were plainly shaken by the grounds of the decision. They were relying on a broad view of the commerce clause to fight the Depression. Their distress only grew when Justice Benjamin Cardozo added a chilling afterthought: the NRA's code making represented "an unconstitutional delegation of legislative power" to the executive branch. Without the ability to make rules and regulations, all the executive agencies of the New Deal might flounder.

### Planning for Agriculture

As with planning for industry, New Deal planning for agriculture relied on private interests—the farmers—to act as the principal planners. Under the Agricultural Adjustment Act of 1933, farmers limited their own production. The government, in turn, paid them for not producing, while a tax on millers, cotton ginners, and other processors financed the payments. In theory, production quotas would reduce surpluses, demand for farm commodities would rise (as would prices), and agriculture would recover.

In practice the Agricultural Adjustment Administration (AAA) did help to increase prices. Unlike the code-ridden NRA, the AAA wisely confined cover-

*Agricultural Adjustment Administration*

age to seven basic commodities. As a way to push prices even higher, the new Commodity Credit Corporation gave loans to farmers who stored their crops rather than sold them—a revival of the Populists' old subtreasury plan (see page 566). Farm income rose from $5.5 billion in 1932 to $8.7 billion in 1935.

Not all the gains in farm income were the result of government actions or free from problems. In the mid-1930s dust storms, droughts, and floods helped to reduce harvests and push up prices. The AAA, moreover, failed to distribute its benefits equally. Large landowners controlled decisions over which plots would be left fallow. In the South this frequently meant cutting the acreage of tenants and sharecroppers or forcing them out. Even when they reduced the acreage that they themselves plowed, big farmers could increase yields, since they had the money and equipment to cultivate more intensively.

In 1936 the Supreme Court voided the Agricultural Adjustment Act. In *Butler v. U.S.*, the six-justice majority concluded that the government had no right to regulate agriculture, either by limiting production or by taxing processors. A hastily drawn replacement, the Soil Conservation and Domestic Allotment Act (1936), addressed the complaints. Farmers were now subsidized for practicing "conservation"—taking soil-depleting crops off the land—and paid from general revenues instead of a special tax. A second Agricultural Adjustment Act in 1938 returned production quotas.

Other agencies tried to help impoverished farmers. The Farm Credit Administration refinanced about a fifth of all farm mortgages. In 1935 the Resettlement Administration gave marginal farmers a fresh start by moving them to better land. Beginning in 1937 the Farm Security Administration furnished low-interest loans to help tenants buy family farms. In neither case did the rural poor have enough political clout to obtain sufficient funds from Congress. Fewer than 5000 families of a projected 500,000 were resettled, and less than 2 percent of tenant farmers received loans.

## A SECOND NEW DEAL (1935–1936)

"Boys—this is our hour," crowed the president's closest advisor, Harry Hopkins, in the spring of 1935. A year earlier voters had broken precedent by returning the party in power to office, giving the Democrats their largest majorities in decades. With the presidential election of 1936 only a year away, Hopkins figured that time was short: "We've got to get everything we want—a works program, social security, wages and hours, everything—now or never."

Hopkins calculated correctly. In 1935 politics, swept along by a torrent of protest, led to a "second hundred days" of lawmaking and a "Second New Deal." The emphasis shifted from planning and cooperation with business to greater regulation of business, broader relief, and bolder reform.

## Voices of Protest

In 1934 a mob of 6000 stormed the Minneapolis city hall, demanding more relief and higher pay for government jobs. In San Francisco longshoremen walked off the job, setting off a citywide strike. By year's end, 1.5 million workers had joined in 1800 strikes. Conditions were improving but not quickly enough, and across the country voices of protest gathered strength.

From the right came the charges of a few wealthy business executives and conservatives that Roosevelt was an enemy of private property and a dictator in the making. In August 1934 they founded the American Liberty

*Liberty League*

League. Despite spending $1 million in anti-New Deal advertising, the League won little support and only helped to convince the president that cooperation with business was failing.

In California discontented voters took over the Democratic party and turned sharply to the left by nominating novelist Upton Sinclair, a Socialist, for governor. Running under the slogan "End Poverty in California"

*End Poverty in California*

(EPIC), Sinclair proposed to confiscate idle factories and land and permit the unemployed to produce for their own use. Republicans mounted a no-holds-barred counterattack, including fake newsreels depicting Sinclair as a Bolshevik, atheist, and free-lover. Sinclair lost the election but won nearly 1 million votes.

Huey P. Long, the flamboyant senator from Louisiana, had ridden to power on a wave of rural discontent against banks, corporations, and political machines. As governor of Louisiana, he pushed through re-

*Huey Long*

forms regulating utilities, building roads and schools, even distributing free school books. Opponents called him a "dictator"; most Louisianans simply called him the "Kingfish." Breaking with Roosevelt in 1933, Long pledged to bring about recovery by making "every man a king." "Share Our Wealth" was a drastic but simple plan: the government would limit the size of all fortunes and confiscate the rest. Every family would then be guaranteed an annual income of $2500 and an estate of $5000, enough to buy a house, an automobile, and a radio (over which Long had already built a national following).

By 1935, one year after its founding, Long's Share Our Wealth organization boasted 27,000 clubs with files containing nearly 8 million names. Democratic National Committee members shuddered at polls showing that Long might capture up to 4 million votes in 1936, enough to put a Republican in the White House. But late in 1935, in the corridors of the Louisiana capitol, Long was shot to death by a disgruntled constituent whose family had been wronged by the Long political machine.

Louisiana Governor and Senator Huey Long promised to "make every man a king," but critics predicted that only Long would wear a crown. The "Kingfish" (a nickname taken from the "Amos 'n' Andy" radio show) made no secret of his presidential ambitions.

Father Charles Coughlin was Long's urban counterpart. Where Long explained the Depression as the result of bloated fortunes, Coughlin blamed the banks. In weekly broadcasts from the Shrine of the Little Flower in suburban Detroit, the "Radio Priest" told his working-class, largely Catholic audience of the international bankers who had toppled the world economy by manipulating gold-backed currencies.

*Charles Coughlin*

Coughlin promised to end the Depression with simple strokes: nationalizing banks, inflating the currency with silver, spreading work. (None would have worked because each would have dampened investment, the key to recovery.) Across the urban North, 30 to 40 million Americans—the largest audience in the world—huddled around their radios to listen. In 1934 Coughlin organized the National Union for Social Justice to pressure both parties. As the election of 1936 approached, the Union loomed on the political horizon.

A less ominous challenge came from Dr. Francis Townsend. The 67-year-old physician had recently retired in California from the public health service. Moved by the plight of elderly Americans without pension plans or medical insurance, Townsend set up Old Age Revolving Pensions, Limited, in 1934. He proposed to have the government pay $200 a month to those 60 years or older who quit their jobs and spent

*Francis Townsend*

the money within 30 days. By 1936 Townsend clubs counted 3.5 million members, most of them small businessmen and farmers at or beyond retirement age.

For all their differences, Sinclair, Long, Coughlin, Townsend, and other critics struck similar chords. Although the solutions they proposed were simplistic, the problems they addressed were serious: a maldistribution of goods and wealth, inadequacies in the money supply, the plight of the elderly. They attacked the growing control of corporations, banks, and government over individuals and communities. And they created mass political movements based on social as well as economic dissatisfaction. When Sinclair supporters pledged to produce for their own use and Long's followers swore to "share our wealth," when Coughlinites damned the "monied interests" and Townsendites thumped their Bibles at foul-ups in Washington, they were also trying to protect their freedom and their communities from the intrusion of big business and big government.

## The Second Hundred Days

By the spring of 1935, the forces of discontent were pushing Roosevelt to more action. And so was Congress. With Democrats accounting for more than two-thirds of both houses, they were prepared to outspend the president in extending the New Deal. The 100 days from April through mid-July, the "second hundred days," produced a legislative barrage that moved the New Deal toward Roosevelt's ultimate destination—"a little to the left of center."

To help the many Americans who were still jobless Roosevelt proposed the Emergency Relief Appropriation Act of 1935, with a record $4.8 billion for relief and employment. Some of the money went to the new National Youth

*Works Progress Administration*

Administration (NYA) for more than 4.5 million jobs for young people. But the lion's share went to the new Works Progress Administration (WPA), where Harry Hopkins mounted the largest work relief program in history. Before its end in 1943, the WPA employed at least 8.5 million people and built or improved over 100,000 schools, post offices, and other public buildings. Constrained from competing with private industry and committed to spending 80 percent of his budget on wages, Hopkins showed remarkable ingenuity. WPA workers taught art classes in a Cincinnati mental hospital, drafted a Braille map for the blind in Massachusetts, and pulled a library by packhorse through the hills of Kentucky.

The ambitious Social Security Act, passed in 1935, sought to help those who could not help themselves: the aged poor, the infirm, dependent children.

*Social security*

In this commitment to the destitute—which the Roosevelt administration believed were actually few in number—it laid the groundwork for the modern welfare state. But social security also acted as an economic stabilizer by furnishing pensions for retirees and insurance for those suddenly laid off from their jobs. A payroll tax on both employer and employee underwrote pensions after age 65, while an employer-financed system of insurance made possible government payments to unemployed workers.

Social security marked a historic reversal in American political values. A new social contract between the government and the people replaced the gospel of self-help and the older policies of laissez faire. At last government acknowledged a broad responsibility to protect the social rights of citizens. The welfare state, foreshadowed in the aid given veterans and their families after the Civil War, was institutionalized, though its coverage was limited. To win the votes of southern Congressmen hostile to African Americans, the legislation excluded farmworkers and domestic servants, doubtless among the neediest Americans but often black and disproportionately southern.

Roosevelt had hoped for social insurance that would cover Americans "from cradle to grave." Congress whittled down his plan, but its labor legislation pushed the president well beyond his goal of providing paternalistic aid for workers, like establishing pension plans and unemployment insurance. New York senator Robert Wagner, the son of a janitor, wanted workers to fight their own battles. In 1933 he had included union recognition in the NRA. When the Supreme Court killed the NRA in 1935, Wagner introduced what became the

*National Labor Relations Act* National Labor Relations Act. (So important had labor support become to Roosevelt that he gave the bill his belated blessing.) The "Wagner Act" created a National Labor Relations Board (NLRB) to supervise the election of unions and ensure union rights to bargain. Most vital, the NLRB had the power to enforce these policies. By 1941, the number of unionized workers had doubled.

Roosevelt responded to the growing hostility of business by turning against the wealthy and powerful in 1935. The popularity of Long's tirades against the rich and Coughlin's against banks sharpened his points of attack. The Revenue Act of 1935 (called the "Wealth Tax Act") threatened to "soak the rich." By the time it worked its way through Congress, however, it levied only moderate taxes on high incomes and inheritances. The Banking Act of 1935 centralized authority over the money market in the Federal Reserve Board. By controlling interest rates and the money supply, government increased its ability to compensate for swings in the economy. The Public Utilities Holding Company Act (1935) limited the size of utility empires. Long the target of progressive reformers, the giant holding companies produced nothing but higher profits for speculators and higher prices for consumers. Diluted like the wealth tax, the utility law was still a political victory for New Dealers. "I am now on your bandwagon again," a Philadelphia voter told the president as the election of 1936 approached.

## The Election of 1936

In June of 1936 Roosevelt traveled to Philadelphia, not to thank the loyal voter who had hopped aboard his bandwagon but to accept the Democratic nomination for a second term as president. "This generation of Americans has a rendezvous with destiny," he told a crowd of 100,000 packed into Franklin Field.

Whatever destiny had in store for his generation, Roosevelt knew that the coming election would turn on a single issue: "It's myself, and people must be either for me or against me."

Roosevelt ignored his Republican opponent, Governor Alfred Landon of Kansas. Despite a bulging campaign chest of $14 million, Landon lacked luster as well as issues. He favored the regulation of business, a balanced budget, and much of the New Deal. For his part Roosevelt turned the election into a contest between haves and have-nots. The forces of "organized money are unanimous in their hate for me," he told a roaring crowd at New York's Madison Square Garden, "and I welcome their hatred."

The strategy deflated Republicans, discredited conservatives, and stole the thunder of the newly formed Union Party of Townsendites, Coughlinites, and old Long supporters. The election returns shocked even experienced observers. Roosevelt won the largest electoral victory ever—523 to 8—and a whopping 60.8 percent of the popular vote. The margin of victory came from those at the bottom of the economic ladder, grateful for help furnished by the New Deal.

A dramatic political realignment was now clearly in place, as important as the Republican rise to power in 1896. The Democrats reigned as the new majority party for the next 30 years. The "Roosevelt coalition" rested on three pillars: traditional Democratic support in the South; the big cities, particularly ethnics and African Americans; and labor, both organized and unorganized. The minority Republicans became the party of big business and small towns.

*Roosevelt coalition*

## THE NEW DEAL AND THE AMERICAN PEOPLE

Before 1939, farmers in the Hill Country of Texas spent their evenings in the light of 25-watt kerosene lamps. Their wives washed eight loads of laundry a week, all by hand. Every day they hauled home 200 gallons—about 1500 pounds—of water from nearby wells. Farms had no milking machines, no washers, no automatic pumps or water heaters, no refrigerators, and no radios. "Living—just living—was a problem," recalled one woman.

The reason for this limited life was simple: the Hill Country had no electricity. Thus no agency of the Roosevelt administration changed the way people lived more dramatically than the Rural Electrification Administration (REA), created in 1935. At the time less than 10 percent of American farms had electricity. Six years later 40 percent did, and by 1950, 90 percent. The New Deal did not always have such a marked impact. And its overall record was mixed. But time and again it changed the lives of ordinary people as government never had before.

*Rural Electrification Administration*

## The New Deal and Western Water

In September 1936, President Roosevelt pushed a button in Washington, D.C., and sent electricity pulsing westward from the towering Boulder Dam in Colorado to cities as far away as Los Angeles. The waters thus diverted irrigated 2.5 million acres, while the dam's floodgates protected millions of people in southern California, Nevada, and Arizona. In its water management programs, the New Deal further extended federal power, literally across the country.

Boulder Dam was one of several multipurpose dams completed under the New Deal in the arid West. The aim was simple: to control whole river systems for regional use. Buchanan Dam on the lower Colorado River, the Bonneville and Grand Coulee dams on the Columbia, and many smaller versions curbed floods, generated cheap electricity, and developed river basins from Texas to Washington state. Beginning in 1938, the All-American Canal diverted the Colorado River to irrigate the Imperial Valley in California.

The environmental price of such rewards soon became evident, as it did with the New Deal's experiment in eastern water use, the Tennessee Valley Authority. The once mighty Columbia River, its surging waters checked by dams, flowed sedately from man-made lake to lake, but without the salmon whose spawning runs were also checked. Blocked by the All-American Canal from its path to the sea, the Colorado River slowly turned salty, until by 1950 its waters were unfit for drinking or irrigation.

## The Limited Reach of the New Deal

In the spring of 1939, the Daughters of the American Revolution refused to permit the black contralto Marian Anderson to sing at Constitution Hall in Washington, D.C. Eleanor Roosevelt quit the DAR in protest, and Secretary of the Interior Harold Ickes began looking for another site. On a nippy Easter Sunday, in the shadow of the Lincoln Memorial, Anderson finally stepped to the microphone and sang to a crowd of 7500. Lincoln himself would not have missed the irony.

In 1932 most African Americans cast their ballots as they had since Reconstruction—for Republicans, the party of Abraham Lincoln and emanci-

*African Americans*

pation. But disenchantment with decades of broken promises was spreading, and by 1934 African Americans were voting for Democrats. "Let Jesus lead you and Roosevelt feed you," a black preacher told his congregation on the eve of the 1936 election. When the returns were counted, three of four black voters had cast their ballots for Roosevelt.

The New Deal accounted for this voting revolution. Sympathetic but never a champion, Roosevelt regarded African Americans as one of many groups whose interests he brokered. Even that was an improvement. Federal offices had been segregated since Woodrow Wilson's day, and in the 1920s black leaders

California's multiethnic workforce is depicted in this detail from Paul Langley
Howard's *California Industrial Scenes.* It was one of several murals painted on
the walls of San Francisco's Coit Tower. The murals were begun in 1934 as a New
Deal relief program for artists.

called Hoover "the man in the lily-White House." Under Roosevelt racial integration slowly returned to government. Supporters of civil rights like Eleanor
Roosevelt and Secretary of the Interior Ickes brought political scientist Clark
Foreman, economist Robert C. Weaver, and other black advisers into the administration. Mary McLeod Bethune, a sharecropper's daughter and founder
of Bethune–Cookman College, ran a division of the National Youth
Administration. Important as both symbols and activists, African American administrators created a "Black Cabinet" to help design federal policy.

Outside of government the Urban League continued to lobby for economic
advancement, and the NAACP pressed to make lynching a federal crime.
(Though publicly against lynching and privately in favor of an antilynching bill,
Roosevelt refused to make it "must" legislation to avoid losing the white southern members of Congress he needed "to save America.") In New York's Harlem,
Reverend John H. Johnson organized the Citizens' League for Fair Play in 1933
to persuade white merchants to hire black clerks. After picketers blocked store-
fronts, hundreds of African Americans got jobs with Harlem retailers and

utility companies. Racial tension over employment and housing continued to run high, and in 1935 Harlem exploded in the only race riot of the decade.

Discrimination persisted under the New Deal. Black newspapers reported hundreds of cases of NRA codes resulting in jobs lost to white workers or wages lower than white rates of pay. Disgusted editors renamed the agency "Negroes Ruined Again." Federal efforts to promote "grass-roots democracy" often gave control of New Deal programs to local governments, where discrimination went unchallenged. New Deal showplaces like the TVA's model town of Norris, Tennessee, and the homestead village of Arthurdale, West Virginia, were closed to African Americans.

African Americans reaped a few benefits from the New Deal. The WPA hired black workers for almost 20 percent of its jobs, even though African Americans made up less than 10 percent of the population. When it was discovered that the WPA was paying black workers less than whites, Roosevelt issued an executive order to halt the practice. Public Works Administrator Ickes established the first quota system for hiring black Americans. By 1941 the percentage of African Americans working for the government exceeded their proportion of the population.

Civil rights never became a serious aspect of the New Deal, but for the nearly 1 million Mexican Americans in the United States, Latino culture some-

*Mexican Americans*

times frustrated meager federal efforts to help. Mexican folk traditions of self-help inhibited some from seeking aid; others remained unfamiliar with claim procedures. Still others failed to meet residency requirements. Meanwhile, low voter turnout hampered their political influence, and discrimination limited economic advancement.

In the Southwest and California, the Civilian Conservation Corps and the Works Progress Administration furnished some jobs, though fewer and for less pay than average. On Capitol Hill, Dennis Chavez of New Mexico, the only Mexican American in the Senate, channeled what funds he could into Spanish-speaking communities. But like African Americans, most Latinos remained mired in poverty. The many Mexican Americans who worked the fields as migratory laborers lay outside the reach of most New Deal programs.

## Tribal Rights

The New Deal renewed federal interest in Indians. Among the most disadvantaged Americans, Indian families on reservations rarely earned more than $100 a year. Their infant mortality rate was the highest in the country; their life expectancy, the shortest; their education level—usually no more than five years—the lowest. Their rate of unemployment was three times the national average.

In the 1930s, Indians had no stronger friend in Washington than John Collier. For years he had fought as a social worker among the Pueblos to

*John Collier and Indians*

restore tribal culture. As the new commissioner of Indian affairs, he reversed the decades-old policy of assimilation and promoted tribal life. Under the Indian Reorganization Act of 1934, elders were urged to celebrate festivals, artists to work in native styles, children to learn the old languages. A special Court of Indian Affairs removed Indians from state jurisdiction, and tribal governments ruled reservations. Perhaps most important, tribes regained control over Indian land. Since the Dawes Act of 1887, the land had been allotted to individual Indians, who were often forced by poverty to sell to whites. By the end of the 1930s, Indian landholding had increased.

Indians split over Collier's policies. The Pueblos, with a strong communal spirit and already functioning communal societies, favored them. The tribes of Oklahoma and the Great Plains tended to oppose them. Individualism, the profit motive, and an unwillingness to share property with other tribe members fed resistance. So did age-old suspicion of all government programs. And some Indians genuinely desired assimilation. The Navajos, under the leadership of J. C. Morgan, rejected the Indian Reorganization Act in 1935. Morgan saw tribal government as a step backward.

## A New Deal for Women

As the tides of change rippled across the country, a new deal for women was unfolding in Washington. The New Deal's welfare agencies offered unprecedented opportunity for social workers, teachers, and other women who had spent their lives helping the downtrodden. They were already experts on social welfare. Several were friends with professional ties, and together they formed a network of activists in the New Deal promoting women's interests and social reform. Led by Eleanor Roosevelt and Labor Secretary Frances Perkins, women served on the consumers' advisory board of the NRA, helped to administer the relief program, and won appointments to the Social Security Board.

In growing numbers women became part of the Democratic party machinery. Under the leadership of social worker Mary W. "Molly" Dewson, the Women's Division of the Democratic National Committee played a critical role in the election. Thousands of women mounted a "mouth-to-mouth" campaign, traveling from door to door to drum up support for Roosevelt and other Democrats. When the ballots were tallied, women formed an important part of the new Roosevelt coalition.

Federal appointments and party politics broke new ground for women, but in general the New Deal abided by existing social standards. Gender equality,

*Progress limited*

like racial equality, was never high on its agenda. One-quarter of all NRA codes permitted women to be paid less than men, while WPA wages averaged $2 a day more for men. The New Deal gave relatively few jobs to women, and when it did, they were often in gender-segregated trades such as sewing. Government employment patterns for women fell below even those in the private sector. The WPA hired nearly half a million women in 1936, roughly 15 percent of all WPA workers, at a time when women constituted almost a quarter of the workforce.

Reflecting old conceptions of reform, New Dealers placed greater emphasis on aiding and protecting women than on employing them. The Federal Emergency Relief Administration built 17 camps for homeless women in 11 states. Social security furnished subsidies to mothers with dependent children, and the WPA established emergency nursery schools (which also became the government's first foray into early childhood education). But even federal protection fell short. Social security, for example, did not cover domestic servants, most of whom were women.

## The Rise of Organized Labor

Although women and minorities discovered that the New Deal had limits to the changes it promoted, a powerful union movement arose in the 1930s by taking full advantage of the new climate. It ended up pushing Roosevelt well beyond

In San Antonio, Texas, Mexican American pecan shellers worked a 54-hour week for only $3. In 1938 they struck for better wages and working conditions. Here Emma Tenayuca, one of their leaders, addresses a group of striking workers.

his limits. At the outset of the Depression barely 6 percent of the labor force belonged to unions. The nation's premier union, the American Federation of Labor (AFL), was historically bound to skilled labor and organized on the basis of craft or skill. It virtually ignored the unskilled workers who made up most of the industrial labor force by the 1930s. Thus the AFL avoided major industries like rubber, automobiles, and steel.

John L. Lewis fought to unionize unskilled laborers. Tough, charismatic, and practical, Lewis headed the United Mine Workers (UMW), an affiliate of the AFL. When he met with Roosevelt in 1933, he received little more than consolation for his shrinking union. Yet the shrewd Lewis returned to the coal fields with a message the president had never given him: "The president wants you to join a union." Within a year the UMW had 400,000 members. Raising his sights, Lewis called for the creation of a Steel Workers' Organizing Committee (SWOC) and for the admission of the United Auto Workers into the AFL.

At the annual AFL convention in Atlantic City in 1935, Lewis demanded a commitment to the "industrial organization of mass production workers." The delegates, mostly from craft unions, voted down the proposal. Near the end of the convention, as he passed "Big Bill" Hutcheson of the carpenters union, angry words passed between the two. Lewis spun and with a single punch sent Hutcheson sprawling in a bloody heap.

The blow signaled the determination of industrial unions to break the AFL's domination of organized labor. A few weeks later, Lewis and the heads of seven other AFL unions announced the formation of the Committee for Industrial Organization (CIO). The AFL suspended the rogue unions in 1936. The CIO, later rechristened the Congress of Industrial Organizations, turned to the unskilled.

*Congress of Industrial Organizations*

## Campaigns of the CIO

CIO representatives concentrated on the mighty steel industry, which had clung to the "open," or nonunion, shop since 1919. In other industries, the rank and file did not wait. Emboldened by the recent passage of the Wagner Act, a group of rubber workers in Akron, Ohio, simply sat down on the job in early 1936. Since the strikers occupied the plants, managers could not replace them with strikebreakers. Nor could the rubber companies call in the military or police without risk to their property. The leaders of the United Rubber Workers Union opposed the "sit-downs," but when the Goodyear Tire & Rubber Company laid off 70 workers, 1400 rubber workers struck on their own. An 11-mile picket line sprang up outside. Eventually Goodyear settled by recognizing the union and accepting its demands on wages and hours.

*Sit-down strikes*

The biggest strikes erupted in the automobile industry. A series of spontaneous strikes at General Motors plants in Atlanta, Kansas City, and Cleveland spread to Fisher Body No. 2 in Flint, Michigan, late in December 1936. Singing the unionists' anthem, "Solidarity Forever," workers took over the plant while wives, friends, and fellow union members handed food and clothing through the windows. Local police tried to break up supply lines, only to be driven off by a hail of nuts, bolts, coffee mugs, and bottles.

In the wake of this "Battle of Running Bulls" (a reference to the retreating police), Governor Frank Murphy finally called out the National Guard, not to arrest but to protect strikers. General Motors surrendered in February 1937. Less than a month later U.S. Steel capitulated without a strike. By the end of the year every automobile manufacturer except Henry Ford had negotiated with the UAW.

Bloody violence accompanied some drives. On Memorial Day 1937, 10 strikers lost their lives when Chicago police fired on them as they marched peacefully toward the Republic Steel plant. And sit-down strikes often alienated an otherwise sympathetic middle class. (In 1939 the Supreme Court outlawed the tactic.) Yet a momentous transfer of power had taken place. By 1940 nearly one worker in three belonged to a union. The unskilled had a powerful voice in the CIO. And the craft unions of the AFL outnumbered them by more than a million. Women's membership in unions tripled between 1930 and 1940, and African Americans also made gains. Independent unions had become a significant part of industrial America.

*Union gains*

Government played an important but secondary role in the industrial union movement by creating a hospitable environment for labor. Roosevelt courted workers, both organized and unorganized, but stood aside in the toughest labor battles. Yet doing nothing in favor of strikers was a vast improvement over the active hostility shown by earlier presidents. The Wagner Act afforded laborers an opportunity to organize and protection if they chose to request it, but nothing more. Leaders such as John L. Lewis, Walter Reuther of the United Auto Workers, and Philip Murray of the Steel Workers' Organizing Committee galvanized workers, who won their own victories.

## "Art for the Millions"

No agency of the New Deal touched more Americans than Federal One, the bureaucratic umbrella of the WPA's arts program. For the first time, thousands of unemployed writers, musicians, painters, actors, and photographers went on the federal payroll. Public projects—from massive murals to tiny guidebooks—would make "art for the millions."

A Federal Writers Project (FWP) produced about a thousand publications. Its 81 state, territorial, and city guides were so popular that commercial publishers happily printed them. A Depression-bred interest in American history prompted the FWP to collect folklore, study ethnic groups, and record the reminiscences of 200 former slaves. Meanwhile, the Federal Music Project (FMP) employed some 15,000 out-of-work musicians. For a token charge, Americans could hear the music of Bach and Beethoven.

*Federal arts programs*

In the Federal Art Project (FAP), watercolorists and draftsmen painstakingly prepared the Index of American Design, which offered elaborate illustrations of American material culture, from skillets to cigar-store Indians. At night artists taught sculpture, painting, clay modeling, and carving in country churches, settlement houses, and schools. Jackson Pollock, Willem de Kooning, and others destined to become important painters survived the Depression by painting for the government.

The most notable contribution of the FAP came in the form of murals. Under the influence of Mexican muralists Diego Rivera and José Clemente

*Muralists* Orozco, American artists covered the walls of thousands of airports, post offices, and other government buildings with wall paintings glorifying local life and work. The rare treatment of class conflict later opened the FAP to charges of communist infiltration, but most of the murals stressed the enduring qualities of American life: family, work, community.

The Federal Theater Project (FTP) reached the greatest number of people—some 30 million—and aroused the most controversy. As its head, Hallie Flanagan made government-supported theater vital, daring, and relevant. Living Newspapers dramatized headlines of the day. Under the direction of Orson Welles and John Houseman an all-black company (one of 16 "Negro Units") set Shakespeare's Macbeth in Haiti, with voodoo priestesses and African drummers. Occasionally frank depictions of class conflict riled congressional conservatives, and beginning in 1938, the House Un-American Activities Committee investigated the FTP as "a branch of the Communistic organization." A year later Congress slashed its budget and brought government-sponsored theater to an end.

The documentary impulse to record life permeated the arts in the 1930s. Novels such as Erskine Caldwell's *Tobacco Road*, feature films like John Ford's

*Documentary realism* *The Grapes of Wrath*, and such federally funded documentaries as Pare Lorentz's *The River* stirred the social conscience of the country. New Dealers had practical motives for promoting documentary realism. They wanted to blunt criticism of New Deal relief measures by documenting the distress. In 1937 Rexford Tugwell established an Information Division in his Resettlement Administration. He put Roy Stryker, his former Columbia University teaching assistant, in charge of its Historical Section. Stryker hired talented photographers to produce an unvarnished record of the Great Depression. Their raw and haunting photographs turned history into both propaganda and art.

## THE END OF THE NEW DEAL (1937–1940)

"I see one-third of a nation ill-housed, ill-clad, ill-nourished," the president lamented in his second inaugural address on January 20, 1937 (the first January inauguration under a new constitutional amendment). Industrial output had doubled since 1932; farm income had almost quadrupled. But full recovery remained elusive. Over 7 million Americans were still out of work, and national income was only half again as large as it had been in 1933, when Roosevelt took office. At the height of his popularity, with bulging majorities in Congress, Roosevelt planned to expand the New Deal. Within a year, however, the New Deal was largely over, drowned in a sea of economic and political troubles—many of them Roosevelt's own doing.

## "Packing" the Courts

As Roosevelt's second term began, only the Supreme Court clouded the political horizon. In its first 76 years the Court had invalidated only two acts of Congress. Between 1920 and 1933 it struck down portions of 22 laws. This new judicial activism, spearheaded by a conservative majority, rested on a narrow view of the constitutional powers of Congress and the president. As the New Deal broadened those powers, the Supreme Court let loose a flood of nullifications.

In 1935 the Court wiped out the NRA on the grounds that manufacturing was not involved in interstate commerce and thus lay beyond federal regulation. In 1936 it canceled the AAA, reducing federal authority under the taxing power and the general welfare clause of the Constitution. In *Moorehead v. Tipaldo* (1936) the Court ruled that a New York minimum-wage law was invalid because it interfered with the right of workers to negotiate a contract. A frustrated Roosevelt complained that the Court had thereby created a " 'no-man's land,' where no government—State or Federal" could act.

Roosevelt was the first president since James Monroe to serve four years without making a Supreme Court appointment. Among federal judges Re-

*Roosevelt's plan* publicans outnumbered Democrats by more than two to one in 1933. Roosevelt intended to redress the balance with legislation that added new judges to the federal bench, including the Supreme Court. The federal courts were overburdened and too many judges "aged or infirm," he declared in February 1937. In the interests of efficiency, said Roosevelt, he proposed to "vitalize" the judiciary with new members. When a 70-year-old judge who had served at least 10 years failed to retire, the president could add another, up to six to the Supreme Court and 44 to the lower federal courts.

Roosevelt badly miscalculated. He unveiled his plan without warning, expecting widespread support. He regarded courts as political, not sacred, institutions and had ample precedent for altering even the Supreme Court. (As recently as 1869 Congress had increased its size to nine.) But most Americans clung to the courts as symbols of stability. Few accepted Roosevelt's efficiency argument, and no one on Capitol Hill (with its share of 70-year-olds) believed that seven decades of life necessarily made one incompetent. Worse still, the proposal ignited conservative–liberal antagonisms within the Democratic party.

"Here's where I cash in my chips," declared the Democratic chairman of the House Judiciary Committee as he abandoned the President.

Suddenly the Court reversed itself. In April, *N.L.R.B. v. Jones and Laughlin Steel Corporation* upheld the Wagner Act by one vote. A month later the justices sustained the Social Security Act as a legitimate exercise of the commerce power. And when Justice Willis Van Devanter, the oldest and most conservative justice, retired later that year, Roosevelt at last made an appointment to the Supreme Court.

With Democrats deserting him, the president accepted a substitute measure that utterly ignored his proposal to appoint new judges. Roosevelt nonetheless claimed victory. After all, the Court shifted course (and eventually he appointed nine Supreme Court justices). But victory came at a high price. The momentum of the 1936 election was squandered, the unity of the Democratic party was destroyed, and opponents learned that Roosevelt could be beaten. A conservative coalition of Republicans and rural Democrats had come together around the first of several anti-New Deal causes.

## The New Deal at Bay

As early as 1936 Secretary of the Treasury Henry Morgenthau began to plead for fiscal restraint. With productivity rising and unemployment falling, it was time to reduce spending, balance the budget, and let business lead the recovery. "Strip off the bandages, throw away the crutches," and let the economy "stand on its own feet," he said.

Morgenthau was preaching to the converted. Although the president had been willing to run budget deficits in a time of crisis, he had never been com-

*John Maynard Keynes*

fortable with them. To be sure, the British economist John Maynard Keynes had actually recommended the kind of deficit spending that Roosevelt had used. Keynes's startling theory called on government not to balance the budget but to spend its way out of depression. When prosperity returned, Keynes argued, government could pay off its debts through taxes. This deliberate policy of "countercyclical" action (spending in bad times, taxing in good) would compensate for swings in the economy.

For the present, however, Roosevelt ignored Keynes and ordered cuts in federal spending early in 1937. He slashed relief rolls by half and virtually halted spending on public works. Within six months, the economy collapsed. Industrial activity plummeted to 1935 levels. At the end of the year unemployment stood

*Roosevelt recession*

at 10.5 million as the "Roosevelt recession" deepened. Finally spenders convinced him to propose a $3.75 billion omnibus measure in April 1938. Facing an election, Congress happily reversed relief cuts, quadrupled farm subsidies, and embarked on a new shipbuilding program. The economy revived but never recovered. Keynesian economics was vindicated, though it would take decades before becoming widely accepted.

With Roosevelt vulnerable, conservatives in Congress struck. They cut back on public housing programs and minimum wage guarantees in the South. The president's successes came where he could act alone, principally in a renewed attack on big business. At his urging, the Justice Department opened investigations of corporate concentration. Even Congress responded by creating the Temporary National Economic Committee to examine corporate abuses and recommend revisions in the antitrust laws. These were small consolations. The president, wrote Interior Secretary Harold Ickes in August 1938, "is punch drunk from the punishment."

Vainly Roosevelt fought back. In the off-year elections of 1938, he tried to purge Democrats who had deserted him. The five senators he targeted for defeat all won. Republicans posted gains in the House and Senate and won 13 governorships. Democrats still held majorities in both houses, but conservatives had the votes to block new programs. With the economy limping toward recovery, the New Deal passed into history, and the nation turned to a new crisis: a looming war abroad.

## The Legacy of the New Deal

The New Deal lasted only five years, from 1933 to 1938, and it never spent enough to end the Depression. Though it pledged itself to the "forgotten" Americans, it failed the neediest among them: sharecroppers, tenant farmers, migrant workers. In many ways, it was quite conservative. It left capitalism intact, even strengthened, and it overturned few cultural conventions. Even its reforms followed the old progressive formula of softening industrialism by strengthening the state.

Yet for all its conservatism and continuities, the New Deal left a legacy of change. Under it, government assumed a broader role in the economy than progressives had ever undertaken. To regulation was now added the complicated task of maintaining economic stability—compensating for swings in the business cycle. In its securities and banking regulations, unemployment insurance, and requirements for wages and hours, the New Deal created stabilizers to avoid future breakdowns. Bolstering the Federal Reserve system and enhancing control over credit strengthened government influence over the economy.

Franklin Roosevelt modernized the presidency. He turned the White House into the heart of government, the place where decisions were made. Americans looked to the president to set the public agenda, spread new ideas, initiate legislation, and assume responsibility for the nation. The power of Congress diminished, but the scope of government grew. In 1932 there were 605,000 federal employees; by 1939 there were nearly a million (and by 1945, after World War II, some 3.5 million). The many programs of the New Deal—home loans, farm subsidies, bank deposit insurance, relief payments and jobs, pension programs, unemployment insurance, aid to mothers with dependent children—

## WHAT THE NEW DEAL DID. . .

|  | RELIEF | RECOVERY | REFORM |
|---|---|---|---|
| FOR THE FARMER: | Rural Electrification Administration (1936) Farm Security Administration (1937) | Agriculture Adjustment Act (1933) | |
| FOR THE WORKER: | | National Industrial Recovery Act (1933) | National Labor Relations Act (1935) Fair Labor Standards Act (1938) |
| FOR THE MIDDLE CLASS: | Home Owner's Loan Act (1934) | | Revenue ("Wealth Tax") Act (1935) Public Utilities Holding Company Act (1935) |
| FOR THE NEEDY: | Federal Emergency Relief Act (1933) Civilian Conservation Corp (1933) Civil Works Administration (1933) Emergency Relief Appropriation Act (1935) National Public Housing Act (1937) | | |
| FOR PROTECTION AGAINST FUTURE DEPRESSIONS: | | | Federal Deposit Insurance Corporation (1933) Securities Exchange Act (1934) Social Security Act (1935) |

touched the lives of ordinary Americans, made them more secure, bolstered the middle class, and formed the outlines of the new welfare state.

The welfare state had limits. Most of its relief measures were designed to last no longer than the crisis. Millions fell through even its more nearly permanent safety nets. Yet the commitment to furnishing minimum standards of life, not the failure to do so, marked a change so dramatic that the poor and working class threw their support to Roosevelt. He was, after all, the first president to try.

At a time when dictators and militarists took hold in Germany, Italy, Japan, and Russia, the New Deal strengthened democracy in America. Roosevelt acted as a democratic broker, responding first to one group, then another. And his "broker state" embraced groups previously spurned: unions, farm organizations, ethnic minorities, women. In short, during the 1930s the United States found a middle way avoiding the extremes of communism and fascism. Still, the broker state also had limits. The unorganized, whether in city slums or in share-croppers' shacks, too often found themselves ignored.

Under the New Deal, the Democratic party became a mighty force in politics. In a quiet revolution, African Americans came into the party's fold, as did workers and farmers. Political attention shifted to bread-and-butter issues. In 1932 people had argued about Prohibition and European war debts. By 1935 they were debating social security, labor relations, tax reform, public housing, and the TVA. With remarkable speed, the New Deal had become a vital part of American life.

---

## COUNTERPOINT   *Assessing the New Deal*

Historians disagree sharply in assessing the New Deal. We have taken the view, shared by many liberal historians, that the New Deal was not radical or socialistic but fell within the American political tradition of pragmatic reform. Historians of the New Left, a group of radical scholars writing in the 1960s, attacked the New Deal for being too conservative and thus failing to aid those most in need—sharecroppers, for example. Instead, they say, New Dealers ended up preserving the inequities of corporate capitalism.

Other scholars have defended the New Deal, noting the obstacles faced by reformers. Some stress the absence of "state capacity," a bureaucracy of necessary size and expertise to carry out the New Deal's massive programs. Others emphasize political constraints: Congress, the Supreme Court, and the public, all of which manifested concern at one time or another over the growth of government. Still others point out that New Dealers themselves were often skeptical about growing deficits, expanding government, and mounting welfare initiatives.

---

SIGNIFICANT EVENTS

1933 — Franklin Roosevelt inaugurated as president; first "100 days" launched; "bank holiday"; repeal of Eighteenth Amendment (Prohibition); Townsend movement begins

1934 — Securities and Exchange Commission; American Liberty League; Indian Reorganization Act; Father Charles Coughlin creates National Union for Social Justice; Huey Long organizes Share Our Wealth Society

1935 — Emergency Relief Appropriation Act; Rural Electrification Administration authorized; *Schecter Poultry Corp. v. United States* invalidates National Recovery Administration; "second hundred days" legislation passed; Huey Long assassinated

1936 — *Butler v. U.S.* ends Agricultural Adjustment Administration; Soil Conservation and Domestic Allotment Act; Congress of Industrial Organizations formed; Roosevelt reelected; United Auto Workers union begins sit-down strikes; John Maynard Keynes's major work, *The General Theory of Employment, Interest, and Money,* published

1937 — Roosevelt announces court "packing" plan; Roosevelt recession

1938 — Fair Labor Standards Act sets minimum wages and maximum hours; Congress establishes Temporary National Economic Committee

# CHAPTER TWENTY-SEVEN

# America's Rise to Globalism

John Garcia, a native Hawaiian, worked at the Pearl Harbor Navy Yard in Honolulu. On Sunday, December 7, 1941, Garcia planned to enjoy a lazy day off. By the time his grandmother rushed in to wake him that morning at eight, he had already missed the worst of it. "The Japanese were bombing Pearl Harbor," he recalled her yelling at him. John listened in disbelief. "I said, 'They're just practicing.'" "No," his grandmother replied. It was real. He catapulted his huge frame from the bed, ran to the front porch, hopped on his motorcycle, and sped to the harbor.

"It was a mess," he remembered. The USS *Shaw* was in flames. The battleship *Pennsylvania*, a bomb nesting one deck above the powder and ammunition, was about to blow. When ordered to put out its fires, he told the navy officer, "There ain't no way I'm gonna go down there." Instead, he spent the rest of the day pulling bodies from the water. There were so many he lost count. Surveying the wreckage the next morning, he noted that the battleship *Arizona* "was a total washout." So was the *West Virginia*. The *Oklahoma* had "turned turtle, totally upside down." It took two weeks to get all the fires out.

The war that had been spreading around the world had, until December 7, spared the United States. The surprise attack on Pearl Harbor suddenly transformed the Pacific into an avenue for potential invasion. Panic spread up and down the West Coast. Crowds in Los Angeles turned trigger-happy. A young police officer named Tom Bradley (who later served as mayor of the city) heard "sirens going off, aircraft guns firing." "Here we are in the middle of the night," he said, "there was no enemy in sight, but somebody thought they saw the enemy." In January 1942 worried officials moved the Rose Bowl from Pasadena, California, to Durham, North Carolina. Though overheated, their fears were not entirely imaginary. Japanese submarines shelled Santa Barbara, while other enemy ships launched balloons carrying incendiary devices. One floated all the way to Iowa without doing any damage.

Although the Japanese never mounted a serious threat to the mainland, in a world with long-range bombers and submarines, no place seemed safe. This was global war, the first of its kind. Arrayed against the Axis powers of Germany, Italy, and Japan were the Allies: Great Britain, the Soviet Union, the United States, China, and the Free French. Their armies fought from the Arctic to the southwestern Pacific, in the great cities of Europe and Asia and the small villages of North Africa and Indochina, in malarial jungles and scorching deserts, on six continents and across four oceans. Perhaps as many as 100 million people took up arms; some 40 to 50 million lost their lives.

Tragedy on such a scale taught the generation of Americans who fought the war that they could no longer isolate themselves from any part of the world, no matter how remote. Manchuria, Ethiopia, and Poland had once seemed far away, yet the road to war had led from those distant places to the United States. Retreat into isolation had not cured the worldwide Depression or preserved the peace. As it waged a global war, the United States began to assume far wider responsibility for managing the world's geopolitical and economic systems.

## THE UNITED STATES IN A TROUBLED WORLD

The outbreak of World War II had its roots in World War I. Many of the victorious as well as the defeated nations resented the peace terms adopted at Versailles. Over the next two decades Germany, the Soviet Union, Italy, Poland, and Japan all sought to achieve on their own what Allied leaders had denied them during the negotiations. War debts imposed at Versailles shackled Germany's economy. As Germany struggled to recover during the Great Depression, so did all of Europe. In central and eastern Europe rivalry among fascists, communists, and other political factions led to frequent violence and instability.

Faced with an unstable world, the United States turned away from collective action. Although their nation possessed the resources at least to ease international tensions, Americans declined to lead in world affairs, remaining outside of the League of Nations.

### Pacific Interests

That did not mean the United States could simply ignore events abroad. In assuming colonial control over the Philippines, Americans had created a potentially dangerous rivalry with Japan over the western Pacific. So also had the American commitment to uphold China's territorial integrity, set out in the "open door" policy of 1900 (page 591). With rival Chinese warlords still fighting among themselves, Japan took the opportunity to capture much-needed overseas raw materials and markets.

The Japanese had long dominated Korea, and during the 1920s they expanded their influence on the Chinese mainland. In 1931 Japanese agents staged an explosion on a rail line in Manchuria (meant to appear as though carried out by Chinese nationalists), which provided Japan with an excuse to occupy the whole province. A year later Japan converted Manchuria into a puppet state called Manchukuo.

Here was a direct threat to the Versailles system. But neither the major powers in Europe nor the United States was willing to risk a war with Japan over China. President Hoover instructed Secretary of State Henry Stimson only to protest that the United States would refuse to recognize Japan's takeover of

*Stimson Doctrine*

Manchuria as legal. The policy of "nonrecognition" became known as the Stimson Doctrine, even though Stimson himself doubted its worth. He was right to doubt. Three weeks later Japan's imperial navy shelled the Chinese port city of Shanghai. When the League of Nations condemned Japan in 1933, the Japanese simply withdrew from the League. The seeds of war in Asia had been sown.

## Becoming a Good Neighbor

Growing tensions in Asia and Europe gave the United States an incentive to improve relations with nations closer to home. By the late 1920s the United States had intervened in Latin America so often that the Roosevelt Corollary (page 628) had become an embarrassment. Slowly, however, American administrations began to moderate those highhanded policies. In 1927, when Mexico confiscated American-owned properties, President Coolidge decided to send an ambassador to settle the dispute rather than the marines. In 1933, when critics compared the American position in Nicaragua to Japan's in Manchuria, Secretary Stimson ordered U.S. troops to withdraw. In such gestures lay the roots of a "Good Neighbor" policy.

Franklin Roosevelt pushed the good neighbor idea. At the seventh Pan-American Conference in 1933, his administration accepted a resolution deny-

*Good Neighbor policy*

ing any country "the right to intervene in the internal or external affairs of another." The following year he negotiated a treaty with Cuba that renounced the American right to intervene under the Platt Amendment (page 628). Henceforth the United States would replace direct military presence with indirect (but still substantial) economic influence.

As the threat of war increased during the 1930s, the United States found a new Latin willingness to cooperate in matters of common defense. By the end of 1940 the administration had worked out defense agreements with every Latin American country but one. The United States faced the threat of war with the American hemisphere largely secured.

## The Diplomacy of Isolationism

During the 1920s Benito Mussolini had appealed to Italian nationalism and fears of communism to gain power in Italy. Spinning his dreams of a new Roman empire, Mussolini embodied the rising force of fascism.

*The rise of fascism*

Then on March 5, 1933, one day after the inauguration of Franklin Roosevelt, the German legislature gave Adolf Hitler control of Germany. Riding a wave of anticommunism and anti-Semitism, Hitler's Nazi party promised to unite all Germans in a Greater Third Reich that would last a thousand years. A week earlier, Japan had withdrawn from the League of Nations. Its militarist leaders were intent on carving out Japan's own empire, which they called the Greater East Asia Co-Prosperity Sphere. The rise of fascism and militarism in Europe and Asia brought the world to war.

As much as Roosevelt wanted the United States to play a leading role in world affairs, he found the nation reluctant to follow. "It's a terrible thing to look over your shoulder when you are trying to lead—and to find no one there," he commented during the mid-1930s. Only when a potential economic interest was involved could the president command wide support for for-

*Recognition of the Soviet Union*

eign initiatives. For example, in 1933 Roosevelt recognized the Communist government of the Soviet Union, hoping it would help contain Japanese expansion in Asia and fascism in Europe. But the move was accepted largely because business leaders welcomed the opportunity to increase Russian–American trade.

For every step Roosevelt took toward internationalism, the Great Depression forced him home again. Programs to revive the economy gained broad support; efforts to resolve crises abroad provoked opposition. The move to noninvolvement in world affairs gained in 1935 after Senator Gerald P. Nye of North Dakota held hearings on the role of bankers and munitions makers in World

*The Nye Committee*

War I. These "merchants of death," Nye's Committee revealed, had made enormous profits during World War I. The committee report implied, but could not prove, that business interests had even steered the United States into war. "When Americans went into the fray," declared Senator Nye, "they little thought that they were there and fighting to save the skins of American bankers who had bet too boldly on the outcome of the war and had two billions of dollars of loans to the Allies in jeopardy."

Nye's charges fed a fierce debate over how the United States should face the growing threat of war. Internationalists like the League of Women Voters and former Secretary of State Henry Stimson favored a policy of collective security: working actively with other nations. Iso-

*Internationalists versus isolationists*

lationists opposed the collective security formula. Two beliefs united them: a firm opposition to war and the conviction that the United States should avoid alliances with other nations. Yet the isolationist camp was a mixed one, with many strange bedfellows. It included liberal reformers and arch-conservatives, a concentration of midwesterners as well as major leaders from both coasts, and a number of Democrats as well as leading Republicans. Pacifists added yet another element to the debate. Powerful groups like the Women's International League for Peace and Freedom insisted that disarmament was the only road to peace.

### Neutrality Legislation

Roused by the Nye Committee hearings, Congress debated a proposal to prohibit the sale of arms to all belligerents in time of war. Internationalists argued that an embargo should apply only to aggressor nations. Otherwise, aggressors could strike when they were better armed than their victims. The president, internationalists suggested, should use the embargo selectively. Isolationists, however, had the votes they needed. The Neutrality Act of 1935 required an impartial embargo of arms to all belligerents. The president had authority only to determine when a state of war existed.

The limitations of formal neutrality became immediately apparent. In October 1935 Mussolini ordered Italian forces into the North African country of Ethiopia. Against tanks and planes, Ethiopian troops fought back with spears and flintlock rifles. Roosevelt immediately invoked neutrality in hopes of depriving Italy of war goods. Unfortunately for Roosevelt, Italy needed not arms but oil, steel, and copper—materials not included under the Neutrality Act. When Secretary of State Cordell Hull called for a "moral embargo" on such goods, Depression-starved American businesses shipped them anyway. With no effective opposition from the League of Nations or the United States, Mussolini quickly completed his conquest. In a second Neutrality Act, Congress added a ban on providing any loans or credits to belligerents.

American isolation also benefited Nazi dictator Adolf Hitler. In March 1936, two weeks after Congress passed the second Neutrality Act, German troops thrust into the demilitarized area west of the Rhine River. This flagrant act violated the Treaty of Versailles. As Hitler shrewdly calculated, Britain and France did nothing, while the League of Nations sputtered out a worthless condemnation. Roosevelt remained aloof. The Soviet Union's lonely call for collective action fell on deaf ears.

Then came an attack on Spain's fledgling democracy. In July 1936 Generalissimo Francisco Franco, made bold by Hitler's success, led a rebellion against the newly elected Popular Front government. Hitler and Mussolini sent supplies, weapons, and troops to Franco's Fascists, while the Soviet Union and Mexico aided the left-leaning government. With Americans sharply divided over whom to support, Roosevelt refused to become involved. Lacking vital support, the Spanish republic fell to Franco in 1939.

*Spanish Civil War*

For its part, Congress searched for a way to allow American trade to continue (and thus to promote economic recovery at home) without drawing the

A company of Nazi youths parades past the *Führer*, Adolf Hitler
(centered in the balcony doorway). Hitler's shrewd use of
patriotic symbols, mass rallies, and marches exploited the
new possibilities of mass politics.

*Cash-and-carry* nation into war itself. Under new "cash-and-carry" provisions in the Neutrality Act of 1937, belligerents could buy supplies other than munitions. But they would have to pay beforehand and carry the supplies on their own ships. If war spread, these terms favored the British, whose navy would ensure that supplies reached England.

But the policy of cash-and-carry did not help China in 1937 when Japanese forces pushed into its southern regions. In order to give China continued access to American goods, Roosevelt refused to invoke the Neu- *Aggression in China* trality Act, which would have cut off trade with both nations. But Japan had far the greater volume of trade with the United States. Since the president lacked the freedom to impose a selective embargo, he could only condemn Japan's invasion.

### Inching toward War

In 1937 the three aggressor nations, Germany, Japan, and Italy, signed the Anti-Comintern Pact. On the face of it, the pact pledged them only to ally against the Soviet Union. But the agreement created a Rome–Berlin–Tokyo axis that provoked growing fear of an even wider war. Roosevelt groped for some way to

contain the Axis powers, delivering in October his first foreign policy speech in
14 months. Seeming to favor firm collective action, he called for
an international "quarantine" of aggressor nations. Although

*Quarantine speech*

most newspapers applauded his remarks, Roosevelt remained
cautious about matching words with deeds. When Japanese planes sank the
American gunboat *Panay* on China's Yangtze River only two months later, he
meekly accepted an apology for the unprovoked attack.

In Europe, the Nazi menace continued to grow as German troops marched
into Austria in 1938—yet another violation of the Versailles Treaty. Hitler then
insisted that the 3.5 million ethnic Germans in the Sudetenland of Czechoslovakia be brought into the Reich. With Germany threatening to invade
Czechoslovakia, the leaders of France and Britain flew to Munich in September
1938, where they struck a deal to appease Hitler. Czechoslovakia would give up
the Sudetenland in return for German pledges to seek no more

*Appeasement at Munich*

territory in Europe. When British Prime Minister Neville
Chamberlain returned to England, he told cheering crowds that
the Munich Pact would bring "peace in our time." Six months later, in open
contempt for the European democracies, Hitler took over the remainder of
Czechoslovakia. "Appeasement" became synonymous with betrayal, weakness,
and surrender.

## Hitler's Invasion

By 1939 Hitler made little secret that he intended to recapture territory Germany
lost to Poland after World War I. What then would the Soviet Union do? If
Soviet leader Joseph Stalin joined the Western powers, Hitler might be blocked.
But Stalin, who coveted eastern Poland, suspected that the West hoped to turn
Hitler against him. On August 24, 1939, Russia and Germany shocked the
world when they announced a nonaggression pact. Its secret protocols freed
Hitler to invade Poland without fear of Soviet opposition. In turn, Stalin could
extend his western borders by bringing eastern Poland, the Baltic states (Latvia,
Estonia, and Lithuania), and parts of Romania and Finland into the Soviet
sphere.

On the hot Saturday of September 1, 1939, German tanks and troops surged
into Poland. "It's come at last," Roosevelt sighed. "God help us all." Within
days France and England declared war on Germany. Stalin

*Hitler invades Poland*

quickly moved into eastern Poland, where German and Russian
armor took just three weeks to crush the Polish cavalry. As Hitler
consolidated his hold on eastern Europe, Stalin invaded Finland.

Once spring arrived in 1940, Hitler moved to protect his sea lanes by capturing Denmark and Norway. Soon after, German panzer divisions supported
by airpower knifed through Belgium and Holland in a *blitzkrieg*—

*German blitzkrieg*

a "lightning war." The Low Countries fell in 23 days, giving the
Germans a route into France. By May a third of a million British

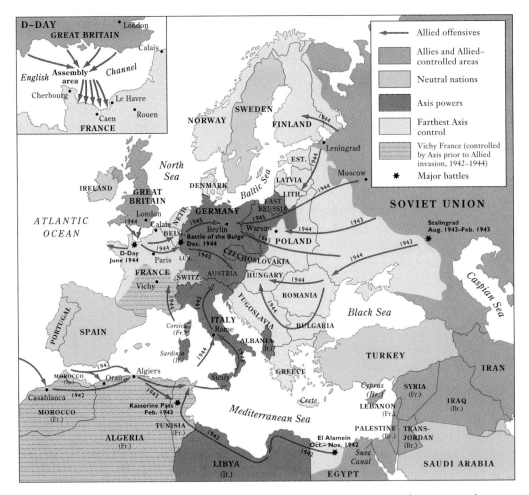

WORLD WAR II IN EUROPE AND NORTH AFRICA   Until 1944 Soviet forces carried
the brunt of the war in Europe, engaging the Axis armies across a huge front.
After winning North Africa, the Allies turned north to knock Italy out of the
war. The final key to defeating Germany was the Anglo-American invasion
of western Europe at Normandy.

and French troops had been driven back onto the Atlantic beaches of Dunkirk.
Only a strenuous rescue effort, staged by the Royal Navy and a flotilla of
English pleasure craft, managed to ferry them to safety, across the Channel to
England. With the British and French routed, German forces marched to Paris.

On June 22, less than six weeks after the German invasion, France capitulated. Hitler insisted that the surrender come in the very railway car in which
Germany had submitted in 1918. William Shirer, an American war correspondent standing 50 yards away, watched the dictator through binoculars: "He
swiftly snaps his hands on his hips, arches his shoulders, plants his feet wide
apart. It is a magnificent gesture of defiance, of burning contempt for this place

and all that it has stood for in the twenty-two years since it witnessed the humbling of the German Empire."

## Retreat from Isolationism

Now, only Great Britain stood between Hitler and the United States. If the Nazis defeated the British fleet, the Atlantic Ocean could easily become a gateway to America. Isolationism suddenly seemed dangerous. By the spring of 1940 Roosevelt had abandoned impartiality in favor of outright aid to the Allies. In May he requested funds to motorize the U.S. army (it had only 350 tanks) and build 50,000 airplanes a year (fewer than 3000 existed, most outmoded). Over isolationist protests he soon persuaded Congress to adopt a bill for the first peacetime draft in history.

In the 1940 presidential election campaign both Roosevelt and his Republican opponent, Wendell Willkie, favored an internationalist course short of war. In defeating Willkie, Roosevelt promised voters that rather than fight, the United States would become "the great arsenal of democracy." The British, however, could no longer pay for arms under the provisions of cash-and-carry. So Roosevelt proposed a scheme to "lease, lend, or otherwise dispose of" arms

*Lend-lease*

and supplies to countries whose defense was vital to the United States. That meant sending supplies to England on the dubious premise that they would be returned when the war ended. Roosevelt likened "lend-lease" to lending a garden hose to a neighbor whose house was on fire. Isolationist Senator Robert Taft thought a comparison to "chewing gum" more apt. After a neighbor used it, "you don't want it back." In March 1941 a large majority in Congress passed the Lend-Lease Act.

Step by step Roosevelt had led the United States to the verge of war with the Nazis. Over the summer of 1941 American destroyers escorted British ships as far as Iceland (though Roosevelt insisted it was a "patrol," not a convoy). The United States extended its defensive sphere to include Greenland and Iceland. Then Hitler, as audacious as ever, broke his alliance with the Soviet Union by launching a surprise invasion of Russia in June 1941. The Allies expected a swift collapse, but when Russian troops mounted a heroic resistance, Roosevelt extended lend-lease to the Soviet Union.

That August Roosevelt secretly met with the new British prime minister, Winston Churchill, on warships off the coast of Newfoundland, in Argentia Bay. Almost every day since England and Germany had gone to war, the two men had exchanged phone calls, letters, or cables. The Argentia meetings cemented this friendship—one key to Allied victory. Roosevelt and Churchill also

*Atlantic Charter*

drew up the Atlantic Charter, a statement of principles that the two nations held in common. The Charter condemned "Nazi tyranny" and embraced the "Four Freedoms": freedom of speech and expression, freedom of worship, freedom from want, and freedom from fear. In effect, the Atlantic Charter was an unofficial statement of war aims.

By mid-1941, American destroyers in the North Atlantic were already stalking German U-boats (submarines) and reporting their whereabouts to British commanders. Given the harsh weather and aggressive American policy, incidents were inevitable. In October a U-boat sank the destroyer *Reuben James*, killing more than 100 American sailors. That act increased public support for the Allied cause. Yet as late as September 1941 eight of ten Americans opposed entering the hostilities. Few in the United States suspected that an attack by Japan, not Germany, would unify America and bring it into the war.

### Disaster in the Pacific

Preoccupied by the fear of German victory in Europe, Roosevelt sought to avoid a showdown with Japan. The navy, the president told his cabinet, had "not got enough ships to go round, and every little episode in the Pacific means fewer ships in the Atlantic." But precisely because American and European attention lay elsewhere, Japan was emboldened to expand militarily into Southeast Asia.

Japanese leaders viewed their Greater East Asia Co-Prosperity Sphere as an Asian version of the Monroe Doctrine. Japan, the preeminent power in the region, would replace the Europeans as a promoter of economic development. To American leaders, however, Japan's actions threatened the policy of keeping an open door to China and preserving that country's independence. By the summer of 1941 Japanese forces controlled the Chinese coast and all major cities. When its army marched into French Indochina (present-day Vietnam) in July, Japan stood ready to conquer all of the Southeast Asian peninsula and the oil-rich Dutch East Indies.

Roosevelt was forced to act. He embargoed trade, froze Japanese assets in American banks, and barred shipments of vital scrap iron and petroleum.

*Embargo* — Japanese leaders indicated a willingness to negotiate with the United States, but diplomats from both sides were only going through the motions. The two nations' goals were totally at odds. Japan demanded that its conquests be recognized; the United States insisted that Japan withdraw from China and renounce the Tripartite Pact with Germany and Italy. As negotiations sputtered on, the Japanese secretly prepared for an attack on American positions in Guam, the Philippines, and Hawaii.

In late November American intelligence located, and then lost, a Japanese armada as it left Japan. Observing strict radio silence, the six carriers and their escorts steamed across the North Pacific. On Sunday morning, December 7, 1941, the first wave of Japanese planes roared down on the Pacific Fleet lying

*Pearl Harbor* — at anchor in Pearl Harbor. For more than an hour the Japanese pounded the ships and nearby airfields. Altogether 19 ships were sunk or battered. Practically all of the 200 American aircraft were damaged or destroyed. Only the aircraft carriers, by chance on maneuvers, escaped the worst naval defeat in American history.

In Washington, Secretary of War Henry Stimson could not believe the news relayed to his office. "My God! This can't be true, this must mean the Philippines." Later that day the Japanese did attack the Philippines, along with Guam, Midway, and British forces in Hong Kong and the Malay peninsula. On December 8, Franklin Roosevelt told a stunned nation that "yesterday, December 7, 1941" was "a date which will live in infamy." America, the "reluctant belligerent," was in the war at last. Three days later Hitler declared war on the "half Judaized and the other half Negrified" people of the United States; Italy quickly followed suit.

---

## COUNTERPOINT    *Did Roosevelt deliberately invite war?*

Had Roosevelt known the attack on Pearl Harbor was coming? Some critics have charged that the president deliberately contrived to bring war about. For months, American intelligence had been cracking some of Japan's secret codes. Much information indicated that Pearl Harbor was at risk. Yet Roosevelt left the fleet exposed, seeming almost to provoke an attack to bring the United States into the war. Was it mere coincidence that the vital aircraft carriers were at sea? That only the obsolete battleships were left at Pearl Harbor?

This argument, however, is based on circumstantial, not documentary, evidence. Roosevelt's defenders (and they include most historians) have countered that he wanted to fight Germany more than Japan. If he really had wished to provoke an incident leading to war, one in Atlantic waters would have served him far better. More important, the intelligence signals intercepted by American code-breakers were confusing. Analysts lost track of the Japanese fleet as it moved toward Hawaii. Secretary of War Stimson had good reason to be astonished when the fleet attacked Pearl Harbor.

---

In the end, cultural misperceptions may have explained the coming of war better than any conspiracy theory. American leaders were surprised by the attack on Pearl Harbor because they could not quite believe that the Japanese were daring or resourceful enough to attack an American stronghold some 4000 miles from Japan. Japanese militarists counted on a surprise attack to give them time to build a line of defense strong enough to discourage weak-willed Westerners from continuing the war. As it turned out, both calculations were wrong.

## A GLOBAL WAR

British Prime Minister Winston Churchill greeted the news of Pearl Harbor with shock but, even more, elation. Great Britain would no longer stand alone in the North Atlantic and the Pacific wars. "We have won the war," he thought, and that night he slept "the sleep of the saved and thankful."

As Churchill recognized, only with the Americans fully committed to war could the Allies make full use of the enormous material and human resources of the United States. Beyond that, the Allies needed to secure an alliance between the Anglo-American democracies and the Soviet Communist dictatorship that could win both the war and the peace to follow.

## Strategies for War

Within two weeks, Churchill was in Washington, meeting with Roosevelt to coordinate production schedules for ships, planes, and armaments. The numbers they announced were so high some critics openly laughed—at first. A year later combined British, Canadian, and American production boards not only met but exceeded the schedules.

Roosevelt and Churchill also planned grand strategy. Outraged by the attack on Pearl Harbor, many Americans thought Japan should be the war's primary target. But the two leaders agreed that Germany posed the greater threat. The Pacific war, they decided, would be fought as a holding action, while the Allies concentrated on Europe. In a global war, arms and resources had to be allocated carefully, for the Allies faced daunting threats on every front.

*Germany first*

## Gloomy Prospects

By summer's end in 1942 the Allies faced defeat. The Nazis stood outside the Soviet Union's three major cities: Leningrad, Moscow, and Stalingrad. In North Africa, General Erwin Rommel, Germany's famed "Desert Fox," swept into Egypt with his Afrika Korps to stand within striking distance of the Suez Canal—a lifeline to the resources of the British empire. German U-boats in the North Atlantic threatened to sever the ocean link between the United States and Britain. U-boat sailors called the first six months of 1942 "the American hunting season," as they sank 400 Allied ships in U.S. territorial waters. So deadly were these "Wolfpacks" that merchant sailors developed a grim humor about sleeping. Those on freighters carrying iron ore slept above decks, since the heavily laden ships could sink in less than a minute. On oil tankers, however, sailors closed their doors, undressed, and slept soundly. If a torpedo hit, no one would survive anyway.

*U-boat war*

In the Far East the supposedly impregnable British base at Singapore fell to Japan in just one week. Furthermore, the Japanese navy destroyed most of the Allied fleet in the western Pacific during the Battle of Java Sea. General Douglas MacArthur, commander of American forces in the Philippines, was forced to flee to Australia in April 1942. In what appeared to be an empty pledge, he vowed, "I shall return." The ill-equipped American and Philippine troops left on Bataan and Corregidor put up

*Fall of the Philippines*

In the face of Japanese occupation, many Filipinos actively supported the American war effort. Valentine Untalan survived capture by the Japanese and went on to serve in the American army's elite Philippine Scouts. Like a growing number of Filipinos, he moved to the United States once the war was over.

a heroic but doomed struggle. By summer no significant Allied forces stood between the Japanese and India or Australia.

The chain of spectacular victories disguised fatal weaknesses within the Axis alliance. Japan and Germany fought separate wars, each on two fronts. They never coordinated strategies. Vast armies in China and Russia drained them of both manpower and supplies. Brutal occupation policies made enemies of conquered populations, which forced Axis armies to use valuable forces to maintain control and move supplies. The Nazis were especially harsh. They launched a major campaign to exterminate Europe's Jews, Slavs, and Gypsies. Resistance movements grew as the victims of Axis aggression fought back. At the war's height 50 countries were among the Allies, who referred to themselves as the United Nations.

## A Grand Alliance

The early defeats also obscured the Allies' strengths. Chief among these were the manpower of the Soviet Union and the productive capacity of the United States. Safe from the fighting, American farms and factories could produce enough food and war materials to supply two separate wars at once. By the end of the war American factories had turned out vast quantities of airplanes, ships, artillery pieces, tanks, and self-propelled guns, as well as 47 million tons of ammunition.

The Allies benefited too from exceptional leadership. The "Big Three"—
Joseph Stalin, Winston Churchill, and Franklin Roosevelt—were able to maintain a unity of purpose that eluded Axis leaders. All three understood the global nature of the war. To a remarkable degree they
managed to set aside their many differences in pursuit of a common goal: the
defeat of Nazi Germany.

*The Big Three*

To be sure, each nation had its own needs. Russian forces faced 3.5 million
Axis troops along a 1600-mile front in eastern Europe. To ease the pressure on
those troops, Stalin repeatedly called upon the Allies to open a second front
in western Europe. So urgent were his demands that one Allied diplomat
remarked that Stalin's foreign minister knew only four words in English: *yes,
no,* and *second front.* But Churchill and Roosevelt felt compelled to turn
Stalin down. In August 1942 the western Allies lacked the massive, well-trained
force needed for a successful invasion of Europe. Churchill himself flew to
Moscow to give Stalin the bad news: no second front in Europe until 1943.
Postponed again until mid-1944, the second front became a source of festering
Russian discontent.

Yet after an initial surge of anger, Stalin accepted Churchill's rationale for
a substitute action. That was to be a British-American invasion of North Africa
at the end of 1942. Code-named Operation Torch, the North
African campaign would bring British and American troops into
direct combat with the Germans and stood an excellent chance of succeeding.
Here was an example of how personal contact among the Big Three ensured
Allied cooperation. The alliance sometimes bent but never broke.

*Operation Torch*

## The Naval War in the Pacific

Despite the Allied decision to defeat Germany first, the earliest successes came in
the Pacific. At the Battle of Coral Sea in May 1942 planes from American aircraft
carriers stopped a large Japanese invading force headed for Port Moresby in New
Guinea. For the first time in history two fleets fought without seeing each other.
The age of naval aviation had arrived. The Japanese fleet actually inflicted greater
damage but decided to turn back to nurse its wounds. Had they captured Port
Moresby, the Japanese could have severed Allied shipping routes to Australia.

To extend Japan's defenses, the Japanese military ordered the capture of
Midway, a small island west of Hawaii. The Americans, in possession of decoded
Japanese transmissions, were ready. On June 3, as the Japanese
main fleet bore down on Midway, American planes sank four enemy carriers, a cruiser, and three destroyers. The Battle of Midway broke
Japanese naval supremacy in the Pacific and stalled Japan's offensive. In August
1942 American forces launched their first offensive, on the Solomon Islands,
east of New Guinea. With the landing of American marines on the island of
Guadalcanal, the Allies started on the bloody road to Japan and victory.

*Midway*

## Turning Points in Europe

By the fall of 1942 the Allies had their first successes in the European war. In Africa, British forces under General Bernard Montgomery broke through Rommel's lines at El Alamein. Weeks later, the Allies launched Operation Torch, the invasion of North Africa. Under the command of General Dwight D. Eisenhower, Allied forces swept eastward through Morocco and Algeria. They were halted in February 1943 at the Kasserine Pass in Tunisia, but General George S. Patton regrouped them and masterminded an impressive string of victories. By May 1943 Rommel had fled from North Africa, leaving behind 300,000 German troops.

Success in North Africa provided a stirring complement to the dogged Russian stand at Stalingrad. From August 1942 until February 1943 Axis and

*Stalingrad*

Soviet armies, each with more than a million troops, fought one of the bloodiest engagements in history. Each side suffered more casualties than the Americans did during the entire war. When it was over, the Germans had lost an army and their momentum; Stalin's forces went on the offensive, moving south and west through the Ukraine toward Poland and Romania.

## Those Who Fought

"The first time I ever heard a New England accent," recalled a midwesterner, "was at Fort Benning. The southerner was an exotic creature to me. The people from the farms. The New York street smarts." Mobilizing for war brought together Americans from all regions, classes, and ethnic backgrounds. More than any other social institution the army acted as a melting pot. It also offered educational opportunities and job skills. "I could be a technical sergeant only I haven't had enough school," reported one Navajo soldier in a letter home to New Mexico. "Make my little brother go to school even if you have to lasso him."

In waging the world's first global war, the U.S. armed forces swept millions of Americans into new worlds and experiences. In 1941, the army had 1.6 million men in uniform. By 1945 it had more than 7 million; the navy, 3.9 million; the army air corps, 2.3 million; and the marines, 600,000. Nineteen-year-olds who had never left home found themselves swept off to Europe or to the South Pacific. At basic training recruits were subjected to forms of regimentation— the army hair cut, foul-mouthed drill sergeants, and barracks life—they had seldom experienced in other areas of America's democratic culture.

As with most wars, the infantry bore the brunt of the fighting and dying. They suffered 90 percent of the battlefield casualties. In all, almost 400,000

*A G.I.'s life*

Americans died and more than 600,000 were wounded. But service in the military did not mean constant combat. Most battles were reasonably short, followed by long periods of waiting and preparation. The army used almost 2 million soldiers just to move supplies. Yet even during the lull in battle, the soldier's biggest enemy, disease, stalked them: malaria, dysentery, typhus, and even plague. In the Pacific theater, the thermometer sometimes rose to over 110 degrees Fahrenheit.

Wherever they fought, American soldiers usually lived in foxholes dug by hand with small shovels. Whenever possible they turned a hole in the ground into a home. "The American soldier is a born housewife," observed war correspondent Ernie Pyle. Between battles, movies were about the only entertainment many troops had. Each film was a tenuous link to a more comfortable world at home, a place American soldiers yearned for with special intensity. It was not a country or an idea for which they fought so much as a set of memories—a house, a car, Mom and Pop.

## Uneasy Recruits

Minorities enlisted in unusually large numbers because the services offered training and opportunities unavailable in civilian life. Still, prejudice against

*African Americans at war*

African Americans and other minorities remained high. The army was strictly segregated and generally assigned black soldiers to noncombatant roles. The navy accepted them only as cooks and servants. At first the air corps and marines would not take them at all. The American Red Cross even kept "black" and "white" blood plasma separated, as if there were a difference. (Ironically, a black physician, Charles Drew, had invented the process allowing plasma to be stored.)

Despite such prejudice, more than a million black men and women served. As the war progressed, leaders of the black community pressured the military to ease segregation and allow black soldiers a more active role. The army did form some black combat units, usually led by white officers, as well as a black air corps unit. By mid-1942 black officers were being trained and graduated from integrated officer candidate schools at the rate of 200 a month. More than 80 black pilots won the Distinguished Flying Cross.

Homosexuals who wished to join the military faced a dilemma. Would their sexual orientation be discovered during the screening process? And if they were

*Choices for homosexuals*

rejected and word got back to their parents or communities, would they be stigmatized? Many took that chance. Charles Rowland, from Arizona, recalled that he and other gay friends "were not about to be deprived the privilege of serving our country in a time of great national emergency by virtue of some stupid regulation about being gay." Those who did pass the screening test found themselves in gender-segregated bases, where life in an overwhelmingly male or female environment allowed many, for the first time in their lives, to meet like-minded gay men and women. They served in all the ways other soldiers did, facing both the dangers of combat and the tedium of military life.

## *Women at War*

World War II brought an end to the military as a male enclave that women entered only as nurses. During the prewar mobilization, Eleanor Roosevelt and other women had campaigned for a regular military organization for women. The War Department came up with a compromise that allowed women to join

*WACs*

the Women's Army Auxiliary Corps (WAAC), but only with inferior status and lower pay. By 1943 the "Auxiliary" had dropped out of the title: WAACs became WACs, with full status, equal ranks, and equal pay. (The navy had a similar force called the WAVEs.)

Women could look with a mixture of pride and resentment on their wartime military service. Thousands served close to the battlefields, working as technicians, mechanics, radio operators, postal clerks, and secretaries. Although filling a vital need, these were largely traditional female jobs that implied a separate and inferior status. Until 1944 women were prevented by law from serving in war zones, even as noncombatants. There were women pilots, but they were restricted to shuttling planes behind the lines. At many posts WAVEs and WACs lived behind barbed wire and could move about only in groups under armed escort.

## WAR PRODUCTION

When Pearl Harbor brought the United States into the war, Thomas Chinn sold his publishing business and devoted full time to war work. Like many Chinese Americans, it was the first time he had worked outside of Chinatown. He served as a supervisor in the Army Quartermaster Market Center, which was responsible for supplying the armed forces with fresh food as it was harvested across California. Chinn found himself coordinating a host of cold storage warehouses all the way from the Oregon border as far south as Fresno. "At times," he recalled, "in order to catch seasonal goods such as fresh vegetables, as many as 200 or 300 railroad cars would be shuttling in and out" of the warehouses.

Food distribution was only one of many areas that demanded attention from the government. After Pearl Harbor, steel, aluminum, and electric power were all in short supply, creating bottlenecks in production lines. Roosevelt recognized the need for more direct government control of the economy.

Although the conversion from peace to war began slowly, the president used a mix of compulsory and voluntary programs to guarantee an ever-increasing supply of food, munitions, and equipment. In the end the United States worked a miracle of production that proved every bit as important to victory as any battle fought overseas. From 1939 to 1945 the gross national product grew from $91 billion to $166 billion. So successful was war production that civilians suffered little deprivation.

## *Mobilizing for War*

Roosevelt first tried to coordinate the war economy by setting up a War Production Board (WPB) under the direction of former Sears, Roebuck president Donald M. Nelson. On paper, Nelson's powers were impressive. The WPB had authority to allocate resources and organize factories in whatever way promoted national defense. In one of its first acts, the WPB ordered an end to all civilian car and truck production. The American people would have no new cars until the war ended.

In practice, Nelson was scarcely the dictator the economy needed. Other federal agencies with their own czars controlled petroleum, rubber, and labor resources, while military agencies continued their own procurement. To end the bottlenecks, the president in 1943 made Supreme Court Justice James F. Byrnes

*Office of War Mobilization*

the dictator the economy needed. His authority as director of the new Office of War Mobilization (OWM) was so great and his access to Roosevelt so direct that he became known as the "assistant president." By assuming control over vital materials such as steel, aluminum, and copper, OWM was able to allocate them more systematically. The bottlenecks disappeared.

Equally crucial, industries both large and small converted their factories to turning out war matériel. The "Big Three" automakers—Ford, General Motors, and Chrysler—generated some 20 percent of all war goods, as auto factories were retooled to make tanks and planes. But small business also played a vital role. A manufacturer of model trains, for example, made bomb fuses.

Henry J. Kaiser, a California industrialist, exemplified the war's creative entrepreneurship. Kaiser rustled up generous government loans for building factories. With generous wages and benefits, including day care for the children of working mothers, he lured workers to his new shipyards on the West Coast. His assembly line techniques reduced the time required to build cargo vessels, known as Liberty ships, from almost a year to only 56 days.

War production also created new industrial centers, especially in the West. When production of aircraft factories peaked in 1944, the industry had 2.1 mil-

*West Coast industry*

lion workers producing almost 100,000 planes. Most of the new factories were located around Los Angeles, San Diego, and Seattle. The demand for workers opened opportunities for many Asian workers who had been limited to jobs within their own ethnic communities. In Los Angeles about 300 laundry workers closed their shops so that they could work on the construction of the ship *China Victory*. By 1943, 15 percent of all shipyard workers around San Francisco Bay were Chinese.

The government relied on large firms such as Ford and General Motors because they had experience with large-scale production. Thus, war contracts helped large corporations increase their dominance over the economy. Workers in companies with more than 10,000 employees amounted to just 13 percent of the workforce in 1939; by 1944 they constituted more than 30 percent. In agriculture a similar move toward bigness occurred. The number of people working on farms dropped by a fifth, yet productivity increased 30 percent, as small farms were consolidated into larger ones that relied on more machinery and artificial fertilizers to increase yields.

Productivity increased for a less tangible reason: pride in work done for a common cause. Civilians volunteered for civil defense, hospitals, and countless scrap drives. Children became "Uncle Sam's Scrappers" and "Tin-Can Colonels" as they scoured vacant lots for valuable trash. Backyard "victory" gardens added 8 million tons of food to the harvest in 1943; car pooling conserved millions of tires. As citizens put off buying new consumer goods, they helped limit inflation. Morale ran high because people believed that every contribution, no matter how small, helped defeat the Axis.

### Science Goes to War

The striking success of aircraft against battleships at Pearl Harbor and Midway was just one way in which technology and science created new strategies of warfare. The Battle of Britain and the European air war spurred the development of a new generation of fighter planes and long-range bombers. To combat enemy bombers and submarines, English and American scientists rushed to perfect electronic detection devices such as radar and sonar, making it possible to hit targets obscured by darkness, fog, or smoke.

Scientific advances saved lives as well as destroying them. Insecticides, pesticides, and drugs limited the spread of infectious diseases like malaria and syphilis. Penicillin saw its first widespread use. Indeed, the health of the nation actually improved during the war. Life expectancy rose by three years overall and by five years for African Americans. Infant mortality was cut by more than a third, and in 1942 the nation recorded its lowest death rate in history. Still, scientific discoveries sometimes had unforeseen consequences. While the pesticide DDT helped control malaria and other insect-borne diseases, its harmful effects on the environment would become clear only years later.

Science made its most dramatic and frightening advances in atomic research. Before the war German scientists had discovered the process of fission: splitting the atom. Leading European physicists who had come to America to escape the Nazis understood all too well the military potential of the German discovery. In 1939 they alerted President Roosevelt to the possibility that fission research would enable the Nazis to develop atomic weapons. Their warning led Roosevelt to commit the United States to the largest research and de-

*Manhattan Project*  velopment effort in history, code-named the Manhattan Project. More than 100,000 scientists, engineers, technicians, and support workers from the United States, Canada, and England worked to build an atomic bomb. Yet even with increased resources, scientists feared they would not win the race to produce a weapon.

## War Work and Prosperity

War production not only ended the Depression, it revived prosperity—but not without stress. Unemployment, which stood at almost 7 million in 1940, virtually disappeared by 1944. Jeff Davies, president of Hoboes of America, reported in 1942 that 2 million of his members were "off the road." Employers, eager to overcome the labor shortage, welcomed handicapped workers. Hearing-impaired people found jobs in deafening factories; dwarfs became aircraft inspectors because they could crawl inside wings and other cramped spaces. By the summer of 1943 nearly 3 million children aged 12 to 17 were working. When the war ended, average income had jumped to nearly $3000, twice what it had been in 1939.

Roosevelt had to find some means to pay the war's enormous cost without triggering severe inflation. His approach mixed conservative and liberal elements: it was voluntary and compulsory, regressive and progressive. The Treasury Department sold war bonds through advertising campaigns rather than enforced savings. Still, Secretary of the Treasury Henry Morgenthau also

*Tax reform* looked to raise money with a new highly progressive tax structure that taxed higher income at a higher rate. Conservatives, however, balked at such sweeping reforms. After six months of wrangling, Congress passed a compromise, the Revenue Act of 1942, which levied a flat 5 percent tax on all annual incomes over $624. That provision struck hardest at low-income workers: in 1942 almost 50 million citizens paid taxes, compared with 13 million the year before.

## Organized Labor

Wartime prosperity brought substantial gains for unions. Still, the tensions between business and labor that characterized the New Deal era continued. In

*War Labor Board* 1941 alone more than 2 million workers walked off their jobs in protest. To end labor strife Roosevelt established the War Labor Board in 1942. Like the similar agency Woodrow Wilson had created during World War I, the new WLB had authority to impose arbitration in any labor dispute.

Despite Roosevelt's attempt to smooth labor relations, dissatisfied railroad workers tied up rail lines in a wildcat strike in 1943. To break the impasse, the

*Coal strike* government seized the railroads and then granted wage increases. That same year the pugnacious John L. Lewis allowed his United Mine Workers to go on strike. "The coal miners of America are hungry," he charged. "They are ill-fed and undernourished." Roosevelt seized the mines and ran them for a time; he even considered arresting union leaders and drafting striking miners. But as Secretary of the Interior Harold Ickes noted, a "jailed miner produces no more coal than a striking miner." In the end the government negotiated a settlement that gave miners substantial new benefits.

Most Americans were less willing to forgive Lewis and his miners. A huge coal shortage along the East Coast had left homes dark and cold. "John L. Lewis—Damn your coal black soul," wrote the military newspaper *Stars and Stripes*. In reaction, Congress easily passed the Smith–Connolly Act of 1943. It gave the president more authority to seize vital war plants shut by strikes and required union leaders to observe a 30-day "cooling-off" period before striking.

Despite these incidents, most workers remained dedicated to the war effort. Stoppages actually accounted for only about one-tenth of one percent of total work time during the war. When workers did strike, it was usually in defiance of their union leadership, and they left their jobs for just a few days.

## Women Workers

With as many as 12 million men in uniform, women (especially married women) became the nation's largest untapped source of labor. During the high unem-

*Womanpower*

ployment years of the Depression, both government and business had discouraged women from competing with men for jobs. Now, magazines and government bulletins began trumpeting "the vast resource of womanpower." Having accounted for a quarter of all workers in 1940, women

During the war, many women proved that they could do work once considered exclusively for males. Lionized with nicknames such as "Rosie the Riveter," women like this aircraft worker dispelled old stereotypes.

amounted to more than a third by 1945. These women were not mostly young and single, as female workers of the past had been. A majority were either married or between 55 and 64 years old.

Many women preferred the relative freedom of work and wages to the confines of home. With husbands off at war, millions of women needed additional income and had more free time. Black women in particular realized dramatic gains in the quality of jobs available to them. Once concentrated in low-paying domestic and farm jobs with erratic hours and tedious labor, some 300,000 rushed into factories that offered higher pay and more regular hours. Whether black or white, working women faced new stresses. The demands of a job were added to domestic responsibilities. The pressures of moving and crowded housing tore at families and communities already fearful for their men at war.

*Social stresses*

Although the war inspired a change in economic roles for women, it did not create a revolution in attitudes about gender. Most Americans assumed that when the war ended, veterans would pick up their old jobs and women would return home. Surveys showed that the vast majority of Americans, whether male or female, continued to believe that child rearing was a woman's primary responsibility. The birthrate, which had fallen during the Depression, began to rise in 1943 as prosperity returned.

## A QUESTION OF RIGHTS

Roosevelt, who had been a government official during World War I, was determined to avoid the patriotic excesses he had witnessed then: mobs menacing immigrants, patriotic appeals to spy on neighbors, raids on pacifist radicals. Even so, the tensions over race, ethnic background, and class differences could not simply be ignored. In a society in which immigration laws discriminated against Asians by race, the war with Japan made life difficult for loyal Asian Americans of all backgrounds. Black and Hispanic workers still faced discrimination in shipyards and airplane factories as much as they had in peacetime industries.

### Italians and Asian Americans

When World War II began, about 600,000 Italian aliens and 5 million Italian Americans lived in the United States. Most still lived in Italian neighborhoods centered around churches, fraternal organizations, and clubs. Some had been proud of Mussolini and supported *Fascismo*. "Mussolini was a hero," recalled one Italian American, "a superhero. He made us feel special." Those attitudes changed abruptly after Pearl Harbor. During the war, Italian Americans unquestioningly pledged their loyalties to the United States.

At first the government treated Italians without citizenship (along with Japanese and Germans) as "aliens of enemy nationality." They could not travel

# EYEWITNESS TO HISTORY

## A Woman Learns Shipyard Welding

I, who hate heights, climbed stair after stair after stair till I thought I must be close to the sun. I stopped on the top deck. I, who hate confined spaces, went through narrow corridors, stumbling my way over rubber-coated leads—dozens of them, scores of them, even hundreds of them. I went into a room about four feet by ten where two shipfitters, a shipfitter's helper, a chipper, and I all worked. I welded in the poop deck lying on the floor while another welder spattered sparks from the ceiling and chippers like giant woodpeckers shattered our eardrums. I, who've taken welding, and have sat at a bench welding flat and vertical plates, was told to weld braces along a baseboard below a door opening. On these a heavy steel door was braced while it was hung to a fine degree of accuracy. I welded more braces along the side, and along the top. I did overhead welding, horizontal, flat, vertical. . . . I made some good welds and some frightful ones. But now a door in the poop deck of an oil tanker is hanging, four feet by six of solid steel, by my welds. Pretty exciting. . . .

I am convinced that it is going to take backbone for welders to stick to their jobs through the summer months. It is harder on them than on any of the other workers—their leathers are so hot and heavy, they get more of the fumes, and their hoods become instruments of torture. . . . It grows unbearably hot under the hood, my glasses fog and blur my vision, and the only thing to do is to stop. . . . Yet the job confirmed my strong conviction—I have stated it before—what exhausts the woman welder is not the work, nor the heat, nor the demands upon physical strength. It is the apprehension that arises from inadequate skill and consequent lack of confidence; and this can be overcome by the right kind of training.

*Enemy aliens* without permission, enter strategic areas, or possess shortwave radios, guns, or maps. By 1942 few Americans believed that German or Italian Americans posed any kind of danger. Eager to keep the support of Italian voters in the 1942 congressional elections, Roosevelt chose Columbus Day, 1942, to lift restrictions on Italian aliens.

The 127,000 Japanese living in the United States, whether aliens or citizens, did not experience similar tolerance. Ironically, prejudices against them were least high in Hawaii, where the war with Japan had begun. Newspapers there expressed confidence in the loyalty of Japanese Americans, who in any case were crucial to the success of Hawaii's economy.

The situation was far more volatile on the mainland. There, Japanese Americans remained largely separated from the mainstream of American life, often because state laws and local custom threw up complex barriers. In the western states where they were concentrated around urban areas, most Japanese Americans could not vote, own land, or live in decent neighborhoods. Approx-

*Issei*

imately 47,000 Japanese aliens, known as *Issei*, were ineligible for citizenship under American law. Only their children could become citizens. Despite such restrictions, some Japanese achieved success in small businesses like landscaping, while many others worked on or owned farms that supplied fruits and vegetables to growing cities.

West Coast politicians pressed the Roosevelt administration to evacuate the Japanese from their communities. It did not seem to matter that about 80,000

*Nisei*

were American citizens, called *Nisei*, and that no evidence indicated that they posed any threat. "A Jap's a Jap . . ." commented General John De Witt, commander of West Coast defenses. "It makes no difference whether he is an American citizen or not." In response, the War Department in February 1942 drew up Executive Order 9066, which allowed the exclusion of any person from designated military areas. Under De Witt's authority, the order was applied only on the West Coast against Japanese Americans. By late February Roosevelt had agreed that both Issei and Nisei would be evacuated. But where would they go?

The army began to ship the entire Japanese community to temporary "assembly centers." Most Nisei were forced to sell their property at far below mar-

*Concentration Camps*

ket value. Furthermore, many army sites did not offer basic sanitation, comfort, or privacy. "We lived in a horse stable," remembered one young girl. Eventually, most Japanese were interned in 10 camps in remote areas of seven western states. No claim of humane intent could change the reality: these were concentration camps. Internees were held in wire-enclosed compounds by armed guards. Tar-papered barracks housed families or small groups in single rooms. Each room had a few cots, some blankets, and a single light bulb. That was home.

Some Japanese Americans protested, especially when government officials circulated a loyalty questionnaire that asked Nisei citizens if they would be willing to serve in the armed forces. "What do they take us for? Saps?" asked Dunks Oshima, a camp prisoner. "First, they change my army status to 4-C [enemy alien] because of my ancestry, run me out of town, and now they want me to volunteer for a suicide squad so I could get killed for this damn democracy." Yet thousands of Nisei did enlist, and many distinguished themselves in combat.

The bleak landscape of this camp at Manzanar, California, was typical of the internment camps to which the government sent Japanese Americans.

Other Japanese Americans challenged the government through the legal system. Fred Korematsu in California and Gordon Hirabayashi in Washington State were arrested when they refused to report for relocation. "As an American citizen, I wanted to uphold the principles of the Constitution," recalled Hirabayashi. But in *Korematsu v. United States* (1944), the Supreme Court upheld the government's relocation program as a wartime necessity. Three justices dissented, criticizing relocation as the "legalization of racism."

*Hirabayashi and Korematsu*

Concentration camps in America did not mirror the horror of Nazi death camps, but they were built on racism and fear. Worse, they violated the traditions of civil rights and liberties for which Americans believed they were fighting.

## Minorities on the Job

Minority leaders saw the irony of fighting a war for freedom in a country in which civil rights were still limited. "A jim crow army cannot fight for a free world," the NAACP declared. Such ideas of racial justice had been the driving force in the life of A. Philip Randolph, long an advocate of greater black militancy. Randolph had already demonstrated his gifts as an organizer and leader of the Brotherhood of Sleeping Car Porters, a strong African American union. During the war he

*A. Philip Randolph*

launched a campaign to gain entrance to defense industries and government agencies, unions, and the armed forces, all of them segregated. "The Administration leaders in Washington will never give the Negro justice," Randolph argued, "until they see masses—ten, twenty, fifty thousand Negroes on the White House lawn." In 1941 he began to organize a march on Washington.

President Roosevelt could have issued executive orders to integrate the government, defense industries, unions, and the armed forces, as Randolph demanded. But it took the threat of the march to make him act. He issued Executive Order 8802 in June, which forbid discrimination by race in hiring either government or defense industry workers. To carry out the policy, Order 8022 established the Fair Employment Practices Commission *FEPC* (FEPC). Despite its promise the new agency had only limited success in breaking down barriers against African Americans and Hispanics. It was one thing to ban discrimination and quite another to enforce that ban in a society still deeply divided by racial prejudice.

Still, the FEPC did open industrial jobs in California's shipyards and aircraft factories, which had previously refused to hire Hispanics. Thousands migrated from Texas, where job discrimination was most *Hispanic war workers* severe, to California, where war work created new opportunities. Labor shortages led the southwestern states to join with the Mexican government under the bracero program to recruit Mexican labor under specially arranged contracts. In Texas, by contrast, antagonism to braceros ran so deep that the Mexican government tried to prevent workers from going there. With support from labor unions, officials in the oil and mining industries routinely blocked Hispanics from training programs and job advancement. Not until late 1943 did the FEPC investigate the situation.

Black Americans experienced similar frustrations. More than half of all defense jobs were closed to minorities. For example, with 100,000 skilled and high-paying jobs in the aircraft industry, blacks held about 200 janitorial positions. The federal agency charged with placing workers honored local "whites only" employment practices. Unions segregated black workers or excluded them entirely. One person wrote to the president with a telling complaint: "Hitler has not done anything to the colored people—it's people right here in the United States who are keeping us out of work and keeping us down."

Eventually the combination of labor shortages, pressures from black leaders, and initiative from government agencies opened the door to more skilled jobs and higher pay. Beginning in 1943 the United States *Jobs for African Americans* Employment Service rejected requests with racial stipulations. Faced with a dwindling labor pool, many employers finally opened their doors. By 1944 blacks, who accounted for almost 10 percent of the population, held 8 percent of the jobs.

## *Urban Unrest*

At the beginning of the war three-quarters of the 12 million black Americans lived in the South. Hispanic Americans, whose population exceeded a million, were concentrated in a belt along the United States–Mexican border. When jobs for minorities opened in war centers, African and Hispanic Americans became increasingly urban. In cities, too, they confronted entrenched systems of segregation that denied them basic rights to decent housing, jobs, and political participation. Competition with white residents for housing and the use of public parks, beaches, and transportation produced explosive racial tensions.

To ease crowding the government funded new housing. In Detroit, federal authorities had picked a site for minority housing along the edge of a Polish

*Detroit riots*

neighborhood. One such project, named in honor of the black abolitionist Sojourner Truth, included 200 units for black families. When the first of them tried to move in, local officials had to send several hundred National Guardsmen to protect the newcomers from menacing Ku Klux Klan members. With a hot summer approaching, riots broke out in June 1943, as white mobs beat up African Americans riding public trolleys or patronizing movie theaters, and black protesters looted white stores. Six thousand soldiers from nearby bases finally imposed a troubled calm, but not before the riot had claimed the lives of 24 black and 9 white residents.

In southern California Anglo hostility toward Latinos focused on pachucos, or "zoot suiters." These young Hispanic men and boys had adopted the stylish fashions of Harlem hipsters: greased hair swept back into a ducktail; broad-shouldered, long-waisted suit coats; baggy pants pegged at the ankles. The Los Angeles city council passed an ordinance making it a crime even to wear a zoot suit. For most "zooters" this style was a modest form of rebellion; for a few it was a badge of criminal behavior; for white servicemen it was a target for racism.

In June 1943 sailors from the local navy base invaded Hispanic neighborhoods in search of zooters who had allegedly attacked servicemen. The self-

*Zoot suit riots*

appointed vigilantes grabbed innocent victims, tore their clothes, cut their hair, and beat them. When Hispanics retaliated, the police arrested them, ignoring the actions of the sailors. Irresponsible newspaper coverage made matters worse. "ZOOTERS THREATEN L.A. POLICE," charged one Hearst paper. A citizens committee created at the urging of California Governor Earl Warren rejected Hearst's inflammatory accusations. Underlying Hispanic anger were the grim realities of poor housing, unemployment, and white racism. All that added up to a level of poverty that wartime prosperity eased but in no way resolved.

Minority leaders acted on the legal as well as the economic front. The Congress of Racial Equality (CORE), a nonviolent civil rights group inspired

*CORE and nonviolence*

by the Indian leader Mohandas K. Gandhi, used sit-ins and other peaceful tactics to desegregate some restaurants and movie theaters. In 1944 the Supreme Court outlawed the "all-white primary," an infamous device used by southerners to exclude blacks from voting in primary elections within the Democratic party. Because Democratic candidates in the South often ran unopposed in the general elections, the primary elections were usually the only true political contests. In *Smith v. Allwright* the Court ruled that since political parties were integral parts of public elections, they could not deny minorities the right to vote in primaries. Such new attitudes opened the door to future gains.

## The New Deal in Retreat

After Pearl Harbor, Roosevelt told reporters that "Dr. New Deal" had retired in favor of "Dr. Win-the-War." Political debates, however, could not be eliminated, even during a global conflict. The increasingly powerful anti–New Deal coalition of Republicans and rural Democrats saw in the war an opportunity to attack programs they had long resented. They quickly ended the Civilian Conservation Corps and the National Youth Administration, reduced the powers of the Farm Security Administration, and blocked moves to extend social security and unemployment benefits. Seeming to approve such measures, voters in the 1942 elections sent an additional 44 Republicans to the House and another 9 to the Senate. The GOP began eyeing the White House.

By the spring of 1944 no one knew whether Franklin Roosevelt would seek an unprecedented fourth term. His health had declined noticeably. Pallid skin, *Election of 1944* sagging shoulders, and shaking hands seemed open signs that he had aged too much to run. In July, one week before the Democratic convention, Roosevelt announced his decision: "All that is within me cries out to go back to my home on the Hudson River. . . . But as a good soldier . . . I will accept and serve." Conservative Democrats, however, made sure that FDR's liberal vice president, Henry Wallace, would not remain on the ticket. In his place they settled on Harry S Truman of Missouri, a loyal Democrat. The Republicans chose the moderate governor of New York, Thomas E. Dewey, to run against Roosevelt, but Dewey never had much of a chance. At the polls, voters gave Roosevelt 25.6 million popular votes to Dewey's 22 million, a clear victory, although the election was tighter than any since 1916. Like its aging leader, the New Deal coalition was showing signs of strain.

## WINNING THE WAR AND THE PEACE

To impress upon newly arrived officers the vastness of the war theater in the Pacific, General Douglas MacArthur laid out a map of the region with the outline of the United States laid over it. Running the war from headquarters in Australia, the distances were about the same as if, in the Western Hemisphere, the center were located in South America. On the same scale, Tokyo would lie far up in northern Canada, Iwo Jima somewhere in Hudson Bay, Singapore in Utah, Manila in North Dakota, and Hawaii off the coast of Scotland.

In a war that stretched from one end of the globe to the other, the Allies had to coordinate their strategies on a grand scale. Which war theaters would receive equipment in short supply? Who would administer conquered territories? Inevitably, the questions of fighting a war slid into discussions of the peace that would follow. What would happen to occupied territories? How would the Axis powers be punished? If a more stable world order could not be created, the cycle of violence might never end. So as Allied armies struggled mile by mile to defeat the Axis, Allied diplomacy concentrated just as much on winning the peace.

## The Fall of the Third Reich

After pushing the Germans out of North Africa in May 1943, Allied strategists agreed to Churchill's plan to drive Italy from the war. Late in July, two weeks after a quarter of a million British and American troops had landed on Sicily, Mussolini fled to German-held northern Italy. Although Italy surrendered early in September, Germany continued to pour in reinforcements. It took the Allies almost a year of bloody fighting to reach Rome, and at the end of the campaign they had yet to break German lines. Along the eastern front, Soviet armies steadily pushed the Germans out of Russia and back toward Berlin.

General Dwight D. Eisenhower, fresh from battle in North Africa and the Mediterranean, took command of Allied preparations for Operation Overlord, *D-Day* the long-awaited opening of a second front in western Europe. By June 1944 all eyes focused on the coast of France, for Hitler, of course, knew the Allies would attack across the English Channel. Allied planners did their best to focus his attention on Calais, the French port city closest to the British Isles. On the morning of June 6, 1944, the invasion began—not at Calais but on the less fortified beaches of Normandy (see the map, page 748). Almost 3 million men, 11,000 aircraft, and more than 2000 vessels took part in D-Day.

As Allied forces hit the beaches, luck and Eisenhower's meticulous planning favored their cause. Still convinced that Calais was the Allied target, Hitler delayed sending in two reserve divisions. His indecision allowed the Allied forces to secure a foothold. Still, the Allied advance from Normandy took almost two months, not several weeks as expected. Once Allied tanks broke through German lines, their progress was spectacular. In August, Paris was liberated, and by mid-September, the Allies had driven the Germans from France and Belgium. *Battle of the Bulge* Hitler's desperate counterthrust in the Ardennes Forest in December 1944 succeeded momentarily, pushing back the Allies along a 50-mile bulge. But the "Battle of the Bulge" cost the Germans their last reserves. After George Patton's forces rescued trapped American units, little stood between the Allies and Berlin.

## Two Roads to Tokyo

In the bleak days of 1942 General Douglas MacArthur—flamboyant and jaunty with his dark sunglasses and corncob pipe—had emerged as America's great military hero. MacArthur believed that the future of America lay in the Far East. The Pacific theater, he argued, not the European, should have top priority. In March 1943 the Combined Chiefs of Staff agreed to his plan for a westward advance along the northern coast of New Guinea toward the Philippines and Tokyo. Naval forces directed by Admiral Chester Nimitz used amphibious warfare to pursue a second line of attack, along the island chains of the central Pacific. American submarines cut Japan's supply lines.

By July 1944 the navy's leapfrogging campaign had reached the Mariana Islands, east of the Philippines. From there B-29 bombers could reach the Japanese home islands. As a result, Admiral Nimitz proposed bypassing the

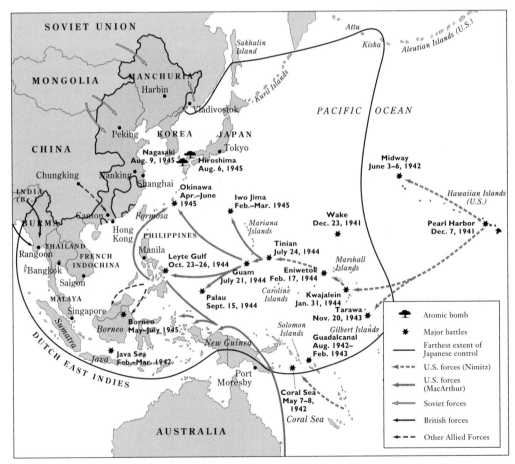

WORLD WAR II IN THE PACIFIC AND ASIA   Extraordinary distances complicated the war in the Pacific. As the map shows, American forces moved on two fronts: the naval war in the central Pacific and General MacArthur's campaign in the southwest Pacific.

*MacArthur returns*

Philippines in favor of a direct attack on Formosa (present-day Taiwan). MacArthur insisted on fulfilling a promise he had made "to eighteen million Christian Filipinos that the Americans would return." President Roosevelt himself came to Hawaii to resolve the impasse, giving MacArthur the green light. Backed by more than 100 ships of the Pacific Fleet, the general splashed ashore on the island of Leyte in October 1944.

*Battle of Leyte Gulf*

The decision to invade the Philippines led to savage fighting until the war ended. As retreating Japanese armies left Manila, they tortured and slaughtered tens of thousands of Filipino civilians. The United States suffered 62,000 casualties redeeming MacArthur's pledge, but a spectacular U.S. Navy victory at the Battle of Leyte Gulf spelled the end of the Japanese Imperial Navy as a fighting force. MacArthur and Nimitz prepared to tighten the noose around Japan's home islands.

## Big Three Diplomacy

While Allied cooperation gained military victories in both Europe and the Pacific, negotiations over the postwar peace proved knottier. Churchill believed that only a stable European balance of power, not an international agency, could preserve peace. In his view the Soviet Union was the greatest threat to upset that balance of power. Premier Joseph Stalin left no doubt that an expansive notion of Russian security defined his war aims. For future protection Stalin expected to annex the Baltic states, once Russian provinces, along with bits of Finland and Romania and about half of prewar Poland. In eastern Europe and other border areas such as Iran, Korea, and Turkey, he wanted "friendly" neighbors. It soon became apparent that "friendly" meant regimes dependent on Moscow.

Early on, Roosevelt had promoted his own version of an international balance of power, which he called the "Four Policemen." Under its framework, the Soviet Union, Great Britain, the United States, and China would guarantee peace through military cooperation. But by 1944 Roosevelt had rejected both this scheme and Churchill's wish to return to a balance of power that hemmed in the Russians. Instead, he looked to bring the Soviet Union into a peacekeeping system based on an international organization similar to the League of Nations. But this time, all the great powers would participate, including the United States. Whether Churchill and Stalin—or the American people as a whole—would accept the idea was not yet clear.

## The Road to Yalta

The outlines and the problems of a postwar settlement emerged during several summit conferences among the Allied leaders. In November 1943, with Italy's

*Teheran Conference*

surrender in hand and the war against Germany going well, Churchill and Roosevelt agreed to make a hazardous trip to Teheran, Iran. There, the Big Three leaders met together for the first time. ("Seems very confident," Roosevelt said of Stalin, "very sure of himself, moves slowly—altogether quite impressive.") The president tried to charm the Soviet premier, teasing Churchill for Stalin's benefit, keeping it up "until Stalin was laughing with me, and it was then that I called him 'Uncle Joe.'"

Teheran proved to be the high point of cooperation among the Big Three. It was there that FDR and Churchill finally committed to the D-Day invasion Stalin had so long sought. In return he promised to launch a spring offensive to pin down German troops on the eastern front. He also reaffirmed his earlier pledge to declare war against Japan once Germany was beaten.

But thorny disagreements over the postwar peace remained. That was clear in February 1945, when the Big Three met at the Russian resort city of Yalta,

*Yalta Conference*

on the Black Sea. By then, Russian, British, and American troops were closing in on Germany. Roosevelt arrived tired, ashen. At 62, limited by his paralysis, he had visibly aged. He came to Yalta mindful that although Germany was all but beaten, Japan still held out in the Pacific. Under no circumstances did he want Stalin to withdraw his promise to enter the fight against Japan or to join a postwar international organization. Churchill remained ever mistrustful of Soviet intentions. The Russians appeared only too eager to fill the power vacuum that a defeated Japan and Germany would leave.

Allied differences were most clearly reflected in their discussions over Poland. Having gone to war to protect Poland, the British wanted to ensure

*Poland*

that it survived as an independent nation. But the presence of Soviet troops there gave Stalin the determining voice. For him, Poland was the historic corridor of invasion used by Russia's enemies. After Soviet troops reentered Poland, he insisted that he would recognize only the Communist-controlled government at Lublin. Stalin also demanded that Russia receive territory in eastern Poland, for which the Poles would be compensated with German lands. That was hardly the "self-determination" the Atlantic Charter called for. Roosevelt proposed a compromise. For the time being, Poland would have a coalition government; after the war, free elections would settle the question of who should rule. The Soviets would also receive the territory they demanded in eastern Poland, and the western boundary would be established later.

Similarly, the Allies remained at odds about Germany's postwar future. Stalin was determined that the Germans would never invade Russia again. Many

*Dividing Germany*

Americans shared his desire to have Germany punished and its war-making capacity eliminated. At the Teheran Conference, Roosevelt and Stalin had proposed that the Third Reich be split into five powerless parts. Churchill, on the other hand, was much less eager to bring low the nation that was the most natural barrier to Russian expansion. The era after World War I, he believed, demonstrated that a healthy European economy required an industrialized Germany.

As with Poland, the Big Three put off making a firm decision. For the time being, they agreed to divide Germany into separate occupation zones (France would receive a zone carved from British and American territory). These four powers would jointly occupy Berlin, while an Allied Control Council supervised the national government.

When the Big Three turned their attention to the Far East, Stalin held a trump card. Fierce Japanese resistance on the islands of Okinawa and Iwo Jima had convinced Roosevelt that only a bloody invasion would force Japan's surrender. He thus secured a pledge from Stalin to declare war within three months of Germany's defeat. The price was high. Stalin wanted to reclaim territories that Russia had lost in the Russo-Japanese War of 1904–1906, as well as control over the Chinese Eastern and South Manchurian railroads.

The agreements reached at Yalta depended on Stalin's willingness to cooperate. In public Roosevelt put the best face on matters. He argued that the new world organization (which Stalin had agreed to support) would "provide the greatest opportunity in all history" to secure a lasting peace. "We shall take responsibility for world collaboration," he told Congress, "or we shall have to bear the responsibility for another world conflict." Privately the president was less optimistic. "When the chips were down," he confessed, he doubted "Stalin would be able to carry out and deliver what he had agreed to."

### The Fallen Leader

The Yalta Conference marked one of the last and most controversial chapters of Franklin Roosevelt's presidency. Critics charged that the concessions to Stalin were far too great: Poland had been betrayed; China sold out; the United Nations crippled at birth. Yet Roosevelt gave to Stalin little that Stalin had not liberated with Russian blood and could have taken anyway. Even Churchill, an outspoken critic of Soviet ambitions, concluded that although "our hopeful assumptions were soon to be falsified . . . they were the only ones possible at the time."

What peace Roosevelt might have achieved can never be known. He returned from Yalta visibly ill. On April 12, 1945, while sitting for his portrait at

*The legacy of FDR*

his vacation home in Warm Springs, Georgia, he complained of a "terrific headache," then suddenly fell unconscious. Two hours later Roosevelt was dead. Not since the assassination of Lincoln had the nation so grieved. Under Roosevelt's leadership government had become a protector, the president a father and friend, and the United States the leader in the struggle against Axis tyranny. Eleanor recalled how many Americans later told her that "they missed the way the President used to talk to them. . . . There was a real dialogue between Franklin and the people."

Harry S Truman faced the awesome task of replacing Roosevelt.* "Who the hell is Harry Truman?" the chief of staff had asked when Truman was nomi-

*Truman*

nated for the vice presidency in 1944. As vice president, Truman had learned almost nothing about the president's postwar plans.

---

*Truman had no middle name, only a middle initial. Thus the *S* appears without a period.

Sensing his own inadequacies, he adopted a tough pose and made his mind up quickly. People welcomed the new president's decisiveness as a relief from Roosevelt's evasive style. Too often, though, Truman acted before the issues were clear. But he at least knew victory in Europe was at hand as Allied troops swept into Germany from the east and west.

### The Holocaust

The horror of war in no way prepared the invading armies for their liberation of the Nazi concentration camps. Hitler, they discovered, had authorized the systematic extermination of all European Jews as well as Gypsies, homosexuals, and others considered deviant. The SS, Hitler's security force, had constructed six extermination centers in Poland. By rail from all over Europe the SS shipped Jews to die in the gas chambers.

No issue of World War II more starkly raised questions of human good and evil than what came to be known as the Holocaust. Tragically, the United States could have done more to save at least some of the 6 million Jews killed. Until the fall of 1941 the Nazis permitted Jews to leave Europe, but few countries would accept them—including the United States. Americans haunted by un-

At Buchenwald in April 1945, Senator Alben Barkley of Kentucky, who became vice president under Harry Truman, viewed firsthand the horror of the Nazis' death camps.

employment feared that a tide of new immigrants would make competition for jobs even worse. Tales of persecution from war refugees had little effect on most citizens: opinion polls showed that more than 70 percent of Americans opposed easing quotas. After 1938 the restrictive provisions of the 1924 Immigration Act were made even tighter.

American Jews wanted to help, especially after 1942 when they learned of the death camps. But they worried that highly visible protests might only ag-

*Anti-Semitism* gravate American anti-Semitism. They were also split over support for Zionists working to establish a Jewish homeland in Palestine. Roosevelt and his advisers ultimately decided that the best way to save Jews was to win the war quickly. That still does not explain why the Allies did not do more: they could have bombed the rail lines to the camps, sent commando forces, or tried to destroy the death factories.

## A Lasting Peace

After 15 years of depression and then war, the Allies sought a new framework to promote international stability. That system, many believed, needed to be

*Postwar organizations* economic as well as political. At a 1944 meeting at Bretton Woods, a resort in New Hampshire, Americans led the way in creating two new economic organizations: the International Monetary Fund (IMF) and the International Bank for Reconstruction and Development, later known as the World Bank. The IMF hoped to promote trade by stabilizing national currencies, while the World Bank was designed to stimulate economic growth by investing in projects worldwide. Later that summer the Allies met at Dumbarton Oaks, a Washington estate, to lay out the structure for the proposed United Nations Organization (UNO, later known simply as the UN). An 11-member Security Council would oversee a General Assembly composed of delegates from all member nations. By the end of the first organizational meeting, held in San Francisco in April 1945, it had become clear that the United Nations would favor the Western powers in most postwar disputes.

While the United Nations was organizing itself in San Francisco, the Axis powers were collapsing in Europe. As Mussolini attempted to escape to Germany, anti-Fascist mobs in Italy captured and slaughtered him like a pig. Adolf Hitler committed suicide in his Berlin bunker on April 30. Two weeks later General Eisenhower accepted the German surrender.

In one final summit meeting, held in July 1945 at Potsdam (just outside of Berlin), President Truman met Churchill and Stalin for the first time. Two is-

*Potsdam Conference* sues dominated the meeting: Germany's political fate and how much the defeated nation would pay in reparations. The three leaders agreed that Germany should be occupied and demilitarized. Stalin insisted that Russia receive a minimum of $10 billion in reparations, regardless of how much it might hurt postwar Germany or the European economy. A complicated compromise allowed Britain and the United States to restrict reparations from their zones. But in large part Stalin had his way. For the foreseeable future, Germany would remain divided into occupation zones, and without a central government of its own.

## Atom Diplomacy

The issue most likely to shape postwar relations never even reached the bargaining table in Potsdam. On July 16, 1945, Manhattan Project scientists detonated their first atomic device. Upon receiving the news in Germany, Truman seemed a changed man—firmer, more confident. He "told the Russians just where they got on and off and generally bossed the whole meeting," observed Churchill. Several questions loomed. Should the United States now use the bomb? Should it warn Japan before dropping it? And perhaps equally vital, should Truman inform Stalin of the new weapon?

Over the spring and early summer of 1945 administration officials discussed the use of atomic weapons. A few scientists had recommended not using the bomb, or at least attempting to convince Japan to surrender by offering a demonstration of the new weapon's power. A high-level committee of administrators, scientists, and political and military leaders dismissed that idea. Rather than tell Stalin directly about the bomb, Truman mentioned obliquely that the United States possessed a weapon of "awesome destructiveness." Stalin showed no surprise, most likely because spies had already informed him about the bomb. Privately, Truman and Churchill decided to drop the first bomb with only a veiled threat of "inevitable and complete" destruction if Japan did not surrender unconditionally. Unaware of the warning's full meaning, officials in Tokyo made no formal reply.

*Stalin and the bomb*

Some historians have charged that Secretary of State James Byrnes, a staunch anti-Communist, believed that a combat demonstration of the bomb would shock Stalin into behaving less aggressively in postwar negotiations. Most evidence, however, indicates that Truman decided to drop the bomb in order to end the war quickly. The victory in the Pacific promised to be bloody. Military leaders estimated that an invasion of Japan would produce heavy Allied casualties.

Before leaving Potsdam, Truman gave the final order for B-29s to drop two atomic bombs on Japan. On August 6 the first leveled four square miles of the city of Hiroshima. Three days later a second exploded over the port of Nagasaki. About 140,000 people died instantly in the fiery blasts. A German priest came upon soldiers who had looked up as the bomb exploded. Their eyeballs had melted from their sockets. Tens of thousands more who lived through the horror began to sicken and die from radiation poisoning.

*Hiroshima and Nagasaki*

The two explosions left the Japanese stunned. Breaking all precedents, the emperor intervened and declared openly for peace. On September 3 a somber Japanese delegation boarded the battleship *Missouri* in Tokyo Bay to sign the document of surrender. World War II had ended.

"World War II changed everything," observed one admiral long after the war. The defeatism of the Depression gave way to the exhilaration of victory. Before the war Americans seldom exerted leadership in international affairs. After it, the world looked to the United States to rebuild the economies of Europe and Asia and to maintain peace. Not only had World War II shown the global interdependence of economic and political systems, but it had also increased that interdependence. Out of the war developed a truly international economy. At home the economy became more centralized and the role of the government larger.

Still, a number of fears loomed, even as victory parades snaked down the nation's main streets. Would the inevitable cutbacks in military spending bring on another Depression? Would Soviet ambitions undo the new global peace, much as fascism and economic instability had undone the peace of Versailles? And then there was the shadow of the atom bomb, looming over the victorious as well as the defeated. The United States might control atomic technology for the present, but what if the weapon fell into unfriendly hands? After World War II launched the atomic age, no nation, not even the United States, was safe anymore.

## SIGNIFICANT EVENTS

| | |
|---|---|
| 1931–1932 | Japan invades Manchuria; Stimson Doctrine |
| 1933 | Roosevelt recognizes the Soviet Union |
| 1935 | Nye Committee hearings; first Neutrality Act |
| 1936 | Second Neutrality Act; Pan-American Conference |
| 1937 | Third Neutrality Act (cash-and-carry); Roosevelt's quarantine speech; *Panay* incident |
| 1938 | Munich meetings |
| 1939 | Fall of Czechoslovakia; Germany signs nonaggression pact with the Soviet Union; World War II begins in Europe |
| 1940 | Germany launches blitzkrieg against Low Countries and France; Roosevelt supports peacetime draft; Roosevelt wins third term |
| 1941 | Congress adopts Lend-Lease Act; A. Philip Randolph plans march on Washington; Roosevelt creates Fair Employment Practices Commission; Germany invades Soviet Union; Roosevelt and Churchill sign Atlantic Charter; Japan occupies Indochina; Roosevelt imposes embargo against Japan; Pearl Harbor attacked; Hitler and Mussolini declare war on the United States |
| 1942 | War Production Board and War Labor Board created; submarine war in the Atlantic; internment of Japanese Americans; Bataan and Corregidor fall; battles of Guadalcanal, Coral Sea, and Midway fought; American and British troops invade North Africa; Manhattan Project begins |
| 1943 | British-American forces invade Italy; Smith–Connolly Act; Office of War Mobilization replaces WPB; race riot in Detroit; zoot suit riots; Big Three meet at Teheran |
| 1944 | War Refugee Board created; D-Day invasion of France; U.S. forces return to Philippines; Dumbarton Oaks and Bretton Woods meetings; *Smith v. Allwright*; Roosevelt wins fourth term; Allies invade Germany |
| 1945 | Yalta Conference; Roosevelt dies; Truman becomes president; Allied troops liberate extermination camps; first United Nations Organization meeting; Germany surrenders; Potsdam Conference; atom bombs dropped on Japan; World War II ends |

## The United States in a Nuclear Age

During the victory celebrations of 1945, the threat of nuclear annihilation seemed improbably distant to most Americans. Although President Truman had become increasingly distrustful of Joseph Stalin, the United States preserved a clear atomic monopoly. The dangers from radioactive fallout impressed only a handful of officials and even fewer members of the public, who were treated to cheery fantasies of the peacetime use of atomics. (A 1947 issue of *Collier's* magazine showed a smiling paraplegic emerging from the mushroom cloud of a nuclear treatment, his wheelchair left behind.)

By 1949, when fallout from Russian atomic tests indicated that the U.S. nuclear monopoly had been broken, a grim global realignment was already well established. Two rival superpowers, the Soviet Union and the United States, had come to dominate world affairs, replacing the players in the old "balance of power" politics that had defined European relations for two centuries.

In area and vastness of resources, the Soviet Union surpassed even the United States, its boundaries encompassing 12 time zones. Given the centuries-long tradition of authoritarian rule (*czar* is the Russian derivative of caesar), the Russian Revolution of 1917 took a firmly centralized approach to modernization. At sometimes frightful cost Stalin brought the Soviet Union to its position as superpower by the end of World War II. By the 1960s both the Russians and the Americans were relying on stockpiles of nuclear weapons to guarantee their security and power.

Nuclear strategists viewed these stockpiles as essential to a policy of deterrence. Neither side, they hoped, would dare launch a missile attack, knowing that any nuclear exchange would end in "mutual assured destruction." Yet that strategy was frightening precisely because the globe could not be neatly divided into communist and noncommunist halves. The world was riven by ethnic, religious, and economic rivalries, and when the prestige of either superpower became critically involved, such regional conflicts threatened to escalate into a full-scale nuclear war.

Over time, both the Soviets and the Americans discovered the limits of projecting their power. For more than a decade, the United States fought an unsuccessful war against North Vietnam before withdrawing in defeat. For another decade, the Soviet Union waged a similarly unsuccessful war in Afghanistan. In both cases, regional rivalries remained strong. In the Middle East, both the Soviets and the Americans found that Arab nationalism and Islamic fundamentalism proved more influential than communist or free-market ideologies.

As the Western world recovered from the devastation of World War II, the peacetime economic expansion that benefited Americans also allowed both West Germany and Japan, their former enemies, to grow into modern industrial states. But the global economy did not expand indefinitely. In America, the boom and development mentality of the 1950s and 1960s was tempered in the 1970s as the environmental costs of air and water pollutants, strip mining, and pesticides became clearer. Similarly, by the mid-1970s major Soviet rivers like the Ural, Volga, and Dnieper were badly polluted by industrial wastes. Smog from coal-fired electrical plants plagued China's northern cities, while damage from acid rain could be charted in neighboring regions.

By the end of the 1980s the natural limits of global growth and the strains of a nuclear standoff were becoming clear. The Soviet empire saw its Eastern European satellite nations break away. The Union of Soviet Socialist Republics itself split into a host of nations divided by ethnic and religious rivalries. Although some Americans cheered at having "won" the cold war, the U.S. economy suffered from an immense federal debt run up in large part by military budgets aimed at checking Soviet power.

The multipolar world emerging in the 1990s reflected a truly global theater of markets, cultures, and politics. Growing industrialization had also created such threats as a hole in the ozone layer and the possibility of a global warming trend. The United States, no longer such a dominant economic power, gratefully left behind 50 years of a long and costly cold war. Its challenge, instead, was to rebuild its decayed public infrastructure, retrain displaced workers, and restore growth without further degrading the global environment. Half a millennium after the civilizations of two hemispheres achieved sustained contact, their ultimate fates have been indivisibly intertwined.

# CHAPTER TWENTY-EIGHT

# Cold War America

The war had been over for almost five months and still troop ships steamed into New York. Timuel Black was packing his duffel below decks when he heard some of the white soldiers shout, "There she is! The Statue of Liberty!"

Black felt a little bitter about the war. He'd been drafted in Chicago in 1943, just after race riots ripped the city. His father, a strong supporter of civil rights, was angry. "What the hell are you goin' to fight in Europe for? The fight is here." He wanted his son to go with him to demonstrate in Detroit, except the roads were blocked and the buses and trains screened to prevent African Americans from coming in to "make trouble."

Instead, Black went off to fight the Nazis, serving in a segregated army. He'd gone ashore during the D-Day invasion and marched through one of the German concentration camps. "The first thing you get is the stench," he recalled. "Everybody knows that's human stench. You begin to see what's happened to these creatures. And you get—I got more passionately angry than I guess I'd ever been." He thought: if it could happen to Jews in Germany, it could happen to black folk in America. So when the white soldiers called to come up and see the Statue of Liberty, Black's reaction was, "Hell, I'm not goin' up there. Damn that." But he went up after all. "All of a sudden, I found myself with tears, cryin' and saying the same thing [the white soldiers] were saying. Glad to be home, proud of my country, as irregular as it is. Determined that it could be better."

At the same time Betty Basye was working as a nurse in California. Her hospital treated soldiers shipped back from the Pacific: "Blind young men. Eyes gone, legs gone. Parts of the face. Burns—you'd land with a fire bomb and be up in flames." She'd joke with the men, trying to keep their spirits up, talking about times to come. She liked to take Bill, one of her favorites, for walks downtown. Half of Bill's face was gone, and civilians would stare. It happened to other patients, too. "Nicely dressed women, absolutely staring, just standing there staring." Some people wrote the local paper, wondering why disfigured vets couldn't be kept on their own grounds and off the streets. Such callousness made Basye indignant. But once the war ended, Basye had to think about her own future. "I got busy after the war," she recalled, "getting married and having my four children. That's what you were supposed to do. And getting your house in suburbia."

Yet as Betty Basye and Timuel Black soon discovered, the return to "normal" life was filled with uncertainties. The first truly global war had left a large part of Europe in ruins and the old balance of power shattered. So great was the rebuilding task that it soon became clear the United States would have a central role in shaping whatever new world order emerged. Isolation seemed neither practical nor desirable in an era where the power of the Soviet Union and communism seemed on the rise.

To blunt the threat of a world shaped by communism, the United States converted not so much to peace as to a "cold war" against its former Soviet ally.

*Effects of the cold war* This undeclared war came to affect almost every aspect of American life. Abroad, it justified a far wider military and economic role for the United States—not just in Europe but in the Middle East and along the Asian Pacific rim, from Korea to Indochina. At home it sent politicians searching the land for communist spies and "subversives," from the State Department to the movie studios of Hollywood.

Trying to deter war in times of peace dramatically increased the role of the military-industrial-university complex formed during World War II. A people who had once resisted government intrusion into individual lives now accepted a large defense establishment. They voted, too, to maintain programs that ensured an active federal role in managing the economy.

## THE RISE OF THE COLD WAR

World War II devastated lands and people almost everywhere outside the Western Hemisphere. As the world struggled to rebuild, power that had once been centered in Europe shifted to nations on its periphery. In place of Germany, France, and England the United States and the Soviet Union emerged as the world's two reigning superpowers—and as mortal enemies. This rivalry was not altogether an equal one. At war's end, the United States had a booming economy, a massive military establishment, and the atomic bomb. By contrast, much of the Soviet Union lay in ruins.

But the defeat of Germany and Japan left no power in Europe or Asia to block the still formidable Soviet army. Many Americans feared that desperate,

*American worries about Soviet intentions* war-weary peoples would find the appeal of communism irresistible. If Stalin intended to extend the Soviet Union's dominion, only the United States had the economic and military might to block him. Events in the critical years of 1945 and 1946 persuaded most Americans that Stalin did have such a plan. The Truman administration concluded that "the USSR has engaged the United States in a struggle for power, or 'cold war', in which our national security is at stake and from which we cannot withdraw short of national suicide." What had happened that led Western leaders to such a dire view of their former Soviet allies? How did such a wide breach open between the two nations?

## American Suspicions

Even before postwar events deepened American suspicions of the Soviets, an ideological gulf had separated the two nations. The October Revolution of

*Roots of the cold war*

1917 shocked most Americans. They had come to view Lenin's Bolshevik revolutionaries with a mixture of fear, suspicion, and loathing. As the communists grasped power, they had often used violence and terror to achieve their ends. As Marxists they rejected both religion and the notion of private property, two institutions central to the American dream. Furthermore, Soviet propagandists had made no secret that they intended to export revolution throughout the world, including the United States.

One event leading to World War II taught Western leaders to resist "appeasement." In 1938 British Prime Minister Neville Chamberlain's attempt to

*Munich analogy*

satisfy Hitler's demands on Czechoslovakia only emboldened the Nazis to expand further (page 747). After the war, Secretary of the Navy James Forrestal applied the Munich analogy to the new Europe. Appeasing Russian demands, he believed, would only seem like an attempt "to buy their understanding and sympathy. We tried that once with Hitler. . . . There are no returns on appeasement." To many of Truman's advisers, the Soviet dictator seemed as much bent on conquest as Hitler.

In April 1946 *Time* magazine portrayed communism as a disease, liable to "infect" unsuspecting populations the world over.

## Communist Expansion

During the war, Stalin did make numerous demands to control territory along the Soviet borders. And with the coming of peace, he continued to push for greater influence. He asked for a role in controlling the Dardanelles, the narrow straits linking Soviet ports on the Black Sea with the Mediterranean Sea (see the map, page 788). In Iran, Soviet forces occupying northern Iran lent support to rebels seeking to break away from the Iranian government. In Greece, local Communists led the fighting to overturn the traditional monarchy.

Asia, too, seemed a target for Communist ambitions. Russian occupation forces in Manchuria were turning over captured Japanese arms to Chinese Communists under Mao Zedong. Russian troops controlled the northern half of Korea. In Vietnam leftist nationalists were fighting against the return of colonial rule.

---

**COUNTERPOINT**    *What Were Stalin's Intentions?*

Despite Russian actions, many historians have argued that American policymakers consistently exaggerated Stalin's ambitions. At war's end, much of the farmland and industry in the Soviet Union lay in ruins. Over the previous two centuries, Russians had seen their lands invaded once by Napoleon (in 1812) and twice by Germany, during the two world wars. In 1945, as the Soviets struggled to rebuild their war-ravaged economy, the United States continued to gain influence and power. When Stalin looked outward, he saw American occupation forces in Europe and Asia ringing the Soviet Union, their military might backed by a newly developed atomic arsenal. American corporations owned or controlled vast oil fields in the Middle East. Along with the French and the British, the United States was a strong presence in Southeast Asia. Given that situation, one could argue that Stalin's actions after the war were primarily defensive, designed to counter what appeared to him a threatening American–European alliance.

In the 1990s, after the breakup of the Soviet Union, historians were able to consult previously closed Russian archives. New evidence suggests that Stalin's position had not been so defensive. Despite the ravages of war, Stalin recognized that in 1945 the Soviet Union was emerging as a more powerful state. With Germany and Japan defeated, Soviet borders to the east and west were secure from invasion. Only to the south did Stalin see a problem, along the border with Iran. Further, he recognized that the people of Britain and the United States had tired of fighting. Their leaders were not about to threaten the Soviet Union with war, at least not in the near term. Equally significant, Soviet spies had informed Stalin that in 1946 the United States possessed only a few atom bombs. For the time being, the nuclear threat was more symbolic than real. These historians thus conclude that Stalin was neither a global expansionist nor a leader fearful that his nation would soon be encircled and broken apart by American imperialists. Rather, he was a political realist eager to advance the interests of the Soviet state and his own regime—so long as his actions did not risk war.

The tensions arising from the conflicting Soviet and American points of view came to a head in the first months of 1946. Stalin announced in February that the Soviet Union would act vigorously to preserve its national security. In a world dominated by capitalism, he warned, future wars were inevitable. The Russian people had to ensure against "any eventuality" by undertaking a new five-year plan for economic development.

Although some Americans thought Stalin was merely rallying Russian support for his domestic programs, others saw their worst fears confirmed. *Time* magazine, an early voice for a "get tough" policy, called Stalin's speech "the most warlike pronouncement uttered by any top-rank statesman since V-J day." "I'm tired of babying the Soviets," remarked President Truman, who in any case seldom wore kid gloves. Even his mother passed along a message: "Tell Harry to be good, be honest, and behave himself, but I think it is now time for him to get tough with someone." In March Winston Churchill warned that the Soviets had dropped an "Iron Curtain" between their satellite nations and the free world. Poland, East Germany, Romania, and Bulgaria lay behind it. Iran, Greece, Turkey, and much of Europe seemed at risk.

*The move to "get tough"*

## A Policy of Containment

As policymakers groped for a way to deal with these developments, the State Department received a diplomatic cable. It was extraordinary both for its length (8000 words) and for its impact in Washington. The author was George Kennan, chargé d'affaires in Moscow and long a student of Soviet conduct. In his "long telegram," Kennan argued that Russian leaders, including Stalin, were so paranoid that it was impossible to reach any useful agreements with them. This temperament could best be explained by "the traditional and instinctive Russian sense of insecurity." When combined with Marxist ideology that viewed capitalism as evil, that insecurity created a potent force for expansion, Kennan argued. Soviet power "moves inexorably along a prescribed path, like a toy automobile wound up and headed in a given direction, stopping only when it meets some unanswerable force."

*George Kennan's "long telegram"*

The response Kennan recommended was "containment." The United States must apply "unalterable counterforce at every point where [the Soviets] show signs of encroaching upon the interests of a peaceful and stable world." The idea of containment was not particularly novel, but Kennan's analysis provided leaders in Washington with a clear strategic plan for responding to Soviet behavior. By applying firm diplomatic, economic, and military counterpressure, the United States could block Russian aggression. Truman wholeheartedly adopted the doctrine of containment.

## The Truman Doctrine

The first major test of Soviet and American wills came in early 1947. As Europe reeled under severe winter storms and a depressed postwar economy, Great
Britain announced that it could no longer support the govern-

*Aid to Greece and Turkey*

ments of Greece and Turkey. Without British aid, the Communist movements within these countries seemed destined to win critical victories. Truman decided that the United States should shore up Greek and Turkish resistance. He asked Congress to provide $400 million in military and economic aid. To gain support he went before Congress in March, determined to "scare hell out of the country." The world was now divided into two hostile camps, the president warned. To preserve the American way of life, the United States must step forward and help "free people" threatened by "totalitarian regimes." This rationale for aid to Greece and Turkey soon became known as the Truman Doctrine.

The Truman Doctrine marked a new level of American commitment to a cold war. Just what responsibility the Soviets had for unrest in Greece and Turkey remained unclear. But Truman had linked communism with rebel movements all across the globe. That committed Americans to a relatively open-ended struggle, in which the president gained expanded powers to act when unrest threatened. Occasionally Congress would regret giving the executive branch so much power, but by 1947 anticommunism had become the dominant theme in American policy, both foreign and domestic.

## The Marshall Plan

For all its importance, the Truman Doctrine did not aid Western Europe. There, national treasuries were empty, city streets stood dark, people starved, and factories were closed. American diplomats warned that without aid to revive the European economy, Communists would seize power in Germany, Italy, and France. If Western Europe fell, the cold war could be lost.

In June 1947 Secretary of State George C. Marshall told a Harvard commencement audience about a plan to ensure the recovery of Europe. He invited all European nations, East or West, to request assistance to rebuild their economies. Unlike Truman, Marshall did not emphasize the communist menace. All the same, his massive aid plan was designed to eliminate conditions that produced the discontent that Communists often exploited. Then, too, humanitarian aid had practical benefits. As Europe recovered, so would its interest in buying American goods. Marshall did not rule out Soviet participation in the massive aid program. Still, he gambled—correctly—that fears of American economic domination would lead the Soviets and their allies to reject his offer.

At first neo-isolationists in Congress argued that the United States could not afford such generosity. But when Communists expelled the non-Communists from Czechoslovakia's government, the cold war seemed to spread. Congress then approved the Marshall Plan, as it became known. The blame for dividing Europe fell on the Soviet Union, not the United States. And the Marshall Plan proved crucial to Western Europe's economic recovery.

## NATO

American efforts to stabilize Europe placed Stalin on the defensive. In 1947 he moved against the moderate government in Hungary, which since 1945 had been chosen through relatively free elections. Soviet forces replaced the gov-

COLD WAR EUROPE   By 1956 the postwar occupation of Europe had hardened into hostile spheres. As a western outpost within the Soviet bloc, West Berlin remained a source of cold war tensions.

ernment with a Communist regime dependent on Moscow. Then in February 1948 Communists toppled the elected government of Czechoslovakia. Shortly after, news came that the popular Czech foreign minister, Jan Masaryk, had fallen to his death from a small bathroom window. Suicide was the official explanation, but many suspected murder.

The spring of 1948 brought another clash between the Soviets and their former allies, this time over Germany. There, the United States, Great Britain,

*Berlin airlift*

and France decided to transform their occupation zones into an independent West German state. The Western-controlled sectors of Berlin, however, lay over 100 miles to the east, well within the Soviet zone. On June 24 the Soviets reacted by blockading land access to Berlin. Truman did not hesitate to respond. "We are going to stay, period." But he did say no when General Lucius Clay proposed to shoot his way through the blockade. Instead, the United States began a massive airlift of supplies that lasted almost a year. In May 1949 Stalin lifted the blockade, conceding that he could not prevent the creation of West Germany.

Stalin's aggressive actions accelerated the American effort to use military means to contain Soviet ambitions. By 1949 the United States and Canada had

*NATO formed*

joined with Britain, France, Belgium, the Netherlands, and Luxembourg to establish the North Atlantic Treaty Organization (NATO) as a mutual defense pact. For the first time since George Washington had warned against the practice in his Farewell Address of 1793, the United States during peacetime entered into entangling alliances with European nations.

Truman's firm handling of the Berlin crisis won him applause from both Democrats and Republicans. They were equally enthusiastic about another

*Israel recognized*

presidential action. Minutes after Jewish residents of Palestine announced their independence in May 1948, Truman recognized the new state of Israel. He had previously supported the immigration of Jews into Palestine, despite the opposition of oil-rich Arab states and diplomats in the State Department. The president sympathized with Jewish aspirations for a homeland. He also faced a tough campaign in 1948 in which Jewish votes would be critical. As British Prime Minister Clement Attlee observed, "There's no Arab vote in America, but there's a heavy Jewish vote and the Americans are always having elections."

### The Atomic Shield versus the Iron Curtain

The Berlin crisis forced Truman to consider the possibility of war. If it came, would atomic weapons again be used? That dilemma raised two other difficult questions. Should the decision to use atomic weapons rest in civilian or military hands? And was it possible to find a way to ease the atomic threat by creating an international system to control nuclear power?

On the question of civilian or military control of the bomb, Truman's response was firm. He was not going to have "some dashing lieutenant colonel

*Atomic Energy Commission*

decide when would be the proper time to drop one." In 1946 Congress seemed to have decided the issue in Truman's favor when it passed the McMahon Act. This bill established the Atomic Energy Commission (AEC) with control of all fissionable materials for both peacetime and military applications. The AEC was a civilian, not a military, agency.

But civilian control was not so complete as Truman had demanded. The wartime head of the Manhattan Project, General Leslie Groves, had been working behind the scenes to give the military a decisive voice in atomic policy. During debate over the bill, Groves had leaked information about a Canadian atomic spy ring delivering secrets to the Soviet Union. That news spread doubts that scientists and civilians could be trusted with key secrets. Thus Groves persuaded Congress to allow the military to review many civilian decisions and even severely limit their actions.

The idea of international control of atomic energy also fell victim to cold war fears. Originally a high-level government committee proposed to Truman that the mining and use of the world's atomic raw materials be supervised by the United Nations. The committee argued that in the long run the United States would be more secure under a system of international control than by relying on its temporary nuclear monopoly. But Truman chose Bernard Baruch, a staunch cold warrior, to draw up the recommendations to the United Nations

*Baruch plan*

in June 1946. Baruch's proposals ensured that the United States would dominate any international atomic agency. The Soviets countered with a plan calling for destruction of all nuclear bombs and a ban on their use. But Baruch had no intention of bargaining. It was either his plan or nothing, he announced. And so it was nothing. The Truman administration never seriously considered the possibility of giving up the American nuclear monopoly.

### Atomic Deterrence

Ironically, because so much secrecy surrounded the bomb, many military planners knew little about it. Even Truman had no idea in 1946 how many bombs the United States possessed. (For the two years after Hiroshima, it was never more than a dozen.) Military planners, however, soon found themselves relying more and more on atomic weapons. The Soviet army had at its command over 260 divisions. The United States, in contrast, had reduced its forces by 1947 to little more than a single division. As the cold war heated up, American military planners were forced to adopt a nuclear strategy in face of the overwhelming superiority of Soviet forces. They would deter any Soviet attack by setting in place a devastating atomic counterattack.

At first, this strategy of nuclear deterrence was little more than a doomsday scenario to incinerate vast areas of the Soviet Union. A 1946 war plan, "Pincher," proposed obliterating 20 Soviet cities if the Soviets attacked Western Europe. By 1948 the war plan "Fleetwood" had raised the tally of cities to 77, with eight bombs aimed for Moscow, seven for Leningrad. Not until "Dropshot," the following year, did planners correct a major flaw in their strategy. If Moscow and Leningrad disappeared, who would be left to surrender? Dropshot recommended sparing those two cities until the second week.

By 1949, then, the cold war framed all aspects of American foreign policy. The Joint Chiefs of Staff had committed themselves to a policy of nuclear deterrence. Western Europe was on its way to economic recovery, thanks to the Marshall Plan. Soviet pressures on Greece and Turkey had abated. Many Americans had hopes that the United States might soon defeat communism.

Yet success brought little comfort. The Soviet Union was not simply a major power seeking to protect its interests and expand where opportunity permitted. In the eyes of many Americans, the Soviets were determined, if they could, to overthrow the United States from either without or within. This was a war being fought not only across the globe but right in America, by unseen agents using subversive means. In this way, the cold war mentality soon came to shape the lives of Americans at home much as it did American policy abroad.

## POSTWAR PROSPERITY

At war's end, many business leaders feared that a sudden drop in government purchases would bring back the depressed conditions of the 1930s. Instead, Americans entered into the longest period of prosperity in the nation's history, lasting until the 1970s. Even the fear of communism could not dampen the simple joys of getting and spending.

Two forces drove the postwar economic boom. One was unbridled consumer and business spending that followed 16 years of depression and war. High war wages had piled up in savings accounts and war bonds. Eager consumers set off to find the new cars, appliances, and foods unavailable during the war. Despite a sharp drop in government spending (from $83 billion in 1945 to only $31 billion in 1946), the gross national product fell less than 1 percent, and employment actually increased. Consumers had taken up the slack.

*Sources of prosperity*

Government spending at the local, state, and federal levels provided another boost to prosperity. The three major growth industries in the decades after World War II were health care, education, and government programs. Each of these was spurred by public spending. Equally important, the federal government poured millions of dollars into the military-industrial sector. The defense budget, which fell to $9 billion in 1947, reached $50 billion by the time Truman left office. Over the longer term, these factors promoting economic growth became clearer. In 1946, though, the road from war to peace seemed rocky, especially for those at the margins of the economy.

## Postwar Adjustments

With millions of veterans looking for peacetime jobs, workers on the home front, especially women and minorities, found themselves out of work. Cultural

*Women workers*

attitudes added to the pressure on these groups to resume more traditional roles. War employment had given many women their first taste of economic independence. As peace came, almost 75 percent of the working women in one survey indicated that they hoped to continue their jobs. But as the troops came home, male social scientists stressed how important it was for women to accept "more than the wife's usual responsibility for her marriage" and offer "lavish—and undemanding—affection" to returning GIs. One marriage counselor urged women to let their husbands know "you are tired of living alone, that you want him now to take charge."

For minorities, the end of the war brought a return of an old labor practice, "last hired, first fired." At the height of the war over 200,000 African

*Minority workers*

Americans and Hispanics had found jobs in shipbuilding. By 1946 that number had dwindled to less than 10,000. The influx of Mexican laborers under the bracero program temporarily halted. In the South, where the large majority of black Americans lived, wartime labor shortages had become surpluses, leaving few jobs available.

At the same time, many black and Hispanic veterans who fought during the war had been treated with greater equality and freedom than they had known

*Push for civil rights*

before enlisting. Thus they often resented returning to a deeply segregated society with limited opportunities. One observer noted that Hispanic veterans in Texas were no longer willing to tolerate discrimination. They "have acquired a new courage, have become more vocal in protesting the restrictions and inequalities with which they are confronted." Benefits received under the GI Bill allowed many Mexican Americans to enter the middle class. When confronted by "haughty, lordly, or unfriendly" businesses, they sometimes organized informal boycotts. Much of the Anglo business community learned to respect this new activism.

Black veterans exerted a similar impact on the civil rights movement. Angered by violence, frustrated by the slow pace of desegregation, they breathed new energy into civil rights organizations like the NAACP and the Congress of Racial Equality. Voting rights was one of the issues they pushed. Registration drives in the South had the greatest success in urban centers like Atlanta. Other black leaders pressed for improved education. In rural Virginia, for example, a young Howard University lawyer, Spottswood Robinson, litigated cases for the NAACP to force improvement in segregated all-black schools. In one county Robinson and the NAACP even won equal pay for black and white teachers.

Out in the countryside, however, segregationists used economic intimidation, violence, and even murder to preserve the "Jim Crow" system. White citizens in rural Georgia lynched several black veterans who had shown the determination to vote. Such instances disturbed President Truman, who saw civil rights as a key ingredient in his reform agenda. The President was especially disturbed when he learned that police in South Carolina had gouged out the eyes of a recently discharged black veteran. Truman responded in December 1946 by appointing a Committee on Civil Rights. A year later it published its report, *To Secure These Rights.*

To Secure
These Rights

Discovering inequities for minorities, the committee exposed a racial caste system that denied African Americans employment opportunities, equal education, voting rights, and decent housing. But every time Truman appealed to Congress to implement the committee's recommendations southern senators threatened to filibuster. That opposition forced the President to resort to executive authority to achieve even modest results. In his most direct attack on segregation, he issued an executive order in July 1948 banning discrimination in the armed forces. Segregationists predicted disaster, but experience soon demonstrated that integrated units fought well and exhibited minimal racial tension.

## The New Deal at Bay

In September 1945 Harry Truman boldly claimed his intention to extend the New Deal into the postwar era. He called for legislation to guarantee full employment, subsidized public housing, national health insurance, and a peacetime version of the Fair Employment Practices Commission to fight job discrimination. But Truman found that inflation, shortages, and labor unrest undermined his ability to pass such liberal legislation. The combination of increased demand and shortages of consumer goods temporarily in short supply triggered a sharp inflation. For two years prices rose as much as 15 percent annually. Consumers blamed the White House for not doing more to ease their burden.

As inflation ate into paychecks, strikes spread across the nation. Autoworkers walked off the job in the fall of 1945; steelworkers, in January 1946; miners, in April. In 1946 some 5 million workers struck, a rate triple that of any previous year. Antiunion sentiment soared. The crisis peaked in May 1946 with a national rail strike, which temporarily paralyzed the nation's transportation network. An angry President Truman asked, "What decent American would pull a rail strike at a time like this?"

*Organized labor*

At first, Truman threatened to seize the railroads and then requested from Congress the power to draft striking workers into the military. The strike was settled before the threat was carried out, but few people, whether conservative or liberal, approved the idea of using the draft to punish political foes. Labor leaders, for their part, became convinced they no longer had a friend at the White House.

With Truman's political stock falling, conservative Republicans and southern Democrats joined to block the president's attempts to revive and extend the

New Deal. All he achieved was a watered-down full-employment bill, which created the Council of Economic Advisors. The bill did establish one key principle: the government rather than the private sector was responsible for maintaining full employment. As the congressional elections of 1946 neared, Republicans pointed to production shortages, the procession of strikes, the mismanagement of the economy. "To err is Truman," proclaimed the campaign buttons—or, more simply, "Had enough?" Many voters had. The Republicans gained control of both houses of Congress. Not since 1928 had the Democrats fared so poorly.

Leading the rightward swing was Senator Robert A. Taft of Ohio, son of former President William Howard Taft. Bob Taft not only wanted to halt the spread

*Taft–Hartley Act*

of the New Deal—he wanted to dismantle it. "We have to get over the corrupting idea we can legislate prosperity, legislate equality, legislate opportunity," he said in dismissing the liberal agenda. Taft especially wished to limit the power of the unions. In 1947 he pushed the Taft–Hartley Act through Congress, over Truman's veto. In the event of a strike, the bill allowed the president to order workers back on the job during a 90-day "cooling-off" period while collective bargaining continued. It also permitted states to adopt "right-to-work" laws, which banned the closed shop by eliminating union membership as a prerequisite for many jobs. Union leaders criticized the new law as a "slave-labor" act. Later, they discovered they could live with it, though it did hurt union efforts to organize, especially in the South.

Despite the conservative backlash, most Americans continued to support the New Deal's major accomplishments: social security, minimum wages, a more active role for government in reducing unemployment. The administration maintained its commitment to setting a minimum wage, raising it again in 1950 from 45 to 75 cents. Social security coverage was broadened to include an additional 10 million workers. Furthermore, a growing list of welfare programs benefited not only the poor but also veterans, middle-income families, the elderly, and students.

The most striking of these was the GI Bill of 1944, which created unparalleled opportunity for returning veterans under the "GI Bill of Rights." Those with more

*The GI Bill*

than two years of service received all tuition and fees plus living expenses for three years of college education. By 1948 the government was paying the college costs of almost half of all male students as over 2 million veterans went to college on the GI Bill. The increase in college graduates encouraged a shift from blue- to white-collar work and self-employment. Veterans also received low-interest loans to start businesses or farms of their own and to buy homes. The GI Bill accelerated trends that would transform American society into a prosperous, better-educated, heavily middle-class suburban nation.

## The Election of 1948

With his domestic program blocked, Harry Truman faced almost certain defeat in the election of 1948. The New Deal coalition that Franklin Roosevelt had held together for so long seemed to be coming apart. On the left Truman was

*Henry Wallace* challenged by Henry Wallace, who had been a capable secretary of agriculture and vice president under Roosevelt, then secretary of commerce under Truman. Wallace wanted to pursue New Deal reforms even more vigorously than Truman did, and he continually voiced his sympathy for the Soviet Union. Disaffected liberals bolted the Democratic party to support Wallace on a third-party Progressive ticket.

Within the southern conservative wing of the party, arch-segregationists resented Truman's moderate civil rights proposals for a voting rights bill and an *Dixiecrats* antilynching law. When the liberal wing of the party passed a civil rights plank as part of the Democratic platform, delegates from several Deep South states stalked out of the convention. They banded together to create the States' Rights or "Dixiecrat" party, with J. Strom Thurmond, the segregationist governor of South Carolina, as their candidate.

With the Democrats divided, the Republicans smelled victory. They sought to control the political center by rejecting the conservative Taft in favor of the more moderate former New York governor, Thomas Dewey. Dewey proved so aloof that he inspired scant enthusiasm. "You have to know Dewey well to really dislike him," quipped one critic. Despite such shortcomings, most observers believed that Dewey would walk away with the race. Pollster Elmo Roper stopped canvassing the voters two months before the election.

Truman, however, would not roll over and play dead. He launched a stinging attack against the "reactionaries" in Congress: that "bunch of old mossbacks . . . gluttons of privilege . . . all set to do a hatchet job on the New Deal." From the rear platform of his campaign train, he made almost 400 speeches in eight weeks. Over and over he hammered away at the "do-nothing" 80th Congress, which, he told farmers, "had stuck a pitchfork" in their backs. Still, on election day odds makers favored Dewey by as much as 20 to 1. Hours before the polls closed the archconservative Chicago *Tribune* happily headlined "Dewey Defeats Truman." But the experts were wrong. Not only did the voters return Truman by over 2 million popular votes, they gave the Democrats commanding majorities in the House and Senate.

The defection of the liberal and conservative extremes had allowed Truman to hold the New Deal coalition together, after all. Jews grateful for his stand on Israel, Catholics loyal to the Democratic party, and ethnics all supported him. He had been the first major presidential candidate to campaign in Harlem. Farmers hurt by falling prices deserted the Republicans. An easing of inflation had reminded middle-income Americans that they had benefited significantly under Democratic leadership. "I have a new car and am much better off than my parents were. Why change?" one suburban voter remarked.

## The Fair Deal

As he began his new term, Harry Truman declared that all Americans were entitled to a "Fair Deal" from their government. He called for a vigorous revival of New Deal programs like national health insurance and regional TVA-style projects. Echoing an old Populist idea, Truman hoped to keep his working coalition together by forging stronger links between farmers and labor. But the conservative coalition of southern Democrats and Republicans in Congress still blocked any significant new initiatives. On the domestic front Truman remained largely the conservator of Franklin Roosevelt's legacy.

## THE COLD WAR AT HOME

Bob Raymondi, a mobster serving a prison term in the late 1940s, was no stranger to racketeering or gangland killings. In fact, he was so feared, he dominated the inmate population at Dannemora Prison. Raymondi made the acquaintance of a group of Communists who had been jailed for advocating the overthrow of the government. He enjoyed talking with people who had some education. When Raymondi's sister learned about his new friends, she was frantic. "My God, Bob," she told him, "You'll get into trouble."

Was something amiss? Many Americans seemed to believe it riskier to associate with Communists than to do so with hardened criminals. Out of a population of 150 million, the Communist party in 1950 could claim a membership of only 43,000. (More than a few of those were FBI undercover agents.) But worry about Communists Americans did. Conservatives still thought of the New Deal as "creeping socialism," only an arm's length short of communism. Leftists, they believed, controlled labor unions, Hollywood, and other interest groups sympathetic to the New Deal. As Stalin extended Soviet control in Eastern Europe and Asia, American fears grew.

### The Shocks of 1949

Nineteen forty-nine proved a pivotal year. American scientists reported in August that rains monitored in the Pacific contained traces of hot nuclear waste.

*The Soviet A-bomb*

Only one conclusion seemed possible: the Soviet Union possessed its own atom bomb. Senator Arthur Vandenberg, a Republican with wide experience in international affairs, summed up the reaction of many to the end of the American nuclear monopoly: "This is now a different world." Truman directed that research into a newer, more powerful hydrogen bomb continue.

Then in December came more bad news. The Nationalist government of Chiang Kai-shek fled mainland China to the offshore island of Formosa

*China falls to the Communists*

(present-day Taiwan). By January 1950 Communist troops under Mao Zedong swarmed into Beijing, China's capital city. Chiang's defeat came as no surprise to the State Department. Officials there had long regarded Chiang and his Nationalists as hopelessly corrupt and inefficient. Despite major American efforts to save his regime and stabilize China, poverty and civil unrest spread. In 1947 full-scale civil war had broken

The fall of China to the forces of Mao Zedong was one of the
chilling cold war shocks of 1949.

out. By February 1949 almost half of Chiang's demoralized troops had defected
to the Communists. So the December defeat was hardly unexpected.

But Republicans, who had formerly supported the president's foreign pol-
icy, now broke ranks. For some time, a group of wealthy conservatives and
Republican senators had resented the administration's preoccupation with
Europe. Time-Life publisher Henry Luce used his magazines to campaign for
a greater concern for Asian affairs, and especially more aid to defeat Mao
Zedong. When Chiang at last collapsed, his American backers charged the
Democrats with letting the Communists win.

Worries that subversives had sold out the country were heightened when
former State Department official Alger Hiss was brought to trial in 1949 for

*The Alger
Hiss case*

perjury. Hiss, an adviser to Roosevelt at the Yalta Conference,
had been accused by former Communist Whittaker Chambers of
passing secrets to the Soviet Union during the 1930s. Though
the evidence in the case was far from conclusive, the jury convicted Hiss for lying about his association with Chambers. And in February 1950 the nation was

further shocked by news from Britain that a high-ranking physicist, Klaus Fuchs, had spied for the Russians while working on the Manhattan Project. Here was clear evidence of conspiracy at work.

## The Loyalty Crusade

As fears of subversion and espionage mounted in the postwar years, President Truman sought ways to protect himself from Republican accusations that he was "soft" on communism. Only days after proposing the Truman Doctrine in March 1947, the president signed an executive order establishing a Federal Employee Loyalty Program designed to guard against any disloyalty by "Reds, phonies, and 'parlor pinks.'" The order required government supervisors to certify the loyalties of those who worked below them, reporting to a system of federal loyalty review boards. The FBI was to follow up any "derogatory information" that came to light.

The system quickly got out of hand. The conservative head of the Loyalty Review Board, Seth Richardson, contended that the government could "discharge any employee for reasons which seem sufficient to the Government, and without extending to such employee any hearing whatsoever." Those accused would have no right to confront their accusers. But a few years' experience showed that it was difficult actually to prove disloyalty on the part of employees. Truman then allowed the boards to fire those who were "potentially" disloyal or "bad security risks," such as alcoholics, homosexuals, and debtors. Suspected employees, in other words, were assumed guilty until proven innocent. After some 5 million investigations, the program identified a few hundred employees who, though not Communists, had at one time been associated with suspect groups. Rather than calm public fears, the loyalty program gave credibility to the growing red scare.

## HUAC and Hollywood

Hollywood, with its wealth, glamour, and highly visible Jewish and foreign celebrities, had long aroused a mixture of attraction and suspicion among traditional Americans. In 1947 the House Committee on Un-American Activities (HUAC) began to investigate communist influences in the film industry. "Large numbers of moving pictures that come out of Hollywood carry the communist line," charged committee member John Rankin of Mississippi.

HUAC called a parade of movie stars, screenwriters, and producers to sit in the glare of its public hearings. Some witnesses were considered "friendly" because, like Gary Cooper and Ronald Reagan, they answered committee questions or supplied names of suspected leftists. Others refused to inform on their colleagues or to answer questions about earlier ties to the Communist party. Eventually 10 uncooperative witnesses, known as the "Hollywood Ten," refused on First Amendment grounds to say whether they were or ever had been Communists. They served prison terms for contempt of Congress.

For all its probing, HUAC never offered convincing evidence that film-makers were in any way subversive. Yet the investigation did have a chilling ef-

*Blacklisting*

fect on the entertainment industry. Nervous Hollywood produc-ers turned out patriotic films like *I Was a Communist for the FBI* (1950) in order to demonstrate their loyalty. The studios also fired any actors suspected of leftist leanings, adopting a blacklist that prevented admitted or ac-cused Communists from finding work. Since no judicial proceedings were in-volved, victims of false charges, rumors, or spiteful accusations found it nearly impossible to clear their names.

Suspicion of aliens and immigrants as subversives led finally to the passage, over Truman's veto, of the McCarran Act (1950). It required all Communists to

*McCarran Act*

register with the attorney general, forbade the entry of anyone who had belonged to a totalitarian organization, and allowed the Justice Department to detain suspect aliens indefinitely during deportation hearings. That same year a Senate committee began an inquiry designed to root out homosexuals holding government jobs. Even one "sex pervert in a Government agency tends to have a corrosive influence upon his fellow em-ployees," warned the committee.

## The Ambitions of Senator McCarthy

By 1950 anticommunism had created a climate of fear, where legitimate con-cerns mixed with irrational hysteria. Senator Joseph R. McCarthy, a mediocre Republican senator from Wisconsin, saw in that fear an opportunity to improve his political fortunes. Before an audience in Wheeling, West Virginia, in February 1950 he waved a sheaf of papers in the air and announced that he had a list of 205—or perhaps 81, 57, or "a lot" of—Communists in the State Department. (No one, including the senator, could remember the number, which he continually changed.) In the following months McCarthy leveled charge after charge. He had penetrated the "iron curtain" of the State De-partment to discover "card-carrying Communists," the "top Russian espionage agent" in the United States, "egg-sucking phony liberals," and "Communists and queers" who wrote "perfumed notes."

It seemed not to matter that McCarthy never substantiated his charges. When examined, his lists contained names of people who had left the State Department long before or who had been cleared by the FBI. Indeed, the FBI provided McCarthy with the little real evidence he did have. In the summer of 1950 a Senate committee headed by Millard F. Tydings of Maryland concluded that McCarthy's charges were "a fraud and a hoax." Such candor among those in government did not last long as "Jolting Joe" (one of McCarthy's favorite

The energetic Roy Cohn (left) served as the key strategist in the crusades of
Senator Joseph McCarthy (center). David Schine (right) joined the
committee at Cohn's urging.

nicknames) during the 1950 elections helped defeat Tydings and several other
of his Senate critics.

In a sense, McCarthyism was the bitter fruit Truman and the Democrats
reaped from their own attempts to exploit the anticommunist mood. McCarthy,

*The Democrats
and
McCarthyism*

more than Truman, tapped the fears and hatreds of traditional
conservatives, Catholic leaders, and neo-isolationists who distrusted things foreign, liberal, or intellectual. They saw McCarthy
and his fellow witch hunters as the protectors of a vaguely defined but deeply felt spirit of Americanism.

By the time Truman stepped down as president, 32 states had laws requiring teachers to take loyalty oaths. Government loyalty boards were asking employees what newspapers they subscribed to or phonograph records they collected. A library in Indiana had banned *Robin Hood* because the idea of stealing
from the rich to give to the poor seemed too leftish. As one historian commented, "Opening the valve of anticommunist hysteria was a good deal simpler
than closing it."

## FROM COLD WAR TO HOT WAR AND BACK

As the cold war heated up during 1949, the Truman administration searched for a more assertive foreign policy. The new approach was developed by the National Security Council (NSC), an agency created by Congress in 1947 as part of a plan to help the executive branch respond more effectively to cold war crises. Rather than merely "contain" the Soviets, as George Kennan had suggested, the National Security Council wanted the United States to "strive for victory." In April 1950 the council sent Truman a document, NSC-68, which came to serve as the framework for American policy over the next 20 years.

NSC-68 called for a dramatic increase in defense spending, from $13 billion to $50 billion a year, to be paid for with a large tax increase. Most of the funds would go to rebuild conventional forces, but the NSC urged that the hydrogen bomb be developed to offset the new Soviet nuclear capacity. Efforts to carry out NSC-68 at first aroused widespread opposition. George Kennan argued that the Soviets had no immediate plans for domination outside the Communist bloc. Fiscal conservatives, both Democrat and Republican, resisted any proposal for higher taxes. All such reservations were swept away on June 25, 1950. "Korea came along and saved us," Secretary of State Dean Acheson later remarked.

*NSC-68*

### *Police Action*

In 1950 Korea was about the last place Americans might have imagined themselves fighting a war. Since World War II the country had been divided along the 38th parallel: the north was controlled by the Communist government of Kim Il Sung, the south by the dictatorship of Syngman Rhee. Preoccupied with China and the rebuilding of Japan, the Truman administration's interest had dwindled steadily after the war. When Secretary of State Acheson discussed American policy in Asia for the National Press Club in January 1950, he did not even mention Korea.

On June 24 Harry Truman was enjoying a leisurely break from politics at the family home in Independence, Missouri. In Korea it was already Sunday morning when Acheson called the president. North Korean troops had crossed the 38th parallel, Acheson reported, possibly to fulfill Kim Il Sung's proclaimed intention to "liberate" South Korea. Soon Acheson confirmed that a full-scale invasion was in progress. The threat of a third world war, this one atomic, seemed agonizingly real. The United States had to respond with enough force to deter aggression, but without provoking a larger war with the Soviet Union or China.

Truman did not hesitate. American troops would fight the North Koreans, though the United States would not declare war. The fighting in Korea would be a "police action" supervised by the United Nations and commanded by General Douglas MacArthur. That move succeeded only because the Soviet delegate, who had veto power, was absent. Stalin had agreed to the attack, but promised only supplies. Neither Russian troops nor prestige would be involved, he had warned Kim.

Truman's forceful response won immediate approval across America. Congress voted to carry out the recommendations of NSC-68. But by the time *Inchon landing* the UN authorized the police action, on June 27, North Korean forces had pinned the South Koreans within an area around Pusan (see the map on the facing page). In a daring counterstroke, General MacArthur launched an amphibious attack behind North Korean lines at Inchon, near the western end of the 38th parallel. Fighting eastward, MacArthur's troops threatened to trap the invaders, who fled back to the North.

## The Chinese Intervene

MacArthur's success led Truman to a fateful decision. With the South liberated, he permitted MacArthur to cross the 38th parallel, drive the Communists from the North, and reunite Korea under Syngman Rhee. Such a victory was just what Truman needed with Senator Joe McCarthy on the attack at home and the 1950 congressional elections nearing. By Thanksgiving American troops had roundly defeated northern forces and were advancing toward the frozen Yalu River, the boundary between Korea and China. MacArthur, made bold by success, promised that the boys would be home by Christmas.

Throughout the fall offensive, however, China's Premier Zhou Enlai cautioned that his country would not tolerate an American presence on its border. Washington officials did not take the warning seriously. Mao Zedong, they assumed, was a Soviet puppet, and Stalin had declared the Korean conflict to be merely a "civil war" and off limits. But on November 26, 400,000 Chinese troops poured across the Yalu, smashing through lightly defended UN lines. At Chosan they trapped 20,000 American and South Korean troops, inflicting one of the worst military defeats in American history. Within three weeks they had driven UN forces back behind the 38th parallel.

So total was the rout that Truman wondered publicly about using the atom bomb. That remark sent a frightened British Prime Minister Clement Attlee flying to Washington to dissuade Truman. The president readily agreed that the war must remain limited and withdrew his nuclear threat.

## Truman versus MacArthur

Military stalemate in Korea brought into the open a simmering feud between General MacArthur and Truman. The general had publicized his differences with Truman, arguing UN forces should bomb Chinese and Russian supply bases across the Korean border, blockade China's coast, and unleash Chiang Kai-shek on mainland China. On March 23 he issued a personal ultimatum to Chinese military commanders demanding total surrender. To his Republican

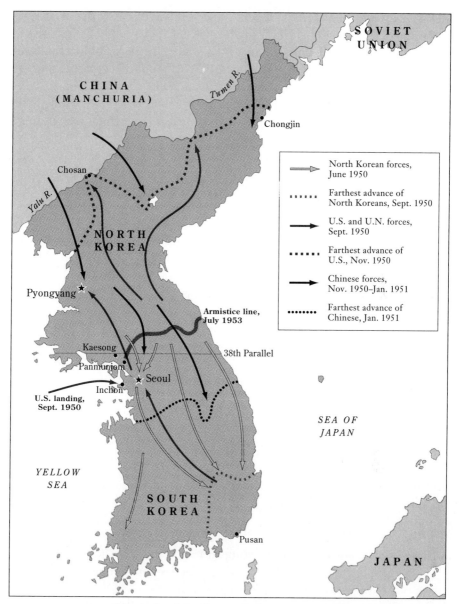

THE KOREAN WAR   MacArthur's landing at Inchon in September 1950 helped UN
forces take the offensive. The drive to the Yalu River provoked
the Chinese to intervene.

congressional supporters he sent a letter declaring, "We must win. There is no
substitute for victory."

To Truman, MacArthur's strategy appeared to be an open invitation to another world war. Equally alarming, the general's insubordination threatened the
tradition that the military remain under clear civilian control. When Truman

made plans to discipline him, General Omar Bradley reported that MacArthur was threatening to resign before Truman could act. "The son of a bitch isn't going to resign on me," Truman retorted. "I want him fired!" Military leaders agreed that MacArthur had to go. On April 11 a stunned nation learned that the celebrated military commander had been relieved of his duties. When MacArthur returned to the states, cheering crowds welcomed him with a ticker-tape parade. Congress gave him the unprecedented opportunity to address a joint session before a national television audience.

Behind the scenes, however, Truman was winning this personal clash. At stake was not simply Truman or MacArthur but the future direction of American foreign policy. MacArthur insisted on an all-out effort in Asia. To Secretary of State Dean Acheson, Europe came first. He asked Congress to see Korea as only one link in a worldwide "collective security system." A wider war in Asia would threaten American interests in Europe. Or as General Omar Bradley argued, a showdown in Asia would lead to "the wrong war, at the wrong place, at the wrong time, and with the wrong enemy." Congressional leaders were persuaded of the need to accompany limited war in Korea with a military buildup in Europe.

Still, the continuing war in Korea took its toll on Truman's political fortunes. After July 1951, the war dragged on and so did the aimless peace talks.

*Korean stalemate*

By March 1952 Truman's popularity had sunk so low that he lost the New Hampshire presidential primary. With that defeat, he announced he would not run for reelection in 1952.

## K1C2: The Election of 1952

The Republican formula for victory in 1952 played on the Truman administration's weaknesses. Those did not include the economy, which remained remarkably healthy. Wage and price controls put in place by the administration prevented the sharp inflation that was expected to follow increased wartime spending. But the Republicans could capitalize on the stalemate over Korea. And several of Truman's advisers had been forced to resign for accepting gifts in return for political favors. The campaign strategy was summed up in the formula K1C2: Korea, corruption, and communism.

Republican party regulars and the conservative wing were committed to Robert Taft, who ran surprisingly well in the party primaries. But former military hero Dwight "Ike" Eisenhower was more popular with voters. His backers maneuvered their candidate to a first-ballot nomination. To heal the breach with the Taft delegates, the convention chose the staunch anticommunist Senator Richard Nixon as Eisenhower's running mate.

The Democrats had no candidate as popular as Eisenhower. They drafted Illinois Governor Adlai E. Stevenson, an unusually eloquent speaker. But, like Dewey before him, Stevenson lacked the common touch. The GOP's campaign against communism and corruption, led by Nixon, forced the Democrats on the defensive. Eisenhower, meanwhile, remained high above the mudslinging and promised voters that if elected, he would go to Korea to seek an end to the war.

The election outcome was never much in doubt. Ike's broad smile and confident manner won him over 55 percent of the vote. "The great problem of America today," he had said during the campaign, "is to take that straight road down the middle." Most Americans who voted for him were comforted to think that was just where they were headed.

And Eisenhower kept his pledge "to go to Korea" and review the situation firsthand. Once in office, he renewed negotiations with North Korea but warned

*Eisenhower and Korea*

that unless the talks made speedy progress, the United States might retaliate "under circumstances of our choosing." The carrot-and-stick approach worked. On July 27, 1953, the Communists and the United Nations forces signed an armistice ending a "police action" in which 54,000 Americans had died. Korea remained divided, almost as it had been in 1950. Communism had been "contained," but at a high price in human lives.

## The Fall of McCarthy

It was less clear whether anticommunism could be contained. When Eisenhower called himself a "modern" Republican, he distinguished himself from what he called the more "hidebound" members of the GOP. Their anticommunist campaigns caused him increasing embarrassment. Senator McCarthy's reckless antics, at first directed at Democrats, began to hit Republican targets as well.

By the summer of 1953 the senator was on a rampage. He dispatched two young staff members, Roy Cohn and David Schine, to investigate the State Department's overseas information agency and the Voice of America radio stations. While there, they insisted on purging government libraries of "subversive" volumes. Some librarians, fearing for their careers, burned a number of books. That drove President Eisenhower to denounce "book burners," though soon after he reassured McCarthy's supporters that he did not advocate free speech for Communists.

The administration's own behavior contributed to the hysteria on which McCarthy thrived. The president launched a loyalty campaign, which he claimed resulted in 3000 firings and 5000 resignations of government employees. It was a godsend to McCarthyites: what further proof was needed that subversives were lurking in the federal bureaucracy? Furthermore, a well-publicized spy

*Rosenberg case*

trial had led to the conviction of Ethel and Julius Rosenberg, a couple accused of passing atomic secrets to the Soviets. Although the evidence was not conclusive, the judge sentenced both Rosenbergs to the electric chair, an unusually harsh punishment even in cases of espionage. When asked to commute the death sentence to life imprisonment, Eisenhower refused and the Rosenbergs were executed in June 1953.

In such a climate—where Democrats remained silent for fear of being called leftists and Eisenhower cautiously refused to "get in the gutter with *that* guy"—

E Y E W I T N E S S    T O    H I S T O R Y

## Harry Truman Disciplines
## His "Big General"

**A**pril 6, 1951

MacArthur shoots another political bomb through Joe Martin, leader of the Republican minority in the House.

This looks like the last straw.

Rank insubordination. Last summer he sent a long statement to the Vets of Foreign Wars—not through the high command back home, but directly! He sent copies to newspapers and magazines particularly hostile to me.

I was furnished a copy from the press room of the White House which had been *accidentally* sent there.

I ordered the release suppressed and then sent him a very carefully prepared directive dated Dec. 5, 1950, setting out Far Eastern policy after I'd flown 14,404 [miles] to Wake Island to see him and reach an understanding face to face.

He told me the war in Korea was over, that we could transfer a regular division to Germany Jan 1st. He was positive Red China would not come in. He expected to support our Far Eastern policy.

---

*The army vs. McCarthy*

McCarthy lost all sense of proportion. When the army denied his staff aide David Schine a commission, McCarthy decided to investigate communism in the army. The new American Broadcasting Company network, eager to fill its afternoon program slots, televised the hearings. The public had an opportunity to see McCarthy badger witnesses and make a mockery of Senate procedures. Soon after, his popularity began to slide and the anticommunist hysteria ebbed as well. The Senate finally moved to censure him. He died three years later, destroyed by alcohol and the habit of throwing so many reckless punches.

With the Democrats out of the White House for the first time since the Depression and with right-wing McCarthyites in retreat, Eisenhower did indeed seem to be leading the nation on a course "right down the middle." Still, it is worth noting how much that sense of "middle" had changed.

I call in Gen. Marshall, Dean Acheson, Mr. Harriman and Gen. Bradley before Cabinet to discuss situation. I've come to the conclusion that our Big General in the Far East must be recalled. I don't express any opinion or make known my decision.

Direct the four to meet again Friday afternoon and go over all phases of the situation.

April 9, 1951

. . . Meet with Acheson, Marshall, Bradley and Harriman. Go over recall orders to MacArthur and suggested public statement. Approve both and decide to send the orders to Frank Pace, Sec. of the Army, for delivery to MacArthur. . . . Gen. Bradley called about 9 P.M. Said there had been a leak. . . . I ordered messages sent at once and directly to MacArthur.

April 10, 1951

Quite an explosion. Was expected but I had to act.
Telegrams and letters of abuse by the dozens.

Harry S Truman, Diary. Reprinted in Robert H. Farrell, ed., *The Private Papers of Harry Truman* (Harper & Row: New York, 1980), pp. 210–211.

Both the Great Depression and World War II made most Americans realize that the nation's economy was closely linked to the international order. The crash in 1929, with its worldwide effects, certainly made that clear. The New Deal demonstrated that Americans were willing to give the federal government power to influence American society in major new ways. And the war led the government to intervene in the economy even more directly.

Thus when peace came in 1945, it became clear that the "middle road" did not mean a return to the laissez-faire economics of the 1920s. Nor would most Americans support the isolationist policies of the 1930s. "Modern" Republicans accepted social welfare programs like social security and recognized that the federal government had the ability to lower unemployment, control inflation, and manage the economy in a variety of ways. Furthermore, the shift from war to peace demonstrated that it was no longer possible to make global war without making a global peace. Under the new balance of power in the postwar world, the United States and the Soviet Union stood alone as "superpowers," with the potential capability to annihilate each other and the rest of the world.

## SIGNIFICANT EVENTS

1945 — Civil war in Greece

1946 — Labor unrest; Kennan's "long telegram"; Stalin and Churchill "cold war" speeches; Republican congressional victories; Atomic Energy Commission created; Baruch plan fails at United Nations

1947 — Truman Doctrine; Taft–Hartley Act; Marshall announces European recovery plan; federal loyalty oath; HUAC investigates Hollywood; National Security Council created; Truman's Committee on Civil Rights issues *To Secure These Rights*

1948 — Marshall Plan adopted; Berlin airlift; Truman upsets Dewey; Truman recognizes Israel

1949 — Soviet A-bomb test; China falls to the Communists; NATO established; Truman orders work on H-bomb

1950 — McCarthy's Wheeling, West Virginia, speech; Korean War begins; McCarran Act; NSC-68 adopted; Alger Hiss convicted

1951 — Truman fires MacArthur; peace talks in Korea

1952 — Eisenhower defeats Stevenson

1953 — UN armistice ends police action in Korea; Rosenbergs executed

1954 — Army–McCarthy hearings; McCarthy censured

# CHAPTER TWENTY-NINE

# The Suburban Era

The company that epitomized the corporate culture of the 1950s was General Motors. GM executives sought to blend in rather than to stand out. They chose their suits in drab colors—dark blue, dark gray, or light gray—to increase their anonymity. Not head car designer Harley Earl. Earl brought a touch of Hollywood into the world of corporate bureaucrats. He had a closet filled with colorful suits. His staff would marvel as he headed off to a board meeting dressed in white linen with a dark blue shirt and *blue suede shoes*, the same shoes that Elvis Presley sang so protectively about.

Mr. Earl—no one who worked for him ever called him Harley—could afford to be a maverick. He created the cars that brought customers into GM showrooms across the country. Before he came to Detroit, engineering sold cars. Advertising stressed mechanical virtues—the steady ride, reliable brakes, or, perhaps, power steering. Earl made style the distinctive feature. Unlike the boxy look other designs favored, an Earl car was low and sleek, suggesting motion even when the car stood still. No feature stood out more distinctively than the fins he first put on the 1948 Cadillac. By the mid-1950s jet planes inspired Earl to design ever more outrageous fins, complemented by huge, shiny chrome grills and ornaments. These features served no mechanical purpose. Some critics dismissed Earl's designs as jukeboxes on wheels.

To Earl and GM that did not matter. Design sold cars. "It gave [customers] an extra receipt for their money in the form of visible prestige marking for an expensive car," Earl said. The "Big Three" auto manufacturers—General Motors, Ford, and Chrysler—raced one another to redesign their annual models, the more outrageous the better. Earl once joked, "I'd put smokestacks right in the middle of the sons of bitches if I thought I could sell more cars." In the lingo of the Detroit stylists, these designs were "gasaroony," an adjective *Popular Mechanics* magazine translated as "terrific, overpowering, weird." The goal was not a better car but what Earl called "dynamic obsolescence," or simply change for change's sake. "The 1957 Ford was great," its designer remarked, "but right away we had to bury it and start another." Even a successful style had to go within a year. "We would design a car to make a man unhappy with his 1957 Ford 'long about the end of 1958." Even though the mechanics of cars changed little from year to year, dynamic obsolescence persuaded Americans in the 1950s to buy new cars in record numbers.

Fins, roadside motels, "gaseterias," drive-in burger huts, interstate highways, shopping centers, and, of course, suburbs—all these were part of a culture of mobility in the 1950s. Americans continued their exodus from rural areas to cities and from the cities to the suburbs. African Americans left the South, heading for industrial centers in the Northeast, in the Midwest, and on the West Coast. Mexican Americans concentrated in southwestern cities, while Puerto Ricans came largely to New York. And for Americans in the Snowbelt, the climate of the West and South (at least when civilized by air conditioning) made the Sunbelt irresistible to ever larger numbers.

The mobility was social, too. As the economy continued to expand, the size of the American middle class grew. In an era of prosperity and peace, some commentators began to speak of a "consensus"—a general agreement in American culture, based on values of the broad middle class. In a positive light consensus reflected the agreement among most Americans about fundamental democratic values. Most citizens embraced the material benefits of prosperity as evidence of the virtue of "the American way." And they opposed the spread of communism abroad.

*The 1950s as an era of consensus*

But consensus had its dark side. Critics worried that too strong a consensus bred a mindless conformity. Were Americans becoming too homogenized? Was there a depressing sameness in the material goods they owned, in the places they lived in, and in the values they held? In addition, wasn't any notion of consensus hollow as long as racism and segregation prevented African Americans and other minorities from fully sharing in American life?

The baby boomers born into this era seldom agonized over such issues. In the White House President Eisenhower radiated a comforting sense that the affairs of the nation and the world were in capable hands. That left teenagers free to worry about what really mattered: a first date, a first kiss, a first job, a first choice for college, and whether or not to "go all the way" in the back seat of one of Harley Earl's fin-swept Buicks.

## THE RISE OF THE SUBURBS

Suburban growth accelerated sharply at the end of World War II. During the 1950s suburbs grew 40 times faster than cities, so that by 1960 half of the American people lived in them. The return of prosperity brought a baby boom and a need for new housing. Automobiles made the suburbs accessible. But the spurt in suburban growth took its toll on the cities, which suffered as the middle class fled urban areas.

## *A Boom in Babies and in Housing*

The Great Depression caused many couples to delay beginning a family. In the 1930s birthrates had reached their low point in American history, about 18 to 19 per thousand. As prosperity returned during the war, birthrates began to rise. By 1952 they had passed 25 per thousand to reach one of the highest fertility rates in the world. New brides were also younger, which translated into unusual fertility. Americans chose to have larger families, as the number with three children tripled and those with four or more quadrupled. "Just imagine how much these extra people, these new markets, will absorb—in food, in clothing, in gadgets, in housing, in services," one journalist predicted.

The boom in marriage and families created a need for housing. At war's end, 5 million families were eager to find anything, tired of living doubled up with other families or in basements or even coal cellars. With the help of the GI Bill and rising incomes, the chance to own a house rather than rent became a reality for over half of American families. And it was the suburbs that offered the kind of residence most Americans idealized: a detached single-family house with a lawn and garden.

In the 1940s inexpensive suburban housing became synonymous with the name of real estate developer William Levitt. From building houses for war

*Levittown, U.S.A.*

workers, Levitt learned how to use mass production techniques. In 1947 he began construction of a 17,000-house community in the New York City suburb of Hempstead. All the materials for a

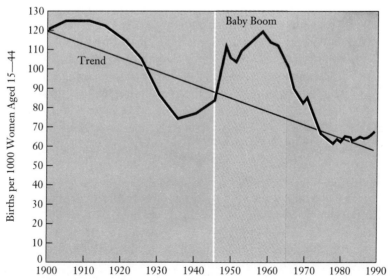

THE UNITED STATES BIRTHRATE, 1900–1989   Over the long term, the nation's birthrate has shown a steady downward trend, which became even sharper during the Depression years. But after World War II, younger marriages and prosperity triggered a baby boom.

Levittown house were precut and assembled at a factory, then moved to the site for assembly. If all went according to schedule, a new house was erected on a cement slab every 16 minutes. Buoyed by his success, Levitt later built developments in Bucks County, Pennsylvania, and Willingboro, New Jersey.

The typical early Levitt house was a "Cape Codder." It boasted a living room, a kitchen, a bath, and two bedrooms on the ground floor and an expansion attic, all for $7990. None of the houses had custom details, insulation, or any features that complicated construction. "The reason we have it so good in this country," Levitt said, "is that we can produce lots of things at low prices through mass production."

Uniformity in house style extended to behavior as well. Levitt discouraged owners from changing colors or adding distinctive features to the house or yard. Buyers promised to cut the grass each week of the summer and not to hang out wash on weekends. African Americans were expressly excluded. Other suburban communities excluded Jews and ethnic Americans through restrictive covenants that dictated who could take up residence.

### Suburbs and Cities Transformed

Single-family houses with spacious lawns required plenty of open land, unlike the row houses built side by side in earlier suburban developments. That meant Levitt and other builders chose vacant areas outside of major urban centers. With the new houses farther from factories, offices, and jobs, the automobile became more indispensable than ever.

As population shifted to suburbs, traffic choked old country roads. To ease congestion, the Eisenhower administration proposed a 20-year plan to build a massive interstate highway system. In rallying support, Eisenhower addressed cold war fears as well, arguing that the new system would help cities evacuate

*The Interstate Highway Act* in case of nuclear attack. In 1956 Congress passed the Interstate Highway Act, setting in motion the largest public works project in history. The federal government picked up 90 percent of the cost through a Highway Trust Fund, financed by special taxes on cars, gas, tires, lubricants, and auto parts.

The Interstate Highway Act had an enormous impact on American life. Average annual driving increased by 400 percent. Shopping centers, linked by the new roads, provided suburbanites with an alternative to the longer trip downtown. By 1960 more than 3840 of them covered as much land as the nation's central business districts. Almost every community had at least one highway strip dotted with drive-in movies, stores, bowling alleys, gas stations, and fast-food joints.

The interstates affected cities in less fortunate ways. The new highway system featured beltways, ring roads around major urban areas. Instead of leading

*Declining cities* traffic downtown, the beltways allowed motorists to avoid the center city altogether. As people took to their cars, intercity rail

Like a freak of evolution run riot, automotive tailfins during the 1950s were elongated
until they reached the monstrous proportions of the 1959 Cadillac,
which also sported bomblike taillights.

service and mass transit declined. Seventy-five percent of all government transportation dollars went to subsidize travel by car and truck; only one percent was
earmarked for urban mass transit. At the same time that middle-class home
owners were moving to the suburbs, many low-paying, unskilled jobs disappeared from the cities. That forced the urban poor into reverse commuting
from city to suburb. All of these trends made cities less attractive places to live
or do business in. With fewer well-to-do taxpayers to draw upon, city governments lacked the tax base to finance public services. A vicious cycle ensued that
proved most damaging to the urban poor, who had few means of escape.

Much of the white population that moved to the suburbs was replaced by
African Americans and Hispanics. They were part of larger migrations, espe-

*Black and
Hispanic
Americans
migrate to cities*

cially of millions of black families leaving the South to search for
work in urban centers. Most headed for the Northeast and Upper
Midwest. While central cities lost 3.6 million white residents,
they gained 4.5 million African Americans. Indeed, by 1960 half
of all black Americans were living in central cities.

Earlier waves of European immigrants had been absorbed by the expanding urban economy. During the 1950s, however, the flight of jobs and middle-
class taxpayers to the suburbs made it difficult for African Americans and

*The suburbs
and race*

Hispanics to follow the same path. In the cities fewer jobs awaited
them, while declining school systems made it harder for newcomers to acculturate. In the hardest-hit urban areas, unemployment rose to over 40 percent.

By contrast, the suburbs remained beyond reach of most minorities. Since
few black or Hispanic families could afford the cost of suburban living, they accounted for less than 5 percent of the population there. The few black suburbs
that existed dated from before the war and had little in common with the newer

white "bedroom communities." Black suburbanites were poorer, held lower-status jobs, lived in more ramshackle housing, and had less education than urban African Americans.

Those who could afford the suburbs discovered that most real estate agents refused to show them houses; bankers would not provide mortgages. And many communities adopted either restrictive covenants or zoning regulations that kept out "undesirable" home buyers. One African American, William Myers, finally managed in 1957 to buy a house from a white family in Levittown, Pennsylvania, but the developers did not sell directly to African Americans until 1960.

## THE CULTURE OF SUBURBIA

In suburban tracts across America, a new appetizer began appearing at trendy dinner parties. Named the California Dip, it was the brainchild of the Lipton Company, which was searching for new ways to market its dehydrated onion soup. Homemakers simply mixed Lipton's soup powder with sour cream and served it up with chips. As one commentator noted,

> Using potato chips as little shovels, you gathered up the deliciously salty but drip-prone liquid and popped it, potato chip and all, into your mouth as quickly and gracefully as possible. There was anxiety in all this—particularly the fear that a great glop of the stuff would land on your tie or the rug—but also immense satisfaction.

As much genius, perhaps, went into the naming of the dip as into the recipe. Sour cream had been a mainstay in ethnic dishes like blintzes (thin Jewish pancakes) and borscht (an Eastern European beet soup). With an all-American name like "California Dip," sour cream's ethnic associations were left behind. The ingredient went mainstream—into the consensus.

The evolving culture of the suburbs reflected a similar process, a shucking off of ethnic associations. In many city neighborhoods, immigrant parents or grandparents lived on the same block or even in the same apartment with their children. In the suburbs, single-family dwellers often left their relatives and in-laws behind, which meant that ethnic lifestyles were less pronounced. The restrictive immigration policies of the 1920s had also reduced the number of newly arrived foreign-born Americans. Thus suburban culture reflected the tastes of the broad, mostly assimilated middle classes.

Class distinctions were more pronounced between suburban communities than within them. The upper middle class clustered in older developments,

*Suburbs and social class*

often centered around country clubs. Working-class suburbs sprouted on the outskirts of large manufacturing centers, where blue-collar families eagerly escaped the city. Within suburbs a more homogeneous suburban culture evolved. "We see eye to eye on most things," commented one Levittown resident, "about raising kids, doing things together with your husband . . . we have practically the same identical background."

## American Civil Religion

If the move out of cities often reduced the ethnic flavor of suburban neighborhoods, most residents held onto their religious beliefs. Religion continued to be a distinctive and segregating factor during the 1950s. Catholics, Protestants, and Jews generally married within their own faiths, and in the suburbs they kept their social distance as well.

Communities that showed no obvious class distinctions were sometimes deeply divided along religious lines. Catholics attended parochial rather than

*Religious divisions*

public schools, formed their own clubs, and socialized less with their Protestant neighbors. Protestant and Catholic members of the same country club usually did not play golf or tennis in the same foursomes. As for Jews, one historian remarked that whereas a gulf divided many Catholics and Protestants, Jews and Gentiles "seem to have lived on the opposite sides of a religious Grand Canyon." Even an outward friendliness masked underlying mistrust and the persistence of old stereotypes.

Although such religious boundaries remained strong, the consensus increased that religion was central to American life. Church membership rose to over 50 percent for the first time in the twentieth century, and by 1957 the census bureau reported that 96 percent of the American people cited a specific affiliation when asked the question "What is your religion?" The religious upswing was supported in part by the prevailing cold war mood, since Communists were avowedly atheists. Cold war fervor led Congress in 1954 to add the phrase "under God" to the Pledge of Allegiance.

Patriotic and anticommunist themes were strong in the preaching of clergy who pioneered the use of television. Billy Graham, a Baptist revival preacher,

*Television ministries*

first attracted national attention at a tent meeting in Los Angeles in 1949. Following in the tradition of nineteenth-century revivalists like Dwight Moody, Graham soon achieved even wider impact by televising his meetings. Though no revivalist, the Roman Catholic Bishop Fulton J. Sheen made the transition from a radio to a television ministry. In his weekly program he extolled traditional values and attacked communism.

Indeed, throughout American culture, the benefits of religion—of *any* religion—were lauded. Historians have referred to this acceptance of generalized religious values as American civil religion. President Eisenhower made the point quite clear. "Our government makes no sense unless it is founded on a deeply religious faith," he proclaimed, "—and I don't care what it is." And every Friday afternoon children watching "The Howdy Doody Show" were exhorted by the show's host, Buffalo Bob, to worship "at the church or synagogue of your choice."

## *"Homemaking" Women in the Workaday World*

The growth of a suburban culture revealed a contradiction in the lives of middle-class women. Never before were their traditional roles as housewives and mothers so central to American society. Yet never before did more women join the workforce outside the home.

For housewives, the single-family suburban home required more labor to keep clean. At the same time, the baby boom left suburban mothers with more children to tend and less help from relatives and grandparents, who less often lived nearby. Increased dependence on automobiles made many a suburban housewife the chauffeur for her family. In the 1920s grocers or milkmen commonly delivered their goods from door to door. By the 1950s delivery services were being replaced by housewives doing "errands."

Yet between 1940 and 1960 the percentage of wives working outside the home doubled from 15 to 30 percent. While some women took jobs simply to help make ends meet, more than financial necessity was involved.

*Working women*

Middle-class married women went to work as often as lower-class wives, and women with college degrees were the most likely to get a job. Two-income families were able to spend far more on extras: gifts, education, recreation, and household appliances. In addition, women found status and self-fulfillment in their jobs, as well as a chance for increased social contacts.

In the automobile-centered suburbs, many women became chauffeurs as well as housewives. The average suburban woman spent one full working day each week driving and doing errands.

More women were going to college, too, but that increased education did not translate into economic equality. The median wage for women was less than half that for men—a greater gap than in any other industrial nation. The percentage of women holding professional jobs actually dropped between 1950 and 1960.

Despite women's wider roles in society, the media most often portrayed them either as sex objects or as domesticated housewives and mothers. A typi-

*Media images of women*

cal article appearing in *Redbook* in 1957 made a heroine of Junior, a "little freckle-faced brunette" who had given up work. As the story closed, Junior nursed her baby at two in the morning, crooning "I'm glad, glad, glad I'm just a housewife." In 1950 Lynn White, the president of Mills College for women, advocated a curriculum that displaced traditional academic subjects with those that were "distinctly feminine," like home economics and crafts.

## The Flickering Gray Screen

In the glow of postwar prosperity, most Americans found themselves with more leisure time and more income. A suburban yard to tend and a young family to raise determined that parents and children would spend much of their free time around the house. The new medium of television fit perfectly into suburban lifestyles. It provided an ideal way to entertain families at home as well as sell them consumer goods.

The entrance of television into the American mainstream came only after World War II. In 1949 Americans owned only a million televisions; by 1960 the figure had jumped to 46 million. Indeed, by then more Americans had televisions than had bathrooms. Soon attendance began dropping for pastimes like moviegoing and professional sports. Over 4000 urban movie theaters closed. Some were replaced in the suburbs by popular drive-ins, which allowed whole families to enjoy movies in the comfort of their cars. But even that novelty failed to attract as many viewers. Restaurant owners also felt the squeeze. When Sid Caesar and Imogene Coca appeared on Saturday nights in "Your Show of Shows," diners rushed home to their television sets.

In 1948 television began its involvement in politics, covering both the Democratic and Republican conventions. Two years later, it televised hearings

*Television and politics*

on organized crime chaired by Senator Estes Kefauver. Some 30 million viewers watched senators grill mobster Frank Costello about his criminal organization and its ties to city governments. Millions more watched Senator Joseph McCarthy's ill-fated attack on the army in 1954. With such a large audience, television clearly had the potential to shape the nation's politics. But by the mid-1950s controversy over news coverage of issues like McCarthyism led the networks to downgrade public affairs programs. As an alternative they turned to Hollywood, which developed telefilm dramas and situation comedies. By 1959 live television was virtually a thing of the past. Westerns, detective shows, and old movies led the ratings.

## THE POLITICS OF CALM

In presiding over these changes in American society, President Dwight David Eisenhower projected an aura of paternal calm. Pursuing "modern Republicanism," the new president sought consensus, not confrontation. No longer would conservatives like Robert Taft call for a repeal of the New Deal and a return to laissez-faire capitalism. Eisenhower declared that he was "conservative when it comes to money and liberal when it comes to human beings."

### The Eisenhower Presidency

Eisenhower had been raised in a large Kansas farm family. His parents, though poor, offered him a warm, caring home steeped in religious faith. In an era of organizational men, Eisenhower succeeded by mastering the military's bureaucratic politics. A graduate of West Point, he was neither a scholar nor an aggressive general like George Patton. In the placid years between the two world wars, the skills "Ike" demonstrated at golf, poker, and bridge often proved as valuable as his military expertise. Yet these genial ways could not hide his ambition or his ability to judge character shrewdly. It took a gifted organizer to coordinate the D-Day invasion and to hold together the egocentric generals who pushed east to Berlin.

As president, Eisenhower resisted conservative demands to dismantle New Deal programs. He even agreed to increases in social security, unemployment insurance, and the minimum wage. He accepted a small public housing program and a modest federally supported medical insurance plan for the needy. But as a conservative, Eisenhower remained uncomfortable with big government. Thus he rejected more far-reaching liberal proposals on housing and universal health care through the social security system.

*Modern Republicanism in practice*

To make modern Republicanism successful, Eisenhower had to woo the newly prosperous Democratic voters joining the middle class. Success in that

President Dwight D. Eisenhower

effort hinged on how well the administration managed the economy. New Deal Democrats had established a tradition of activism: when the economy faltered, they used deficit spending and tax cuts to stimulate it. Eisenhower preferred to reduce federal spending and the government's role in the economy. When a recession struck in 1953–1954, the administration was concerned more with balancing the budget and holding inflation in line than with reducing unemployment through government spending.

Eisenhower was similarly pragmatic in other areas. When major projects called for federal leadership, as with the Highway Act, he supported them. In 1954 he signed the St. Lawrence Seaway Act, which joined the United States and Canada in an ambitious engineering project to open the Great Lakes to ocean shipping. Like the highway program, the Seaway was fiscally acceptable because the funding came from user tolls and taxes rather than from general revenues.

Farm policy was one area where Eisenhower's pragmatic approach faltered. Farmers made up a major Republican voting bloc. For the president to abolish

*Farm policy*

the price supports established under the New Deal was to commit political suicide. On the other hand, crop surpluses continued to fill government silos with unwanted grain. Eisenhower's secretary of agriculture, Ezra Taft Benson, proposed lowering support payments so that farmers would not overproduce basic commodities like corn, cotton, and wheat. Benson also established a soil bank program to pay farmers for reducing acreage.

In the end, however, the effects of modern technology made it difficult to regulate agricultural production. Even when farmers cut back acreage, they discovered that automated harvesters, fertilizers, and new varieties of plants actually increased farm outputs. In an age of continuing centralization, more and more small farms were being replaced by agribusinesses. As power became more concentrated in these large commercial farming businesses, so did their political power to protect farm subsidies.

Despite occasional setbacks Eisenhower remained popular. Although he suffered a major heart attack in 1955, voters gladly reelected him in 1956. But

*The limits of modern Republicanism*

poor economic performance took its toll on the Republican party. In the wake of the 1954 recession the Democrats gained a 29-member majority in the House and a 1-vote edge in the Senate. Never again would Eisenhower work with a Republican majority in Congress. In 1958, when recession again dragged down the economy, the Democrats took a 68-seat majority in the House and a 12-vote advantage in the Senate. Modern Republicanism did not put down deep roots beyond Eisenhower's White House.

---

COUNTERPOINT    *Assessing Eisenhower*

In 1962, when historians rated presidential performance, Eisenhower scored near the bottom, barely ahead of Ulysses S Grant. As president, he had kept a low political profile. Critics complained that he conceived of himself as a mere figurehead, like a constitiutional monarch. Certainly, Eisenhower was reluctant to challenge the aggressive anticommunism of Senator Joseph McCarthy, and as we shall see, he only reluctantly moved to defend the civil rights of African Americans. Critics also attacked Ike's firm belief in letting the business community chart its own course without closer government regulation. Secretary of Defense Charles Wilson, former president of General Motors, expressed the administration's probusiness creed, proclaiming that "What was good for our country was good for General Motors and vice versa."

More recently, historians have been inclined to place Eisenhower among the most capable of American presidents. His aloof manner, some argue, disguised a president whose "hidden hand" acted vigorously behind the scenes. While in public Eisenhower let others speak for him (and take the heat), in private he made decisions and set directions. Ike was not activist in the energetic tradition of either Roosevelt. Then again, the three presidents who followed him took "bold" actions that were quite controversial: John Kennedy's invasion of Cuba, Lyndon Johnson's war in Vietnam, and Richard Nixon's political overreaching. In this light Eisenhower's modern Republicanism seems no longer like inactive government, but like a mature appreciation of the limits of the presidency.

## The Conglomerate World

Large businesses welcomed the administration's probusiness attitudes as well as the era's general prosperity. Wages for the average worker rose over 35 percent between 1950 and 1960. At the same time, the economic distress of the 1930s had led corporate executives to devise new ways to minimize the danger of economic downturns. In various ways, each of the approaches sought to minimize shocks in specific markets by expanding the size of corporations in different ways.

One expansion strategy took the form of diversification. In the 1930s, a giant like General Electric had concentrated largely in one industrial area: equip-

*Diversification and conglomeration*

ment for generating electric power and light. When the Depression struck, GE found its markets evaporating. The company responded by entering markets for appliances, X-ray machines, and elevators—all products developed or enhanced by the company's research labs. In the postwar era General Electric diversified even further, into nuclear power, jet engines, and television. Diversification was most practical for large industrial firms, whose size allowed them to support extensive research and development.

Conglomeration often turned small companies into giants. Unlike earlier horizontal and vertical combinations, conglomerate mergers could join companies with seemingly unrelated products. Over a 20-year period International Telephone and Telegraph branched out from its basic communications business into baking, hotels and motels, car rental, home building, and insurance. Corporations also became multinational by expanding their overseas operations or buying out potential foreign competitors. Large integrated oil companies like Mobil and Standard Oil of New Jersey (Exxon) developed huge oil fields in the Middle East and markets around the free world.

One aid to managing these modern corporate giants was the advent of electronic data processing. In the early 1950s computers were virtually unknown in

*Early computers*

private industry. But banks and insurance companies saw calculating machines as an answer to their need to manipulate huge quantities of records and statistical data. Manufacturers, especially in the petroleum, chemical, automotive, and electronics industries, began to use computers to monitor their production lines, quality control, and inventory.

## NATIONALISM IN AN AGE OF SUPERPOWERS

Along the Iron Curtain of Eastern Europe and across the battle lines of northern Asia, the Soviet-American cold war settled into an uneasy stalemate. But World War II had also disrupted Europe's colonial relationships. As nationalists in the Middle East, Africa, and Southeast Asia fought to gain independence, the two superpowers competed for their allegiance. Across the globe the Eisenhower administration sought ways to prevent the Soviet Union from capturing national independence movements. To do so, it sometimes used the threat of nuclear war to block communist expansion in Europe or Asia.

### *To the Brink?*

Eisenhower, no stranger to world politics, shared the conduct of foreign policy with his secretary of state, John Foster Dulles. Coming from a family of mis-

*John Foster Dulles*

sionaries and diplomats, Dulles had within him a touch of both. He viewed the Soviet–American struggle in almost religious terms, as a fight between good and evil. Eisenhower was less hostile toward the Soviets. In the end, the two men's differing temperaments led to a policy that seesawed from confrontation to conciliation.

The administration was determined to turn Truman's containment strategy into a more dynamic offensive. Dulles wanted the United States to aid in liberating the "captive peoples" of Eastern Europe and other communist nations. On the other hand, Eisenhower was equally determined to cut back military spending and troop levels in order to keep the budget balanced. The president was sometimes irked at the "fantastic programs" the Pentagon kept proposing. "If we demand too much in taxes in order to build planes and ships," he argued, "we will tend to dry up the accumulations of capital that are necessary to provide jobs for the million or more new workers that we must absorb each year."

Rather than rely on costly conventional forces, Eisenhower and Dulles used the threat of massive nuclear retaliation to intimidate the Soviets into behaving less aggressively. Dulles insisted that Americans should not shrink from the

*The policy of massive retaliation*

threat of nuclear war: "If you are scared to go to the brink, you are lost." And as Secretary of Treasury George Humphrey put it, a nuclear strategy was much cheaper—"a bigger bang for the buck." Henceforth American foreign policy would have a "new look," though behind the more militant rhetoric lay an ongoing commitment to containment.

### Brinksmanship in Asia

Moving beyond talk of "brinksmanship" to concrete action did not prove easy. When Dulles announced American intentions to "unleash" Chiang Kai-shek to

*Taiwan and mainland China*

attack mainland China from his outpost on Taiwan (formerly Formosa), China threatened to invade Taiwan. At that, Eisenhower ordered the Seventh Fleet into the area to protect rather than unleash Chiang. If the Communists attacked, Dulles warned bluntly, "we'll have to use atomic weapons."

Nuclear weapons also figured in the American response to a crisis in Indochina. There, Vietnamese forces led by Ho Chi Minh were fighting the French, who had returned at the end of World War II to reestablish their colonial rule. Between 1950 and 1954, the United States provided France with over $1 billion in military aid in Vietnam. Eisenhower worried that if Vietnam fell to a Communist revolutionary like Ho, other nations of Southeast Asia would follow. "You have a row of dominoes set up," the president warned, "you knock over the first one [y]ou could have the beginning of a disintegration that would have the most profound influences."

Worn down by a war they seemed unable to win, the French in 1954 tried to force a final showdown with Ho Chi Minh's army at Dien Bien Phu. With

*Vietnamese victory at Dien Bien Phu*

Vietnamese and Chinese communist troops holding the surrounding hilltops, the French garrison there could not have chosen a worse place to do battle. Desperate, the French pleaded for more American aid. Admiral Arthur Radford, head of the Joint Chiefs of Staff, proposed a massive American air raid, perhaps even using tactical nuclear weapons. But again Eisenhower pulled back. The idea of American involvement in another Asian war aroused opposition from both allies and domestic political leaders.

Finally the garrison at Dien Bien Phu collapsed under the seige. In May, at an international peace conference in Geneva, Switzerland, the French negotiated the terms of their withdrawal. Ho Chi Minh agreed to pull his forces north of the 17th parallel, temporarily dividing the nation into North and South Vietnam. Because of Ho's broad popularity, he seemed assured an easy victory in elections scheduled for within the next two years. Dulles, however, viewed any communist victory as unacceptable, even if the election was democratic. He convinced Eisenhower to support a South Vietnamese government under Ngo Dinh Diem. Dulles insisted that Diem was not bound by the Geneva Accords to hold any election—a position the autocratic Diem eagerly supported. To help keep him in power, the United States sent a military mission to train South Vietnam's army. The commitment was small, but a decade later it would return to haunt Americans.

## The Superpowers

Korea, Taiwan, Indochina—to Dulles and Eisenhower, the crises in Asia and elsewhere could all be traced back to the Soviet dictatorship. Although nationalist movements around the globe were leading nations like India to declare themselves neutral or nonaligned, Dulles continually warned them that they could not sit on the fence. They must choose either the "free world" or the communist bloc. Throughout the 1950s the secretary of state crisscrossed the globe, setting up mutual defense pacts patterned on NATO, to solidify American security. Yet in all this, it was becoming harder to decide what the motives of the Soviets themselves might be.

Joseph Stalin had died in March 1953, after becoming increasingly isolated, arbitrary, vengeful, and perhaps simply mad. Power soon fell to Nikita

*Nikita Khrushchev*

Khrushchev, a party stalwart with a formidable intellect and peasant origins in the farm country of the Ukraine. In some ways Khrushchev resembled another farm-belt politician, Harry Truman. Both were unsophisticated yet shrewd, earthy in their sense of humor, energetic, short-tempered, and largely inexperienced in international affairs. Khrushchev kept American diplomats off balance. At times genial and conciliatory, he would suddenly become demanding and boastful.

Khrushchev moderated some of the excesses of the Stalin years. At home, he gradually shifted the Soviet economy toward production of consumer goods. Internationally, he called for an easing of tensions and reduced forces in Europe, hoping to make Western Europeans less dependent on the United States. In Washington the administration was unsure of how to receive the new overtures. The spirit of McCarthyism still reigned, so that compromise with the Soviets involved great political risk. It was actually Winston Churchill who suggested that the Russians might be serious about negotiating. In 1955 the Americans, British, French, and Soviets met in a summit conference at Geneva, Switzerland. While little came of the summit other than a cordial "spirit of Geneva," the meeting hinted that a cooling in the arms race was possible.

## Nationalism Unleashed

The spirit of Geneva did not long survive new nationalist upheavals. Khrushchev's moderation encouraged nationalists in Soviet-controlled Eastern Europe to

*Revolt in Hungary*

push for greater independence. Riots erupted in Poland, while in Hungary students took to the streets demanding that a coalition government replace the puppet regime established by Stalin. At first, Moscow accepted the new Hungarian government and began to remove Soviet tanks. But when Hungary announced it was withdrawing from the Warsaw Pact, the tanks rolled back into Budapest to crush the uprising in October 1956. The United States protested but did nothing to help liberate the "captive nations." For all its tough talk, the "new look" foreign policy recognized that the Soviets possessed a sphere of influence where the United States would not intervene.

At the same time that nationalism erupted in Eastern Europe Dulles faced a series of crises in the Middle East. When a nationalist government in Iran seemed to lean toward the Soviets, he obtained Eisenhower's approval to launch a covert CIA operation in 1953 to oust its leader, Mohammad Mossadeq, and restore a firm ally, the Shah Mohammad Reza Pahlavi. Meanwhile, for several years Egyptian leader Gamal Abdel Nasser, a nationalist, had been attempting to modernize his country and rebuild his army. Dulles tried to befriend Nasser by offering American aid to build the Aswan Dam, a massive power project on the Nile River. But when Nasser formed an Arab alliance against the young state of Israel and continued to pursue economic ties with the Warsaw bloc, Dulles withdrew the American pledge on Aswan. In 1956 Nasser angrily countered by seizing the British-owned Universal Suez Canal Company. The company ran the waterway through which tankers carried most of Europe's oil.

*Nationalism in Iran and Egypt*

Events then moved quickly. Israel, alarmed at Nasser's Arab alliance, invaded the Sinai peninsula of Egypt on October 29—the same day Hungary announced it was leaving the Warsaw Pact. Three days later French and British forces seized the canal in an attempt to restore their own interests and prestige. Angered that his allies had not consulted him, Eisenhower joined the Soviet Union in supporting a United Nations resolution condemning Britain, France, and Israel and demanding an immediate cease-fire. By December American pressures forced Britain and France to remove their forces. Few events placed so much strain on the Western alliance as the Suez crisis. At the same time, Nasser had demonstrated to the industrial powers the potential force of Third World nationalism.

Given the unstable situation in the Middle East, Eisenhower convinced Congress to give him the authority to use force against any communist attack in that region. What became known as the Eisenhower Doctrine in effect allowed the president in times of crisis to preempt Congress's power to declare war. In 1958 he used that power to send U.S. marines into Lebanon, a small nation that claimed to have been infiltrated by Nasser's supporters. Since no fighting had yet occurred, sunbathers on the beaches of Beirut, Lebanon's capital, were startled as 5000 combat-clad marines stormed ashore. In the end, the crisis blew over, and the American forces withdrew. Dulles claimed that the United States had once again turned back the communist drive into the emerging nations. In reality, nationalism more than communism had been at the root of Middle Eastern turmoil.

*Eisenhower Doctrine*

Nationalist forces were also in ferment in Latin America, where only 2 percent of the people controlled 75 percent of the land. Given this unequal distribution of wealth and a rapidly growing population, social tensions were rising. Yet any move toward more democratic government seemed unlikely. Repressive dictatorships exercised power, and foreign interests—especially American ones—dominated Latin American economies. In 1954, Eisenhower authorized the CIA to send a band of Latin American mercenaries into Guatemala to overthrow a nationalist government there. Although the government was democratically elected, it had seized 400,000 acres from United Fruit, a U.S. corporation. The new military dictatorship promptly returned the confiscated lands to United Fruit.

Similar economic tensions were reflected in Cuba, where the United States owned 80 percent of the country's utilities and operated a major naval base at Guantánamo Bay. Cuban dictator Fulgencio Batista had close ties both to the U.S. government and to major crime figures who operated gambling, prostitution, and drug rings in Havana. A disgruntled middle-class lawyer, Fidel Castro, gained the support of impoverished peasants in Cuba's mountains and, in January 1959, drove Batista from power.

*Castro's revolution in Cuba*

At first many Americans applauded the revolution, welcoming Castro when he visited the United States. But Eisenhower was distinctly cool to the cigar-smoking Cuban, who dressed in green military fatigues and sported a full beard. By summer Castro had filled key government positions with Communists, launched a sweeping agricultural reform, and confiscated American properties. Retaliating, Eisenhower embargoed Cuban sugar and mobilized opposition to Castro in other Latin American countries. Cut off from American markets and aid, Castro turned to the Soviet Union.

## The Response to Sputnik

Castro's turn to the Soviets seemed all the more dangerous because of Soviet achievements in their missile program. In 1957 they stunned America by launching into outer space the first satellite, dubbed *Sputnik*. By 1959, the Soviets had crash-landed a much larger payload on the moon. If the Russians could target the moon, surely they could launch nuclear missiles against America. In contrast, the American space program suffered so many delays and mishaps that rockets exploding on launch were nicknamed "flopniks" and "kaputniks."

How had the Soviets managed to catch up with American technology so quickly? Some Americans blamed the schools, especially weak programs in science and math. In 1958 Eisenhower joined with Congress to enact a National Defense Education Act, designed to strengthen graduate education and the teaching of science, math, and foreign languages. At the same time, crash programs were undertaken to build basement fallout shelters to protect Americans in case of a nuclear attack. Democrats charged that the administration had allowed the United States to face an unacceptable "missile gap."

## *Thaws and Freezes*

Throughout this series of crises, each superpower found it difficult to interpret the other's motives. The Russians exploited nationalist revolutions where they could—less successfully in Egypt, more so in Cuba. "We will bury you," Khrushchev admonished Americans, though it was unclear whether he meant through peaceful competition or military confrontation. More menacingly, in November 1958 he demanded that the Western powers withdraw all troops from West Berlin within six months. Berlin would then become a "free city," and the Western powers could negotiate further access to it only with East Germany, a government the West had refused to recognize. When Eisenhower flatly rejected the ultimatum, Khrushchev backed away from his hard-line stance.

*Controversy over Berlin*

Rather than adopt a more belligerent course, Eisenhower determined to use the last 18 months of his presidency to improve Soviet–American relations. The shift in policy was made easier because Eisenhower knew from American intelligence (but could not admit publicly) that the "missile gap" was not real. While willing to spend more on missile development, he refused to heed the calls for a crash defense program at any cost. Instead, he took a more conciliatory approach by inviting Khrushchev to visit the United States in September 1959. Though the meetings produced no significant results, they eased tensions. And

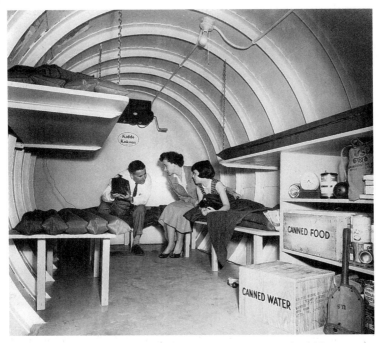

The nuclear arms race inspired many Americans to build basement fallout shelters in case of an attack.

E Y E W I T N E S S     T O     H I S T O R Y

## Growing Up with the Threat of Atomic War

And so whenever the civil defense sirens interrupted my school days with their apocalyptic howls, I folded my papers neatly and filed into the hallway and squatted in front of the lockers with my head between my knees and my hands on the back of my neck, like everyone else. . . .

In those days we did not know if we would survive from month to month. . . . Everyone was thinking about large questions and What Is to Be Done? . . . Should you shoot a person who seeks safety in your shelter? That was a question we debated in church, without satisfaction. Our pastor recalled the parable of the Good Samaritan, but it didn't seem appropriate to the occasion. "I can see letting one or two guys in," said a member of the congregation, "but what about ten? fifty? You've got to draw a line somewhere." Another woman, slightly ecstatic, said we were all going to die in the blast and meet Jesus, so what's the problem? . . .

Properly prepared, we were told, the rest of us could expect a 97 percent chance of survival—a figure universally recognized as a lie. Nonetheless, we kept a small store of canned goods in our house, and Mother stored bottled water in the closet. We had a small store of candles, flashlight batteries, and a transistor radio with the Conelrad stations marked with the nuclear triangles. Parents were told not to rescue their children from school; presumably we were safe in the hallways. The mother of a friend of mine told him if she *ever* came to school to get him, he was to go with her and never mind what the teachers or the principal might say. One day he was gazing out the window of his classroom and saw his mother drive up, and he jumped out the window and ran to her car. She was bringing his lunch money.

Lawrence Wright, *In the New World: Growing Up with America, 1960-1984* (New York, Knopf, 1987), pp. 53–55. Copyright © 1983, 1986, 1987 by Lawrence Wright. Reprinted by permission of Alfred A. Knopf, Inc.

---

Khrushchev undertook a picturesque tour across America, swapping comments about manure with Iowa farmers, reacting puritanically to movie cancan dancers, and grousing when his visit to the new capitalist marvel, Disneyland, was canceled for security reasons.

In May, Eisenhower's plans for a return visit to the Soviet Union were abruptly canceled. Only weeks earlier the Russians had shot down a high-

*The U-2 incident*

altitude U-2 American spy plane over Soviet territory. At first Eisenhower claimed the plane had strayed off course during weather research, but Khrushchev sprang his trap: the CIA pilot, Gary Powers, had been captured alive. The president then admitted that he had personally authorized the U-2 overflights for reasons of national security.

That episode ended Eisenhower's hopes that his personal diplomacy might create a true thaw in the cold war. Yet a less mature president might have led the United States into more severe conflict or even war. Eisenhower was not readily impressed by the promises of new weapon systems. He left office with a warning that too much military spending would lead to "an unwarranted influence, whether sought or unsought" by the "military–industrial complex" at the expense of democratic institutions.

## CIVIL RIGHTS AND THE NEW SOUTH

The struggle of African Americans for equality during the postwar era is filled with ironies. By the time barriers to legal segregation in the South began to fall, millions of black families were leaving for regions where discrimination was less easily challenged in court. The South they left behind was in the early stages of an economic boom. The cities where many migrated had entered a period of decline. Yet, as if to close a circle, the rise of large black voting blocs in major cities created political pressures that forced the nation to dismantle the worst legal and institutional barriers to racial equality. For black Americans, it might be said that these were the best and the worst of times.

### The Changing South and African Americans

Before World War II, 80 percent of African Americans lived in the South. Most raised cotton as sharecroppers and tenant farmers. But the war created a labor

*Mechanizing cotton farms*

shortage at home, as millions went off to fight and others to armament factories. This shortage gave cotton growers an incentive to mechanize cotton picking. In 1950 only 5 percent of the crop was picked mechanically; by 1960 it was at least half. Farmers began to consolidate land into larger holdings. Tenant farmers, sharecroppers, and hired labor of both races left the countryside for the city.

The national level of wages also profoundly affected southern labor. When federal minimum wage laws forced lumber or textile mills to raise their pay scales, the mills no longer expanded. In addition, steel and other industries with strong national unions and manufacturers with plants around the country set wages by national standards. That brought southern wages close to the national average by the 1960s. As the southern economy grew, what had for many years been a distinct regional economy became more diversified and more integrated into the national economy.

As wages rose and unskilled work disappeared, job opportunities for black southerners declined. Outside of cotton farming, the lumber industry provided the largest number of jobs for young black men. There, the number of black teenagers hired by lumber mills dropped 74 percent between 1950 and 1960. New high-wage jobs were reserved for white southerners, since outside industries arriving in the South made no effort to change local patterns of discrimination. So the ultimate irony arose. As per capita income rose and industrialization brought in new jobs, black laborers poured out of the region in search of work. They arrived in cities that showed scant tolerance for racial differences and little willingness or ability to hire unskilled black labor.

## The NAACP and Civil Rights

In the postwar era the National Association for the Advancement of Colored People led the legal fight against racial segregation. Their hard-hitting campaign reflected the increased national political influence African Americans achieved as they migrated out of the South. No longer could northern politicians readily ignore the demands black leaders made for greater equality. At first, however, the NAACP focused its campaign on the courts.

Thurgood Marshall was the association's leading attorney. Marshall had attended law school in the 1930s at Howard University in Washington. There,

*Thurgood Marshall*

the law school's dean, Charles Houston, was in the midst of revamping the school and turning out sharp, dedicated lawyers. Not only was Marshall sharp, but he had the common touch as well. "Before he came along," one observer noted,

> the principal black leaders—men like Du Bois and James Weldon Johnson and Charles Houston—didn't talk the language of the people. They were upper-class and upper-middle-class Negroes. Thurgood Marshall was of the people. . . . Out in Texas or Oklahoma or down the street here in Washington at the Baptist church, he would make these rousing speeches that would have 'em all jumping out of their seats. . . . "We ain't gettin' what we should," was what it came down to, and he made them see that.

During the late 1930s and early 1940s Marshall toured the South (in "a little old beat-up '29 Ford"), typing out legal briefs in the back seat, trying to get teachers to sue for equal pay, and defending blacks accused of murder in a Klan-infested county in Florida. He was friendly with whites and not shy, and black citizens who had never even considered the possibility that a member of their race might win a legal battle "would come for miles, some of them on muleback or horseback, to see 'the nigger lawyer' who stood up in white men's courtrooms."

For years NAACP lawyers worked hard to organize local chapters, to support members of the community willing to risk their jobs, property, and lives in order to challenge segregation. But they waged a moderate, pragmatic campaign. They chose not to attack head-on the Supreme Court decision (*Plessy v. Ferguson*, 1896) that permitted "separate but equal" segregated facilities. They simply demonstrated that a black college or school might be separate, but it was hardly equal if it lacked a law school or even indoor plumbing.

## *The* Brown *Decision*

In 1950 the NAACP changed tactics: it would now try to convince the Supreme Court to overturn the separate but equal doctrine itself. Oliver Brown of Topeka, Kansas, was one of the people who provided a way. Brown was dissatisfied that his daughter Linda had to walk past an all-white school on her way to catch the bus to her segregated black school. A three-judge federal panel rejected Brown's suit because the schools in Topeka, while segregated, did meet the legal standards for equality. The NAACP appealed the case to the Supreme Court and, in 1954, won a striking decision. *Brown v. Board of Education of Topeka* overturned the lower court ruling and overthrew the doctrine of "separate but equal."

Marshall and his colleagues succeeded in part because of a change in the Court itself. The year before, President Eisenhower had appointed Earl Warren, a liberal Republican from California, as chief justice. Warren, a forceful advocate, managed to persuade the last of his reluctant judicial colleagues that segregation as defined in *Plessy* rested on an insupportable theory of racial supremacy. The Court ruled unanimously that separate facilities were inherently unequal. To keep black children segregated solely on the basis of race, it ruled, "generates a feeling of inferiority as to their status in the community that may affect their hearts and minds in a way unlikely ever to be undone."

*Overruling Plessy*

At the time of the *Brown* decision, 21 states and the District of Columbia operated segregated school systems. All had to decide, in some way, how to comply with the new ruling. The Court allowed some leeway, handing down a second ruling in 1955 that required states to carry out desegregation "with all deliberate speed." Some border states reluctantly decided to comply, but in the Deep South, many pledged diehard defiance. In 1956, a "Southern Manifesto" was issued by 19 United States senators and 81 representatives: they intended to use "all lawful means" to reestablish legalized segregation.

## *A New Civil Rights Strategy*

The *Brown* decision did not end segregation, but it combined with political and economic forces to usher in a new era of southern race relations. In December

*Rosa Parks arrested*

1955 Rosa Parks, a 43-year-old black civil rights activist, was riding the bus home in Montgomery, Alabama. When the driver ordered her to give up her seat for a white man, as Alabama Jim Crow laws required, she refused. Police took her to jail and eventually fined her $14.

Determined to overturn the law, black leaders organized a boycott of Montgomery buses, whose riders were largely black. Many in the white community responded angrily to this challenge. No local insurance agent would insure cars used to carpool black workers. A bomb exploded in the house of the Reverend Martin Luther King, Jr., the key boycott leader. Ninety black leaders were arrested for organizing the boycott. Still they held out until November 23, 1956, when the Supreme Court ruled that bus segregation was illegal.

The triumph was especially sweet for Martin Luther King, Jr., whose leadership in Montgomery brought him national fame. Before becoming a minister

*Martin Luther King, Jr.*

at the Dexter Street Baptist Church, King had had little personal contact with the worst forms of white racism. He had grown up in the relatively affluent middle-class black community of Atlanta, Georgia, the son of one of the city's most prominent black ministers. He attended Morehouse College, an academically respected black school in Atlanta, and Crozer Theological Seminary in Philadelphia, before entering the doctoral program in theology at Boston University. As a graduate student, King embraced the pacifism and nonviolence of the Indian leader Mohandas Gandhi and the activism of Christian reformers of the progressive era. King accepted the call to Dexter Street in 1954 with the idea of becoming a theologian after he served his active ministry and finished his dissertation.

As boycott leader, it was King's responsibility to rally black support without triggering violence. Since local officials were all too eager for any excuse to use force, King's nonviolent approach proved an effective strategy. King offered his audience two visions. First, he reminded them of the many injustices they had been forced to endure. The boycott, he asserted, was a good way to seek redress. Then he counseled his followers to avoid the actions of their oppressors: "In our protest there will be no cross burnings. No white person will be taken from his home by a hooded Negro mob and brutally murdered." And he evoked the Christian and republican ideals that would become the themes of his civil rights crusade. "If we protest courageously, and yet with dignity and Christian love," he said, "when the future history books are written, somebody will have to say, 'There lived a race of people, of black people, of people who had the moral courage to stand up for their rights. And thereby they injected a new meaning into the history of civilization.'"

Indeed, the African Americans of Montgomery did set an example of moral courage that rewrote the pages of American race relations. The firm stand of Montgomery's black community caught the attention of the national news media. King and his colleagues were developing the tactics needed to launch a more aggressive phase of the civil rights movement.

## *Little Rock and the White Backlash*

The civil rights spotlight moved the following year to Little Rock, Arkansas. There, white officials had reluctantly adopted a plan to integrate the schools with a most deliberate lack of speed. Nine black students were scheduled to enroll in September 1957 at the all-white Central High School. Instead, the school board urged them to stay home. Governor Orval Faubus, generally a moderate on race relations, called out the Arkansas National Guard on the excuse of maintaining order. President Eisenhower tacitly supported Faubus in his defiance of court-ordered integration by remarking that "you cannot change people's hearts merely by laws."

Still, the Justice Department could not simply let Faubus defy the federal courts. It won an injunction against the governor, but when the nine blacks returned on September 23, a mob of 1000 abusive white protesters greeted them. So great was national attention to the crisis that President Eisenhower felt compelled to send in 1000 federal troops and take control of the National Guard. For one year the Guard preserved order until Faubus, in a last-ditch maneuver, closed all the schools. Only in 1959, under the pressure of another federal court

Angry white students menace black students during the integration crisis at Little Rock's Central High School.

ruling, did the Little Rock schools reopen and resume the plan for gradual integration.

In the face of such attitudes, King and other civil rights leaders recognized that the skirmishes of Montgomery and Little Rock were a beginning, not the end. Cultural attitudes and customs were not about to give way overnight.

## CRACKS IN THE CONSENSUS

The fifties, then, were not a time of consensus on civil rights. In other ways, too, the era could hardly be painted as a decade of undisturbed calm. Intellectuals and social critics spoke out against the stifling features of a conformist corporate culture. Even a moderate like Eisenhower had warned of giving too much power to military, governmental, and industrial bureaucracies. At the fringes of American society, the "beatniks" rejected conformity, while the more mainstream rock 'n' roll movement broadcast its own brand of youthful rebellion. Such cultural ferment undercut the notion that the fifties were merely a decade of consensus.

### Critics of Mass Culture

In Levittown, New Jersey, a woman who had invited her neighbors to a cocktail party eagerly awaited them dressed in newly fashionable Capri pants—a tight-fitting calf-length style. Alas, one early-arriving couple glimpsed the woman through a window. What on earth was the hostess wearing? *Pajamas?* Who in their right mind would entertain in pajamas? The couple sneaked home, afraid they had made a mistake about the day of the party. They telephoned another neighbor, who anxiously called yet others on the guest list. The neighbors finally mustered enough courage to attend the party. But when the hostess later learned of their misunderstanding, she put her Capri pants in the closet for good. Levittown was not ready for such a change in fashion.

Was America turning into a vast suburban wasteland, where the neighbors' worries over Capri pants would stifle all individuality? Many "highbrow" intellectuals worried openly about the effects of mass culture: the homogenized lifestyle created by mass consumption, conformity, and mass media. Critics like Dwight Macdonald sarcastically attacked the culture of the suburban middle classes: Reader's Digest Condensed Books or uplifting film spectacles like *The Ten Commandments*. "Midcult," Macdonald called it, which was his shorthand for uninspired middlebrow culture.

Other critics charged that the skyscrapers and factories of giant conglomerates housed an impersonal world. In large, increasingly automated workplaces, skilled laborers seemed little more than caretakers of machines. Large corporations required middle-level executives to submerge their personal goals

*David Riesman's The Lonely Crowd* — in the processes and work routines of a large bureaucracy. David Riesman, a sociologist, condemned stifling conformity in *The Lonely Crowd* (1950). In nineteenth-century America, Riesman argued, Americans had been "inner directed." It was their own consciences that formed their values and drove them to seek success. In contrast, modern workers had developed a personality shaped not so much by inner convictions as by the opinions of their peers. The new "other-directed" society of suburbia preferred security to success. "Go along to get along" was its motto. In a bureaucratized economy, it was important to please others, to conform to the group, and to cooperate.

William Whyte carried Riesman's critique from the workplace to the suburb in *The Organization Man* (1956). Here he found rootless families, shifted *William Whyte's Organization Man* — from town to town by the demands of corporations. (IBM, went one standard joke, stood for "I've Been Moved.") The typical "organization man" was sociable but not terribly ambitious. He sought primarily to "keep up with the Joneses" and the number of consumer goods they owned. He lived in a suburban "split-level trap," as one critic put it, one among millions of "haggard" men, "tense and anxious" women, and "the gimme kids."

No doubt such portraits were overdrawn and overly alarmist. (Where, after all, did Riesman's nineteenth-century inner-directed Americans get their values, if not from the society around them?) But such critiques indicated the problems of adjustment faced by those working within large bureaucratic organizations and living in suburbs that were decentralized and self-contained.

### Juvenile Delinquency, Rock and Roll, and Rebellion

Young Americans were among suburbia's sharpest critics. Dance crazes, outlandish clothing, slang, rebelliousness, and sexual precociousness—all these behaviors challenged middle-class respectability. More than a few educators warned that America had spawned a generation of rebellious "juvenile delinquents." Psychologist Frederic Wertheim told a group of doctors, "You cannot understand present-day juvenile delinquency if you do not take into account the pathogenic and pathoplastic [infectious] influence of comic books." Others laid the blame on films and the lyrics of popular music.

The center of the new teen culture was the high school. Whether in consolidated rural school districts, new suburban schools, or city systems, the large, *Teenage culture* — comprehensive high schools of the 1950s were often miniature melting pots where middle-class students were exposed to, and often adopted, the style of the lower classes. They wore jeans and T-shirts, challenged authority, and defiantly smoked cigarettes, much like the motorcycle gang leader portrayed by Marlon Brando in the film *The Wild One* (1954).

In many ways the debate over juvenile delinquency was an argument about social class and, to a lesser degree, race. When adults complained that "delinquent" teenagers dressed poorly, lacked ambition, were irresponsible and sexually promiscuous, these were the same arguments traditionally used to denigrate other outsiders—immigrants, the poor, and African Americans. Nowhere were these racial and class undertones more evident than in the hue and cry that greeted the arrival of rock and roll.

Before 1954 popular music had been divided into three major categories: pop, country and western, and rhythm and blues. A handful of major record companies with almost exclusively white singers dominated the pop charts. On one fringe of the popular field was country and western, often split into cowboy musicians like Roy Rogers and Gene Autry and the hillbilly style associated with Nashville. The music industry generally treated rhythm and blues as "race music," whose performers and audience were largely black. Each of these musical traditions, it is worth noting, grew out of regional cultures. As the West and the South merged into the national culture, so these musical subcultures were gradually integrated into the national mainstream.

By the mid-1950s the distinctiveness of the three styles began to blur. Singers on the white pop charts recorded a few songs from country and from

*The rock revolution*

rhythm and blues. The popularity of crossovers such as "Sh-boom," "Tutti-Frutti," and "Earth Angel" indicated that a major shift in taste and market was under way. Lyrics still reflected the pop field's preoccupation with young love, marriage, and happiness, but the music reflected the rawer, earthier style of rhythm and blues. Country and western singer Bill Haley brought the new blend to the fore in 1954 with "Shake, Rattle, and Roll," the first rock song to reach the top ten on the pop charts.

And then—calamity! Millions of middle-class roofs nearly blew off with the appearance in 1955 of the rhythmic and raucous Elvis Presley. By background, Elvis was a country boy whose musical style combined elements of gospel, country, and blues. But it was his hip-swinging, pelvis-plunging performances that electrified teenage audiences. To more conservative adults, Presley's long hair, sideburns, and tight jeans seemed menacingly delinquent, an expression of hostile rebellion. What they often resented but rarely admitted was that Elvis looked lower class, sounded black, and really could sing.

Beyond the frenetic rhythms of rock and roll, and even further beyond the pale of suburban culture, a subculture flourished known as the beat generation.

*The "beats"*

In run-down urban neighborhoods and college towns this motley collection of artists, intellectuals, musicians, and middle-class students dropped out of mainstream society. In dress and behavior the "beatniks" self-consciously rejected what they viewed as the excessive spiritual bankruptcy of America's middle-class culture. Cool urban "hipsters"—especially black jazz musicians like John Coltrane or Sonny Rollins—were their models. They read poetry, listened to jazz, explored Oriental philosophy, and experimented openly with drugs, mystical religions, and sex.

The "beats" viewed themselves as driven to the margins of society by the culture of abundance, materialism, and conformity. "I saw the best minds of my generation destroyed by madness, starving hysterical naked," wrote Allen Ginsberg in his 1955 poem *Howl*. They had become "angelheaded hipsters . . . who in poverty and tatters and hollow-eyed and high sat up smoking in the supernatural darkness of cold-water flats floating across the tops of cities contemplating jazz." Jack Kerouac tapped the frenzied energy beneath the beatniks' cool facade in *On the Road* (1957), a novel based on his travels across the country with his friend Neal Cassady. Kerouac finished the novel in one three-week binge, feeding a 120-foot roll of paper through his typewriter and spilling out tales of pot, jazz, crazy sex, and all-night raps undertaken in a search for "IT"— the ultimate transcendental moment when mind and experience mesh.

The dreams of Kerouac and Ginsberg came from a world starkly different from that of the manicured lawns of suburbia. The world of the suburbs seemed content, middle-of-the-road, prosperous. The beats seemed restless, nonconformist, beyond the fringe. Yet the 1960s would demonstrate that the suburban era contained enough cracks in the consensus to launch an era of rebellion and reform. Those upheavals would test the limits of a liberal, even radical vision of American society. The fringes and the middle-of-the-roaders were perhaps not so far apart as they seemed.

## SIGNIFICANT EVENTS

| | |
|---|---|
| 1947 | Levittown construction begins |
| 1950 | David Riesman's *The Lonely Crowd* published; Kefauver crime hearings |
| 1952 | Fertility rate in the United States reaches new high |
| 1954 | *Brown v. Board of Education*; St. Lawrence Seaway Act; CIA overthrows government in Guatemala; Geneva summit |
| 1955 | Montgomery bus boycott; Elvis Presley ignites rock and roll |
| 1956 | Interstate Highway Act; Eisenhower reelected; Suez crisis; "Southern Manifesto" |
| 1957 | *Sputnik* launched; Little Rock crisis; Eisenhower Doctrine |
| 1958 | Marines sent into Lebanon; Berlin crisis; National Defense Education Act |
| 1959 | Castro seizes power in Cuba; Khrushchev visits United States |
| 1960 | Soviet Union captures CIA pilot; Paris summit canceled |
| 1961 | Eisenhower's farewell address warns of military–industrial complex |

# CHAPTER THIRTY

# Liberalism and Beyond

Six-year-old Ruby knew the lessons. She was to look straight ahead—not to one side or the other—and especially not at *them*. She was to keep walking. Above all, she was not to look back once she'd passed, because that would encourage them. Ruby knew these things, but it was hard to keep her eyes straight. The first day of school, her parents came, along with federal marshals to keep order. And all around hundreds of angry white people were yelling things like, "You little nigger, we'll get you and kill you." Then she was within the building's quiet halls and alone with her teacher. She was the only person in class: none of the white students had come. As the days went by during that autumn of 1960, the marshals stopped walking with her but the hecklers still waited. And once in a while Ruby couldn't help looking back, trying to see if she recognized the face of one woman in particular.

Ruby's parents were not social activists. They signed their daughter up for the white school in this New Orleans neighborhood because "we thought it was for all the colored to do, and we never thought Ruby would be alone." Her father's white employer fired him; letters and phone calls threatened the family. Through it all Ruby seemed to take things in stride, though her parents worried that she was not eating well. Often she left her school lunch untouched or refused anything other than packaged food such as potato chips. It was only after a time that the problem was traced to the hecklers. "They tells me I'm going to die, and that it'll be soon. And that one lady tells me every morning I'm getting poisoned soon, when she can fix it." Ruby was convinced that the woman owned the variety store nearby and would carry out her threat by poisoning the family's food.

*Desegregation in New Orleans, 1960*

Over the course of a year, white students gradually returned to class and life settled into a new routine. By the time Ruby was 10, she had developed a remarkably clear perception of herself. "Maybe because of all the trouble going to school in the beginning I learned more about my people. Maybe I would have anyway; because when you get older you see yourself and the white kids; and you find out the difference. You try to forget it, and say there is none; and if there is you won't say what it be. Then you say it's my own people, and so I can be proud of them instead of ashamed."

The new ways were not easy for white southerners either—even those who saw the need for change. One woman, a teacher from Atlanta, recalled the summer 10 years earlier, when she went to New York City to take courses in education. There were black students in her dormitory, an integrated situation she was not used to. One day as she stepped from her shower, so did a black student from the nearby stall. "When I saw her I didn't know what to do," the woman recalled. "I felt sick all over, and frightened. What I remember—I'll never forget it—is that horrible feeling of being caught in a terrible trap, and not knowing what to do about it. . . . My sense of propriety was with me, though—miraculously—and I didn't want to hurt the woman. It wasn't *her* that was upsetting me. I knew that, even in that moment of sickness and panic." So she ducked back into the shower until the other woman left.

It took most of the summer before she felt comfortable eating with black students. Back in Atlanta, she told no one about her experiences. "At that time people would have thought one of two things: I was crazy (for being so upset and ashamed) or a fool who in a summer had become a dangerous 'race mixer.'" She continued to love the South and to defend its traditions of dignity, neighborliness, and honor, but she saw the need for change. And so in 1961 she volunteered to teach one of the first integrated high school classes in Atlanta. "I've never felt so useful," she concluded after two years; ". . .not just to the children but to our whole society. American as well as Southern. Those children, all of them, have given me more than I've given them."

## A LIBERAL AGENDA FOR REFORM

For Americans in all walks of life, the changes that swept the United States in the 1960s were wrenching. From the schoolrooms and lunch counters of the South to the college campuses of the North, from eastern slums to western migrant labor camps, American society was in ferment.

On the face of it, such agitation seemed to be a dramatic reversal of the placid fifties. Turbulence and change had overturned stability and consensus. Yet the events of the 1960s grew naturally out of the social conditions that preceded them.

### The Social Structures of Change

The prosperity of the 1950s encouraged a confidence that problems like poverty and discrimination might finally be solved. At the same time, that prosperity did not reach all areas of the nation equally. While suburbs flourished, urban areas decayed. While more white Americans went to college, more African Americans found themselves out of work on southern farms or desperate for jobs in northern ghettos. As Mexican American migrant workers picked grapes in California or followed the harvest north from Texas, they saw their employers resist every attempt to unionize and improve their wages. Yet the general prosperity remained for all to see. And the success of the NAACP in wringing a policy of integration from the Supreme Court gave minorities new hopes that they too could win the rights due them.

The expansive years of the 1950s, in other words, proved to be a seedbed for reform movements of the 1960s. Time and again, the dissenters challenged the political system to deal with what the 1950s had done—and what had been left undone. As one friend of Martin Luther King predicted in 1958, "If the young people are aroused from their lethargy through this fight, it will affect broad circles throughout the country. . . ."

Inevitably, these forces for change brought hope and energy to the liberal tradition. Like the New Dealers and the Progressives before them, liberals of

*The liberal tradition*

the 1960s did not wish to overturn capitalism. They looked primarily to tame its excesses, taking a pragmatic approach to reforming American society. Like Franklin Roosevelt, they believed that the government should play an active role in managing the economy in order to soften the boom-and-bust swings of capitalism. Like Progressives from the turn of the century, liberals looked to improve society by applying the intelligence of "experts."

The confidence of liberals that poverty could be eliminated and the good society achieved sometimes verged on arrogance—as the end of the decade would prove. Yet during the early sixties, the optimism of liberal politicians and thinkers was both heady and energizing.

## The Election of 1960

The first president to ride these currents of reform was John Fitzgerald Kennedy, at 43 the youngest ever elected to the office. On the face of it, Kennedy's 1960 campaign promised to bring change to Washington. The nation needed to find "new frontiers," he proclaimed. Kennedy's rhetoric was noble, but the direction in which he would take the nation was far from clear.

Aside from political issues, there was a social one to be met. Jack Kennedy was a Roman Catholic out of Irish Boston, and no Catholic had ever been

*Kennedy's Catholicism*

elected president. Conservative Protestants, many concentrated in the heavily Democratic South, were convinced that a Catholic president would never be "free to exercise his own judgment" if the pope ordered otherwise. Kennedy confronted the issue head-on, addressing an association of hostile ministers in Houston. "I believe in an America where the separation of church and state is absolute," he said, "—where no Catholic prelate would tell the President (should he be Catholic) how to act, and no Protestant minister would tell his parishioners how to vote." House Speaker

Sam Rayburn, an old Texas pol, was astonished by Kennedy's bravura performance. "My God! . . . He's eating them blood raw."

Kennedy's opponent, Vice President Richard Nixon, ran on his political experience and staunch anti-Communism. His campaign faltered in October as unemployment rose. Nixon was also hurt by a series of televised debates with Kennedy—the first broadcast nationally. Despite his debating skill, Nixon was overtired, and his "Lazy Shave" makeup failed to hide his five-o'clock shadow. Election Day saw the largest turnout in 50 years: 64 percent of all voters. Out of 68.3 million ballots cast, Kennedy won by a margin of just 118,000. The whisker-thin victory was made possible by strong Catholic support in key states. "Hyphenated" Americans—Hispanic, Jewish, Irish, Italian, Polish, and German—voted Democratic in record numbers, while much of the black vote that had gone to Eisenhower in 1956 returned to the Democratic fold.

### The Hard-Nosed Idealists of Camelot

Many observers compared the Kennedy White House to Camelot, King Arthur's magical court. A popular musical of 1960 pictured Camelot as a land where skies were fair, men brave, women pretty, and the days full of challenge. With similar vigor, Kennedy surrounded himself with bright, energetic liberal advisers. Touch football games on the White House lawn displayed a rough-and-tumble playfulness, akin to Arthur's jousting tournaments of old.

In truth, Kennedy was not a liberal by temperament. Handsome and intelligent, he possessed an ironic, self-deprecating humor. Yet in Congress, he had led an undistinguished career, supported Senator Joe McCarthy, and earned a reputation as a playboy. Once Kennedy set his sights on the White House, however, he revealed an astonishing capacity for political maneuver and organization. To woo the liberals, he surrounded himself with a distinguished group of intellectuals and academics.

Robert Strange McNamara typified the pragmatic, liberal bent of the new Kennedy team. Steely and brilliant, McNamara was one of the postwar breed of young executives known as the "whiz kids." As a Harvard Business School professor and later as president of Ford Motors, he specialized in using new quantitative tools to streamline business. As the new secretary of defense, McNamara intended to find more flexible and efficient ways of conducting the cold war.

*McNamara and the whiz kids*

Kennedy liked men like this—witty, bright, intellectual—because they seemed comfortable with power and were not afraid to use it. If Khrushchev spoke of waging guerrilla "wars of liberation," Americans could play that game too. The president's leisure reading reflected a similar adventurous taste: the popular James Bond spy novels. Agent 007, with his license to kill, was sophisticated, a cool womanizer (as Kennedy himself continued to be), and ready to use the latest technology to deal with Communist villains. Ironically, Bond demon-

The urbane John F. Kennedy was associated with both King Arthur and the spy James Bond (played by Sean Connery, right). Kennedy and his advisers prided themselves on their pragmatic, hard-nosed idealism. But while Bond used advanced technology and covert operations to save the world, in real life such approaches had their downside, as the growing civil war in Vietnam would demonstrate.

strated that there could be plenty of glamour in being "hard-nosed" and pragmatic. That illicit pleasure was the underside, perhaps, of Camelot's high ideals.

## NEW FRONTIERS

Abroad, Kennedy was convinced that the cold war had shifted from the traditional battlefronts of Europe to the developing nations in Asia, Africa, and Latin America. That meant the United States needed a more flexible range of military and economic options.

The Alliance for Progress, announced in the spring of 1961, indicated the Kennedy approach. He promised to provide $20 billion in foreign aid over 10

*Alliance for Progress and the Peace Corps*

years—about four times the aid given to Latin America under Eisenhower. In return, Latin American nations would agree to reform unfair tax policies and begin agricultural land reforms. If successful, the Alliance would discourage future Castro-style revolutions. With similar fanfare, the administration set up the Peace Corps. This program sent idealistic young men and women to Third World nations to provide technical, educational, and public health services. Under the Alliance, most Peace Corps volunteers were assigned to Latin America.

To back the new economic policies with military muscle, the Pentagon directed jungle warfare schools, both in North Carolina and in the Canal Zone. The programs were designed to train Latin American police and paramilitary groups, as well as American special forces like the Green Berets. If the Soviets or their allies entered wars of liberation, United States commandos would be ready to fight back.

Kennedy believed, too, that the Soviets had made space the final frontier of the cold war. Only a few months after the president's inauguration, a Russian

*The cold war's race to the moon*

cosmonaut orbited the world for the first time. In response, Kennedy challenged Congress to authorize a manned space mission to the moon that would land by the end of the decade. In February 1962 John Glenn circled the earth three times in a "fireball of a ride." Gradually, the American space program gained on the Russians.

### Cold War Frustrations

In more down-to-earth ways, high ideals did not translate easily into practical results. Latin American governments eagerly accepted aid, but they were less willing to carry out reforms. During the first five years of the Alliance for Progress, nine Latin American governments were overthrown by military coups. The Peace Corps, for its part, helped thousands of Third World farmers on a people-to-people basis. But individual Peace Corps workers could do little to change corrupt policies on a national level.

Nor did Kennedy succeed in countering "wars of liberation." The Eisenhower administration had authorized the CIA to overthrow Fidel Castro's

*Bay of Pigs invasion*

Communist regime in Cuba, 90 miles south of Florida. Eager to establish his own cold war credentials, Kennedy approved an attack by a 1400-member army of Cuban exiles in April 1961. The invasion turned into a mismanaged disaster. The poorly equipped rebel forces landed at the swampy Bay of Pigs, and no discontented rebels flocked to their support. Within two days Castro's army had rounded them up. Taking responsibility for the fiasco, Kennedy suffered a bitter humiliation.

Kennedy's advisers took a similar covert approach in South Vietnam. There, the American-backed Prime Minister, Ngo Dinh Diem (see page 822), grew

*Vietnam*

more unpopular by the month. South Vietnamese Communists, known as the Vietcong, waged a guerrilla war against Diem with support from North Vietnam. Buddhists and other groups backed the rebellion, since Diem, a Catholic, ruthlessly persecuted them. In May 1961, a month after the Bay of Pigs invasion, Kennedy secretly ordered 500 Green Berets and military advisers to Vietnam to prop up Diem. By 1963 the number of "military advisers" had risen to more than 16,000.

As the situation degenerated, Diem's corruption and police-state tactics made it unlikely he could defeat the Vietcong. Thus the Kennedy administration tacitly encouraged the military to stage a coup. The plotters captured Diem and, to Washington's surprise, shot him in November 1963. Despite Kennedy's policy of pragmatic idealism, the United States found itself mired in a Vietnamese civil war, which it had no clear strategy for winning.

## Confronting Khrushchev

Vietnam and Cuba were just two areas in the Third World where the Kennedy administration sought to battle Communist forces. But the conflict between the United States and the Soviet Union soon overshadowed developments in Asia, Africa, and Latin America.

In June 1961, a summit held in Vienna gave the president his first chance to take the measure of Nikita Khrushchev. For two long days, Khrushchev was *The Berlin Wall* brash and belligerent. East and West Germany must be reunited, he demanded. The problem of Berlin, where dissatisfied East Germans were fleeing to the city's free western zone, must be settled within six months. Kennedy left Vienna worried that the Soviet leader perceived him as weak and inexperienced. By August events in Berlin confirmed his fears. The Soviets threw up a heavily guarded wall sealing off the enclave of West Berlin from the rest of the eastern zone. Despite American protests, the wall stayed up.

Tensions with the Soviet Union also led the administration to rethink the American approach to nuclear warfare. Under the Dulles doctrine of massive *Flexible response doctrine* retaliation, almost any incident threatened to trigger a full launch of nuclear missiles. Kennedy and McNamara sought to establish a "flexible response doctrine" that would limit the level of a first nuclear strike and thus leave room for negotiation.

But what if the Soviets were tempted to launch a first-strike attack to knock out American missiles? McNamara's flexible response policy required that enough American missiles survive in order to retaliate. So McNamara began a program to bury missile sites underground and develop submarine-launched missiles. The new flexible response policies resulted in a 15 percent increase in the 1961 military budget, compared with only 2 percent increases during the last two years of Eisenhower's term.

## The Missiles of October

The peril of nuclear confrontation became dramatically clear in the Cuban missile crisis of October 1962. President Kennedy had warned repeatedly that the United States would treat any attempt to place offensive weapons in Cuba as an unacceptable threat. For his part, Khrushchev promised that the Soviets had no such intention. Thus Kennedy was outraged when a CIA flight over Cuba confirmed that offensive missile sites were being constructed. "He can't do that to me," the president snapped.

For a week, top security advisers met secretly to plan a response. Military advisers urged air strikes against the missile sites, but Kennedy worried that the strikes might trigger nuclear war. Indeed, recent evidence from Soviet archives indicates that, unknown to American officials, Soviet commanders in Cuba

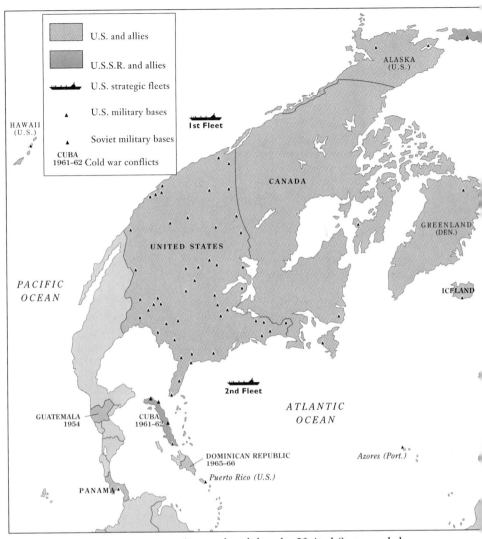

THE WORLD OF THE SUPERPOWERS   Across the globe, the United States and the Soviet Union stood astride a network of military bases and regional alliances that marked the extent of their powers. Around these strategic perimeters, centers of conflict continued to emerge.

possessed the authority to launch short-range nuclear missiles if American forces attacked. In the end Kennedy chose the more restrained option of imposing a naval quarantine to intercept "all offensive military equipment under shipment to Cuba." On October 22, Americans were stunned when the president announced news of the crisis and his response. Tensions mounted as Soviet vessels approached the line of American ships, then stopped or reversed course.

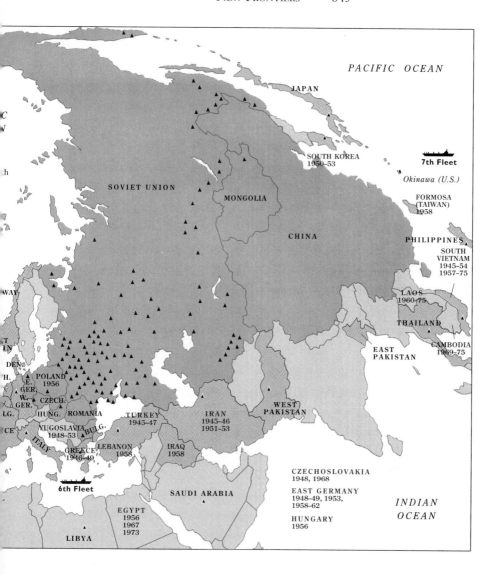

PACIFIC OCEAN

JAPAN

SOUTH KOREA
1950-53

7th Fleet

Okinawa (U.S.)

SOVIET UNION

MONGOLIA

FORMOSA
(TAIWAN)
1958

CHINA

PHILIPPINES

SOUTH
VIETNAM
1945-54
1957-75

LAOS
1960-75

THAILAND

EAST
PAKISTAN

CAMBODIA
1969-75

WAY

DEN.

H.

POLAND
1956
E.
GER.
W.
GER.
CZECH.

LG.

HUNG. ROMANIA

TURKEY
1945-47

IRAN
1945-46
1951-53

WEST
PAKISTAN

CE

ITALY

YUGOSLAVIA
1948-53
BULG.

GREECE
1946-49
LEBANON
1958

IRAQ
1958

6th Fleet

SAUDI ARABIA

CZECHOSLOVAKIA
1948, 1968

EAST GERMANY
1948-49, 1953,
1958-62

HUNGARY
1956

INDIAN
OCEAN

EGYPT
1956
1967
1973

LIBYA

Meanwhile, Kennedy scrambled to resolve the crisis through diplomatic channels. On October 26 he received a rambling message from Khrushchev agreeing to remove the missiles in return for an American promise not to invade Cuba. The next day came a more troubling message, insisting the United States must also dismantle its missile bases in Turkey, which bordered on the Soviet Union. Unwilling to strike that deal publicly, Kennedy decided to ignore the second letter and accept the offer in the first. When the Soviets agreed, the face-off ended on terms that saved either side from overt humiliation.

The nuclear showdown prompted Kennedy and his advisers to seek ways to control the nuclear arms race. "We all inhabit this small planet," he warned in

*Nuclear test
ban treaty* June 1963. "We all breathe the same air. We all cherish our children's future. And we are all mortal." The administration negotiated a nuclear test ban with the Soviets, outlawing all aboveground nuclear tests. At the same time Kennedy's prestige soared for "standing up" to the Soviets.

## The (Somewhat) New Frontier at Home

It proved more difficult to take bold initiatives at home than abroad. Kennedy and his advisors had no broad vision for reform. They preferred to tackle problems one by one. In making domestic policy Kennedy found himself hemmed in by a Democratic Congress dominated by conservatives. As a result, the president's legislative achievements were modest. He passed a bill providing some financial aid to depressed industrial and rural areas. But on key issues, including aid to education and medical health insurance, Kennedy made no headway.

He wavered, too, on how to manage the economy. The president's liberal advisers favored increased government spending to reduce unemployment, even

*Relations with
business and
big steel* if that meant a budget deficit. Even so, Kennedy believed that prosperity for big business spelled growth for the whole nation. Thus the president asked Congress to ease antitrust restrictions and grant investment credits and tax breaks—actions that pleased corporate interests. But he was convinced that the government needed to limit the power of both large corporations and unions to set prices and wages. The alternative was an inflationary spiral, in which wage increases would spark price increases, followed by even higher wage demands.

To prevent that, the Council of Economic Advisors proposed that wage increases be given to workers only if their increased productivity kept prices stable. In April 1962 the United Steel Workers, like most other major unions, agreed to a contract that held down wage increases. The large steel corporations, however, broke their part of the informal bargain by sharply raising steel prices. Angered, Kennedy called for investigations into price fixing and shifted Pentagon purchases to smaller steel companies that had not raised prices. The intense pressure caused the big companies to drop the price increases but soured relations between the president and the business community.

## The Reforms of the Warren Court

With Kennedy's promise of new frontiers blocked by a conservative Congress, the Supreme Court broke the logjam. Chief Justice Earl Warren turned what was traditionally the least activist branch of government into a center of liberal reform. Until Warren's retirement in 1969, the Court continued to hand down landmark decisions in broad areas of civil liberties and civil rights.

In 1960 the rights of citizens accused of a crime but not yet convicted were often unclear. Those too poor to afford lawyers could be forced to go to trial

I was sentenced to the state Penitentiary
by the Circuit Court of Bay County, state of
Florida. The present proceeding was commenced
on a petition for a writ of Habeus Corpus
to the Supreme Court of the state of
Florida to vacate the sentence, on the
grounds that I was made to stand
Trial without the aid of counsel, and, at all
times of my incarseretion. The said Court
refused to appoint counsel and therefore
deprived me of Due process of law. and violate
my rights in the Bill of Rights and the
constitution of the United States.

_Clarence Earl Gideon_

5th day of Jan 1962 Petitioner.

_Laurence C. Dugga_

NOTary Public

Notary Public
My Comm. 10, 1962
Bonded by American Surety Co. of N.Y.

Gideon's Letter to the Supreme Court
John F. Davis, Clerk, Supreme Court of the United States

Clarence Earl Gideon, a prisoner in a Florida jail, used this handwritten letter to bring his successful appeal to the Supreme Court. In the *Gideon* case the court ruled that even poor defendants have the right to legal counsel.

*Protection of due process*

without representation. Often they were not informed of their constitutional rights when arrested. In a series of decisions, the Court ruled that the Fourteenth Amendment provided broad guarantees of due process under the law. *Gideon v. Wainwright* (1963), an appeal launched by a Florida prisoner, made it clear that all citizens were entitled to legal counsel in any case involving a possible jail sentence. In *Escobedo v. Illinois* (1964) and *Miranda v. Arizona* (1966), the Court declared that individuals detained for a crime must be informed of the charges against them, of their right to remain silent, and of their right to have an attorney present during questioning. Though these decisions applied to all citizens, they were primarily intended to benefit the poor, who were most likely to be in trouble with the law and least likely to understand their rights.

Other decisions promoted a more liberal social climate. In *Griswold v. Connecticut* (1964) the Warren Court overturned a nineteenth-century law banning the sale of contraceptives or medical advice about their use.

*Liberal social decisions*

The Court also demonstrated its distaste for censorship by greatly narrowing the legal definition of obscenity. A book had to be "utterly without redeeming social value" to permit censorship. And the Court strengthened the constitutional separation of church and state by ruling in *Engle v. Vitale* that prayers could not be read in public schools.

Banning official school prayer may have been one of the Court's most controversial decisions; *Baker v. Carr* was one of its most far-reaching. Most states had not redrawn their legislative districts to reflect the growth of urban and suburban population since the nineteenth century. The less populated (and most often conservative) rural areas elected the most legislators. In *Baker v. Carr* the Court ruled that the states must redraw legislative lines to follow as closely as possible the principle of "one person, one vote."

## THE CIVIL RIGHTS CRUSADE

In Greensboro, North Carolina, in 1960, four black students attending a local college read a pamphlet describing the 1955 bus boycott in Montgomery, Alabama. They decided it was time to make their own protest against segregation. Proceeding to the "whites only" lunch counter at a local store, they sat politely waiting for service. "The waitress looked at me as if I were from outer space," recalled one of the protesters. Rather than serve them, the manager closed the counter. Word of the action spread, and within two weeks, the courage of the Greensboro students had inspired 15 sit-ins across the South. By year's end, 50,000 people had demonstrated; 3000 had gone to jail.

Nothing did more to propel the liberalism of the 1960s—and, in the end, to push beyond it—than the campaign for civil rights. By the late 1950s a new generation of southern African Americans, many having moved from farms to cities, increasingly rejected their second-class citizenship. But how could they overturn the legal framework of segregation in the South? How could they overturn the racism evident in everyday life across the nation?

### Riding to Freedom

During the 1950s the push for desegregation had centered on court actions launched by the NAACP and the Urban League. Martin Luther King's Southern Christian Leadership Conference (SCLC) hinted at newer, more direct challenges to the social order. Since organizing the Montgomery boycott, King had continued to advocate nonviolent protest: "To resist without bitterness; to be cursed and not reply; to be beaten and not hit back." A second key organization, the Congress of Racial Equality (CORE), was even more willing to force confrontations with the segregationist system. Another group, the Student Non-Violent Coordinating Committee (SNCC, pronounced "Snick"), grew out of the Greensboro sit-in. SNCC represented the militant, younger generation of black activists, impatient with the slow pace of reform.

*The SCLC, CORE, and SNCC*

In May 1961 CORE director James Farmer led a group of black and white "freedom riders" on a bus trip from Washington to New Orleans. They intended to focus national attention on the inequality of segregated facilities. Violent southern mobs gave the freedom riders the kind of attention they feared. In South Carolina, thugs beat divinity student John Lewis as he tried to enter an all-white waiting room. Mobs in Anniston and Birmingham, Alabama, assaulted the freedom riders as police ignored the violence. One of the buses was burned.

Sensitive to the power of conservative southern Democrats, President Kennedy tried to avoid sending federal forces to protect the demonstrators. But his hopes were dashed. From a phone booth outside the bus terminal, John Doar, a Justice Department official in Montgomery, relayed the horror to Attorney General Robert Kennedy:

> Now the passengers are coming off. They're standing on a corner of the platform. Oh, there are fists, punching! A bunch of men led by a guy with a bleeding face are beating them. There are no cops. It's terrible! It's terrible! There's not a cop in sight. People are yelling, "There those niggers are! Get 'em, get 'em!" It's awful.

Appalled, Robert Kennedy ordered in 400 federal marshals, who barely managed to hold off the crowd. Martin Luther King, addressing a meeting in town, phoned the attorney general to say that their church had been surrounded by a mob of several thousand—jeering, throwing rocks, and carrying firebombs. Kennedy later recalled, "I said that we were doing the best that we could and that he'd be as dead as Kelsey's nuts if it hadn't been for the marshals and the efforts that we made."

Both Kennedys understood that civil rights was the most divisive issue the administration faced. The president needed the votes of African Americans and liberals to win reelection. Yet an active federal role threatened to drive white southerners from the Democratic party. Thus Kennedy hedged on his promise to introduce civil rights legislation. He assured black leaders that executive orders would eliminate discrimination in the government and in businesses filling government contracts. He appointed several blacks to high positions and five, including Thurgood Marshall, to the federal courts. But the freedom riders, by their bold actions, forced the Kennedys to do more.

### Civil Rights at High Tide

By the fall of 1961 Robert Kennedy had persuaded SNCC to shift its energies to voter registration, which he assumed would stir less violence. Voting booths, Kennedy noted, were not like schools, where people would protest, "We don't want our little blond daughter going to school with a Negro."

As SNCC and CORE workers arrived in southern towns in the spring of 1962, they discovered that voting rights was not a peaceful issue. Over two years in Mississippi they registered only 4000 out of 394,000 black adults. Angry

# E Y E W I T N E S S    T O    H I S T O R Y

## *A Mississippi College Student Attends the NAACP Convention*

I n mid September [1962] I was back on campus. But didn't very much happen until February when the NAACP held its annual convention in Jackson [Mississippi]. They were having a whole lot of interesting speakers: Jackie Robinson, Floyd Patterson, Curt Flood, Margaretta Belafonte, and many others. I wouldn't have missed it for anything. I was so excited that I sent one of the leaflets home to Mama and asked her to come.

Three days later I got a letter from Mama with dried-up tears on it, forbidding me to go to the convention. It went on for more than six pages. She said if I didn't stop that shit she would come to Tougaloo and kill me herself. She told me about the time I last visited her, on Thanksgiving, and she had picked me up at the bus station. She said she picked me up because she was scared some white in my hometown would try to do something to me. She said the sheriff had been by, telling her I was messing around with that NAACP group. She said he told her if I didn't stop it, I could not come back there any more. He said that they didn't need any of those NAACP people messing around in Centreville. She ended the letter by saying that she had burned the leaflet I sent her. "Please don't send any more of that stuff here. I don't want nothing to happen to us here," she said. "If you keep that up, you will never be able to come home again."

I was so damn mad after her letter, I felt like taking the NAACP convention to Centreville. I think I would have, if it had been in my power to do so. The remainder of the week I thought of nothing except going to the convention. I didn't know exactly what to do about it. I didn't want Mama or any one at home to get hurt because of me.

I had felt something was wrong when I was home. During the four days I was there, Mama tried to do everything she could to keep me in the house.

racists countered with legal harassment, jailings, beatings, bombings, and murders. Terrorized workers who called for protection found it woefully lacking. FBI agents often stood by taking notes while SNCC volunteers were assaulted. Undaunted, the workers fanned out across the countryside to speak with farmers and sharecroppers who had never dared ask for the vote.

When I said I was going to see some of my old classmates, she pretended she was sick and said I would have to cook. I knew she was acting strangely, but I hadn't known why. I thought Mama just wanted me to spend most of my time with her, since this was only the second time I had been home since I entered college as a freshman.

Things kept running through my mind after that letter from Mama. My mind was so active, I couldn't sleep at night. I remembered the one time I did leave the house to go to the post office. I had walked past a bunch of white men on the street on my way through town and one said "Is that the gal goin' to Tougaloo?" He acted kind of mad or something, and I didn't know what was going on. I got a creepy feeling, so I hurried home. When I told Mama about it, she just said, "A lotta people don't like that school." I knew what she meant. Just before I went to Tougaloo, they had housed the Freedom Riders there. The school was being criticized by whites throughout the state.

The night before the convention started, I made up my mind to go, no matter what Mama said. I just wouldn't tell Mama or anyone from home. Then it occurred to me—how did the sheriff or anyone at home know I was working with the NAACP chapter on campus? Somehow they had found out. Now I knew I could never go to Centreville safely again. I kept telling myself that I didn't really care too much about going home, that it was more important to me to go to the convention.

I was there from the very beginning. Jackie Robinson was asked to serve as moderator. This was the first time I had seen him in person. I remembered how when Jackie became the first Negro to play Major League baseball, my uncles and most of the Negro boys in my hometown started organizing baseball leagues. It did something for them to see a Negro out there playing with all those white players. Jackie was a good moderator, I thought. He kept smiling and joking. People felt relaxed and proud. They appreciated knowing and meeting people of their own race who had done something worth talking about.

Anne Moody, *Coming of Age in Mississippi* (New York: Dell, 1968), pp. 261–62. Copyright © 1968 by Anne Moody. Used by permission of Doubleday, a division of Bantam Doubleday Publishing Group.

*Meredith enters University of Mississippi*

Confrontation increased when a federal court ordered the segregated University of Mississippi to admit James Meredith, a black applicant. When Governor Ross Barnett personally blocked Meredith's registration in September 1962, Kennedy ordered several hundred federal marshals to escort Meredith into a university dormitory.

The marshals were met by a mob on campus, which shot out street lights and threw rocks and bottles. The president finally sent in federal troops, but not before 2 people were killed and 375 wounded.

In Mississippi, President Kennedy had begun to lose control of the civil rights issue. The House of Representatives, influenced by television coverage of the violence, introduced a number of civil rights measures. And in 1963 Martin Luther King led a group to Birmingham, Alabama, to force a showdown against segregation. From a prison cell there, he produced one of the most eloquent documents of the civil rights movement, his "Letter from Birmingham Jail." Addressed to local ministers who had called for an end to confrontation, King defended the use of civil disobedience. The choice, he warned, was not between obeying the law and nonviolently breaking it to bring about change. It was between his way and streets "flowing with blood," as frustrated black citizens turned toward more militant ideologies.

*"Letter from Birmingham Jail"*

On August 28, 1963, more than 250,000 demonstrators joined the great civil rights march on Washington. The day belonged to the Reverend Martin Luther King Jr., who movingly called on black and white Americans to join together in a color-blind society.

Once freed, King led new demonstrations. Television cameras were on hand that May as Birmingham police chief "Bull" Connor, a man with a short fuse, unleashed attack dogs, club-wielding police, and fire hoses powerful enough to peel the bark off trees. When segregationist bombs went off in African American neighborhoods, black mobs retaliated with their own riot, burning a number of shops and businesses owned by white citizens. In the following 10 weeks, more than 750 riots erupted in 186 cities and towns, both North and South. King's warning of streets "flowing with blood" no longer seemed far-fetched.

Kennedy sensed that he could no longer compromise on civil rights. "If [an American with dark skin] cannot enjoy the full and free life all of us want," he asked Americans, "then who among us would be content to have the color of his skin changed and stand in his place? Who among us would then be content with counsels of patience and delay?" The president followed his words with support for a strong civil rights bill to end segregation and protect black voters. When King announced a massive march on Washington for August 1963, Kennedy objected that it would undermine support for his bill. "I have never engaged in any direct action movement which did not seem ill-timed," King replied. Faced with the inevitable, Kennedy convinced the organizers to use the event to promote the administration's bill, much to the disgust of militant CORE and SNCC factions.

On August 28 some 250,000 people gathered at the Lincoln Memorial to march and sing in support of civil rights and racial harmony. Appropriately, *The march on Washington* the day belonged to King. In the powerful tones of a southern preacher, he reminded the crowd that the Declaration of Independence was a promise that applied to all people, black and white. "I have a dream," he told them, that one day "all of God's children, black men and white men, Jews and Gentiles, Protestants and Catholics, will be able to join hands and sing in the words of the old Negro spiritual, 'Free at last! Free at last! Thank God Almighty, we are free at last!'"

## The Fire Next Time

While liberals applauded Kennedy's civil rights stand and appreciative African Americans rejoined the Democratic party, many southern whites and northern ethnics deserted. The president scheduled a trip to Texas to recoup some southern support. On November 22, 1963, the people of Dallas lined *Assassination* the streets for his motorcade. Suddenly, a sniper's rifle fired several times. Kennedy slumped into his wife's arms, fatally wounded. His assassin, Lee Harvey Oswald, was caught several hours later. Oswald seemed a mysterious figure. Emotionally unstable, he had spent several years in the Soviet Union. But his actions were never fully explained, because only two days after his arrest—in full view of television cameras—he was gunned down by a disgruntled nightclub operator named Jack Ruby.

In the face of such violence, many Americans came to doubt that gradual reform or nonviolence could hold the nation together. Many younger black leaders observed that civil rights received the greatest national coverage when white, not black, demonstrators were killed. They wondered too how Lyndon Johnson, a consummate southern politician, would approach the civil rights programs.

The new president, however, saw the need for action. Just as the Catholic issue had tested Kennedy's ability to lead, Johnson knew that without strong

*Civil Rights Act of 1964*

leadership on civil rights, "I'd be dead before I could ever begin." On his first day in office, he promised one civil rights leader after another that he would pass Kennedy's bill. Despite a southern filibuster in the Senate, the Civil Rights Act of 1964 became law. Embodying the provisions of the Kennedy bill, it barred discrimination in public accommodations like lunch counters, bus stations, and hotels. It also prohibited employers from discriminating by race, color, religion, sex, or national origin.

The Civil Rights Act, however, did not strike down literacy tests and other laws used to prevent black citizens from voting. With King and other black

*Voting Rights Act of 1965*

leaders keeping up the pressure, President Johnson persuaded Congress to pass a strong Voting Rights Act in August 1965. The act outlawed literacy tests and permitted federal officials to monitor elections in many southern districts. With some justice Johnson called the act "one of the most monumental laws in the entire history of American freedom." Within a five-year period black registration in the South jumped from 35 to 65 percent.

## Black Power

But even the new civil rights laws did not strike at the de facto segregation found outside the South. This was segregation not spelled out in laws but practiced through unwritten custom. In large areas of America, African Americans were locked out of suburbs, kept out of decent schools, barred from clubs, and denied all but the most menial jobs. Nor did the Voting Rights Act deal with the sources of urban black poverty. The median income for urban black residents was about half of what white residents earned.

In such an atmosphere, militants sharply questioned the liberal goal of integration. Since the 1940s the Black Muslim religious sect, dedicated to complete separation from white society, had attracted as many as 100,000 members, mostly young men. During the early 1960s the sect drew wider attention through the

*Malcolm X*

efforts of Malcolm X. Provocative, shrewd, and charismatic, Malcolm had learned the language of the downtrodden from his own experience as a former hustler, gambler, and prison inmate. His militancy alarmed whites, though by 1965 he was in fact becoming more moderate. He accepted integration, but emphasized black community action. After breaking with the Black Muslims, Malcolm was gunned down by rivals.

But by 1965, even CORE and SNCC had begun to give up working with white liberals for nonviolent change. If black Americans were to liberate themselves fully, militants argued, they could not merely accept rights "given" to them by whites: they had to claim them. Some members began carrying guns to defend themselves. In 1966 Stokely Carmichael of SNCC gave the militants a slogan—"Black Power"—and the defiant symbol of a gloved fist raised in the air.

In its moderate form, the black power movement encouraged African Americans to recover their cultural roots, their African heritage, and a new sense of identity. African clothes and natural hairstyles became popular. On college campuses black students pressed universities to hire black faculty, create black studies programs, and provide segregated social and residential space.

For black militants, on the other hand, violence became a revolutionary tool. The Black Panther party of Oakland, California, called on the black com-

*Black Panthers* munity to arm. Panther leader Huey Newton and his followers openly brandished shotguns and rifles as they patrolled the streets protecting blacks from police harassment. After a gun battle with police left a wounded Newton in jail, Eldridge Cleaver assumed leadership of the party. Cleaver later attracted the attention of whites with his searing autobiography, *Soul on Ice*. But even at the height of their power, the Panthers never counted more than 2000 members nationwide.

## Violence in the Streets

No ideology shaped the reservoir of frustration and despair that existed in the ghettos. Often, a seemingly minor incident like an arrest or an argument on the streets would trigger an eruption of violence. A mob would gather, and police cars and white-owned stores would be firebombed or looted. Riots broke out in Harlem and Rochester, New York, in 1964; the Watts area of Los Angeles in 1965; Chicago in 1966; and Newark and Detroit in 1967. It took nearly 5000 troops to end the bloodiest rioting in Detroit, where 40 died, 2000 were injured, and 5000 were left homeless.

To most white Americans the violence was unfathomable and inexcusable. Martin Luther King, still pursuing the tactics of nonviolence, was saddened by the destruction but came to understand the anger behind it. Touring Watts only days after the riots, he was approached by a band of young blacks. "We won," they told him proudly. "How can you say you won," King countered, "when thirty-four Negroes are dead, your community is destroyed, and whites are using the riot as an excuse for inaction?" The youngsters were unmoved. "We won because we made them pay attention to us."

For Lyndon Johnson, ghetto violence and black militance mocked his efforts to achieve racial progress. The Civil Rights and Voting Rights acts were essential parts of the "Great Society" he hoped to build. In that effort he had achieved a legislative record virtually unequaled by any other president in the

nation's history. What Kennedy had promised, Johnson delivered. But the anger exploding in the nation's cities exposed serious flaws in the theory and practice of liberal reform.

## LYNDON JOHNSON AND THE GREAT SOCIETY

Like the state he hailed from, Lyndon Baines Johnson was in all things bigger than life. His gifts were greater, his flaws more glaring. Insecurity was his Achilles heel and the engine that drove him. If Kennedy had been good as president, Johnson would be "the greatest of them all, the whole bunch of them." His folksy style often verged on the offensive: after a 1965 operation, he shocked a national audience by lifting his shirt to expose a jagged scar and corpulent belly. The president was sometimes driven to ask why so few people genuinely liked him; once a courageous diplomat actually answered: "Because, Mr. President, you are not a very likable man."

Johnson was born in the hill country outside Austin, Texas, where the dry, rough terrain only grudgingly yielded up a living. He arrived in Washington in 1932 as an ardent New Dealer who loved the political game. As majority leader of the Senate after 1954, Johnson was regarded as a moderate conservative who knew what strings to pull to get the job done. On an important bill, he latched onto the undecided votes until they succumbed to the famous "Johnson treat-

*The Johnson treatment* — ment," a combination of arguments, threats, rewards, and patriotic appeals. (Once, before meeting with Johnson, President Eisenhower pleaded with his attorney general, William Rogers, to run interference: "Bill, if Lyndon tries to get around my desk, block him off. I can't stand it when he grabs me by the lapel.")

Despite his compulsion to control every person and situation, Johnson was best at hammering out compromises among competing interest groups. To those who served him well he could be loyal and generous. And as president, he cared sincerely about society's underdogs. His support for civil rights, aid to the poor, education, and the welfare of the elderly came from genuine conviction. He made the betterment of such people the goal of his administration.

### The Origins of the Great Society

In the first months after the assassination, Johnson acted as the conservator of the Kennedy legacy. "Let us continue," he told a grief-stricken nation. Liberals who had dismissed Johnson as an unprincipled power broker came to respect the energy he showed in quickly steering Kennedy's Civil Rights Act and tax cut legislation through Congress.

Kennedy had come to believe that prosperity alone would not ease the plight of America's poor. In 1962 Michael Harrington's book *The Other America*

*Michael Harrington's The Other America*

brought attention to the persistence of poverty despite the nation's affluence. Harrington focused attention on the hills of Appalachia that stretched from western Pennsylvania south to Alabama. In some counties a quarter of the population survived on a diet of flour and dried-milk paste supplied by federal surplus food programs. Under Kennedy, Congress had passed a new food stamp program as well as laws designed to revive the economies of poor areas. Robert Kennedy also headed a presidential committee to fight juvenile delinquency in urban slums by involving the poor in "community action" programs.

It fell to Lyndon Johnson to fight Kennedy's "war on poverty." By August 1964 this master politician had driven through Congress the most sweeping social welfare bill since the New Deal. The Economic Opportunity Act addressed almost every major cause of poverty. It included training programs such as the Job Corps, which brought poor and unemployed recruits to rural or urban camps to learn new job skills. It granted loans to rural families and urban small businesses as well as aid to migrant workers. The price tag for these programs was high—almost $1 billion to fund the new Office of Economic Opportunity (OEO).

*Economic Opportunity Act*

The speed Johnson demanded led inevitably to confusion, conflict, and waste. Officials at OEO often found themselves in conflict with other cabinet departments, as well as state and local officials. For example, OEO workers organized voter registration drives in order to oust corrupt city officials. Others led rent strikes to force improvements in public housing. The director of city housing in Syracuse, New York, reacted typically: "We are experiencing a class struggle in the traditional Karl Marx style in Syracuse, and I do not like it." Such battles for bureaucratic turf undermined federal poverty programs.

Lyndon Johnson had difficulty playing second fiddle to anyone, even as vice president under John F. Kennedy (right).

## The Election of 1964

In 1964, however, these long-term flaws were not yet evident. Johnson's political stock remained high as he announced his ambition to forge a "Great Society," in which poverty and racial injustice no longer existed. The chance to fulfill his dreams seemed open to him, for the Republicans nominated Senator Barry Goldwater of Arizona as their presidential candidate. Though ruggedly handsome and refreshingly candid, Goldwater believed that government should not dispense welfare, subsidize farmers, or aid public education. Few Americans subscribed to such conservative views. Many worried, too, at Goldwater's willingness to give military commanders the power to launch tactical nuclear weapons without presidential authority.

Thus the election produced the landslide Johnson craved. Carrying every state except Arizona and four in the Deep South, he received 61 percent of the vote. Democrats gained better than two-to-one majorities in the Senate and House. The president moved rapidly to exploit the momentum of his 1964 majority.

## The Great Society

In January 1965 Johnson announced a legislative vision that would extend welfare programs on a scale beyond even Franklin Roosevelt's New Deal. By the end of 1965, some 50 bills had been passed, many of them major pieces of legislation.

As a former teacher, Johnson made education the cornerstone of his program. Stronger schools would compensate the poor for their disadvantaged homes, he believed. Under the Elementary and Secondary School Act, students in low-income school districts were to receive educational equipment, money for books, and enrichment programs like Project Headstart for nursery-age children. As schools scrambled to create programs that would tap federal money, they sometimes spent more to pay middle-class educational professionals than to teach lower-income students.

*Programs in education*

Johnson also pushed through the Medicare Act, to provide the elderly with health insurance to cover their hospital costs. Studies had shown that older people used hospitals three times more than other Americans and generally had incomes only half as large. Since Medicare made no provision for the poor who were not elderly, Congress also passed a program called Medicaid. Participating states would receive matching grants from the federal government to pay the medical expenses of those on welfare or those too poor to afford medical care.

*Medicare and Medicaid*

In many ways, Medicare and Medicaid worked. Over the next two decades, their benefits helped to lower significantly the number of elderly poor. But as more patients used hospital services, Medicare budgets rose. In addition, nothing in the act restricted hospitals or doctors from raising their fees or charging for care they had once given for free. The cost of the programs soared by more than 500 percent in the first 10 years.

The Great Society also reformed immigration policy, striking down a discriminatory quota system based on national origins that had been in effect since

*Immigration*

1924 (page 675). Only about 150,000 immigrants a year had been allowed to enter the United States, almost all from northern Europe. The Immigration Act of 1965 abolished the national origins system. Now, 170,000 people a year would be admitted on a first-come, first-served basis. Racial provisions restricting Asian immigration were eliminated, although new limits were placed on immigration from the Western Hemisphere.

Nor did Johnson, in his efforts to outdo the New Deal, slight the environment. By the mid-1960s many Americans had become increasingly concerned

*The environment*

about smog from factories and automobiles; lakes and rivers polluted by detergents, pesticides, and industrial wastes; and the disappearance of wildlife. In 1964 Congress had already passed the National Wilderness Preservation System Act to set aside 9.1 million acres of wilderness as "forever wild." Congress first established pollution standards for interstate waterways and a year later provided funds for sewage treatment and water purification. Legislation also tightened standards on air pollution. Despite opposition from entrenched interests, the new standards did result in a gradual improvement in water and air quality in many areas.

For all he had done, Johnson wanted more. In 1966 he pushed through bills to raise the minimum wage, improve auto safety, aid mass transit, and develop "model cities." But in time opposition mounted. "Doesn't matter what kind of majority you come in with," Johnson had predicted early on. "You've got just one year when they treat you right, and before they start worrying about themselves." Even so, Johnson pushed major legislation through Congress as late as 1968.

Historians have difficulty measuring the Great Society's impact. It produced more legislation and more reforms than the New Deal. It also carried a higher

*Evaluating the Great Society*

price tag than anyone predicted. Economic statistics suggested that general prosperity, boosted by the tax cut bill, did more to fight poverty than all the OEO programs. Conservatives and radicals alike objected that the liberal welfare state was intruding into too many areas of people's lives.

For all that, the Great Society proved to be the high-water mark of a trend toward activist government that had grown steadily since the progressive era and the Great Depression. While Americans continued to pay lip service to the notion that government should remain small and interfere little in citizens' lives, no strong movement emerged to eliminate Medicare or Medicaid. Few Americans disputed the right of the government to regulate industrial pollution or to control the excesses of large corporations or powerful labor unions. In this sense, the tradition of liberalism prevailed, whatever Johnson's failings.

## THE COUNTERCULTURE

In 1964 some 800 students from Berkeley, Oberlin, and other colleges met in western Ohio to be trained for the voter registration campaign in the South. Middle-class students who had grown up in peaceful white suburbs found themselves being instructed by protest-hardened SNCC coordinators. The lessons were sobering. When beaten by police, the SNCC staff advised, assume the fetal position—hands protecting the neck, elbows covering the temples. That minimized injuries from nightsticks. A few days later, grimmer news arrived. Three volunteers who had left for Mississippi two days earlier had already been arrested by local police. Now they were reported "missing." Six weeks later, their mangled bodies were found, bulldozed into the earthworks of a freshly finished dam.

By the mid-1960s conservatives, civil rights organizations, and the poor were not the only groups rejecting liberal solutions. Dissatisfied members of the middle class—and especially the young—had joined them. The students who returned to campus from the voter registration campaign that summer of 1964 were the shock troops of a much larger movement.

### Activists on the New Left

More than a few students had become disillusioned with the slow pace of reform. Tom Hayden, from a working-class family in a suburb of Detroit, went to college at the University of Michigan, then traveled to Berkeley, and soon joined civil rights workers in Mississippi. Along with other radical students, Hayden helped form Students for a Democratic Society (SDS). Members of SDS gave up on change through the electoral system. Direct action was needed if the faceless, bureaucratic society of the "organization man" were to be made truly democratic. SDS advocated sit-ins, protest marches, and confrontation.

*Students for a Democratic Society*

---

COUNTERPOINT    *What Triggered the Upheavals of the 1960s?*

Historians have debated the causes of the turbulent 1960s. Some scholars have favored a generational explanation. The United States has undergone periodic cycles of reform as each new generation has come of age—about once every 30 years. Thus the twentieth century began with progressive reformers pushing for change, only to give way to the "normalcy" of the 1920s, which in turn was succeeded by the activist New Deal. Similarly, the "consensus" decade of the 1950s preceded liberalism's high tide in the 1960s. In that light, the Port Huron Statement can be read as a call for new cycle of reform led by the nation's baby boomers, who grew up during the 1950s. "There had to be a critical mass of students, and enough economic fat to cushion them," suggested one historian.

Other historians are more leery of the "generational" approach. Consider some of the figures who played pivotal roles in the decade's social reforms: civil rights advocates like Martin Luther King and Cesar Chavez, feminist Betty Friedan, environmentalist Rachel Carson, consumer advocate Ralph Nader, drug promoter Timothy Leary, and rock stars like Bob Dylan and the Beatles. All were born before or during World War II and were not a part of the baby boom generation. In fact, it is possible to argue that by and large baby boomers served mainly as foot soldiers in a crusade led by a generation that came of age during the consensus years of the 1950s.

In the end, it may be more useful to focus on specific catalytic events that bonded different generations. Mississippi Freedom Summer was such an event. Young student volunteers gave up their surburban dress for overalls and work shirts of the sort worn by poor African American laborers in the Mississippi Delta. Volunteers and local folks shared in the terror of frequent harassment and even possible death. Once SNCC volunteers returned to their college campuses, they themselves became catalysts for much of the turmoil that followed. That is not to say necessarily that they "caused" the rebellion of the 1960s. But they did help shape much of the discontent stirring beneath the veneer of campus conformity.

These discontents surfaced most dramatically in the Free Speech Movement at the University of California's Berkeley campus. To most liberals, Berkeley was

*Free Speech Movement*

the gem of the California state system. Like so many other universities, it had educated a generation of GIs following World War II. But to people like Tom Hayden and the SDS, Berkeley was a bureaucratic monster, enrolling more than 30,000 students who filed into large impersonal halls to endure lectures from remote professors. In the fall of 1964, Berkeley officials declared off limits the one small area in which political organizations had been allowed to advertise their causes. When university police tried to remove a recruiter for CORE, thousands of angry students surrounded the police car for 32 hours.

To Mario Savio, a graduate student in philosophy and veteran of the Mississippi Freedom summer, the issue was clear: "In our free-speech fight, we have come up against what may emerge as the greatest problem of our nation—depersonalized, unresponsive bureaucracy." When the university's president, Clark Kerr, threatened to expel Savio, 6000 students took control of the administration building, stopped classes with a strike, and convinced many faculty members to join them. Kerr backed down, placing no limits to free speech on campus except those that applied to society at large. But the lines between students and administrators had been drawn. The rebellious spirit spread to other major universities like Michigan, Yale, and Columbia, and then to campuses across the nation.

## The Rise of the Counterculture

Other youthful rebels were less interested in political dissent. Instead, they condemned American society as materialistic and shallow. These alienated students began to grope toward spiritual, nonmaterial goals. "Turn on to the scene, tune in to what is happening, and drop out of high school, college, grad school, junior executive," advised Timothy Leary, a Harvard psychology professor who dropped out himself. Those who heeded Leary's call to spiritual renewal rejected politics for a lifestyle of experimentation with music, sex, and drugs. Observers labeled their movement a "counterculture."

The counterculture of the 1960s had much in common with earlier religious revival and utopian movements. It admired the quirky individualism of

*Communal living*

Henry David Thoreau. Like Thoreau, it turned to Asian philosophies such as Zen Buddhism. Like Brook Farm and other nineteenth-century utopian communities, the new "hippie" communes sought perfection along the fringes of society. Communards "learned how to scrounge materials, tear down abandoned buildings, use the unusable," as one member of the "Drop City" commune put it. Sexual freedom became a means to liberate members of the counterculture from the repressive inhibitions that distorted the lives of their "uptight" parents. Drugs appeared to offer access to a higher state of consciousness or pleasure.

The early threads of the sixties counterculture led back to the fifties and the subculture of the beat generation (page 835). For the beats, unconventional

This couple at their wedding reflect many of the motifs of the counterculture—long hair, casual dress, informal setting, and racial equality.

*The drug scene*    drugs had long been a part of the scene, but now their use expanded dramatically. Timothy Leary began experimenting with hallucinogenic mushrooms in Mexico and soon moved on to LSD. The drug "blew his mind," he announced, and he became so enthusiastic in making converts that Harvard blew him straight out of its hallowed doors. By 1966 Leary was lecturing across the land on the joys of drug use.

Where Leary's approach to LSD was cool and contemplative, novelist Ken Kesey (*One Flew Over the Cuckoo's Nest*) embraced it with antic frenzy. His ragtag company of druggies and freaks formed the "Merry Pranksters" at Kesey's home outside San Francisco. Writer Tom Wolfe chronicled their travels in *The Electric Kool-Aid Acid Test*, as the Pranksters headed east on a psychedelic school bus in search of Leary. Their example inspired others to drop out.

## The Rock Revolution

In the 1950s rock and roll defined a teen culture preoccupied with young love, cars, and adult pressures. One exception was the Kingston Trio, which in 1958 popularized folk music and historical ballads, especially among college audiences. As the interest in folk music grew, the lyrics increasingly focused on social or political issues. Joan Baez, with a voice one critic found as pure and clear "as air in autumn," dressed simply, wore no makeup, and rejected the commercialism of popular music. She joined folk singer Bob Dylan in the civil rights march on Washington in 1963, singing "We Shall Overcome" and "Blowin' in the Wind." Such folk singers reflected the activist side of the counterculture as they sought to provoke their audiences to political commitment. Dylan, who

*Bob Dylan*    had played his songs of social protest on an unamplified guitar, shocked fans in 1965 by donning a black leather jacket and shifting to a "folk rock" style featuring an electric guitar. His new songs seemed to suggest that the old America was almost beyond redemption.

In 1964 a new sound, imported from England, exploded on the American scene. The Beatles, four musicians from Liverpool, attracted frenzied teen audiences who screamed and swooned as the "mod" crooners sang "I Want to Hold Your Hand." Along with other English groups, like the Rolling Stones, the Beatles reconnected American audiences with the rhythm-and-blues roots of rock and roll. And, like Dylan, their style influenced pop culture almost as much as their music. After a pilgrimage to India to study transcendental meditation, they returned to produce *Sergeant Pepper's Lonely Hearts Club Band*, possibly the most influential album of the decade. It blended sound effects with music, alluded to trips taken with "Lucy in the Sky with Diamonds" (LSD), and concluded, "I'd love to turn you on." Out in San Francisco, bands like the Grateful Dead pioneered "acid rock" with long pieces aimed to echo drug-induced states of mind.

The debt of white rock musicians to rhythm and blues led to increased integration in the music world. Before the 1960s black rhythm-and-blues bands played primarily to black audiences, in segregated clubs or over black radio stations. Black artists like Little Richard, Chuck Berry, and Ray Charles wrote many hit songs made popular by white performers. The civil rights movement

*Soul* and a rising black social and political consciousness gave rise to "soul" music. Blacks became "soul brothers" and "soul sisters," and for the first time their music was played on major radio stations. One black disc jockey described soul as "the last to be hired, first to be fired, brown all year round, sit-in-the-back-of-the-bus feeling." Soul was the quality that expressed black pride and separatism. Out of Detroit came the Motown sound, which combined elements of gospel, blues, and big band jazz.

### The West Coast Scene

The heady visibility of the counterculture also signaled an increasing importance of the West Coast in American popular culture. In the 1950s the shift of television production from the stages of New York to the film lots of Hollywood helped establish Los Angeles as a communications center. San Francisco became notorious as a center of the beat movement. By 1963 the "surfing sound" of West Coast rock groups like the Beach Boys and Jan and Dean had made southern California's preoccupation with surfing and cars into a national fad. And Mario Savio and his Free Speech Movement attracted the attention of the nation.

Before 1967 Americans were only vaguely aware of another West Coast phenomenon, the "hippies." But in January a loose coalition of drug freaks, Zen

*Hippies and Haight-Ashbury* cultists, and political activists banded together to hold the first well-publicized "Be-In." The beat poet Allen Ginsberg was on hand to offer spiritual guidance. The Grateful Dead and Jefferson Airplane, acid rock groups based in San Francisco, provided entertainment. An unknown organization called the Diggers somehow managed to supply free food and drink, while the notorious Hell's Angels motorcycle gang policed the occasion. In that way the Bay Area emerged as a spiritual center of the counterculture. Politically conscious dropouts gravitated toward Berkeley. Flower children who cared less about politics moved into Haight-Ashbury, a run-down San Francisco neighborhood of apartments and Victorian houses, where head shops sold drug paraphernalia, wall posters, and Indian bedspreads. Haight-Ashbury became a model replicated across the nation.

In the summer of 1969 all the positive forces of the counterculture converged on Bethel, New York, in the Catskill Mountains resort area, to celebrate

*Woodstock* the promise of peace, love, and freedom. The Woodstock Music Festival attracted 400,000 people to the largest rock concert ever organized. For one long weekend the audience and performers joined to form an ephemeral community based on sex, drugs, and rock and roll. Even then, the counterculture was dying. Violence intruded on the laid-back urban communities hippies had formed. Organized crime and drug pushers muscled in on the lucrative trade in LSD, amphetamines, and marijuana. Bad drugs and addiction took their toll. Free sex often became an excuse for rape, exploitation, and loveless gratification.

Much that had once seemed outrageous in the hippie world was readily absorbed into the marketplace. Rock groups became big business enterprises commanding huge fees. Yogurt, granola, and herbal teas appeared on supermarket shelves. Ironically, much of the world that hippies forged was embraced and tamed by the society they had rejected.

By the late 1960s most dreams of human betterment seemed shattered— whether John Kennedy's New Frontier, Lyndon Johnson's Great Society, or the communal society of the hippie counterculture. Recession and inflation brought an end to the easy affluence that made liberal reform programs and alternative lifestyles seem so easily affordable. Poverty and unemployment menaced even middle-class youth who had found havens in communes, colleges, and graduate schools. Racial tensions divided black militants and the white liberals of the civil rights movement into sometimes hostile camps.

But the Vietnam War more than any other single factor destroyed the promise of Camelot and the Great Society. After 1965 the nation divided sharply as the American military role in Southeast Asia grew. Radicals like the SDS condemned a capitalist system that promoted race and class conflict at home and imperialism abroad. Conservatives who supported the war called for a return to traditional values and law and order. Both the left and the right attacked the liberal center. Their combined opposition helped to undermine the consensus Lyndon Johnson had worked so hard to build.

## SIGNIFICANT EVENTS

1958 — Kingston Trio popularizes folk music

1960 — Kennedy–Nixon debates; Greensboro sit-ins; Kennedy elected president

1961 — Alliance for Progress; Peace Corps begun; Bay of Pigs invasion; Kennedy steps up U.S. role in Vietnam; Vienna summit; Berlin Wall built; CORE freedom rides begin

1962 — John Glenn orbits earth; Michael Harrington's *The Other America* published; Cuban missile crisis; James Meredith desegregates University of Mississippi; *Engel v. Vitale; Baker v. Carr*

1963 — Diem assassinated in Vietnam; nuclear test ban treaty; University of Alabama desegregation crisis; Kennedy introduces Civil Rights Bill; March on Washington; *Gideon v. Wainwright;* Kennedy assassinated

1964 — *Escobedo v. Illinois; Griswold v. Connecticut;* Civil Rights Act passed; Harlem and Rochester race riots; Johnson enacts Kennedy tax cuts; Economic Opportunity Act; VISTA established; Wilderness Preservation System Act; Johnson defeats Goldwater; Berkeley "Free Speech" Movement; Beatles introduce British rock

1965 — Johnson launches the Great Society; Voting Rights Act; Watts riots; Malcolm X assassinated; Medicare and Medicaid acts; Elementary and Secondary School Act; Immigration Act; escalation in Vietnam

1966 — *Miranda v. Arizona;* Stokely Carmichael of SNCC coins "Black Power" slogan; Model Cities Act

1967 — Black Panthers battle Oakland, California, police; first "Be-In"

1968 — Fair Housing Act

1969 — Woodstock Music Festival; American astronauts land on moon

# CHAPTER THIRTY-ONE

# The Vietnam Era

Vietnam from afar: it looked like an emerald paradise. Thomas Bird, an army rifleman sent there in 1965, recalled his first impression: "A beautiful white beach with thick jungle background. The only thing missing was naked women running down the beach, waving and shouting 'Hello, hello, hello.'" Upon landing, Bird and his buddies were each issued a "Nine-Rule" card outlining proper behavior toward the Vietnamese. "Treat the women with respect, we are guests in this country and here to help these people."

But who were they helping and who were they fighting? When American troops searched out Vietcong forces, the VC generally disappeared into the jungle beyond the villages and rice fields. John Muir, a Marine rifleman, walked into a typical hamlet with a Korean lieutenant. To Muir the place looked ordinary, but the Korean had been in Vietnam a while. "We have a little old lady and a little old man and two very small children," he pointed out. "According to them, the rest of the family has been spirited away . . . either been drafted into one army or the other. So there's only four of them and they have a pot of rice that's big enough to feed fifty people. And rice, once it's cooked, will not keep. They gotta be feeding the VC." Muir watched in disbelief as the lieutenant set the house on fire. The roof "started cooking off ammunition because all through the thatch they had ammunition stored."

GIs soon learned to walk down jungle trails with a cautious shuffle, looking for a wire or a piece of vine that seemed too straight. "We took more casualties from booby traps than we did from actual combat," recalled David Ross, a medic. "It was very frustrating because how do you fight back against a booby trap? You're just walking along and all of a sudden your buddy doesn't have a leg. Or you don't have a leg." Yet somehow the villagers would walk the same paths and never get hurt. Who was the enemy and who the friend?

The same question was being asked half a globe away, on the campus of Kent State University in May 4, 1970. By then the Vietnam War had dragged

*Kent State*

on for more than five years, driving President Lyndon Johnson from office and embroiling his successor, Richard Nixon, in controversy. When Nixon expanded the war beyond Vietnam into Cambodia, protest erupted even at Kent State, just east of Akron, Ohio. Opposition to the war had become so intense in this normally apolitical community that 300 students had torn the Constitution from a history text and, in a formal ceremony, buried it. "President Nixon has murdered it," they charged. That evening demonstrators spilled into the nearby town, smashed shop windows, and returned to campus to burn down an old army ROTC building. Governor James Rhodes ordered in 750 of the National Guard. Student dissidents were the "worst type of people we harbor in America," he announced. "We are going to eradicate the problem."

By background and education, the National Guard troops were little different from the students they had come to police. Almost all were white, between 18 and 30, and from Ohio. But Guard veterans who had fought in World War II or Korea particularly disapproved of students who avoided their military obligation. As his troops arrived at Kent, Guard Commander General Robert

A student lies dead at Kent State, May 1970. Who was the enemy, who was the friend?

Canterbury remarked that "these students are going to have to find out what law and order is all about."

When demonstrators assembled for a rally on the college commons, the Guard ordered them to disperse. Whether they had the authority to do so was debatable. The protesters stood their ground. Then the guardsmen advanced, wearing full battle gear and armed with M-1 rifles, whose high-velocity bullets had a horizontal range of almost two miles. Some students scattered; a few picked up rocks and threw them. The guardsmen suddenly fired into the crowd, many of whom were students passing back and forth from classes. Incredulous, a young woman knelt over Jeffrey Miller; he was dead. By the time calm was restored, three other students had been killed and nine more wounded, some caught innocently in the Guard's indiscriminate fire.

News of the killings swept the nation. At Jackson State, a black college in Mississippi, antiwar protesters seized a women's dormitory. On May 14 state po-

*Jackson State* lice surrounding the building opened fire without provocation, killing two more students and wounding a dozen. In both inci-

dents the demonstrators had been unarmed. The events at Kent State and Jackson State turned sporadic protests against the American invasion of Cambodia into a nationwide student strike. Many students believed the ideals of the United States had been betrayed by those forces of law and order sworn to protect them.

Who was the friend and who the enemy? Time and again the war in Vietnam led Americans to ask that question. Not since the Civil War had the nation been so deeply divided. As the war dragged on, debate moved off college campuses and into the homes of middle Americans, where sons went off to fight and the war came home each night on the evening news. As no other war had, Vietnam seemed to stand the nation on its head. When American soldiers shot at Vietnamese "hostiles," who could not always be separated from "friendlies," or when National Guardsmen fired on their neighbors across a college green, who were the enemies and who were the friends?

## THE ROAD TO VIETNAM

"The enemy must fight his battles far from his home base for a long time," one Vietnamese strategist wrote. "We must further weaken him by drawing him into protracted campaigns. Once his initial dash is broken, it will be easier to destroy him." The enemy in question was not American soldiers nor the French, but the Mongol invaders of A.D. 1284. For several thousand years Vietnam had struggled periodically to fight off foreign invasions. Buddhist culture had penetrated eastward from India. More often Indochina faced invasion and rule by the Chinese from the north. After 1856 the French entered as a colonial power, bringing with them a strong Catholic tradition.

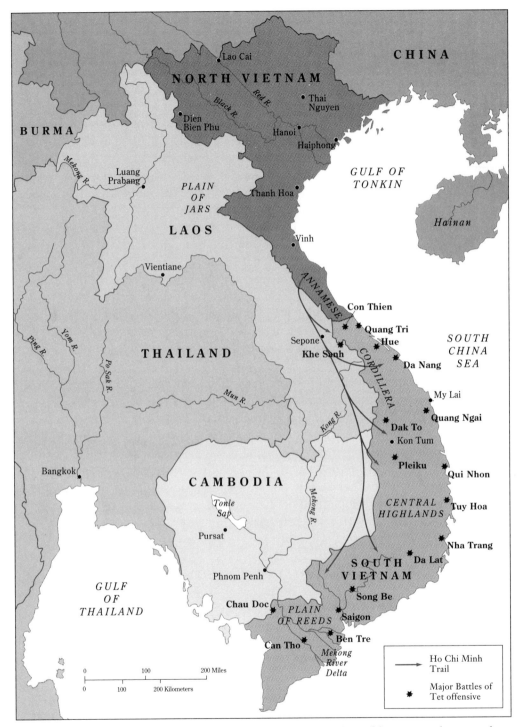

THE WAR IN VIETNAM   For the United States, one strategic problem was to locate and destroy the supply routes known as the Ho Chi Minh Trail. Rugged mountains and triple canopy jungles hid much of the trail from aerial observation and attack.

Ho Chi Minh was one Vietnamese who hoped to throw off French influence as well as the Chinese. Since the end of World War I, he had worked to
*Ho Chi Minh* create an independent Vietnam. After World War II, he organized a guerrilla war against the French, which finally led to their defeat at Dien Bien Phu in 1954 (page 822). He agreed at the Geneva peace conference to withdraw his forces north of the 17th parallel, in return for a promise to hold free elections in both the North and the South. Having supported what they saw as a French struggle against communism, the Americans wanted to block Ho. They helped install Ngo Dinh Diem in South Vietnam and supported his decision not to hold elections, which Ho's forces seemed sure to win. Frustrated South Vietnamese Communists—the Vietcong—renewed their guerrilla war. "I think the Americans greatly underestimate the determination of the Vietnamese people," Ho remarked in 1962, as President Kennedy was committing more American advisers to South Vietnam.

## Lyndon Johnson's War

For Kennedy, Vietnam had been just one of many anti-Communist skirmishes his activist advisers wanted to fight. As attention focused increasingly on
*Domino theory* Vietnam, Kennedy accepted President Eisenhower's "domino theory": if the pro-Western Catholic government fell to the Communists, the other nations of Southeast Asia would collapse one after the other. But even 16,000 American "advisers" had been unable to help the unpopular Diem, who was overthrown by the military in November 1963. When Kennedy was assassinated in the same month as Diem, the problem of Vietnam was left to Lyndon Johnson.

Johnson's political instincts told him to keep the Vietnam War at arm's length. He felt like a catfish, he remarked, who had "just grabbed a big juicy worm with a right sharp hook in the middle of it." Johnson's heart was in his Great Society programs. Yet fear of the political costs of defeat in Vietnam led him steadily toward deeper American involvement. He shared the assumption of Kennedy holdovers like National Security Advisor McGeorge Bundy and Defense Secretary Robert McNamara that Vietnam was a key cold war test.

Until August 1964 American advisers had focused on training and supporting the South Vietnamese army, which fought the Vietcong reluctantly. North Vietnam, for its part, had been infiltrating men and supplies along the Ho Chi Minh Trail, a network of jungle routes threading through Laos and Cambodia into the highlands of South Vietnam. But American support seemed to be having little impact. The Vietcong controlled some 40 percent of South Vietnam. Johnson strategists decided to relieve the South by increasing pressure on North Vietnam itself.

American ships patrolling the Gulf of Tonkin began to provide cover for secret South Vietnamese raids against the North. On August 2, three North

*Tonkin Gulf incident*

Vietnamese patrol boats exchanged fire with the American destroyer *Maddox*, neither side hurting the other. Two nights later, in inky blackness and a heavy thunderstorm, a second incident occurred. But a follow-up investigation could not be sure whether enemy ships had even been near the scene. President Johnson was not pleased. "For all I know our navy might have been shooting at whales out there," he remarked privately.

Whatever his doubts, the president publicized the incidents as "open aggression on the high sea" and ordered retaliatory air raids on North Vietnam. He did not disclose that the navy and South Vietnamese forces had been conducting secret military operations at the time. When Johnson then asked for the authority to take "all necessary measures" to "repel any armed attack" on American forces and to "prevent future aggression," Congress overwhelmingly passed what became known as the Tonkin Gulf Resolution.

Senator Ernest Gruening of Alaska, one of only two lawmakers to vote no, objected that the resolution gave the president "a blank check" to declare war, a power the Constitution specifically reserved to Congress. Johnson insisted— no doubt sincerely at the time—that he had limited aims. But as pressure for an American victory increased, the president exploited the powers the resolution gave him.

## Rolling Thunder

*Escalation*

In January 1965 Johnson received a disturbing memorandum from McGeorge Bundy and Robert McNamara, two of his most trusted advisers on foreign policy. "Both of us are now pretty well convinced that our present policy can lead only to disastrous defeat," they said. The United States should either increase its attack—*escalate* was the term coined in 1965— or simply withdraw. In theory escalation would increase military pressure to the point at which further resistance would cost more than the enemy was willing to pay. By taking gradual steps, the United States would demonstrate its resolve to win while leaving the door open to negotiations.

But the theory that made so much sense in the White House did not work well in practice. Each stage of American escalation only hardened the resolve of the Vietcong and North Vietnamese. When a Vietcong mortar attack in February killed seven Marines stationed at Pleiku airbase, Johnson ordered U.S. planes to begin bombing North Vietnam. Privately, McGeorge Bundy admitted that Pleiku was only an excuse. "Pleikus are like streetcars," he remarked; "there's one every ten minutes."

*Air strikes*

Restricted air strikes did not satisfy more hawkish leaders. Retired Air Force Chief of Staff Curtis LeMay complained, "We are swatting flies when we should be going after the whole manure pile." In March Johnson ordered Operation Rolling Thunder, a systematic bombing campaign aimed at bolstering confidence in South Vietnam and cutting the flow of supplies from the North. At the same time, he declared his willingness to negotiate an end to the war once North Vietnamese troops had left the South.

Rolling Thunder achieved none of its goals. American pilots could seldom spot the Ho Chi Minh Trail under its dense jungle canopy. Even when bombs hit, North Vietnamese crews kept the supplies moving by filling bomb craters or improvising pontoon bridges from bamboo stalks. Equally discouraging, South Vietnamese leaders spent their energy on political intrigue. One military government after another proved equally inept.

Once the Americans established bases from which to launch the new air strikes, these too became targets for guerrilla attacks. General William West-

*Combat troops* moreland, the chief of American military operations in Vietnam, requested combat troops to defend the bases. Johnson sent in 3500 Marines, almost without considering the implication of his decision. With the crucial decision to commit combat troops, the urge to shore up and protect those already there became stronger. Another 40,000 soldiers arrived in May and 50,000 more by July.

Johnson, as before, downplayed the escalation, because he feared a political backlash. McNamara ordered the decision carried out in a "low-keyed manner," both to prevent Soviet or Chinese intervention and "to avoid undue concern and excitement in the Congress and in domestic public opinion." By the end of 1965 almost 185,000 American troops had landed—and still the call for more continued. In 1968, at the height of the war, 536,000 American troops were being supported with helicopters, jet aircraft, and other advanced military technologies. This was "escalation" with a vengeance.

## SOCIAL CONSEQUENCES OF THE WAR

The impact of the war fell hardest on the baby-boom generation of the 1950s. As these young people came of age, draft calls for the armed services were rising. At the same time, the civil rights movement and the growing counterculture were encouraging students to question the goals of establishment America. Whether they fought in Vietnam or protested at home, supported the government or demonstrated against it, eventually these baby boomers—as well as Americans of all ages—were forced to take a stand on Vietnam.

### The Soldiers' War

Most Americans sent to Vietnam were chosen by the draft. The Selective Service System, as it was called, favored the middle and upper classes. College

*Composition of U.S. forces* students could avoid service, as well as those in "critical" occupations like teachers and engineers. As the war escalated, the draft was changed, so that some students were called up through a lottery system. Still, those who knew the medical requirements might be able to produce a doctor's affidavit certifying a weak knee, flat feet, or bad eyes—all grounds for flunking the physical. Of the 1200 men in Harvard's class of 1970, only 56 served in the military, and only 2 of them in Vietnam.

The poorest and least educated were also likely to escape service, because the Armed Forces Qualification Test and the physical often screened them out. Thus the sons of blue-collar America were most likely to accept Uncle Sam's letter of induction. Once in uniform, the sons of Hispanic and black Americans who had fewer skills were more often assigned to combat duty. The draft also made it a relatively young man's war. The average age of soldiers serving in Vietnam was 19, compared with the average of 26 for World War II.

Most American infantry came to Vietnam ready and willing to fight. But physical and psychological hardships took their toll. An American search-and-destroy mission would fight its way into a Communist-controlled hamlet, clear and burn it, and move on—only to be ordered back days or weeks later because the enemy had moved in again. Since success could not be measured in terri-

*Body counts*

tory gained, the measure became the "body count": the number of Vietcong killed. Unable to tell who was friendly and who was hostile, GIs regularly took out their frustrations on innocent civilians. Officers counted those victims to inflate the numbers that suggested the Americans were winning.

Most Americans assumed that superior military technology could guarantee success. But technology alone could not tell friend from foe. Since

*Technology and its limits*

the Vietcong routinely mixed with the civilian population, the chances for deadly error increased. Bombs of napalm (jellied gasoline) and white phosphorus rained liquid fire from the skies, coating everything from village huts to the flesh of fleeing humans. To clear jungle canopies and expose Vietcong camps and roads, American planes spread more than 100 million pounds of defoliants. The forests destroyed totaled more than one-third of South Vietnam's timberlands—an area approximately the size of the state of Rhode Island. The long-term health and ecological effects were severe.

The miracles of modern technology also made the war more demanding. Helicopters could whisk GIs from one firefight to another or from the front lines of a steaming jungle back to Saigon. There they could catch overnight flights to Hawaii or the mainland. The sudden shift from the hell of war to civilian peace could be wrenching. "I fell asleep [on the plane to New York] and woke up yelling, probably a nightmare," recalled John Kerry, later a senator from Massachusetts. "The other passengers moved away from me—a reaction I noticed more and more in the months ahead. . . . The feeling toward [Vietnam vets] was, 'Stay away—don't contaminate us with whatever you've brought back from Vietnam.'"

By 1967 the war was costing more than $2 billion a month. The United States dropped more bombs on Vietnam than it had during all of World

Vietnam's difficult terrain of mountains, jungles, and rice paddies made helicopters especially useful to move troops quickly.

War II. After one air attack on a Communist-held provincial capital, American troops walked into the smoldering ruins. "We had to destroy the town in order to save it," an officer explained. As the human and material costs of the war increased, that statement stuck in the minds of many observers. What sense was there in a war that saved people by burning their homes?

### The War at Home

As the war dragged on, such questions provoked anguished debate among Americans, especially on college campuses. Faculty members held "teach-ins"

*Teach-ins*

to explain the issues to concerned students. Scholars familiar with Southeast Asia questioned every major assumption the president used to justify escalation. The United States and South Vietnam had brought on the war, they charged, by violating the Geneva accords of 1954. Moreover, the Vietcong were an indigenous rebel force with legitimate grievances against Saigon's corrupt government. The war was a civil war among the Vietnamese, not an effort by Soviet or Chinese Communists to conquer Southeast Asia, as Eisenhower, Kennedy, and Johnson had claimed.

By 1966 national leaders had similarly divided into opposing camps of "hawks" and "doves." The hawks argued that America must win in Vietnam to

*Hawks and doves*

save Southeast Asia from communism, to preserve the nation's prestige, and to protect the lives of American soldiers fighting the war. Most Americans supported those views. The doves were nonetheless a prominent minority. African Americans as a group were far less likely than white Americans to support the war. Some resented the diversion of resources from the cities to the war effort. Many black Americans' heightened sense of racial consciousness led them to identify with the Vietnamese people. Martin Luther King, SNCC, and CORE all opposed the war. Heavyweight boxing champion Muhammad Ali, a black Muslim, refused on religious grounds to serve in the army, even though the decision cost him his title.

By 1967 college students and faculty turned out in crowds to express their outrage: "Hey, hey, LBJ, how many kids have you killed today?" More than

*Antiwar demonstrations* 300,000 people attended the demonstration organized in April 1967 in New York City. Some college protesters even burned their draft cards in defiance of federal law. In the fall more violent protests erupted as antiwar radicals stormed a draft induction center in Oakland, California. The next day 55,000 protesters ringed the Pentagon in Washington. Again, mass arrests followed.

Student protests forced policymakers and citizens to take a sobering look at the war. Key moderates became increasingly convinced the United States could not win the war. Senator William Fulbright of Arkansas was among them. Having helped President Johnson push the Tonkin Gulf Resolution through the Senate, Fulbright now held hearings sharply critical of American policy. The hawkish publisher of *Time* and *Life* magazines, Henry Luce, turned his editorials against the war in 1967.

Defense Secretary Robert McNamara became the most dramatic defector. For years the statistically minded secretary had struggled to quantify the suc-

Lyndon Johnson once shocked reporters by lifting his shirt to show them a surgical scar. In the whimsical hands of cartoonist David Levine, the scar took the shape of Vietnam.

*McNamara loses faith*

cess of the war effort. But by 1967 McNamara had become skeptical. If Americans were killing 300,000 Vietnamese, enemy forces should be shrinking. Instead, intelligence estimates indicated that North Vietnamese infiltration had risen from 35,000 a year in 1965 to 150,000 by the end of 1967. McNamara came to have deep moral qualms. "The picture of the world's greatest superpower killing or seriously injuring 1,000 noncombatants a week, while trying to pound a tiny, backward nation into submission on an issue whose merits are hotly disputed, is not a pretty one," he advised.

Johnson thought of himself as a moderate on the war. He weighed doves like McNamara against hawks who pressed to escalate further. But since the president did not want to be remembered as the first American leader who lost a war, he sided more with the hawks. And so McNamara resigned.

## COUNTERPOINT   *Whose War?*

In 1995 Robert McNamara published a memoir that stunned long-time defenders of the war and confirmed the beliefs of those who had opposed it. The war had been a great mistake, he concluded. The Johnson administration could—and should—have avoided sending hundreds of thousands of Americans into the conflict. Moreover, McNamara implied that if Kennedy had lived, he would not have escalated the war as Lyndon Johnson had. In other words, even though presidents from Truman through Kennedy had involved the United States in Southeast Asia, Vietnam was truly Lyndon Johnson's war. Some historians have argued that by the summer of 1963, Kennedy had become convinced that American forces had to be withdrawn gradually but that politically he dared not do so until after the election of 1964. "If I tried to pull out now from Vietnam," one aide recalls him saying, "we would have another Joe McCarthy red scare on our hands."

Other historians have been skeptical. They argue that even in 1965, no official of importance suggested that the United States should allow Vietnam to fall to the Communists. Senators Fulbright and Mike Mansfield, who criticized Johnson by 1968, all backed the Tonkin Gulf resolution in 1965. Further, historians have evidence that President Kennedy would have escalated the war, though perhaps not as quickly. "We want the war to be won, the Communists to be contained, and the Americans to go home," Kennedy asserted only two months before his death; ". . . But we are not there to see a war lost." As one historian concluded, "The widespread and prevailing opinion in the administration, Congress, and the press and among the mass of Americans was that the United States simply could not walk away from Vietnam and sacrifice a pro-Western country to Communist aggression." In his view Vietnam was America's war: a product of the cold war mentality that had arisen over the previous two decades, not the act of a single, stubborn president.

As the war's annual cost soared to more than $50 billion a year, it fueled a rising inflation. Medicare, education, housing, and other Great Society programs raised the domestic budget sharply too. Through it all Johnson refused to raise taxes, even though wages and prices rose rapidly. From 1965 to 1970 inflation jumped from about 2 percent to around 4 percent. The economy was headed for trouble.

*Inflation*

## THE UNRAVELING

Almost all the forces dividing America seemed to converge in 1968. Until January of that year, most Americans had reason to believe General Westmoreland's estimate of the war. There was, he suggested, "light at the end of the tunnel." Johnson and his advisers, whatever their private doubts, in public painted an optimistic picture. With such optimism radiating from Washington, few Americans were prepared for the events on the night of January 30, 1968.

### *Tet Offensive*

As the South Vietnamese began their celebration of Tet, the Vietnamese lunar New Year, Vietcong guerrillas launched a series of concerted attacks. Assault targets included Saigon's major airport, the South Vietnamese presidential palace, and Hue, the ancient Vietnamese imperial capital. Perhaps most unnerving to Americans, 19 crack Vietcong commandos blasted a hole in the wall of the American embassy compound in Saigon and stormed in. They fought in the courtyard until all 19 lay dead. One reporter, stunned by the carnage, compared the courtyard to a butcher shop.

Tet must rank as one of the great American intelligence failures, on a par with the failure to anticipate Japan's attack on Pearl Harbor or China's intervention in the Korean War. For nearly half a year the North Vietnamese had lured American troops away from Vietnam's cities into pitched battles at remote outposts like Khe Sanh and Con Thien. As American forces dispersed, the Vietcong infiltrated major population areas of Saigon and the Mekong Delta region. A few audacious VC, disguised as South Vietnamese soldiers, even hitched rides on American jeeps and trucks. Though surprised by the Tet offensive, American and South Vietnamese troops repulsed most of the assaults. General Westmoreland announced that the Vietcong had "very deceitfully" taken advantage of the Vietnamese holiday "to create maximum consternation" and that their "well-laid plans went afoul."

In a narrow military sense, Westmoreland was right. The enemy had been driven back, sustaining perhaps 40,000 deaths. Only 1100 American and 2300 South Vietnamese soldiers had been killed—a ratio of more than 10 to 1 (though 12,500 civilians died). But Americans at home received quite another message. Tet created a "credibility gap" between the ad-

*Stalemate*

ministration's optimistic reports and the war's harsh reality. Westmoreland, Johnson, and other officials had repeatedly claimed that the Vietcong were on their last legs. Yet as Ho Chi Minh had coolly informed the French after World War II, "You can kill ten of my men for every one I kill of yours . . . even at those odds, you will lose and I will win." Highly respected CBS news anchor Walter Cronkite drew a gloomy lesson of Tet for his national audience: "To say that we are mired in stalemate seems the only realistic, yet unsatisfactory, conclusion."

The Tet offensive sobered Lyndon Johnson as well as his new secretary of defense, Clark Clifford. Clifford was a Johnson loyalist and a stalwart believer in the war. But as he reviewed the American position in Vietnam, he could get no satisfactory answers from the Joint Chiefs of Staff, who had requested an additional 206,000 troops. "How long would it take to succeed in Vietnam?" Clifford recalled asking them.

*Clark Clifford*

> They didn't know. How many more troops would it take? They couldn't say. Were two hundred thousand the answer? They weren't sure. Might they need more? Yes, they might need more. Could the enemy build up [their own troop strength] in exchange? Probably. So what was the plan to win the war? Well, the only plan was that attrition would wear out the Communists, and they would have had enough. Was there any indication that we've reached that point? No, there wasn't.

Clifford decided to build a case for deescalation. To review policy, he formed a panel of "wise men," respected pillars of the cold war establishment that included Dean Acheson, Harry Truman's secretary of state; Henry Cabot Lodge, a Republican and former ambassador to South Vietnam; and several retired generals. The war could not be won, they concluded, and Johnson should seek a negotiated settlement.

Meanwhile, the antiwar forces had found a political champion in Senator Eugene McCarthy from Wisconsin. McCarthy was something of a senatorial maverick who wrote poetry in his spare time. He announced that no matter how long the odds, he intended to challenge Lyndon Johnson in the 1968 Democratic primaries. Idealistic college students got haircuts and shaves in order to look "clean for Gene." Thus transformed, they canvassed New Hampshire voters. Johnson won the primary vote, but his margin was so slim (300 votes) that it amounted to a stunning defeat. To the anger of McCarthy supporters, Robert Kennedy, John Kennedy's younger brother, quickly announced his own antiwar candidacy.

*"Clean for Gene"*

"I've got to get me a peace proposal," the president told Clifford. White House speechwriters finally put together an announcement that bombing raids against North Vietnam would be halted, at least partially, in hopes that peace talks could begin. They were still trying to write an ending when Johnson told them, "Don't worry; I may have a little ending of my own." On March 31 he supplied it, announcing: "I have concluded that I

*LBJ withdraws*

should not permit the presidency to become involved in the partisan divisions that are developing in this political year. . . . Accordingly I shall not seek, and I will not accept, the nomination of my party for another term as your president."

The announcement shocked nearly everyone. The Vietnam War had pulled down one of the savviest, most effective politicians of the era. North Vietnam responded to the speech by sending delegates to a peace conference in Paris, where negotiations quickly bogged down. And American attention soon focused on the chaotic situation at home, where all the turbulence, discontent, and violence of the 1960s seemed to be coming together.

## The Shocks of 1968

On April 4 Martin Luther King, Jr., traveled to Memphis to support striking sanitation workers. He was relaxing on the balcony of his motel when James

*King and Kennedy killed*

Earl Ray, an escaped convict, fatally shot him with a sniper's rifle. King's campaign of nonviolence was overshadowed by the violent reaction to his murder. Riots broke out in ghetto areas of the nation's capital; by the end of the week, disturbances rocked 125 more neighborhoods across the country. Almost before Americans could recover, a disgruntled Arab nationalist, Sirhan Sirhan, assassinated Robert Kennedy on the evening of June 5. Running in opposition to the war, Kennedy had just won a crucial primary victory in California.

The deaths of King and Kennedy pained Americans deeply. In their own ways, both men exemplified the liberal tradition, which reached its high-water mark in the 1960s. King had retained his faith in a Christian theology of nonviolence. He sought reform for the poor of all races without resorting to the language of the fist and the gun. Robert Kennedy had come to reject the war his brother had supported, and he seemed genuinely to sympathize with the poor and minorities. At the same time, he was popular among traditional white ethnics and blue-collar workers. Would the liberal political tradition have flourished longer if these two charismatic figures had survived the turbulence of the sixties?

Once violence silenced the clearest liberal voices, it became clear that Democrats would choose Hubert Humphrey to replace Lyndon Johnson.

*A tumultuous Democratic convention*

Humphrey had begun his career as a progressive and a strong supporter of civil rights. But as Johnson's loyal vice president, he was intimately associated with the war and the old-style liberal reforms that could never satisfy radicals. The Republicans had chosen Richard Nixon, a traditional anti-Communist (now reborn as the "new," more moderate Nixon). As much as radicals disliked Johnson, they truly abhorred Nixon, "new" or old.

Chicago, where the Democrats met for their convention, was the fiefdom of Mayor Richard Daley, long a symbol of machine politics and backroom deals. Daley was determined that the dissatisfied radicals who poured into Chicago would not disrupt "his" Democratic convention. The radicals were equally determined that they would. For a week the police skirmished with demonstrators: police clubs, riot gear, and tear gas versus the demonstrators' eggs, rocks, and balloons filled with paint and urine. When Daley refused to allow a peaceful march past the convention site, the radicals marched anyway, and then the police, with the mayor's blessing, turned on the crowd in what a federal commission later labeled a police riot. In one pitched battle, many officers took off their badges and waded into the crowd, nightsticks swinging, chanting "Kill, kill, kill." Reporters, medics, and other innocent bystanders were injured; at 3 A.M. police invaded candidate Eugene McCarthy's hotel headquarters and pulled some of his assistants from their beds.

With feelings running so high, President Johnson did not dare appear at his own party's convention. Theodore White, a veteran journalist covering the assemblage, scribbled his verdict in a notebook as police chased hippies down Michigan Avenue. "The Democrats are finished," he wrote.

### Whose Silent Majority?

Radicals were not the only Americans alienated from the political system in 1968. Governor George Wallace of Alabama sensed the frustration among the "average man on the street, this man in the textile mill, this man in the steel mill, this barber, this beautician, the policeman on the beat." In running for president, Wallace sought the support of blue-collar workers and the lower middle classes.

Wallace had first come to national attention in 1963, when he barred integration of the University of Alabama. Briefly, he pursued the Democratic presidential nomination in 1964. For the race in 1968 he formed his

*George Wallace*

own American Independent party with the hawkish General Curtis LeMay as his running mate. (LeMay spoke belligerently of bombing North Vietnam "back to the stone age.") Wallace's enemies were the "liberals, intellectuals, and long hairs [who] have run this country for too long."

Wallace did not simply appeal to law and order, militarism, and white backlash; he was too sharp for that. With roots in southern Populism, he called for federal job-training programs, stronger unemployment benefits, national health insurance, a higher minimum wage, and a further extension of union rights. Polls in September revealed that many Robert Kennedy voters had shifted to Wallace. A quarter of all union members backed him.

In fact, Wallace had tapped true discontent among the working class. Many blue-collar workers despised hippies and peace marchers, yet wanted the United States out of Vietnam. And they were suspicious, as Wallace was, of the upper-class "establishment" that held power. "We can't understand how all those rich kids—the kids with beards from the suburbs—how they got off when my son

# EYEWITNESS TO HISTORY

## A Disabled Vietnam Veteran Joins a Los Angeles Antiwar Demonstration

The noon traffic is moving along Wilshire Boulevard just as if the line of veterans and ordinary citizens picketing Nixon's campaign headquarters were not there. "Join us!" we cry. "Stop the war!" Heavy curtains are drawn over the windows of the campaign headquarters where volunteers are working for the reelection of the president. We have been there for two days and not one of the volunteers has ever looked out, the people in their cars pass us quickly, intent on their steering wheels. Who are these people going to work, going to lunch as if nothing is more important than that? "Here!" I scream. "Look at the war!" They never so much as turn their heads. I wheel out into traffic, pushing myself in front of cars. "Take a good look at the war!" I cry, racing my wheel chair in front of a truck. I do not think—or even care—about getting killed. I am screaming at them to look at me. Up on the rooftop of the headquarters the hidden police cameras are taking pictures, and I know that all by myself I have at least succeeded in stopping traffic.

One by one the other demonstrators are breaking from the line. They sit down among the cars, banging their picket sticks and yelling, their voices hoarse. . . . We have taken the streets. People are honking their horns now, workers and secretaries hanging out their windows, bus drivers shouting their approval. Some of the demonstrators are dancing and I grab both wheels of my chair, then let go with one hand and raise my middle finger in the air as a salute to the cops and the FBI. I spin on my two wheels in front of everyone, as the shouting goes on for the war to end, for the killing to be stopped forever. I keep doing my wheelies as the police look on with envy and utter contempt, frozen on their side of the street. They seem torn between wanting to kill us and wanting to tear off their uniforms and throw away their guns. "Come join us!" we shout to them, but they do not take us up on our invitation.

had to go over there and maybe get his head shot off," one blue-collar parent complained.

Richard Nixon too sought the votes of these traditionally Democratic voters, especially disaffected southern Democrats. The Republicans, of course, had

*Nixon and the "silent majority"* been reviled by the Populists of old as representatives of the money power, monopoly, and the old-line establishment. But Nixon himself had modest roots. His parents owned a general store in Whittier, California, where he had worked to help the family out. At Duke Law School he was so pinched for funds he lived in an abandoned toolshed. His dogged hard work earned him the somewhat dubious nickname of "iron pants." If ever there had been a candidate who could claim to be self-made, it was Nixon. And he well understood the disdain ordinary laborers felt for "kids with beards from the suburbs" who seemed always to be insisting, protesting, *demanding*. Nixon believed himself a representative of the "silent majority," as he later described it, not a vocal minority.

He thus set two fundamental requirements for his campaign: to distance himself from President Johnson on Vietnam and to turn Wallace's "average Americans" into a Republican majority. The Vietnam issue was delicate, because Nixon had generally supported the president's efforts to end the war. He told his aide Richard Whalen, "I've come to the conclusion that there's no way to win the war. But we can't say that, of course. In fact, we have to seem to say the opposite." For most of his campaign he hinted that he had a secret plan to end the war but steadfastly refused to disclose it. He pledged only to find an honorable solution. As for Wallace's followers, Nixon promised to promote "law and order" while cracking down on "pot," pornography, protest, and permissiveness.

Hubert Humphrey had the more daunting task of surmounting the ruins of the Chicago convention. All through September antiwar protesters dogged his *The 1968 election* campaign with "Dump the Hump" posters. Although Humphrey picked up steam late in the campaign (partly by cautiously criticizing Johnson's war policies), the last-minute surge was not enough. Nixon captured 43.4 percent of the popular vote to 42.7 percent for Humphrey and 13.5 percent for Wallace. Some voters had punished the Democrats not just for the war but also for supporting civil rights. The majority of the American electorate had turned its back on liberal reform.

## THE NIXON ERA

In Richard Nixon, Americans had elected two men to the presidency. On the public side, he appeared as the traditional small-town conservative who cherished individual initiative, chamber-of-commerce capitalism, Fourth-of-July patriotism, and middle-class Victorian values. The private Nixon was a troubled man. His language among intimates was caustic and profane. He waxed bitter toward those he saw as enemies. Never a natural public speaker, he was physically rather awkward—a White House aide once found toothmarks on a "child-proof" aspirin cap the president had been unable to pry open. But Nixon seemed to search out challenges—"crises" to face and conquer.

## Vietnamization—and Cambodia

A settlement of the Vietnam "crisis" thus became one of Nixon's first priorities. He found a congenial ally in National Security Advisor Henry Kissinger. Kissinger, an intensely ambitious Harvard academic, shared with the new president a global vision of foreign affairs. Like Nixon, Kissinger had a tendency to pursue his ends secretly, circumventing the traditional channels of government such as the Department of State.

*Henry Kissinger*

Nixon and Kissinger wanted to bring the war to an end, but insisted on "peace with honor." That meant leaving a pro-American South Vietnamese government behind. The strategy Nixon adopted was "Vietnamization," which involved a carrot and a stick. On its own initiative, the United States began gradually withdrawing troops as a way to advance the peace talks in Paris. The burden of fighting would shift to the South Vietnamese army. Critics likened this strategy to little more than "changing the color of the corpses." All the same, it helped reduce antiwar protests at home. As the media shifted their focus to the peace talks, the public had the impression the war was winding down.

Using the stick, President Nixon hoped to drive the North Vietnamese into negotiating peace on American terms. Quite consciously, he traded on his reputation as a cold warrior who would stop at nothing. As he explained to his chief of staff, Robert Haldeman,

> I call it the Madman Theory, Bob. I want the North Vietnamese to believe that I've reached the point where I might do anything to stop the war. We'll just slip the word to them that, "for God's sake, you know Nixon is obsessed about Communists. We can't restrain him when he's angry—and he has his hand on the nuclear button"—and Ho Chi Minh himself will be in Paris in two days begging for peace.

To underline his point, in the spring of 1969 Nixon launched a series of bombing attacks against North Vietnamese supply depots inside neighboring Cambodia. Johnson had refused to widen the war in this manner, fearing domestic reaction. Nixon simply kept the raids secret.

The North Vietnamese refused to cave in to the bombing. Ho Chi Minh's death in 1969 changed nothing. His successors continued to reject any offer that did not end with complete American withdrawal and an abandonment of the South Vietnamese military government. Once again Nixon turned up the heat. Over the opposition of his secretaries of defense and state, he ordered American troops into Cambodia to wipe out North Vietnamese bases there. On April 30, 1970, he announced the "incursion" of American troops, proclaiming that he would not allow "the world's most powerful nation" to act "like a pitiful helpless giant."

*Cambodian invasion*

The wave of protests that followed included the fatal clashes between authorities and students at Kent State and Jackson State as well as another march on Washington by 100,000 protesters. Even Congress was upset enough to repeal the Tonkin Gulf Resolution, a symbolic rejection of Nixon's invasion. After two months American troops left Cambodia, having achieved little.

## Fighting a No-Win War

For a time, Vietnamization seemed to be working. As more American troops went home, the South Vietnamese forces improved modestly. But for American GIs still in the country, morale became a serious problem. Obviously the United States was gradually pulling out its forces. After Tet, it was clear there would be no victory. So why were the "grunts" in the field still being asked to put their lives on the line? The anger surfaced increasingly in incidents known as "fragging," in which GIs threw fragmentation grenades at officers who pursued the war too aggressively.

Nor could the army isolate itself from the trends dividing American society. Just as young Americans "turned on" to marijuana and hallucinogens, so soldiers in Vietnam used drugs. The Pentagon estimated that by 1971 nearly a third of American troops there had experimented with either opium or heroin, easily obtained in Southeast Asia.

Black GIs brought with them the black power issues from home. One white medic noticed that Muhammad Ali's refusal to be drafted caused the blacks in
his unit "to question why they were fighting the Honky's war
*GIs and black power*
against other Third World people. I saw very interesting relationships happening between your quick-talking, sharp-witted Northern blacks and your kind of easygoing, laid-back Southern blacks. . . . Many Southern blacks changed their entire point of view by the end of their tour and went home extremely angry."

The problem with morale only underlined the dilemma facing President Nixon. As the troops became restive, domestic opposition to the war grew and the North Vietnamese refused to yield.

## The Move toward Détente

Despite Nixon's insistence on "peace with honor," Vietnam was not a war he had chosen to fight. And both Kissinger and Nixon recognized that by 1968 the United States no longer had the resources to exercise unchallenged dominance across the globe. The Soviet Union remained their prime concern. Ever since Khrushchev had backed down at the Cuban missile crisis in 1962, the Soviets had steadily expanded their nuclear arsenal. Furthermore, the growing economies of Japan and Western Europe challenged American leadership in world trade. Continued instability in Southeast Asia, the Middle East, and other Third World areas threatened the strength of the non-Communist bloc. Thus Vietnam diverted valuable military and economic resources from more critical areas.

In what the White House labeled the "Nixon Doctrine," the United States would shift some of the military burden for containment to other allies: Japan

*Nixon Doctrine* in the Pacific, the shah of Iran in the Middle East, Zaire in central Africa, and the apartheid government in South Africa. Over the next six years American foreign military sales jumped from $1.8 billion to $15.2 billion. At the same time, Nixon and Kissinger looked for new ways to contain Soviet power not simply by the traditional threat of arms but through negotiations to ease tensions. This policy was named, from the French, détente.

Kissinger and Nixon looked to create "linkages" among many cold war issues. For example, the arms race burdened the Soviet economy. To ease that pressure, they would make concessions to the Soviets on nuclear arms. The Soviets in return would have to limit their arms buildup and, in a linked concession, pressure North Vietnam to negotiate an end to the war. To add lever-*The China card* age, Nixon and Kissinger developed a "China card." The United States would stop treating Communist Mao Zedong as an archenemy and, instead, open diplomatic relations with the Chinese. Fearful of a more powerful China, the Soviets would be more conciliatory toward the United States.

It took a shrewd diplomatist to sense an opportunity to shift traditional cold war policy. Conservative Republicans denounced the idea of recognizing Mao's government, even after 20 years. They believed that the Soviets responded only to force and that they were united with China in a monolithic Communist conspiracy. Now Richard Nixon, the man who had built a career fighting commu-

Richard Nixon's trip to China included this visit to the Great Wall. Perhaps precisely because he had been so staunch an anticommunist, Nixon appreciated the enormous departure his trip marked in Sino-American relations.

nism, made overtures to the Communist powers. Kissinger slipped off to China on a secret mission (he was nursing a stomachache, his aides assured the press) and then reappeared having arranged a trip to China for the president. During that visit in early 1972, Nixon pledged to normalize relations, a move the public enthusiastically welcomed.

A new overture to the Soviet Union followed the China trip. Eager to acquire American grain and technology, Soviet Premier Leonid Brezhnev invited Nixon to Moscow in May 1972. Nixon saw in the Soviet market a chance to ease American trade deficits by selling surplus wheat to the Russians. But the meeting's most important result was the signing of the first Strategic Arms

*SALT I*

Limitation Treaty (SALT I). In the agreement, both sides pledged not to develop a new system of antiballistic missiles (ABMs), which would have accelerated the costly arms race. And they agreed to limit the number of intercontinental ballistic missiles (ICBMs) each side would deploy.

Both the China and the Moscow visits strengthened Nixon's reputation as a global strategist. Americans were pleased at the prospect of lower cold war tensions. But it was not clear that the linkages achieved in Moscow and Beijing would help extricate the United States from Vietnam.

### Nixon's New Federalism

As a Republican, Nixon wanted to scale back many New Deal and Great Society programs. "After a third of a century of power flowing from the people and the states to Washington," he proclaimed, "it is time for a New Federalism in which power, funds, and responsibility will flow from Washington to the states and to the people."

The New Federalism involved a system of revenue sharing, where Washington gave money in block grants to state and local governments. Instead of

*Revenue sharing*

the funds being earmarked for specific purposes, localities could decide which problems needed attention and how best to attack them. Congress passed a revenue sharing act in 1972, which distributed $30 billion over the following five years. A similar approach influenced aid to individuals. In contrast, liberal programs from the New Deal to the Great Society often provided specific services to individuals: job retraining programs, Head Start programs for preschoolers, food supplement programs for nursing mothers. Republicans argued that such a "service strategy" too often assumed that federal bureaucrats best understood what the poor needed. Nixon favored an "income strategy" instead, which simply gave recipients money and allowed them to spend it as they saw fit. Such grants were meant to encourage individual initiative, increase personal freedom, and reduce government bureaucracy.

Even if Nixon was determined to reverse the liberalism of the 1960s, critics were wrong to dismiss him as a knee-jerk conservative. His appeal to local

*Nixon reforms*

authority and individual initiative in some ways echoed the New Left's rhetoric of "power to the people." In 1970 he signed a bill establishing an Occupational Safety and Health Agency (OSHA) to enforce health and safety standards in the workplace. And although the president was no crusader for the environment, he did support a Clean Air Act to reduce car exhaust emissions, as well as a Clean Water Act to make polluters liable for their negligence and to deal with disastrous oil spills.

## Stagflation

Ironically, a worsening economy forced Nixon to adopt liberal remedies. By 1970 the nation had entered its first recession in a decade. Traditionally a recession brought a decrease in demand for goods and a rise in unemployment as workers were laid off. Manufacturers then cut prices in order to encourage demand for their goods and cut wages in order to preserve profit margins. But in the recession of 1970, while unemployment rose as economists would have expected, wages and prices were also rising in an inflationary spiral—a condition described as "stagflation."

Unfriendly Democrats labeled the phenomenon "Nixonomics," although in truth Lyndon Johnson had brought on inflation by refusing to raise taxes to pay for the war and for Great Society social programs. In addition, wages continued their inflationary rise partly because powerful unions had negotiated automatic cost-of-living increases into their contracts. Similarly, in industries dominated by a few large corporations, like steel and oil, prices did not follow the market forces of a recession. So prices and wages continued to rise as demand and employment fell.

Mindful that his own "silent majority" were the people most pinched by the slower economy, Nixon decided that unemployment posed a greater threat than inflation. Announcing "I am now a Keynesian," he adopted a deficit budget de-

*Wage and price controls*

signed to stimulate the growth of jobs. More surprising, in August 1971 he announced that to provide short-term relief, wages and prices would be frozen for 90 days. For a Republican to advocate wage and price controls was near heresy, almost as heretical as Nixon's overtures to China. For a year federal wage and price boards enforced the ground rules for any increases until the economy grew again. Controls were lifted in January 1973. As in foreign policy, Nixon had reversed long-cherished economic policies to achieve practical results.

## "SILENT" MAJORITIES AND VOCAL MINORITIES

During the 1968 campaign Richard Nixon had noticed a placard carried by a hopeful voter: "Bring Us Together." That became his campaign theme. Yet of necessity political coalitions cannot bring everyone together. Their goal is simply to assemble a majority on Election Day. Nixon recognized quite well that in the three-way race of 1968, his 43 percent did not add up to a majority. But when Wallace's vote was added, the total came to an impressive 60 percent. If Nixon could add discontented southerners and blue-collar workers to the traditional GOP base, he could win again in 1972.

These groups resented much that the civil rights movement had done to overcome racial inequalities. To add to that resentment, the civil rights movement inspired other minorities to demand greater equality for themselves. Just as the civil rights campaign gave way to black power militancy, so too other minority activists adopted increasingly disruptive tactics to press their causes. Their new, more assertive visibility was crucial to Nixon's attempt to form his own countermajority.

### Hispanic Activism

Part of that increased visibility resulted from a new wave of immigration from Mexico and Puerto Rico after World War II and, in the case of Cubans, after the 1959 revolution that brought Castro to power. Historical, cultural, ethnic, and geographic differences among the three major Hispanic groups made it difficult to develop a common political agenda. Still, some activists did seek greater Hispanic unity.

Cesar Chavez (center left) mobilized the largely Hispanic migrant workers into the United Farm Workers Union. In 1969 a call for boycotts against grapes and lettuce gained Chavez and the union national attention.

After World War II a weak island economy and the lure of prosperity on the mainland brought more than a million Puerto Ricans into New York City.

*Puerto Rican migration*

As citizens of the United States, they could move freely to the mainland and back home again. That dual consciousness discouraged many from establishing deep roots stateside. Equally important, the newcomers were startled to discover that, whatever their status at home, on the mainland they were subject to racial discrimination and most often segregated into urban slums. In 1964 approximately half of all recent immigrants lived below the poverty level, according to the Puerto Rican Forum. Light-skinned migrants escaped those conditions by blending into the middle class as "Latin Americans." The Puerto Rican community thereby lost some of the leadership it needed to assert its political rights.

Still, during the 1960s, the urban barrios gained greater political consciousness as groups like *Aspira* adopted the strategies of civil rights activists and organizations like the Black and Puerto Rican Caucus created links with other minority groups. The Cubans who arrived in the United States after 1959—some 350,000 over the course of the decade—forged fewer ties with other Hispanics. Most settled around Miami. An unusually large number came from Cuba's professional, business, and government class and were racially white and politically conservative.

Mexican Americans, on the other hand, constituted the largest segment of the Hispanic population. Until the 1940s most were farmers and farm laborers in Texas, New Mexico, and California. But during the 1950s, the process of mechanization had affected them, just as it had black southerners. By 1969 about 85 percent of Mexican Americans had settled in cities. With urbanization came a slow improvement of the range and quality of jobs they held. A body of skilled workers, middle-class professionals, and entrepreneurs emerged.

In 1960, frustrated by years of neglect by major parties, Hispanic political leaders from the region formed the Mexican American Political Association. MAPA declared its intent to be "proudly Mexican American, openly political, and necessarily bipartisan." By 1964 four Mexican Americans had been elected to Congress, but the growing activism across the nation altered traditional Hispanic approaches to politics. Younger Mexican Americans began to call

*Cesar Chavez*

themselves Chicanos. In 1965 Cesar Chavez gained national attention by his efforts to organize migrant laborers into the United Farm Workers. He led them in *La Huelga*—The Strike—which they supported with a national boycott of California lettuce and grapes.

By the late 1960s Mexican Americans had clearly established greater ethnic consciousness. Like African Americans, Chicanos saw themselves as a people whose culture had been taken from them. Their heritage had been rejected, their labor exploited, and their opportunity for advancement denied. The new ethnic militancy led to the formation of *La Raza Unida* (The Race United). This third-party movement sought to gain power in communities in which Mexican

Americans were a majority and to extract concessions from the Democrats and Republicans. The more militant "Brown Berets" adopted the paramilitary tactics and radical rhetoric of the Black Panthers.

## The Choices of American Indians

Like African Americans and Hispanics, Indians began to protest; yet the unique situation of Native Americans (as many had begun to call themselves) set them apart from other minorities. A largely hostile white culture had in past centuries sought to either exterminate or assimilate American Indians. Ironically, the growing strength of the civil rights movement created another threat to Indian tribal identities. Liberals came to see the reservations not as oases of Indian culture but as rural ghettos. During the 1950s they joined conservatives eager to repeal the New Deal and western state politicians eyeing tribal resources to

*Termination*

adopt a policy of "termination." The Bureau of Indian Affairs would reduce federal services, gradually sell off tribal lands, and push Indians into the "mainstream" of American life. Although most full-blooded Indians objected to the policy, some people of mixed blood and Indians already assimilated into white society supported the move. The resulting relocation of approximately 35,000 Indians accelerated a shift from rural areas to cities. The urban Indian population, which had been barely 30,000 in 1940, reached more than 300,000 by the 1970s.

The social activism of the 1960s inspired Indian leaders to shape a new political agenda. In 1968 urban activists in Minneapolis created AIM, the American

*American Indian Movement*

Indian Movement. A year later similarly minded Indians living around San Francisco Bay formed Indians of All Tribes. Because the Bureau of Indian Affairs refused to address the problems of urban Indians, more militant members of the organization dramatized their dissatisfaction by seizing the abandoned federal prison on Alcatraz Island in San Francisco Bay.

The Alcatraz action inspired a national Pan-Indian rights movement. Richard Oakes, a Mohawk Indian from New York, declared that the Alcatraz protest was not "a movement to liberate the island, but to liberate ourselves."

*Occupation of Wounded Knee*

Then in 1973, AIM organizers Russell Means and Dennis Banks led a dramatic takeover of a trading post at Wounded Knee, on a Sioux reservation in South Dakota. Ever since white cavalry had gunned down over a hundred Sioux in 1890 (page 542), Wounded Knee had symbolized for Indians the betrayal of white promises and the bankruptcy of reservation policy. Even more, Wounded Knee now demonstrated the problems that Indian activists faced. When federal officers surrounded the trading post, militants discovered that other Indians did not support their tactics and were forced to leave. A Pan-Indian movement was difficult to achieve when so many tribes were determined to go their own ways, as distinct, self-regulating communities. Thus even activists who supported the Pan-Indian movement found themselves splintering. During the 1970s more than 100 different organizations were formed to unite various tribes pursuing political and legal agendas at the local, state, and federal levels.

### Gay Rights

In 1972, Black Panther leader Huey Newton observed that homosexuals "might be the most oppressed people" in American society. Certainly Newton was qualified to recognize oppression when he saw it. But by then a growing number of homosexuals had embraced liberation movements that placed them among minorities demanding equal rights.

Even during the "conformist" 1950s, gay men founded the Mattachine Society (1951) to fight antihomosexual attacks and to press for a wider public acceptance of their lifestyle. Lesbians formed a similar organization, the Daughters of Bilitis, in 1955. Beginning in the mid-1960s, more radical gay and lesbian groups began organizing to raise individual consciousness and to establish a gay culture in which they felt free. One group called for "acceptance as full equals . . . basic rights and equality as citizens; our human dignity; . . . [our] right to love whom we wish."

The movement's defining moment came on Friday, June 27, 1969, when New York police raided the Stonewall Inn, a Greenwich Village bar. Such raids

*Stonewall incident*

were common enough: gay bars were regularly harassed by the police in an attempt to control urban "vice." This time the patrons fought back, first with taunts and jeers, then with paving stones and parking meters. Increasingly, gay activists called on homosexuals to "come out of the closet" and publicly affirm their sexuality. In 1974 gays achieved a major symbolic victory when the American Psychiatric Association removed homosexuality from its list of mental disorders.

### Social Policies and the Court

Many of the blue-collar and southern Democratic voters Nixon sought to attract especially resented the use of school busing to achieve court-ordered de-

*School busing*

segregation. Fifteen years after *Brown v. Board of Education* had ruled that racially separate school systems must be desegregated, many localities still had not complied. In white neighborhoods, parents opposed having their children bused to more distant, formerly all-black schools, as part of a plan to achieve racial balance. Although black parents for their part worried about the reception their children might receive in hostile white neighborhoods, by and large they supported busing as a means to better education.

Under Nixon, federal policy on desegregation took a 180-degree turn. In 1969 when lawyers for Mississippi asked the Supreme Court to delay an integration plan, the Nixon Justice Department supported the state. The Court rejected that proposal, holding in *United States v. Jefferson County Board of Education* that all state systems, including Mississippi's, had an obligation "to terminate dual systems at once and to operate now and hereafter only unitary schools." Two years later, in *Swann v. Charlotte–Mecklenburg Board of Education* (1971), the Court further ruled that busing, balancing ratios, and redrawing school district lines were all acceptable ways to achieve integration.

To end the Court's liberal activism, Nixon looked to fill vacancies with more conservative justices. He replaced Chief Justice Earl Warren in 1969 with

*Nixon and the Court*

Warren Burger, a jurist who had no wish to break new ground. When another vacancy occurred in 1969, Nixon tried twice to appoint conservative southern judges with reputations for opposing civil rights and labor unions. Congress rejected both. In the end, Nixon chose Minnesotan Harry Blackmun, a moderate judge of unimpeachable integrity. Two additional conservative appointments guaranteed that the Court would no longer lead the fight for minority rights. But neither would it reverse the achievements of the Warren Court.

## Us versus Them

In so many of his battles, as in the struggle to shape the Supreme Court, Nixon portrayed those who opposed him as foes of traditional American values. Just as Nixon had tended to equate liberal reformers with Communist "pinkos" during the 1950s, now his administration blurred the lines between honest dissent and radical criminals. In doing so, it reflected a side of the president that tended to see issues in terms of "us against them."

With Nixon's consent (and Lyndon Johnson's before him), the FBI and intelligence agencies conducted a covert and often illegal war against dissent. Attorney General John Mitchell and his Justice Department aggressively prosecuted civil rights activists, antiwar groups like Vietnam Veterans Against the War, socially liberal members of the Catholic clergy, the Black Panthers, SDS activists, and leaders of the peace movement. In its war on the drug culture of hippies and radicals, the administration proposed a bill that would allow police to stage "no-knock" raids and use "preventive detention" to keep suspected criminals in jail without bail.

In the political arena, Nixon gave Vice President Spiro Agnew the task of mudslinging that Nixon had once performed for Eisenhower. Agnew launched an alliterative assault on the administration's adversaries. He referred to the press and television news commentators as "nattering nabobs of negativism" and "troubadours of trouble" who contributed to the "creeping permissiveness that afflicted America." In the campaign between "us" and "them," the national press corps was clearly "them," a hostile establishment slanting the news.

## Triumph

As the election of 1972 approached, Nixon's majority seemed to be falling into place, especially after the Democrats nominated Senator George McGovern of South Dakota. Under new party rules, which McGovern had helped write, the delegate selection process was opened to all party members. No longer would party bosses handpick the delegates. Minorities, women, and young people all received proportional representation. McGovern's nomination gave Nixon the split between "us" and "them" he sought. The Democratic platform embraced all the activist causes that the silent majority resented. It called for immediate withdrawal from Vietnam, abolition of the draft, amnesty for war resisters, and a minimum guaranteed income for the poor.

*George McGovern*

By November the only question that remained to be settled was the size of Nixon's majority. An unsolved burglary at the Watergate complex in Washington, D.C., while vaguely linked to the White House, had not touched the president. Nixon even captured some antiwar votes by announcing on election eve that peace in Vietnam was at hand. When the smoke cleared, only liberal Massachusetts and the heavily black District of Columbia gave McGovern a majority. Nixon received almost 61 percent of the popular vote.

An overwhelming victory did not bring peace to Richard Nixon. He still felt that he had scores to settle with his political opponents. "We have not used the power in the first four years, as you know," he remarked to Haldeman during the campaign. "We haven't used the Bureau [FBI] and we haven't used the Justice Department, but things are going to change now. And they are going to change and they're going to get it, right?" Haldeman could only agree.

### THE END OF AN ERA

Nixon was particularly frustrated because peace in Vietnam still eluded him. The North Vietnamese refused any settlement that left the South Vietnamese government. Nixon wanted to subdue the enemy through force, but he recognized that it would have been political suicide to send back American troops. Instead, he ordered North Vietnam's major port, Haiphong, mined and blockaded in May 1972, along with a sustained bombing campaign. Then on December 18 the president launched an even greater wave of attacks, as American planes dropped more bombs on the North in 12 days than they had during the entire campaign from 1969 to 1971.

Once again, Kissinger returned to Paris, hoping that the combination of threats and conciliation would bring a settlement. Ironically South Vietnamese officials had thrown up the greatest stumbling blocks, for they were rightly convinced that General Thieu's regime would not last once the United States

*Peace treaty* departed. But in January 1973 a treaty was finally arranged, smoothed by Kissinger's promise of aid to the North Vietnamese to help in postwar reconstruction. By March the last American units were home.

"The enemy must fight his battles . . . [in] protracted campaigns," wrote the Vietnamese strategist in 1284. For all concerned the American phase of the Vietnam Wars had been bloody and wearying. Between 1961 and 1973 the war claimed 57,000 American lives and left more than 300,000 wounded. The cost to Southeast Asia in lives and destruction was almost impossible to calculate. More than a million Vietnamese soldiers and perhaps half a million civilians died. Some 6.5 million South Vietnamese became refugees, along with 3 million Cambodians and Laotians.

At a frightful price in human lives and material destruction, Nixon could claim the "peace with honor" he had insisted on. But experienced observers predicted that South Vietnam's days were numbered. (Indeed they were: the Communist armies united the two Vietnams in 1975.) By any real measure of military success the Vietcong peasant guerrillas and their lightly armed North Vietnamese allies had held off—and in that sense defeated—the world's greatest military power.

Truman may have started the United States down the road to Vietnam by promoting the doctrine of containment all across the globe. Certainly Eisenhower and Kennedy increased American involvement. But fairly or not, Vietnam is remembered as Lyndon Johnson's war. He committed both the material and the human resources of the United States to defeat communism in Southeast Asia. That decision to escalate eventually destroyed the political consensus that had unified Americans since the late 1940s. And ironically, it was Richard Nixon, the ardent cold warrior, who recognized that the United States did not have the inexhaustible resources to contain communism everywhere. To end the war in Vietnam, he had to open new relations with the People's Republic of China and the Soviet Union. Where containment assumed a bipolar world, Nixon's policy of détente saw the world as multipolar.

*Vietnam in the perspective of the cold war*

Liberal dreams died with Vietnam, too. The war in Southeast Asia shattered the optimism of the early sixties: the belief that the world could be remade with the help of brilliant intellectuals and federal programs. The war also eroded the prosperity upon which the optimism of the postwar era had rested. After 1973 the economy slid into a long recession that forced Americans to recognize they had entered an era of limits both at home and abroad. Lyndon Johnson, who sought to preserve both liberal dreams and the cold war consensus, died on January 22, 1973, one day before the American war in Vietnam ended.

## SIGNIFICANT EVENTS

1945 — Ho Chi Minh unifies Vietnam

1954 — French defeat at Dien Bien Phu; Geneva accords

1963 — Diem assassinated; United States has 16,000 "advisers" in Vietnam

1964 — Tonkin Gulf incident; Tonkin Gulf Resolution

1965 — Rolling Thunder begins bombing of North Vietnam; antiwar "teach-ins" on college campuses; Cesar Chavez leads national campaign on behalf of farmworkers

1967 — March on the Pentagon; Johnson's advisers oppose war

1968 — U.S. troop levels in Vietnam peak at 536,000; Tet offensive; peace talks begin in Paris; Eugene McCarthy challenges Johnson in New Hampshire primary; Johnson withdraws from race; Martin Luther King, Jr., assassinated; Robert Kennedy enters race and is assassinated; riots at Democratic Convention in Chicago; George Wallace candidacy; Nixon wins election

1969 — Secret bombing of Cambodia; Vietnamization leads to reduction of American forces; Nixon Doctrine

1970 — U.S. troops invade Cambodia; killings at Kent State and Jackson State; antiwar march on Washington; Clean Air and Water acts; creation of OSHA; recession creates stagflation; repeal of Tonkin Gulf Resolution

1971 — Nixon adopts wage and price controls; *Swann v. Charlotte–Mecklenburg Board of Education*

1972 — Nixon trip to China; détente with Soviet Union; SALT I; Revenue Sharing Act; Watergate break-in; Nixon reelected; mining of Haiphong Harbor; Christmas bombings of North Vietnam

1973 — Vietnam peace treaty; AIM supporters occupy Wounded Knee

# CHAPTER THIRTY-TWO

# The Age of Limits

In July 1969, tens of thousands of spectators gathered at Cape Kennedy to witness the launching of *Apollo 11*, the first manned space flight to the moon. Among the crowd was a mule-cart procession led by civil rights leader Ralph Abernathy. The Reverend Abernathy had brought his Poor People's March to dramatize the problem of poverty. The *Saturn 5*'s thunderous ignition proved so awesome that it caught Abernathy up just as it did the millions of Americans who watched on television. He found himself praying for the safety of the crew. Days later, he too celebrated when astronauts Neil Armstrong and Buzz Aldrin walked across a lunar landscape.

The triumph had been epochal. And yet some uncertainty lingered over what it all meant. One scientist took comfort that after Apollo the human race could always go elsewhere, no matter how much a mess was made of the planet earth. That was no small consideration given the increasing problems of smog, water pollution, and toxic wastes. There had been some dramatic warnings. In 1967 an oil tanker spilled 100,000 tons of oil into the English Channel. Detergents used to clean up the spill left the area clean but without plant and animal life for years after.

Such dangers worried city officials in Santa Barbara, California, an outpost of paradise along the Pacific Coast. In the channel stretching between there and Los Angeles, 90 miles to the south, oil companies had drilled some 925 wells in the coastal tidelands. State efforts to impose stringent regulations on federal oil leases offshore had failed. The Department of the Interior repeatedly assured local officials they had "nothing to fear." That changed on January 28, 1969, when Union Oil Company's well A-21 blew a billow of thick crude oil into the channel. Crews quickly capped the hole, only to discover that pressure from the well had opened a fissure in the ocean floor, through which natural gas and oil were seeping to the surface. "It looked like a massive, inflamed abscess bursting with reddish-brown pus," one observer commented.

In the 11 days it took to seal the leak, more than 200,000 barrels of oil had left a slick extending some 800 miles. Tarry goo coated beaches, boats, and wildlife as far south as San Diego. "Cormorants and grebes dived into the oily swells for fish, most never to surface alive. All along the mucky shoreline, birds lay dead or dying, unable to raise their oil-soaked feathers," one reporter wrote. Detergents used to clean up the spill claimed the coast's population of limpets, abalones, lobsters, sea urchins, mussels, and clams, as well as some fish.

Santa Barbara, not *Apollo 11*, served as a portent of the coming decade. Having reached the moon, Americans discovered more pressing concerns closer to home. A political scandal spread so far that, for the first time in American history, a president was forced to resign from office. Renewed war in the Middle East sent the price of oil and gasoline skyrocketing. Pollution from factory smokestacks, poisonous pesticides, and oil spills like the one at Santa Barbara led some scientists to warn of a "drastic ecological imbalance" that threatened the health of the earth itself. Americans began to doubt that technological know-how could solve any problem or that economic growth was both inevitable and beneficial. Elliot Richardson, the Nixon administration's secretary of health, education and welfare (HEW), remarked, "We must recognize, as we have with both foreign affairs and natural resources, that resources we thought were boundless . . . are indeed severely limited."

## THE LIMITS OF REFORM

Like the space program, the reform movements of the early 1960s sprang from an optimistic faith in the perfectibility of society. But as the war in Vietnam dragged on, American society seemed to become more fragmented. And as inflation dogged the economy and unemployment grew, Americans set their sights lower. According to social observer Tom Wolfe, in the 1970s the self-obsessed "Me Generation" displaced the crusading New Left.

Some elements of the reform movement kept alive the idea of restructuring society. Environmentalists, feminists, and consumer advocates used many of the same strategies of nonviolent protest and legal maneuver that worked so effectively in the civil rights crusade. But unlike much of the radicalism of the 1960s, these movements each had long been associated with the American reform tradition. Though they often pursued radical goals, their leadership was likely to come from the political mainstream. Consumer advocates, environmentalists, and feminists all won major victories, even if they failed to achieve the transformation of society they sought.

### Consumerism

In 1965 a thin, intense young man shocked the automotive world by publishing *Unsafe at Any Speed.* The author, Ralph Nader, argued that too many automobiles were unsafe even in minor accidents. Nader's particular target was the

*Ralph Nader's Unsafe at Any Speed* Chevrolet Corvair, a rear-engined small car built by General Motors. Crash reports indicated that the Corvair sometimes rolled over in routine turns and quickly lost control when it skidded. Even more damning, Nader accused General Motors of being aware of the flaw, from its own internal engineering studies.

GM, the corporate Goliath, at first decided that rather than defend the Corvair, it would attack Nader, this countercultural David. It sent out private investigators to dig up dirt from his personal life. They discovered no hippie disguised in a suit, but the hard-working son of Lebanese immigrants, who had fulfilled the American dream. Nader had graduated from Princeton and Harvard Law School, wore his hair short, and never used drugs. And when he discovered GM's conspiracy against him, he sued.

GM's embarrassed president publicly apologized, but by then Nader was a hero and *Unsafe at Any Speed* a bestseller. In 1966 Congress passed legislation (the National Traffic and Motor Vehicle Safety Act), which *Highway Safety Act* for the first time required safety standards for cars, tires, and roads. Nader used $425,000 from his successful lawsuit to launch his Washington-based Center for the Study of Responsive Law (1969) with a staff of five lawyers and a hundred college volunteers. "Nader's Raiders," as the group became known, investigated a range of issues, including water pollution, congressional reform, fraud in old-age homes, and auto safety.

Nader's Raiders were part of a diverse consumer movement that ranged from modest reformers to radicals. The radicals viewed the free market system as deeply flawed. Only with a thorough overhaul carried out by an active, interventionist government could citizen-consumers be empowered. Nader suggested both the radicals' tone and their agenda when he called on corporations "to stop stealing, stop deceiving, stop corrupting politicians with money, stop monopolizing, stop poisoning the earth, air and water, stop selling dangerous products, stop exposing workers to cruel hazards. . . ."

More moderate reformers viewed the problem in terms of making the existing market economy more open and efficient. To be better consumers, people needed better information about unsafe toys, dangerous food additives, and defective products. These reformers also exposed unethical marketing strategies like hidden credit costs that plagued the poor. Many consumer organizations concentrated on a single issue, such as auto safety, smoking, insurance costs, or health care.

Diversity of goals broadened the movement's appeal but also fragmented support. Nader was never able to establish consumerism as a mass political movement. Its strongest supporters remained within the ranks of the upper middle classes. Then, too, a weak economy created fears that more government regulations would add to inflation. Still, the consumer movement had placed its agenda in the mainstream of political debate, and powerful consumer groups continued to represent the public interest.

## Environmentalism

The Santa Barbara oil spill was hardly the first warning that Americans were abusing the environment. As early as 1962 marine biologist Rachel Carson had warned in *Silent Spring* of the environmental damage done by the pesticide DDT. Though chemical companies tried to discredit her as a woman and an eccentric scientist, 40 state legislatures passed laws restricting DDT. Certainly, no one with a sense of irony could help but marvel that the oil-polluted Cuyahoga River running through Cleveland, Ohio, had burst into flames. Smog from auto emissions, nuclear fallout, dangerous pesticides, hazardous consumer goods, and polluted rivers were the not-so-hidden costs of a society wedded to technology and unbridled economic growth.

The environmental movement of the 1960s drew heavily on the field of ecology. Since the early twentieth century this biological science had demon-

*Barry Commoner and ecology*

strated how closely life processes throughout nature depend on one another. Barry Commoner in his book *The Closing Circle* (1971) argued that modern society courted disaster by recklessly trying to "improve on nature." American farmers, for example, had shifted from animal manures to artificial fertilizers to increase farm productivity. But the change also raised costs, left soil sterile, and poisoned nearby water sources. After laundry detergents artificially "whitened" clothes, they created foamy scum in lakes and rivers while nourishing deadly algae blooms. Industry profited in the short run, Commoner argued, but in the long run the environment was going bankrupt.

By the 1970s, environmentalists were organizing to implement what microbiologist René Dubos called a "new social ethic." They brought a lawsuit in an effort to block the building of an 800-mile oil pipeline across Alaska's fragile wilderness. In addition, they successfully lobbied in Congress to defeat a bill authorizing support for the supersonic plane, the SST, whose high-altitude flights appeared to be depleting the earth's ozone layer. Similarly, environmental groups fought a proposed jet airport that threatened south Florida's water supply and the ecology of Everglades National Park.

Even President Nixon, normally a friend of business and real estate interests, responded to the call for tougher environmental regulations. His administration banned all domestic use of DDT and supported the National Environmental Policy Act of 1969. The act required environmental impact statements for most public projects and made the government responsible for representing the public interest. Nixon also established the Environmental

*EPA established*

Protection Agency to enforce the law. Echoing Barry Commoner, he announced, "We must learn not how to master nature but how to master ourselves, our institutions, and our technology."

By the spring of 1970 a healthy environment had become a popular cause. Senator Gaylord Nelson of Wisconsin suggested a national "Earth Day" to cel-

*Earth Day*

ebrate the new consciousness. On April 22, 1970, for at least a few hours pedestrians replaced exhaust-belching cars on downtown city streets, millions of schoolchildren planted trees and picked up trash, college students demonstrated, and Congress adjourned. But at least one member of Congress recognized the movement's more radical implications: "The Establishment sees this as a great big anti-litter campaign. Wait until they find out what it really means . . . to clean up our earth."

Earth Day did not signal a consensus on an environmental ethic. President Nixon, for one, was unwilling to restrict economic development, including the oil industry's Alaskan pipeline. Despite a long series of court challenges, construction began in 1973. "We are not going to allow the environmental issue . . . to destroy the system," he announced in 1972.

Nixon's political instincts were shrewd. Conflict between social classes underlay the environmental debate. To those he courted for his silent majority, the issue came down to jobs versus the environment. "Out of work? Hungry? Eat an environmentalist," declared one bumper sticker. During the 1960s many middle Americans came to resent the veterans of the counterculture, civil rights, and antiwar movements who now found an outlet in environmental activism. But so long as pollution threatened, the environmental movement would not go away. From conservative hunters in Ducks Unlimited to mainstream nature lovers in the Wilderness Society to radical "enviro-freaks" in Earth First, numerous groups fought to save the environment.

---

## COUNTERPOINT   *Interpreting the Environmental Movement*

Because historians have often been sympathetic to the goals of environmentalists, they have tended to interpret the movement somewhat uncritically. Mainstream accounts often point out flattering continuities with the progressive movement, such as a reliance on the authority of science. Biology, for example, caused progressives to discard once-popular theories of human exceptionalism and to see nature not as a simple warehouse of useful resources but as a series of interlinking systems. In similar ways, environmentalists have relied on ecological studies to provide a more sophisticated understanding of how those systems were interacting.

Recently some historians have become more critical of environmentalism. One confessed, "Where once I saw a movement founded in science, now I see a utopian political program." He compared modern environmentalism to the temperance crusade at the turn of the century. Although temperance advocates were divided over how to attack alcohol abuse, the more extreme factions successfully promoted prohibition and the Eighteenth Amendment. It was a utopian experiment that, in the end, was doomed to fail. Similarly, some environmental reformers have called for "global schemes of economic and political control," according to this point of view. Environmentalist Paul Ehrlich's popular book *The Population Bomb* (1968), for example, warned of the dire consequences of overpopulation. Ehrlich suggested that voluntary efforts at family planning were likely to fail and that the state might have to step in to control birthrates, especially in developing nations.

The parallel between the environmentalists and the temperance reformers is instructive. Progressivism, we have seen, displayed a mix of reform and control. Its middle- and upper-middle-class advocates worried about what the unruly masses might do without the guidance of "experts." A similar tension can be seen in the environmental movement, whose professional, white-collar advocates during the 1960s and 1970s paid scant attention to the environmental problems specific to poor urban residents. Only in the 1980s did a number of new organizations focus greater attention on the effects of hazardous industrial sites on lower-class neighborhoods or the danger of pesticides to migrant workers.

## Feminism

Organized struggle for women's rights and equality in the United States began before the Civil War. Sustained political efforts had won women the vote in 1920. But the women's movement of the 1960s and 1970s began to push for equality in broader, deeper ways.

Writer Betty Friedan was one of the earliest to voice dissatisfaction with the cultural attitudes that flourished after World War II. Even though more women were entering the job market, the media routinely glorified house-wives and homemakers, while discouraging those who aspired to independent careers. In *The Feminine Mystique* (1963) Friedan identified the "problem that has no name," a dispiriting boredom or emptiness in the midst of affluent lives. "Our culture does not permit women to accept or gratify their basic need to grow and fulfill their potentialities as human beings."

The Feminine Mystique

*The Feminine Mystique* gave new life to the women's rights movement. The Commission on the Status of Women appointed by President Kennedy proposed the 1963 Equal Pay Act and helped add gender to the forms of discrimination outlawed by the 1964 Civil Rights Act. Women also assumed an important role in both the civil rights and antiwar movements. They accounted for half the students who went south for the "Freedom Summers" in 1964 and 1965.

Even women who joined the protests of the 1960s found themselves belit-tled and limited to providing menial services such as cooking and laundry. Casey Hayden, a veteran of Students for a Democratic Society and the civil rights or-ganization SNCC, told her male comrades that the "assumptions of male supe-riority are as widespread . . . and every much as crippling to the woman as the assumptions of white superiority are to the Negro."

By 1966 activist women were less willing to remain silent. Friedan joined a group of 24 women and 2 men who formed the National Organization

E Y E W I T N E S S    T O    H I S T O R Y

## Recounting the Early Days of the Feminist Movement

I remember meeting with a group of women in Missouri who, because they had come in equal numbers from the small town and from its nearby campus, seemed to be split between wives with white gloves welded to their wrists and students with boots who talked about "imperialism" and "oppression." Planning for a child care center had brought them together, but the meeting seemed hopeless until three of the booted young women began to argue among themselves about a young male professor, the leader of the radicals on campus, who accused all women unwilling to run mimeograph machines of not being sufficiently devoted to the cause. As for child care centers, he felt their effect of allowing women to compete with men for jobs was part of the "feminization" of the American male and American culture. "He sounds just like my husband," said one of the white-gloved women, "only he wants me to have bake-sales and collect door-to-door for his Republican Party."

The young women had sense enough to take it from there. What did boots or white gloves matter if they were all getting treated like servants and children? Before they broke up, they were discussing the myth of the vaginal orgasm and planning to meet every week. "Men think we're whatever it is we do for men," complained one of the housewives. "It's only by getting together with other women that we'll ever find out who we are."

Gloria Steinem, "Sisterhood," *Ms.* magazine (Spring 1972), p. 49. Reprinted by permission.

---

*National Organization for Women*

for Women (NOW). In arguing that "sexism" was much like racism, they persuaded President Johnson in 1967 to include women along with African Americans, Hispanics, and other minorities as a group covered by federal affirmative action programs.

Many social trends in American society gave women more freedom in their lives, both to work outside the home and to control their individual destinies. After 1957 the birthrate began a rapid decline; improved methods of contraception, such as the birth control pill, permitted smaller families. By 1970 more than 40 percent of all women, an unprecedented number, were employed outside the home.

The creation of *Ms.* magazine in 1972 gave feminists a means to reach a broader audience. The cover of its first issue used the image of a many-armed Hindu goddess to satirize the many roles of the modern housewife.

Education also spurred the shift from home to the job market, since higher educational levels allowed women to enter an economy oriented increasingly to white-collar service industries rather than blue-collar manufacturing.

## Equal Rights and Abortion

As its influence grew, the feminist movement translated women's grievances into a political agenda. In 1967 NOW proclaimed a "Bill of Rights" that called for maternity leave for working mothers, federally supported day-care facilities, child-care tax deductions, and equal education and job training. But feminists divided on two other issues: the passage of an Equal Rights Amendment to the Constitution and a repeal of state antiabortion laws.

At first, support seemed strong for an Equal Rights Amendment that forbade all discrimination on the basis of gender. In 1972 both the House and the Senate passed the Equal Rights Amendment (ERA) virtu-
*ERA and Roe v. Wade* ally without opposition. Within a year 28 of the necessary 38 states had approved the ERA. It seemed only a matter of time before 10 more state legislatures would complete its ratification. Many in the women's movement also applauded the Supreme Court's decision, in *Roe v. Wade* (1973), to strike down 46 state laws restricting a woman's access to abortion. In his opinion for the majority, Justice Harry Blackmun observed that a woman in the nineteenth century had "enjoyed a substantially broader right to terminate a pregnancy than she does in most states today." As legal abortion in the first three months of pregnancy became more readily available, the

rate of maternal deaths from illegal operations, especially among minorities, declined.

But the early success of the Equal Rights Amendment and the feminist triumph in *Roe v. Wade* masked underlying divisions among women's groups. *Roe v. Wade* triggered a sharp backlash from many Catholics, Protestant fundamentalists, and socially conservative women.

*Women divided*

Their opposition inspired a crusade for a "right to life" amendment to the Constitution. A similar conservative reaction breathed new life into the "STOP ERA" crusade of Phyllis Schlafly, an Illinois political organizer. Although Schlafly was a professional working woman herself, she believed that women should embrace their traditional role as homemakers subordinate to their husbands. "Every change [that the ERA] requires will deprive women of a right, benefit, or exemption that they now enjoy," she argued.

In the middle ground stood women (and a considerable number of men) who wanted to use the political system, rather than a constitutional amendment, to correct the most glaring inequalities between the sexes. Within a year after Congress passed the ERA, the National Women's Political Caucus conceded that the momentum to ratify was waning. Although Congress in 1979 extended the deadline for state legislatures to act for another three years, it became clear that the amendment would fail. Determined feminists vowed to continue the fight, but they too had discovered the limits of the 1970s.

The environmental, consumer, and feminist movements may have lost ground after the early 1970s, but that is not to say they failed. Rather, each crusade fell short in its effort to forge a consensus. There would be no sweeping new ecological consciousness, no consumer-directed economy, and no absolute gender equality. Indeed, none of the movements could ever agree on just what those ideas should mean in practice. But the advocates of reform had created new organizations, like NOW and Friends of the Earth, that became regular and active players in the political process. Within government the Environmental Protection Agency, the Federal Trade Commission, and other agencies had been given a mandate to enforce the court decisions and reform legislation. In that way these social movements had renewed the activist tradition of progressivism and the New Deal.

*The activist legacy*

## POLITICAL LIMITS: WATERGATE

To Richard Nixon, his 1972 reelection offered sweet revenge. In 49 of the 50 states he had defeated George McGovern, the candidate of liberal environmentalists, consumer advocates, feminists, and the youthful counterculture. Yet while Nixon sought to stem the liberal tide, he continued to concentrate federal power away from Congress and the Court and more in an "imperial presidency." That trend had been under way since the early twentieth century, but the cold war with its sense of ongoing crisis had accelerated the shift.

## The President's Enemies

Encouraged by his victory, Nixon determined to use the power of his office even more broadly. The president wanted to destroy the radical counterculture that he saw as a menace to American society. Members of his staff began compiling an "enemies list"—including everyone from CBS correspondent Daniel Schorr to actress and antiwar activist Jane Fonda. Some on the list were targeted for audits by the Internal Revenue Service or similar harassment.

Then in June 1971 the *New York Times* published a secret, often highly critical military study of the Vietnam War, soon dubbed the Pentagon Papers. Nixon was so irate he authorized his aide John Ehrlichman to organize a team known as "the plumbers" to find and plug security leaks. The government prosecuted Daniel Ellsberg, the disillusioned official who had leaked the Pentagon Papers. The plumbers also went outside the law: they illegally burglarized the office of Ellsberg's psychiatrist in hopes of finding personally damaging material.

*The plumbers*

When Congress passed a number of programs Nixon opposed, he simply refused to spend the appropriated money. Some members of Congress claimed that the practice, called impoundment, violated the president's constitutional duty to execute the laws of the land. By 1973 Nixon had used impoundment to cut some $15 billion out of more than 100 federal programs. The courts eventually ruled that impoundment was illegal. But the president continued his campaign to consolidate power and reshape the more liberal social policies of Congress to his own liking.

*Impoundment*

Conviction of the need for firm action in a crisis, suspicion of his "enemies" —such traits made it easier for Richard Nixon to break or bend the rules in the service of what he believed was a good cause. In the end, his refusal to acknowledge the limits of power brought him down.

## Break-In

Nixon's fall began with what seemed a minor event. In June 1972 burglars entered the Democratic National Committee headquarters, located in Washington's plush Watergate apartment complex. The *Washington Post* assigned this routine story to a couple of cub reporters, Bob Woodward and Carl Bernstein. But the five burglars proved an unusual lot. They wore business suits, carried walkie-talkies as well as bugging devices and tear-gas guns, and had more than $2000 in crisp new hundred-dollar bills. One of the burglars had worked for the CIA. Another was carrying an address book whose phone numbers included that of a Howard Hunt at the "W. House."

Woodward and Bernstein sensed that this was no simple break-in. When Woodward called the mysterious "W. House" number, he discovered that Hunt

*A "third rate burglary"* was indeed a White House consultant. Nixon's press secretary dismissed the break-in as "a third rate burglary attempt" and warned that "certain elements may try to stretch this beyond what it is." In August, Nixon himself announced that after a thorough investigation, White House counsel John Dean had concluded that "no one on the White House staff . . . was involved in this very bizarre incident. What really hurts in matters of this sort is not the fact that they occur," the president continued. "What really hurts is if you try to cover up."

Matters were not so easily settled, however. Woodward and Bernstein traced some of the burglars' money back to the Nixon reelection campaign, which had a secret "slush fund" to pay for projects to harass the Democrats. The dirty tricks included forged letters, false news leaks, and spying on Democratic campaign workers. But by election time, Woodward and Bernstein had run out of fresh leads.

## To the Oval Office

In January 1973 the five burglars plus former White House aides E. Howard Hunt, Jr., and G. Gordon Liddy went on trial before Judge John Sirica. Sirica, a no-nonsense judge tagged with the nickname "Maximum John," was not satisfied with the defendants' guilty plea. He wanted to know whether anyone else had directed the burglars and why "these hundred dollar bills were floating around like coupons."

Facing a stiff jail sentence, one of the Watergate burglars cracked. He admitted that other government officials had been involved, that the defendants had been bribed to plead guilty, and that they had perjured themselves. The White House then announced on April 17 that all previous administration statements on the Watergate scandal had become "inoperative." Soon after, the president accepted the resignations of his two closest aides, H. R. Haldeman and John Ehrlichman. He also fired John Dean, his White House counsel, after Dean agreed to cooperate with prosecutors.

Over the summer of 1973 a string of administration officials testified at televised Senate hearings. Each witness took the trail of the burglary and its *Senate hearings* cover-up higher into White House circles. Then White House counsel John Dean gave his testimony. Young, with a Boy Scout's face, Dean declared in a quiet monotone that the president had personally been involved in the cover-up as recently as April. The testimony stunned the nation. Still, it remained Dean's word against the president's—until Senate committee staff discovered, almost by chance, that since 1970 Nixon had been secretly recording all conversations and phone calls in the Oval Office. The reliability of Dean's testimony was no longer central, for the tapes could tell all.

Obtaining that evidence proved no easy task. In an effort to restore confidence in the White House, Nixon agreed to the appointment of a special

*Special prosecutor*

prosecutor, Harvard law professor Archibald Cox, to investigate the new Watergate disclosures. When Cox subpoenaed the tapes, the president refused to turn them over, citing executive privilege and matters of national security. The courts, however, overruled this position.

As that battle raged and the astonished public wondered if matters could possibly get worse, they did. Evidence unrelated to Watergate revealed that Vice President Spiro Agnew had systematically solicited bribes, not just as governor of Maryland but while serving in Washington. To avoid jail, he agreed to resign the vice presidency in October and to plead no contest to a single charge of federal income tax evasion. Under provisions of the Twenty-Fifth Amendment, Nixon appointed Representative Gerald R. Ford of Michigan to replace Agnew.

Meanwhile, when Special Prosecutor Cox demanded the tapes, the president offered to submit written summaries instead. Cox no longer had any reason to trust the president and rejected the offer. On Saturday night, October 20, Nixon ordered Attorney General Elliot Richardson to fire Cox. Rather than comply, Richardson and his deputy secretary both resigned, leaving the third in

*"Saturday Night Massacre"*

command to do the dirty work. Reaction to the "Saturday Night Massacre" was overwhelming: 150,000 telegrams poured into Washington, and by the following Tuesday, 84 House members had sponsored 16 different bills of impeachment. The beleaguered president agreed to hand over the tapes. And he appointed Texas lawyer Leon Jaworski as a new special prosecutor. By April 1974, Jaworski's investigations led him to request additional tapes. Again the president refused, although he grudgingly supplied some 1200 pages of typed transcripts of the tapes.

Even the transcripts damaged the president's case. Littered with cynicism and profanity, they revealed Nixon talking with his counsel John Dean about how to "take care of the jackasses who are in jail." When Dean estimated it might take a million dollars to shut them up, Nixon replied, "We could get that. . . . You could get a million dollars. And you could get it in cash. I know where it could be gotten." When the matter of perjury came up, Nixon suggested a way out: "You can say, 'I don't remember.' You can say, 'I can't recall.'"

Even those devastating revelations did not produce the "smoking gun" demanded by the president's defenders. When Special Prosecutor Jaworski peti-

*United States v. Nixon*

tioned the Supreme Court to order release of additional tapes, the Court in *United States v. Nixon* ruled unanimously in Jaworski's favor.

## Resignation

The end came quickly. The House Judiciary Committee adopted three articles of impeachment, charging that Nixon had obstructed justice, had abused his constitutional authority in improperly using federal agencies to harass citizens, and had hindered the committee's investigation.

The tapes produced the smoking gun. Conversations with Haldeman on June 23, 1972, only a few days after the break-in, showed that Nixon knew the

*The smoking gun*

burglars were tied to the White House staff and knew that his attorney general had acted to limit an FBI investigation. Not willing to be the first president convicted in a Senate impeachment trial, Nixon resigned on August 8, 1974. The following day Gerald Ford became president. "The Constitution works," Ford told a relieved nation. "Our long national nightmare is over."

Had the system worked? In one sense, yes. The wheels of justice had turned, even if slowly. For the first time a president had been forced to leave office. Four cabinet officers, including Attorney General John Mitchell, the highest law officer in the nation, were convicted of crimes. Twenty-five Nixon aides eventually served prison terms ranging from 25 days to more than 4 years. Yet the corrupt compaign practices that financed Watergate continue to plague the political system. The system works, as the Founding Fathers understood, only when citizens and public servants respect the limits of government power.

## A FORD, NOT A LINCOLN

Gerald Ford inherited a presidential office badly diminished by the Watergate scandals. As the first unelected president, he had no popular mandate. He was little known outside Washington and his home district around Grand Rapids, Michigan. Ford's success as the House minority leader came from personal popularity, political reliability, and party loyalty, qualities that suited a member of Congress better than an unelected president.

Yet Ford's easy manner and modest approach to government came as a relief after the mercurial styles of Johnson and Nixon. By all instincts a conservative, Ford was determined to continue Nixon's foreign policy of cautious détente and a domestic program of social and fiscal conservatism.

### Kissinger and Foreign Policy

As Nixon's star fell, that of Secretary of State and National Security Advisor Henry Kissinger rose. Kissinger viewed himself as a realist, a man for whom order and stability were more important than principle. Quoting the German writer Goethe, he acknowledged, "If I had to choose between justice and disorder, on the one hand, and injustice and order on the other, I would always choose the latter."

Kissinger had struggled to prevent Vietnam and Watergate from eroding the president's power to conduct foreign policy. He believed Congress was too

*War Powers Act*

sensitive to public opinion and special-interest groups to pursue consistent long-term policies. But after Vietnam congressional leaders were eager to curtail presidential powers. The War Powers Act of 1973 required the president to consult Congress whenever possible before committing troops, to send an explanation for his actions within 2 days, and to withdraw any troops after 60 days unless Congress voted to retain them. Such limits often led Kissinger to take a covert approach to foreign policy, as he did in an attempt to quell political ferment in Chile.

In 1970 Chile ranked as one of South America's few viable democracies. When a coalition of Socialists, Communists, and radicals elected Salvador

*Overthrow of Allende*

Allende Gossens as president that year, the Central Intelligence Agency viewed his victory as dangerous to the United States. To drive Allende from power, Kissinger resorted to economic pressure, bribery of the Chilean congress, and the encouragement of a military coup. By 1973 a conservative Chilean coalition with CIA backing had driven the Socialists from power, attacked the presidential palace, and murdered Allende. Kissinger argued that the United States had the right to destroy this democracy because Communists themselves threatened an even longer-term dictatorship.

## Economic Limits and American Diplomacy

Kissinger recognized that a weakening economy limited American ability to dominate the affairs of the non-Communist world. That weakness came not merely from the soaring inflation generated by the Vietnam War and Johnson's Great Society programs. Key American industries were crippled by inefficient production, products of poor quality, and high wages. They faced mounting competition from more efficient manufacturers in Europe and in nations along the Pacific rim, such as Japan, South Korea, and Taiwan. Reacting to these changes, American-based multinational corporations moved high-wage jobs overseas to take advantage of lower costs and cheap labor. The AFL–CIO complained that the United States would soon become "a country stripped of industrial capacity . . . , a nation of citizens busily buying and selling cheeseburgers and root beer floats."

War in the Middle East soon made inflation at home even worse. On October 6, 1973, Syria and Egypt launched a devastating surprise attack against

*Yom Kippur War and the energy crisis*

Israel, on the Jewish holy day of Yom Kippur. The Soviet Union airlifted supplies to the Arabs; the United States countered by resupplying its Israeli allies while pressing the two sides to accept a cease-fire. The seven Arab members of the Organization of Petroleum Exporting Countries (OPEC) imposed a boycott of oil sales to countries seen as friendly to Israel. Lasting from October 1973 until March 1974, the boycott staggered the economies of Western Europe and Japan, which imported 80 to 90 percent of their oil from the Middle East.

The United States, too, was far more dependent on foreign oil than most Americans had appreciated. With just 7 percent of the world's population, the United States consumed about 30 percent of its energy. In November 1973

President Nixon warned the nation, "We are heading toward the most acute shortage of energy since World War II." Americans felt the crunch in every aspect of their lives. In some places motorists hoping to buy a few gallons of gas waited for hours in lines miles long.

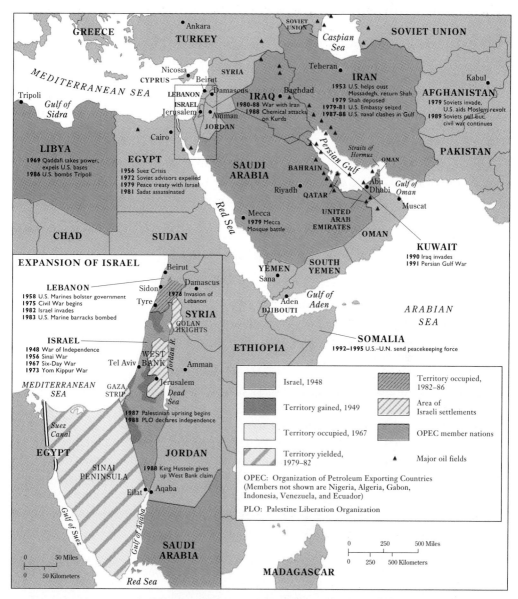

OIL AND CONFLICT IN THE MIDDLE EAST, 1948–1995   With so much of the world's oil supply coming from the Middle East, political stability in the region is vital to the health of the global economy. Yet the conflict between Israel and the Arab states, the regional political unrest, and the cold war rivalry after World War II have all contributed to the area's chronic instability.

Kissinger sought economic relief at home by promoting stability in the Middle East. If the Arab states saw the United States as neutral in their conflict with Israel, they would be less likely to resort to future oil blackmail. And as American prestige rose, Kissinger could move to reduce Soviet influence in the region. Egypt's President Anwar Sadat had recently expelled 10,000 Russian advisers from his country. From January to April 1974 Kissinger intermittently flew back and forth in "shuttle diplomacy" between Sadat's government in Cairo and the Israeli government in Jerusalem. He persuaded Israel to withdraw its troops from the west bank of the Suez Canal and arranged a disengagement between Israel and Syria in the Golan Heights.

Still, Kissinger's whirlwind efforts could not stem the erosion of American power. By the spring of 1975, the American-backed government in South

*South Vietnam falls*

Vietnam faced certain defeat at the hands of North Vietnam. President Ford asked Congress for $1 billion in aid to South Vietnam, Cambodia, and Laos, but Congress refused to spend money on a lost cause. As North Vietnamese forces marched into Saigon in April, desperate South Vietnamese civilian and military leaders rushed to escape Communist retribution.

## Détente

Vietnam, Chile, the Yom Kippur War, and other crises demonstrated that the spirit of détente had not ended the rivalry between the Soviets and the Americans to win influence in the Third World. Seeking to ease tensions, Ford met with Soviet leader Leonid Brezhnev in November 1974. Since economic stagnation also dogged the Soviet Union, Brezhnev came to this summit, in Vladivostok, eager for more American trade. Ford and Kissinger wanted a limit on nuclear weapons that preserved the current American advantage. Though many issues could not be resolved, the two sides agreed in principle to a framework for a second Strategic Arms Limitation Treaty.

A similar hope to extend détente brought Ford and Brezhnev together with European leaders at Helsinki, Finland, in August 1975. There they agreed to rec-

*Helsinki summit*

ognize the political boundaries that had divided Eastern and Western Europe since 1945. For the first time the United States sent an ambassador to East Germany. In return Brezhnev eased restrictions on the rights of Soviet Jews to emigrate.

## The Limits of a Post-Watergate President

After only a month in office Gerald Ford granted Richard Nixon a pardon for any crimes he had committed during Watergate. That attempt to put the scandals in the past only managed to reopen the wounds. Pardon meant no prosecution of the former president, leaving charges unanswered and crimes unpun-

After having won a Nobel Peace Prize in 1973 for his role in ending the Vietnam War, Henry Kissinger (left) entered the Ford administration as something of a hero. But his efforts to improve relations with the Soviet Union by strengthening détente aroused the ire of the Republican right wing, while liberals accused Kissinger of being too secretive and friendly to dictators. Here, he briefs President Ford on a train, on the way to a 1974 summit meeting in Vladivostok in the Soviet Union.

ished. The move was especially controversial because at the same time, Ford refused to provide any similar full pardon to draft resisters from the Vietnam War. (He did offer a conditional amnesty, but only after review by a government panel. Most resisters rejected the offer.)

If Ford was willing to forgive and forget presidential sins, Congress was not, especially after reports surfaced of misconduct by the nation's intelligence agen-

*Intelligence abuses*

cies. Investigations revealed that the CIA had routinely violated its charter by spying on American citizens at home. It had opened private mail, infiltrated domestic protest organizations—even conducted experiments on unwitting subjects using the hallucinogenic drug LSD. Abroad, the CIA had been involved in the assassination or attempted murder of foreign leaders in Cuba, Chile, South Vietnam, the Dominican Republic, and the Congo. The FBI had also used illegal means to infiltrate and disrupt domestic dissidents, including an attempt by J. Edgar Hoover to drive Martin Luther King to suicide. In an effort to bring the executive branch under control, the Senate created an oversight committee to monitor the intelligence agencies.

## Fighting Inflation

By the time Ford gave Congress his first State of the Union message in January 1975, he faced twin scourges: inflation and recession. Inflation had climbed to almost 14 percent, and unemployment exceeded 7 percent. At the heart of the economic crisis lay rising energy costs. Imports of Middle Eastern oil were needed to supply the nation's increasing thirst for energy. The price of that oil had jumped from $2 to almost $14 a barrel.

*Recession*

The 1975 Energy Policy and Conservation Act authorized the Federal Energy Administration to order utilities to burn abundant (though more polluting) coal rather than expensive oil. In addition, the act ordered the auto industry to improve the energy efficiency of the engines it produced. And as a final—but environmentally dangerous—stopgap measure, the government encouraged the rapid development of nuclear power plants.

*Energy policy*

The energy-driven recession struck hardest at the older industrial centers of the Northeast and Upper Midwest, which imported most of their energy. Housing and plants built in the days of cheap energy proved wasteful and inefficient. Nixon's and Ford's cutbacks in federal spending fell hardest on major cities with shrinking tax bases, outmoded industries, and heavy social service costs. The crisis for "rust belt" cities came to a head in October 1975, when New York City announced that it faced bankruptcy. New York's plight reflected the wrenching adjustments Americans faced in an era of economic limits.

## The Election of 1976

In the 1976 presidential campaign the greatest debates occurred within rather than between the major parties. Ford's challenge came from former California governor, movie actor, and television pitchman Ronald Reagan. The polished Reagan won crowds with an uncompromising but amiable conservatism, and Ford barely squeaked by Reagan to win the nomination.

Before 1976 few Democrats had ever heard of presidential hopeful James Earl (Jimmy) Carter. That allowed Carter, a peanut farmer and former governor of Georgia, to run as a Washington outsider, an advantage after the Watergate scandals. As a southerner and a born-again Christian he appealed to many voters who had recently left the Democratic party.

Since both candidates rejected Great Society activism, party loyalty determined the outcome. Most voters backed their party's candidate, giving Carter 50.1 percent of the vote. Carter's overwhelming margin among African Americans (90 percent) carried the South and offset Ford's margin among white voters, especially in the western states. Resounding Democratic majorities in Congress indicated more accurately than the presidential race how much the weak economy had hurt Ford's campaign.

*Jimmy Carter*

## JIMMY CARTER: RESTORING THE FAITH

Jimmy Carter looked to invest the White House with a new simplicity and directness. Rather than the usual Inauguration Day ride down Pennsylvania Avenue in the presidential limousine, the new president and his wife Rosalynn walked. He shunned the formal morning coat and tails for a business suit. But Congress too was determined to see that the executive branch would no longer be so imperial. Because the president and many of his staff were relative newcomers, Carter found his program stymied by Washington's special-interest politics.

### The Search for Direction

Carter struggled, often unsuccessfully, to give his presidency a clear sense of direction. Although the president was able to absorb tremendous amounts of information, too often he focused on details. That left his larger goals obscure. Carter's key appointments reflected this confusion. In foreign policy, for

The support of African Americans proved critical to Carter's victory in 1976. Here he and his wife Rosalynn worship with Coretta Scott King, Andrew Young, and other black leaders.

example, a rivalry arose between National Security Advisor Zbigniew Brzezinski and Secretary of State Cyrus Vance. Brzezinski harbored the staunch cold warrior's preoccupation with containing the Communist menace. Vance believed negotiations with the Communist bloc were both possible and potentially profitable. Stronger economic ties would reduce the risk of superpower conflict. Carter gravitated in both directions.

The President found that it was no easy task to make government more efficient, responsive to the people, and ethical. His first push for efficiency—a call for the elimination of 19 expensive pork-barrel water projects—angered many in Congress, including the leaders of his own party. They promptly threatened to bury his legislative program. Even the weather seemed to conspire against Carter, when the winter of 1976–1977 proved to be one of the most severe in modern history. Supplies of heating fuels dwindled, and prices shot up. Like Ford, Carter preferred voluntary restraint to mandatory rules for conserving energy and controlling fuel costs. The nation had to adopt energy conservation measures as the "moral equivalent of war," he announced in April 1977.

The President correctly sensed that conservation was the cheapest, most practical way to reduce dependence on foreign oil. But homilies about "helping our neighbors" did not persuade Congress. Most controversial were new taxes to discourage wasteful consumption. The American way, as domestic oil pro-

*Department of Energy*

ducers were quick to argue, was to produce more, not to live with less. Most Americans were too wedded to gas-guzzling cars, air conditioners, and warm houses to accept limits as long as fuel was available. Although Congress did agree to establish a cabinet-level Department of Energy, it rejected most of Carter's energy program.

By 1978 the "moral equivalent of war" was sounding more like its acronym: MEOW. Renewed administration efforts resulted in a weak National Energy Act of modest tax incentives and deregulation of natural gas prices. As a result, the nation was ill-prepared for the dislocation in international oil markets that followed the 1978 revolution against the shah of Iran. Oil shortages allowed OPEC to raise prices nearly 15 percent. Carter could only complain that such hikes were unfair while asking Americans to lower thermostats to 65 degrees, take only essential car trips, and "drive 55."

Many Americans saw nuclear energy as the best alternative. But on March 28, 1979, a valve stuck in the cooling system of the Three Mile Island nuclear

*Three Mile Island*

power plant near Harrisburg, Pennsylvania. A cloud of radioactive gas floated into the atmosphere, and for a time, officials worried that the plant's nuclear fuels might overheat, causing a meltdown of the reactor core. About 100,000 nearby residents fled their homes. The debate that followed revealed that public utilities had often constructed nuclear power plants before installing adequate safeguards or solving the problem of where to dispose of the nuclear radioactive wastes produced by the plants. By the time of the accident at Three Mile Island, many energy experts believed that nuclear plants were at best a temporary response to the nation's long-term needs.

## A Sick Economy

Long lines at the gas pumps were a symbol of a sick economy built on cheap energy. As OPEC hiked prices inflation shot from just below 6 percent in 1976 to almost 14 percent by 1979. Other factors also helped drive up the price of goods and services, including higher minimum wages, import protection for key industries like steel, and new social security taxes. So too did declines in the productivity of American labor, where output for each workhour kept dropping. And as productivity dropped, so did the competitiveness of American industry in world markets.

"Hard choices" were needed to restore the economy to health, the *Wall Street Journal* argued. That might mean higher taxes and cuts in popular programs like social security or subsidy payments to farmers. Yet Carter called only for voluntary restraints on prices and wages, while seeking to restore the strength of the dollar in international trade. But even before the president's economic remedies could be tried, OPEC raised the price of oil again. Energy costs rose almost 60 percent. Interest rates shot up to almost 20 percent. Such high rates struck hard at American consumers addicted to buying on credit. Mortgage money disappeared. With the Federal Reserve raising interest rates to dampen inflation, the recession grew worse. As the economy slumped, so did Carter's political future. At the same time he found himself bedeviled by crises abroad.

## Leadership, Not Hegemony

Carter approached foreign policy with a set of ambitious, yet reasonable, goals. Like Nixon and Kissinger, he accepted the fact that in a postcolonial world, American influence could not be heavy-handed. The United States had to exert "leadership without hegemony." Unlike Nixon and Kissinger, Carter believed that a knee-jerk fear of Soviet ambition had led Americans to support too many right-wing dictators, simply because they claimed to be anti-Communist. Carter reasserted the nation's moral purpose by giving a higher priority to preserving human rights.

*Human rights*

Though this policy was often jeered at by foreign policy "realists," it did make a difference. At least one Argentinian Nobel Peace Prize winner, Adolfo Pérez Esquivel, claimed he owed his life to it. So did hundreds of others in countries like the Philippines, South Korea, Argentina, and Chile, where dissidents were routinely tortured and murdered. The Carter administration exerted economic pressures to promote more humane policies.

Debate over American influence in the Third World soon focused on the Panama Canal, long a symbol of American intervention in Latin America. Most Americans were under the impression that the United States owned the canal—or if it didn't, at least deserved to. Senator S. I. Hayakawa of California spoke for defenders of the American imperial tradition when he argued, "It's ours. We stole it fair and square." In reality the

*Panama Canal*

United States held sovereignty over a 10-mile-wide strip called the Canal Zone and administered the canal under a perpetual lease. Since the 1960s Panamanians had resented, and sometimes rioted against, the American presence. Secretary of State Vance believed conciliation would reduce anti-American sentiment in the region. He convinced Carter in 1977 to sign treaties that would return the canal to Panama by 1999. The United States did reserve the right to defend and use the waterway.

From 1979 on, however, it was not Vance but National Security Advisor Zbigniew Brzezinski who dominated the administration's foreign policy.

*Brzezinski in charge*

Brzezinski preferred a hard-line anti-Communist approach, even in Latin America. Unrest troubled all the region's struggling nations, especially Nicaragua. Its dictator, Anastasio Somoza, proved so corrupt and greedy that he alienated the normally conservative propertied classes. The United States, at Brzezinski's urging, continued to support Somoza, but with cooperation from Nicaragua's business leaders, the Sandinistas toppled him. They then rejected American aid in favor of a nonaligned status and closer ties to Cuba. Hard-line American anti-Communists grew especially alarmed when the Sandinistas began supplying leftist rebels in neighboring El Salvador. To contain the threat, Carter agreed to assist the brutal right-wing dictatorship in El Salvador while encouraging the overthrow of the leftist government in Nicaragua.

## Saving Détente

The United States was not the only superpower with a flagging economy and problems in the Third World. The Soviet Union struggled with an aging leadership and an economy that produced guns but little butter. Even though the Russians led the world in oil production, income from rising oil prices was drained off by an inefficient economy. Support for impoverished allies in Eastern Europe, Cuba, and Vietnam and attempts to extend Soviet influence in the Middle East and Africa proved costly.

Economic weakness made the Soviets receptive to greater cooperation with the United States. In that spirit President Carter and Soviet premier Leonid Brezhnev in 1977 issued a joint statement on a Middle East peace. But domestic opposition to any Soviet role as a peacemaker in the Middle East was immediate and powerful. Carter quickly rendered his understanding with Brezhnev inoperative.

*A revived China card*

tive. The Soviets then renewed arms shipments to Israel's archenemy, Syria. And in that troubled environment, Zbigniew Brzezinski flew off to Beijing to revive the "China card": Kissinger's old hope of playing the two Communist superpowers against each other. The United States extended formal recognition to China in 1979, and trade doubled within a year.

For the Russians the China card was a blow to détente. A potential Japanese–Chinese–American alliance threatened their Asian border. In an attempt to save détente Brezhnev met Carter at Vienna in 1979. Following through on the summit with President Ford, their talks produced an arms con-

*SALT II*

trol treaty—SALT II—to limit nuclear launchers and missiles with multiple warheads (MIRVs). But neither the Americans nor the Soviets would agree to scrap key weapons systems. Conservative critics saw the SALT agreements as another example of the bankruptcy of détente. Nuclear "parity" (an equal balance of weapons on the American and the Soviet sides) was to them yet another insulting symbol of declining American power. They successfully blocked ratification of the treaty in the Senate.

Such hostility to détente caused Carter to adopt Brzezinski's harder line. Confrontation and a military buildup replaced the Vance policy of negotiation and accommodation. The president expanded the defense budget, built American bases in the Persian Gulf region, and sent aid to anti-Communist dictators whatever their record on human rights. The Soviet Union responded with similar hostility.

## The Middle East: Hope and Hostages

What the unstable Balkans were to Europe before World War I, the Middle East promised to be for the superpowers in the 1970s and 1980s. Oil and the Soviets' nearby southern border gave the area its geopolitical importance. The United States had strong ties to oil-rich Saudi Arabia, a commitment to the survival of Israel, and a determination to prevent the Soviet Union from extending its influence into the area. That commitment was tested each time war broke out between Israel and its Arab neighbors in 1948, 1956, 1967, and 1973.

Preservation of the peace was one key to American policy. As a result, Americans were greatly encouraged when President Anwar Sadat of Egypt

*Camp David accords*

made an unprecedented trip to Israel to meet with Prime Minister Menachem Begin. To encourage the peace process, Carter invited Begin and Sadat to Camp David in September 1978. After 13 difficult days of heated debate, Carter brought the two archrivals to an agreement. Israel agreed to withdraw from the Sinai peninsula, which it had occupied since defeating Egypt in 1967; Carter compensated Israel by offering $3 billion in military aid. Begin and Sadat shared a Nobel Peace Prize that might just as fairly have gone to Carter.

The shah of Iran, with his American-equipped military forces, was another key to American hopes for stability in the Middle East. A strong Iran, after all,

*The Iranian Revolution*

blocked Soviet access to the Persian Gulf and its oil. But in the autumn of 1978, the shah's regime was challenged by Iranian Islamic fundamentalists. They objected to the Western influences flooding their country, especially the tens of thousands of American advisers. Brzezinski urged Carter to support the shah with troops if necessary; Vance recommended meetings with the revolutionary leaders, distance from the shah, and military restraint.

Carter waffled between the two approaches. He encouraged the shah to use force but refused any American participation. When the shah's regime collapsed

Jimmy Carter brought together Israeli Prime Minister Menachem
Begin (right) and Egypt's Anwar Sadat (left). Together at Camp David
they hammered out a "Framework for Peace in the Middle East."

in February 1979, fundamentalists established an Islamic republic, led by a religious leader, the Ayatollah Ruhollah Khomeini. The new government was particularly outraged when Carter admitted the ailing shah to the United States for
cancer treatment. In November student revolutionaries stormed the American
embassy in Teheran, occupying it and taking 53 hostages. In the face of this
insult the United States seemed helpless to act. Would Muslim Shiite fundamentalists spread their revolution to neighboring Arab states? Worse yet, would
the Soviets prey upon a weakened Iran?

In fact, the Soviets were equally worried that religious zeal might spread to
their own restless minorities, especially to Muslims within their borders. In

*U.S.S.R.
invasion of
Afghanistan*

December 1979 Leonid Brezhnev ordered Soviet troops to
subdue anti-Communist Muslim guerrillas in neighboring Afghanistan. President Carter condemned the invasion, but the actions he took to protest were largely symbolic, especially the decision to withdraw the American team from the 1980 Olympic games in Moscow.
And he announced a Carter Doctrine: the United States would intervene unilat-
erally if the Soviet Union threatened American interests in the Persian Gulf.

### A President Held Hostage

Even more than the 53 Americans in Teheran, the president himself seemed to
have been taken hostage by events. His ratings in national polls sank to record
lows (77 percent negative). Carter responded by reviving the cold war rhetoric

of the 1950s and accelerating the development of nuclear weapons. But where the CIA in 1953 had successfully overthrown an Iranian government, an airborne rescue mission launched in 1980 ended in disaster. Eight Marines died when two helicopters and a plane collided in Iran's central desert. Cyrus Vance, a lonely voice of moderation, finally resigned.

By 1980 the United States was mired in what Carter himself described as "a crisis of confidence." Turmoil in Vietnam, Central America, and the Middle

*Crisis of confidence*

East produced a nightmare of waning American power. Economic dislocations at home revived fears of a depression. None of these problems had begun with Jimmy Carter. The inflationary cycle and declining American productivity had their roots in the Vietnam era. And ironically, America's declining influence abroad reflected long-term success in bringing economic growth to Europe and the Pacific rim.

In that sense, Carter's failure was largely symbolic. But the uneasiness of the late 1970s reflected a widespread disillusionment with liberal social programs, and even with pragmatic "engineers" like Carter. Had the government become a drag on the American dream? Tom Wolfe's "Me Generation" seemed to be rejecting Carter's appeals to sacrifice. It turned instead to promoters of self-help therapy, fundamentalist defenders of the faith, and staunch conservatives who promised both spiritual and material renewal for the 1980s.

## SIGNIFICANT EVENTS

1962 ┼ Rachel Carson's *Silent Spring* published

1965 ┼ Ralph Nader's *Unsafe at Any Speed* published

1966 ┼ National Traffic and Motor Vehicle Safety Act; NOW established

1969 ┼ *Apollo 11* moon mission; Santa Barbara oil spill; National Environmental Policy Act

1970 ┼ First Earth Day; Environmental Protection Agency created

1971 ┼ Barry Commoner's *The Closing Circle* published; *Pentagon Papers* published

1972 ┼ Congress passes Equal Rights Amendment; Woodward and Bernstein investigate Watergate burglary

1973 ┼ *Roe v. Wade*; Senate hearings on Watergate; Spiro Agnew resigns; Saturday Night Massacre; OPEC oil boycott triggers U.S. recession

1974 ┼ *United States v. Nixon*; House adopts articles of impeachment; Nixon resigns; Ford becomes president; Kissinger Arab–Israeli "shuttle diplomacy"; Ford pardons Nixon; CIA and FBI abuses exposed

1975 ┼ Thieu government falls in South Vietnam; Helsinki summit; Energy Policy and Conservation Act; New York City faces bankruptcy

1976 ┼ Carter elected president

1977 ┼ Department of Energy established; Panama Canal treaties signed

1978 ┼ Revolution in Iran; Camp David meetings on the Middle East

1979 ┼ Three Mile Island crisis; United States recognizes People's Republic of China; SALT II agreement; Iran hostage crisis; Soviet Union invades Afghanistan

1980 ┼ Inflation and recession hurt economy; Carter adopts sanctions against the Soviet Union; U.S. hostage mission fails

1982 ┼ Ratification of ERA fails

# CHAPTER THIRTY-THREE

# A Nation Still Divisible

In the early 1970s San Diego city officials looked out at a downtown that was growing seedier each year, as stores and shoppers fled to more than a dozen suburban malls that ringed the city. Nor was San Diego's experience unusual. Across the nation many downtown retail centers were disintegrating, becoming virtual ghost towns at the close of the business day. But San Diego found a way to bounce back. The city launched a $3 billion redevelopment plan, calling for a convention center, a marina, hotels, and apartment complexes.

At the core of the plan was Horton Plaza, an ambitious mall designed to look like a quaint Italian hill town. When it opened in 1985, its stucco facades and Renaissance arches lured customers to upscale stores like Banana Republic, prosperous jewelers, and leisure sporting goods shops. Jugglers and clowns wandered the mall's twisting thoroughfares, while guitarists serenaded passersby. Horton Plaza soon ranked just behind the zoo and Sea World as San Diego's prime tourist attractions.

For all its extravagance, Horton Plaza was hardly an innovation. The first enclosed mall, Southdale Center, had been completed nearly 20 years earlier in Edina, Minnesota, near Minneapolis. With chilling winters and 100 days a year of rain, shopping conditions in Edina were hardly ideal. Southdale provided an alternative: a climate-controlled marketplace where shoppers could browse or get a bite to eat without dodging cars or inhaling exhaust fumes. At first, retailers had worried that customers who couldn't drive by or park in front of their stores wouldn't stop and shop. But the success of the new malls quickly dispelled such fears. By 1985, when Horton Plaza opened, Minnesota's Southdale had expanded to a three-level complex with 144 stores. Nationwide, there were more shopping centers (25,000) than either school districts or hospitals.

With their soaring atriums and splashing fountains, malls became for consumers the cathedrals of American material culture. Shopping on Sunday rivaled churchgoing as the weekly family ritual. Where American youth culture centered on high schools in the 1950s and on college campuses in the 1960s, in the 1970s and 1980s it had gravitated toward mall fast-food stores and video amusement arcades. Older people in search of moderate exercise discovered that the controlled climate was ideal for "mall walking." Malls even had their counterculture: "mall rats" who "hung out" and survived by shoplifting.

*Malls as the symbol of an age*

The new cathedrals of consumption served as an appropriate symbol of a society that in the 1980s and 1990s turned from protests and crusades to more private paths of spiritual fulfillment. Confronted by an age of limits, some turned to evangelical religion, with its emphasis on the conversion of "born-again" individuals. Others extolled the virtues of the traditional family and lauded private charity and volunteerism as an alternative to activist social policies of a modern welfare state. Along less orthodox paths, the "human potential movement" focused on techniques like yoga, transcendental meditation, and "bioenergetics" to bring spiritual fulfillment.

So it was not surprising, perhaps, that in 1980 Ronald Reagan chose to evoke Puritan John Winthrop's seventeenth-century vision of an American "city on a hill"—that city Winthrop hoped would inspire the rest of the world. For conservatives, the image carried strong religious overtones. The Puritans, after all, sought to create a Christian commonwealth that was both well-ordered and moral. Reagan's vision, of course, had been updated. It embraced nineteenth-century ideals of "manifest destiny." (America should "stand tall," he insisted, as the world's number one military power.) And Reagan affirmed the laissez-faire ideals of the late nineteenth century, encouraging citizens to promote the public good through the pursuit of private wealth. "Government is not the solution to our problem," he asserted. "Government is the problem."

Critics contended that Reagan was no more likely than the Puritans to succeed with his revolution. History, they argued, had shown that private enterprise was unable to prevent or regulate the environmental damage caused by acid rain, oil spills, or toxic waste dumps. Furthermore, a severely limited federal government would prove unable to cope with declining schools, urban violence, or the AIDS epidemic. To many liberals the Reagan agenda amounted to a flight from public responsibility into a fantasy world no more authentic than the Italian hill town nestled in downtown San Diego. John Winthrop's austere vision risked being transformed into a city on a hill with climate control, where the proprietors of Muzak-filled walkways banished all problems beyond the gates of the parking lots.

Yet conservatives in the 1980s and 1990s demonstrated the abiding attraction of their ideals. Although an economic downturn brought the Democrats into the White House in 1992, Republican control of Congress after the elections of 1994 and 1996 kept alive the campaign for a born-again America.

## THE CONSERVATIVE REBELLION

In 1964 billboards for conservative candidate Barry Goldwater had proclaimed across America: "In Your Heart You Know He's Right." Beneath one of the billboards an unknown Democratic wag unfurled his own banner: "Yes—Extreme Right." Most citizens voted with the wag, perceiving Goldwater's platform as too conservative, too extreme, too dangerous for the times.

By 1980 rising prices, energy shortages, and similar economic uncertainties fed a growing resistance to a liberal agenda. Hard-pressed workers resented in-

*Issues of the 1970s and 1980s*

creased competition from minorities, especially those supported by affirmative action quotas and government programs. Citizens resisted the demands for higher taxes to support social welfare spending. The traditional family, too, seemed under siege, as divorce rates and births to single mothers soared. Sexually explicit media, an outspoken gay rights movement, and the availability of legal abortions struck many religious conservatives as part of a wholesale assault on decency. Increasingly the political agenda was determined by those who wanted to restore a strong family, traditional religious values, patriotism, and limited government.

### *Born Again*

At one center of the conservative rebellion was the call for a revival of religion. It came most insistently from white Protestant evangelicals. Fundamentalist Protestants had since the 1920s increasingly separated themselves from the older, more liberal denominations. In the decades after World War II their membership grew dramatically—anywhere from 400 to 700 percent, compared with less than 90 percent for main-line denominations. By the 1980s they had become a significant third force in Christian America, after Roman Catholics and traditional Protestants. The election of Jimmy Carter, himself a born-again Christian, reflected their newfound visibility.

Like fundamentalists of the 1920s, the evangelicals of the 1980s resisted the trend toward more secular ideas, especially in education. They pressed states

*Evangelicals*

and the federal government to adopt a "school prayer" amendment allowing officially sanctioned prayer in classrooms. They urged the teaching of "creationism" as an alternative to Darwinian evolution. Frustrated with public schools, they created private Christian academies to insulate their children from the influence of "secular humanism." Fundamentalists applied this term to the modernist notions of a materially determined world in which all truths were relative and in which circumstances rather than moral precepts determined ethical behavior.

Although evangelicals condemned the secularism of the modern media, they used broadcast technology to sell their message. Cable and satellite broadcasting brought "televangelists" to national audiences. The Reverend Pat Robertson introduced his "700 Club" over the Christian Broadcast Network from Virginia Beach, Virginia. Another "700 Club" regular, Jim Bakker, launched a spinoff program called the "Praise the Lord Club"—PTL for short. Within a few years PTL had the largest audience of any daily show in the world.

But it was the Reverend Jerry Falwell, spiritual leader of the Thomas Road Baptist Church in Lynchburg, Virginia, who first made the step from religious to political activism. In 1979 Falwell formed the Moral Majority, Inc., an organization to attract campaign contributions and examine candidates around the country on issues important to Christians. In the 1980 election the Moral Majority sent out more than a billion pieces of mail in an attempt to unseat liberals in Congress.

*The Moral Majority*

## The Catholic Conscience

American Catholics faced their own decisions about the lines between religion and politics. In the 1960s Catholic social activism reflected a movement that had arisen out of the church council known as Vatican II (1962–1965). The council sought to revitalize the church and to reappraise its role in the modern world. The reforms of Vatican II invited greater participation by ordinary church members and encouraged closer ties to other Christians and to Jews.

Disturbed by these currents, Catholic conservatives found support for their views when the magnetic John Paul II became pope in 1979. Pope John Paul reined in the modern trends inspired by Vatican II. The pope resisted a wider role for women and stiffened Church policy against birth control. That put him at odds on such issues with a majority of American Catholics.

*Catholic conservatism*

Though conservative Catholics and Protestant evangelicals were sometimes wary of one another, they shared certain views. Both groups lobbied the government to provide federal aid to parochial schools and fundamentalist academies. And on the issue of abortion, Pope John Paul reaffirmed the church's teaching that all life began at conception, so that any abortion amounted to the murder of the unborn. Evangelicals, long suspicious of the power of secular technology and science, attacked abortion as another instance in which science had upset the natural moral order of life.

---

COUNTERPOINT    *Defining the New Conservatism*

It is not an easy task to pinpoint the wellsprings of the conservative rebellion. Some analysts, focusing on the movement's political leadership, have viewed matters cynically. They argue that Ronald Reagan, George Bush, and other Republican leaders are simply members of the established business elite, who have tapped the resentments of ordinary people in order to provide others of their class with tax and regulatory relief. "Hot button" issues like school prayer, abortion, and gun control can be used "as a means to ignite people who do not normally support Republicans," in the words of one conservative political

Many conservative Christians adopted the militant style of 1960s radicals to protest issues like abortion. Here they clash with pro-choice demonstrators outside Faneuil Hall in Boston.

adviser. Such an analysis emphasizes the differences within the conservative movement. On the one side, libertarians and free-enterprising businessmen would keep the government out of regulating public morals as well as out of regulating the economy. On the other side, cultural conservatives urge the government to take an active role in restoring morality.

Other historians stress the cultural roots that unite conservatives: the rejection of a liberalism that brought activism to government and a secular perspective to society at large. Conservatives of all stripes, one can argue, uphold the values of a purer, idealized past, one free from government interference and invigorated by a clear moral order. In 1955, when William F. Buckley, Jr., began his conservative magazine, *National Review*, he proclaimed it his job to "stand athwart History and shout Stop!" In the eyes of some historians, it is this fixation on a past—an idealized one, at that—that unites the new right. "People became conservatives," suggested one analyst, "when they experienced 'the horrible feeling' that a society they took for granted might suddenly cease to exist."

## The Media as Battleground

Both evangelists and political conservatives viewed the mass media as an establishment that was politically liberal and morally permissive. Certainly by the 1980s American popular culture had come to portray sex and violence more explicitly than ever, as well as to treat openly such sensitive social issues as racial and ethnic prejudice. Because the media—and especially television—played such a prominent role in American life, it became a battleground where conservatives and liberals clashed.

The conflict could be seen in producer Norman Lear's situation comedy *All in the Family*, introduced in 1971. Its main character, Archie Bunker, was a blue-

*Topical sitcoms*

collar father seething with fears and prejudices. Americans were supposed to laugh at Archie's outrageous references to "Hebes," "Spics," and "Commie crapola," but many in the audience were not laughing. Some minority leaders charged that by making Archie lovable, the show legitimized the very prejudices it seemed to attack.

M∗A∗S∗H, a popular sitcom launched in 1972, was more clearly liberal in tone. Although set in a medical unit during the Korean War, its real inspiration was the growing disillusionment with the Vietnam war. M∗A∗S∗H twitted bureaucracy, authority, pretense, bigotry, and snobbery. For conservatives, the antiauthoritarian bent of such shows seemed to spill over into newspaper and television reporting. On the other hand, feminists and minority groups complained that television portrayed them through stereotypes, when it bothered to portray them at all.

Perhaps inevitably, the wars for the soul of prime time spilled into the political arena. Norman Lear, Archie Bunker's creator, went on to form People for the American Way, a lobbying group that campaigned for more diversity in American life and attempted to counteract pressure groups like the Moral Majority. Conservatives, looking to make a stronger political impact, in 1980 embraced an amiable former movie actor who had long preached their gospel.

## The Election of 1980

Jimmy Carter might be born again, but Ronald Reagan spoke the language of true conservatism. "I think there is a hunger in this land for a spiritual revival, a return to a belief in moral absolutes," he told his followers. Such a commitment to fundamentalist articles of faith was more important than the fact that Reagan actually had no church affiliation and seldom attended services.

The defection of many evangelical Protestants meant that the Democrats had lost the majority of white Southern voters. The Republican Party became

*Reagan supporters*

the home of most conservatives. When undecided voters saw Reagan as the candidate with the power to lead, the race turned into a landslide. Equally impressive, Republicans won their first majority in the Senate since 1954. They cited the margin of victory as a popular mandate for a conservative agenda.

On that count, the verdict was not clear. Only 52 percent of the eligible electorate went to the polls, the lowest total in 32 years. "It's a fed-up vote," argued Carter's political analyst Patrick Caddell. Still, the New Deal Democratic coalition had been splintered. Although Reagan's majority was greatest among white voters over 45 who earned more than $50,000 a year, he made striking gains among union workers, southern white Protestants, Catholics, and Jews.

## PRIME TIME WITH RONALD REAGAN

Ronald Reagan brought the bright lights of Hollywood to Washington. His managers staged one of the most extravagant inaugurations in the nation's history. Nancy Reagan became the most fashion-conscious first lady since Jackie Kennedy, while the new administration made the conspicuous display of wealth once again a sign of success and power. During Reagan's first term sales of stretch limousines doubled every year. Poverty rates rose, too, as the gulf between rich and poor widened.

### *The Great Communicator*

Ronald Reagan brought a simple message to Washington. "It is time to reawaken the industrial giant, to get government back within its means, and to lighten our punitive tax burden," he announced on inauguration day. Commentators began referring to the president as "the great communicator," because of his mastery of television and radio.

Reagan used his skill as an actor to obscure contradictions between his rhetoric and reality. With his jaunty wave and jutting jaw, he projected phys-

*The Reagan style*

ical vitality and the charismatic good looks of John Kennedy. Yet at age 69, he was the oldest president to take office, and none since Calvin Coolidge had slept so soundly or so much.

Reagan had begun his political life as a New Deal Democrat, but by the 1950s he had become an ardent anti-Communist, Republican. In 1966 he began two terms as governor of California with a promise to pare down government programs and balance budgets. In fact, spending jumped sharply during his term in office.

Similar inconsistencies marked Reagan's leadership as president. Outsiders applauded his "hands-off" management: Reagan set the tone and direction, let-

As president, Ronald Reagan often evoked the image of a cowboy hero. Yet the Reagan revolution in practice led to sharply increased federal spending and federal deficits.

ting his advisers take care of the details. On the other hand, many within the administration, like Secretary of the Treasury Donald Regan, were shocked to find the new president remarkably ignorant about and uninterested in important matters of policy. "The Presidential mind was not cluttered with facts," Regan lamented. Yet Reagan's cheerful ability to deflect responsibility for mistakes earned him a reputation as the "Teflon president," since no criticism seemed to stick.

In addition, Reagan was blessed by remarkably good luck. The deaths of three aging Soviet leaders, from 1982 through 1985, compounded that country's economic weakness and reduced Russian influence abroad. *Reagan's fortune* Members of the OPEC oil cartel quarreled among themselves, exceeded production quotas, and thus forced oil prices lower. That removed a major inflationary pressure on the American economy. And when a would-be assassin shot the president in the chest on March 30, 1981, the wound was not life threatening. His courage in the face of danger impressed even his critics.

## *The Reagan Agenda*

As president, Reagan's primary goal was to weaken big government. His budget would become an instrument to reduce bureaucracy and to undermine activist federal agencies in the areas of civil rights, environmental and consumer protection, poverty programs, the arts, and education. In essence, the new president wanted to return government to the size and responsibility it possessed in the 1950s before the reforms of Kennedy and Johnson.

At the heart of the Reagan revolution was a commitment to "supply-side" economics, a program that in many ways resembled the trickle-down economic theories of the Harding-Coolidge era. Supply-side theorists argued that high taxes and government regulation stifled enterprising businesses and economic expansion. The key to revival lay in a large tax cut, a politically popular though economically controversial proposal. Such a cut threatened to reduce revenues and increase an already large deficit. Not so, argued economist Arthur Laffer. The economy would be so stimulated that tax revenues would actually rise, even though the tax rate was cut.

*Supply-side economics*

The president's second target for action was inflation, the "silent thief" that had burdened the economy during the Ford-Carter years. Reagan resisted certain traditional cures for inflation: tight money, high interest rates, and wage and price controls. He preferred two approaches unpopular with Democrats: higher unemployment and weakened unions to reduce labor costs.

Lower public spending, a favorite Republican remedy, might have seemed one likely method of reducing inflation. But the third element of Reagan's agenda was a sharp rise in military outlays: a total of $1.5 trillion to be spent over five years. The president wanted to create an American military presence with the strength to act unilaterally anywhere in the world to beat back Communist threats. This was a remarkably expansive goal: Presidents Nixon, Ford, and Carter had all looked to scale back American commitments, either through détente or by shifting burdens to allies in Western Europe. Reagan recognized no such limits. And rather than emphasize either nuclear defense or conventional weapons, Defense Secretary Caspar Weinberger successfully lobbied Congress for both.

*Military buildup*

## The Reagan Revolution in Practice

The administration soon found an opportunity to "hang tough" when air traffic controllers went on strike, claiming that understaffing and long working hours threatened air safety. Because the controllers were civil service employees, the strike was technically illegal. Without addressing the merits of the controllers' complaints, Reagan simply fired them for violating their contract. The defeat of the air controllers signaled a broader attack on unions. When a recession enveloped the nation, major corporations wrung substantial concessions on wages and work rules. Organized labor witnessed a steady decline in membership and political power.

The president's war against government regulation took special aim at environmental rules. Conservatives, especially in the West, dismissed the environmental lobby as "nature lovers." Preservation of wild lands restricted mining, cattle grazing, farming, and real estate development—all powerful western industries. Reagan appointed westerner James Watt, an outspoken champion of this "sagebrush rebellion," to head the Interior Department. Watt, in turn, devoted himself to opening federal

*Environmental controversy*

E Y E W I T N E S S     T O     H I S T O R Y

## The President's Budget Director
## Discusses the "Reagan Revolution"

L ike all revolutionaries, we wanted to get our program out of the fringe cell group where it had been hatched and into the mainstream. . . . So we pitched it in tones that were music to every politician's ears. We highlighted the easy part—the giant tax cut. The side of the doctrine that had to do with giving to the electorate, not taking from it.

My blueprint for sweeping, wrenching change in national economic governance would have hurt millions of people in the short run. . . . It meant complete elimination of subsidies to farmers and businesses. It required an immediate end to welfare for the able-bodied poor. It meant no right to draw more from the Social Security fund than retirees had actually contributed, which was a lot less than most were currently getting.

These principles everywhere clashed with the political reality. Over the decades, the politicians had lured tens of millions of citizens into milking . . . cows, food stamps, Social Security, the Veterans Hospitals, and much more. . . . For the Reagan Revolution to add up, they had to be cut off. The blueprint was thus riddled with the hardship and unfairness of unexpected change. Only an iron chancellor would have tried to make it stick. Ronald Reagan wasn't that by a long shot.

Even [after I criticized the administration publicly] my private exoneration at lunch in the Oval Office by a fatherly Ronald Reagan showed why a Reagan Revolution couldn't happen. He should have been roaring mad like the others—about either the bad publicity or my admission of a flawed economic plan.

But Ronald Reagan proved to be too gentle and sentimental for that. He always went for the hard luck stories. He sees the plight of real people before anything else. Despite his right-wing image, his ideology and philosophy always takes a back seat when he learns that some individual human being might be hurt.

That's also why he couldn't lead a real revolution in American economic policy.

lands for private development, including lumbering and offshore oil drilling. After offending Indians, African Americans, Jews, the handicapped, as well as many Republicans, Watt was forced to resign in 1983, but the administration continued to oppose environmental initiatives.

Most important to conservatives, Reagan had by the summer of 1981 pushed his supply-side legislation through Congress. The Economic Recovery Tax Act pro-

*Tax cuts*

vided a 25 percent across-the-board reduction for all taxpayers. The president hailed it, along with recently passed budget cuts, as an antidote to "big government's" addiction to spending and a stimulus to the economy.

## The Impact of Reaganomics

The impact of Reagan's supply-side economics (nicknamed "Reaganomics" by the press) was mixed. By 1982 a recession had pushed unemployment above 10 percent. But the following year marked the beginning of an economic expansion that lasted through Reagan's presidency, thanks in part to increased federal spending and lowered interest rates. Then, too, falling energy costs and improved industrial productivity contributed to renewed prosperity.

Even so, the Reagan tax cut was one of a series of policy changes that brought about a substantial transfer of wealth from poor and lower-middle-class workers to the upper middle classes and the rich. For the wealthiest Americans, the 1980s were the best of times. The top 1 percent commanded a greater share of the nation's wealth (37 percent) than at any time since 1929. Their earnings averaged about $560,000 per year, as opposed to $20,000 or less for the bottom 40 percent. What counterculture hippies were to the 1960s, high-salaried "yuppies" (young, upwardly mobile professionals) were to the 1980s.

On the surface, the buoyant job market seemed to signal a more general prosperity as well. By the end of Reagan's second term, more than 14.5 million jobs had been created for Americans. Yet these jobs were spread unevenly by region,

*Factors encouraging the transfer of wealth*

class, and gender. More than 2 million were in finance, insurance, real estate, and law, all services used more by the wealthy than the poor. In highly paid "Wall Street" jobs—those involving financial services—more than 70 percent went to white males, only 2 percent to African Americans. New employment for women was concentrated in the areas of health, education, social services, and government, where approximately 3 million jobs opened, most dependent on government support. New jobs for the poor (more than 3 million) were largely restricted to minimum-wage, part-time, dead-end jobs in hotels, fast-food restaurants, and retail stores.

Because Reaganomics preached the virtues of free markets and free trade, the administration did little to discourage high-wage blue-collar jobs from flowing to cheap labor markets in Mexico and Asia. Furthermore, Reagan aimed the sharpest edge of his budget axe at programs for the poor: food stamps, Aid to Families with Dependent Children, Medicaid, school lunches, and housing

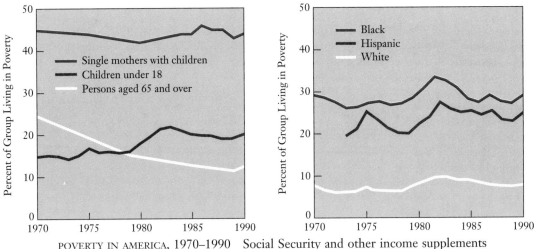

POVERTY IN AMERICA, 1970–1990   Social Security and other income supplements account for the reduced level of poverty among those over 65. For all other traditionally impoverished groups the Reagan–Bush years left them slightly worse off.

assistance. The programs trimmed back least were middle-class entitlements like Social Security and Medicare. Those programs affected Americans over 65 who, as social activist Michael Harrington observed, as a general class "are not now, and for a long time have not been, poor."

As more income flowed toward the wealthy and as jobs were lost to overseas competitors, the percentage of Americans below the poverty level rose from 11.7 percent in 1980 to 15 percent by 1982. There the level remained through the Bush administration. Reagan's successful war on inflation, which dropped to less than 2 percent by 1986, contributed to a rise in unemployment. Even during the recovery, the figure dropped below 6 percent of the workforce only in the months before the 1988 election. (By contrast, the highest rate under Jimmy Carter was 5.9 percent.) Thus the Reagan boom was an uneven one, despite continued economic expansion.

## The Military Buildup

The heart of the Reagan revolution was a sharp rise in military spending. Outlays rose from less than $200 billion under Presidents Ford and Carter to almost $300 billion in 1985. The largest increases were for expensive strategic nuclear weapons systems.

Huge costs were not the only source of criticism. When Reagan's tough-talking defense planners spoke about "winning" a nuclear exchange, they revived the antinuclear peace movement across Europe and America. The bishops of the American Catholic church announced their opposition to nuclear

*Star Wars*

war. Scientists warned that the debris in the atmosphere from an atomic exchange might create a "nuclear winter" fatal to all life on earth. Other critics singled out runaway Pentagon costs. Stories of $600 toilet seats and $7000 coffee pots made headlines, but more serious were the failures of entire multi-billion-dollar weapons systems. One of the president's favorite programs was the Strategic Defense Initiative, or SDI. Nicknamed "Star Wars," after a popular science fiction film, it spent billions of dollars trying to establish a space-based missile defense system. Most scientists contended that the project was as fantastic as the movie.

The combination of massive defense spending and substantial tax cuts left the federal government awash in red ink. Annual deficits climbed to more than $200 billion. Furthermore, with interest rates so high, the value of the dollar soared on world markets, pushing up the cost of American exports. As American exports declined, imports from abroad (such as Japanese autos) competed more successfully in America. The United States, a creditor nation since World War I, had by 1986 become the world's largest debtor.

*Growing deficits*

The spending excesses of the Reagan agenda would come to haunt his conservative successors. For the time being, however, Ronald Reagan's popularity seemed unassailable. In 1984 he easily won a second term, gaining 59 percent of the vote in his run against Democrat Walter Mondale of Minnesota. (Mondale's running mate, Geraldine Ferraro of New York, was the first female candidate for the vice presidency.) Reagan remained his sunny, unflappable self, seeming to enjoy the presidency immensely. "The 75-year-old man is hitting home runs," rhapsodized *Time* magazine at the beginning of his second term. In reality, Reagan would soon be tested by a series of crises arising out of his aggressive foreign policy.

## STANDING TALL IN A CHAOTIC WORLD

Reagan brought to the conduct of foreign policy the same moral stance that shaped his approach to domestic affairs. Reagan wanted the United States to stand tall: to adopt a policy that drew bold, clear lines as a means of restoring American prestige. But turmoil abroad demonstrated that bold policies were not always easy to carry out. And because the president remained indifferent to most day-to-day details, he was at the mercy of those officials who put into effect his aggressive anti-Communist foreign policy.

### Terrorism in the Middle East

In the Middle East, the passions of religious factions suggested how difficult it was to impose order, even for a superpower like the United States. In 1982 President Reagan sent American marines into Lebanon as part of a European-American peacekeeping force. His hope was to bring a measure of stability to a region torn by civil war. But in trying to mediate between Lebanon's religious and political sects, the American "peacekeepers" found themselves dragged into the fighting. Terrorists retaliated by blowing up a U.S. Marine barracks in October 1983, killing 239. The president then ordered American troops withdrawn.

Just as hostage-taking in Iran had frustrated the Carter administration, terrorist attacks by Islamic fundamentalists bedeviled Reagan. In 1985 terrorists took new hostages in Lebanon; others hijacked American airline flights, killed an American hostage on a Mediterranean cruise ship, and bombed a nightclub where American soldiers met in West Germany. Reagan's public response was always uncompromising: "Let terrorists beware: . . . our policy will be one of swift and effective retribution."

But against whom should the United States seek revenge? American intelligence agencies found it extremely difficult to collect reliable information on the many political and terrorist factions. In 1986 the president sent bombers to attack targets in Libya, whose anti-American leader Colonel Muammar Qadhafi had links to terrorists. But so did the more powerful states of Syria and Iran.

## Mounting Frustrations in Central America

At first, a policy of standing tall seemed easier closer to home. In 1983, the administration launched an invasion of Grenada, a small Caribbean island whose government was challenged by pro-Castro revolutionaries. U.S. forces crushed the rebels, but the invasion was largely a symbolic gesture.

*Grenada invasion*

More frustrating to the president, Nicaragua's left-wing Sandinista government had established increasingly close ties with Cuba. In 1981 Reagan extended aid to the antigovernment "Contra" forces. When critics warned that Nicaragua could become another Vietnam, the president countered that the Contras were "freedom fighters," battling in the spirit of America's Founding Fathers. Although the Contras did include some moderate democrats and disillusioned Sandinistas, most of their leaders had served the brutal Somoza dictatorship that the Sandinistas had toppled in 1979.

Reagan might have sought a negotiated settlement between the Contras and the Sandinistas; instead he allowed CIA to help the Contras mine Nicaraguan harbors, in hopes of overthrowing the Sandinistas outright. When some of the mines exploded, damaging foreign ships in violation of international law, even some conservative senators were dismayed.

*Boland Amendment*

Congress adopted an amendment sponsored by Representative Edward Boland of Massachusetts, explicitly forbidding the CIA or "any other agency or entity involved in intelligence activities" from spending money to support the Contras "directly or indirectly." The president signed the Boland Amendment, though only grudgingly.

## The Iran-Contra Connection

Thus by mid-1985 Reagan policymakers felt two major frustrations. First, Congress had forbidden support of the Contras in Nicaragua. And second,

Iranian-backed terrorists continued to hold American hostages in Lebanon. In the summer of 1985 a course of events was set in motion that eventually linked these two issues.

The president let his advisers know that he wanted to find a way to free the remaining hostages. National Security Advisor Robert McFarlane suggested opening a channel to "moderate factions" in the Iranian government. If the United States sold Iran a few weapons, the grateful moderates might use their influence in Lebanon to free the hostages. But an agreement to exchange arms for hostages would violate the president's often-repeated vow never to pay ransom to terrorists. Still, Reagan apparently approved the initiative. Over the following year, four secret arms shipments were made to Iran. One hostage was set free.

Reagan's secretaries of state and defense both had strongly opposed the trading of arms for hostages. "This is almost too absurd to comment on," Defense Secretary Weinberger protested. Thus, both men were kept largely uninformed of the arms shipments, precisely because their opposition was well known. McFarlane's successor, Admiral John Poindexter, had the president sign a secret intelligence "finding" that allowed him and his associates to pursue their mission without informing anyone in Congress or even the secretaries of defense and state. Since the president ignored the details of foreign policy, McFarlane, Poindexter, and their aides had assumed the power to act on their own.

*Arms for hostage deals*

The man most often pulling the strings seemed to be Lieutenant Colonel Oliver "Ollie" North, a junior officer under McFarlane and later Poindexter. A Vietnam veteran with a flair for the dramatic, North was impatient with bureaucratic rules and procedures. He and McFarlane had already discovered a way to evade the Boland Amendment, in order to secretly aid the Nicaraguan Contras. McFarlane told Saudi Arabia and several other American allies that the Contras desperately needed funds. As a favor, the Saudis deposited at least $30 million in Swiss bank accounts he used to launder the money. North then arranged to spend the money to buy the weapons that were delivered to Central America.

The two secret strands came together in January 1986. North hit upon the idea that the profits made selling arms to Iran could be siphoned off to buy weapons for the Contras. The Iranian arms dealer who brokered the deal thought it a great idea. "I think this is now, Ollie, the best chance, because . . . we never get such good money out of this," he laughed, as he was recorded on a tape North himsef made. "We do everything. We do hostages free of charge; we do all terrorists free of charge; Central America free of charge."

### Cover Blown

The secrecy that surrounded both operations through much of 1986 abruptly lifted when reports of the Iranian arms deal were leaked to a Lebanese

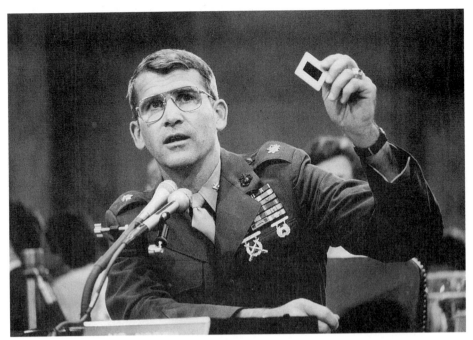

As Colonel Oliver North himself admitted during the Iran–Contra
hearings, he purposefully misled Congress about the Reagan
administration's secret aid to the Contras.

newspaper. Astonished reporters besieged the administration. How did secret
arms sales to a terrorist regime benefit the president's antiterrorist campaign,
they asked. Further inquiry revealed the link between the arms sales and the
Contras. Attorney General Edwin Meese moved so slowly to investigate that
North and his secretary had time to shred crucial documents. Still, enough evidence remained to make the dimensions of the illegal operations clear.

The press immediately began referring to the scandal as "Irangate," com-
paring it to Richard Nixon's Watergate scandal. But Irangate raised more trou-

*Irangate*

bling issues. Watergate sprang from political tricks that ran amok.
The president had led the cover-up to save his own political skin.
The Irangate hearings, held during the summer of 1987, left the role of the
president unexplained. Admiral Poindexter testified that he had kept Reagan in
ignorance, "so that I could insulate him from the decision and provide some future deniability for the president if it ever leaked out. . . ." In that way, Iran-
Contra revealed a presidency out of control. An unelected segment within the
government had taken upon itself the power to pursue its own poilicies beyond
legal channels. In doing so, Reagan, North, Poindexter, and McFarlane sub-
verted the constitutional system of checks and balances.

## From Cold War to Glasnost

Since few in Congress wanted to impeach a popular president, the Iran-Contra hearings came to a sputtering end. Reagan's popularity returned, in part because of substantial improvement in Soviet-American relations.

In 1985 a fresh spirit entered the Kremlin. Unlike the aged leaders who preceded him, Mikhail Gorbachev was young, saw the need for reform within the

*Mikhail Gorbachev*

Soviet Union, and rivaled Reagan as a shaper of world opinion. Gorbachev's fundamental restructuring, or *perestroika*, set about improving relations with the United States, reducing military commitments, and adopting a policy of openness (*glasnost*) about problems in the Soviet Union. In October, the two leaders held a summit meeting in Reykjavík, Iceland. Gorbachev dangled the possibility of abolishing all nuclear weapons. Reagan seemed receptive to the idea, apparently unaware that if both sides eliminated all nuclear weapons, Soviet conventional forces would far outnumber NATO troops in Europe. In the end, the president refused to sacrifice his Star Wars system for so radical a proposal.

Despite the immediate impasse, negotiations continued. In December 1987 Reagan traveled to Moscow to sign the Intermediate Nuclear Force treaty, which eliminated an entire class of intermediate-range nuclear missiles with ranges of 600 to 3400 miles. Both sides agreed to allow on-site inspections of missile bases and the facilities where missiles would be destroyed. That agreement greatly eased cold war tensions.

## The Election of 1988

As the election of 1988 approached, the president could claim credit for improved relations with the Soviet Union. Loyalty to Reagan made Vice President George Bush the Republican heir. Bush appealed most to party professionals, white Protestants, and the affluent middle class that had benefited from Reaganomics.

The Democratic challenger, Governor Michael Dukakis of Massachusetts, tried to call attention to weaknesses in the American economy. An alarming number of savings and loan institutions had failed, and Dukakis recognized that poor and even many middle-class Americans had lost ground during the 1980s. But under attack from Bush the lackluster Dukakis appeared weak. With the economy reasonably robust, Bush won by a comfortable margin, taking 54 percent of the popular vote. The Reagan agenda remained on track.

## AN END TO THE COLD WAR

President George Herbert Walker Bush was born to both privilege and politics. The son of a powerful Connecticut senator, he attended an exclusive boarding school and the ivy-league Yale University. That background made him part of the Eastern establishment often condemned by more populist Republicans. Yet once the oil business lured Bush to Texas, he moved to the right, becoming a Goldwater Republican when he ran for the Senate in 1964. Although he once supported Planned Parenthood and a woman's right to abortion, Bush eventually adopted the conservative right-to-life position. In truth, however, foreign policy interested him far more than domestic politics.

## A Post–Cold War Foreign Policy

To the astonishment of most western observers, Mikhail Gorbachev's reform policies led not only to the collapse of the Soviet empire but to the breakup of the Soviet Union itself. In December 1988, Gorbachev spoke in the United Nations of a "new world order." To that end he began liquidating the Soviet cold war legacy, as the last Russian troops began leaving Afghanistan and then Eastern Europe.

Throughout 1989 Eastern Europeans began to test their newfound freedom. In Poland, Hungary, Bulgaria, Czechoslovakia, and most violently in Romania, Communist dictators fell from power. Nothing inspired the world more than the stream of celebrating East Germans pouring through the Berlin Wall in November 1989. Within a year the Wall, a symbol of Communist oppression, had been torn down and Germany reunified. Although Gorbachev struggled to keep together the 15 republics that made up the U.S.S.R., the forces of nationalism and reform pulled the Soviet Union apart. The Baltic republics—Lithuania, Latvia, and Estonia—declared their independence in 1991. Then in December, the Slavic republics of Ukraine, Belarus, and Russia formed a new Commonwealth of Independent States. By the end of December eight more of the former Soviet republics had joined the loose federation. Boris Yeltsin, the charismatic president of Russia, became the Commonwealth's dominant figure. With no Soviet Union left to preside over, Gorbachev resigned as president.

*The fall of Communism*

President Bush responded cautiously to these momentous changes. Although the president increasingly supported Gorbachev's reforms, he distrusted the more popular yet unpredictable maverick, Yeltsin. Even if Bush had wished to launch a campaign to aid Eastern Europe and the new Commonwealth states, soaring deficits and a stagnant American economy limited his options. The administration seemed to support the status quo in Communist China, too. When in June 1989 China's aging leadership crushed students rallying for democratic reform in Beijing's Tiananmen Square, Bush muted American protests.

The fall of the Soviet Union signaled the end of a cold war that, more than once, had threatened a nuclear end to human history. At a series of summits with Russian leaders, the United States and its former rivals agreed to sharp reductions in their stockpiles of nuclear weapons. The Strategic Arms Reduction Treaty (or START), concluded in July 1991, far sur-

*START Treaty*

President George Bush met with Soviet President Mikhail Gorbachev at a Moscow summit meeting in 1991. Clearly the policy of *glasnost* extended to American beverages: the Kremlin's conference table is stocked with Coke.

passed the limits negotiated in earlier SALT talks. By June 1992 Bush and Yeltsin had agreed to even sharper cuts.

## The Persian Gulf War

With two superpowers no longer facing off against each other, what would the "new world order" look like? If anything, regional crises loomed larger. President Bush moved to project American power more forcefully in the Middle East. But civil wars in Eastern Europe and Africa demonstrated that a world order beyond the shadow of the cold war might be more chaotic and unpredictable than ever.

Instability in the Middle East brought Bush's greatest foreign policy challenge. From 1980 to 1988 Iran and Iraq had battered each other in a debilitat-

*Saddam Hussein* ing war. During those years the Reagan administration assisted Iraq with weapons and intelligence, until at last it won a narrow victory over Iran's fundamentalists. But Iraq's ruthless dictator, Saddam Hussein, had run up enormous debts. To ease his financial crisis, Saddam cast a covetous eye on his neighbor, the small oil-rich sheikdom of Kuwait. In August 1990, 120,000 Iraqi troops invaded and occupied Kuwait, catching the Bush administration off guard. Would Saddam stop there?

"We committed a boner with regard to Iraq and our close friendship with Iraq," admitted Ronald Reagan. Embarrassed by having supported the pro-Iraqi policy, Bush was determined to thwart Saddam's invasion of Kuwait. The president successfully coordinated a United Nations–backed economic boycott. Increasing the pressure further, he deployed half a million American troops in Saudi Arabia and the Persian Gulf. By November Bush had won a resolution from the Security Council permitting the use of military force if Saddam did not withdraw.

On January 17, 1991, planes from France, Italy, Britain, Saudi Arabia, and the United States began bombing Baghdad and Iraqi bases. Operation Desert

*Operation Desert Storm*

Storm had begun. After weeks of merciless pounding from the air, ground operations shattered Saddam's vaunted Royal Guards in less than 100 hours. By the end of February Kuwait was liberated and nothing stood between Allied forces and Baghdad. Bush was unwilling to go that far—and most other nations in the coalition agreed. If Hussein were toppled, it was not clear who in Iraq would fill the vacuum of power. But long after the war ended, the United States still worried about Saddam and his potential possession of biological and atomic weapons.

### Domestic Doldrums

Victory in the Gulf War so boosted the president's popularity that aides brushed aside the need for any bold domestic program. "Frankly, this president doesn't need another single piece of legislation, unless it's absolutely right," asserted John Sununu, his cocky chief of staff. That attitude suggested a lack of direction that proved fatal to Bush's reelection hopes.

At first, Bush envisioned a domestic program that would soften the harsher edges of the Reagan revolution. He promised to create a "kinder, gentler" nation.

*Environmental issues*

Yet pressures from conservative Republicans kept the new president from straying too far in the direction of reform. Although Bush appointed a well-respected conservationist, William Reilly, to head the Environmental Protection Agency, Reilly often found his programs opposed by others in the administration. When delegates from 178 nations met at an "Earth Summit" in Rio de Janiero in 1992, the president opposed efforts to draft stricter rules to lessen the threat of global warming. Bush did sign into law the sweeping Clean Air Act passed by Congress in 1990. But soon after, Vice President Dan Quayle established a "Council on Competitiveness" to rewrite environmental regulations that corporations found burdensome.

### The Conservative Court

Although Presidents Reagan and Bush both spoke out against abortion, affirmative action, the banning of prayer in public schools, and other liberal social positions, neither made action a legislative priority. Even so, both presidents shaped social policy through their appointments to the Supreme Court. Reagan placed three members on the bench, including in 1981 Sandra Day O'Connor, the first woman to sit on the high court. Bush nominated two justices. As more liberal members of the Court retired (including William Brennan and Thurgood Marshall), the decisions handed down became distinctly more conservative.

On two occasions, the Senate challenged this trend. In 1987, it rejected Robert Bork, a nominee whose opposition to long-established Court policies on privacy and civil rights led even some Republicans to oppose him. But this fight proved so exhausting that the Senate quickly approved President Reagan's alternate choice, Antonin Scalia. Scalia proved to be the Court's most conservative member.

In 1991 the Senate also hotly debated President Bush's nomination of Clarence Thomas, an outspoken black conservative and former member of the

*The Clarence Thomas hearings*

Reagan administration. The confirmation hearings became even more heated when Anita Hill, a woman who had worked for Thomas, testified that he had sexually harassed her. Because Hill was a professor of law and herself a Reagan conservative, her often graphic testimony riveted millions of television viewers. Suddenly the hearings raised new issues. Women's groups blasted the all-male Judiciary Committee for keeping Hill's allegations private until reporters uncovered the story. Thomas and his defenders accused his opponents of using a disgruntled woman to help conduct a latter-day lynching. In the end the Senate narrowly voted to confirm, and Thomas joined Scalia as one of the Court's most conservative members.

Evidence of the Court's changing stance came most clearly in its attitude toward affirmative action, those laws that gave preferred treatment to minority groups in order to remedy past racial discrimination. State and federal courts and legislatures had used techniques like busing and the setting of quotas as ways to overturn past injustices. In 1978, however, even before Reagan's appointments, the Court began to set limits on affirmative action. In *Bakke v. Regents of the University of California* (1978), the majority ruled that college admissions staffs could not set fixed quotas, although they could still use race as a guiding factor in trying to create a more diverse student body. Increasingly, the Court made it easier for white citizens to challenge affirmative action programs. At the same time it set higher standards for those who wished to put forward a claim of discrimination. "An amorphous claim that there has been past discrimination in a particular industry cannot justify the use of an unyielding racial quota," wrote Justice O'Connor in 1989. By 1996 a federal circuit court had gone so far as to state (in *Hopwood v. State of Texas et al.*) that race could not be a factor in college admissions.

Court decisions on abortion and religion in public schools demonstrated a similar desire to set limits on the established precedents. *Planned Parenthood v. Casey* (1992) upheld a woman's constitutional right to an abortion, but it also allowed states to place new restrictions on the procedure. Other Court decisions let stand laws restricting abortions and even abortion counseling by clinics or hospitals receiving federal funds. And while the Court affirmed that religious teachings or prayer could have no official status in public schools, it allowed students to engage in voluntary prayer as well as to form religious clubs meeting after school.

## Disillusionment and Anger

Ronald Reagan had given a sunny face to conservatism. He assured voters that if taxes were cut, the economy would revive and deficits fall. Yet after a decade of conservative leadership, the deficit had ballooned and state and local governments were larger than ever. A growing number of Americans felt that the institutions of government had come seriously off track.

A series of longer-term crises contributed to this disillusionment. One of the most threatening centered on the nation's savings and loan institutions. By *S&L crisis* the end of the 1980s these "thrifts" were failing at the highest rate since the Great Depression. To help banks, the Reagan administration and Congress had cut back federal regulations, allowing savings banks to invest their funds more speculatively. Reagan's advisers ignored the warnings that fraud and mismanagement were increasing sharply. Only during the Bush administration did it become clearer that the cost of restoring solvency would run into hundreds of billions of taxpayers' dollars.

The late 1980s also brought a public health crisis. Americans were spending a higher percentage of their resources on medical care than citizens in other *Health crises* nations, yet they were no healthier. As medical costs soared, more than 30 million Americans had no health insurance. The crisis was worsened by a fatal disorder that physicians began diagnosing in the early 1980s: Acquired Immune Deficiency Syndrome, or AIDS. With no cure available, the disease threatened to take on epidemic proportions, not only in the United States but across the globe. Yet because the illness at first struck hardest at the male homosexual community and intravenous drug abusers, many groups in American society resisted addressing the problem.

The anger felt in the country had a social edge as well. In 1991 Los Angeles police were videotaped while arresting a black motorist for speeding and drunken *Los Angeles riots* driving. The tape showed Rodney King being struck more than 50 times by officers wielding nightsticks. When a suburban white jury acquitted the officers, the black community of central Los Angeles exploded. Stores were looted, some 600 buildings were set ablaze, and more than 50 people were killed. Clearly, the anger in central Los Angeles over racism was also fueled by the stresses of high unemployment, urban poverty, and economic decline.

Bank failures, skyrocketing health costs, an increase in unemployment and poverty—by themselves none of these problems could derail the conservative rebellion that had swept Ronald Reagan into office. Still, the crises demonstrated how pivotal government had become in providing social services and limiting the abuses of powerful private interests in a highly industrialized society. Neither the Reagan nor the Bush administrations had developed a clear way to address such problems without the intervention of government—the sort of intervention envisioned by a more activist Republican, Teddy Roosevelt, at the turn of the century.

## The Election of 1992

In the end, George Bush's inability to rein in soaring government deficits proved most damaging to his reelection prospects. "Read my lips! No new taxes," he had pledged to campaign audiences in 1988. But the president and

*Gramm-Rudman Act*

Congress were at loggerheads over how to reach the holy grail of so many conservatives: a balanced budget. In 1985 Congress had passed the Gramm–Rudman Act, establishing a set of steadily increasing limits on federal spending. These limits were meant to force Congress and the president to make hard choices needed to reach a balanced budget. If they did not, automatic across-the-board cuts would go into effect. By 1990 the law's automatic procedures were threatening programs like Medicare, which Republicans and Democrats alike supported. Facing such unpopular cuts, Bush agreed to a package of new taxes along with budget cuts. Conservatives felt betrayed, and in the end, the deficit grew larger all the same.

As the election of 1992 approached, unemployment stood at more than 8 percent, penetrating to areas of the economy not affected by most recessions. Statistics

*White-collar unemployment*

showed that real wages for middle-class families had not increased since the early 1970s and had actually declined during Bush's presidency. Many Reagan Democrats seemed ready to return to the party of Franklin Roosevelt, who had mobilized an activist government in a time of economic depression. Other disillusioned voters were drawn to the maverick candidacy of Texas computer billionaire H. Ross Perot. The blunt-talking Perot demanded a government run like a business, but free of big-business lobbyists.

Meanwhile, the Democrats gave their nomination to Governor Bill Clinton of Arkansas, who hammered away at Bush for failing to revive the economy. "It's

*"It's the economy . . ."*

the economy, stupid!" read the sign tacked up at headquarters, to remind Clinton workers of the campaign's central theme. Clinton painted himself as a new kind of Democrat: moderate, willing to work with business, and not a creature of liberal interest groups.

The Bush campaign badly miscalculated by allowing the most conservative members of the party to dominate the Republican convention. On election day, Clinton captured 43 percent of the popular vote (to Bush's 38 and Perot's 19) in the largest turnout—55 percent—in 20 years. The election of four women to the Senate, including the first African American woman, Carol Moseley Braun, indicated that gender had become an electoral factor.

## THE CLINTON PRESIDENCY

Did Clinton's victory in 1992 signal a reversal of fortune for the conservatives? Sixty-two percent of the electorate had voted against the Republicans, but only 43 percent had voted for the man who now looked to lead the nation.

Still, William Jefferson Clinton intended to bring change. He shared with his wife, Hillary Rodham Clinton, a love for politics and government as well as a determination to address problems neglected by the "hands-off" policies of Reagan and Bush. An activist executive could accomplish much, he insisted, "even a president without a majority mandate coming in, if the president has a disciplined, aggressive agenda. . . ." Certainly Clinton's agenda was ambitious. Beyond seeking to revive the economy and rein in the deficit, he called for systematic reform of the welfare and health care systems, as well as measures to lessen the increasing violence in American life.

## The New World Disorder

Determined to focus on domestic issues, Clinton hoped to pay less attention to foreign affairs. Yet the "new world order" hailed by both Mikhail Gorbachev and George Bush seemed more than ever to be disrupted by regional conflicts.

In sub-Saharan Africa, corruption and one-party rule had severely weakened most economies, tribal violence mounted, and AIDS became epidemic. Brutal civil wars broke out in both Somalia and Rwanda. Clinton did sup-

*Civil wars in Somalia and Rwanda*

port President Bush's decision in December 1992 to send troops to aid famine-relief efforts in Somalia. But when U.S. troops withdrew in 1994, a stable government had not been established. Similary, the United States as well as European nations remained reluctant to intervene in Rwanda, where over a million people were massacred in 1994.

In Yugoslavia, Serbs fought Croats and Muslims who had broken off to form the independent state of Bosnia-Herzegovina. Western Europeans and Americans were dismayed by the systematic slaughter and rape of Muslims that Serbs justified in the name of "ethnic cleansing." In November 1995 the United States hosted peace talks between the warring factions in Dayton, Ohio. The resulting Dayton Accord called for Bosnia to remain a single nation, but governed as two separate republics. To help guarantee the peace, Clinton sent 20,000 American ground troops to Bosnia as part of an international peace-keeping mission.

Instability closer to home posed greater political problems for the president. With the economies of both Cuba and Haiti in shambles, desperate refugees

*Intervention in Haiti*

built boats and homemade rafts in their attempts to reach the United States. Thousands who arrived on American shores severely taxed the ability of local governments, especially in Florida. Instability in Haiti pushed the president to take a bold approach. In 1991 Haitian military leaders had forced their country's elected president, Jean-Bertrand Aristide, to leave the country. When a U.N.–sponsored economic embargo failed to oust the military regime, the Security Council in 1994 approved an invasion of Haiti by a multinational force. American troops proved crucial in convincing the military to leave and in reinstalling Aristide. The following year a smaller U.N. force replaced the Americans.

Whether in Africa, Eastern Europe, or the Caribbean, such regional crises demonstrated that a new global "world order" would be difficult to maintain. Despite the president's willingness to intervene in Haiti, his foreign policy marked a pulling back from the high-spending, high-profile style of the Reagan era. Clearly, Clinton believed his most important work remained at home.

## Recovery—but Reform?

The president emphasized his domestic priorities in his first appearance before a joint session of Congress in February 1993. In a graceful performance, Clinton improvised nearly half of his speech when his teleprompter broke down, a feat that would have eluded either Ronald Reagan or George Bush. The new president proposed a program of economic recovery that combined deficit reduction with a package of investments to stimulate the economy and repair the nation's decaying infrastructure.

But the president's facility for public speaking by no means ensured his command of Congress. Republicans filibustered to death the stimulus portion of Clinton's program. In August 1993 a compromise budget bill passed by only a single vote in the Senate. Still, it was a remarkable achievement. During the Reagan-Bush years deficits had

*Clinton's successes*

President Bill Clinton's most ambitious attempt at reform was to overhaul the nation's health care system to provide all Americans with basic health care (along with a card to guarantee it). But powerful interest groups opposed the legislation, which went down to defeat.

risen sharply, despite conservative rhetoric about balancing the budget. As prosperity returned to the economy, annual budget deficits steadily dwindled.

The budget bill victory provided Clinton with some momentum in other battles. In the fall he hammered together a bipartisan coalition to pass NAFTA, the North American Free Trade Agreement. With the promise of greater trade and jobs, the pact linked the United States more closely with Canada and Mexico. The president even helped supporters of gun control overcome the powerful opposition of the National Rifle Association to pass the Brady Bill, requiring a five-day waiting period on gun purchases.

Clinton's most ambitious reform was health care—and in that area he stumbled. A task force led by Hillary Rodham Clinton developed a plan designed to

*Health care reform*

provide health coverage for all Americans, including the 37 million who in 1994 remained uninsured. The plan proposed more far-reaching changes than a Republican proposal merely to reform insurance laws in order to make private medical coverage more readily available. If the bill had passed, the president and the Democratic majority in Congress might have staked their claim to a government that actively responded to some of the long-term problems facing American society. But the failure of health care reform heightened the perception of an ill-organized adminstration and a well-entrenched Democratic-controlled Congress content with the status quo.

## Revolution Reborn

The 1994 midterm elections confirmed the public's anger over political gridlock. For the first time since the Eisenhower years, Republicans captured majorities in both the House and the Senate. The combative new speaker of the house, Newt Gingrich of Georgia, proclaimed himself a "genuine revolutionary," and vowed to complete what Ronald Reagan had begun. Gingrich used the first hundred days of the new Congress to bring to a vote ten popular proposals from his campaign document, "The Contract with America." The proposals included a balanced budget amendment, tax cuts, and term limits for all members of Congress. Term limits was the only one of the ten proposals not passed by the House.

"When you look back five years from now," enthused Republican Governor Tommy Thompson of Wisconsin, "you're going to say they came, they saw,

*The revolution stumbles*

they conquered." But as Republicans assembled their budget, the public became increasingly worried. To pay for a $245 billion tax cut (and still balance the federal budget by the year 2002), Gingrich and his followers proposed scaling back Medicare expenditures and allowing Medicare premiums to double. Republicans also sought to roll back environmental legislation that had been passed over the previous quarter century. Their proposals reduced protection for endangered species, relaxed pollution controls set up by the Clean Water Act, and gave mining, ranching, and logging interests greater freedom to develop public lands.

When President Clinton threatened to veto the congressional budget, Republicans pushed for confrontation. Twice they forced the federal government to shut down. The result was a public relations disaster for the self-proclaimed revolutionaries, who were forced to back down.

At the same time, President Clinton began moving steadily toward the political center. In 1995, he proposed his own route toward a balanced budget by 2002. Similarly, in August 1996 the president signed into law a sweeping reform of welfare. The law owed as much to Republican ideas as it did to his. For the first time in sixty years, the social welfare policies of the liberal democratic state were being substantially reversed. The bill ended guarantees of federal aid to poor children, turning over such programs to the states. Food stamp spending was cut, and the law placed a five-year limit on payments to any family. Most adults receiving payments had to find work within two years.

*Clinton moves to the center*

As the election of 1996 approached, the Republican revolution had been chastened. At the same time, Clinton had adroitly adopted many issues that Republicans once called their own. Following a lackluster primary campaign, the Republicans nominated former Senator Bob Dole, an aging political technician, to run for president. In vain Dole and his running mate Jack Kemp sought to stir voters with promises of a 15 percent tax cut. With the economy robust, voters reelected Clinton by a comfortable margin (49 percent to Dole's 40 percent, with Ross Perot taking under 10 percent). Bill Clinton became the first Democrat since Franklin Roosevelt to win a second term in the White House.

## Morality and Politics

Clinton seemed to draw several lessons from his first four years in office. Republican victories in 1994 led him to accept much of the conservative rhetoric. "The era of 'big government' is over," he proclaimed. The defeat of his health care proposal led him to avoid large and complicated reforms.

Instead, Clinton looked to achieve more progressive reform through a succession of smaller, incremental changes. Some changes were largely symbolic, such as his promotion of school uniforms to promote discipline and civility. Other reforms were substantive. He championed a bill designed to make health insurance more readily available to citizens who had changed or lost their jobs. Even more ambitious, in 1997 a proposal to provide health insurance for children passed with his support. The president's cautious approach, combined with a prosperous economy, led Clinton's popularity in polls to rise above 60 percent.

*Incremental reforms*

But the president confronted a potential political disaster in January 1998: allegations that he had carried on an extramarital affair with a 21-year-old White House intern, and then pressed her to deny the affair under oath. Reporters raised the possibility that associates of the president had solicited jobs for the intern in return for her silence.

Accusations of personal misconduct by the president were not new. A long-running controversy, known as the Whitewater affair, centered on special treat-

*Presidential scandals*

ment that the Clintons might have received in a failed real estate venture during the early 1980s. In 1994 a panel of federal judges appointed Special Prosecutor Kenneth Starr to investigate. Starr prosecuted and convicted several friends of the president for fraud. Even so, four years of investigation produced little evidence implicating the president in any illegal activities.

Feverish press coverage of the alleged White House infidelity reignited controversy over the president's conduct. Clinton already faced a lawsuit accusing him of sexual harrassment while he served as governor of Arkansas. In response to the intern scandal, Special Prosecutor Starr enlarged his investigation. News reports suggested Starr was seeking to prove that the White House had participated in a cover-up, both of this scandal and of Whitewater. Television commentators spoke ominously of the president's resignation or, failing that, his impeachment.

To the amazement of Clinton's foes, the president's popularity ratings rose. A federal judge dismissed the sexual harrassment suit in March 1998. Unemployment reached new lows, while the stock market hit record highs. Preferring prosperity to political turmoil, the public refused to link the president's personal conduct with his job performance. In addition, Starr found himself embroiled in controversy. His aggressive pursuit of witnesses dismayed even some of his staunch supporters. Unless the investigation produced convincing evidence of legal wrongdoing, President Clinton appeared likely to serve out his second term, regardless of what Americans believed about his private life.

## A NATION OF NATIONS IN THE TWENTY-FIRST CENTURY

When George Washington took the oath of office in 1789, he understood all too well the odds against the survival of the United States. History offered no example of such a large and diverse republic ever enduring for long. As the United States approaches the twenty-first century, its population and territory have grown even larger and ever more diverse. More than 250 million inhabit a nation exceeding 3.6 million square miles. Such size and diversity would have astonished Washington. Given the present state of the world, in which ethnic, religious, and nationalist rivalries threaten so many nations, the survival of the American republic should perhaps astonish us as well.

How well the republic has dealt with the conflicts among its diverse citizenry has depended on the ability of different groups to participate equally and openly in the political system. The republic's most dramatic failure came with the Civil War. That breakdown occurred, it might be argued, because enslaved African Americans were forbidden any participation in the system—indeed, were treated as the property of other Americans who could and did exercise political power. Many pivotal moments in American history have turned on the attempts of groups to exercise effective political power—whether western Populists or eastern immigrants, militant suffragettes or concerned evangelicals. In a nation where half the people have moved over the past decade and immigration has reached new highs, diversity and mobility define the social fabric. As a consequence, the debate over equal participation will continue.

## The New Immigration

During the 1980s, more than 7 million immigrants entered the country legally—more than in any decade in American history except 1901–1910. Adding another 300,000 to 500,000 illegal immigrants each year, the total was even greater than the 8.8 million arriving in the first decade of the century.

Latin American immigrants accounted for as much as 40 percent of the yearly influx, as they had since the 1960s. But in addition to Mexicans, Cubans,

*Latin immigrants*

and Puerto Ricans, the Latino population in the 1980s included communities of Dominicans and Central Americans. Like immigrants at the turn of the century, established Hispanic families provided housing for newer immigrants, who were often single. The newcomers hoped to save money from their weekly paychecks to send to relatives in Mexico or Central America. However, in an economy increasingly divided between skilled jobs in the service sectors and low-paying unskilled jobs, Latinos lagged behind Anglos and black Americans in education. Often, the lack of adequate English-language skill discouraged success.

The political climate of the 1990s alarmed many Latinos. The welfare reform bill passed in 1996 prohibited legal immigrants who had not become citizens from receiving most federal welfare benefits. Furthermore, pressures to restrict immigration were rising, especially in California. In response, applications by legal immigrants to become U.S. citizens rose sharply: from almost 446,000 in 1995 to 1.2 million in 1996.

Once the Immigration Act of 1965 eliminated the national origins quota system, immigration from Asia increased heavily. By 1990 about 7.3 million

*Asian Americans*

Asian Americans lived in the United States. Like earlier immigrants from Europe, those from the Pacific rim came in waves. Some, like the Vietnamese "boat people" of the late 1970s, were driven from their homes by economic or political turmoil. Others were drawn to reunite families or realize greater opportunities in the Western Hemisphere. "My brother-in-law left his wife in Taiwan and came here as a student to get a Ph.D. in engineering," explained Subi Lin Felipe. "After he received his degree, he got a job in San Jose. Then he brought in a sister and his wife, who brought over one of her brothers and me. And my brother's wife then came."

Professional Asian-Indians emigrated in search of better jobs. Doctors and nurses constituted a large percentage of the early Korean immigrants. But

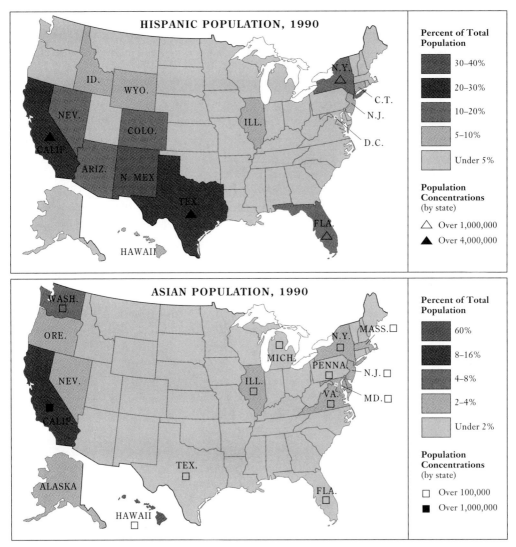

HISPANIC AND ASIAN POPULATIONS   Hispanics and Asians made up the two fastest-growing population groups in the United States over the past several decades. Demographers predict that Hispanics will soon displace African Americans as the nation's single largest minority group.

letters home soon attracted a more diverse population, which concentrated in small businesses. The presence of other Asian Americans and an international atmosphere drew many Asians to New York City, but climate made Hawaii and California particulary popular destinations. Of more than 800,000 Korean-Americans, about a quarter lived around Los Angeles in 1990. So, too, the 1.4 million Japanese-Americans settled primarily in California and Hawaii. By contrast, the federal government attempted to disperse around the country nearly half a million Vietnamese (as well as Cambodians and Laotians) who fled after the American withdrawal from Southeast Asia.

The relative success of many Asian Americans has led the media often to stereotype them as a "model minority"; yet the experience of Asian immigrants remains widely diverse, encompassing high-income Filipino-American doctors and low-income agricultural laborers, Japanese-Americans who are poor and elderly as well as those who are younger, upwardly mobile technicians. Ethnic tensions, made worse by job losses and an American trade deficit with Asian countries, gave rise periodically to acts of violence. During the 1992 Los Angeles riots, for example, Korean shops were often the targets of looters and arsonists.

*A "model minority"*

## Equality Still Denied

By the 1980s the African American community had seemingly split in two. A significant minority was successfully living the American dream. Almost three times more black Americans held public office in the 1970s and 1980s than had in the 1960s. They made substantial strides in the professions, management, sports, and entertainment. The earnings of black households rose faster than those for whites in the 1970s and 1980s, although they remained 20 percent lower.

But the surge of African Americans into middle-class occupations tended to disguise the persistence of poverty tied to race. In the 1970s and 1980s, more young families were counted among the nation's poor. Those families were increasingly headed by single women. More than 40 percent of all black families (versus 12 percent for whites) were headed by women, and the number was growing. To make matters worse, the largest numbers of black families were concentrated in urban areas hard hit by the recessionary economy. Black unemployment, particularly severe among teenagers and young adults, was twice the national average. More shocking still, the infant mortality rate for African Americans was double the white average and worse than that for some Third World nations. Homicide was the leading cause of death for black males between 15 and 34, and in that group about 20 percent had prison records. These were the cruelest realities of poverty.

*The persistence of poverty*

One event starkly dramatized the ongoing currents of racial tension in America: the murder trial of O. J. Simpson. Born into a ghetto family, Simpson had become first a football legend, then a movie star and television personality. He seemed to defy all notions that race prejudice restricted African Americans. But in June 1994 police charged Simpson with the murders of his white wife, Nicole, and a friend. During televised proceedings Simpson's attorneys transformed what seemed to be a strong prosecution case into a debate over whether Simpson had been the victim of systematic police racism. The defense revealed that the lead police officer in the case lied on the stand about his own prejudices and his use of racial slurs. After a trial

*The OJ case*

lasting almost a year, a jury took just four hours to acquit. Regardless of Simpson's guilt or innocence, the trial demonstrated the lines of race dividing American society. The vast majority of whites believed Simpson guilty; most African Americans thought he was innocent. White and black Americans disagreed because they held differing opinions of whether the American system of justice permitted a fair trial for all its citizens.

In the United States, where diversity—and therefore conflict—remains central to its history, the debate continues over how strongly government should intervene to manage the conflicts of a modern industrial state. For better or worse, the long-term trend has been clear. As economic power became more concentrated in the late nineteenth century and as cycles of boom and bust periodically wracked the nation, government has increased its powers to curb the excesses of the market and to provide both economic protection and social guarantees for its citizens. Undoubtedly the debate will continue, as it has for the past 200 years, over how to make diversity the strength, not the weakness, of a nation of nations.

## SIGNIFICANT EVENTS

1978 — *Bakke v. Regents of the University of California*

1979 — Moral Majority established

1980 — Ronald Reagan elected president

1981 — Reagan breaks air controllers' strike; Economic Recovery Tax Act; United States begins aiding Nicaraguan Contras

1982 — Attack on U.S. Marine barracks in Lebanon

1983 — Invasion of Grenada

1984 — Boland Amendment passed; Reagan reelected

1985 — Gramm–Rudman Act; United States begins secret arms-for-hostages negotiations with Iran

1986 — Reykjavík summit

1987 — Iran-Contra hearings

1988 — George Bush elected president

1989 — Fall of the Berlin Wall

1990 — Iraq invades Kuwait; Clean Air Act

1991 — Operation Desert Storm launched; Strategic Arms Reduction Treaty (START) concluded; Clarence Thomas hearings; 11 former republics of the Soviet Union become the Commonwealth of Independent States

1992 — Los Angeles riots; *Planned Parenthood v. Casey;* Bill Clinton elected president

1993 — Deficit-reduction budget passed; North American Free Trade Agreement approved

1994 — Health care reform fails; Republicans win control of Congress

1995 — O. J. Simpson acquitted in murder trial; Dayton accords signed

1996 — Welfare reform legislation signed; Clinton defeats Dole

1998 — Scandal over President Clinton's personal conduct

# APPENDIX

## THE DECLARATION OF INDEPENDENCE

*In Congress, July 4, 1776,*

THE UNANIMOUS DECLARATION OF THE
THIRTEEN UNITED STATES OF AMERICA

When, in the course of human events, it becomes necessary for one people to dissolve the political bands which have connected them with another, and to assume, among the powers of the earth, the separate and equal station to which the laws of nature and of nature's God entitle them, a decent respect to the opinions of mankind requires that they should declare the causes which impel them to the separation.

We hold these truths to be self-evident, that all men are created equal; that they are endowed by their Creator with certain unalienable rights; that among these, are life, liberty, and the pursuit of happiness. That, to secure these rights, governments are instituted among men, deriving their just powers from the consent of the governed; that, whenever any form of government becomes destructive of these ends, it is the right of the people to alter or to abolish it, and to institute a new government, laying its foundation on such principles, and organizing its powers in such form, as to them shall seem most likely to effect their safety and happiness. Prudence, indeed, will dictate that governments long established, should not be changed for light and transient causes; and, accordingly, all experience hath shown, that mankind are more disposed to suffer, while evils are sufferable, than to right themselves by abolishing the forms to which they are accustomed. But, when a long train of abuses and usurpations, pursuing invariably the same object, evinces a design to reduce them under absolute despotism, it is their right, it is their duty, to throw off such government and to provide new guards for their future security. Such has been the patient sufferance of these colonies, and such is now the necessity which constrains them to alter their former systems of government. The history of the present King of Great Britain is a history of repeated injuries and usurpations, all having, in direct object, the establishment of an absolute tyranny over these States. To prove this, let facts be submitted to a candid world:

He has refused his assent to laws the most wholesome and necessary for the public good.

He has forbidden his governors to pass laws of immediate and pressing importance, unless suspended in their operation till his assent should be obtained; and, when so suspended, he has utterly neglected to attend to them.

He has refused to pass other laws for the accommodation of large districts of people, unless those people would relinquish the right of representation in the legislature; a right inestimable to them, and formidable to tyrants only.

He has called together legislative bodies at places unusual, uncomfortable, and distant from the depository of their public records, for the sole purpose of fatiguing them into compliance with his measures.

He has dissolved representative houses repeatedly for opposing, with manly firmness, his invasions on the rights of the people.

He has refused, for a long time after such dissolutions, to cause others to be elected; whereby the legislative powers, incapable of annihilation, have returned to the people at large for their exercise; the state remaining, in the meantime, exposed to all the danger of invasion from without, and convulsions within.

He has endeavored to prevent the population of these States; for that purpose, obstructing the laws for naturalization of foreigners, refusing to pass others to encourage their migration hither, and raising the conditions of new appropriations of lands.

He has obstructed the administration of justice, by refusing his assent to laws for establishing judiciary powers.

He has made judges dependent on his will alone, for the tenure of their offices, and the amount and payment of their salaries.

He has erected a multitude of new offices, and sent hither swarms of officers to harass our people, and eat out their substance.

He has kept among us, in time of peace, standing armies, without the consent of our legislatures.

He has affected to render the military independent of, and superior to, the civil power.

He has combined, with others, to subject us to a jurisdiction foreign to our Constitution, and unacknowledged by our laws; giving his assent to their acts of pretended legislation:

For quartering large bodies of armed troops among us:

For protecting them by a mock trial, from punishment, for any murders which they should commit on the inhabitants of these States:

For cutting off our trade with all parts of the world:

For imposing taxes on us without our consent:

For depriving us, in many cases, of the benefit of trial by jury:

For transporting us beyond seas to be tried for pretended offences:

For abolishing the free system of English laws in a neighboring province, establishing therein an arbitrary government, and enlarging its boundaries, so as to render it at once an example and fit instrument for introducing the same absolute rule into these colonies:

For taking away our charters, abolishing our most valuable laws, and altering, fundamentally, the powers of our governments:

For suspending our own legislatures, and declaring themselves invested with power to legislate for us in all cases whatsoever.

He has abdicated government here, by declaring us out of his protection, and waging war against us.

He has plundered our seas, ravaged our coasts, burnt our towns, and destroyed the lives of our people.

He is, at this time, transporting large armies of foreign mercenaries to complete the works of death, desolation, and tyranny, already begun, with circumstances of cruelty and perfidy scarcely paralleled in the most barbarous ages, and totally unworthy the head of a civilized nation.

He has constrained our fellow citizens, taken captive on the high seas, to bear arms against their country, to become the executioners of their friends, and brethren, or to fall themselves by their hands.

He has excited domestic insurrections amongst us, and has endeavored to bring on the inhabitants of our frontiers, the merciless Indian savages, whose known rule of warfare is an undistinguished destruction of all ages, sexes, and conditions.

In every stage of these oppressions, we have petitioned for redress, in the most humble terms; our repeated petitions have been answered only by repeated injury. A prince, whose character is thus marked by every act which may define a tyrant, is unfit to be the ruler of a free people.

Nor have we been wanting in attention to our British brethren. We have warned them from time to time, of attempts made by their legislature to extend an unwarrantable jurisdiction over us. We have reminded them of the circumstances of our emigration and settlement here. We have appealed to their native justice and magnanimity, and we have conjured them, by the ties of our common kindred, to disavow these usurpations, which would inevitably interrupt our connections and correspondence. They, too, have been deaf to the voice of justice and consanguinity. We must, therefore, acquiesce in the necessity which denounces our separation, and hold them as we hold the rest of mankind, enemies in war, in peace, friends.

We, therefore, the representatives of the United States of America, in general Congress assembled, appealing to the Supreme Judge of the world for the rectitude of our intentions, do, in the name, and by the authority of the good people of these colonies, solemnly publish and declare, that these united colonies are, and of right ought to be, free and independent states: that they are absolved from all allegiance to the British Crown, and that all political connection between them and the state of Great Britain is and ought to be, totally dissolved; and that, as free and independent states, they have full power to levy war, conclude peace, contract alliances, establish commerce, and to do all other acts and things which independent states may of right do. And, for the support of this declaration, with a firm reliance on the protection of Divine Providence, we mutually pledge to each other our lives, our fortunes, and our sacred honor.

The foregoing Declaration was, by order of Congress, engrossed, and signed by the following members:

# JOHN HANCOCK

| **New Hampshire** | **New York** | **Delaware** | **North Carolina** |
|---|---|---|---|
| Josiah Bartlett | William Floyd | Caesar Rodney | William Hooper |
| William Whipple | Philip Livingston | George Reed | Joseph Hewes |
| Matthew Thornton | Francis Lewis | Thomas M'Kean | John Penn |
| | Lewis Morris | | |
| | | | |
| **Massachusetts Bay** | **New Jersey** | **Maryland** | **South Carolina** |
| Samuel Adams | Richard Stockton | Samuel Chase | Edward Rutledge |
| John Adams | John Witherspoon | William Paca | Thomas Heyward, Jr. |
| Robert Treat Paine | Francis Hopkinson | Thomas Stone | Thomas Lynch, Jr. |
| Elbridge Gerry | John Hart | Charles Carroll, | Arthur Middleton |
| | Abraham Clark | of Carrollton | |
| | | | |
| **Rhode Island** | **Pennsylvania** | **Virginia** | **Georgia** |
| Stephen Hopkins | Robert Morris | George Wythe | Button Gwinnett |
| William Ellery | Benjamin Rush | Richard Henry Lee | Lyman Hall |
| | Benjamin Franklin | Thomas Jefferson | George Walton |
| **Connecticut** | John Morton | Benjamin Harrison | |
| Roger Sherman | George Clymer | Thomas Nelson, Jr. | |
| Samuel Huntington | James Smith | Francis Lightfoot Lee | |
| William Williams | George Taylor | Carter Braxton | |
| Oliver Wolcott | James Wilson | | |
| | George Ross | | |

*Resolved*, That copies of the Declaration be sent to the several assemblies, conventions, and committees, or councils of safety, and to the several commanding officers of the continental troops; that it be proclaimed in each of the United States, at the head of the army.

# THE CONSTITUTION OF THE UNITED STATES OF AMERICA[1]

We the People of the United States, in Order to form a more perfect Union, establish Justice, insure domestic Tranquility, provide for the common defence, promote the general Welfare, and secure the Blessings of Liberty to ourselves and our Posterity, do ordain and establish this CONSTITUTION for the United States of America.

## ARTICLE 1

**Section 1.**  All legislative Powers herein granted shall be vested in a Congress of the United States, which shall consist of a Senate and House of Representatives.

**Section 2.**  The House of Representatives shall be composed of Members chosen every second Year by the People of the several States, and the Electors in each State shall have the Qualifications requisite for Electors of the most numerous Branch of the State Legislature.

No Person shall be a Representative who shall not have attained to the Age of twenty-five Years, and been seven Years a Citizen of the United States, and who shall not, when elected, be an Inhabitant of that State in which he shall be chosen.

[Representatives and direct Taxes[2] shall be apportioned among the several States which may be included within this Union, according to their respective Numbers, which shall be determined by adding to the whole Number of free Persons, including those bound to Service for a Term of Years, and excluding Indians not taxed, three fifths of all other Persons.][3] The actual Enumeration shall be made within three Years after the first Meeting of the Congress of the United States, and within every subsequent Term of ten Years, in such Manner as they shall by Law direct. The Number of Representatives shall not exceed one for every thirty Thousand, but each State shall have at Least one Representative; and until such enumeration shall be made, the State of New Hampshire shall be entitled to chuse three, Massachusetts eight, Rhode-Island and Providence Plantations one, Connecticut five, New York six, New Jersey four, Pennsylvania eight, Delaware one, Maryland six, Virginia ten, North Carolina five, South Carolina five, and Georgia three.

When vacancies happen in the Representation from any State, the Executive Authority thereof shall issue Writs of Election to fill such Vacancies.

The House of Representatives shall chuse their Speaker and other Officers; and shall have the sole Power of Impeachment.

**Section 3.**  The Senate of the United States shall be composed of two Senators from each State, chosen by the Legislature thereof, for six Years; and each Senator shall have one Vote.

Immediately after they shall be assembled in Consequence of the first Election, they shall be divided as equally as may be into three Classes. The Seats of the Senators of the first Class shall be vacated at the Expiration of the second Year, of the second Class at the Expiration of the fourth Year, and of the third Class at the Expiration of the sixth Year, so that one-third may be chosen every second Year; and if Vacancies happen by Resignation, or otherwise, during the Recess of the Legislature of any State, the Executive thereof may make temporary Appointments until the next Meeting of the Legislature, which shall then fill such Vacancies.

---

[1]This version follows the original Constitution in capitalization and spelling. It is adapted from the text published by the United States Department of the Interior, Office of Education.

[2]Altered by the Sixteenth Amendment.

[3]Negated by the Fourteenth Amendment.

No Person shall be a Senator who shall not have attained to the Age of thirty Years, and been nine Years a Citizen of the United States, and who shall not, when elected, be an Inhabitant of that State for which he shall be chosen.

The Vice President of the United States shall be President of the Senate, but shall have no vote, unless they be equally divided.

The Senate shall chuse their other Officers and also a President pro tempore, in the absence of the Vice President, or when he shall exercise the Office of President of the United States.

The Senate shall have the sole Power to try all Impeachments. When sitting for that purpose they shall be on Oath or Affirmation. When the President of the United States is tried, the Chief Justice shall preside: And no person shall be convicted without the Concurrence of two thirds of the Members present.

Judgment in Cases of Impeachment shall not extend further than to removal from Office, and disqualification to hold and enjoy any Office of honor, Trust, or Profit under the United States: but the Party convicted shall nevertheless be liable and subject to Indictment, Trial, Judgment, and Punishment, according to Law.

**Section 4.**   The Times, Places and Manner of holding Elections for Senators and Representatives, shall be prescribed in each State by the Legislature thereof; but the Congress may at any time by Law make or alter such Regulations, except as to the Places of Chusing Senators.

The Congress shall assemble at least once in every Year, and such Meeting shall be on the first Monday in December, unless they shall by Law appoint a different Day.

**Section 5.**   Each House shall be the Judge of the Elections, Returns and Qualifications of its own Members, and a Majority of each shall constitute a Quorum to do Business; but a smaller number may adjourn from day to day, and may be authorized to compel the Attendance of absent Members, in such Manner, and under such Penalties, as each House may provide.

Each House may determine the Rules of its Proceedings, punish its Members for disorderly Behaviour, and, with the Concurrence of two thirds, expel a Member.

Each House shall keep a Journal of its Proceedings, and from time to time publish the same, excepting such Parts as may in their Judgment require Secrecy; and the Yeas and Nays of the Members of either House on any question shall, at the Desire of one fifth of those Present, be entered on the Journal.

Neither House, during the Session of Congress, shall, without the Consent of the other, adjourn for more than three days, nor to any other Place than that in which the two Houses shall be sitting.

**Section 6.**   The Senators and Representatives shall receive a Compensation for their Services, to be ascertained by Law, and paid out of the Treasury of the United States. They shall in all Cases, except Treason, Felony, and Breach of the Peace, be privileged from Arrest during their Attendance at the Session of their respective Houses, and in going to and returning from the same; and for any Speech or Debate in either House, they shall not be questioned in any other Place.

No Senator or Representative shall, during the Time for which he was elected, be appointed to any civil Office under the Authority of the United States, which shall have been created, or the Emoluments whereof shall have been increased, during such time; and no Person holding any Office under the United States shall be a Member of either House during his continuance in Office.

**Section 7.**   All Bills for raising Revenue shall originate in the House of Representatives; but the Senate may propose or concur with Amendments as on other bills.

Every Bill which shall have passed the House of Representatives and the Senate, shall, before it become a Law, be presented to the President of the United States; If he approve he shall sign it, but if not he shall return it, with his Objections, to that House in which it shall have originated, who shall enter the Objections at large on their Journal, and proceed to reconsider it. If after such Reconsideration two thirds of that House shall agree to pass the bill, it shall be sent, together with the objections, to the other House, by which it shall likewise be reconsidered, and if approved by two thirds of that House, it shall become a Law. But in all such Cases the Votes of both Houses shall be determined by Yeas and Nays, and the Names of the Persons voting for and against the Bill shall be entered on the Journal of each House respectively. If any Bill shall not be returned by the President within ten Days (Sundays excepted) after it shall have been presented to him, the Same shall be a Law, in like Manner as if he had signed it, unless the Congress by their Adjournment prevent its Return, in which Case it shall not be a Law.

Every Order, Resolution, or Vote to which the Concurrence of the Senate and House of Representatives may be necessary (except on a question of Adjournment) shall be presented to the President of the United States; and before the Same shall take Effect, shall be approved by him, or being disapproved by him, shall be repassed by two thirds of the Senate and House of Representatives, according to the Rules and Limitations prescribed in the Case of a Bill.

**Section 8.** The Congress shall have Power To lay and collect Taxes, Duties, Imposts and Excises, to pay the Debts and provide for the common Defence and general Welfare of the United States; but all Duties, Imposts and Excises shall be uniform throughout the United States;

To borrow money on the credit of the United States;

To regulate Commerce with foreign Nations, and among the several States, and with the Indian Tribes;

To establish an uniform rule of Naturalization, and uniform Laws on the subject of Bankruptcies throughout the United States;

To coin Money, regulate the Value thereof, and of foreign Coin, and fix the Standard of Weights and Measures;

To provide for the Punishment of counterfeiting the Securities and current Coin of the United States;

To establish Post Offices and post Roads;

To promote the Progress of Science and useful Arts, by securing for limited Times to Authors and Inventors the exclusive Right to their respective Writings and Discoveries;

To constitute Tribunals inferior to the Supreme Court;

To define and punish Piracies and Felonies committed on the high Seas, and Offenses against the Law of Nations;

To declare War, grant Letters of Marque and Reprisal, and make Rules concerning Captures on Land and Water;

To raise and support Armies, but no Appropriation of Money to that Use shall be for a longer Term than two Years;

To provide and maintain a Navy;

To make Rules for the Government and Regulation of the land and naval forces;

To provide for calling forth the Militia to execute the Laws of the Union, suppress Insurrections and repel Invasions;

To provide for organizing, arming, and disciplining the Militia, and for governing such Part of them as may be employed in the Service of the United States, reserving to the States respectively, the Appointment of the Officers, and the Authority of training the Militia according to the discipline prescribed by Congress;

To exercise exclusive Legislation in all Cases whatsoever, over such District (not exceeding ten Miles square) as may, by Cession of particular States, and the acceptance of Congress, become the Seat of the Government of the United States, and to exercise like Authority over all Places purchased by the Consent of the Legislature of the State in which the Same shall be, for the Erection of Forts, Magazines, Arsenals, Dock-yards, and other needful Buildings;—And

To make all Laws which shall be necessary and proper for carrying into Execution the foregoing Powers, and all other Powers vested by this Constitution in the Government of the United States, or in any Department or Officer thereof.

**Section 9.** The Migration or Importation of such Persons as any of the States now existing shall think proper to admit, shall not be prohibited by the Congress prior to the Year one thousand eight hundred and eight, but a tax or duty may be imposed on such Importation, not exceeding ten dollars for each Person.

The privilege of the Writ of Habeas Corpus shall not be suspended, unless when in Cases of Rebellion or Invasion the public Safety may require it.

No bill of Attainder or ex post facto Law shall be passed.

No capitation, or other direct, Tax shall be laid unless in Proportion to the Census or Enumeration herein before directed to be taken.

No Tax or Duty shall be laid on Articles exported from any State.

No Preference shall be given by any Regulation of Commerce or Revenue to the Ports of one State over those of another: nor shall Vessels bound to, or from, one State, be obliged to enter, clear, or pay Duties in another.

No Money shall be drawn from the Treasury, but in Consequence of Appropriations made by Law; and a regular Statement and Account of the Receipts and Expenditures of all public Money shall be published from time to time.

No Title of Nobility shall be granted by the United States: And no Person holding any Office of Profit or Trust under them, shall, without the Consent of the Congress, accept of any present, Emolument, Office, or Title, of any kind whatever, from any King, Prince, or foreign State.

**Section 10.** No State shall enter into any Treaty, Alliance, or Confederation; grant Letters of Marque and Reprisal; coin Money; emit Bills of Credit; make any Thing but gold and silver Coin a Tender in Payment of Debts; pass any Bill of Attainder, ex post facto Law, or Law impairing the Obligation of Contracts, or grant any Title of Nobility.

No State shall, without the Consent of the Congress, lay any Imposts or Duties on Imports or Exports, except what may be absolutely necessary for executing its inspection Laws; and the net Produce of all Duties and Imposts, laid by any State on Imports or Exports, shall be for the use of the Treasury of the United States; and all such Laws shall be subject to the Revision and Control of the Congress.

No state shall, without the Consent of Congress, lay any duty of Tonnage, keep Troops, or Ships of War in time of Peace, enter into any Agreement or Compact with another State, or with a foreign Power, or engage in War, unless actually invaded, or in such imminent Danger as will not admit of delay.

# ARTICLE II

**Section 1.** The executive Power shall be vested in a President of the United States of America. He shall hold his Office during the Term of four years, and, together with the Vice President, chosen for the same Term, be elected, as follows:

Each State shall appoint, in such Manner as the Legislature thereof may direct, a Number of Electors, equal to the whole Number of Senators and Representatives to which the State may be entitled in the Congress: but no Senator or Representative, or Person holding an Office of Trust or Profit under the United States, shall be appointed an Elector.

[The Electors shall meet in their respective States, and vote by Ballot for two persons, of whom one at least shall not be an Inhabitant of the same State with themselves. And they shall make a List of all the Persons voted for, and of the Number of Votes for each; which List they shall sign and certify, and transmit sealed to the Seat of the Government of the United States, directed to the President of the Senate. The President of the Senate shall, in the Presence of the Senate and House of Representatives, open all the Certificates, and the Votes shall then be counted. The Person having the greatest Number of Votes shall be the President, if such Number be a Majority of the whole Number of Electors appointed; and if there be more than one who have such Majority, and have an equal Number of Votes, then the House of Representatives shall immediately chuse by Ballot one of them for President; and if no Person have a Majority, then from the five highest on the List the said House shall in like Manner chuse the President. But in chusing the President, the Votes shall be taken by States, the Representation from each State having one Vote; a quorum for this Purpose shall consist of a Member or Members from two-thirds of the States, and a Majority of all the States shall be necessary to a Choice. In every Case, after the Choice of the President, the Person having the greatest Number of Votes of the Electors shall be the Vice President. But if there should remain two or more who have equal votes, the Senate shall chuse from them by Ballot the Vice President.][4]

The Congress may determine the Time of chusing the Electors, and the Day on which they shall give their Votes; which Day shall be the same throughout the United States.

No person except a natural-born Citizen, or a Citizen of the United States, at the time of the Adoption of this Constitution, shall be eligible to the Office of President; neither shall any Person be eligible to that Office who shall not have attained to the Age of thirty-five years, and been fourteen Years a Resident within the United States.

In Case of the Removal of the President from Office, or of his Death, Resignation, or Inability to discharge the Powers and Duties of the said Office, the same shall devolve on the Vice President, and the Congress may by Law provide for the Case of Removal, Death, Resignation, or Inability, both of the President and Vice President, declaring what Officer shall then act as President, and such Officer shall act accordingly, until the disability be removed, or a President shall be elected.

The President shall, at stated Times, receive for his Services a Compensation, which shall neither be increased nor diminished during the Period for which he shall have been elected, and he shall not receive within that Period any other Emolument from the United States, or any of them.

Before he enter on the execution of his Office, he shall take the following Oath or Affirmation:— "I do solemnly swear (or affirm) that I will faithfully execute the Office of President of the United States, and will, to the best of my Ability, preserve, protect, and defend the Constitution of the United States."

**Section 2.** The President shall be Commander in Chief of the Army and Navy of the United States, and of the Militia of the several States, when called into the actual Service of the United States; he may require the Opinion, in writing, of the principal Officer in each of the executive Departments, upon any subject relating to the Duties of their respective Offices, and he shall have Power to Grant Reprieves and Pardons for Offenses against the United States, except in Cases of Impeachment.

He shall have Power, by and with the Advice and Consent of the Senate, to make Treaties, provided two-thirds of the Senators present concur; and he shall nominate, and by and with the Advice and Consent of the Senate, shall appoint Ambassadors, other public Ministers and Consuls, Judges of the Supreme Court, and all other Officers of the United States, whose Appointments are not herein otherwise provided for, and which shall be established by Law: but the Congress may by Law vest the Appointment of such inferior Officers, as they think proper, in the President alone, in the Courts of Law, or in the Heads of Departments.

The President shall have Power to fill up all Vacancies that may happen during the Recess of the Senate, by granting Commissions which shall expire at the End of their next Session.

**Section 3.** He shall from time to time give to the Congress Information of the State of the Union, and recommend to their Consideration such Measures as he shall judge necessary and expedient; he may, on extraordinary occasions, convene both Houses, or either of them, and in Case of Disagreement between them, with respect to the Time of Adjournment, he may adjourn them to such Time as he shall think proper; he shall receive Ambassadors and other public Ministers; he shall take care that the Laws be faithfully executed, and shall Commission all the Officers of the United States.

**Section 4.** The President, Vice President and all civil Officers of the United States, shall be removed from Office on Impeachment for, and Conviction of, Treason, Bribery, or other high Crimes and Misdemeanors.

---

[4]Revised by the Twelfth Amendment.

# ARTICLE III

**Section 1.** The judicial Power of the United States, shall be vested in one supreme Court, and in such inferior Courts as the Congress may from time to time ordain and establish. The Judges, both of the supreme and inferior Courts, shall hold their Offices during good Behaviour, and shall, at stated Times, receive for their Services, a Compensation, which shall not be diminished during their Continuance in Office.

**Section 2.** The judicial Power shall extend to all Cases, in Law and Equity, arising under this Constitution, the Laws of the United States, and Treaties made, or which shall be made, under their Authority;—to all Cases affecting ambassadors, other public ministers and consuls;—to all cases of admiralty and maritime Jurisdiction;—to Controversies to which the United States shall be a Party;—to Controversies between two or more States;—between a State and Citizens of another State;[5]—between Citizens of different States—between Citizens of the same State claiming Lands under Grants of different States, and between a State, or the Citizens thereof, and foreign States, Citizens, or Subjects.

In all Cases affecting Ambassadors, other public Ministers and Consuls, and those in which a State shall be Party, the supreme Court shall have original Jurisdiction. In all the other Cases before mentioned, the supreme Court shall have appellate Jurisdiction, both as to Law and Fact, with such Exceptions, and under such Regulations as the Congress shall make.

The trial of all Crimes, except in Cases of Impeachment, shall be by Jury; and such Trial shall be held in the State where the said Crimes shall have been committed; but when not committed within any State, the Trial shall be at such Place or Places as the Congress may by Law have directed.

**Section 3.** Treason against the United States, shall consist only in levying War against them, or in adhering to their Enemies, giving them Aid and Comfort. No Person shall be convicted of Treason unless on the Testimony of two Witnesses to the same overt Act, or on Confession in open Court.

The Congress shall have power to declare the Punishment of Treason, but no Attainder of Treason shall work Corruption of Blood, or Forfeiture except during the Life of the Person attainted.

# ARTICLE IV

**Section 1.** Full Faith and Credit shall be given in each State to the public Acts, Records, and judicial Proceedings of every other State. And the Congress may by general Laws prescribe the Manner in which such Acts, Records and Proceedings shall be proved, and the Effect thereof.

**Section 2.** The Citizens of each State shall be entitled to all Privileges and Immunities of Citizens in the several States.

A Person charged in any State with Treason, Felony, or other Crime, who shall flee from Justice, and be found in another State, shall on demand of the executive Authority of the State from which he fled, be delivered up, to be removed to the State having Jurisdiction of the crime.

No Person held to Service or Labour in one State, under the Laws thereof, escaping into another, shall, in Consequence of any Law or Regulation therein, be discharged from such Service or Labour, but shall be delivered up on Claim of the Party to whom such Service or Labour may be due.

---

[5]Qualified by the Eleventh Amendment.

**Section 3.**   New States may be admitted by the Congress into this Union; but no new State shall be formed or erected within the Jurisdiction of any other State; nor any State be formed by the Junction of two or more States, or parts of States, without the Consent of the Legislatures of the States concerned as well as of the Congress.

The Congress shall have Power to dispose of and make all needful Rules and Regulations respecting the Territory or other Property belonging to the United States; and nothing in this Constitution shall be so construed as to Prejudice any Claims of the United States, or of any particular State.

**Section 4.**   The United States shall guarantee to every State in this Union a Republican Form of Government, and shall protect each of them against Invasion; and on Application of the Legislature, or of the Executive (when the Legislature cannot be convened) against domestic Violence.

## ARTICLE V

The Congress, whenever two-thirds of both Houses shall deem it necessary, shall propose Amendments to this Constitution, or, on the Application of the Legislatures of two-thirds of the several States, shall call a Convention for proposing Amendments, which, in either Case, shall be valid to all Intents and Purposes, as part of this Constitution, when ratified by the Legislatures of three-fourths of the several States, or by Conventions in three-fourths thereof, as the one or the other Mode of Ratification may be proposed by the Congress; Provided that no Amendment which may be made prior to the Year One thousand eight hundred and eight shall in any Manner affect the first and fourth Clauses in the Ninth Section of the first Article; and that no State, without its Consent, shall be deprived of its equal Suffrage in the Senate.

## ARTICLE VI

All Debts contracted and Engagements entered into, before the Adoption of this Constitution, shall be as valid against the United States under this Constitution, as under the Confederation.

This Constitution, and the Laws of the United States which shall be made in Pursuance thereof; and all Treaties made, or which shall be made, under the Authority of the United States, shall be the supreme Law of the Land; and the Judges in every State shall be bound thereby, any Thing in the Constitution or Laws of any State to the Contrary notwithstanding.

The Senators and Representatives before mentioned, and the Members of the several State Legislatures, and all executive and judicial Officers, both of the United States and of the several States, shall be bound by Oath or Affirmation to support this Constitution; but no religious Tests shall ever be required as a qualification to any Office or public Trust under the United States.

## ARTICLE VII

The Ratification of the Conventions of nine States shall be sufficient for the Establishment of this Constitution between the States so ratifying the same.

Done in Convention by the Unanimous Consent of the States present the Seventeenth Day of September in the Year of our Lord one thousand seven hundred and Eighty seven, and of the Independence of the United States of America the Twelfth. In Witness whereof We have hereunto subscribed our Names.[6]

---

[6]These are the full names of the signers, which in some cases are not the signatures on the document.

# GEORGE WASHINGTON

PRESIDENT AND DEPUTY FROM VIRGINIA

**New Hampshire**
John Langdon
Nicholas Gilman

**New Jersey**
William Livingston
David Brearley
William Paterson
Jonathan Dayton

**Delaware**
George Read
Gunning Bedford, Jr.
John Dickinson
Richard Bassett
Jacob Broom

**North Carolina**
William Blount
Richard Dobbs
 Spaight
Hugh Williamson

**Massachusetts**
Nathaniel Gorham
Rufus King

**Connecticut**
William Samuel
 Johnson
Roger Sherman

**New York**
Alexander Hamilton

**Pennsylvania**
Benjamin Franklin
Thomas Mifflin
Robert Morris
George Clymer
Thomas FitzSimons
Jared Ingersoll
James Wilson
Gouverneur Morris

**Maryland**
James McHenry
Daniel of
 St. Thomas Jenifer
Daniel Carroll

**Virginia**
John Blair
James Madison, Jr.

**South Carolina**
John Rutledge
Charles Cotesworth
 Pinckney
Charles Pinckney
Pierce Butler

**Georgia**
William Few
Abraham Baldwin

*Articles in Addition to, and Amendment of, the Constitution of the United States of America, Proposed by Congress, and Ratified by the Legislatures of the Several States, Pursuant to the Fifth Article of the Original Constitution*[7]

## [AMENDMENT I]

Congress shall make no law respecting an establishment of religion, or prohibiting the free exercise thereof; or abridging the freedom of speech, or of the press; or the right of the people peaceably to assemble, and to petition the Government for a redress of grievances.

## [AMENDEMENT II]

A well regulated Militia, being necessary to the security of a free State, the right of the people to keep and bear Arms shall not be infringed.

## [AMENDMENT III]

No Soldier shall, in time of peace, be quartered in any house, without the consent of the Owner, nor in time of war, but in a manner to be prescribed by law.

## [AMENDMENT IV]

The right of the people to be secure in their persons, houses, papers, and effects, against unreasonable searches and seizures, shall not be violated, and no Warrants shall issue, but upon proba-

---

[7]This heading appears only in the joint resolution submitting the first ten amendments, known as the Bill of Rights.

ble cause, supported by Oath or affirmation, and particularly describing the place to be searched, and the persons or things to be seized.

## [AMENDMENT V]

No person shall be held to answer for a capital or otherwise infamous crime, unless on a present-ment or indictment of a Grand Jury, except in cases arising in the land or naval forces, or in the Militia, when in actual service in time of War or public danger; nor shall any person be subject for the same offence to be twice put in jeopardy of life or limb; nor shall be compelled in any crim-inal case to be a witness against himself, nor be deprived of life, liberty, or property, without due process of law; nor shall private property be taken for public use, without just compensation.

## [AMENDMENT VI]

In all criminal prosecutions, the accused shall enjoy the right to a speedy and public trial, by an impartial jury of the State and district wherein the crime shall have been committed, which dis-trict shall have been previously ascertained by law, and to be informed of the nature and cause of the accusation; to be confronted with the witnesses against him; to have compulsory process for obtaining witnesses in his favour, and to have the Assistance of Counsel for his defence.

## [AMENDMENT VII]

In suits at common law, where the value in controversy shall exceed twenty dollars, the right of trial by jury shall be preserved, and no fact tried by a jury, shall be otherwise reexamined in any Court of the United States, than according to the rules of the common law.

## [AMENDMENT VIII]

Excessive bail shall not be required, nor excessive fines imposed, nor cruel and unusual punish-ments inflicted.

## [AMENDMENT IX]

The enumeration of the Constitution, of certain rights, shall not be construed to deny or dispar-age others retained by the people.

## [AMENDMENT X]

The powers not delegated to the United States by the Constitution, nor prohibited by it to the States, are reserved to the States respectively, or to the people.
    [Amendments I–X, in force 1791.]

## [AMENDMENT XI][8]

The Judicial power of the United States shall not be construed to extend to any suit in law or equity, commenced or prosecuted against one of the United States by Citizens of another State, or by Citizens or Subjects of any Foreign State.

## [AMENDMENT XII][9]

The Electors shall meet in their respective States and vote by ballot for President and Vice-President, one of whom, at least, shall not be an inhabitant of the same State with themselves; they shall name in their ballots the person voted for as President, and in distinct ballots the person voted for as Vice-President, and they shall make distinct lists of all persons voted for as President, and of all persons voted for as Vice-President, and of the number of votes for each, which lists they shall sign and certify, and transmit sealed to the seat of the government of the United States, directed to the President of the Senate;—The President of the Senate shall, in the presence of the Senate and House of Representatives, open all the certificates and the votes shall then be counted;—The person having the greatest number of votes for President, shall be the President, if such number be a majority of the whole number of Electors appointed; and if no person have such majority, then from the persons having the highest numbers not exceeding three on the list of those voted for as President, the House of Representatives shall choose immediately, by ballot, the President. But in choosing the President, the votes shall be taken by states, the representation from each state having one vote; a quorum for this purpose shall consist of a member or members from two-thirds of the states, and a majority of all the states shall be necessary to a choice. And if the House of Representatives shall not choose a President whenever the right of choice shall devolve upon them, before the fourth day of March next following, then the Vice-President shall act as President, as in the case of the death or other constitutional disability of the President.—The person having the greatest number of votes as Vice-President, shall be the Vice-President, if such number be a majority of the whole number of Electors appointed, and if no person have a majority, then from the two highest numbers on the list, the Senate shall choose the Vice-President; a quorum for the purpose shall consist of two-thirds of the whole number of Senators, and a majority of the whole number shall be necessary to a choice. But no person constitutionally ineligible to the office of President shall be eligible to that of Vice-President of the United States.

## [AMENDMENT XIII][10]

**Section 1.**  Neither slavery nor involuntary servitude, except as a punishment for crime whereof the party shall have been duly convicted, shall exist within the United States, or any place subject to their jurisdiction.

**Section 2.**  Congress shall have power to enforce this article by appropriate legislation.

## [AMENDMENT XIV][11]

**Section 1.**  All persons born or naturalized in the United States, and subject to the jurisdiction thereof, are citizens of the United States and of the State wherein they reside. No State shall

---

[8]Adopted in 1798.
[9]Adopted in 1804.
[10]Adopted in 1865.
[11]Adopted in 1868.

abridge the privileges or immunities of citizens of the United States; nor shall any State deprive any person of life, liberty, or property, without due process of law; nor deny to any person within its jurisdiction the equal protection of the laws.

**Section 2.** Representatives shall be apportioned among the several States according to their respective numbers, counting the whole number of persons in each State, excluding Indians not taxed. But when the right to vote at any election for the choice of electors for President and Vice-President of the United States, Representatives in Congress, the Executive and Judicial officers of a State, or the members of the Legislature thereof, is denied to any of the male inhabitants of such State, being twenty-one years of age, and citizens of the United States, or in any way abridged, except for participation in rebellion, or other crime, the basis of representation therein shall be reduced in the proportion which the number of such male citizens shall bear to the whole number of male citizens twenty-one years of age in such State.

**Section 3.** No person shall be a Senator or Representative in Congress, or elector of President and Vice-President, or hold any office, civil or military, under the United States, or under any State, who, having previously taken an oath, as a member of Congress, or as an officer of the United States, or as a member of any State legislature, or as an executive or judicial officer of any State, to support the Constitution of the United States, shall have engaged in insurrection or rebellion against the same, or given aid or comfort to the enemies thereof. But Congress may by a vote of two-thirds of each House, remove such disability.

**Section 4.** The validity of the public debt of the United States, authorized by law, including debts incurred for payment of pensions and bounties for services in suppressing insurrection or rebellion, shall not be questioned. But neither the United States nor any State shall assume or pay any debts or obligation incurred in aid of insurrection or rebellion against the United States, or any claim for the loss or emancipation of any slave; but all such debts, obligations, and claims shall be held illegal and void.

**Section 5.** The Congress shall have the power to enforce, by appropriate legislation, the provisions of this article.

# [AMENDMENT XV][12]

**Section 1.** The right of citizens of the United States to vote shall not be denied or abridged by the United States or by any State on account of race, color, or previous condition of servitude—

**Section 2.** The Congress shall have power to enforce this article by appropriate legislation.

# [AMENDMENT XVI][13]

The Congress shall have power to lay and collect taxes on incomes, from whatever source derived, without apportionment among the several States, and without regard to any census or enumeration.

---

[12]Adopted in 1870.
[13]Adopted in 1913.

## [AMENDMENT XVII][14]

The Senate of the United States shall be composed of two Senators from each State, elected by the people thereof, for six years; and each Senator shall have one vote. The electors in each State shall have the qualifications requisite for electors of the most numerous branch of the State legislatures.

When vacancies happen in the representation of any State in the Senate, the executive authority of such State shall issue writs of election to fill such vacancies: *Provided,* That the legislature of any State may empower the executive thereof to make temporary appointments until the people fill the vacancies by election as the legislature may direct.

This amendment shall not be so construed as to affect the election or term of any Senator chosen before it becomes valid as part of the Constitution.

## [AMENDMENT XVIII][15]

**Section 1.**  After one year from the ratification of this article the manufacture, sale, or transportation of intoxicating liquors within, the importation thereof into, or the exportation thereof from the United States and all territory subject to the jurisdiction thereof for beverage purposes is hereby prohibited.

**Section 2.**  The Congress and the several States shall have concurrent power to enforce this article by appropriate legislation.

**Section 3.**  This article shall be inoperative unless it shall have been ratified as an amendment to the Constitution by the legislatures of the several States, as provided in the Constitution, within seven years from the date of the submission hereof to the States by the Congress.

## [AMENDMENT XIX][16]

The right of citizens of the United States to vote shall not be denied or abridged by the United States or by any State on account of sex.

Congress shall have power to enforce this article by appropriate legislation.

## [AMENDMENT XX][17]

**Section 1.**  The terms of the President and Vice-President shall end at noon on the 20th day of January, and the terms of Senators and Representatives at noon on the 3d day of January, of the years in which such terms would have ended if this article had not been ratified; and the terms of their successors shall then begin.

---

[14]Adopted in 1913.

[15]Adopted in 1918.

[16]Adopted in 1920.

[17]Adopted in 1933.

**Section 2.** The Congress shall assemble at least once in every year, and such meeting shall begin at noon on the 3d day of January, unless they shall by law appoint a different day.

**Section 3.** If, at the time fixed for the beginning of the term of the President, the President elect shall have died, the Vice-President elect shall become President. If a President shall not have been chosen before the time fixed for the beginning of his term or if the President elect shall have failed to qualify, then the Vice-President elect shall act as President until a President shall have qualified; and the Congress may by law provide for the case wherein neither a President elect nor a Vice-President elect shall have qualified, declaring who shall then act as President, or the manner in which one who is to act shall be selected, and such person shall act accordingly until a President or Vice-President shall have qualified.

**Section 4.** The Congress may by law provide for the case of the death of any of the persons from whom the House of Representatives may choose a President whenever the right of choice shall have devolved upon them, and for the case of the death of any of the persons from whom the Senate may choose a Vice-President whenever the right of choice shall have devolved upon them.

**Section 5.** Sections 1 and 2 shall take effect on the 15th day of October following the ratification of this article.

**Section 6.** This article shall be inoperative unless it shall have been ratified as an amendment to the Constitution by the legislatures of three-fourths of the several States within seven years from the date of its submission.

# [AMENDMENT XXI][18]

**Section 1.** The eighteenth article of amendment to the Constitution of the United States is hereby repealed.

**Section 2.** The transportation or importation into any State, Territory, or possession of the United States for delivery or use therein of intoxicating liquors, in violation of the laws thereof, is hereby prohibited.

**Section 3.** This article shall be inoperative unless it shall have been ratified as an amendment to the Constitution by conventions in the several States, as provided in the Constitution, within seven years from the date of the submission hereof to the States by the Congress.

# [AMENDMENT XXII][19]

No person shall be elected to the office of the President more than twice, and no person who has held the office of President, or acted as President, for more than two years of a term to which some other person was elected President shall be elected to the office of the President more than once.

But this Article shall not apply to any person holding the office of President when this Article was proposed by the Congress, and shall not prevent any person who may be holding the office of President, or acting as President, during the term within which this Article becomes operative from holding the office of President or acting as President during the remainder of such term.

---

[18]Adopted in 1933.
[19]Adopted in 1961.

This article shall be inoperative unless it shall have been ratified as an amendment to the Constitution by the legislatures of three-fourths of the several states within seven years from the date of its submission to the states by the Congress.

## [AMENDMENT XXIII][20]

**Section 1.**   The District constituting the seat of Government of the United States shall appoint in such manner as the Congress may direct:

A number of electors of President and Vice-President equal to the whole number of Senators and Representatives in Congress to which the District would be entitled if it were a State, but in no event more than the least populous State; they shall be in addition to those appointed by the States, but they shall be considered, for the purpose of the election of President and Vice-President, to be electors appointed by a State; and they shall meet in the District and perform such duties as provided by the twelfth article of amendment.

**Section 2.**   The Congress shall have power to enforce this article by appropriate legislation.

## [AMENDMENT XXIV][21]

**Section 1.**   The right of citizens of the United States to vote in any primary or other election for President or Vice-President, for electors for President or Vice-President, or for Senator or Representative in Congress, shall not be denied or abridged by the United States or any state by reason of failure to pay any poll tax or other tax.

**Section 2.**   The Congress shall have the power to enforce this article by appropriate legislation.

## [AMENDMENT XXV][22]

**Section 1.**   In case of the removal of the President from office or of his death or resignation, the Vice-President shall become President.

**Section 2.**   Whenever there is a vacancy in the office of the Vice-President, the President shall nominate a Vice-President who shall take office upon confirmation by a majority vote of both Houses of Congress.

**Section 3.**   Whenever the President transmits to the President Pro Tempore of the Senate and the Speaker of the House of Representatives his written declaration that he is unable to discharge the powers and duties of his office, and until he transmits to them a written declaration to the contrary, such powers and duties shall be discharged by the Vice-President as Acting President.

**Section 4.**   Whenever the Vice-President and a majority of either the principal officers of the executive departments or of such other body as Congress may by law provide, transmit to the President Pro Tempore of the Senate and the Speaker of the House of Representatives their written declaration that the President is unable to discharge the powers and duties of his office, the Vice-President shall immediately assume the powers and duties of the office as Acting President.

---

[20]Adopted in 1961.

[21]Adopted in 1964.

[22]Adopted in 1967.

Thereafter, when the President transmits to the President Pro Tempore of the Senate and the Speaker of the House of Representatives his written declaration that no inability exists, he shall resume the powers and duties of his office unless the Vice-President and a majority of either the principal officers of the executive departments or of such other body as Congress may by law provide, transmit within four days to the President Pro Tempore of the Senate and the Speaker of the House of Representatives their written declaration that the President is unable to discharge the powers and duties of his office. Thereupon Congress shall decide the issue, assembling within forty-eight hours for that purpose if not in session. If the Congress, within twenty-one days after receipt of the latter written declaration, or, if Congress is not in session, within twenty-one days after Congress is required to assemble, determines by two-thirds vote of both Houses that the President is unable to discharge the powers and duties of his office, the Vice-President shall continue to discharge the same as Acting President; otherwise, the President shall resume the powers and duties of his office.

## [AMENDMENT XXVI][23]

**Section 1.**   The right of citizens of the United States, who are eighteen years of age or older, to vote shall not be denied or abridged by the United States or by any State on account of age.

**Section 2.**   The Congress shall have power to enforce this article by appropriate legislation.

## [AMENDMENT XXVII][24]

No law, varying the compensation for the services of the Senators and Representatives, shall take effect, until an election of Representatives shall have intervened.

---

[23]Adopted in 1971.
[24]Adopted in 1992.

# PRESIDENTIAL ELECTIONS

| Year | Candidates | Parties | Popular Vote | % of Popular Vote | Electoral Vote | % Voter Participation |
|------|-----------|---------|-------------|------------------|---------------|----------------------|
| 1789 | **George Washington** | | | | 69 | |
| | John Adams | | | | 34 | |
| | Other candidates | | | | 35 | |
| 1792 | **George Washington** | | | | 132 | |
| | John Adams | | | | 77 | |
| | George Clinton | | | | 50 | |
| | Other candidates | | | | 5 | |
| 1796 | **John Adams** | Federalist | | | 71 | |
| | Thomas Jefferson | Dem.-Rep. | | | 68 | |
| | Thomas Pinckney | Federalist | | | 59 | |
| | Aaron Burr | Dem.-Rep. | | | 30 | |
| | Other candidates | | | | 48 | |
| 1800 | **Thomas Jefferson** | Dem.-Rep. | | | 73 | |
| | Aaron Burr | Dem.-Rep. | | | 73 | |
| | John Adams | Federalist | | | 65 | |
| | Charles C. Pinckney | Federalist | | | 64 | |
| | John Jay | Federalist | | | 1 | |
| 1804 | **Thomas Jefferson** | Dem.-Rep. | | | 162 | |
| | Charles C. Pinckney | Federalist | | | 14 | |
| 1808 | **James Madison** | Dem.-Rep. | | | 122 | |
| | Charles C. Pinckney | Federalist | | | 47 | |
| | George Clinton | Dem.-Rep. | | | 6 | |
| 1812 | **James Madison** | Dem.-Rep. | | | 128 | |
| | DeWitt Clinton | Federalist | | | 89 | |
| 1816 | **James Monroe** | Dem.-Rep. | | | 183 | |
| | Rufus King | Federalist | | | 34 | |
| 1820 | **James Monroe** | Dem.-Rep. | | | 231 | |
| | John Quincy Adams | Indep.-Rep. | | | 1 | |
| 1824 | **John Quincy Adams** | Dem.-Rep. | 108,740 | 31.0 | 84 | 26.9 |
| | Andrew Jackson | Dem.-Rep. | 153,544 | 43.0 | 99 | |
| | Henry Clay | Dem.-Rep. | 47,136 | 13.0 | 37 | |
| | William H. Crawford | Dem.-Rep. | 46,618 | 13.0 | 41 | |
| 1828 | **Andrew Jackson** | Democratic | 647,286 | 56.0 | 178 | 57.6 |
| | John Quincy Adams | National Republican | 508,064 | 44.0 | 83 | |
| 1832 | **Andrew Jackson** | Democratic | 688,242 | 54.5 | 219 | 55.4 |
| | Henry Clay | National Republican | 473,462 | 37.5 | 49 | |
| | William Wirt | Anti-Masonic | 101,051 | 8.0 | 7 | |
| | John Floyd | Democratic | | | 11 | |

| Year | Candidates | Parties | Popular Vote | % of Popular Vote | Electoral Vote | % Voter Partici- pation |
|------|-----------|---------|-------------|-------------------|----------------|------------------------|
| 1836 | **Martin Van Buren** | Democratic | 765,483 | 50.9 | 170 | 57.8 |
|      | William H. Harrison | Whig | | | 73 | |
|      | Hugh L. White | Whig | 739,795 | 49.1 | 26 | |
|      | Daniel Webster | Whig | | | 14 | |
|      | W. P. Mangum | Whig | | | 11 | |
| 1840 | **William H. Harrison** | Whig | 1,275,016 | 53.0 | 234 | 80.2 |
|      | Martin Van Buren | Democratic | 1,129,102 | 47.0 | 60 | |
| 1844 | **James K. Polk** | Democratic | 1,338,464 | 49.6 | 170 | 78.9 |
|      | Henry Clay | Whig | 1,300,097 | 48.1 | 105 | |
|      | James G. Birney | Liberty | 62,300 | 2.3 | | |
| 1848 | **Zachary Taylor** | Whig | 1,360,967 | 47.4 | 163 | 72.7 |
|      | Lewis Cass | Democratic | 1,222,342 | 42.5 | 127 | |
|      | Martin Van Buren | Free Soil | 291,263 | 10.1 | | |
| 1852 | **Franklin Pierce** | Democratic | 1,601,117 | 50.9 | 254 | 69.6 |
|      | Winfield Scott | Whig | 1,385,453 | 44.1 | 42 | |
|      | John P. Hale | Free Soil | 155,825 | 5.0 | | |
| 1856 | **James Buchanan** | Democratic | 1,832,955 | 45.3 | 174 | 78.9 |
|      | John C. Fremont | Republican | 1,339,932 | 33.1 | 114 | |
|      | Millard Fillmore | American | 871,731 | 21.6 | 8 | |
| 1860 | **Abraham Lincoln** | Republican | 1,866,452 | 39.8 | 180 | 81.2 |
|      | Stephen A. Douglas | Democratic | 1,375,157 | 29.5 | 12 | |
|      | John C. Breckinridge | Democratic | 847,953 | 18.1 | 72 | |
|      | John Bell | Constitutional Union | 590,631 | 12.6 | 39 | |
| 1864 | **Abraham Lincoln** | Republican | 2,206,938 | 55.0 | 212 | 73.8 |
|      | George B. McClellan | Democratic | 1,803,787 | 45.0 | 21 | |
| 1868 | **Ulysses S. Grant** | Republican | 3,013,421 | 52.7 | 214 | 78.1 |
|      | Horatio Seymour | Democratic | 2,706,829 | 47.3 | 80 | |
| 1872 | **Ulysses S. Grant** | Republican | 3,596,745 | 55.6 | 286 | 71.3 |
|      | Horace Greeley | Democratic | 2,843,446 | 43.9 | 66 | |
| 1876 | **Rutherford B. Hayes** | Republican | 4,036,298 | 48.0 | 185 | 81.8 |
|      | Samuel J. Tilden | Democratic | 4,300,590 | 51.0 | 184 | |
| 1880 | **James A. Garfield** | Republican | 4,453,295 | 48.5 | 214 | 79.4 |
|      | Winfield S. Hancock | Democratic | 4,414,082 | 48.1 | 155 | |
|      | James B. Weaver | Greenback-Labor | 308,578 | 3.4 | | |
| 1884 | **Grover Cleveland** | Democratic | 4,879,507 | 48.5 | 219 | 77.5 |
|      | James G. Blaine | Republican | 4,850,293 | 48.2 | 182 | |
|      | Benjamin F. Butler | Greenback-Labor | 175,370 | 1.8 | | |
|      | John P. St. John | Prohibition | 150,369 | 1.5 | | |
| 1888 | **Benjamin Harrison** | Republican | 5,477,129 | 47.9 | 233 | 79.3 |
|      | Grover Cleveland | Democratic | 5,537,857 | 48.6 | 168 | |
|      | Clinton B. Fisk | Prohibition | 249,506 | 2.2 | | |
|      | Anson J. Streeter | Union Labor | 146,935 | 1.3 | | |

| Year | Candidates | Parties | Popular Vote | % of Popular Vote | Electoral Vote | % Voter Partici-pation |
|------|-----------|---------|-------------|------------------|---------------|----------------------|
| 1892 | **Grover Cleveland** | Democratic | 5,555,426 | 46.1 | 277 | 74.7 |
|      | Benjamin Harrison | Republican | 5,182,690 | 43.0 | 145 | |
|      | James B. Weaver | People's | 1,029,846 | 8.5 | 22 | |
|      | John Bidwell | Prohibition | 264,133 | 2.2 | | |
| 1896 | **William McKinley** | Republican | 7,104,779 | 52.0 | 271 | 79.3 |
|      | William J. Bryan | Democratic | 6,502,925 | 48.0 | 176 | |
| 1900 | **William McKinley** | Republican | 7,218,491 | 51.7 | 292 | 73.2 |
|      | William J. Bryan | Democratic; Populist | 6,356,734 | 45.5 | 155 | |
|      | John C. Wooley | Prohibition | 208,914 | 1.5 | | |
| 1904 | **Theodore Roosevelt** | Republican | 7,628,461 | 57.4 | 336 | 65.2 |
|      | Alton B. Parker | Democratic | 5,084,223 | 37.6 | 140 | |
|      | Eugene V. Debs | Socialist | 402,283 | 3.0 | | |
|      | Silas C. Swallow | Prohibition | 258,536 | 1.9 | | |
| 1908 | **William H. Taft** | Republican | 7,675,320 | 51.6 | 321 | 65.4 |
|      | William J. Bryan | Democratic | 6,412,294 | 43.1 | 162 | |
|      | Eugene V. Debs | Socialist | 420,793 | 2.8 | | |
|      | Eugene W. Chafin | Prohibition | 253,840 | 1.7 | | |
| 1912 | **Woodrow Wilson** | Democratic | 6,293,454 | 42.0 | 435 | 58.8 |
|      | Theodore Roosevelt | Progressive | 4,119,538 | 28.0 | 88 | |
|      | William H. Taft | Republican | 3,484,980 | 24.0 | 8 | |
|      | Eugene V. Debs | Socialist | 900,672 | 6.0 | | |
|      | Eugene W. Chafin | Prohibition | 206,275 | 1.4 | | |
| 1916 | **Woodrow Wilson** | Democratic | 9,129,606 | 49.4 | 277 | 61.6 |
|      | Charles E. Hughes | Republican | 8,538,221 | 46.2 | 254 | |
|      | A. L. Benson | Socialist | 585,113 | 3.2 | | |
|      | J. Frank Hanly | Prohibition | 220,506 | 1.2 | | |
| 1920 | **Warren G. Harding** | Republican | 16,143,407 | 60.4 | 404 | 49.2 |
|      | James M. Cox | Democratic | 9,130,328 | 34.2 | 127 | |
|      | Eugene V. Debs | Socialist | 919,799 | 3.4 | | |
|      | P. P. Christensen | Farmer-Labor | 265,411 | 1.0 | | |
| 1924 | **Calvin Coolidge** | Republican | 15,718,211 | 54.0 | 382 | 48.9 |
|      | John W. Davis | Democratic | 8,385,283 | 28.8 | 136 | |
|      | Robert M. La Follette | Progressive | 4,831,289 | 16.6 | 13 | |
| 1928 | **Herbert C. Hoover** | Republican | 21,391,381 | 58.2 | 444 | 56.9 |
|      | Alfred E. Smith | Democratic | 15,016,443 | 40.9 | 87 | |
| 1932 | **Franklin D. Roosevelt** | Democratic | 22,821,857 | 57.4 | 472 | 56.9 |
|      | Herbert C. Hoover | Republican | 15,761,841 | 39.7 | 59 | |
|      | Norman Thomas | Socialist | 881,951 | 2.2 | | |
| 1936 | **Franklin D. Roosevelt** | Democratic | 27,751,597 | 60.8 | 523 | 61.0 |
|      | Alfred M. Landon | Republican | 16,679,583 | 36.5 | 8 | |
|      | William Lemke | Union | 882,479 | 1.9 | | |

| Year | Candidates | Parties | Popular Vote | % of Popular Vote | Electoral Vote | % Voter Partici- pation |
|------|-----------|---------|--------------|-------------------|----------------|--------------------------|
| 1940 | Franklin D. Roosevelt | Democratic | 27,307,819 | 54.8 | 449 | 62.5 |
|      | Wendell L. Wilkie | Republican | 22,321,018 | 44.8 | 82 | |
| 1944 | Franklin D. Roosevelt | Democratic | 25,606,585 | 53.5 | 432 | 55.9 |
|      | Thomas E. Dewey | Republican | 22,014,745 | 46.0 | 99 | |
| 1948 | Harry S Truman | Democratic | 24,105,812 | 50.0 | 303 | 53.0 |
|      | Thomas E. Dewey | Republican | 21,970,065 | 46.0 | 189 | |
|      | J. Strom Thurmond | States' Rights | 1,169,021 | 2.0 | 39 | |
|      | Henry A. Wallace | Progressive | 1,157,172 | 2.0 | | |
| 1952 | Dwight D. Eisenhower | Republican | 33,936,234 | 55.1 | 442 | 63.3 |
|      | Adlai E. Stevenson | Democratic | 27,314,992 | 44.4 | 89 | |
| 1956 | Dwight D. Eisenhower | Republican | 35,590,472 | 57.6 | 457 | 60.6 |
|      | Adlai E. Stevenson | Democratic | 26,022,752 | 42.1 | 73 | |
| 1960 | John F. Kennedy | Democratic | 34,227,096 | 49.7 | 303 | 62.8 |
|      | Richard M. Nixon | Republican | 34,107,646 | 49.6 | 219 | |
|      | Harry F. Byrd | Independent | 501,643 | | 15 | |
| 1964 | Lyndon B. Johnson | Democratic | 43,129,566 | 61.1 | 486 | 61.7 |
|      | Barry M. Goldwater | Republican | 27,178,188 | 38.5 | 52 | |
| 1968 | Richard M. Nixon | Republican | 31,785,480 | 44.0 | 301 | 60.6 |
|      | Hubert H. Humphrey | Democratic | 31,275,166 | 42.7 | 191 | |
|      | George C. Wallace | American Independent | 9,906,473 | 13.5 | 46 | |
| 1972 | Richard M. Nixon | Republican | 47,169,911 | 60.7 | 520 | 55.2 |
|      | George S. McGovern | Democratic | 29,170,383 | 37.5 | 17 | |
|      | John G. Schmitz | American | 1,099,482 | 1.4 | | |
| 1976 | Jimmy Carter | Democratic | 40,830,763 | 50.1 | 297 | 53.5 |
|      | Gerald R. Ford | Republican | 39,147,793 | 48.0 | 240 | |
| 1980 | Ronald Reagan | Republican | 43,899,248 | 51.0 | 489 | 52.6 |
|      | Jimmy Carter | Democratic | 35,481,432 | 41.0 | 49 | |
|      | John B. Anderson | Independent | 5,719,437 | 7.0 | 0 | |
|      | Ed Clark | Libertarian | 920,859 | 1.0 | 0 | |
| 1984 | Ronald Reagan | Republican | 54,451,521 | 58.8 | 525 | 53.3 |
|      | Walter Mondale | Democratic | 37,565,334 | 40.5 | 13 | |
| 1988 | George H. Bush | Republican | 48,881,221 | 53.9 | 426 | 48.6 |
|      | Michael Dukakis | Democratic | 41,805,422 | 46.1 | 111 | |
| 1992 | William J. Clinton | Democratic | 44,908,254 | 43.0 | 370 | 55.9 |
|      | George H. Bush | Republican | 39,102,343 | 37.4 | 168 | |
|      | H. Ross Perot | Independent | 19,741,065 | 18.9 | 0 | |
| 1996° | William J. Clinton | Democratic | 47,401,054 | 49.3 | 379 | 49 |
|      | Robert Dole | Republican | 39,197,350 | 40.7 | 159 | |
|      | H. Ross Perot | Reform | 8,085,285 | 8.4 | 0 | |

°Preliminary figures

# JUSTICES OF THE SUPREME COURT

| | Term of Service | Years of Service | Life Span | | Term of Service | Years of Service | Life Span |
|---|---|---|---|---|---|---|---|
| John Jay | 1789–1795 | 5 | 1745–1829 | Lucius Q. C. Lamar | 1888–1893 | 5 | 1825–1893 |
| John Rutledge | 1789–1791 | 1 | 1739–1800 | Melville W. Fuller | 1888–1910 | 21 | 1833–1910 |
| William Cushing | 1789–1810 | 20 | 1732–1810 | David J. Brewer | 1890–1910 | 20 | 1837–1910 |
| James Wilson | 1789–1798 | 8 | 1742–1798 | Henry B. Brown | 1890–1906 | 16 | 1836–1913 |
| John Blair | 1789–1796 | 6 | 1732–1800 | George Shiras, Jr. | 1892–1903 | 10 | 1832–1924 |
| Robert H. Harrison | 1789–1790 | — | 1745–1790 | Howell E. Jackson | 1893–1895 | 2 | 1832–1895 |
| James Iredell | 1790–1799 | 9 | 1751–1799 | Edward D. White | 1894–1910 | 16 | 1845–1921 |
| Thomas Johnson | 1791–1793 | 1 | 1732–1819 | Rufus W. Peckham | 1895–1909 | 14 | 1838–1909 |
| William Paterson | 1793–1806 | 13 | 1745–1806 | Joseph McKenna | 1898–1925 | 26 | 1843–1926 |
| John Rutledge* | 1795 | — | 1739–1800 | Oliver W. Holmes | 1902–1932 | 30 | 1841–1935 |
| Samuel Chase | 1796–1811 | 15 | 1741–1811 | William R. Day | 1903–1922 | 19 | 1849–1923 |
| Oliver Ellsworth | 1796–1800 | 4 | 1745–1807 | William H. Moody | 1906–1910 | 3 | 1853–1917 |
| Bushrod Washington | 1798–1829 | 31 | 1762–1829 | Horace H. Lurton | 1909–1914 | 4 | 1844–1914 |
| Alfred Moore | 1799–1804 | 4 | 1755–1810 | Charles E. Hughes | 1910–1916 | 5 | 1862–1948 |
| John Marshall | 1801–1835 | 34 | 1755–1835 | Edward D. White | 1910–1921 | 11 | 1845–1921 |
| William Johnson | 1804–1834 | 30 | 1771–1834 | Willis Van Devanter | 1911–1937 | 26 | 1859–1941 |
| H. Brockholst Livingston | 1806–1823 | 16 | 1757–1823 | Joseph R. Lamar | 1911–1916 | 5 | 1857–1916 |
| Thomas Todd | 1807–1826 | 18 | 1765–1826 | Mahlon Pitney | 1912–1922 | 10 | 1858–1924 |
| Joseph Story | 1811–1845 | 33 | 1779–1845 | James C. McReynolds | 1914–1941 | 26 | 1862–1946 |
| Gabriel Duval | 1811–1835 | 24 | 1752–1844 | Louis D. Brandeis | 1916–1939 | 22 | 1856–1941 |
| Smith Thompson | 1823–1843 | 20 | 1768–1843 | John H. Clarke | 1916–1922 | 6 | 1857–1945 |
| Robert Trimble | 1826–1828 | 2 | 1777–1828 | William H. Taft | 1921–1930 | 8 | 1857–1930 |
| John McLean | 1829–1861 | 32 | 1785–1861 | George Sutherland | 1922–1938 | 15 | 1862–1942 |
| Henry Baldwin | 1830–1844 | 14 | 1780–1844 | Pierce Butler | 1922–1939 | 16 | 1866–1939 |
| James M. Wayne | 1835–1867 | 32 | 1790–1867 | Edward T. Sanford | 1923–1930 | 7 | 1865–1930 |
| Roger B. Taney | 1836–1864 | 28 | 1777–1864 | Harlan F. Stone | 1925–1941 | 16 | 1872–1946 |
| Philip P. Barbour | 1836–1841 | 4 | 1783–1841 | Charles E. Hughes | 1930–1941 | 11 | 1862–1948 |
| John Catron | 1837–1865 | 28 | 1786–1865 | Owen J. Roberts | 1930–1945 | 15 | 1875–1955 |
| John McKinley | 1837–1852 | 15 | 1780–1852 | Benjamin N. Cardozo | 1932–1938 | 6 | 1870–1938 |
| Peter V. Daniel | 1841–1860 | 19 | 1784–1860 | Hugo L. Black | 1937–1971 | 34 | 1886–1971 |
| Samuel Nelson | 1845–1872 | 27 | 1792–1873 | Stanley F. Reed | 1938–1957 | 19 | 1884–1980 |
| Levi Woodbury | 1845–1851 | 5 | 1789–1851 | Felix Frankfurter | 1939–1962 | 23 | 1882–1965 |
| Robert C. Grier | 1846–1870 | 23 | 1794–1870 | William O. Douglas | 1939–1975 | 36 | 1898–1980 |
| Benjamin R. Curtis | 1851–1857 | 6 | 1809–1874 | Frank Murphy | 1940–1949 | 9 | 1890–1949 |
| John A. Campbell | 1853–1861 | 8 | 1811–1889 | Harlan F. Stone | 1941–1946 | 5 | 1872–1946 |
| Nathan Clifford | 1858–1881 | 23 | 1803–1881 | James F. Byrnes | 1941–1942 | 1 | 1879–1972 |
| Noah H. Swayne | 1862–1881 | 18 | 1804–1884 | Robert H. Jackson | 1941–1954 | 13 | 1892–1954 |
| Samuel F. Miller | 1862–1890 | 28 | 1816–1890 | Wiley B. Rutledge | 1943–1949 | 6 | 1894–1949 |
| David Davis | 1862–1877 | 14 | 1815–1886 | Harold H. Burton | 1945–1958 | 13 | 1888–1964 |
| Stephen J. Field | 1863–1897 | 34 | 1816–1899 | Fred M. Vinson | 1946–1953 | 7 | 1890–1953 |
| Salmon P. Chase | 1864–1873 | 8 | 1808–1873 | Tom C. Clark | 1949–1967 | 18 | 1899–1977 |
| William Strong | 1870–1880 | 10 | 1808–1895 | Sherman Minton | 1949–1956 | 7 | 1890–1965 |
| Joseph P. Bradley | 1870–1892 | 22 | 1813–1892 | Earl Warren | 1953–1969 | 16 | 1891–1974 |
| Ward Hunt | 1873–1882 | 9 | 1810–1886 | John Marshall Harlan | 1955–1971 | 16 | 1899–1971 |
| Morrison R. Waite | 1874–1888 | 14 | 1816–1888 | William J. Brennan, Jr. | 1956–1990 | 33 | 1906– |
| John M. Harlan | 1877–1911 | 34 | 1833–1911 | Charles E. Whittaker | 1957–1962 | 5 | 1901–1973 |
| William B. Woods | 1880–1887 | 7 | 1824–1887 | Potter Stewart | 1958–1981 | 23 | 1915– |
| Stanley Matthews | 1881–1889 | 7 | 1824–1889 | Byron R. White | 1962–1993 | 31 | 1917– |
| Horace Gray | 1882–1902 | 20 | 1828–1902 | Arthur J. Goldberg | 1962–1965 | 3 | 1908–1990 |
| Samuel Blatchford | 1882–1893 | 11 | 1820–1893 | Abe Fortas | 1965–1969 | 4 | 1910–1982 |

|  | Term of Service | Years of Service | Life Span |  |  | Term of Service | Years of Service | Life Span |
|---|---|---|---|---|---|---|---|---|
| Thurgood Marshall | 1967–1991 | 24 | 1908–1993 | *William H. Rehnquist* | 1986– | – | 1924– |
| *Warren C. Burger* | 1969–1986 | 17 | 1907– | Antonin Scalia | 1986– | – | 1936– |
| Harry A. Blackmun | 1970–1994 | 24 | 1908– | Anthony M. Kennedy | 1987– | – | 1936– |
| Lewis F. Powell, Jr. | 1972–1987 | 15 | 1907– | David H. Souter | 1990– | – | 1939– |
| William H. Rehnquist | 1972– | – | 1924– | Clarence Thomas | 1991– | – | 1948– |
| John P. Stevens III | 1975– | – | 1920– | Ruth Bader Ginsburg | 1993– | – | 1933– |
| Sandra Day O'Connor | 1981– | – | 1930– | Stephen G. Breyer | 1994– | – | 1938– |

°Appointed and served one term, but not confirmed by the Senate.
Note: Chief justices are in italics.

# A SOCIAL PROFILE OF THE AMERICAN REPUBLIC

## POPULATION

| Year | Population | Percent Increase | Population Per Square Mile | Percent Urban/ Rural | Percent Male/ Female | Percent White/ Nonwhite | Persons Per Household | Median Age |
|------|-----------|------------------|---------------------------|----------------------|----------------------|-------------------------|----------------------|-----------|
| 1790 | 3,929,214 |      | 4.5  | 5.1/94.9  | NA/NA     | 80.7/19.3 | 5.79 | NA   |
| 1800 | 5,308,483 | 35.1 | 6.1  | 6.1/93.9  | NA/NA     | 81.1/18.9 | NA   | NA   |
| 1810 | 7,239,881 | 36.4 | 4.3  | 7.3/92.7  | NA/NA     | 81.0/19.0 | NA   | NA   |
| 1820 | 9,638,453 | 33.1 | 5.5  | 7.2/92.8  | 50.8/49.2 | 81.6/18.4 | NA   | 16.7 |
| 1830 | 12,866,020 | 33.5 | 7.4  | 8.8/91.2  | 50.8/49.2 | 81.9/18.1 | NA   | 17.2 |
| 1840 | 17,069,453 | 32.7 | 9.8  | 10.8/89.2 | 50.9/49.1 | 83.2/16.8 | NA   | 17.8 |
| 1850 | 23,191,876 | 35.9 | 7.9  | 15.3/84.7 | 51.0/49.0 | 84.3/15.7 | 5.55 | 18.9 |
| 1860 | 31,443,321 | 35.6 | 10.6 | 19.8/80.2 | 51.2/48.8 | 85.6/14.4 | 5.28 | 19.4 |
| 1870 | 39,818,449 | 26.6 | 13.4 | 25.7/74.3 | 50.6/49.4 | 86.2/13.8 | 5.09 | 20.2 |
| 1880 | 50,155,783 | 26.0 | 16.9 | 28.2/71.8 | 50.9/49.1 | 86.5/13.5 | 5.04 | 20.9 |
| 1890 | 62,947,714 | 25.5 | 21.2 | 35.1/64.9 | 51.2/48.8 | 87.5/12.5 | 4.93 | 22.0 |
| 1900 | 75,994,575 | 20.7 | 25.6 | 39.6/60.4 | 51.1/48.9 | 87.9/12.1 | 4.76 | 22.9 |
| 1910 | 91,972,266 | 21.0 | 31.0 | 45.6/54.4 | 51.5/48.5 | 88.9/11.1 | 4.54 | 24.1 |
| 1920 | 105,710,620 | 14.9 | 35.6 | 51.2/48.8 | 51.0/49.0 | 89.7/10.3 | 4.34 | 25.3 |
| 1930 | 122,775,046 | 16.1 | 41.2 | 56.1/43.9 | 50.6/49.4 | 89.8/10.2 | 4.11 | 26.4 |
| 1940 | 131,669,275 | 7.2  | 44.2 | 56.5/43.5 | 50.2/49.8 | 89.8/10.2 | 3.67 | 29.0 |
| 1950 | 150,697,361 | 14.5 | 50.7 | 64.0/36.0 | 49.7/50.3 | 89.5/10.5 | 3.37 | 30.2 |
| 1960 | 179,323,175 | 18.5 | 50.6 | 69.9/30.1 | 49.3/50.7 | 88.6/11.4 | 3.33 | 29.5 |
| 1970 | 203,302,031 | 13.4 | 57.4 | 73.5/26.5 | 48.7/51.3 | 87.6/12.4 | 3.14 | 28.0 |
| 1980 | 226,545,805 | 11.4 | 64.0 | 73.7/26.3 | 48.6/51.4 | 86.0/14.0 | 2.76 | 30.0 |
| 1990 | 248,709,873 | 9.8  | 70.3 | NA        | 48.7/51.3 | 80.3/19.7 | 2.63 | 32.9 |
| 2000* | 276,382,000 | 7.1 | 75.8 | NA        | 48.9/51.1 | 82.6/17.4 | NA   | NA   |

NA = Not available.
*Projections.

## VITAL STATISTICS (rates per thousand)

| Year | Births | Year | Births | Deaths° | Marriages° | Divorces° |
|------|--------|------|--------|---------|------------|-----------|
| 1800 | 55.0 | 1900 | 32.3 | 17.2 | NA   | NA  |
| 1810 | 54.3 | 1910 | 30.1 | 14.7 | NA   | NA  |
| 1820 | 55.2 | 1920 | 27.7 | 13.0 | 12.0 | 1.6 |
| 1830 | 51.4 | 1930 | 21.3 | 11.3 | 9.2  | 1.6 |
| 1840 | 51.8 | 1940 | 19.4 | 10.8 | 12.1 | 2.0 |
| 1850 | 43.3 | 1950 | 24.1 | 9.6  | 11.1 | 2.6 |
| 1860 | 44.3 | 1960 | 23.7 | 9.5  | 8.5  | 2.2 |
| 1870 | 38.3 | 1970 | 18.4 | 9.5  | 10.6 | 3.5 |
| 1880 | 39.8 | 1980 | 15.9 | 8.8  | 10.6 | 5.2 |
| 1890 | 31.5 | 1990 | 16.7 | 8.6  | 9.8  | 4.6 |

NA = Not available.
°Data not available before 1900.

## LIFE EXPECTANCY (in years)

| Year | Total Population | White Females | Nonwhite Females | White Males | Nonwhite Males |
|------|------|------|------|------|------|
| 1900 | 47.3 | 48.7 | 33.5 | 46.6 | 32.5 |
| 1910 | 50.1 | 52.0 | 37.5 | 48.6 | 33.8 |
| 1920 | 54.1 | 55.6 | 45.2 | 54.4 | 45.5 |
| 1930 | 59.7 | 63.5 | 49.2 | 59.7 | 47.3 |
| 1940 | 62.9 | 66.6 | 54.9 | 62.1 | 51.5 |
| 1950 | 68.2 | 72.2 | 62.9 | 66.5 | 59.1 |
| 1960 | 69.7 | 74.1 | 66.3 | 67.4 | 61.1 |
| 1970 | 70.9 | 75.6 | 69.4 | 68.0 | 61.3 |
| 1980 | 73.7 | 78.1 | 73.6 | 70.7 | 65.3 |
| 1990 | 75.4 | 79.3 | 76.3 | 72.6 | 68.4 |

## REGIONAL ORIGIN OF IMMIGRANTS (percent)

| Years | Total Number of Immigrants | Europe Total Europe | North and West | East and Central | South and Other | Western Hemisphere | Asia |
|------|------|------|------|------|------|------|------|
| 1821–1830 | 143,389 | 69.2 | 67.1 | – | 2.1 | 8.4 | — |
| 1831–1840 | 599,125 | 82.8 | 81.8 | – | 1.0 | 5.5 | — |
| 1841–1850 | 1,713,251 | 93.8 | 92.9 | 0.1 | 0.3 | 3.6 | — |
| 1851–1860 | 2,598,214 | 94.4 | 93.6 | 0.1 | 0.8 | 2.9 | 1.6 |
| 1861–1870 | 2,314,824 | 89.2 | 87.8 | 0.5 | 0.9 | 7.2 | 2.8 |
| 1871–1880 | 2,812,191 | 80.8 | 73.6 | 4.5 | 2.7 | 14.4 | 4.4 |
| 1881–1890 | 5,246,613 | 90.3 | 72.0 | 11.9 | 6.3 | 8.1 | 1.3 |
| 1891–1900 | 3,687,546 | 96.5 | 44.5 | 32.8 | 19.1 | 1.1 | 1.9 |
| 1901–1910 | 8,795,386 | 92.5 | 21.7 | 44.5 | 6.3 | 4.1 | 2.8 |
| 1911–1920 | 5,735,811 | 76.3 | 17.4 | 33.4 | 25.5 | 19.9 | 3.4 |
| 1921–1930 | 4,107,209 | 60.3 | 31.7 | 14.4 | 14.3 | 36.9 | 2.4 |
| 1931–1940 | 528,431 | 65.9 | 38.8 | 11.0 | 16.1 | 30.3 | 2.8 |
| 1941–1950 | 1,035,039 | 60.1 | 47.5 | 4.6 | 7.9 | 34.3 | 3.1 |
| 1951–1960 | 2,515,479 | 52.8 | 17.7 | 24.3 | 10.8 | 39.6 | 6.0 |
| 1961–1970 | 3,321,677 | 33.8 | 11.7 | 9.4 | 12.9 | 51.7 | 12.9 |
| 1971–1980 | 4,493,300 | 17.8 | 4.3 | 5.6 | 8.4 | 44.3 | 35.2 |
| 1981–1990 | 7,338,000 | 10.4 | 5.9 | 4.8 | 1.1 | 49.3 | 37.3 |

Dash indicates less than 0.1 percent.

## RECENT TRENDS IN IMMIGRATION (in thousands)

| | 1961–1970 | 1971–1980 | 1981–1990 | 1991 | Percent 1961–1970 | Percent 1971–1980 | Percent 1981–1990 |
|---|---|---|---|---|---|---|---|
| All countries | 3,321.7 | 4,493.3 | 7,338.0 | 1,827.2 | 100.0 | 100.0 | 100.0 |
| Europe | 1,123.5 | 800.4 | 761.5 | 146.7 | 33.8 | 17.8 | 10.4 |
| Austria | 20.6 | 9.5 | 18.9 | 3.5 | 0.6 | 0.2 | 0.3 |
| Hungary | 5.4 | 6.6 | 5.9 | 0.9 | 0.2 | 0.1 | 0.1 |
| Belgium | 9.2 | 5.3 | 6.6 | 0.7 | 0.3 | 0.1 | 0.1 |
| Czechoslovakia | 3.3 | 6.0 | 5.4 | 0.6 | 0.1 | 0.1 | 0.1 |
| Denmark | 9.2 | 4.4 | 2.8 | 0.6 | 0.3 | 0.1 | 0.1 |
| France | 45.2 | 25.1 | 92.1 | 4.0 | 1.4 | 0.6 | 1.3 |
| Germany | 190.8 | 74.4 | 159.0 | 10.9 | 5.7 | 1.7 | 2.2 |
| Greece | 86.0 | 92.4 | 31.9 | 2.9 | 2.6 | 2.1 | 0.4 |
| Ireland | 33.0 | 11.5 | 67.2 | 4.6 | 1.0 | 0.3 | 0.9 |
| Italy | 214.1 | 129.4 | 12.3 | 30.3 | 6.4 | 2.9 | 0.2 |
| Netherlands | 30.6 | 10.5 | 4.2 | 1.3 | 0.9 | 0.2 | 0.1 |
| Norway | 15.5 | 3.9 | 83.2 | 0.6 | 0.5 | 0.1 | 1.1 |
| Poland | 53.5 | 37.2 | 40.3 | 17.1 | 1.6 | 0.8 | 0.5 |
| Portugal | 76.1 | 101.7 | 20.5 | 4.6 | 2.3 | 2.3 | 0.3 |
| Spain | 44.7 | 39.1 | 11.1 | 2.7 | 1.3 | 0.9 | 0.2 |
| Sweden | 17.1 | 6.5 | 8.0 | 1.2 | 0.5 | 0.1 | 0.1 |
| Switzerland | 18.5 | 8.2 | 57.6 | 1.0 | 0.6 | 0.2 | 0.8 |
| USSR | 2.5 | 39.0 | 18.7 | 31.6 | 0.1 | 0.9 | 0.3 |
| United Kingdom | 213.8 | 137.4 | 159.4 | 16.8 | 6.4 | 3.1 | 2.2 |
| Yugoslavia | 20.4 | 30.5 | 37.3 | 2.8 | 0.6 | 0.7 | 0.5 |
| Other Europe | 9.1 | 18.9 | 7.7 | 1.2 | 0.2 | 0.2 | 0.0 |
| Asia | 427.6 | 1,588.2 | 2,738.1 | 342.2 | 12.9 | 35.2 | 37.3 |
| China | 34.8 | 124.3 | 298.9 | 24.0 | 1.0 | 2.8 | 4.1 |
| Hong Kong | 75.0 | 113.5 | 98.2 | 15.9 | 2.3 | 2.5 | 1.3 |
| India | 27.2 | 164.1 | 250.7 | 42.7 | 0.8 | 3.7 | 3.4 |
| Iran | 10.3 | 45.1 | 116.0 | 9.9 | 0.3 | 1.0 | 1.6 |
| Israel | 29.6 | 37.7 | 44.2 | 5.1 | 0.9 | 0.8 | 0.6 |
| Japan | 40.0 | 49.8 | 47.0 | 5.6 | 1.2 | 1.1 | 0.6 |
| Korea | 34.5 | 267.6 | 333.8 | 25.4 | 1.0 | 6.0 | 4.5 |
| Philippines | 98.4 | 355.0 | 548.7 | 68.8 | 3.0 | 7.9 | 7.5 |
| Turkey | 10.1 | 13.4 | 23.4 | 3.5 | 0.3 | 0.3 | 0.3 |
| Vietnam | 4.3 | 172.8 | 281.0 | 14.8 | 1.1 | 3.8 | 3.8 |
| Other Asia | 36.5 | 176.1 | 631.4 | 126.4 | 1.1 | 3.8 | 8.6 |
| America | 1,716.4 | 1,982.5 | 3,615.6 | 1,297.6 | 51.7 | 44.3 | 49.3 |
| Argentina | 49.7 | 29.9 | 27.3 | 4.2 | 1.5 | 0.7 | 0.4 |
| Canada | 413.3 | 169.9 | 158.0 | 19.9 | 12.4 | 3.8 | 2.2 |
| Colombia | 72.0 | 77.3 | 122.9 | 19.3 | 2.2 | 1.7 | 1.7 |
| Cuba | 208.5 | 264.9 | 144.6 | 9.5 | 6.3 | 5.9 | 2.0 |
| Dominican Rep. | 93.3 | 148.1 | 252.0 | 42.4 | 2.8 | 3.3 | 3.4 |
| Ecuador | 36.8 | 50.1 | 56.2 | 10.0 | 1.1 | 1.1 | 0.8 |
| El Salvador | 15.0 | 34.4 | 213.5 | 46.9 | 0.5 | 0.8 | 2.9 |
| Haiti | 34.5 | 56.3 | 138.4 | 47.0 | 1.0 | 1.3 | 1.9 |
| Jamaica | 74.9 | 137.6 | 208.1 | 23.0 | 2.3 | 3.1 | 2.8 |
| Mexico | 453.9 | 640.3 | 1,655.7 | 947.9 | 13.7 | 14.3 | 22.6 |
| Other America | 264.4 | 373.8 | 639.3 | 128.4 | 7.9 | 8.3 | 8.7 |
| Africa | 29.0 | 80.8 | 176.8 | 33.5 | 0.9 | 1.8 | 2.4 |
| Oceania | 25.1 | 41.2 | 45.2 | 7.1 | 0.8 | 0.9 | 0.6 |

Figures may not add to total due to rounding.

## AMERICAN WORKERS AND FARMERS

| Year | Total Number of Workers (thousands) | Percent of Workers Male/Female | Percent of Female Workers Married | Percent of Workers in Female Population | Percent of Workers in Labor Unions | Farm Population (thousands) | Farm Population as Percent of Total Population |
|------|------|------|------|------|------|------|------|
| 1870 | 12,506 | 85/15 | NA | NA | NA | NA | NA |
| 1880 | 17,392 | 85/15 | NA | NA | NA | 21,973 | 43.8 |
| 1890 | 23,318 | 83/17 | 13.9 | 18.9 | NA | 24,771 | 42.3 |
| 1900 | 29,073 | 82/18 | 15.4 | 20.6 | 3 | 29,875 | 41.9 |
| 1910 | 38,167 | 79/21 | 24.7 | 25.4 | 6 | 32,077 | 34.9 |
| 1920 | 41,614 | 79/21 | 23.0 | 23.7 | 12 | 31,974 | 30.1 |
| 1930 | 48,830 | 78/22 | 28.9 | 24.8 | 7 | 30,529 | 24.9 |
| 1940 | 53,011 | 76/24 | 36.4 | 27.4 | 27 | 30,547 | 23.2 |
| 1950 | 59,643 | 72/28 | 52.1 | 31.4 | 25 | 23,048 | 15.3 |
| 1960 | 69,877 | 68/32 | 59.9 | 37.7 | 26 | 15,635 | 8.7 |
| 1970 | 82,049 | 63/37 | 63.4 | 43.4 | 25 | 9,712 | 4.8 |
| 1980 | 108,544 | 58/42 | 59.7 | 51.5 | 23 | 6,051 | 2.7 |
| 1990 | 117,914 | 55/45 | 58.4 | 44.3 | 16 | 4,591 | 1.8 |

## THE ECONOMY AND FEDERAL SPENDING

| Year | Gross National Product (GNP) (in billions) | Foreign Trade (in millions) Exports | Foreign Trade (in millions) Imports | Balance of Trade | Federal Budget (in billions) | Federal Surplus/Deficit (in billions) | Federal Debt (in billions) |
|------|------|------|------|------|------|------|------|
| 1790 | NA | $ 20 | $ 23 | $ −3 | $ 0.004 | $ +0.00015 | $ 0.076 |
| 1800 | NA | 71 | 91 | −20 | 0.011 | +0.0006 | 0.083 |
| 1810 | NA | 67 | 85 | −18 | 0.008 | +0.0012 | 0.053 |
| 1820 | NA | 70 | 74 | −4 | 0.018 | −0.0004 | 0.091 |
| 1830 | NA | 74 | 71 | +3 | 0.015 | +0.100 | 0.049 |
| 1840 | NA | 132 | 107 | +25 | 0.024 | −0.005 | 0.004 |
| 1850 | NA | 152 | 178 | −26 | 0.040 | +0.004 | 0.064 |
| 1860 | NA | 400 | 362 | −38 | 0.063 | −0.01 | 0.065 |
| 1870 | $ 7.4 | 451 | 462 | −11 | 0.310 | +0.10 | 2.4 |
| 1880 | 11.2 | 853 | 761 | +92 | 0.268 | +0.07 | 2.1 |
| 1890 | 13.1 | 910 | 823 | +87 | 0.318 | +0.09 | 1.2 |
| 1900 | 18.7 | 1,499 | 930 | +569 | 0.521 | +0.05 | 1.2 |
| 1910 | 35.3 | 1,919 | 1,646 | +273 | 0.694 | −0.02 | 1.1 |
| 1920 | 91.5 | 8,664 | 5,784 | +2,880 | 6.357 | +0.3 | 24.3 |
| 1930 | 90.7 | 4,013 | 3,500 | +513 | 3.320 | +0.7 | 16.3 |
| 1940 | 100.0 | 4,030 | 7,433 | −3,403 | 9.6 | −2.7 | 43.0 |
| 1950 | 286.5 | 10,816 | 9,125 | +1,691 | 43.1 | −2.2 | 257.4 |
| 1960 | 506.5 | 19,600 | 15,046 | +4,556 | 92.2 | +0.3 | 286.3 |
| 1970 | 992.7 | 42,700 | 40,189 | +2,511 | 195.6 | −2.8 | 371.0 |
| 1980 | 2,631.7 | 220,783 | 244,871 | +24,088 | 590.9 | −73.8 | 907.7 |
| 1990 | 5,524.5 | 421,730 | 487,129 | −65,399 | 1,251.8 | −220.5 | 3,233.3 |

## AMERICAN WARS

| | U.S. Military Personnel (thousands) | Personnel as % of Population | U.S. Deaths | U.S. Wounds | Direct Cost 1990 Dollars (millions) |
|---|---|---|---|---|---|
| American Revolution | | | | | |
|   Apr. 1775–Sept. 1783 | 184–250 | 9–12 | 4,004 | 6,004 | $100–140 |
| War of 1812 | | | | | |
|   June 1812–Feb. 1815 | 286 | 3 | 1,950 | 4,000 | 87 |
| Mexican War | | | | | |
|   May 1846–Feb. 1848 | 116 | 0.5 | 13,271 | 4,102 | 82 |
| Civil War: Union | 3,393 | 14 | 360,222 | 275,175 | 2,302 |
| Civil War: Confederacy | | | | | |
|   Apr. 1861–Apr. 1865 | 1,034 | 11 | 258,000 | NA | 1,032 |
| Spanish-American War | | | | | |
|   Apr. 1898–Aug. 1898 | 307 | 0.4 | 2,446 | 1,662 | 270 |
| World War I | | | | | |
|   Apr. 1917–Nov. 1918 | 4,714 | 5 | 116,516 | 204,002 | 32,740 |
| World War II | | | | | |
|   Dec. 1941–Aug. 1945 | 16,354 | 12 | 405,399 | 670,846 | 360,000 |
| Korean War | | | | | |
|   June 1950–June 1953 | 5,764 | 4 | 54,246 | 103,284 | 50,000 |
| Vietnam War | | | | | |
|   Aug. 1964–June 1973 | 8,400 | 4 | 47,704 | 219,573 | 140,644 |
| Persian Gulf War | | | | | |
|   Jan. 1991–Feb. 1991 | 467 | 0.1 | 293 | 467 | NA |

# BIBLIOGRAPHY

## CHAPTER 17: RECONSTRUCTING THE UNION

### General Histories
James McPherson, *Ordeal by Fire: The Civil War and Reconstruction* (1982); Kenneth M. Stampp, *The Era of Reconstruction, 1865–1877* (1965).

### National Politics
Herman Belz, *Emancipation and Equal Rights: Politics and Constitutionalism in the Civil War Era* (1978); Michael Les Benedict, *A Compromise of Principle: Congressional Republicans and Reconstruction* (1974); W. R. Brock, *An American Crisis: Congress and Reconstruction, 1865–1867* (1963); John and LaWanda Cox, *Politics, Principles, and Prejudice, 1865–1866* (1963); James M. McPherson, *The Struggle for Equality: Abolitionists and the Negro in the Civil War and Reconstruction* (1964); Hans L. Trefousse, *The Radical Republicans: Lincoln's Vanguard for Racial Justice* (1969).

### Reconstruction and the Constitution
William Gillette, *The Right to Vote: Politics and the Passage of the Fifteenth Amendment* (1965); Harold M. Hyman, *A More Perfect Union: The Impact of the Civil War and Reconstruction on the Constitution* (1973); Joseph James, *The Framing of the Fourteenth Amendment* (1956); William E. Nelson, *The Fourteenth Amendment: From Political Principle to Judicial Doctrine* (1988).

### The Black Experience in Reconstruction
James D. Anderson, *The Education of Blacks in the South, 1860–1935* (1988); Herbert G. Gutman, *The Black Family in Slavery and Freedom, 1750–1925* (1976); Janet Sharp Hermann, *The Pursuit of a Dream* (1981); Howard Rabinowitz, ed., *Southern Black Leaders in Reconstruction* (1982); Vernon L. Wharton, *The Negro in Mississippi, 1865–1890* (1947); Joel Williamson, *After Slavery: The Negro in South Carolina during Reconstruction* (1966).

### Reconstruction in the South
Richard N. Current, *Those Terrible Carpetbaggers: A Reinterpretation* (1988); William C. Harris, *Day of the Carpetbagger: Republican Reconstruction in Mississippi* (1979); Michael Perman, *Reunion without Compromise: The South and Reconstruction, 1865–1868* (1973); George C. Rable, *But There Was No Peace: The Role of Violence in the Politics of Reconstruction* (1984); James Sefton, *The United States Army and Reconstruction, 1865–1877* (1967); Ted Tunnell, *Crucible of Reconstruction: War, Radicalism, and Race in Louisiana, 1862–1877*

(1974); Allen Trelease, *White Terror: The Ku Klux Klan Conspiracy and Southern Reconstruction* (1967); Sarah Woolfolk Wiggins, *The Scalawag in Alabama Politics, 1865–1881* (1977).

### Social and Economic Reconstruction
George R. Bentley, *A History of the Freedmen's Bureau* (1955); Eric Foner, *Nothing But Freedom: Emancipation and Its Legacy* (1983); Steven Hahn, *The Roots of Southern Populism: Yeoman Farmers and the Transformation of the Georgia Upcountry, 1850–1890* (1983); Jacqueline Jones, *Soldiers of Light and Love: Northern Teachers and Georgia Blacks, 1865–1873* (1980); Donald Nieman, *To Set the Law in Motion: The Freedmen's Bureau and the Legal Rights of Blacks, 1865–1868* (1979); Claude F. Oubre, *Forty Acres and a Mule: The Freedmen's Bureau and Black Landownership* (1978); Lawrence N. Powell, *New Masters: Northern Planters during the Civil War and Reconstruction* (1984); Roger L. Ransom and Richard Sutch, *One Kind of Freedom: The Economic Consequences of Emancipation* (1977); Mark W. Summers, *Railroads, Reconstruction, and the Gospel of Prosperity* (1984).

### The End of Reconstruction
Paul Buck, *The Road to Reunion, 1865–1900* (1937); Keith Ian Polakoff, *The Politics of Inertia: The Election of 1876 and the End of Reconstruction* (1973); C. Vann Woodward, *Reunion and Reaction: The Compromise of 1877 and the End of Reconstruction* (1951).

### Biographies
Fawn M. Brodie, *Thaddeus Stevens: Scourge of the South* (1959); David Donald, *Charles Sumner and the Rights of Man* (1970); William S. McFeely, *Yankee Stepfather: General O. Howard and the Freedmen* (1968) and *Grant: A Biography* (1981); Brooks D. Simpson, *Let Us Have Peace: Ulysses S. Grant and the Politics of War and Reconstruction, 1861–1868* (1991); Hans L. Trefousse, *Andrew Johnson: A Biography* (1989).

## CHAPTER 18: THE NEW INDUSTRIAL ORDER

### General Studies
Daniel Boorstin, *The Americans: The Democratic Experience* (1973); John A. Garraty, *The New Commonwealth* (1968); Ray Ginger, *The Age of Excess* (1963); Samuel P. Hays, *The Response to Industrialism, 1885–1914* (1957); Edward C.

Kirkland, *Industry Comes of Age: Business, Labor, and Public Policy, 1860–1897* (1967); Martin V. Melosi, *Coping with Abundance: Energy and Environment in Industrial America* (1985); Robert Wiebe, *The Search for Order, 1877–1920* (1968).

### The Economy
Frederick Lewis Allen, *The Great Pierpont Morgan* (1949); W. Elliot Brownlee, *Dynamics of Ascent: A History of the American Economy*, rev. ed. (1979); Stuart Bruchey, *Growth of the Modern American Economy* (1975); Milton Friedman and Anna Schwartz, *Monetary History of the United States, 1867–1960* (1963); Robert L. Heilbroner, *The Economic Transformation of America* (1977); Robert Higgs, *The Transformation of the American Economy, 1865–1914* (1971); Susan Previant Lee and Peter Passell, *A New Economic View of American History* (1979); Harold G. Vatter, *The Drive to Industrial Maturity: The United States Economy, 1860–1914* (1975).

### The Railroads
Alfred D. Chandler, Jr., *The Railroads: The Nation's First Big Business* (1965); Robert Fogel, *Railroads and American Economic Growth* (1964); Julius Grodinsky, *Jay Gould* (1957); Gabriel Kolko, *Railroads and Regulation, 1877–1916* (1965); Albro Martin, *James J. Hill and the Opening of the Northwest* (1976) and *Railroads Triumphant: The Growth, Rejection, and Rebirth of a Vital American Force* (1992); John F. Stover, *American Railroads* (1970).

### The Rise of Big Business
Alfred Chandler, Jr., *Strategy and Structure: Chapters in the History of American Industrial Enterprise* (1962), *The Visible Hand: The Managerial Revolution in American Business* (1977) and *Scale and Scope: The Dynamics of Industrial Capitalism* (1990); Thomas Cochrane, *Business in American Life* (1972); Naomi Lamoreaux, *The Great Merger Movement in American Business, 1895–1904* (1985); Harold C. Livesay, *Andrew Carnegie and the Rise of Big Business* (1975); Alan Nevins, *Study in Power: John D. Rockefeller*, 2 vols. (1953); Glenn Porter, *The Rise of Big Business* (1973); Martin J. Sklar, *The Corporate Reconstruction of American Capitalism, 1890–1916: The Market, Law and Politics* (1988); Richard Tedlow, *The Rise of the American Business Corporation* (1991); Alan Trachtenberg, *The Incorporation of America* (1982); Joseph Wall, *Andrew Carnegie* (1970); Olivier Zunz, *Making America Corporate, 1870–1920* (1990).

### Invention and Industry
Robert Bruce, *Alexander Graham Bell and the Conquest of Solitude* (1973); Robert Conot, *A Streak of Luck* (1979); Ruth Schwartz Cowan, *A Social History of American Technology* (1996); Siegfried Giedion, *Mechanization Takes Command* (1948); David Hounshell, *From the American System to Mass Production, 1800–1932* (1984); John F.

Kasson, *Civilizing the Machine* (1976); Carolyn Marvin, *When Old Technologies Were New: Thinking about Electric Communication in the Late Nineteenth Century* (1988); David Nye, *Electrifying America: Social Meanings of a New Technology, 1890–1940* (1990); Harold Passer, *The Electrical Manufacturers, 1875–1900* (1953); Leonard S. Reich, *The Making of Industrial Research: Science and Business at GE and Bell, 1876–1926* (1985); Nathan Rosenberg, *Technology and American Economic Growth* (1972); Peter Temin, *Iron and Steel in Nineteenth Century America* (1964); Frederick A. White, *American Industrial Research Laboratories* (1961).

### Capitalism and Its Critics
Robert Bannister, *Social Darwinism: Science and Myth in Anglo-American Social Thought* (1979); Robert H. Bremner, *American Philanthropy* (1988); Carl N. Degler, *In Search of Human Nature: The Decline and Revival of Darwinism in America* (1991); Sidney Fine, *Laissez Faire and the General Welfare State: A Study of Conflict in American Thought, 1865–1900* (1956); Louis Galambos, *The Public Image of Big Business in America, 1880–1940: A Quantitative Study of Social Change* (1975); Richard Hofstadter, *Social Darwinism in American Thought*, rev. ed. (1955); Edward C. Kirkland, *Dream and Thought in the Business Community, 1860–1900* (1956); Ellen Condliffe Lagemann, *The Politics of Knowledge: The Carnegie Corporation, Philanthropy, and Public Policy* (1989); T. Jackson Lears, *No Place of Grace: Antimodernism and the Transformation of American Culture, 1880–1920* (1981); George E. Pozzetta, ed., *Americanization, Social Control, and Philanthropy* (1991); John Thomas, *Alternative America: Henry George, Edward Bellamy, Henry Demarest Lloyd, and the Adversary Tradition* (1983).

### The Culture of Work
American Social History Project, *Who Built America? Working People and the Nation's Economy, Politics, Culture, Society*, Volume Two: *From the Gilded Age to the Present* (1992); Cindy Sondik Aron, *Ladies and Gentlemen of the Civil Service: Middle-Class Workers in Victorian America* (1987); James R. Barrett, *Work and Community in the Jungle: Chicago's Packinghouse Workers, 1894–1922* (1990); John Bodnar, *Immigration and Industrialization: Ethnicity in an American Mill Town* (1977); John T. Cumbler, *Working Class Community in Industrial America: Work, Leisure, and Struggle in Two Industrial Cities, 1880–1930* (1979); David Emmons, *The Butte Irish: Class and Ethnicity in an American Mining Town, 1875–1925* (1989); Michael Frisch and Daniel Walkowitz, eds., *Working-Class America: Essays on Labor, Community, and American Society* (1983); James R. Green, *World of the Worker: Labor in Twentieth Century America* (1980); Herbert Gutman, *Work, Culture and Society in Industrializing America: Essays in American Working-Class History* (1976); Tamara Hareven, *Family, Time, and Industrial*

*Time: The Relationship between the Family and Work in a New England Industrial Community* (1982); William H. Harris, *The Harder We Run: Black Workers since the Civil War* (1982); Jacqueline Jones, *Labor of Love, Labor of Sorrow: Black Women, Work and the Family, from Slavery to the Present* (1985); Susan Kennedy, *If All We Did Was to Weep at Home: A History of White Working Class Women in America* (1979); Walter Licht, *Working for the Railroad: The Organization of Work in the Nineteenth Century* (1983); Joanne J. Meyerowitz, *Women Adrift: Independent Wage Earners in Chicago, 1880–1930* (1988); David Montgomery, *Workers' Control in America: Studies in the History of Work, Technology, and Labor Struggles* (1979); Daniel Nelson, *Managers and Workers: Origins of the New Factory System* (1975); Richard Jules Oestreicher, *Solidarity and Fragmentation: Working People and Class Consciousness in Detroit, 1875–1900* (1986); Daniel T. Rodgers, *The Work Ethic in Industrial America, 1850–1920* (1978); Stephan Thern-strom, *The Other Bostonians: Poverty and Progress in the American Metropolis, 1880–1970* (1973).

**The Labor Movement**
Eric Arnesen, *Waterfront Workers of New Orleans: Race, Class, and Politics, 1863–1923* (1991); Paul Avrich, *The Haymarket Tragedy* (1984); Mary H. Blewett, *Men, Women, and Work: Class, Gender, and Protest in the New England Shoe Industry, 1880–1910* (1988); Jeremy Brecher, *Strike!* (1977); Mari Jo Buhle, *Women and American Socialism, 1870–1920* (1981); Melvyn Dubofsky, *Industrialism and the American Worker, 1865–1920* (1975) and *We Shall Be All: A History of the Industrial Workers of the World* (1969); Philip Foner, *Women and the American Labor Movement*, 2 vols. (1979); James R. Grossman, *Land of Hope: Chicago, Black Southerners, and the Great Migration* (1989); William H. Harris, *The Harder We Run: Black Workers since the Civil War* (1982); Stuart Kaufman, *Samuel Gompers and the Origins of the American Federation of Labor* (1973); Paul Krause, *The Battle for Homestead: Politics, Culture and Steel* (1992); Susan Levine, *Labor's True Women: Carpet Weavers, Industrialization, and Labor Reform in the Gilded Age* (1984); Gwendolyn Mink, *Old Labor and New Immigrants in American Political Development: Union, Party, and State, 1875–1920* (1986); David Montgomery, *The Fall of the House of Labor: The Workplace, the State, and American Labor Activism, 1865–1925* (1987); Leon Fink, *Workingmen's Democracy: The Knights of Labor and American Politics* (1983) Alice Kessler-Harris, *Out to Work: A History of Wage-Earning Women in the United States* (1982); Nick Salvatore, *Eugene V. Debs: Citizen and Socialist* (1982); David Shannon, *The Socialist Party* (1955); Sheldon Stromquist, *A Generation of Boomers: The Pattern of Railroad Labor Conflict in Nineteenth-Century America* (1987); Lloyd Ulman, *The Rise of the National Trade Union: The Development and Significance of*

*Its Structure, Governing Institutions, and Economic Policies* (1955).

## CHAPTER 19: THE RISE OF AN URBAN ORDER

**General Studies**
Howard B. Chudacoff, *The Evolution of American Urban Society*, rev. ed., (1981); William Cronon, *Nature's Metropolis: Chicago and the Great West* (1991); Charles Glabb and A. Theodore Brown, *A History of Urban America*, rev. ed., (1976); Blake McKelvey, *The Urbanization of America, 1860–1915* (1963); Allan Pred, *Spatial Dynamics of U.S. Urban Growth, 1800–1914* (1971); John Stilgoe, *Borderland: The Origins of the American Suburb, 1820–1929* (1988); Stephan Thernstrom and Richard Sennett, eds., *19th Century Cities: Essays in the New Urban History* (1969); Sam Bass Warner, Jr., *Streetcar Suburbs* (1962) and *The Urban Wilderness* (1972).

**Immigration and Immigrants**
John Bodnar, *The Transplanted: A History of Immigrants in Urban America* (1985); Josef Barton, *Peasants and Strangers: Italians, Rumanians and Slovaks in an American City* (1975); John J. Bukowczyk, *And My Children Did Not Know Me: A History of Polish Americans* (1987); Sucheng Chan, *Asian Americans: An Interpretive History* (1991); Jack Chen, *The Chinese of America* (1970); Roger Daniels, *Coming to America: A History of Immigration and Ethnicity in American Life* (1990); Hasia A. Diner, *Erin's Daughters in America: Irish Immigrant Women in the Nineteenth Century* (1983); Leonard Dinnerstein, Roger Nichols, and David Reimers, *Natives and Strangers* (1979); John Duff, *The Irish in the United States* (1971); Mario Garcia, *Desert Immigrants: The Mexicans of El Paso, 1880–1920* (1981); Susan A. Glenn, *Daughters of the Shtetl: Life and Labor in the Immigrant Generation* (1990); Richard Griswold del Castillo, *La Familia: Chicano Families in the Urban Southwest, 1848 to the Present* (1984); Irving Howe, *World of Our Fathers: The Journey of the East European Jews to America and the Life They Found and Made* (1976); Yuji Ichioka, *The Issei: The World of the First Generation Japanese Americans, 1885–1924* (1988); Jenna Weissman Joselit, *The Wonders of America: Reinventing Jewish Culture, 1880–1950* (1994); Edward Kantowicz, *Polish-American Politics in Chicago* (1975); Thomas Kessner, *The Golden Door: Italian and Jewish Immigrant Mobility in New York City, 1880–1915* (1977); Alan M. Kraut, *The Huddled Masses: The Immigrant in American Society, 1880–1921* (1982); Michael La Sorte, *La Merica: Images of Italian Greenhorn Experience* (1985); Joseph Lopreato, *Italian Americans* (1970); Kerby A. Miller, *Emigrants and Exiles: Ireland and the Irish Exodus to North America* (1985); Ewa Morawska, *For Bread and Butter: The Life-Worlds of East Central Europeans in Johnstown, Pennsyl-*

*vania, 1890–1940* (1985); James Stuart Olsen, *The Ethnic Dimension in American History*, vol. II (1979); Moses Rischin, *The Promised City: New York's Jews* (1962); Jacob Riis, *How the Other Half Lives* (1890); Howard M. Sachar, *A History of Jews in America* (1992); Ronald Takaki, *Strangers from a Different Shore: A History of Asian Americans* (1989) and *A Different Mirror: A History of Multicultural America* (1993); Philip Taylor, *The Distant Magnet: European Emigration to the U.S.A.* (1971); Virginia Yans-McLaughlin, *Family and Commu-nity: Italian Immigrants in Buffalo, 1880– 1930* (1977), and as ed., *Immigration Reconsidered: History, Sociology, Politics* (1990); Anzia Yezierska, *Bread Givers* (1925); Olivier Zunz, *The Changing Face of Inequality: Urbanization, Industrial Development, and Immigrants in Detroit, 1880– 1920* (1982).

**Nativism and Race**
Leonard Dinnerstein, *Anti-Semitism in America* (1994); Louis Harlan, *Booker T. Washington: The Making of a Black Leader, 1856–1901* (1972) and *Booker T. Washington: The Wizard of Tuskegee, 1901–1915* (1983); John Higham, *Strangers in the Land: Patterns of American Nativism, 1880–1925* (1955) and *Send These to Me* (1975); Kenneth Kusmer, *A Ghetto Takes Shape: Black Cleveland, 1870–1930* (1976); Stanley Lieberson, *A Piece of the Pie: Blacks and White Immigrants Since 1880* (1980); Gilbert Osofsky, *Harlem: The Making of a Ghetto* (1966); Joel Perlman, *Ethnic Differences: Schooling and Social Structure among the Irish, Italians, Jews, and Blacks in an American City, 1880– 1935* (1988); Elizabeth Hafkin Pleck, *Black Migration and Poverty, Boston, 1865–1900* (1979); Allan H. Spear, *Black Chicago* (1967); Donald Spivey, *Schooling for the New Slavery: Black Industrial Education, 1868–1915* (1978).

**Politics and Poverty**
John Allswang, *Bosses, Machines, and Urban Voters* (1977); Robert H. Bremmer, *From the Depths: The Discovery of Poverty in the United States* (1956); Alexander B. Callow, ed., *The City Boss in America* (1976); Lyle Dorsett, *The Pendergast Machine* (1968); Steven P. Erie, *Rainbow's End: Irish- Americans and the Dilemmas of Urban Machine Politics, 1840–1985* (1988); Leo Hershkowitz, *Tweed's New York: Another Look* (1977); Zane Miller, *Boss Cox's Cincinnati* (1968); James T. Patterson, *America's Struggle against Poverty* (1981); Thomas Philpott, *The Slum and the Ghetto* (1978); William L. Riordon, *Plunkitt of Tammany Hall* (1963); Lloyd Wendt and Herman Kogan, *Bosses in Lusty Chicago*, 2d ed. (1971).

**Reform**
Jane Addams, *Twenty Years at Hull-House* (1910); Ruth Bordin, *Woman and Temperance: The Quest for Power and Liberty, 1860–1900* (1981); Paul Boyer, *Urban Masses and Moral Order in America, 1820–1920* (1978); Allen Davis, *Spearheads for Reform: The Social Settlements and the Progressive Movement, 1890–1914* (1967) and *American Heroine: The Life and Legend of Jane Addams* (1973); Marvin Lazerson, *Origins of the Urban School* (1971); Eric Monkonnen, *Police in Urban America, 1860–1920* (1981); David Pivar, *Purity Crusade: Sexual Morality and Social Control, 1868–1900* (1973); James Reed, *The Birth Control Movement and American Society: From Private Vice to Public Virtue* (1983); Barbara Rosencrantz, *Public Health and the State* (1972); Martin Schiesl, *The Politics of Efficiency: Municipal Administration and Reform in America* (1977); David Tyack, *The One Best System: A History of American Urban Education* (1974); Morris Vogel, *The Invention of the Modern Hospital: Boston, 1870–1930* (1980); James C. Whorton, *Crusaders for Fitness: The History of American Health Reformers* (1982).

**Urban Life, Work, and Culture**
Cindy Aron, *Ladies and Gentlemen of the Civil Service: Middle Class Workers in Victorian America* (1987); Gunther Barth, *City People: The Rise of Modern City Culture in 19th Century America* (1980); Susan Porter Benson, *Counter Cultures: Saleswomen, Managers, and Customers in Department Stores, 1890–1940* (1986); Allan Brandt, *No Magic Bullet: A Social History of Venereal Disease in the United States Since 1880*, rev. ed. (1985); Robert Cross, *The Church and the City* (1967); Ronald Davies, *A History of Music in American Life*, Volume II: *The Gilded Years, 1865– 1920* (1980); Lewis A. Erenberg, *Steppin' Out: New York Nightlife and the Transformation of American Culture, 1890–1930* (1981); Ellen Garvey, *The Adman in the Parlor: Magazines and the Gendering of Consumer Culture, 1880s to 1910s* (1996); James Gilbert, *Perfect Cities: Chicago Utopias of 1893* (1991); Thomas J. Gilfoyle, *City of Eros: New York City, Prostitution, and the Commercialization of Sex, 1790–1920* (1992); Tamara K. Hareven and Randolph Langenbach, *Amoskeag: Life and Work in an American Factory* (1978); Neil Harris, *Humbug: The Art of P. T. Barnum* (1973); Lawrence Kasson, *Amusing the Million: Coney Island at the Turn of the Century* (1978) and *Rudeness & Civility: Manners in Nineteenth-Century Urban America* (1990); William Leach, *Land of Desire: Merchants, Power, and the Rise of a New American Culture* (1993); Lawrence Levine, *Highbrow/Lowbrow: The Emergence of Cultural Hierarchy in America* (1988); Richard Lingeman, *Theodore Dreiser: At the Gates of the City, 1871–1907* (1986); John Lucas and Ronald Smith, *Saga of American Sport* (1978); Henry F. May, *Protestant Churches and Urban America* (1949); Katherine Morello, *The Invisible Bar: The Woman Lawyer in America, 1638 to the Present* (1986); Joseph Musselman, *Music in the Cultured Generation: A Social History of Music in America, 1870–1900* (1971); David Nasaw, *Schooled to Order: A Social History of Public Schooling in the United States* (1979), *Children of the City: At*

*Work and at Play* (1986), and *Going Out: The Rise and Fall of Public Amusements* (1993); Kathy Peiss, *Cheap Amusements: Working Women and Leisure in Turn-of-the-Century New York* (1986); Roy Rosenzweig, *Eight Hours for What We Will: Workers & Leisure in an Industrial City, 1870–1920* (1983); Russel Nye, *The Unembarrassed Muse: The Popular Arts in America* (1970); Thomas J. Schlereth, *Victorian American: Transformations in Everyday Life, 1876–1915* (1991); Robert H. Walker, *Life in the Age of Enterprise, 1865–1900* (1967).

### Women, Family, and Social Mores
Elaine S. Abelson, *When Ladies Go A-Thieving: Middle-Class Shoplifters in the Victorian Department Store* (1990); Allan M. Brandt, *No Magic Bullet: A Social History of Venereal Disease since 1880* (1985); John D'Emilio and Estelle B. Freedman, *Intimate Matters: A History of Sexuality in America* (1988); Harvey Green, *The Light of the Home: An Intimate View of the Lives of Women in Victorian America* (1983); John S. Haller and Robin M. Haller, *The Physician and Sexuality in Victorian America* (1986); N. Ray Hiner and Joseph Hawes, eds., *Growing Up in America: Children in Historical Perspective* (1985); David Katzman, *Seven Days a Week: Women and Domestic Service in Industrializing America* (1978); Judith Leavitt, *Brought to Bed: Childbearing in America, 1750–1950* (1988); Elizabeth Lunbeck, *The Psychiatric Persuasion: Knowledge, Gender, and Politics in Modern America* (1994); Elaine May, *Great Expectations: Marriage and Divorce in Post-Victorian America* (1980); Steven Mintz, *A Prison of Expectations: The Family in Victorian Culture* (1983); Steven Mintz and Susan Kellogg, *Domestic Revolutions: A Social History of American Family Life* (1988); Ellen Rothman, *Hands and Hearts: A History of Courtship in America* (1984); Gar Scharnhorst, *Charlotte Perkins Gilman* (1985); Carroll Smith-Rosenberg, *Disorderly Conduct: Visions of Gender in Victorian America* (1986); Susan Strasser, *Never Done: A History of American Housework* (1983).

## CHAPTER 20: AGRARIAN DOMAINS: THE SOUTH AND THE WEST

### The New South: History, Politics, and Culture

Edward L. Ayers, *The Promise of the New South: Life after Reconstruction* (1992) and *Southern Crossing: A History of the American South, 1877–1906* (1995); Orville Vernon Burton, *In My Father's House* (1985); W. J. Cash, *The Mind of the South* (1941); Thomas D. Clark and Albert Kirwan, *The South since Appomattox* (1967); David L. Carlton, *Mill and Town in South Carolina, 1880–1920* (1982); John M. Cooper, *Walter Hines Page: The Southerner as American, 1855–1918* (1977); Pete Daniel, *Breaking the Land: The Transformation of Cotton, Tobacco, and Rice Cultures since 1880* (1985); Carl N. Degler, *The Other South: Southern Dissenters in the Nineteenth Century* (1974); Robert Durden, *The Self-Inflicted Wound: Southern Politics in the Nineteenth Century* (1985); John S. Ezell, *The South since 1865* (1975); Paul Gaston, *The New South Creed: A Study in Southern Mythmaking* (1970); Richard Gray, *Writing the South: The Idea of an American Region* (1986); Patrick H. Hearden, *Independence and Empire: The New South's Cotton Mill Campaign, 1865–1920* (1982); J. Morgan Kousser, *The Shaping of Southern Politics: Suffrage Restriction and Establishment of the One Party South* (1974); J. Morgan Kousser and James McPherson, eds., *Region, Race, and Reconstruction* (1982); Lawrence Karsen, *The Rise of the Urban South* (1985); I. A. Newby, *Plain Folk in the New South: Social Change and Cultural Persistence, 1880–1915* (1989); Raymond B. Nixon, *Henry W. Grady: Spokesman of the New South* (1969); Ted Ownby, *Subduing Satan* (1990); David M. Potter, *The South and the Concurrent Majority* (1972); Allen Tullos, *Habits of Industry: White Culture and the Transformation of the Carolina Piedmont* (1989); Marjorie Spruill Wheeler, *New Women of the New South: The Leaders of the Woman Suffrage Movement in the Southern States* (1993); Charles R. Wilson, *Baptized in Blood: The Religion of the Lost Cause, 1865–1920* (1980); C. Vann Woodward, *Tom Watson: Agrarian Rebel* (1938), and *The Origins of the New South* (1951).

### The Southern Economy and Race

David Carlton, *Mill and Town in South Carolina, 1880–1920* (1982); Pete Daniel, *Breaking the Land: The Transformation of Cotton, Tobacco, and Rice Cultures since 1880* (1985); Steven Hahn, *The Roots of Southern Populism: Yeoman Farmers and the Transformation of the Georgia Upcountry, 1850–1890* (1983); Louis T. Harlan, *Booker T. Washington: The Making of a Black Leader, 1865–1901* (1972); Robert Higgs, *Competition and Coercion: Blacks in the American Economy, 1865–1890* (1977); Gerald David Jaynes, *Branches without Roots: Genesis of the Black Working Class in the American South, 1862–1882* (1986); Neil R. McMillen, *Dark Journey: Black Mississippians in the Age of Jim Crow* (1989); J. M. McPherson, *The Abolitionist Legacy: From Reconstruction to the NAACP* (1975); August Meier, *Negro Thought in America, 1880–1915: Racial Ideologies in the Age of Booker T. Washington* (1963); Howard Rabinowitz, *Race Relations in the Urban South, 1865–1890* (1978); Roger Ransom and Richard Sutch, *One Kind of Freedom: The Economic Consequences of Emancipation* (1977); Donald Spivey, *Schooling for the New Slavery: Black Industrial Education* (1978); J. F. Stover, *The Railroads of the South* (1955); Edward Wheeler, *Uplifting the Race: The Black Minister in the New South, 1865–1902* (1986); Joel Williamson, *The Crucible of Race: Black-White Relations in the American South since Emancipation* (1984) and *After Slavery* (1965); C. Vann Woodward, *The Strange Career of Jim Crow*, 3d rev. ed. (1974); Gavin Wright, *Old South, New South: Revolutions in the Southern Economy since the Civil War* (1986).

## Opening of the West

Walton Bean, *California* (1978); Thomas Berger, *Little Big Man* (1964); Ray A. Billington, *Westward Expansion* (1967); Thomas D. Clark, *Frontier America*, rev. ed. (1969); William Cronon, *Nature's Metropolis: Chicago and the Great West* (1991); William Cronon, George Miles, and Jay Gitlin, *Under an Open Sky: Rethinking America's Western Past* (1992); Sarah Deutsch, *No Separate Refuge: Culture, Class, and Gender on an Anglo-Hispanic Frontier in the American Southwest, 1880–1940* (1987); Robert Hine, *The American West*, 2d rev. ed. (1984); Paul Hutton, ed., *Soldiers West: Biographers from the Military Frontier* (1987); Howard Lamar, *The Reader's Encyclopedia of the American West* (1977) and *The Far Southwest, 1846–1912* (1966); Patricia Nelson Limerick, *The Legacy of Conquest: The Unbroken Past of the American West* (1987); Gerald McFarland, *A Scattered People: An American Family Moves West* (1985); Leo Marx, *The Machine in the Garden* (1964); Donald W. Meinig, *The Southwest: Three People in Geographical Change, 1600–1970* (1971); Frederick Merk, *History of the Westward Movement* (1978); Clyde A. Milner II, *A New Significance: Re-Envisioning the History of the American West* (1996); Clyde A. Milner II, Carol A. O'Connor, and Martha A. Sandweiss, eds., *The Oxford History of the American West* (1994); Roderick Nash, *Wilderness and the American Mind*, 3d ed. (1982); Earl Pomery, *The Pacific Slope* (1968); Richard Slotkin, *The Fatal Environment: The Myth of the West in the Age of Industrialization* (1985) and *Gunfighter Nation: The Myth of the Frontier in Twentieth-Century America* (1992); Wallace Stegner, *Beyond the Hundredth Meridian: John Welsey Powell and the Second Opening of the West* (1954); Henry Nash Smith, *Virgin Land* (1950); Jane Tompkins, *West of Everything: The Inner Life of Westerns* (1992); Mark Twain, *Roughing It* (1872); Elliott West, *The Way to the West: Essays on the Central Plains* (1995); Richard White, *"It's Your Misfortune and None of My Own": A New History of the American West* (1992); Donald Worster, *Rivers of Empire: Water, Aridity, and the Growth of the American West* (1992) and *Under Western Skies: Nature and History in the American West* (1992).

## The Peoples of the West

Rudolfo Acuna, *Occupied America: A History of Chicanos* (1981); Ralph Andrist, *The Long Death: The Last Days of the Sioux Nation* (1964); Robert Athearn, *In Search of Canaan: Black Migration in Kansas, 1879–1880* (1978); Gunther Barth, *Bitter Strength: A History of the Chinese in the United States, 1850–1870* (1964); Gretchen Bataille and Charles Silet, *The Pretend Indians: Images of Native Americans in the Movies* (1980); Beverly Beeton, *Women Vote in the West: The Woman Suffrage Movement, 1869–1896* (1986); Robert Berkhofer, Jr., *The White Man's Indian* (1978); Dee Brown, *Bury My Heart at Wounded Knee: An Indian History of the American War* (1970); Anne M. Butler, *Daughters of Joy, Sisters of Misery: Prostitutes in the American West, 1865–1890* (1985); Colin G. Calloway, ed., *Our Hearts Fell to the Ground: Plains Indian Views of How the West Was Lost* (1996); Edward Curtis, *The North American Indian* (1972); David Dary, *Cowboy Culture* (1981); Everett Dick, *Sod House Frontier* (1954); Carol Fairbanks, *Prairie Women: Images in American and Canadian Fiction* (1986); John Mack Faragher, *Women and Men on the Overland Trail* (1979); Christine Fisher, ed., *Let Them Speak for Themselves: Women in the American West, 1849–1900* (1977); Joe B. Frantz and Julian Choate, *The American Cowboy: The Myth and Reality* (1955); Carl Guarneri and David Alvarez, *Religion and Society in the American West* (1987); Julie Roy Jeffrey, *Frontier Women: The Trans-Mississippi West, 1840–1880* (1979); Alvin Josephy, *The Indian Heritage in America* (1969); William Katz, *The Black West* (1971); Polly W. Kaufman, *Women Teachers on the Frontier* (1984); William Leckie, *The Buffalo Soldiers: A Narrative History of the Negro Cavalry* (1967); Frederick Luebke, *Ethnicity on the Great Plains* (1980); Janet A. McDonnell, *The Dispossession of the American Indian, 1887–1934* (1991); M. S. Meier and Feliciano Rivera, *The Chicanos: A History of the Mexican Americans* (1972); David Montejano, *Anglos and Mexicans in the Making of Texas, 1836–1986* (1987); Sandra Myres, *Western Women and the Frontier Experience, 1880–1915* (1982); James S. Olsen and Raymond Wilson, *Native Americans in the Twentieth Century* (1984); Nell Painter, *The Exodusters: Black Migration to Kansas after Reconstruction* (1976); Peggy Pascoe, *Relations of Rescue: The Search for Female Moral Authority in the American West, 1874–1939* (1990); Paul Prucha, *American Indian Policy in Crisis* (1976); Harriet and Fred Rochlin, *Pioneer Jews: A New Life in the Far West* (1984); Mari Sandoz, *Cheyenne Autumn* (1954); William Savage, *The Cowboy Hero: His Image in American History and Culture* (1979) and as ed., *Cowboy Life* (1975); Kent Steckmesser, *The Western Hero in History and Legend* (1965); Elinor Pruitt Stewart, *Letters of a Woman Homesteader* (1913, 1914); Joanna Stratton, *Pioneer Women: Voices of the Kansas Frontier* (1981); John Tebbel and Keith Jennison, *The American Indian Wars* (1960); Robert Utley, *High Noon in Lincoln: Violence on the Western Frontier* (1987), *The Indian Frontier of the American West, 1846–1890* (1984) and *Frontier Regulars: The United States Army and the Indian, 1866–1890* (1984); Sylvia Van Kirk, *Many Tender Ties: Women in Fur Trade Society* (1983); Wilcomb Washburn, *The Indian in America* (1975).

## The Western Economy

Lewis Atherton, *Cattle Kings* (1961); Gunther Barth, *Instant Cities* (1975); Edward Dale, *The Range Cattle Industry*, rev. ed., (1969); David Dary, *Entrepreneurs of the Old West* (1986); Alan

Derickson, *Workers' Health, Workers' Democracy: The Western Miners' Struggle, 1891–1925* (1988); Robert Dykstra, *The Cattle Towns* (1968); Gilbert Fite, *The Farmer's Frontier* (1966); David Emmons, *The Butte Irish: Class and Ethnicity in an American Mining Town, 1875–1925* (1989); Paul Gates, *History of Public Land Development* (1968); William Greever, *The Bonanza West: The Story of the Western Mining Rushes* (1963); Gene M. Gressley, *Bankers and Cattlemen* (1966); Robert West Howard, *The Great Iron Trail: The Story of the First Transcontinental Railroad* (1963); Donald Jackson, *Gold Dust* (1980); Richard Lingenfelter, *The Hardrock Miners: A History of the Mining Labor Movement in the American West, 1863–1893* (1974); Rodman Paul, *The Far West and the Great Plains in Transition, 1865–1900* (1988); Mari Sandoz, *Old Jules* (1962) and *The Buffalo Hunters: The Story of the Hide Men* (1978); Fred A. Shannon, *The Farmer's Last Frontier, 1860–1897* (1945); J. M. Skaggs, *The Cattle Trailing Industry* (1973); George R. Taylor and Irene Neu, *The American Railroad Network, 1861–1890* (1956); James Ward, *Railroads and the Character of America, 1820–1887* (1986); Walter Prescott Webb, *The Great Plains* (1931); Donald Worster, *Rivers of Empire* (1985); Mark Wyman, *Hard Rock Epic: Western Miners and the Industrial Revolution, 1860–1910* (1979).

## CHAPTER 21: THE POLITICAL SYSTEM UNDER STRAIN

### General Studies

James Bryce, *The American Commonwealth*, 2 vols. (1888); Sean Cashman, *America and the Gilded Age: From the Death of Lincoln to the Rise of Theodore Roosevelt* (1984); John Dobson, *Politics in the Gilded Age* (1978); Harold Faulkner, *Politics, Reform, and Expansion, 1890–1900* (1959); John Garraty, *The New Commonwealth, 1877–1890* (1968); Richard Hofstadter, *The Age of Reform: From Bryan to FDR* (1955); Nancy Eleanor Flexner, *Century of Struggle: The Women's Rights Movement in the United States* (1959); Morton Keller, *Affairs of State: Public Life in the Late 19th Century America* (1977); H. Wayne Morgan, *From Hayes to McKinley: National Party Politics, 1877–1896* (1969), and as ed., *The Gilded Age* (1970); Nell Irvin Painter, *Standing at Armageddon: The United States, 1877–1919* (1987); Stephen Skowronek, *Building a New American State: The Expansion of National Administrative Capacities* (1982); Robert Wiebe, *The Search for Order, 1877–1929* (1967).

### Ideology and Politics

Kenneth Davison, *The Presidency of Rutherford B. Hayes* (1972); Margaret Forster, *Significant Sisters: The Grass-roots of Active Feminism, 1839–1939* (1986); Lewis Gould, *The Presidency of William McKinley* (1981); David C. Hammack, *Power and Society: Greater New York at the Turn of the Century* (1982); S. P. Hirshon, *Farewell to the Bloody Shirt:*

*Northern Republicans and the Southern Negro, 1877–1893* (1962); Ari Hoogenboom, *Rutherford B. Hayes: Warrior and President* (1995); Richard Jensen, *The Winning of the Midwest: Social and Political Conflict, 1888–1896* (1971); David Jordan, *Roscoe Conkling of New York* (1971); Paul Kelppner, *The Cross of Culture: A Social Analysis of Midwestern Politics, 1850–1900* (1970) and *The Third Electoral System, 1853–1892: Voters, Parties, and Political Cultures* (1979); Robert Marcus, *Grand Old Party: Political Structure in the Gilded Age* (1971); Robert McCloskey, *American Conservatism in the Age of Enterprise* (1951); Michael McGerr, *The Decline of Politics: The American North, 1865–1928* (1988); Allan Nevins, *Grover Cleveland: A Study in Courage* (New York, 1932); Arnold Paul, *Conservative Crisis and the Rule of Law: Attitudes of Bar and Bench, 1887–1895* (1969); Allan Peskin, *Garfield* (1978); Thomas Reeves, *Gentlemen Boss: The Life of Chester Alan Arthur* (1975); Martin Ridge, *Ignatius Donnelly* (1962); David Rothman, *Politics and Power: The United States Senate, 1869–1901* (1966); Martin J. Sklar, *The Corporate Reconstruction of American Capitalism, 1890–1916* (1988); Homer E. Socolofsky and Allan B. Spetter, *The Presidency of Benjamin Harrison* (1987); Richard Welch, *The Presidencies of Grover Cleveland* (1988); R. Hal Williams, *Years of Decision: American Politics in the 1890s* (1978).

### Protest and Reform

Geoffrey Blodgett, *The Gentle Reformers* (1966); William Dick, *Labor and Socialism in America* (1972); John Diggins, *The American Left in the Twentieth Century* (1973); Louis Harlan, *Booker T. Washington: The Making of a Black Leader, 1856–1901* (1972) and *Booker T. Washington: The Wizard of Tuskegee* (1983); Ari Hoogenboom, *Outlawing the Spoils: A History of the Civil Service Movement, 1865–1883* (1961); John Laslett, *Labor and the Left* (1970); Charles Lofgren, *The Plessy Case: A Legal-Historical Interpretation* (1987); Walter Nugent, *Money and American Society* (1968); Theda Skocpol, *Protecting Soldiers and Mothers: The Political Origins of Social Policy in the United States* (1992); John Sproat, *The Best Men: Liberal Reformers in the Gilded Age* (1968); Irwin Unger, *The Greenback Era: A Social and Political History of American Finance, 1865–1879* (1964); C. Vann Woodward, *The Strange Career of Jim Crow*, 3d rev. ed. (1974).

### Populism

Peter Argersinger, *Populism and Politics: William Alfred Peffer and the People's Party* (1974); Gene Clanton, *Populism: The Humane Preferences, 1890–1900* (1991); Gerald H. Gaither, *Blacks and the Populist Revolt* (1977); Lawrence Goodwyn, *Democratic Promise: The Populist Movement in America* (1976) and *The Populist Moment: A Brief History of the Agrarian Revolt* (1978); Steven Hahn, *The Roots of Southern Populism: Yeoman Farmers and the Transformation of the Georgia Upcountry*

(1983); Sheldon Hackney, *Populism to Progressivism in Alabama* (1969); John Hicks, *The Populist Revolt* (1931); Robert W. Larson, *Populism in the Mountain West* (1986); Robert C. McMath, Jr., *Populist Vanguard: A History of the Southern Farmers' Alliance* (1975) and *American Populism: A Social History, 1877–1898* (1993); Scott G. McNall, *The Road to Rebellion: Class Formation and Kansas Populism, 1865–1900* (1988); Theodore R. Mitchell, *Political Education in the Southern Farmers' Alliance, 1887–1900* (1987); Bruce Palmer, *Man over Money* (1980); Norman Pollack, *The Populist Response to Industrial America* (1962) and *The Just Polity: Populism, Law, and Human Welfare* (1987); Theodore Saloutos, *Farmer Movements in the South, 1865–1933* (1960); Barton Shaw, *The Wool-Hat Boys: Georgia's Populist Party* (1984); John L. Shover, *First Majority–Last Minority: The Transforming of Rural Life in America* (1976); Lala Carr Steelman, *The North Carolina Farmers' Alliance* (1985); C. Vann Woodward, *Tom Watson, Agrarian Rebel* (1938); Allan Weinstein, *Prelude to Populism: Origins of the Silver Issue* (1970).

**The Depression of 1893 and the Election of 1896**
Paolo Coletta, *William Jennings Bryan*, 3 vols. (1964–1969); Robert F. Durden, *The Climax of Populism: The Election of 1896* (1965); Ray Ginger, *Altgeld's America* (1958); Paul W. Glad, *McKinley, Bryan, and the People* (1964) and *The Trumpet Soundeth* (1960); Charles Hoffman, *The Depression of the Nineties: An Economic History* (1970); J. Rogers Hollingsworth, *The Whirligig of Politics: The Democracy of Cleveland and Bryan* (1963); Stanley Jones, *The Presidential Election of 1896* (1964); Louis Koenig, *Bryan* (1971); Samuel McSeveney, *The Politics of Depression* (1972); Carlos A. Schwantes, *Coxey's Army: An American Odyssey* (1985).

**The New American Empire**
Richard Bannister, *Social Darwinism* (1979); Robert Beisner, *From the Old Diplomacy to the New, 1865–1900* (1975); Charles Campbell, *The Transformation of American Foreign Relations, 1865–1900* (1976) and *From Revolution to Rapprochement: The United States and Great Britain, 1783–1903* (1974); Richard Challener, *Admirals, Generals and American Foreign Policy, 1889–1914* (1973); John Dobson, *America's Ascent: The United States Becomes a Great Power, 1880–1914* (1978); John Lewis Gaddis, *Russia, the Soviet Union, and the United States*, 2d ed. (1990); John A. S. Grenville and George Young, *Politics, Strategy, and American Diplomacy* (1967); Richard Hofstadter, *Social Darwinism in American Thought*, rev. ed. (1959); Michael Hunt, *Ideology and American Foreign Policy* (1984); Ronald Jensen, *The Alaska Purchase and Russian-American Relations* (1970); Walter LaFeber, *The New Empire: An Interpretation of American Expansion, 1860–1898* (1963) and *The*

*American Age* (1989); David Pletcher, *The Awkward Years* (1962); Emily Rosenberg, *Spreading the American Dream* (1982); Tom Terrill, *The Tariff, Politics, and American Foreign Policy, 1874–1901* (1973); Mira Wilkins, *The Emergence of the Multinational Enterprise* (1970); William A. Williams, *The Tragedy of American Diplomacy*, rev. ed. (1962) and *Empire as a Way of Life: An Essay on the Causes and Character of America's Present Predicament* (1982).

**The Question of Imperialism**
David Anderson, *Imperialism and Idealism: American Diplomats in China, 1861–1898* (1986); William Becker, *The Dynamics of Business-Government Relations* (1982); Robert L. Beisner, *Twelve against Empire* (1968); Phillip Darby, *Three Faces of Imperialism: British and American Approaches to Asia and Africa, 1870–1970* (1987); Philip S. Foner, *The Spanish-Cuban-American War and the Birth of American Imperialism*, 2 vols. (1972); Frank Friedel, *The Splendid Little War* (1958); Willard Gatewood, Jr., *Black Americans and the White Man's Burden, 1898–1903* (1975); Kenneth Hagan, *American Gunboat Diplomacy, 1877–1889* (1973); David Healy, *U.S. Expansionism* (1970); Michael Hunt, *Ideology and U.S. Foreign Policy* (1987); Frederick Merk, *Manifest Destiny and Mission in American History* (1963); Wolfgang Mommsen and Jurgen Osterhammel, eds., *Imperialism and After* (1986); H. Wayne Morgan, *America's Road to Empire: The War with Spain and Overseas Expansion* (1965); Thomas J. Osborne, *Empire Can Wait: American Opposition to Hawaiian Annexation, 1893–1898* (1981); Ernest Paolino, *The Foundations of American Empire* (1973); Thomas Paterson, ed., *Imperialism and Anti-Imperialism* (1973); Bradford Perkins, *The Great Rapprochement* (1968); Julius Pratt, *The Expansionists of 1898* (1936); Tony Smith, *The Pattern of Imperialism: The United States, Great Britain and the Late Industrializing World since 1815* (1982); Richard Turk, *The Ambiguous Relationship: Theodore Roosevelt and Alfred Thayer Mahan* (1987).

**The United States and Asia**
David Anderson, *Imperialism and Idealism: American Diplomacy in China, 1861–1898* (1985); Jongsuk Chay, *Diplomacy of Asymmetry: Korean-American Relations to 1910* (1990); Warren Cohen, *America's Response to China*, rev. ed. (1980); Michael Hunt, *The Making of a Special Relationship: The United States and China to 1914* (1983); Jane Hunter, *The Gospel of Gentility: American Women Missionaries in Turn-of-the-Century China* (1984); Akira Iriye, *Across the Pacific* (1967) and *Pacific Estrangement: Japanese and American Expansion, 1897–1911* (1972); Stanley Karnow, *In Our Image* (1989); Yur-Bok Lee and Wayne Patterson, eds., *One Hundred Years of Korean-American Relations, 1882–1982* (1986); Brian M. Linn, *The U.S. Army and Counterinsurgency in the Philippine War, 1899–*

1902 (1989); Ernest May and John Fairbanks, eds., *America's China Trade in Historical Perspective* (1986); Glenn May, *Social Engineering in the Philippines* (1980); Thomas McCormick, *China Market: America's Quest for Informal Empire, 1893–1901* (1968); Charles Neu, *The Troubled Encounter* (1975); Gary Okihiro, *Cane Fires: The Anti-Japanese Movement in Hawaii, 1865–1945* (1991); Peter Stanley, *A Nation in the Making: The Philippines and the United States* (1974); Randall Stross, *The Hard Earth: American Agriculturalists on Chinese Soil, 1898–1937* (1986); James Thomson, Peter Stanley, and John Perry, *Sentimental Imperialists: The American Experience in East Asia* (1981); Robert Welch, Jr., *Response to Imperialism: The United States and the Philippine-American War, 1899–1902* (1979); Marilyn B. Young, *Rhetoric of Empire: American China Policy, 1895–1901* (1968).

**The United States and the Americas**
Robert Brown, *Canada's National Policy, 1883–1900* (1964); Kenneth Bourne, *Britain and the Balance of Power in North America, 1815–1908* (1967); Walter LaFeber, *Inevitable Revolutions: The United States in Central America*, rev. ed. (1993); Lester Langley, *The Banana Wars* (1983) and *The United States and the Caribbean, 1900–1970* (1980); Louis Perez, Jr., *Cuba under the Platt Amendment, 1902–1934* (1986) and *Cuba between Empires, 1878–1902* (1983); Dexter Perkins, *The Monroe Doctrine, 1867–1907* (1937); Ramon Ruiz, *Cuba* (1968); Karl Schmitt, *Mexico and the United States, 1821–1973* (1974); Josefina Vazquez and Lorenzo Meyer, *The United States and Mexico* (1985).

# CHAPTER 22: THE PROGRESSIVE ERA

**General Studies**
John Chambers II, *The Tyranny of Change: America in the Progressive Era, 1900–1917* (1980); John M. Cooper, Jr., *The Pivotal Decades: The United States, 1900–1920* (1990); Alan Dawley, *Struggles for Justice: Social Responsibility and the Liberal State* (1991); Arthur Ekrich, *Progressivism in America* (1974); Peter Filene, "An Obituary for 'the Progressive Movement,'" *American Quarterly* 22 (1970); Lewis Gould, ed., *The Progressive Era* (1974); Richard Hofstadter, *The Age of Reform: From Bryan to FDR* (1955); James T. Kloppenberg, *Uncertain Victory: Social Democracy and Progressivism in European and American Thought, 1870–1920* (1986); Gabriel Kolko, *The Triumph of Conservativism* (1963); Arthur Link and Richard L. McCormick, *Progressivism* (1985); William O'Neill, *The Progressive Years* (1975); Dan Rogers, "In Search of Progressivism," *Reviews in American History* 10 (1982); James Weinstein, *The Corporate Ideal in the Liberal States, 1900–1918* (1969); Robert Wiebe, *Businessmen and Reform: A Study of the Progressive Movement* (1962).

**The Progressive Impulse**
Daniel Aaron, *Men of Good Hope: A Story of American Progressives* (1951); Richard Abrams, *The Burdens of Progress* (1978); Walter M. Brasch, *Forerunners of Revolution: Muckrakers and the American Social Conscience* (1990); Robert H. Bremner, *From the Depths: The Discovery of Poverty in the United States* (1956); Mina Julia Carson, *Settlement Folk: Social Thought and the American Settlement Movement, 1885–1930* (1990); David Chalmers, *The Social and Political Ideas of the Muckrakers* (1964); Clarke Chambers, *Paul U. Kellog and the Survey* (1971); Robert Crunden, *Ministers of Reform: The Progressives' Achievements in American Civilization, 1889–1920* (1982); Charles Forcey, *The Crossroads of Liberalism: Croly, Weyl, Lippmann and the Progressive Era, 1900–1925* (1961); William Hutchinson, *The Modernist Impulse in American Protestantism* (1976); Rivka Shpak Lissak, *Pluralism and Progressives: Hull House and the New Immigrants, 1890–1919* (1989); Roy Lubove, *The Professional Altruist: The Emergence of Social Work as a Career, 1880–1930* (1965); D. W. Marcell, *Progress and Pragmatism: James, Dewey, Beard and the American Idea of Progress* (1974); Daniel Nelson, *Frederick W. Taylor and the Rise of Scientific Management* (1980); David Nobel, *The Progressive Mind, 1890–1917* rev. ed. (1981); Martin Schiesl, *The Politics of Efficiency: Municipal Administration and Reform in America, 1880–1920* (1977); Robert B. Westbrook, *John Dewey and American Democracy* (1991); Morton White, *Social Thought in America: The Revolt against Formalism*, (1949); Harold Wilson, *McClure's Magazine and the Muckrakers* (1970).

**Social Reform, Radical Politics, and Minority Rights**
Mari Jo Buhle, *Women and American Socialism, 1870–1920* (1981); Allen F. Davis, *American Heroine: The Life and Legend of Jane Addams* (1973); James R. Green, *Grass-Roots Socialism: Radical Movements in the Southwest, 1895–1943* (1978); Louis Harlan, *Separate and Unequal: Public School Campaigns and Racism in the Southern Seaboard States, 1900–1915* (1968); Charles F. Kellogg, *NAACP: A History of the National Association for the Advancement of Colored People, 1909–1920* (1967); David L. Lewis, *W. E. B. Dubois: Biography of a Race* (1994); Roy Lubove, *The Progressives and the Slums: Tenement House Reform in New York City* (1962); James McPherson, *The Abolitionist Legacy: From Reconstruction to the NAACP* (1975); David Musto, *The American Disease: Origins of Narcotics Control* (1973); Elliot M. Rudwick, *W. E. B. DuBois* (1968); Nick Salvatore, *Eugene V. Debs: Citizen and Socialist* (1982); James Timberlake, *Prohibition and the Progressive Campaign* (1963); John D. Weaver, *The Brownsville Raid* (1970); James Weinstein, *The Decline of Socialism in America, 1912–1925* (1967); Nancy Weiss, *The National Urban League, 1910–1940* (1974).

## Women's Rights, Gender, and Sexuality

Paula Baker, *Gender and the Transformation of Politics: Public and Private Life in New York, 1870–1930* (1989); George Chester, *Gay New York: Gender, Urban Culture, and the Making of the Gay Male World, 1890–1940* (1994); Ellen Chesler, *Woman of Valor: Margaret Sanger and the Birth Control Movement in America* (1992); Nancy F. Cott, *The Grounding of Modern Feminism* (1987); Nancy Dye, *As Equals and Sisters: Feminism, the Labor Move-ment, and the Women's Trade Union League of New York* (1980); Linda Gordon, *Woman's Body, Woman's Right: A Social History of Birth Control* (1976), *Heroes of Their Own Lives: The Politics and History of Family Violence, 1880–1960* (1988), and *Pitied but Not Entitled: Single Mothers and the History of Welfare* (1994); David Kennedy, *Birth Control in America: The Career of Margaret Sanger* (1970); Aileen Kraditor, *Ideas of the Woman Suffrage Movement* (1965); Ellen Lagemann, *A Generation of Women: Education in the Lives of Progres-sive Reformers* (1979); Christine Lunardini, *From Equal Suffrage to Equal Rights: Alice Paul and the National Women's Party* (1986); David Morgan, *Suffragists and Democrats: The Politics of Woman Suffrage in America* (1972); Robyn Muncy, *Creating a Female Dominion in American Reform, 1890–1935* (1991); William O'Neil, *Divorce in the Progressive Era* (1967); Dorothy Richardson, *The Long Day: The Story of a New York Working Girl* (1905); Ruth Rosen, *The Lost Sisterhood: Prostitutes in America, 1900–1918* (1982); Rosalind Rosenberg, *Beyond Separate Spheres: Intellectual Roots of Modern Feminism* (1982); Anne Firor Scott, *Natural Allies: Women's Associations in American History* (1992); Anne Firor Scott and Andrew MacKay Scott, *One Half the People: The Fight for Woman Suffrage* (1982); Meredith Tax, *The Rising of the Women: Feminist Solidarity and Class Conflict, 1880–1917* (1980).

## Education, the New Professionalism, and Entertainment

Burton Bledstein, *The Culture of Professionalism* (1976); Darlene Clark Hine, *Black Women in White: Racial Conflict and Cooperation in the Nursing Profession, 1890–1950* (1989); Lawrence Cremin, *The Transformation of the School: Progressivism in American Education* (1961); John DiMeglio, *Vaudeville U.S.A.* (1973); Lewis Erenberg, *Steppin' Out: New York Nightlife and the Transformation of American Culture, 1890–1930* (1981); James Farrell, *Inventing the American Way of Death, 1830–1920* (1980); Thomas Haskell, *The Emergence of Professional Social Science* (1977); Bruce Kuklick, *The Rise of American Philosophy* (1977); Martin Laforse and James Drake, *Popular Culture and American Life: Selected Topics in the Study of American Popular Culture* (1981); Cathy Peiss, *Cheap Amusements: Working Women and Leisure in Turn-of-the-Century New York* (1986); Robert Sklar, *Movie-Made America: A Social History of the American Movies* (1975); Paul Starr, *The Social Transformation of American Medicine* (1982); David Tyack and Elizabeth Hansot, *Managers of Virtue: Public School Leadership in America, 1820–1980* (1982); Lawrence Vesey, *The Emergence of the American University* (1970).

## Local and State Reform

Richard Abrams, *Conservatism in a Progressive Era: Massachusetts Politics, 1900–1912* (1964); John D. Buenker, *Urban Liberalism and Progressive Reform* (1973); Thomas E. Cronin, *Direct Democracy: The Politics of Initiative, Referendum and Recall* (1989); James Crooks, *Politics and Progress: The Rise of Urban Progressivism in Baltimore, 1895–1911* (1968); Dewey Grantham, *Southern Progressivism: The Reconciliation of Progress and Tradition* (1983); Melvin Holli, *Reform in Detroit: Hazen S. Pingree and Urban Politics* (1969); J. Joseph Huthmacher, "Urban Liberalism and Progressive Reform," *Mississippi Valley Historical Review* (1962); Jack Kirby, *Darkness at Dawning: Race and Reform in the Progressive South* (1972); Richard L. McCormick, *From Realignment to Reform: Political Change in New York State, 1893–1910* (1981); George Mowry, *The California Progressives* (1951); Bradley Rice, *Progressive Cities: The Commission Government Movement in America, 1901–1920* (1977); Jack Tager, *The Intellectual as Urban Reformer: Brand Whitlock and The Progressive Movement* (1968); David P. Thelen, *The New Citizenship: Origins of Progressivism in Wisconsin* (1972).

## National Politics and Public Policy

Donald Anderson, *William Howard Taft* (1973); John M. Blum, *The Republican Roosevelt* (1954) and *Woodrow Wilson and the Politics of Morality* (1954); John Milton Cooper, Jr., *The Warrior and the Priest: Woodrow Wilson and Theodore Roosevelt* (1983); Stephen R. Fox, *The American Conservation Movement: John Muir and His Legacy* (1981); John Gable, *The Bull Moose Years* (1978); Alexander George and Juliette George, *Woodrow Wilson and Colonel House: A Personality Study* (1956); Lewis Gould, *Reform and Regulation: American Politics, 1900–1916* (1978) and *The Presidency of Theodore Roosevelt* (1991); Samuel P. Hays, *Conservation and the Gospel of Efficiency: The Progressive Conservation Movement, 1890–1920* (1959); James Holt, *Congressional Insurgents and the Party System* (1969); Arthur Link, *Woodrow Wilson*, 5 vols. (1947–1965); Albro Martin, *Enterprise Denied: Origins of the Decline of American Railroads, 1897–1917*; David McCullough, *Mornings on Horseback* (1981); Robert T. McCulley, *Banks and Politics during the Progressive Era: The Origins of the Federal Reserve System* (1992); Michael McGerr, *The Decline of Popular Politics: The American North, 1865–1928* (1986); Edmund Morris, *The Rise of Theodore Roosevelt* (1979); George Mowry, *The Era of Theodore Roosevelt* (1958); James Penick, *Progressive Politics and Conservation: The Ballinger-Pinchot Affair* (1968); Harold Pinkett, *Gifford Pinchot: Private and Public Forester* (1970); Edwin Weinstein, *Woodrow Wilson* and Colonel House: A Personality Study (1956); Craig West, Banking Reform and the Federal Reserve, 1863–1923 (1977); Clifton Yearley, The Money Machines (1970).

## CHAPTER 23: THE UNITED STATES AND THE OLD WORLD ORDER

### General Studies
Paul Abrahams, The Foreign Expansion of American Finance and Its Relationship to Foreign Economic Policies of the United States, 1907–1921 (1976); Robert Beisner, From the Old Diplomacy to the New, 1865–1900 (1975); John Dobson, America's Ascent: The United States Becomes a Great Power, 1880–1914 (1978); Morrell Heald and Lawrence Kaplan, Culture and Diplomacy (1977); Peter Karsten, The Naval Aristocracy (1972); Robert Osgood, Ideals and Self-Interest in America's Foreign Relations (1953); Emily Rosenberg, Spreading the American Dream: American Economic and Cultural Expansion, 1890–1945 (1982); Robert Schulzinger, American Diplomacy in the Twentieth Century (1984); Tom Terrill, The Tariff, Politics, and American Foreign Policy, 1874–1901 (1973); Rubin Weston, Racism and U.S. Imperialism, 1865–1946 (1971); Mira Wilkins, The Emergence of the Multinational Enterprise (1970).

### Roosevelt, Taft, and Wilson
Howard K. Beale, Theodore Roosevelt and the Rise of America to World Power (1956); David Burton, Theodore Roosevelt: Confident Imperialist (1968); Robert W. Cherney, A Righteous Cause: The Life of William Jennings Bryan (1985); Richard H. Collin, Theodore Roosevelt, Culture, Diplomacy, and Expansion (1985); John Cooper, Jr., Walter Hines Page (1977); Lloyd Gardner, Wilson and Revolutions, 1913–1921 (1976) and William Jennings Bryan: Missionary Isolationist (1983); Arthur Link, Wilson: The Diplomatist (1957) and Woodrow Wilson: Revolution, War, and Peace (1968); Frederick Marks III, Velvet on Iron: The Diplomacy of Theodore Roosevelt (1979); Ralph E. Minger, William Howard Taft and United States Foreign Policy (1975).

### Asia, the Pacific, and Latin America
Warren Cohen, America's Response to China, rev. ed. (1980); David Healy, Gunboat Diplomacy in the Wilson Era: The U.S. Navy in Haiti, 1915–1916 (1976) and Drive to Hegemony: The United States in the Caribbean, 1898–1917 (1988); Akira Iriye, Pacific Estrangement: Japanese and American Expansion, 1897–1911 (1972); Jerry Israel, Progressivism and the Open Door: America and China, 1905–1921 (1971); Lester Langley, Struggle for the American Mediterranean (1980) and The United States and the Caribbean, 1900–1970 (1980); Glenn May, Social Engineering in the Philippines (1980); Robert McClellan, The Heathen Chinese: A Study

of American Attitudes toward China (1971); David McCullough, The Path between the Seas: The Creation of the Panama Canal, 1870–1914 (1977); Dana Munro, Intervention and Dollar Diplomacy in the Caribbean, 1900–1920 (1964); Charles Neu, The Troubled Encounter (1975); Robert Smith, The United States and Revolutionary Nationalism in Mexico, 1916–1932 (1972); Peter Stanley, A Nation in the Making: The Philippines and the United States, 1899–1921 (1974).

### From Neutrality to War
Thomas Baily and Paul Ryan, The Lusitania Disaster (1975); John Coogan, The End of Neutrality: The United States, Britain, and Maritime Rights, 1899–1915 (1981); John Cooper, The Vanity of Power: American Isolationism and the First World War (1969); Patrick Devlin, Too Proud to Fight: Woodrow Wilson's Neutrality (1974); Ross Gregory, The Origins of American Intervention in the First World War (1977); Burton Kaufman, Efficiency and Expansion: Foreign Trade Organization in the Wilson Administration (1974); Roland Marchand, The American Peace Movement and Social Reform, 1898–1918 (1972); Ernest R. May, The World War and American Isolation, 1914–1917 (1957); Jeffrey Safford, Wilsonian Maritime Diplomacy (1977).

### The First World War Abroad
Arthur Barbeau and Henri Florette, The Unknown Soldiers: Black American Troops in World War I (1974); J. Gary Clifford, The Citizen Soldiers (1972); Edward Coffman, The War to End All Wars: The American Military Experience in World War I (1968); Frank Freidel, Over There: The Story of America's First Great Overseas Crusade (1964); Paul Fussell, The Great War and Modern Memory (1975); John Gifford, The Citizen Soldiers (1972); Otis Graham, The Great Campaigns (1971); Maurine Greenwald, Women, War, and Work (1980); James Joll, The Origins of the First World War (1984); N. Gordon Levin, Jr., Woodrow Wilson and World Politics: America's Response to War and Revolution (1968); Laurence Stallings, The Doughboys: The Story of the AEF, 1917–1918 (1963); David F. Trask, The AEF and Coalition Warmaking, 1917–1918 (1973); Frank Vandiver, Black Jack: The Life and Times of John J. Pershing, 2 vols. (1977); Russell Weigley, The American Way of War (1973).

### The Home Front
Daniel R. Beaver, Newton D. Baker and the American War Effort, 1917–1919 (1966); John W. Chambers, To Raise an Army: The Draft Comes to Modern America (1987); Valerie Jean Connor, The National War Labor Board: Stability, Social Justice, and the Voluntary State in World War I (1983); Robert Cuff, The War Industries Board: Business-Government Relations during World War I (1973); Maurine W. Greenwald, Women, War, and Work (1980); Keith Grieves, The Politics of Manpower, 1914–1918 (1988); Frank L. Grubb, Samuel

Gompers and the Great War (1982); Carol Gruber, Mars and Minerva: World War I and the Uses of Higher Learning in America (1975); Ellis Hawley, The Great War and the Search for Modern Order (1979); Robert Haynes, A Night of Violence: The Houston Riot of 1917 (1976); David M. Kennedy, Over Here: The First World War and American Society (1980); Seward Livermore, Politics Is Adjourned: Woodrow Wilson and the War Congress, 1917–1918 (1966); Frederick Luebke, Bonds of Loyalty: German Americans and World War I (1974); Paul Murphy, World War I and the Origins of Civil Liberties (1979); Richard Polenberg, Fighting Faiths: The Abrams Case, the Supreme Court, and Free Speech (1987); Walton Rawls, Wake Up America! World War I and the American Poster (1987); Ronald Schaffer, America in the Great War: The Rise of the War Welfare State (1991); Jordan Schwarz, The Speculator: Bernard M. Baruch in Washington, 1917–1965 (1981); Dale N. Shook, William G. McAdoo and the Development of National Economic Policy, 1913–1918 (1987); Barbara Steinson, American Women's Activism in World War I (1982); John A. Thompson, Reformers and War: Progressive Publicists and the First World War (1987); Joe William Trotter, Jr., ed., The Great Migration in Historical Perspective (1991); Stephen Vaughn, Holding Fast the Inner Lines: Democracy, Nationalism, and the Committee on Public Information (1979); James Weinstein, The Decline of Socialism in America, 1912–1923 (1967); Neil A. Wynn, From Progressivism to Prosperity: World War I and American Society (1986).

**Versailles**
Thomas Bailey, Woodrow Wilson and the Great Betrayal (1945) and Woodrow Wilson and the Lost Peace (1944); Robert Ferrell, Woodrow Wilson and World War I (1985); Inga Floto, Colonel House at Paris (1980); John Gaddis, Russia, the Soviet Union, and the United States (1978); Lloyd Gardner, Safe for Democracy: The Anglo-American Response to Revolution, 1913–1923 (1984); Thomas J. Knock, To End All Wars: Woodrow Wilson and the Quest for a New World Order (1992); Arno Mayer, Politics and Diplomacy of Peacemaking: Containment and Counterrevolution at Versailles (1965); Charles Mee, Jr., The End of Order, Versailles, 1919 (1980); Ralph Stone, The Irreconcilables: The Fight against the League of Nations (1970); William C. Widenor, Henry Cabot Lodge and the Search for an American Foreign Policy (1980).

**Aftermath**
David Brody, Labor in Crisis: The Steel Strike of 1919 (1965); Stanley Coben, A. Mitchell Palmer: Politician (1963); Stanley Cooperman, World War I and the American Mind (1970); Roberta Feuerlicht, Justice Crucified (1977); Dana Frank, Purchasing Power: Consumer Organizing, Gender, and the Seattle Labor Movement, 1919–1929 (1994); Robert Murray, The Red Scare (1955); Burl Noggle, Into the Twenties (1977); Stuart Rochester,

American Liberal Disillusionment in the Wake of World War I (1977); Francis Russell, A City in Terror (1975); William Tuttle, Jr., Race Riot: Chicago in the Red Summer of 1919 (1970); Stephen Ward, ed., The War Generation: Veterans of the First World War (1975).

## CHAPTER 24: THE NEW ERA

**General Studies**
Frederick Lewis Allen, Only Yesterday: An Informal History of the 1920s (1931); John Braeman et al., eds., Change and Continuity in Twentieth Century America: The 1920s (1968); Ann Douglas, Terrible Honesty: Mongrel Manhattan in the 1920s (1995); Lynn Dumenil, Modern Temper: American Culture and Society in the 1920s (1995); Ellis Hawley, The Great War and the Search for a Modern Order (1979); John Hicks, The Republican Ascendancy, 1921–1933 (1960); Isabel Leighton, ed., The Aspirin Age (1949); William Leuchtenburg, The Perils of Prosperity, 1914–1932 (1958); Donald McCoy, Coming of Age (1973); Geoffrey Perrett, America in the Twenties (1982); Arthur Schlesinger, Jr., The Crisis of the Old Order (1957); David Shannon, Between the Wars: America, 1919–1940 (1979).

**Economics, Business, and Labor**
Irving Bernstein, The Lean Years: A History of the American Worker, 1920–1933 (1960); David Brody, Steelworkers in America (1960) and Workers in Industrial America (1980); Lizabeth Cohen, Making a New Deal: Industrial Workers in Chicago, 1919–1939 (1990); Alfred D. Chandler, Jr., Strategy and Structure: Chapters in the History of American Industrial Enterprise (1962); Ed Cray, Chrome Colossus: General Motors and Its Times (1980); Gilbert Fite, George Peek and the Fight for Farm Parity (1954); James Flink, The Car Culture (1975); Louis Galambos, Competition and Cooperation (1966); James Gilbert, Designing the Industrial State (1972); Allan Nevins and Frank Hill, Ford, 3 vols. (1954–1963); Jim Potter, The American Economy between the Wars (1974); John Rae, American Automobile (1965) and The Road and the Car in American Life (1971); George Soule, Prosperity Decade (1947); Keith Sward, The Legend of Henry Ford (1948); Leslie Woodcock Tentler, Wage Earning Women: Industrial Work and Family Life in the United States, 1900–1930 (1979); Bernard Weisberger, The Dress Maker (1979); Robert Zieger, Republicans and Labor, 1919–1929 (1969) and American Workers, American Unions, 1920–1980 (1986).

**Mass Society and Mass Culture**
Erick Barnouw, A Tower of Babel: A History of American Broadcasting in the United States to 1933 (1966); Daniel Boorstin, The Americans: The Democratic Experience (1973); Paul Carter, Another Part of the Twenties (1977); Robert Creamer, Babe (1974); Kenneth Davis, The Hero: Charles A.

*Lindbergh* (1954); Stuart Ewen, *Captains of Consciousness: Advertising and the Social Roots of the Consumer Culture* (1976); Richard Wrightman Rox and T. J. Jackson Lears, eds., *The Culture of Consumption: Critical Essays in American History, 1880–1980* (1983); Jackson Lears, *Fables of Abundance: A Cultural History of Advertising in America* (1994); Robert Lynd and Helen Lynd, *Middletown: A Study in Modern Culture* (1929); Roland Marchand, *Advertising the American Dream: Making Way for Modernity, 1920–1940* (1985); Lary May, *Screening Out the Past* (1980); Leonard Mosley, *Lindbergh: A Biography* (1976); Otis Pease, *The Responsibilities of American Advertising* (1959); Daniel Pope, *The Making of Modern Advertising* (1983); Randy Roberts, *Jack Dempsey, The Manassa Mauler* (1979); Philip Rosen, *The Modern Stentors: Radio Broadcasting and the Federal Government, 1920–1933* (1980); Robert Sklar, *Movie-Made America: A Cultural History of American Movies* (1975); Kevin Starr, *Material Dreams: Southern California through the 1920s* (1990); Susan Strasser, *Satisfaction Guaranteed: The Making of the American Mass Market* (1990).

## High Culture
Carlos Baker, *Hemingway* (1956); Malcolm Cowley, *Exile's Return* (1934); Robert Crunden, *From Self to Society: Transition in Modern Thought, 1919–1941* (1972); Frederick Hoffman, *The Twenties* (1949); Arthur Mizner, *The Far Side of Paradise* (1951); Roderick Nash, *The Nervous Generation: American Thought, 1917–1930* (1969); Mark Shorer, *Sinclair Lewis* (1961); Marvin Singleton, *H. L. Mencken and the "American Mercury" Adventure* (1962).

## Women, Youth, and Minorities
Lois Banner, *American Beauty* (1983); Susan D. Becker, *The Origins of the Equal Rights Amendment* (1981); Kathlenn M. Blee, *Women of the Klan: Racism and Gender in the 1920s* (1991); Dorothy M. Brown, *Setting a Course: American Women in the 1920s* (1987); William Chafe, *The American Women: Her Changing Social, Economic, and Political Roles, 1920–1970* (1972); Nancy Cott, *The Grounding of Modern Feminism* (1987); David Cronon, *Black Moses: The Story of Marcus Garvey* (1955); Melvin Patrick Ely, *The Adventures of Amos 'n' Andy: A Social History of an American Phenomenon* (1991); Paula Fass, *The Damned and Beautiful: American Youth in the 1920s* (1977); Linda Gordon, *Woman's Body, Woman's Right: A Social History of Birth Control in America* (1976); Peter Gottlieb, *Making Their Own Way: Southern Blacks' Migration to Pittsburgh, 1916–1930* (1987); Florette Henri, *Black Migration: Movement North, 1900–1920* (1975); Nathan Huggins, *Harlem Renaissance* (1971); Jacqueline Jones, *Labor of Love, Labor of Sorrow: Black Women, Work, and Family, from Slavery to the Present* (1985); J. Stanley Lemons, *The Woman Citizen: Social Feminism in the 1920s* (1973); David Levering

Lewis, *When Harlem Was in Vogue* (1981); Glenna Matthews, *"Just a Housewife!" The Rise and Fall of Domesticity in America* (1987); Cary D. Mintz, *Black Culture and the Harlem Renaissance* (1988); Wilson Moses, *The Golden Age of Black Nationalism, 1850–1925* (1988); Kathy H. Ogren, *The Jazz Revolution: Twenties America and the Meaning of Jazz* (1989); Arnold Rampersed, *The Life of Langston Hughes*, 2 vols. (1986–1988); Ricardo Romo, *East Los Angeles: History of a Barrio* (1983); George J. Sanchez, *Becoming Mexican American: Ethnicity, Culture and Identity in Chicano Los Angeles, 1900–1945* (1993); Lois Scharf, *To Work and to Wed* (1980); Virginia Scharff, *Taking the Wheel: Women and the Coming of the Motor Age* (1991); Alan Spear, *Black Chicago* (1967); Judith Stein, *The World of Marcus Garvey: Race and Class in Modern Society* (1986); Joe William Trotter, Jr., *Black Milwaukee: The Making of an Industrial Proletariat* (1985); Theodore Vincent, *Black Power and the Garvey Movement* (1971); Winifred Wandersee, *Women's Work and Family Values, 1920–1940* (1981).

## Political Fundamentalism
Paul Avrich, *Sacco-Vanzetti: The Anarchist Background* (1991); David Burner, *The Politics of Provincialism* (1968); David Chalmers, *Hooded Americanism: The History of the Ku Klux Klan* (1965); Norman Clark, *Deliver Us from Evil* (1976); Robert Divine, *American Immigration Policy* (1957); Norman Furniss, *The Fundamentalist Controversy, 1918–1933* (1954); Ray Ginger, *Six Days or Forever? Tennessee v. John Scopes* (1958); Joseph Gusfeld, *Symbolic Crusade* (1963); John Higham, *Strangers in the Land: Patterns of American Nativism, 1860–1925* (1955); Kenneth Jackson, *The Ku Klux Klan in the City, 1915–1930* (1967); Don Kirschner, *City and Country: Rural Responses to Urbanization in the 1920s* (1970); Shawn Lay, ed., *The Invisible Empire in the West: Toward a New Historical Appraisal of the Ku Klux Klan of the 1920s* (1992); Nancy MacLean, *Behind the Mask of Chivalry: The Making of the Second Ku Klux Klan* (1994); George Maraden, *Fundamentalism and American Culture* (1980); Leonard J. Moore, *Citizen Klansmen: The Ku Klux Klan in Indiana, 1921–1928* (1991); Andrew Sinclair, *Prohibition: The Era of Excess* (1962); William Wilson, *Coming of Age: Urban America, 1915–1945* (1974).

## Politics, Public Policy, and the Election of 1928
Kristi Andersen, *The Creation of a Democratic Majority* (1979); Paula Edler, *Governor Alfred E. Smith: The Politician as Reformer* (1983); James Giglio, *H. M. Daugherty and the Politics of Expediency* (1978); Oscar Handlin, *Al Smith and His America* (1958); Ellis Hawley, *Herbert Hoover as Secretary of Commerce: Studies in New Era Thought and Practice* (1974); Robert Himmelberg, *The Origins of the National Recovery Administration: Business, Government, and the Trade Association Issue, 1921–1933* (1976); J. Joseph Huthmacher,

*Massachusetts People and Politics, 1919–1933* (1959); Alan Lichtman, *Prejudice and the Old Politics* (1979); Richard Lowitt, *George Norris*, 2 vols. (1971); Donald McCoy, *Calvin Coolidge* (1967); Robert Murray, *The Harding Era* (1969) and *The Politics of Normalcy* (1973); Burl Noggle, *Teapot Dome* (1962); Elisabeth Perry, *Belle Moskowitz: Feminine Politics and the Exercise of Power in the Age of Alfred E. Smith* (1987); George Tindall, *The Emergence of the New South* (1967); Eugene Trani and David Wilson, *The Presidency of Warren G. Harding* (1977).

## CHAPTER 25: CRASH AND DEPRESSION

### General Studies
Frederick Lewis Allen, *Since Yesterday* (1939); John A. Garraty, *The Great Depression* (1987); Robert McElvaine, *The Great Depression: America, 1929–1941* (1984); Broadus Mitchell, *Depression Decade* (1947); Arthur Schlesinger, Jr., *The Crisis of the Old Order* (1957); T. H. Watkins, *The Great Depression: America in the 1930s* (1991).

### The Great Crash and the Origins of the Great Depression
Michael A. Bernstein, *The Great Depression: Delayed Recovery and Economic Change in America, 1929–1939* (1987); Lester Chandler, *America's Greatest Depression, 1929–1941* (1970); Milton Friedman and Ana Schwartz, *The Great Contraction, 1929–1933* (1965); John Kenneth Galbraith, *The Great Crash*, rev. ed. (1988); Susan Kennedy, *The Banking Crisis of 1933* (1973); Charles Kindleberger, *The World in Depression* (1973); Robert Sobel, *The Great Bull Market: Wall Street in the 1920s* (1968); Peter Temin, *Did Monetary Forces Cause the Great Depression?* (1976); Gordon Thomas and Max Morgan-Witts, *The Day the Bubble Burst: The Social History of the Wall Street Crash of 1929* (1979).

### Depression Life
Edward Anderson, *Hungry Men* (1935); Robert Angel, *The Family Encounters the Depression* (1936); Ann Banks, *First Person America* (1980); Caroline Bird, *The Invisible Scar* (1966); The Federal Writers' Project, *These Are Our Lives* (1939); John Garraty, *Unemployment in History: Economic Thought and Public Policy* (1978); Mirra Komarovsky, *The Unemployed Man and His Family* (1940); Robert Lynd and Helen Lynd, *Middletown in Transition* (1937); Robert McElvaine, ed. *Down & Out in the Great Depression* (1983); Harvey Levenstein, *Paradox of Plenty: A Social History of Eating in Modern America* (1993); H. Wayne Morgan, *Drugs in America: A Social History, 1800–1980* (1981); David Musto, *The American Disease, Origins of Narcotics Control*, rev. ed. (1988); Lois Scharf, *To Work and to Wed: Female Employment, Feminism, and the Great Depression* (1980); Tom Terrill and Jerrold Hirsch, eds., *Such as Us:*

*Southern Voices of the Thirties* (1978); Studs Terkel, *Hard Times: An Oral History of the Great Depression* (1970); Winifred Wandersee, *Women's Work and Family Values, 1920–1940* (1981); Susan Ware, *Holding Their Own: American Women in the 1930s* (1982); Jeane Westin, *Making Do: How Women Survived the '30s* (1976).'

### Ethnicity and Race
Rodolfo Acuna, *Occupied America*, rev. ed. (1981); Ralph Bunche, *The Political Status of the Negro in the Age of FDR* (1973); Dan Carter, *Scottsboro: A Tragedy of the American South* (1969); Sarah Deutsch, *No Separate Refuge: Culture, Class, and Gender on an Anglo-Hispanic Frontier in the American Southwest, 1880–1940* (1987); Abraham Hoffman, *Unwanted Mexican-Americans in the Great Depression* (1974); Richard Polenberg, *One Nation Divisible: Class, Race, and Ethnicity in the United States since 1938* (1980); Bernard Sternsher, ed., *The Negro in Depression and War* (1969); Robert Weisbrot, *Father Divine and the Struggle for Racial Equality* (1983); Nancy Weiss, *The National Urban League* (1974); Raymond Wolters, *Negroes and the Great Depression* (1970).

### Depression Culture
Daniel Aaron, *Writers on the Left* (1961); James Agee, *Let Us Now Praise Famous Men* (1941); Andrew Bergman, *We're in the Money: Depression America and Its Films* (1971); Eileen Eagan, *Class, Culture and the Classroom* (1981); Neal Gabler, *An Empire of Their Own: How the Jews Invented Hollywood* (1988); Lawrence Levine, *The Unpredictable Past: Explorations in American Cultural History* (1993); Jeffrey Meikle, *Twentieth Century Limited: Industrial Design in America, 1925–1939* (1979); Richard Pells, *Radical Visions and American Dreams: Culture and Social Thought in the Depression Years* (1973); Thomas Schatz, *The Genius of the System: Hollywood Filmmaking in the Studio Era* (1988); John Steinbeck, *The Grapes of Wrath* (1939); William Stott, *Documentary Expressionism and Thirties America* (1973); Warren Susman, *Culture as History: The Transformation of American Society in the Twentieth Century* (1984); Twelve Southerners, *I'll Take My Stand: The South and the Agrarian Tradition* (1937).

### Radicalism and Protest
Irving Bernstein, *The Lean Years: A History of the American Worker, 1920–1933* (1960); Robert Cohen, *When the Old Left Was Young: Student Radicals and America's First Mass Student Movement, 1929–1941* (1993); Roger Daniels, *The Bonus March* (1971); John Hevener, *Which Side You On? The Harlan County Coal Miners, 1931–1939* (1978); Harvey Klehr, *The Heyday of American Communism: The Depression Decade* (1984); Donald Lisio, *The President and Protest: Hoover, Conspiracy, and the Bonus Riot* (1974); Mark Naison, *Communists in Harlem during the Depression* (1983); Theodore Saloutos and John Hicks, *Twentieth*

Century Populism: Agrarian Protest in the Middle West, 1900–1939 (1951); John Shover, Cornbelt Rebellion: The Farmers' Holiday Association (1965).

## The Hoover Years
David Burner, Herbert Hoover: A Public Life (1979); Roger Daniels, The Bonus March (1971); Martin Fausold, The Presidency of Herbert C. Hoover (1985); Martin Fausold and George Mazuzun, eds., The Hoover Presidency (1974); George Nash, The Life of Herbert Hoover (1983); James Olson, Herbert Hoover and the Reconstruction Finance Corporation (1977); Albert Romasco, The Poverty of Abundance: Hoover, the Nation, the Depression (1965); Elliot A. Rosen, Hoover, Roosevelt, and the Brains Trust: From Depression to New Deal (1977); Jordan Schwarz, The Interregnum of Despair (1970); Joan Hoff Wilson, Herbert Hoover: Forgotten Progressive (1975).

## CHAPTER 26: THE NEW DEAL

### General Studies
John Braeman et al., The New Deal, 2 vols. (1975); Paul Conkin, The New Deal (1967); Steve Fraser and Gary Gerstle, eds., The Rise and Fall of the New Deal Order, 1930–1980 (1989); Otis Graham, Jr., Encore for Reform: The Old Progressives and the New Deal (1967); Barry Karl, The Uneasy State (1983); William Leuchtenburg, Franklin D. Roosevelt and the New Deal, 1932–1940 (1963); Robert McElvaine, The Great Depression: America, 1929–1941 (1984); Gerald Nash, The Great Depression and World War II (1979); Harvard Sitkoff, ed., Fifty Years Later: The New Deal Evaluated (1985).

### Franklin and Eleanor
James Burns, Roosevelt: The Lion and the Fox (1956); Rochelle Chadakoff, ed., Eleanor Roosevelt's My Day: Her Acclaimed Columns, 1936–1945 (1989); Blanche Wiesen Cook, Eleanor Roosevelt, Volume One, 1884–1933 (1992); Kenneth Davis, FDR, 4 vols. (1972–1993); Frank Freidel, Franklin D. Roosevelt, 4 vols. (1952–1973) and Franklin D. Roosevelt: A Rendezvous with Destiny (1990); Joseph Lash, Eleanor and Franklin (1971); Ted Morgan, FDR: A Biography (1985); Eleanor Roosevelt, This Is My Story (1937) and This I Remember (1949); Lois Scharf, Eleanor Roosevelt: First Lady of American Liberalism (1987); Arthur Schlesinger, Jr., The Age of Roosevelt, 3 vols. (1957–1960); Rexford Tugwell, The Democratic Roosevelt: A Biography of Franklin D. Roosevelt (1957); Geoffrey Ward, Before the Trumpet: Young Franklin Roosevelt (1985) and A First Class Temperament: The Emergence of Franklin Roosevelt (1989).

### The New Deal and New Dealers
Anthony J. Badger, The New Deal: The Depression Years, 1933–1940 (1989); Barton J. Bernstein, "The New Deal: The Conservative Achievements of New Deal Reform," in Barton J. Bernstein, ed.,

Towards a New Past: Dissenting Essays in American History (1968); Michael Beschloss, Kennedy and Roosevelt: The Uneasy Alliance (1980); John Blum, From the Morgenthau Diaries, 3 vols. (1959–1965); Harold Ickes, The Secret Diaries of Harold L. Ickes, 3 vols. (1953–1954); Peter Irons, The New Deal Lawyers (1982); Joseph Lash, Dealers and Dreamers: A New Look at the New Deal (1988); Katie Lockheim, ed., The Making of the New Deal: The Insiders Speak (1983); Richard Lowitt, George W. Norris: The Triumph of a Progressive, 1933–1944 (1978); George Martin, Madame Secretary: Frances Perkins (1976); George McJimsey, Harry Hopkins: Ally of the Poor and Defender of Democracy (1987); Raymond Moley, After Seven Years (1939); Frances Perkins, The Roosevelt I Knew (1946); Samuel Rosenman, Working for Roosevelt (1952); Jordan Schwarz, Liberal: Adolf A. Berle and the Vision of an American Era (1987) and The New Dealers: Power Politics in the Age of Roosevelt (1993); Robert Sherwood, Roosevelt and Hopkins: An Intimate History (1948); Bernard Sternsher, Rexford Tugwell and the New Deal (1964); Susan Ware, Beyond Suffrage: Women and the New Deal (1981) and Partner and I: Molly Dewson, Feminism, and New Deal Politics (1987); T. H. Watkins, The Righteous Pilgrim: The Life and Times of Harold L. Ickes (1990).

### Recovery and Reform
Bernard Belush, The Failure of the NRA (1975); Donald R. Brand, Corporatism and the Rule of Law: A Study of the National Recovery Administration (1988); Walter L. Creese, TVA's Public Planning: The Vision, the Reality (1990); Colin Gordon, New Deals: Business, Labor, and Politics in America, 1920–1935 (1994); Ellis Hawley, The New Deal and the Problems of Monopoly (1966); Barry Karl, Executive Reorganization and Reform in the New Deal (1963); Susan E. Kennedy, The Banking Crisis of 1933 (1973); Mark Leff, The Limits of Symbolic Reform: The New Deal and Taxation, 1933–1939 (1984); Thomas McCraw, TVA and the Public Power Fight (1970); James Olson, Saving Capitalism: The RFC and the New Deal, 1933–1940 (1988); Michael Parrish, Securities Regulation and the New Deal (1970); Richard Polenberg, Reorganizing Roosevelt's Government (1966); Albert Romasco, The Politics of Recovery: Roosevelt's New Deal (1983).

### Agriculture and Conservation
Sidney Baldwin, Poverty and Politics: The Rise and Decline of the Farm Security Administration (1967); David Conrad, The Forgotten Farmers: The Story of Sharecroppers in the New Deal (1965); James Gregory, American Exodus: The Dust Bowl Migration and Okie Culture in California (1989); Richard Kirkendall, Social Scientists and Farm Politics in the Age of Roosevelt (1966); Richard Lowitt, The New Deal and the West (1984); Percy H. Merrill, Roosevelt's Forest Army: A History of the Civilian Conservation Corps, 1933–1942 (1981); Paul Mertz, The New Deal and Southern Rural Poverty (1978); Van Perkins, Crisis in Agriculture (1969); Donald

Worster, *Dust Bowl: The Southern Plains in the 1930s* (1979) and *Rivers of Empire: Water, Aridity, and the Growth of the American West* (1986).

**Relief and the Rise of the
Semi-Welfare State**
Searle Charles, *Minister of Relief* (1963) [about Harry Hopkins]; Paul Conkin, *FDR and the Origins of the Welfare State* (1967); Phoebe Cutler, *The Public Landscape of the New Deal* (1986); Linda Gordon, *Pitied but Not Entitled: Single Mothers and the History of Welfare* (1994); Richard Lowitt and Maurine Beasley, eds., *One Third of a Nation: Lorena Hickok Reports on the Great Depression* (1981); Roy Lubove, *The Struggle for Social Security* (1968); Jerre Mangione, *The Dream and the Deal: The Federal Writers' Project, 1935–1943* (1972); Jane deHart Matthews, *The Federal Theater, 1935–1939* (1967); Richard McKinzie, *The New Deal for Artists* (1973); Barbara Melosh, *Engendering Culture: Manhood and Womanhood in New Deal Public Art and Theater* (1991); Francis O'Connor, ed., *Art for the Millions: Essays from the 1930s by Artists and Administrators of the WPA Federal Art Project* (1973); Karen Benker Orhn, *Dorothea Lange and the Documentary Tradition* (1980); Marlene Park and Gerald Markowitz, *Democratic Vistas: Post Offices and Public Art in the New Deal* (1984); John Salmond, *The Civilian Conservation Corps* (1967); Bonnie Schwartz, *The Civil Works Administration, 1933–1934* (1984).

**Dissent and Protest**
Alan Brinkley, *Voices of Protest: Huey Long, Father Coughlin, and the Great Depression* (1982); Donald Grubbs, *Cry from Cotton: The Southern Tenant Farmers Union and the New Deal* (1971); Abraham Holzman, *The Townsend Movement* (1963); Glen Geansonne, *Gerald L. K. Smith: Minister of Hate* (1988); Robin D. G. Kelly, *Hammer and Hoe: Alabama Communists during the Great Depression* (1990); R. Alan Lawson, *The Failure of Independent Liberalism, 1930–1941* (1971); Greg Mitchell, *The Campaign of the Century: Upton Sinclair's Epic Race for Governor of California and the Birth of Media Politics* (1992); Mark Naison, *Communists in Harlem during the Depression* (1983); Leo Ribuffo, *The Old Christian Right: The Protestant Far Right from the Great Depression to the Cold War* (1983); Vicki Ruiz, *Cannery Women/Cannery Lives: Mexican Women, Unionization, and the California Food Processing Industry, 1930–1950* (1987); Charles Tull, *Father Coughlin and the New Deal* (1965); T. Harry Wiliams, *Huey Long* (1969); Frank Warren, *Liberals and Communism: The "Red Decade" Revisited* (1966) and *An Alternative Vision: The Socialist Party in the 1930s* (1976); George Wolfskill, *Revolt of the Conservatives: A History of the American Liberty League, 1934–1940* (1962).

**Labor**
Jerold Auerback, *Labor and Liberty: The La Follette Committee and the New Deal* (1966); John Barnard, *Walter Reuther and the Rise of the Auto Workers* (1983); Irving Bernstein, *Turbulent Years: A History*

*of the American Worker, 1933–1941* (1969); Lizabeth Cohen, *Making a New Deal: Industrial Workers in Chicago, 1919–1939* (1990); Melvyn Dubofsky and Warren Van Tine, *John L. Lewis: A Biography* (1977); Sidney Fine, *Sit-Down: The General Motors Strike of 1936–1937* (1969); Steven Fraser, *Labor Will Rule: Sidney Hillman and the Rise of American Labor* (1991); Peter Friedlander, *The Emergence of a UAW Local* (1975); Nelson Lichenstein, *"The Most Dangerous Man in Detroit": Walter Reuther and the Fate of American Labor* (1995); August Meier and Elliott Rudwick, *Black Detroit and the Rise of the UAW* (1979); David Milton, *The Politics of U.S. Labor: From the Great Depression to the New Deal* (1980); Ronald Schatz, *The Electrical Workers* (1983); Robert H. Zieger, *John L. Lewis* (1988).

**New Deal Politics**
John Allswang, *The New Deal in American Politics* (1978); Frank Freidel, *FDR and the South* (1965); J. Joseph Huthmacher, *Senator Robert Wagner and the Rise of Urban Liberalism* (1968); Gregg Mitchell, *The Campaign of the Century: Upton Sinclair's Race for Governor and the Birth of Media Politics* (1992); James Patterson, *Congressional Conservatism and the New Deal* (1967) and *The New Deal and the States* (1969); William Leuchtenburg, "The Origins of Franklin D. Roosevelt's 'Court Packing' Plan," in Philip Kurland, ed., *The Supreme Court Review* (1966).

**Minorities**
Laurence Kelly, *The Assault on Assimilation: John Collier and the Origins of Indian Policy Reform, 1920–1954* (1983); Harry A. Kersey, Jr., *The Florida Seminoles and the New Deal, 1933–1942* (1989); John Kirby, *Black Americans in the Roosevelt Era: Liberalism and Race* (1980); Carey McWilliams, *North from Mexico* (1949); Donald Parman, *The Navajoes and the New Deal* (1976); Kenneth Philp, *John Collier's Crusade for Indian Reform, 1920–1934* (1977); Francis Prucha, *The Indians in American Society: From the Revolutionary War to the Present* (1985); Mark Reisler, *By the Sweat of Their Brow: Mexican Immigrant Labor in the United States, 1900–1940* (1976); Harvard Sitkoff, *A New Deal for Blacks* (1978); Raymond Walters, *Negroes and the Great Depression: The Problem of Economic Recovery* (1970); Graham D. Taylor, *The New Deal and American Indian Tribalism: The Administration of the Indian Reorganization Act, 1934–1945* (1980); Nancy Weiss, *Farewell to the Party of Lincoln: Black Politics in the Age of FDR* (1983); Robert Zangrando, *The NAACP Crusade against Lynching* (1980).

# CHAPTER 27: AMERICA'S RISE TO GLOBALISM

**The Roosevelt Era and the Coming of World War II**
Dorothy Borg, *The United States and the Far Eastern Crisis of 1933–1938* (1964); James

MacGregor Burns, *Roosevelt: The Lion and the Fox* (1956); Wayne S. Cole, *Roosevelt and the Isolationists, 1932–1945* (1983); Robert Dallek, *Franklin D. Roosevelt and American Foreign Policy, 1932–1945* (1979); Charles DeBenedetti, *The Peace Reform Movement in American History* (1980); John Findling, *Close Neighbors, Distant Friends: United States–Central American Relations* (1987); Lloyd Gardner, *Economic Aspects of New Deal Diplomacy* (1964) and *The Great Powers Partition Europe, from Munich to Yalta* (1993); Irwin Gellman, *Good Neighbor Diplomacy* (1979); Patrick Headen, *Roosevelt Confronts Hitler: America's Entry into World War II* (1987); Edwin Herzstein, *Roosevelt and Hitler: Prelude to War* (1989); Akira Iriye and Warren Cohen, eds., *American, Chinese, and Japanese Perspectives on Asia, 1931–1949* (1990); Warren Kimball, *The Most Unsordid Act: Lend Lease, 1939–1941* (1969); Walter LaFeber, *Inevitable Revolutions: The United States in Central America* (1993); Douglas Little, *Malevolent Neutrality: The United States, Great Britain, and the Origins of the Spanish Civil War* (1985); Arthur Morse, *While Six Million Died* (1968); Arnold Offner, *The Origins of the Second World War* (1975); Gordon Prange, *At Dawn We Slept* (1981); Michael Slackman, *Target: Pearl Harbor* (1990); John Toland, *Infamy* (1982); Jonathan Utley, *Going to War with Japan, 1937–1941* (1985); Roberta Wohlstetter, *Pearl Harbor: Warning and Decision* (1962); Bryce Wood, *The Making of the Good Neighbor Policy* (1961); David Wyman, *The Abandonment of the Jews* (1984).

**War and Strategy**
John Dower, *War without Mercy: Race and Power in the Pacific War* (1986); David Eisenhower, *Eisenhower at War, 1943–1945* (1986); Richard B. Frank, *Guadalcanal* (1990); B. H. Liddell Hart, *History of the Second World War* (1970); Max Hastings, *OVERLORD: D-Day and the Battle of Normandy* (1984); Akira Iriye, *Power and Culture: The Japanese-American War, 1941–1945* (1981); D. Clayton James with Anne Sharp Wells, *A Time for Giants: Politics of the American High Command during World War II* (1987); John Keegan, *The Second World War* (1989); Eric Larabee, *Commander in Chief: Franklin Delano Roosevelt, His Lieutenants, and Their War* (1987); William Manchester, *American Caesar* (1979); Karal Ann Marling and John Wetenhall, *Iwo Jima* (1991); Ken McCormick and Hamilton Perry, *Images of War: The Artists' Vision of World War II* (1990); Nathan Miller, *War at Sea: A Naval History of World War II* (1995); Samuel Eliot Morison, *The Two Ocean War* (1963); Bernard C. Nalty, *Strength for the Fight: A History of Black Americans in the Military* (1986); Geoffrey Perret, *There's a War to Be Won: The United States Army and World War II* (1991) and *Winged Victory: The American Air Force in World War II* (1993); Forrest Pogue, *George C. Marshall*, 3 vols. (1963–1975); Paul P. Rogers, *The Good Years: MacArthur and Sutherland* (1990); Ronald Schaffer, *Wings of Judgment: American*

*Bombing in World War II* (1985); Michael Sherry, *The Rise of American Air Power* (1987); Bradley Smith, *The Shadow Warriors: O.S.S. and the Origins of the C.I.A.* (1983); Ronald Spector, *The Eagle against the Sun: The American War with Japan* (1985); James Stokesbury, *A Short History of World War II* (1980).

**The Home Front at War**
Michael Adams, *The Best War Ever: Americans and World War II* (1994); Karen T. Anderson, *Wartime Women: Sex Roles, Family Relations, and the Status of American Women during World War II* (1981); Matthew Baigall and Julia Williams, eds., *Artists against War and Fascism* (1986); M. Joyce Baker, *Images of Women on Film: The War Years, 1941–1945* (1981); David Brinkley, *Washington Goes to War* (1988); John Costello, *Virtue under Fire: How World War II Changed Our Social and Sexual Attitudes* (1985); George Q. Flynn, *The Draft, 1940–1973* (1993); Paul Fussell, *Wartime* (1989); Sherna Berger Gluck, *Rosie the Riveter Revisited: Women, the War, and Social Change* (1987); Doris Kearns Goodwin, *No Ordinary Time, Franklin and Eleanor Roosevelt: The Homefront in World War II* (1994); Susan Hartmann, *The Home Front and Beyond: American Women in the 1940s* (1982); Maurice Isserman, *Which Side Were You On? The American Communist Party during the Second World War* (1982); Clayton Koppes and Gregory Black, *Hollywood Goes to War* (1987); Ruth Milkman, *Gender at Work: The Dynamics of Job Segregation by Sex during World War II* (1987); Gerald Nash, *The American West Transformed: The Impact of the Second World War* (1985); Richard Polenberg, *War and Society: The United States, 1941–1945* (1972); David Robertson, *Sly and Able: A Political Biography of James F. Byrnes* (1994); George H. Roeder, Jr., *The Censored War: American Visual Experience during World War II* (1993); Studs Turkel, *The Good War: An Oral History of World War II* (1984); William Tuttle, *Daddy's Gone to War: The Second World War in the Lives of America's Children* (1993); Harold Vatter, *The American Economy in World War II* (1985).

**Minorities and the War**
Robert Abzug, *Inside the Vicious Heart: Americans and the Liberation of the Nazi Concentration Camps* (1985); Allan Bérubé, *Coming Out under Fire: Gay Men and Women in World War Two* (1990); Richard Breitman and Alan Kraut, *American Refugee Policy and European Jewry, 1933–1945* (1987); A. Russell Buchanan, *Black Americans in World War II* (1977); Dominic Capeci, Jr., *Race Relations in Wartime Detroit* (1984) and *The Harlem Race Riot of 1943* (1977); Richard Dalfiume, *Desegregation of the U.S. Armed Forces* (1969); Clete Daniel, *Chicano Workers and the Politics of Fairness: The Fair Employment Practices Commission and the Southwest 1941–1945* (1990); Roger Daniels, *Concentration Camps U.S.A.* (1981) and *Prisoners without Trials: The Japanese-Americans in World War II* (1993); Leonard Dinnerstein, *America and the Survivors of the*

*Holocaust* (1982); Masayo Umezawa Duus, *Unlikely Liberators: The Men of the 100th and 442nd* (1987); Lee Finkel, *Forum for Protest: The Black Press during World War II* (1975); Peter Irons, *Justice at War: The Story of the Japanese American Internment Cases* (1983); Deborah Lipstadt, *Beyond Belief: The American Press and the Coming of the Holocaust, 1933–1945* (1986); Mauricio Mazon, *The Zoot Suit Riots* (1984); Phillip McGuire, ed., *Taps for a Jim Crow Army: Letters from Black Soldiers in World War II* (1982); Sandra Taylor, *Jewel of the West: Japanese-American Internment at Topaz* (1993); Patrick Washburn, *A Question of Sedition: The Federal Government and the Investigation of the Black Press during World War II* (1986); Neil Wynn, *The Afro-American and the Second World War* (1976); Norman Zucker and Naomi Flink Zucker, *The Guarded Gate: The Reality of American Refugee Policy* (1987).

**Atoms and Diplomacy**
Gar Alperovitz, *The Decision to Use the Bomb* (1995); Edward M. Bennett, *Franklin D. Roosevelt and the Search for Victory: American-Soviet Relations, 1935–1945* (1990); Henry Blumenthal, *Illusion and Reality in Franco-American Diplomacy, 1914–1945* (1982); McGeorge Bundy, *Danger and Survival: Choices about the Atom Bomb in the First Fifty Years* (1988); James MacGregor Burns, *Roosevelt: The Soldier of Freedom* (1970); Winston Churchill, *The Second World War*, 6 vols. (1948–1953); Herbert Feis, *Roosevelt, Churchill, Stalin: The War They Waged and the Peace They Sought* (1957), *Between War and Peace: The Potsdam Conference* (1960), and *The Atomic Bomb and the End of World War II* (1966); John L. Gaddis, *The United States and the Origins of the Cold War* (1972); Fraser J. Harbutt, *The Iron Curtain: Churchill, America, and the Origins of the Cold War* (1986); George Herring, *Aid to Russia, 1941–1946* (1977); John Hersey, *Hiroshima* (1946); Richard Hewlett and Oscar Anderson, *The New World* (1962); "Hiroshima in History and Memory: A Symposium," *Diplomatic History*, vol. 19, No. 2, Spring, 1995, 197–365; Godfrey Hodgson, *The Colonel: The Life and Wars of Henry Stimson* (1990); Warren Kimball, ed., *Churchill and Roosevelt: The Complete Correspondence, 1939–1945* (1984); Gabriel Kolko, *The Politics of War* (1968); William Roger Louis, *Imperialism at Bay: The United States and the Decolonization of the British Empire, 1941–1945* (1978); Mark H. Lytle, *The Origins of the Iranian-American Alliance, 1941–1953* (1987); David Painter, *Oil and the American Century: The Political Economy of U.S. Foreign Oil Policy, 1941–1954* (1986); Richard Rhodes, *The Making of the Atomic Bomb* (1986); Keith Sainsbury, *Roosevelt, Stalin, Churchill, and Chiang Kai-shek, 1943: The Moscow, Cairo, and Tehran Conferences* (1985); Gaddis Smith, *American Diplomacy during the Second World War, 1941–1945* (1985); Michael B. Stoff, *Oil, War, and American Security: The Search for a National Policy on Foreign Oil, 1941–1947* (1980), and as ed., *The Manhattan Project: A Documentary Introduction* (1991); Randall B. Woods, *A Changing of the Guard: Anglo-American Relations, 1941–1946* (1990).

**CHAPTER 28: COLD WAR AMERICA**

**The Postwar Era**
Paul Boyer, *By the Bomb's Early Light* (1986); H. W. Brands, *The Devil We Knew: America and the Cold War* (1993); Robert Ferrell, *Harry S Truman: A Life* (1994); Eric Goldman, *The Crucial Decade and After* (1960); Landon Jones, *Great Expectations: America and the Babyboom Generation* (1980); George Lipsitz, *Class and Culture in Postwar America* (1981); James O'Connor, ed., *American History/American Television* (1983); William O'Neill, *American High* (1986); Richard Pells, *The Liberal Mind in a Conservative Age* (1985); Dana Polan, *Power and Paranoia: History, Narrative, and the American Cinema, 1940–1950* (1986); Leila Rupp and Verta Taylor, *Survival in the Doldrums: The American Women's Rights Movement, 1945 to the 1960s* (1987); Mark Silk, *Spiritual Politics: Religion and America since World War II* (1988); Jules Tygiel, *Baseball's Great Experiment: Jackie Robinson and His Legacy* (1983); Martin Walker, *The Cold War: A History* (1994).

**The Cold War in the West**
Dean Acheson, *Present at the Creation* (1969); Stephen Ambrose, *The Rise to Globalism* (1983); Douglas Brinkley, ed., *Dean Acheson and the Making of American Foreign Policy* (1993); Richard Wightman Fox, *Reinhold Niebuhr: A Biography* (1985); Richard Freeland, *The Truman Doctrine and the Origins of McCarthyism* (1970); John L. Gaddis, *Strategies of Containment* (1982) and *The Long Peace: Inquiries into the History of the Cold War* (1987); Lloyd Gardner, *Architects of Illusion* (1970); David Green, *The Containment of Latin America* (1971); Gregg Herken, *The Winning Weapon* (1980); Michael Hogan, *The Marshall Plan: America, Britain, and the Reconstruction of Western Europe, 1947–1952* (1987); Walter Isaacson and Evan Thomas, *The Wise Men* (1986); Fred Kaplan, *The Wizards of Armageddon* (1983); Laurence Kaplan, *The United States and NATO* (1984); George Kennan, *Memoirs*, 2 vols. (1967, 1972); Bruce Kuniholm, *The Origins of the Cold War in the Near East* (1980); Mark H. Lytle, *The Origins of the Iranian-American Alliance, 1941–1953* (1987); James Miller, *The United States and Italy, 1940–1950* (1986); Ronald Pruessen, *John Foster Dulles* (1982); Cheryl Rubenberg, *Israel and the American National Interest* (1986); Gaddis Smith, *Dean Acheson* (1972) and *The Last Years of the Monroe Doctrine, 1945–1993* (1994); Adam Ulam, *The Rivals* (1971); Lawrence Wittner, *American Intervention in Greece, 1943–1949* (1982); Randall B. Woods and Howard Jones, *Dawning of the Cold War* (1991).

### The Cold War in Asia

Robert Blum, *Drawing the Line: The Origin of the American Containment Policy in East Asia* (1982); Bruce Cumings, *The Origins of the Korean War* (1980) and vol. 2 (1990), and as ed., *Child of Conflict: The Korean-American Relationship, 1943–1953* (1983); William Head, *America's China Sojourn* (1983); Gary Hess, *The United States' Emergence as a Southeast Asian Power, 1940–1950* (1987); Akira Iriye, *The Cold War in Asia* (1974); Burton Kaufman, *The Korean War* (1986); Michael Schaller, *The United States and China in the Twentieth Century* (1979) and *The American Occupation of Japan: The Coming of the Cold War to Asia* (1985); John W. Spanier, *The Truman–MacArthur Controversy and the Korean War* (1959); William Stueck, Jr., *The Road to Confrontation* (1981) and *The Korean War: An International History* (1995); Nancy Tucker, *Patterns in the Dust: Chinese-American Relations and the Recognition Controversy, 1949–1950* (1983).

### The Domestic Cold War

Michael Belknap, *Cold War Political Justice: The Smith Act, the Communist Party, and American Civil Liberties* (1977); David Caute, *The Great Fear* (1978); Bernard F. Dick, *Radical Innocence: A Critical Study of the Hollywood Ten* (1988); Stanley I. Kutler, *The American Inquisition: Justice and Injustice in the Cold War* (1982); Robert Lamphere and Tom Shachtman, *The FBI-KGB War* (1986); Victor Navasky, *Naming Names* (1980); Robert Newman, *Owen Lattimore and the "Loss" of China* (1992); William O'Neill, *A Better World: Stalinism and the American Intellectuals* (1983); Michael Oshinsky, *A Conspiracy So Immense: The World of Joe McCarthy* (1983); Ronald Radosh and Joyce Radosh, *The Rosenberg File* (1983); Thomas Reeves, *The Life and Times of Joe McCarthy* (1982); Richard Rovere, *Senator Joe McCarthy* (1959); Ellen Schrecker, *No Ivory Tower: McCarthyism and the Universities* (1984); Athan Theoharis, *Seeds of Repression: Harry S. Truman and the Origins of McCarthyism* (1971); Allen Weinstein, *Perjury: The Hiss-Chambers Case* (1978); Robert Williams, *Klaus Fuchs: Atom Spy* (1987).

### The Truman Administration

Jack Ballard, *The Shock of Peace: Military and Economic Demobilization after World War II* (1983); Clark Clifford with Richard Holbrooke, *Counsel to the President, A Memoir* (1991); Richard Dalfiume, *Desegregation of the U.S. Armed Forces* (1969); Andrew Dunar, *The Truman Scandals and the Politics of Morality* (1984); Robert Ferrell, *Harry S. Truman and the Modern American Presidency* (1983); Donald Fixico, *Termination and Relocation: Federal Indian Policy, 1945–1960* (1986); David Goldfield, *Black, White, and Southern: Race Relations and Southern Culture* (1990); Alton Lee, *Truman and Taft-Hartley* (1966); Allen Matusow, *Farm Politics and Policies in the Truman Years* (1967); Donald McCoy, *The Presidency of Harry S. Truman* (1984); Donald McCoy and Richard Ruetten, *Quest and Response: Minority Rights and the Truman Administration* (1973); Merle Miller, *Plain Speaking* (1973); Richard Miller, *Truman: The Rise to Power* (1986); Allen Yarnell, *Democrats and Progressives: The 1948 Presidential Election as a Test of Postwar Liberalism* (1974).

## CHAPTER 29: THE SUBURBAN ERA

### General

Paul Carter, *Another Part of the Fifties* (1983); John Diggins, *The Proud Decades: America in War and Peace, 1941–1960* (1988); James Gilbert, *A Cycle of Outrage* (1986); Godfrey Hodgson, *America in Our Time* (1976); Martin Jezer, *The Dark Ages: Life in the United States, 1945–1960* (1982); William Leuchtenberg, *A Troubled Feast* (1979); Douglas Miller and Marion Nowak, *The Fifties: The Way We Really Were* (1977); Ronald Oakley, *God's Country: America in the 1950s* (1986); Stephen Whitfield, *The Culture of the Cold War* (1991).

### American Life and Culture

Erik Barnouw, *Tube of Plenty: The Evolution of American Television* (1975); James L. Baughman, *The Republic of Mass Culture: Journalism, Filmmaking, and Broadcasting in America since 1941* (1992); Daniel Bell, *The End of Ideology* (1960); Carl Belz, *The Story of Rock* (1972); Wini Breines, *Young, White, and Miserable: Growing Up Female in the Fifties* (1992); Victoria Byerly, *Hard Times Cotton Mill Girls* (1986); Bruce Cook, *The Beat Generation* (1970); Stephanie Coontz, *The Way We Never Were: American Families and the Nostalgia Trap* (1992); John D'Emilio and Estelle Freedman, *Intimate Matters: A History of Sexuality in America* (1988); Colin Escott, *Good Rockin' Tonight: Sun Records and the Birth of Rock and Roll* (1991); Betty Friedan, *The Feminine Mystique* (1963); Neil Gabler, *Winchell: Gossip, Power and the Culture of Celebrity* (1994); John Kenneth Galbraith, *The Affluent Society* (1958); Herbert Gans, *The Levittowners* (1967); Carol George, *God's Salesman: Norman Vincent Peale and the Power of Positive Thinking* (1994); Serge Gilbaut, *How New York Stole the Idea of Modern Art* (1983); Charlie Gillett, *The Sound of the City: The Rise of Rock and Roll* (1970); William Graebner, *Coming of Age in Buffalo: Youth and Authority in the Postwar Era* (1990); Will Herberg, *Protestant-Catholic-Jew* (1956); Thomas Hine, *Populux* (1986); Kenneth Jackson, *Crabgrass Frontier: The Suburbanization of the United States* (1985); Wendy Kozol, *Life's America: Family and Nation in Postwar Photojournalism* (1994); William Martin, *A Prophet with Honor: The Billy Graham Story* (1991); C. Wright Mills, *The Power Elite* (1956) and *White Collar* (1951); George Nash, *The Conservative Intellectual Movement in America* (1976); Richard Pells, *The Liberal Mind in a Conservative Age* (1985); David Potter, *People of Plenty* (1956); David Riesman, *The Lonely Crowd* (1950); Lynn Spiegel,

*Make Room for TV: Television and the Family Ideal in Postwar America* (1992); Gaye Tuchman et al., eds., *Hearth and Home: Images of Women in the Mass Media* (1978); Ed Ward et al., *Rock of Ages: The Rolling Stone History of Rock and Roll* (1986); Carol Warren, *Madwives: Schizophrenic Women in the 1950s* (1987); William Whyte, *The Organization Man* (1956).

**Foreign Policy in the Eisenhower Era**
Stephen Ambrose, *Ike's Spies: Eisenhower and the Espionage Establishment* (1981); Blanche Weisen Cook, *The Declassified Eisenhower* (1981); Robert Divine, *Eisenhower and the Cold War* (1981) and *Blowin' in the Wind: The Nuclear Test Ban Debate, 1954–1960* (1978); Townsend Hoopes, *The Devil and John Foster Dulles* (1973); Richard Immerman, *The CIA in Guatemala* (1982); Madeline Kalb, *The Congo Cables: The Cold War in Africa from Eisenhower to Kennedy* (1982); Frederick Marks III, *Power and Peace: The Diplomacy of John Foster Dulles* (1993); Richard Melanson and David Mayers eds., *Reevaluating Eisenhower: American Foreign Policy in the 1950s* (1987); Thomas Paterson, *Contesting Castro: The United States and the Triumph of the Cuban Revolution* (1994); Richard Rhodes, *Dark Sun: The Making of the Hydrogen Bomb* (1995); Evan Thomas, *The Very Best Men: Four Who Dared: The Early Years of the CIA* (1995); Richard Welch, Jr., *Response to Revolution: The United States and the Cuban Revolution, 1954–1961* (1985).

**Civil Rights**
Numan Bartley, *The Rise of Massive Resistance: Race and Politics in the South during the 1950s* (1969); Jack Bloom, *Class, Race, and the Civil Rights Movement* (1987); Taylor Branch, *Parting the Waters: America in the King Years, 1954–1963* (1988); James Duram, *Moderate among Extremists: Dwight D. Eisenhower and the School Desegregation Crisis* (1981); David Garrow, *Bearing the Cross* (1986); Henry Louis Gates, Jr., *Colored People: A Memoir* (1994); Vincent Harding, *There Is a River: The Black Struggle for Freedom in America* (1981); Elizabeth Huckaby, *The Crisis at Central High: Little Rock, 1957–1958* (1980); Richard Kluger, *Simple Justice: The History of Brown v. Board of Education and Black America's Struggle for Equality* (1975); Anthony Lewis et al., *Portrait of a Decade* (1964); August Meier and Elliott Rudwick, *CORE: A Study in the Civil Rights Movement, 1942–1968* (1975); Stephen Oates, *Let the Trumpet Sound: The Life and Times of Martin Luther King, Jr.* (1982); Bernard Schwartz, *Inside the Warren Court* (1983); Harvard Sitkoff, *The Struggle for Black Equality, 1954–1992* (1992); Juan Williams, *Eyes on the Prize: America's Civil Rights Years, 1954–1965* (1987); C. Vann Woodward, *The Strange Career of Jim Crow* (1974).

**Domestic Politics**
Stephen Ambrose, *Eisenhower the President* (1984); Piers Brendon, *Ike* (1986); Jeff Broadwater,

*Eisenhower and the Anti-Communist Crusade* (1992); Larry Burt, *Tribalism in Crisis: Federal Indian Policy, 1953–1961* (1982); Barbara Clowse, *Brainpower for the Cold War: The Sputnik Crisis and the National Defense Education Act of 1958* (1981); Donald Fixico, *Termination and Relocation: Federal Indian Policy, 1945–1960* (1986); Fred Greenstein, *The Hidden Hand Presidency: Eisenhower as Leader* (1982); Chester Pach, *The Presidency of Dwight D. Eisenhower* (1991); Mark Rose, *Interstate Express Highway Politics, 1939–1989* (1991); Gary Wills, *Nixon Agonistes* (1970).

## CHAPTER 30: LIBERALISM AND BEYOND

**General**
John M. Blum, *Years of Discord: American Politics and Society, 1961–1974* (1991); David Faber, *The Age of Great Dreams: America in the 1960s* (1994), and as ed., *The Sixties: From Memory to History* (1994); Richard Goodwin, *Remembering America: A Voice from the Sixties* (1988); Godfrey Hodgson, *America in Our Time* (1976); Edward P. Morgan, *The 60s Experience: Hard Lessons about Modern America* (1991); David Steigenwald, *The Sixties and the End of the Modern Era* (1995); Lawrence Wright, *The New World: Growing Up in America, 1960–1984* (1988).

**The Counterculture and New Left**
Serge Denisoff, *Great Day Coming: Folk Music and the American Left* (1971); Morris Dickstein, *The Gates of Eden* (1976); Todd Gitlin, *The Whole World Is Watching: The Mass Media in the Making and Unmaking of the New Left* (1981); Richard Goldstein, *Reporting the Counterculture* (1989); Paul Goodman, *Growing Up Absurd* (1960); Emmett Grogan, *Ringolevio* (1972); Maurice Isserman, *If I Had a Hammer . . . : The Death of the Old Left and the Birth of the New Left* (1987); Judy Kaplan and Linn Shapiro, *Red Diaper Babies: Children on the Left* (1985); Martin Lee and Bruce Shlain, *Acid Dreams: The CIA, LSD, and the Sixties Rebellion* (1985); Christine Mamiya, *Pop Art and the Consumer Culture: American Super Market* (1992); Timothy Miller, *The Hippies and American Values* (1991); W. J. Rorabaugh, *Berkeley at War: The 1960s* (1989); Theodore Roszak, *The Making of a Counter Culture* (1969); Kirkpatrick Sale, *SDS* (1973), Mark Spitz, *Dylan: A Biography* (1989); Students for a Democratic Society, *The Port Huron Statement* (1962); Hunter Thompson, *Hell's Angels* (1967) and *Fear and Loathing in Las Vegas* (1971); Ed Ward et al., *Rock of Ages: The Rolling Stone History of Rock and Roll* (1986); Tom Wolfe, *Electric Kool-Aid Acid Test* (1968).

**The Civil Rights Revolution**
Michael Belknap, *Federal Law and Southern Order: Racial Violence and Constitutional Conflict in the Post-Brown South* (1987); Derrick Bell, *And We Are Not Saved: The Elusive Quest for Racial Justice* (1987);

Jack Bloom, *Class, Race, and the Civil Rights Movement* (1987); Eric Burner, *And Gently He Shall Lead Them: Robert Parris Moses and Civil Rights in Mississippi* (1994); Stokely Carmichael and Charles Hamilton, *Black Power* (1967); Clayborne Carson, *In Struggle: SNCC and the Black Awakening of the 1960s* (1981); Dan T. Carter, *The Politics of Rage: George Wallace and the New Conservatism* (1995); William Chafe, *Civilities and Civil Rights* (1980); John Dittmar, *Local People: The Struggle for Civil Rights in Mississippi* (1994); Michael Eric Dyson, *Making Malcolm: The Myth and Meaning of Malcolm X* (1995); David Garrow, *The FBI and Martin Luther King* (1981); Hugh Davis Graham, *Civil Rights and the Presidency: Race and Gender in American Politics, 1960–1972* (1992); Otto Kerner et al., *The Report of the National Advisory Commission on Civil Disorders* (1968); Doug McAdam, *Freedom Summer* (1988); Malcolm X (with Alex Haley), *The Autobiography of Malcolm X* (1966); Adam Nossiter, *Of Long Memory: Mississippi and the Murder of Medgar Evers* (1994); Stephen Oates, *Let the Trumpet Sound: The Life and Times of Martin Luther King, Jr.* (1982); Hugh Pearson, *The Shadow of the Panther: Huey Newton and the Price of Black Power in America* (1994); Bruce Perry, *Malcolm* (1992); Bernard Schwartz, *Inside the Warren Court* (1983); Harvard Sitkoff, *The Struggle for Black Equality, 1954–1992* (1993); Mark Stern, *Calculating Visions: Kennedy, Johnson, and Civil Rights* (1992); Harris Wofford, *Of Kennedy and Kings* (1980); Eugene Wolfenstein, *The Victims of Democracy: Malcolm X and the Black Revolutionaries* (1981); Miles Wolff, *Lunch at the 5 & 10* (1990).

**The Kennedys and Lyndon Johnson**
David Burner and Thomas West, *The Torch Is Passed: The Kennedy Brothers and American Liberalism* (1984); Paul Ronnie Dugger, *The Politician* (1982); John Giglio, *The Presidency of John F. Kennedy* (1991); Lyndon Johnson, *Vantage Point* (1971); Gerald Posner, *Case Closed: Lee Harvey Oswald and the Assassination of John F. Kennedy* (1993); Thomas Reeves, *A Question of Character: A Life of John F. Kennedy* (1992); Arthur Schlesinger, Jr., *The Thousand Days* (1965) and *Robert Kennedy and His Times* (1978); Earl Warren et al., *The Report of the Warren Commission* (1964); Theodore White, *The Making of the President, 1960* (1961).

**Politics and Foreign Policy in the Kennedy – Johnson Era**
Graham Allison, *Essence of Decision: Explaining the Cuban Missile Crisis* (1971); James Anderson and Jared Hazelton, *Managing Macroeconomic Policy: The Johnson Presidency* (1986); Michael Beschloss, *The Crisis Years, Kennedy and Khrushchev, 1960–1963* (1991); H. W. Brands, *The Wages of Globalism: Lyndon Johnson and the Limits of American Power* (1994); Warren Cohen, *Dean Rusk* (1980); Hugh Graham Davis, *Uncertain Trumpet* (1984); Greg Duncan, *Years of Poverty, Years of*

*Plenty* (1984); Trumbell Higgins, *Perfect Failure: Kennedy, Eisenhower and the Bay of Pigs* (1987); Diane Kunz, ed., *The Diplomacy of the Crucial Decade: American Foreign Policy in the 1960s* (1995); Richard Mahoney, *JFK: Ordeal in Africa* (1983); Walter McDougall, . . . *The Heavens and the Earth: A Political History of the Space Age* (1985); Charles Murray, *Losing Ground: American Social Policy, 1950–1980* (1984); Thomas Noer, *Cold War and Black Liberation: The United States and White Rule in Africa, 1948–1968* (1985); Gerald Rice, *The Bold Experiment: JFK's Peace Corps* (1985); R. B. Smith, *An International History of the Vietnam War: The Kennedy Strategy* (1985); Mary Ann Watson, *The Expanding Vista, American Television in the Kennedy Years* (1990); Tom Wicker, *JFK and LBJ* (1968); Bryce Wood, *The Dismantling of the Good Neighbor Policy* (1985).

## CHAPTER 31: THE VIETNAM ERA

**The United States and the Vietnam War**
Christian Appy, *Working Class War: American Combat Soldiers and Vietnam* (1993); Loren Baritz, *Backfire: A History of How American Culture Led Us into Vietnam and Made Us Fight the Way We Did* (1985); Larry Berman, *Planning a Tragedy* (1982); Larry Cable, *Conflict of Myths: The Development of American Counterinsurgency Doctrine and the Vietnam War* (1986); Mark Clodfelter, *The Limits of Airpower* (1989); Lloyd Gardner, *Pay Any Price: Lyndon Johnson and the War for Vietnam* (1995); Francis Fitzgerald, *Fire in the Lake* (1972); Leslie Gelb and Richard Betts, *The Irony of Vietnam: The System Worked* (1979); Mike Gravel et al., *The Pentagon Papers* (1975); David Halberstam, *The Best and the Brightest* (1972) and *The Making of Quagmire* (1987); Le Ly Hayslip, *When Heaven and Earth Changed Places* (1989), and with James Hayslip, *Child of War, Woman of Peace* (1993); George Herring, *LBJ and Vietnam* (1994); George Kahin, *Intervention* (1986); Stanley Karnow, *Vietnam* (1983); Gabriel Kolko, *Anatomy of a War* (1985); Andrew Krepinevich, Jr., *The Army and Vietnam* (1986); David Levy, *The Debate Over Vietnam* (1991); Kathryn Marshall, *In the Combat Zone: An Oral History of Women in the Vietnam War, 1966–1975* (1987); Harold G. Moore and Joseph Galloway, *We Were Soldiers Once . . . and Young* (1992); Tim Page, *Nam* (1983); Bruce Palmer, Jr., *The 25-Year War* (1984); Archimedes Patti, *Why Viet Nam?* (1983); Norman Podhoretz, *Why We Were in Vietnam* (1982); Al Santoli, *Everything We Had: An Oral History of the Vietnam War by Thirty-Three American Soldiers Who Fought It* (1981); Neil Sheehan, *A Bright Shining Lie: John Paul Vann and America in Vietnam* (1988); Ronald Spector, *The United States Army in Vietnam* (1983) and *After Tet: The Bloodiest Year in Vietnam* (1993); Harry Summers, Jr., *On Strategy: A Critical Analysis of the Vietnam War* (1981); Wallace Terry, *Bloods: An Oral History of the Vietnam War by Black Veterans*

(1984); William Turley, *The Second Indochina War: A Short Political and Military History* (1986); Jim Wilson, *The Sons of Bardstown* (1994).

**Dissent against the War**
William Berman, *William Fulbright and the Vietnam War* (1988); David Caute, *The Year of the Barricades, 1968* (1988); Charles DeBenedetti and Charles Chatfield, *An American Ordeal: The Antiwar Movement and the Vietnam Era* (1990); Gloria Emerson, *Winners and Losers* (1976); David Farber, *Chicago '68* (1988); Myra MacPherson, *Long Time Passing: Vietnam and the Haunted Generation* (1984); Kim McQuaid, *The Anxious Years* (1989); Norman Mailer, *Armies of the Night* (1968) and *Miami and the Siege of Chicago* (1969); James Miller, *Democracy Is in the Streets* (1987); Melvin Small, *Covering Dissent: The Media and the Anti-Vietnam War Movement* (1994); William Strauss, *Chance and Circumstance* (1978); Amy Swerdlow, *The Women's Strike for Peace: Traditional Motherhood and Radical Politics in the 1960s* (1993); Lawrence Wittner, *Rebels against War: The American Peace Movement, 1933–1983* (1984) Nancy Zaroulis and Gerald Sullivan, *Who Spoke Up? American Protest against the War in Vietnam* (1984).

**The Nixon Presidency before Watergate**
Stephen Ambrose, *Nixon, the Triumph of a Politician, 1962–1972* (1989); John Erlichmann, *Witness to Power* (1982); Raymond Garthoff, *Détente and Confrontation: American–Soviet Relations from Nixon to Reagan* (1985); H. R. Haldeman, *The Haldeman Diaries: Inside the Nixon White House* (1994); Seymour Hersh, *The Price of Power: Kissinger in the Nixon White House* (1983); Walter Isaacson, *Kissinger* (1992); Henry Kissinger, *The White House Years* (1979) and *Years of Upheaval* (1982); Robert Litwack, *Détente and the Nixon Doctrine* (1984); Morris Morley, *The United States and Chile* (1975); Richard Nixon, *RN* (1978); William Shawcross, *Sideshow: Nixon, Kissinger, and the Destruction of Cambodia* (1978); Robert Sutter, *The China Quandary* (1983); Theodore White, *The Making of the President, 1968* (1969); Tom Wicker, *One of Us: Richard Nixon and the American Dream* (1991).

**Minorities: Background and Politics**
Rodolfo Acuna, *Occupied America* (1981); Mario Barerra, *Race and Class in the Southwest* (1979); John Burma, ed., *Mexican-Americans in the United States* (1970); Albert Camarillo, *Hispanics in a Changing Society* (1979); Tony Castro, *Chicano Power* (1974); Vine Deloria, *Behind the Veil of Broken Treaties* (1974); Patrick Gallagher, *The Cuban Exile* (1980); Hazel W. Hertzberg, *The Search for an American Indian Identity: Modern Pan-Indian Movements* (1971); Peter Iverson, *The Navajo Nation* (1981); Virginia Sanchez Korrol, *From Colonia to Community* (1983); Darcy McNickle, *Native American Tribalism* (1973); Joan

Moore and Harry Pachon, *Hispanics in the United States* (1985); Joan Moore et al., *Homeboys* (1978); Roger Nichols, *The American Indian: Past and Present* (1986); James Olsen and Raymond Wilson, *Native Americans in the Twentieth Century* (1984); A. Petit, *Images of the Mexican-American in Fiction and Film* (1980); Ronald Taylor, *Chavez and the Farm Workers* (1975); Arnulfo Trejo, ed., *The Chicanos: As We See Ourselves* (1979); Karl Wagenheim, *Puerto Rico: A Profile* (1975).

## CHAPTER 32: THE AGE OF LIMITS

**American Society and the Economy in the 1970s**
Barry Bluestone and Bennett Harrison, *The Deindustrialization of America* (1982); Paul Boyer, *When Time Shall Be No More: Prophecy Belief in Modern American Culture* (1992); Peter Calleo, *The Imperious Economy* (1982); Barry Commoner, *The Politics of Energy* (1979); Ronald Formisano, *Boston against Busing: Race, Class, and Ethnicity in the 1960s and 1970s* (1991); Christopher Lasch, *The Culture of Narcissism* (1978); Michael Lienesch, *Redeeming America: Piety and Politics in the New Christian Right* (1993); J. Anthony Lukas, *Common Ground: A Turbulent Decade in the Lives of Three American Families* (1986); George Marsden, *Fundamentalism and Evangelicalism* (1991); Martin Melosi, *Coping with Abundance: Energy and Environment in Industrial America* (1985); Timothy O'Neill, *Bakke and the Politics of Equality* (1985); Daniel Yergin, *The Prize* (1991).

**Environmentalism**
Rachel Carson, *Silent Spring* (1962); Barry Caspar and Paul Wellstone, *Powerline* (1981); Albert Cowdry, *This Land, This South: An Environmental History* (1983); Thomas Dunlap, *DDT: Scientists, Citizens, and Public Policy* (1981); Robert Booth Fowler, *The Greening of Protestant Thought* (1995); Ian McHarg, *Design with Nature* (1969); Daniel Martin, *Three Mile Island* (1980); Lester Milbrath, *Environmentalists: Vanguard for a New Society* (1984); Roderick Nash, *The Rights of Nature* (1989); Marc Reisner, *Cadillac Desert: The American West and Its Disappearing Water* (1986); Kirkpatrick Sale, *The Green Revolution, The American Environmental Movement, 1962–1993* (1993); Philip Shabecoff, *A Fierce Green Fire: The American Environmental Movement* (1993); Andrew Szasz, *EcoPopulism: Toxic Waste and the Movement for Environmental Justice* (1994); James Trefethen, *An American Crusade for Wildlife* (1975); Donald Worster, *Rivers of Empire: Water, Aridity, and the Growth of the American West* (1985).

**Feminism, Sexual Politics, and the Family**
Barry D. Adam, *The Rise of a Gay and Lesbian Movement* (1987); Rae Andre, *Homemakers: The Forgotten Workers* (1981); Peter Berger and Brigitte Berger, *The War over the Family: Capturng*

the Middle Ground (1983); Mary Frances Berry, Why ERA Failed: Politics, Women's Rights, and the Amending Process of the Constitution (1986) and The Politics of Parenthood: Childcare, Women's Rights and Feminism (1993); Susan Brownmiller, Against Our Will: Men, Women, and Rape (1975); Robert Coles and Geoffrey Stokes, Sex and the American Teenager (1985); Angela Davis, Women, Race, and Class (1981); Susan Douglas, Where the Girls Are: Growing Up Female with the Mass Media (1994); John D'Emilio, Sexual Politics, Sexual Communities: The Making of a Homosexual Minority in the United States, 1940–1970 (1983); Martin Duberman, Stonewall (1993); Andrea Dworkin, Right-Wing Women (1983); Barbara Ehrenreich, The Hearts of Men: American Dreams and the Flight from Commitment (1983); Susan Estebrook, If All We Did Was to Weep at Home: A History of White Working-Class Women in America (1979); Shulamith Firestone, The Dialectic of Sex: The Case for the Feminist Revolution (1970); Jo Freeman, The Politics of Women's Liberation (1975); David Garrow, Liberty and Sexuality: The Right and Privacy in the Making of Roe v. Wade (1994); Carol Gilligan, In Another Voice: Psychological Theory and Women's Development (1982); Germaine Greer, The Female Eunuch (1972); Alice Kessler Harris, Out to Work (1982); Gloria Hull et al., But Some of Us Are Brave: Black Women's Studies (1982); Christopher Lasch, Haven in a Hostile World (1979); Kristen Luker, Abortion and the Politics of Motherhood (1984); Norma McCorvey, I Am Roe: My Life, Roe v. Wade and Freedom of Choice (1994); Kate Millett, Sexual Politics (1970); Steven Mintz and Susan Kellogg, Domestic Revolutions: A Social History of American Family Life (1988); Robin Morgan, ed., Sisterhood Is Powerful: An Anthology (1970); Maureen Muldoon, The Abortion Debate in the United States and Canada: A Source Book (1991); La Frances Rodgers-Rose, ed., The Black Woman (1980); Gloria Steinem, Outrageous Acts and Everyday Rebellions (1983).

### Politics and Diplomacy in the Age of Limits

Stephen Ambrose, Nixon: Ruin and Recovery, 1973–1990 (1991); James Bill, The Eagle and the Lion: The Tragedy of American–Iranian Relations (1987); Zbigniew Brzezinski, Power and Principle (1983); James Cannon, Time and Chance: Gerald Ford's Appointment with History, 1913–1974 (1993); Jimmy Carter, Keeping the Faith (1982); Rosalynn Carter, First Lady from Plains (1984); John Dean, Blind Ambition (1976); John Dumbull, The Carter Presidency: A Re-evaluation (1993); Gerald Ford, A Time to Heal (1979); Raymond Garthoff, Détente and Confrontation: American–Soviet Relations from Nixon to Reagan (1985); Millicent Gates and Bruce Geelhoed, The Dragon and the Snake: An American Account of the Turmoil in China, 1976–1977 (1986); Michael Hogan, The Panama Canal in American Politics (1986); Henry Jackson, From the Congo to Soweto: U.S. Foreign Policy toward Africa since 1960 (1982); Burton

Kaufman, The Presidency of James Earl Carter, Jr. (1993); Walter LaFeber, The Panama Canal, rev. ed. (1989); J. Anthony Lukas, Nightmare: The Underside of the Nixon Years (1988); Richard Pipes, U.S.–Soviet Relations in the Era of Détente (1981); William Quandt, Camp David (1986); A. James Reichley, Conservatives in an Age of Change: The Nixon and Ford Administrations (1981); Robert Schulzinger, Henry Kissinger: Doctor of Diplomacy (1989); Gary Sick, All Fall Down (1985); John Sirica, To Set the Record Straight (1979); Seth Tillman, The U.S. in the Middle East (1982); Cyrus Vance, Hard Choices (1983); Theodore White, Breach of Faith (1975); Bob Woodward and Carl Bernstein, All the President's Men (1974) and The Final Days (1976).

## CHAPTER 33: A NATION STILL DIVISIBLE

### Contemporary American Society

Bruce Bawer, A Place at the Table: The Gay Individual and American Society (1994); Robert Bellah et al., Habits of the Heart: Individualism and Commitment in American Life (1985) and The Good Society (1991); Dallas Blanchard, The Anti-Abortion Movement (1994); Stephen Carter, The Culture of Disbelief: How American Law and Politics Trivialize Religious Devotion (1993); William Dietrich, In the Shadow of the Rising Sun: The Political Roots of American Economic Decline (1991); Thomas Byrne Edsall, The New Politics of Inequality (1984); Barbara Ehrenreich, Fear of Falling: The Inner Life of the Middle Class (1989) and The Worst Years of Our Lives (1990); Susan Faludi, Backlash: The Undeclared War against American Women (1991); Elizabeth Fee and Daniel Fox, eds., AIDS: The Burdens of History (1992); Henry Louis Gates, Jr., Loose Canons: Notes on the Culture Wars (1993); Michael Goldfield, The Decline of Organized Labor in the United States (1987); Otis Graham, Jr., Losing Time: The Industrial Policy Debate (1992); Michael Harrington, The New American Poverty (1984); Richard Herrnstein and Charles Murray, The Bell Curve: Intelligence and Class Structure in American Life (1994); Robert Hughes, Culture of Complaint: The Fraying of America (1993); Paul Krugman, Peddling Prosperity: Economic Sense and Nonsense in the Age of Diminished Expectations (1994); Frank Levy, Dollars and Dreams: The Changing American Income Distribution (1987); Steve Levy, Insanely Great: The Life and Times of Macintosh, the Computer That Changed Everything (1994); Jane Maysbridge, Why We Lost the ERA (1986); Joseph Nocera, A Piece of the Action: How the Middle Class Joined the Money Class (1994); Juliet Schor, The Overworked American: The Unexpected Decline of Leisure (1991); Studs Terkel, The Great Divide (1988); Thomas Toch, In the Name of Excellence: The Struggle to Reform the Nation's Schools (1991); James Trabor and Eugene Gallagher, Why Waco? Cults in the Battle for Religious Freedom (1995).

## Politics from Reagan to Clinton

Charles Allen, *The Comeback Kid: The Life and Career of Bill Clinton* (1992); Earl Black and Merle Black, *The Vital South: How Presidents Are Elected* (1992); Sidney Blumenthal, *The Rise of the Counter-Establishment from Conservative Ideology to Political Power* (1988), and with Thomas Byrne Edsall, eds., *The Reagan Legacy* (1988); Paul Boyer, ed., *Reagan as President: Contemporary Views of the Man, His Politics, and His Policies* (1990); William Brennan, *America's Right Turn from Nixon to Bush* (1994); Barbara Bush, *Barbara Bush: A Memoir* (1994); Michael Deaver, *Behind the Scenes* (1987); Theodore Draper, *A Very Thin Line: The Iran–Contra Affairs* (1991); Elizabeth Drew, *On the Edge: The Clinton Presidency* (1994); Ken Gross, *Ross Perot: The Man Behind the Myth* (1992); David Hoeveler, Jr., *Watch on the Right: Conservative Intellectuals in the Reagan Era* (1991); Peter Irons, *Brennan vs. Rehnquist: The Battle for the Constitution* (1994); Jonathan Kwitny, *The Crimes of Patriots: A True Tale of Dope, Dirty Money, and the CIA* (1987); Jonathan Lash, *A Season of Spoils: The Story of the Reagan Administration's Attack on the Environment* (1984); Theodore Lowi, *The End of the Republican Era* (1995); Mary Matlin and James Carville, *All's Fair: Love, War, and Running for President* (1994); *The New Yorker,* "Special Politics Issue," October 21 & 28, 1996; Kevin Phillips, *The Politics of Rich and Poor: Wealth and the American Electorate in the Reagan Aftermath* (1990) and *Boiling Point: Republicans: Democrats and the Decline of Middle Class Prosperity* (1993); John Podhoretz, *Hell of a Ride: Backstage at the White House Follies, 1989–1993* (1993); Dan Quayle, *Standing Firm: A Vice-Presidential Memoir* (1994); Donald Regan, *For the Record* (1988); Tom Rosenstiel, *Strange Bedfellows: How Television and the Presidential Candidates Changed American Politics, 1992* (1993); Randy Shilts, *And the Band Played On: Politics, People and the AIDS Epidemic* (1987); David Stockman, *The Triumph of Politics: The Inside Story of the Reagan Revolution* (1986); Stephen Vaugh, *Ronald Reagan in Hollywood: Movies and Politics* (1994); Gary Wills, *Reagan's America* (1987); Daniel Wirls, *The Politics of Defense in the Reagan Era* (1992); Bob Woodward, *The Agenda: Inside the Clinton White House* (1994).

## Foreign Policy into the 1990s

Michael Beschloss and Strobe Talbot, *At the Highest Levels: The Inside Story of the End of the Cold War* (1993); Raymond Bonner, *Weakness and Deceit: U.S. Policy and El Salvador* (1984); William Broad, *Teller's War: The Top Secret Story behind the Star Wars Deception* (1992); Bradford Burns, *At War with Nicaragua* (1987); Leslie Cockburn, *Out of Control* (1987); Christopher Coker, *The United States and South Africa, 1968–1985* (1986); Thomas Friedman, *From Beirut to Jerusalem* (1989); John Lewis Gaddis, *The United States and the End of the Cold War* (1992); Roy Gutman, *Banana Diplomacy* (1988); Alexander Haig, Jr., *Caveat: Realism, Reagan, and Foreign Policy* (1984); Delip Hiro, *Desert Shield to Desert Storm* (1992); Bruce Jentleson, *Pipeline Politics: The Complex Political Economy of East–West Trade* (1986); Robert Kaplan, *Balkan Ghosts* (1993); Walter LaFeber, *Inevitable Revolutions* (1993); John Mueller, *Policy and Opinion in the Gulf War* (1994); Robert Pastor, *Condemned to Repetition: The United States and Nicaragua* (1987); Jonathan Schell, *The Fate of the Earth* (1982); David Schoenbaum, *The United States and the State of Israel* (1993); Strobe Talbott, *Deadly Gambits: The Reagan Administration and the Stalemate in Nuclear Arms Control* (1984); Sanford Ungar, *Africa* (1985); William Vogele, *Stepping Back: Nuclear Arms Control and the End of the Cold War* (1994). Thomas Walker, ed., *Reagan versus the Sandinistas* (1987); Bob Woodward, *Veil: The Secret Wars of the CIA* (1987).

## Minorities and American Culture

Ken Auletta, *The Underclass* (1982); Richard Bernstein, *Multiculturalism and the Battle for America's Future* (1994); Ellis Cose, *The Rage of the Privileged Class: Why Are Middle Class Blacks Angry?* (1994); Roger Daniels et al., eds., *Japanese-Americans: From Relocation to Redress* (1986); Reynolds Farley and Walter Allen, *The Color Line and the Quality of Life in America* (1987); Lawrence Fuchs, *The American Kaleidoscope: Race, Ethnicity, and the Civic Culture* (1990); Douglas Glasgow, *The Black Underclass* (1980); Andrew Hacker, *Two Nations: Black and White, Separate, Hostile, Unequal* (1992); Denis Heyck, ed., *Barrios and Borderlands: Cultures of Latinos and Latinas in the United States* (1993); Bill Ong Hing, *Making and Remaking Asian America through Immigration Policy, 1850–1990* (1993); David Hollinger, *Postethnic America: Beyond Multiculturalism* (1995); Christopher Jencks, *The Homeless* (1994); Jonathan Kozol, *Savage Inequalities: Children in America's Schools* (1991); Oscar Martinez, *Border People: Life and Society in the U.S.–Mexico Border Lands* (1994); Joan Moore and Harry Pachon, *Hispanics in the United States* (1985); Adolph Reed, *The Jesse Jackson Phenomenon: The Crisis of Purpose in Afro-American Politics* (1986); Sam Roberts, *Who Are We? A Portrait of America Based on the Latest U.S. Census* (1994); Arthur Schlesinger, Jr., *The Disuniting of America* (1991); Peter Skerry, *Mexican-Americans: The Ambivalent Minority* (1993); Robert C. Smith, *Racism in the Post–Civil Rights Era: Now You See It, Now You Don't* (1995); The Staff of the Chicago Tribune, *The American Millstone: An Examination of the Nation's Permanent Underclass* (1986); Shih-Shan Henry Tsai, *The Chinese Experience in America* (1986); William Wei, *The Asian American Movement* (1993).

# Credits

*Chapter 17* 441: Library of Congress; 447: General Research Division. The New York Public Library. Astor, Lenox and Tilden Foundations; 456: Stock Montage; 458: Rutherford B. Hayes Presidential Center.

*Chapter 18* 488: Library of Congress; 491: Courtesy MetLife Archive; 495: Collection of Lee Baxandall.

*Chapter 19* 500: George Wesley Bellows, *Cliff Dwellers*. Los Angeles County Museum of Art, Los Angeles County Funds; 505: National Archives, photo courtesy Rudolph Vetter/Interpretive Photography; 509: Albert H. Wiggins Collection, by Courtesy of the Trustees of the Boston Public Library; 511: Photo reproduced courtesy Thomas W. Chinn. From *Bridging the Pacific: SF Chinatown and Its People* by Thomas W. Chinn. © 1989 Chinese Historical Society of America, San Francisco; 523: Drawing by Charles Dana Gibson.

*Chapter 20* 533: Billy Graham Center Museum.

*Chapter 21* 563: Courtesy of Cornell University Library, Ithaca, NY; 569: Courtesy Dover Publications, NY; 582: Hawaii State Archives; 585: Chicago Historical Society; 587: Huntsville Public Library.

*Chapter 22* 595: Brown Brothers; 602: San Diego Historical Society, Ticor Collection, Photograph Collection; 613: Library of Congress; 617: The Bancroft Library, University of California, Berkeley.

*Chapter 23* 640: Trustees of the Imperial War Museum, London; 641: Culver; 644: National Archives, U.S. War Department.

*Chapter 24* 659: Bettmann; 669 & 674: Bettmann; 678: Paul Cadmus, *To the Lynching!* 1935. Pencil and watercolor on paper. 20 1/2 x 15 1/4 inches. Collection of Whitney Museum of American Art. Purchase 36.32.

*Chapter 25* 688: Library of Congress; 689: Library of Congress; 695: Brown Brothers; 701: Library of Congress; 708: The Butler Institute of American Art, Youngstown, OH.

*Chapter 26* 713: Franklin D. Roosevelt Library; 715: UPI/ Bettmann; 723: UPI/ Bettmann; 728: John Langly Howard (b. 1902), California Industrial Scenes, Coit Tower, S.F., PWAP, 1934. Don Beatty © 1983; 731: U.T. The Institute of Texan Cultures, The San Antonio Light Collection.

*Chapter 27* 746: UPI/ Bettmann; 753: James W. Davidson. Private collection; 761: Library of Congress; 765; Eliot Elisofon, Life Magazine © Time Warner Inc.; 774: National Archives, U.S. Army Signal Corps.

*Chapter 28* 784: Time map by R.M. Chapin, Jr.; 797: Bettmann; 800: Eve Arnold/Magnum.

*Chapter 29* 813: Courtesy Cadillac Motor Cars; 816: © The Curtis Publishing Company; 818: AP/Wide World; 826: AP/Wide World; 832: Burt Glinn/ Magnum.

*Chapter 30* 841(left): UPI/Corbis/Bettmann; 841(right): Photofest; 852: UPI/ Corbis/ Bettmann; 857: Richard Pipes; 862: Leonard Freed/ Magnum.

## EYEWITNESS CREDITS

# Index

Note: Page numbers in *italics* indicate illustrations and their captions; page numbers followed by *M* indicate maps and their captions.

*History of the Standard Oil Company* (Tarbell), 599
Hitler, Adolf, 657, 709, 744, *746*, 769
  death of, 775
  invasions, 747–749, 748*M*
  violation of Versailles Treaty, 745
  *See also* Germany; World War II
Hoboes of America, 760
Ho Chi Minh, 656, 822, 871, 879, 884
Ho Chi Minh Trail, 870*M*, 871
Holding companies, 483
"Hollywood Ten," 798–799
Holmes, Oliver Wendell, Jr., 598, 647, 652
Holocaust, *774*, 774–775, 782
Home Insurance Building, 504
Homemaking, importance in Great Depression, 696
Home Owners' Loan Act, 717
Homestead Act of 1862, 537, 550
Homestead steel mill, 482, 487–488, 567
Homestead steel strike (1892), 598
Homosexuals
  AIDS and, 944
  in armed services, 756
  gay rights movement, 892
  Holocaust and, 774
  investigation of, 799
  urban life and, 517
Hoover, Herbert, 681, 743
  election of 1928, 684–685, 685*M*
  election of 1932, 710
  personal habits, 705
  presidency of, 682
  *See also* Great Depression
Hoover, J. Edgar, 913
Hoovervilles (shantytowns), *695*
Hopkins, Harry, 712, 717, 721–722, 724
Hopkins, Johns, 519
*Hopwood v. State of Texas et al* (1996), 943
Horizontal growth of businesses, 480–481
Horses, 503, 536, 547
House, Edward, 637
House Committee on Un-American Activities (HUAC), 798–799
Houseman, John, 734
Housing, 811, 812
Houston, Charles, 829
Houston race riots (1917), 642
Howard, Paul Langley, *728*
Howard University, 792, 829
"Howdy Doody Show," 815
*Howl* (Ginsberg), 835–836
*How the Other Half Lives* (Riis), 600
HUAC (House Committee on Un-American Activities), 798–799
Hudson, T. S., 469, 477, 497
Huerta, Victoriano, 632
Hughes, Charles Evans, 637, 653, 681
Hughes, Langston, 674
Hull, Cordell, 745
Hull House, 510, 609, 695, 704
"Human potential movement," 924
Human resources, of "New South," 526, 527
Human rights issues, of Carter administration, 917–918
Humphrey, George, 822
Humphrey, Hubert, 880, 883
Hungary, Soviet occupation of (1947), 788–789
Hunt, E. Howard, 906, 907
Hunting, for sport, 531–532
Huntington, Collis, 574–575
Hurston, Zora Neale, 674
Hussein, Saddam, 941–942
Hutcheson, "Big Bill," 732
Hydrogen bomb, 796, 801

ICBMs (Intercontinental ballistic missiles), 887
ICC (Interstate Commerce Commission), 615
Ickes, Harold, 727, 728, 729, 737, 760
"If We Must Die" (McKay), 674
Illinois Vice Commission (1916), 608
IMF (International Monetary Fund), 775
Immigrants
  characteristics of, 501, 502
  city life and, 510–514, *511*
  education for, 518–519
  prejudice against, 606
Immigration, 466
  differing reasons for, 514
  illegal, 951
  immigrant aid societies, 512
  Mexican immigrants, 544–545, 889
  from Puerto Rico, 889
  reasons for 1880s immigration, 501–502, *502*
  reform of policy, 859
  restriction of, 607
  since 1980s, 951–953, 952*M*
  workers, 475–476
Immigration Act (1924), 775
Immigration Act (1965), 859, 951
Immigration restriction, 675–676
Immigration Restriction League, 508, 607
Impeachment, of Nixon, 908–909
Imperialism, 576–592
  Age of Imperialism, 467
  chronology of, 593
  foreign policy, 578–579
  in Latin America, 580–581
  in Pacific, 581–582, *582*
  scramble for empire, 576–578, 577*M*
  Seward's diplomacy, 579–580
  Venezuelan crisis, 583
Impoundment, 906
Inchon (Korea), 802, 803*M*
Income tax, graduated, 618–619, 622, 760
Index of American Design, 734
Indianapolis (Indiana), KKK capital in 1920s, 677
Indian Reorganization Act of 1934, 730
Indians of All Tribes, 891
Individuality, mass culture and, 833
Indochina, history of, 869
Industrialization, 466–497
  chronology of, 497
  cities and (*See* Cities and urbanization)
  corporate greed and, 595
  development of industrial systems, 469–476
    corporations, 474–475
    investment capital, 474
    labor resources, 475–476, *476*
    resources and technology, *471*, 471–472
    systematic invention, 472–473
    transportation and communication, 473–474
  drawbacks of "New South," 530
  growth of big business, 480–486
    consumer goods, 480–481
    corporate critics, 484–485
    costs of, 486, *486*
    mergers and holding companies, 483–484
    petroleum industry, 482–483
    social Darwinism and, 484
    steel industry, 481–482
  imperialism and, 555, 578
  labor unions (*See* Labor unions)
  railroads (*See* Railroads)
  Reconstruction and, 453
  roots of progressivism and, 597
  urbanization and (*See* Cities and urbanization)
  workers and, 487–492